BARRON'S

HOW TO PREPARE FOR THE

AP

WORLD HISTORY EXAMINATION

John McCannon, Ph.D.
Department of History,
University of Saskatchewan

BARRON'S

About the author: John McCannon earned a Ph.D. in history from the University of Chicago in 1994. He has taught Russian history, modern European history, and world history at several universities in the United States and Canada. He is the author of *Red Arctic: Polar Exploration* and *The Myth of the North in the Soviet Union, 1932–1939*. Professor McCannon is now a faculty member in the Department of History at the University of Saskatchewan.

About the contributor: Pamela Jordan received a Ph.D. in political science from the University of Toronto in 1997. In addition to her academic background, she has worked as a news writer for Facts on File News Services, Inc., and as executive director of a nongovernmental organization affiliated with the United Nations. Dr. Jordan is now teaching international studies courses at the University of Saskatchewan.

Acknowledgments:
This book is dedicated to Pamela Jordan, a co-author in every sense of the word. Without her formidable research skills, her invaluable written contributions to the manuscript, and her sharp editorial eye, this book could never have come into being.

Both the author and contributor would like to thank David Rodman, whose editorial supervision made the preparation of this manuscript a smooth and easy process. We are also grateful to Bill Kuchler for art direction, to Debby Becak for production assistance, and to the anonymous reviewer of this manuscript for his insightful and encouraging comments.

All inquiries should be addressed to:
Barron's Educational Series, Inc.
250 Wireless Boulevard
Hauppauge, New York 11788
http://www.barronseduc.com

Library of Congress Catalog Card No. 2001043330

International Standard Book No. 0-7641-1816-1

Library of Congress Cataloging-in-Publication Data
McCannon, John, 1967–
    How to prepare for AP world history / John McCannon, Pam Jordan.
        p.   cm.
    Includes bibliographical references and index.
    ISBN 0-7641-1816-1 (alk. paper)
    1. World history—Study and teaching.   2. World history—Examinations—Study guides.
  3. Advanced placement programs (Education).   I. Title: How to prepare for advanced
placement world history.   II. Jordan, Pam.   III. Title.
D21 .M33   2002
907'.6—dc21   2001043330

Printed in the United States of America
9 8 7

CONTENTS

UNIT ONE

Introduction

SECTION A

How to Use This Book

This volume is designed to assist students in preparing for the Advanced Placement Examination in World History. It provides:

- A guide to the Advanced Placement Examination in World History (Unit One).
- Review chapters that outline the major developments and periods of world history (Units Two through Six).
- Two complete model Advanced Placement Examinations in World History, with answer keys for the multiple-choice questions, and sample answers and commentary for the essays (Unit Seven).

TO TEACHERS AND STUDENTS

This book can be a useful supplement to classwork and study materials. For readers who are not taking—or have never taken—a course in world history, this volume can serve as an independent study aid. Ideally, however, this book will be used in conjunction with an actual academic course in world history, or by students who have taken such a course and are attempting to review.

Unit One, Sections B through F, offers strategies that students may find useful in approaching the various types of questions they will encounter on the Advanced Placement Examination in World History. These include multiple-choice questions, the document-based essay question, the change-over-time essay question, and the comparative essay question.

Units Two through Six contain review chapters. Each unit is dedicated to one of the major historical periods covered by the exam. There are five to eight chapters within each unit. Each chapter deals with a major geographical area or historical topic. Every chapter is followed by a set of 10 multiple-choice questions; these will allow students to review material immediately after having read it. Each unit is preceded by a historical overview. A major review section, consisting of 20 multiple-choice questions and three essay questions, follows each of these five units.

TO THE TEACHER

The review chapters contained within this book can be used as supplements to summarize or reinforce particular teaching units and classroom or homework assignments. Unit overviews and chapter introductions assist students in looking at historical events from a broad perspective. The unit overviews also strive to place historical events and developments in the comparative context that the World History exam will emphasize heavily. The multiple-choice questions at the end of each chapter and each unit focus the learning.

The sample examinations in Unit Seven can be used near the end of the academic year as a culmination of a world history course. The sample exams also serve as good practice for the actual Advanced Placement exam.

Unit One should be covered with students at the beginning of a world history course, then at several points afterward. The sooner students are familiar with the structure of the Advanced Placement Examination in World History, as well as the examination's procedures, the more comfortable they will be with the exam process itself.

TO THE STUDENT

This book can be used as an independent review device, even if you are not currently taking an Advanced Placement course in world history. Even for students who have never taken an academic or Advanced Placement course in world history, this book can prove helpful. It is optimal, however, if you are using this book while taking a course in world history, or if you have taken a world history course in the past and are using this book as a refresher.

It is best to use this book over a long period of time, rather than trying to cram at the last minute. You will want to absorb information and ideas slowly and thoroughly.

At the beginning, read Unit One, on the structure of the Advanced Placement exam and the types of questions asked by it. To do well on the Advanced Placement exam, it is crucial to know the procedure and follow directions closely. The sooner and better you make yourself familiar with the rules and procedures, the more comfortable you will be with them, and the more natural they will feel when you take the actual test.

Also pay special attention to unit overviews and chapter introductions. These will help you to see world history from a "big picture" perspective. They also place trends and facts in a comparative context. Your ability to compare and contrast different eras and parts of the world will be tested extensively by the Advanced Placement exam.

If you plan to use this volume as a review device, as practice for the Advanced Placement exam, do not wait until late April or May. Try to reserve time in late March or early April to go over review chapters and do sample questions on material you have already studied in class and homework assignments. You may want to save one of the model Advanced Placement exams for early May, then use it as a last-minute practice round.

GENERAL NOTES

Dates are given according to the standard Western calendar, with one exception. The abbreviations B.C.E. and C.E. are used, rather than the traditional B.C. ("before Christ") and A.D. (*anno domini,* or "year of our Lord"). Standing for "before common era" and "common era," respectively, the use of B.C.E. and C.E. is more neutral and more secular, showing more respect to those world cultures whose traditions are not based on Christianity. It should be noted that the Western calendar is only one of many systems used for measuring time. According to the Hebrew calendar, for example, year 1 is the equivalent of 3760 B.C.E. Year 1 of the Muslim calendar, by contrast, is 622 C.E.

Dates with no designation—those that appear simply as numerals—are assumed to be C.E.

Names and terms from a variety of languages are used throughout this book. Many of these languages—such as Russian, Chinese, Arabic, Japanese, and Hebrew—use different alphabets, rather than the Latin script used by English speakers. There is no single way of transliterating, or converting, one alphabet to another.

When referring to people or terms transliterated from non-Latin scripts, this book will try to use versions that are both linguistically accurate and easily recognizable. Students should be aware that there are several variants of certain well-known names and terms. For example, Genghis Khan versus Chinggis Khan (or Jenghiz Khan), Mao Tse-tung versus Mao Zedong, Mohammed versus Muhammad, or Sundiata versus Son-Jara. Students may encounter some or all of these different versions in different textbooks and readings.

SECTION B

The Advanced Placement Examination in World History: An Overview

Following is an outline of the Advanced Placement Examination in World History. Also included are a description of the grading system, a discussion of the historical periods covered on the examination, and a list of the major themes that the examination will emphasize.

FORMAT

The Advanced Placement exam lasts a total of 3 hours and 5 minutes.

Students will be allowed 55 minutes in order to complete 70 multiple-choice questions.

For the completion of the free-response, or essay, section of the examination, 130 minutes will be allotted. The free-response section of the test will consist of the following three types of questions:

- *Document-based question (DBQ):* 50 minutes total. A mandatory period of 10 minutes will be devoted to the reading and selection of documents. Students will then write their answers in the remaining 40 minutes.
- *Change-over-time essay question (COT):* 40 minutes will be allowed for a thematic essay that touches on at least two of the time periods covered in the exam.
- *Comparative essay question:* 40 minutes will be given to a comparative question that will focus on broad issues and deal with at least two societies.

For each of the essay questions, it is recommended that students spend 5 minutes planning their answers, then write their answers in the next 35 minutes.

GRADING

Grades for the Advanced Placement Examination in World History will be calculated as follows:

- The 70 multiple-choice questions: one half of the total grade.
- The 3 free-response questions: one half of the total grade. Each of the free-response questions is weighed equally; therefore, each is worth 16.66 percent of the total grade. Each essay will receive a grade of 0 (the worst) to 9 (the best).

After grading, each exam will be assigned a score of 1 through 5. The higher the number, the better the score. Scores can be interpreted as follows:

5. Extremely well qualified. Accepted by the majority of colleges and universities for some kind of academic credit or benefit.
4. Well qualified. Accepted by many colleges and universities for some kind of academic credit or benefit.
3. Qualified. Accepted by many colleges and universities for some kind of academic credit or benefit, but often of a limited nature.
2. Possibly qualified. Accepted by a few colleges and universities for credit or benefit, generally quite limited.
1. No recommendation. Not accepted anywhere.

Different universities and colleges have different policies regarding Advanced Placement exams. Students should contact the school of their choice to determine what benefit, if any, a particular score will result in at that institution.

TIME FRAME

The Advanced Placement Examination in World History focuses mainly on global developments since 1000 C.E. Some attention will be paid to broad trends taking place during the Foundations period (prehistory to 1000 C.E.). The percentage of questions pertaining to each era is approximately as follows:

- Foundations period (prehistory to 1000 C.E.): 14 percent of questions
- 1000 to 1450: 23 percent of questions
- 1450 to 1750: 20 percent of questions
- 1750 to 1914: 20 percent of questions
- 1914 to the present: 23 percent of questions

THEMES

By its very nature, the Advanced Placement World History exam is extremely broad and ambitious in scope. More so than most exams of this type, the World History exam seeks to test students not merely on their ability to memorize information, but on their critical and interpretive skills, as well as their ability to examine and analyze historical issues from a "big-picture" perspective. Both multiple-choice and free-response questions will emphasize social, economic, and cultural trends; issues of gender and ethnic identity; interrelationships and exchanges among various civilizations; and the ability to compare different historical eras and societies.

Topics such as battles, the lives of monarchs and political leaders, and the careers of individual "great figures" will receive some coverage on the Advanced Placement World History exam, but less than on traditional history exams. It will be necessary to place such events, lives, and careers in their broader political, economic, cultural, and social contexts.

A note about coverage of European and United States history: One of the declared purposes of the Advanced Placement world history course is to focus more academic attention on areas of the world other than Europe and North America. Accordingly, no more than 30 percent of the questions (multiple-choice or free-response) will cover topics in European history. The United States will be included only as part of topics that are global or comparative in nature, such as colonization, foreign affairs, war, and the globalization of trade and culture. There will be no coverage of the internal politics of the United States.

The six overarching themes outlined formally by the Advanced Placement world history course are as follows. These themes are intended to assist students in focusing their study efforts in a way that enables them to analyze broad trends and make insightful comparisons across time and place.

- The impact of interaction among major societies, such forms of interaction including trade, systems of international exchange, war, and diplomacy.
- The relationship of change and continuity across the periods of world history outlined by the Advanced Placement course.
- The impact of technology and demography on people and the environment, including issues such as population growth and decline, disease, manufacturing, migrations, agriculture, and weaponry.
- Systems of social organization and gender structure.
- Cultural and intellectual developments and interactions among and within societies.
- Changes over time in the functions and structures of states and in attitudes toward states. This includes discussion of various types of political organization, principally the nation-state.

SECTION C

Multiple-Choice Question Strategies

The Advanced Placement Examination in World History will require you to answer 70 multiple-choice questions. Each question will have five answer choices. Your goal is to pick the ONE answer that BEST responds to the question.

You will be given 55 minutes to complete this section of the test.

Multiple-choice questions will cover political-diplomatic topics, economic and social topics, and intellectual and cultural topics. The percentage of questions devoted to each historical period will be roughly the same as that described in Unit One, Section B (foundations period, 14 percent; 1000–1450, 23 percent; 1450–1750, 20 percent; 1750–1914, 20 percent; 1914–present, 23 percent).

As a general rule, you must answer 50 percent of the multiple-choice questions correctly in order to qualify for an overall score of 3 ("qualified"). This assumes that you complete the free-response (essay) portions of the exam acceptably. You receive a point for each correct answer. If you answer a question incorrectly, you lose one fourth of a point. If you skip a question altogether, leaving it blank, you lose no points, but you gain nothing, either.

TIPS FOR THE MULTIPLE-CHOICE QUESTIONS

There are a number of guidelines to keep in mind when taking the multiple-choice section of the Advanced Placement exam. They are as follows:

- *Remember that you are looking for the BEST answer to the question.* This calls for reading the question carefully. On occasion, there may seem to be more than one acceptable answer. If so, is the question calling for the "most important"? Or "most influential"? Or some other qualifying factor? For example, a question asking you to choose the IMMEDIATE cause of World War I might give you a choice among "the assassination of the Archduke Francis Ferdinand," "the Anglo-German naval race," and "competition over colonies in Africa." All three factors helped cause World War I. But because the question asks for the most immediate cause, the BEST answer is "the assassination of the Archduke Francis Ferdinand," because the other two responses deal with long-term causes.
- *Be aware that some questions include the answers "none of the above" and "all of the above."* If either is one of the responses, you must evaluate all the others carefully. "None of the above" prevents you from making vague guesses. "All of the above" keeps you from settling for the most obviously correct answer. If you can determine that a second answer is also

correct, then you are fairly safe in assuming that "all of the above" is the right response (although you should check the other two answers as well).

- *Do not make too many wild guesses.* Remember that you are penalized one fourth of a point for every incorrect answer, but nothing for a question left blank. You may lose more points due to wrong answers than you gain by blind guessing.
- *Do not leave too many questions blank.* This may seem like a contradiction of the previous item, but you must also remember that not answering a question means giving up the opportunity to gain points. A good rule of thumb is that if you can narrow the number of likely answers to two, you should pick one of them, even if you are not sure.
- *Read the question twice:* first quickly, to get a general sense, then slowly, to absorb the details.
- *Read all five answers.* As with the questions, read through quickly, then go over the answers a second time, more slowly.
- *As you turn to a new question, start by eliminating obviously incorrect answers.* This will help you focus your attention on the two or three possibly correct answers. If you eliminate any answers at all, and one of the responses is "all of the above," then you have really eliminated two answers, because "all of the above" obviously cannot be correct if even one of the responses is wrong.
- *Beware of statements and answers that contain the words* always *and* never. Such absolute statements are almost always incorrect (note the use of the word *almost* here). You should feel secure in eliminating such answers right away. Look for answers that contain the phrases *frequently, most often, generally*, and so on.
- *Trust your intuition—up to a point.* Most teachers and exam-preparation specialists say that your first choice is generally the correct one. If you have read the question and the answers carefully, you should probably stick with your first choice, unless you have a specific, concrete reason for changing your mind. On the other hand, this rule of thumb should not be used as an excuse for lazy reading or sloppy thinking. Do not make your first choice until you have read and thought about the question and answers carefully.

TYPES OF MULTIPLE-CHOICE QUESTIONS

There are many types of multiple-choice questions, each of which attempts to test a different skill or different way of thinking. A list of the major types would include the following:

- Identification
- Analytical
- Quotation-based
- Image interpretation
- Map-based
- Graph and chart identification

IDENTIFICATION QUESTIONS

Identification questions test your mastery of information and command of facts. Some are quite simple: you either know the fact the question is based on, or you do not. Who did what? Which religion or philosophy does a certain principle belong to? What happened when? Other identification questions are a little more complicated, with some analysis mixed in.

Of the multiple-choice questions offered on the Advanced Placement exam, about 35 to 40 percent are likely to be of the identification type. Some examples follow.

1. Which Qing emperor is considered to be one of the greatest rulers in Chinese history?

   (A) Yuan Shikai
   (B) Kangxi
   (C) Hong Xiuquan
   (D) Qianlong
   (E) Yongle

2. This city became one of West Africa's greatest centers of trade and Islamic scholarship from the thirteenth to the fifteenth centuries.

   (A) Timbuktu
   (B) Zimbabwe
   (C) Mogadishu
   (D) Zanzibar
   (E) Mombasa

3. Which of the following would best fit in with the beliefs of a practicing Buddhist?

   (A) Justice should be based on the principle of an eye for an eye, a tooth for a tooth.
   (B) Each individual should place his or her trust in a personal savior in order to ensure a place in heaven.
   (C) At the end of the world, God will judge all sinners and condemn them to eternal torment.
   (D) Yogic discipline and mastery of the body helps to improve the quality of one's spirit.
   (E) People are born and reborn into lives of suffering, but can escape this cycle by attaining enlightenment.

ANSWERS: 1. **B** 2. **A** 3. **E**

The first two questions are "pure" identification. They require only that you know a specific fact. The third question is more analytical, in that you must think about the basic tenets of Buddhism. But it still boils down to a slightly complicated way of asking you to pick one correct "fact" that matches what the question asks.

ANALYTICAL QUESTIONS

Analytical questions are somewhat more complicated than identification questions. Rather than simply testing your factual knowledge, they require you to think about historical relationships, to understand cause and effect, to place events and developments in proper chronological order, and to ponder more abstract points.

Approximately 20 to 25 percent of the multiple-choice section of the examination is made up of analytical questions. Examples follow.

1. Which of the following is NOT true of most human societies during the Stone Age?

(A) Despite limitations on their techno-logical aptitude, Stone Age humans designed many innovative and clever tools.

(B) Biological differences between men and women gave rise to a gender division of labor in most Stone Age societies.

(C) Human beings tended to be more aggressive during the Stone Age than during later periods in history.

(D) Human beings settled North and South America later than they did Africa, Asia, and Europe.

(E) Human societies developed complex forms of tribal organization, religious ritual, and oral traditions during the Stone Age.

2. Which of the following broad social, diplomatic, and economic effects can be attributed to World War II?

I. In many Western nations, such as Great Britain and the United States, women received the vote shortly after the war.

II. Late in the war, the United States took the lead in creating an international system of rules and agencies to foster free trade after the war.

III. The war dramatically reduced Europe's global influence, making it difficult for nations such as Great Britain and France to retain control over their empires.

IV. The war concentrated strategic might and economic power in the hands of the United States and the Soviet Union, which were now superpowers.

(A) I, II, and III
(B) II and III
(C) I, III, and IV
(D) II, III, and IV
(E) all of the above

3. Which of the following lists is in the correct chronological order?

(A) the calling of the Estates General, the storming of the Bastille, the execution of Louis XVI, the Declaration of the Rights of Man and the Citizen

(B) the calling of the Estates General, the storming of the Bastille, the Declaration of the Rights of Man and the Citizen, the execution of Louis XVI

(C) the storming of the Bastille, the calling of the Estates General, the Declaration of the Rights of Man and the Citizen, the execution of Louis XVI

(D) the Declaration of the Rights of Man and the Citizen, the storming of the Bastille, the execution of Louis XVI, the calling of the Estates General

(E) none of the above

ANSWERS: 1. **C** 2. **D** 3. **B**

QUOTATION-BASED QUESTIONS

This type of question is comparatively rare. Only 10 percent or less of multiple-choice questions will be of this sort. You will be required to read a short quotation about an event, person, or phenomenon. You will then choose which answer best relates to the quotation. An example follows.

1. "A fierce conqueror, he is often perceived in the West as a vicious barbarian. It is true that he and his horseback warriors accomplished their conquests by means of horrible violence. However, warlords and generals in the West were capable of equally horrible atrocities. And while this leader and his people were, in the beginning, primitive, they proved surprisingly capable, by means of cultural borrowing, of developing a legal system, bureaucracy, and communications system suitable for governing vast stretches of Eurasia for decades."

   The individual referred to in this quotation is

   (A) Xerxes I
   (B) Genghis Khan
   (C) Mehmet II
   (D) Oda Nobunaga
   (E) Abbas the Great

ANSWER: 1. **B**

IMAGE INTERPRETATION

A few questions will ask you to identify or interpret images. These may include paintings, cartoons, photographs, architectural works, or other artworks. You may be asked to determine the message or purpose of the image, or you may be required to identify the artist who created it, the movement it belongs to, or the civilization it comes from.

Less than 10 percent of multiple-choice questions will be of this type. A sample follows.

1. The sculpture pictured is most likely

   (A) a personal likeness commissioned by a wealthy patron.
   (B) an example of Asian influence on Western art.
   (C) an experiment in modernist abstraction.
   (D) a ritual object with religious significance crafted in Africa.
   (E) an artistic protest against the dehumanizing effects on women caused by male domination.

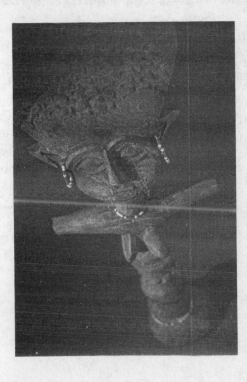

ANSWER: 1. **D**

MAP-BASED QUESTIONS

Some questions will require you to use map-reading skills. Map-related questions typically fall into two categories. One type of map question will ask you to identify what the map depicts. The other type will ask you to analyze the map and draw conclusions from the information contained on it.

In either case, map questions require fairly basic skills and general information. There is an excellent chance that, by careful reading and thought, you can gain points by focusing on these questions.

Less than 10 percent of multiple-choice questions will be map-based. One example follows.

1. What historical development does the map depict?

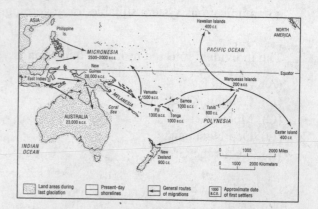

   (A) The expansion of Chinese trade routes
   (B) James Cook's voyages of discovery
   (C) Japan's military assault on the South Pacific
   (D) Thor Heyerdahl's *Kon-Tiki* expedition
   (E) The migration of Polynesian peoples throughout the Pacific

ANSWER: 1. **E**

GRAPH AND CHART INTERPRETATION

A number of questions will make use of graphs and charts. Even more so than with map-based questions, the information needed to answer the question is generally contained within the chart or graph.

Less than 10 percent of questions will be of this type. A sample follows.

1. What is the most likely explanation for the rise in population of the cities included on the chart?

   (A) industrialization
   (B) foreign immigration
   (C) increased levels of pollution in the countryside
   (D) the elimination of diseases such as tuberculosis and polio
   (E) more advanced forms of birth control

Year	Cities (Pop. in thousands)				
	London	Paris	Antwerp	Berlin	Moscow
1800	960	600	60	170	250
1850	2,700	1,400	90	500	360
1900	6,500	3,700	280	2,700	1,000

ANSWER: 1. **A**

SECTION D

Document-Based Question Strategies

The free-response section of the Advanced Placement Examination in World History lasts for 130 minutes. During this time, you will be required to write three essays: a document-based question (DBQ), a change-over-time (COT) question, and a comparative essay.

The first essay you will write is the DBQ. The DBQ is also the most complicated of the essay types you will encounter. The directions for the DBQ are complex and specific, and in order to do well on the essay, it is imperative that you follow them.

This section will start by outlining some general tips for successful essay writing. These can be applied to the other types of essays you will write, not just the DBQ. This section will then go on to explain the specific procedures to be followed in completing the DBQ.

GENERAL TIPS FOR ESSAY WRITING

Unlike the multiple-choice questions, which are graded by machine, the written portions of Advanced Placement exams are evaluated by hand. To mark the written portions of the exam given in each subject area, several hundred high-school teachers and university professors gather in June, generally on a college campus, for about a week.

In the course of that week, an Advanced Placement reader is likely to mark well over a thousand essays. He or she is conscientious, careful, and well trained in the Advanced Placement method of grading. Still, since your reader will be looking over so many essays in such a short time, it is up to you to make sure that the quality of your work stands out.

One way to impress your reader is to follow some basic dos and don'ts. Most of the following items may seem like elementary common sense, and by themselves, they will not guarantee you a good grade. After all, you must know your material and write well about it. However, it is surprising how many students violate one or more of these rules. Because of this, what would otherwise be good essays quite often receive lower grades than they otherwise could have earned. By keeping these dos and don'ts in mind, not just for the DBQ, but for all of your essays, you will make it easier for your reader to appreciate your work—and more likely that he or she will assign you a high score.

- *Develop a thesis and state it clearly*. The guidelines that all Advanced Placement readers follow for all essay questions stress this explicitly. You must make some kind of argument or draw some kind of concrete conclusion, and you must let your reader know you are doing it. Some students go so far as to underline their thesis statements or write sentences such as "My thesis is . . ." You do not need to do this, and it is not considered good writing (although it is preferable to omitting a thesis statement altogether). The best method for presenting a thesis statement is to write a short introductory paragraph. Included in that paragraph, often as the last sentence, will be your thesis statement. Good ways to open your thesis statement include "I will argue that . . ." "Based on the historical evidence, it is clear that . . ." "A close reading of the documents leads one to the conclusion that . . ."

- *Read the directions and follow them closely.* Remember that you are writing three different types of essays. Each type has its own specific set of rules. Advanced Placement readers are trained to judge your work based on how well you follow those rules. Even if your essay is beautifully composed, with perfect grammar and spelling, and shows crystal-clear logic and an impressive command of factual knowledge, it will lose points if you do not follow the directions. If you want more detail on the guidelines followed by Advanced Placement readers in grading essays, see the College Board/Educational Testing Service's web page, at *www.collegeboard.org/ap*.

- *Look at the question's key verb.* Answer the question based on that key verb. Questions will ask you to *defend* or *refute* (argue for or against); *assess the validity of* (judge the truth of); *evaluate* (determine the worth of, discuss advantages and disadvantages); *describe*, *discuss*, or *detail* (tell about, consider points of view); *outline* (list); *explain* (offer reasons for, make clear); *analyze* or *examine* (look at in detail, consider relationships, take into account cause and effect); and *compare* and *contrast* (show differences and similarities). The last item on this list—compare and contrast—will be especially important on the World History exam.

- *Write neatly and clearly.* Remember that your reader will be marking hundreds of essays. Your reader will not be inclined to grade generously if he or she has to struggle just to understand what you are saying. Grading guidelines state that "substance takes precedence over neatness," but neatness certainly helps the exam reader appreciate more fully what you are trying to say.

- *Make sure to divide your essay into paragraphs.* Paragraphs should be clearly indented. Correct and effective use of paragraphs shows the reader that you know how to think and write in an organized fashion.

- *Turn in an answer of an appropriate length.* There is no hard-and-fast rule as to how long your essay should be. To begin with, how long your essay is depends largely on how large or small your handwriting is. Also, quantity does not always mean quality. It is possible to make a good argument and back it up well with a minimal amount of writing, and it is equally possible to write a bad essay that rambles on and on for pages. However, an essay that is less than two pages long will generally be regarded with suspicion by the reader. Assuming that your handwriting is of an average size, a good MINIMUM length to aim for is two FULL pages. Three, even four, pages is optimal.

- *If you have time, reread your essay.* If necessary, revise it. Cross out mistakes or awkward phrasings. If new information or a good idea occurs to you, add it. Try to do so neatly, although remember that "substance takes precedence over neatness."

Organization is just as important as any of the foregoing points. Your essay should have an introduction. As noted previously, your thesis, stated explicitly, should appear here. Your essay should be divided into paragraphs. Make sure your reader can tell where your paragraphs begin and end (indent clearly or skip a line between paragraphs).

Paragraphs should correspond with specific points or arguments you wish to make. These points and arguments should serve somehow to back up or prove your thesis. You should have at least three main points, although there can be more. If you have time, write a conclusion to sum up your arguments or make some general remarks about the topic you have just written about.

APPROACHING THE DOCUMENT-BASED QUESTION (DBQ)

As previously noted, the DBQ will be not only the first essay you write, but also the one with the most elaborate rules. It is, therefore, extremely important for you to be familiar with the procedure.

A total of 50 minutes will be alloted for the DBQ. The first 10 minutes will be devoted to reading the documents. You will not be allowed to write your essay during this time. After the document-reading period, you will be given 40 minutes to complete your essay. It is recommended that you spend 5 to 10 minutes thinking about and organizing your response, then use the last 30 to 35 minutes to write.

You will be provided with anywhere from four to twelve documents. Most of them will be traditional written documents: excerpts from books and essays; transcriptions of speeches or radio and television addresses; government papers; and so on. Sometimes song lyrics, poetry, or popular-culture material may be included. Occasionally, you will see a painting, cartoon, or some type of visual image. The authors or speakers may be famous, or they may not be at all well known.

The purpose of the DBQ is to assess your ability to understand, evaluate, and comment on primary documents. Therefore, you must not only write a good essay with a clear thesis, but you must actively incorporate all or almost all of the documents provided into your response. You must also comment on what OTHER documents (or types of documents), NOT included, might be useful in shedding light on the question.

Graders will judge your essay based on how well you do the following:

- *Define and support your thesis.* Address all parts of the question. As is noted subsequently, your thesis will have much to do with how you group your documents.
- *Include the documents in your essay.* At the least, you need to include all (for full credit) or all but one (for partial credit) of the documents.
- *Use the documents.* In addition to including the documents, you must use them as evidence to support your thesis. Listing documents is not enough. You must attribute them (link them with the author or speaker), identify their point of view, and analyze them. You must show a clear understanding of the documents and what they mean.
- *Group the documents.* The most effective way to analyze the documents is to group them together into various types, showing how certain documents are alike and different. Your thesis will most likely determine how you group your documents.
- *Bring in relevant historical content and evidence.* Can you place the documents (or some of them) and their authors in a wider context? Can you comment insightfully on the individuals or events to which some or all of the documents are related?
- *Identify additional types of documents that might be useful supplements to the ones provided for you.* The DBQ asks you to demonstrate your historical judgment by commenting on what is missing from the picture presented to you. If you could have OTHER documents provided to you, what types would you find useful in answering your question? This needs to be done at least TWO times, if not three.

Of the foregoing requirements, a few deserve additional attention because they must be done in specific ways to avoid losing points.

Attribution. Do NOT simply refer to "Document 1," "#5," or "doc. 3" in your essay. When you make use of a document, you must identify the source clearly. This can be as simple as mentioning the name of the speaker or writer, as well as making a brief reference to the title. You may also refer to the number of the document, as long as you do it IN ADDITION to providing other information. Do this EVERY time you introduce a document. For example, referring to the sample documents that follow, you could attribute as follows: "As Nasser, in the 'Philosophy of the Revolution' (Doc. #2), argues, . . ." or "In the interview given by Teodora Gomes (#8), . . ."

Point of view. Simply attributing the documents is not sufficient, even if it is necessary. You must also comment on point of view. In other words, what is the bias or perspective of the author, speaker, or artist? This may be clear from the speaker's or writer's nationality, ethnicity, gender, social class, religion, or political affiliation. If the speaker or writer is famous, his or her point of view may be easy to describe. If he or she is not well known, you will have to read the document closely to determine its point of view. For partial credit, you must analyze the point of view of two or three documents. For full credit, especially if there are fewer than seven or eight documents, you must do this for all (or almost all) of the documents.

Grouping documents. One of the skills you MUST demonstrate is an ability to group documents into useful and meaningful categories. Can the documents be grouped by national origin (generally a weak approach)? By chronology (also weak, as a rule)? From a class perspective? According to a political philosophy or outlook? By purpose? By gender? According to cultural attitudes? There is no single right or wrong way to do this, so you can be creative here. However, your groupings must make sense, and the DBQ will be designed in such a way that some methods of grouping will be more appropriate than others. Also, the NUMBER of groups is important. Some questions allow you to divide the documents into as few as two categories. This is rare, however, and you should not do it unless you are specifically instructed that you may do so. Nine times out of ten, it is safest to come up with a MINIMUM of THREE categories. Four is acceptable as well. Five or more is difficult and unwieldy. Remember that, unless you are explicitly allowed to do so in the instructions, you may not have a group that contains only one document.

Thesis. Don't forget your thesis. Most often, your thesis will determine the way you group your documents. Conveniently, each category of document—especially if you have three or four categories—can be used as a main point in the body of your essay.

SAMPLE QUESTION

1. In the modern world, major political and social changes have been brought about by many different means: national liberation, revolution, reformism, parliamentary action, and so forth. Using the documents presented below, discuss the various methods of political and social transformation that they call for or advocate.

DOCUMENT 1

Source: Vladimir Lenin, Russian revolutionary leader and head of the Soviet state, *What Is To Be Done?* (1902).

A small, compact core of the most reliable, experienced, and hardened workers, with responsible representatives in the principal districts and connected by all the rules of strict secrecy with the organization of revolutionaries, can . . . perform all the functions of a trade union organization. . . .

I assert: 1) that no revolutionary movement can endure without a stable organization of leaders that maintains continuity . . . 3) that such an organization must consist chiefly of people professionally engaged in revolutionary activity; 4) that in an autocratic state, the more we confine the membership of such an organization to people who are professionally engaged in revolutionary activity and have been professionally trained in the art of combatting the political police, the more difficult it will be to wipe out such an organization. . . .

Only a gross failure to understand Marxism . . . could prompt the opinion that the rise of a mass, spontaneous working-class movement relieves us of the duty of creating a good organization of revolutionaries. On the contrary, this movement imposes this duty upon us, because the spontaneous struggle of the proletariat will not become its genuine "class struggle" until this struggle is led by a strong organization of revolutionaries.

DOCUMENT 2

Source: Gamal Abdel Nasser, Arab nationalist and president of Egypt, "The Philosophy of the Revolution."

As I often sit in my study and think quietly of this subject, I ask myself: "What is our positive role in this troubled world, and where is the scene in which we can play that role?"

Can we ignore that there is a Muslim world to which we are tied by bonds which are not only forged by religious faith, but also tightened by the facts of history? . . . It is not in vain that our country lies to the southwest of Asia, close to the Arab world, whose life is intermingled with ours. . . . It is not in vain that Islamic civilization and Islamic heritage, which the Mongols ravaged in their conquest of the old Islamic capitals, retreated and found refuge in Egypt, where they found shelter and safety as a result of the counterattack with which Egypt repelled the invasion of these Tartars at Ein Galout.

All these are fundamental facts, whose roots lie deeply in our life. Whatever we do, we cannot forget them or run away from them.

DOCUMENT 3

Source: Mikhail Bakunin, nineteenth-century anarchist, "Principles of Revolution" (1869).

We recognize no other activity but the work of extermination, but we admit that the forms in which this activity will show itself will be extremely varied—poison, the knife, the rope, etc. In this struggle, revolution sanctifies everything alike.

DOCUMENT 4

Source: Sun Yat-sen, Chinese nationalist leader, founder of the Kuomintang, "Manifesto of the Nationalist Party" (1905).

We proclaim to the world in utmost sincerity the outline of the present revolution and the fundamental plan for the future administration of the nation. 1) *Drive out the Tartars*. The extreme cruelties and tyrannies of the Manchu government have now reached their limit. With the righteous army poised against them, we will overthrow that government, and restore our sovereign rights. 2) *Restore China*. . . . 3) *Establish the Republic*. . . . 4) *Equalize land ownership*. The good fortune of civilization is to be shared equally by all the people of the nation. We should improve our social and economic organization, and assess the value of all the land in the country.

The above four points will be carried out in three steps in due order. The first period is government by military law. . . . The second period is that of government by a provisional constitution. . . . The third period will be government under the constitution.

DOCUMENT 5

Source: Kwame Nkrumah, leader of Ghana's independence movement, "The African Personality," speech delivered to a conference of independent African states (April 13, 1958).

Africa is the last remaining stronghold of colonialism. Unlike Asia, there are on the continent of Africa more dependent territories than independent sovereign nations. Therefore we, the free independent states of Africa, have a responsibility to hasten the total liberation of Africa.

I believe that there are lessons from the past that will help us in discharging this sacred duty. . . .

We, the delegates of this conference, in promoting our foreign relations, must endeavor to seek the friendship of all and the enmity of none. We must stand for international peace and security, in conformity with the United Nations charter.

This will enable us to assert our own African personality and to develop our own ways of life, our own customs, traditions, and cultures. . . .

As independent states, it is in our mutual interest to explore trade possibilities between our respective countries, while at the same time enlarging our trade with the rest of the world. In this connection, we should exchange our own efforts to develop our economies, and so strengthen our political independence. . . .

We must also examine ways and means to broaden and strengthen our association with one another through such means as the exchange of students and the visits of cultural, scientific, and technical missions . . . and the establishment of libraries specializing in various aspects of African history and culture which may become centers of research. . . .

If we can as independent African states show by our own efforts that we can settle our own problems in Africa, then we shall be setting an example to others. . . . For this reason it may be necessary for this conference to examine the possibility of setting up some sort of machinery to maintain the links we shall forge here and to implement the decisions we shall reach. . . .

Today we are one. . . . An injury to one is an injury to all of us. From this conference must go out a new message: "Hands off Africa! Africa must be free!"

DOCUMENT 6

Source: Gloria Steinem, American feminist, "Far from the Opposite Shore" (1978).

Even the late suffragists, the ones who are most often labeled reformers because of their concentration on the vote, used radical tactics. Yes, they lobbied politely, sometimes, and took tea with their friends in Congress, but they also picketed the White House and engaged in the civil disobedience that those same congressmen abhorred. . . .

Chaining themselves to the White House fence, going to jail, declaring a hunger strike, being cruelly force-fed: those events are now famous. But the range of tactics [also] included humor, theatrics, passive resistance, [and] persuasion.

DOCUMENT 7

Source: Mao Tse-tung, leader of the Chinese Communist Party, "The Peasant Movement in Hunan" (1926).

In a very short time, . . . several hundred million peasants will rise like a mighty storm. . . . There are three alternatives. To march at their head and lead them? To trail behind them, gesticulating and criticizing? Or to stand in their way and oppose them?

Every revolutionary comrade should know that the national revolution requires a great change in the countryside. The Revolution of 1911 did not bring about this change, hence its failure. This change is now taking place, and it is an important factor for the completion of the revolution. Every revolutionary comrade must support it, or he will be taking the stand of counterrevolution.

DOCUMENT 8

Source: Teodora Ignacia Gomes, member of the African Party for the Independence of Guinea and Cape Verde, interview given to journalist (1974).

If we construct a society without exploitation of man by man, then of course women will be free in that society. Our struggle for national liberation is one way of assuring the liberation of women, because by doing the same work as men, or by doing work that ensures the liberation of our country, a woman will convince herself that she is able to do the same work as men. . . . This is important because it convinces women that they have potential and shows men what that potential is.

DOCUMENT 9

Source: Henry David Thoreau, American philosopher and activist, *On the Duty of Civil Disobedience* (1848).

Can there not be a government in which majorities do not virtually decide right and wrong, but conscience?

. . . How does it become a man to behave toward this American government today? I answer that he cannot without disgrace be associated with it. I cannot for an instant recognize that political organization as *my* government which is the *slave's* government also.

All men recognize the right of revolution; that is, the right to refuse allegiance to and to resist the government, when its tyranny or its inefficiency are great and unendurable.

. . . I do not hesitate to say, that those who call themselves abolitionists should at once effectually withdraw their support, both in person and property, from the government of Massachusetts, and not wait till they constitute a majority of one. . . .

Under a government which imprisons any unjustly, the true place for a just man is also a prison. . . . A minority is powerless while it conforms to the majority . . . but it is irresistible when it clogs by its whole weight. If the alternative is to keep all just men in prison, or give up war and slavery, the State will not hesitate which to choose. If a thousand men were not to pay their tax-bills this year, that would not be a violent and bloody measure, as it would be to pay them, and enable the State to commit violence and shed innocent blood.

DOCUMENT 10

Source: Fidel Castro, Cuban revolutionary and national leader, "Fidel Castro Speaks on Marxism-Leninism," television address (December 1, 1961).

Do I have any doubt about Marxism and do I feel that certain interpretations were wrong and have to be revised? No, I do not have the slightest doubt!

What occurs to me is precisely the opposite: the more experience we gain from life, the more we learn what imperialism is . . . the more we have to face up to that imperialism. . . . [T]he more we dig deeper and uncover the bloody claws of imperialism, the crimes they commit against humanity, the more we feel sentimentally Marxist, emotionally Marxist, and the more we see and discover all the truths contained in the doctrine of Marxism. The more we have to face the reality of a revolution and the class struggle . . . the more convinced we become of all the truths Marx and Engels wrote and the truly ingenious interpretations of scientific socialism Lenin made.

We had to choose between remaining under the domination, under the exploitation, and, furthermore, the insolence of imperialism, to go on putting up with Yankee ambassadors giving the orders here, keeping our country in the state of poverty it was in, or making an anti-imperialist revolution, making a socialist revolution. There was no alternative. We chose the only honorable road. . . . [T]here was no room for any other position.

DOCUMENT 11

Source: Marie-Aimée Helie-Lucas, participant in the Algerian War of Independence against French colonization, paper delivered at the International Symposium on Women and the Military System (1987).

[We] "liberated" women were in the kitchen, or sewing clothes (or flags?), carrying parcels, typing. Nevertheless, since there was "no humble task in the revolution," we did not dispute the roles we had.

This is the real harm which comes with liberation struggles: The overall task of women during liberation is seen as symbolic. Faced with colonization, the people have to build a national identity based on their own values, traditions, religion, language, and culture. Women bear the heavy burden of safeguarding this threatened identity. And this burden exacts its price.

DOCUMENT 12

Source: Mohandas K. Gandhi, member of the Indian National Congress and leader of the Indian independence movement, letter to Russian novelist Leo Tolstoy (1909).

These Indians [living in South Africa] have for several years labored under various legal disabilities. The prejudice against color and in some respect against Asiatics is intense in that colony. . . . The climax was reached three years ago, with a law which I and many others considered to be degrading and calculated to unman those to whom it was applicable. I felt that submission to a law of this nature was inconsistent with the spirit of true religion. I and some of my friends were and still are firm believers in the doctrine of non-resistance to evil. The result has been that nearly one-half of the Indian population [of Transvaal], that was unable to stand the heat of the struggle, to suffer the hardships of imprisonment, have withdrawn from the Transvaal rather than submit to a law which they have considered degrading. Of the other half, nearly 2,500 have for conscience's sake allowed themselves to be imprisoned, some as many as five times. . . . The struggle still continues, and one does not know when the end will come. This, however, some of us at least have seen most clearly, that passive resistance will and can succeed where brute force must fail.

POSSIBLE ANSWER:

On many occasions throughout modern history, when normal political and legal means have failed to bring about necessary or desired change, political groups, social movements, and individuals have turned to more drastic or more radical forms of transformation.

The documents included in this question all relate to various changes—national liberation, decolonization, the overthrow of oppressive regimes, the inclusion of women in politics, and the abolition of unjust laws—brought about by various means *other* than governmental reform or parliamentary action. As discussed in this essay, these means include the formation of nationalist or pan-cultural movements, revolution inspired by radical ideologies, and civil disobedience. In such cases, when any of these means is necessary to solve a social or political problem, it is a clear sign that the preexisting system—be it monarchy, democracy, or colonizing power—has, in a fundamental sense, failed.

[Note how the introduction provides a thesis (even a secondary thesis, about how the means of change discussed here result from large-scale political or social failure). The thesis is simple, based on a grouping of the means of political and social change into three categories. Be aware, however, that in the body of the essay, the documents themselves will be grouped into FOUR categories.]

One group of documents—#4, #2, and #5—provides examples of how nationalist movements have sought to bring about change. In his "Manifesto of the Nationalist Party" (#4), Chinese nationalist Sun Yat-sen, father of the Chinese Republic that replaced the Qing Dynasty in 1911, addresses the problem of how to remove an oppressive regime. "The Philosophy of the Revolution" (#2), by Egyptian leader Gamal Nasser, and "The African Personality" (#5), a speech given by African nationalist Kwame Nkrumah, focus on what to do *after* liberation has been achieved.

Although Sun Yat-sen speaks of land reform and constitutional rule in his manifesto, his primary emphasis is on nationalism (hence the name of his party, the Kuomintang, or Nationalist Party) and the sharp differentiation between ethnic Chinese and the foreign Manchu, or Qing, overlords who ruled them. Did this nationalist approach succeed? Only partly. The Manchus indeed fell in 1911, and a republic was formed. But democracy did not appear—even Sun himself had argued that military control over the government would be necessary for a time—and, as Mao Tse-tung observes in "The Peasant Movement in Hunan" (#7), the new republic did not succeed in bringing about change in the countryside. In the end, the Chinese Republic collapsed into authoritarianism, warlordism, anarchy, and civil war.

Nasser, one of the most charismatic and successful leaders of the postwar Middle East, became renowned for his reliance on national sentiment, rather than democratic rule, to rally his newly liberated Egyptians to his cause. And not just Egyptians. Writing from the perspective of an anti-Western (especially anti-British) leader of a country recently freed from foreign dominance, as well as a country at the crossroads of the Middle East and Islamic North Africa, Nasser discusses his goal of collective action as a means for Muslim states to assert themselves against the previously hegemonic Western world. This appeal was only partly successful. Although Nasser created a strong, modern, independent (if somewhat authoritarian) Egypt, he largely failed in his goal of fostering a wide movement of pan-Arab nationalism, a goal toward which "The Philosophy of the Revolution" is directed.

Nkrumah, leader of Ghana, the first of Britain's colonies in sub-Saharan Africa to gain freedom, also discusses multinational and regional cooperation as a means by which newly decolonized states can make their way in the modern world. Nkrumah's pan-Africanism, however, although well intentioned, was too utopian to succeed in an Africa plagued by too much ethnic, tribal, and linguistic diversity, not to mention the inefficiency, corruption, and violence that made up the legacy of European colonization.

[These first paragraphs discuss the first group of documents. Note how the essay attributes each document in several ways: by number, author, AND title. To be on the safe side, do this as much as possible. Also note how the documents are not just listed or summarized. They are discussed in the context of the thesis, their political ideals are evaluated in terms of success or failure, and they are supplemented with relevant historical information. A detailed point of view is provided in the case of Nasser. Because there are so many documents in this DBQ, it is not necessary to provide detailed point of view for every document. If there were fewer documents, you would need to provide point of view for almost all of them, in order to get full credit.]

From a different perspective, a second cluster of documents illustrates not a type of political action but, instead, a problem common to many revolutions and national liberation movements: the failure or unwillingness to recognize or reward the efforts of women. As early as the French Revolution, despite the fact that they played a brave and important role in the transformation of their country, women were not included among the "Men" and "Citizens" to whom the revolutionary government's declaration of rights applied—and, indeed, women in France did not even get the vote until near the end of World War II.

Likewise, the difficulty women have experienced in gaining benefits from the revolutions and movements they have worked for is shown in documents #8 and #11. Teodora Gomes, a freedom activist agitating for the independence of Guinea and Cape Verde, speaks in an interview (#8) of the importance of ensuring that issues of women's equality are included in the struggle for decolonization. Although she does not directly state that there is a problem, the fact that she finds it necessary to speak of the matter at all indicates that a problem most likely does exist.

In a presentation given at an international symposium on women and military affairs (#11), Marie-Aimée Helie-Lucas is much more forthright and bitter about this problem. Helie-Lucas's bitterness stems from her point of view: that of a woman who took part in the Algerian War of Independence from France, but was deeply disappointed in how women's concerns were ignored and how their contributions were undervalued. Also, she states, too many women were kept in traditional roles, such as cooking, sewing, and domestic labor, during the war. As in the French Revolution more than a century and a half before, Algerian women, according to Helie-Lucas, did not receive the rewards they deserved as participants in their country's efforts to free itself. To back up Helie-Lucas's complaints, as well as Gomes's more subtly expressed concerns, it would be helpful to have documents containing figures detailing the number of women taking part in national liberation movements, as well as descriptions of what kind of work they were doing outside the home. Male commentary on the role of women in such movements would be illuminating, if only for purposes of contrast.

[These paragraphs deal with a second group of documents, but not the second form of social and political change mentioned in the introduction. This is clearly stated, to avoid confusing the reader. Also, the opening sentence clearly marks the transition to "a second cluster of documents," to show the reader that the essay is well organized. Note how historical content is used to flesh out the documents. For the second time, in the case of Helie-Lucas, point of view is addressed directly. Also, in speaking of other forms of documents that would be helpful, this paragraph fulfills another requirement of the DBQ rules.]

One of the more frequent—and dramatic—forms of social and political change in the modern world has been revolution, often animated by radical, very commonly Marxist, ideology. A third group of documents, consisting of #3, #1, #7, and #10, speaks to this means of change. In "Principles of Revolution" (#3), the nineteenth-century prophet of anarchism, the Russian radical Mikhail Bakunin, advocates the most extreme form of political transformation: revolution carried out by any means necessary, including violence. Bakunin was driven to this view partly by his own personality, partly by his frustration at the apparent impossibility of democratic and legal change in nations as repressive as the German states, the Habsburg Empire of Austria-Hungary, and his native Russia. In arguing that "revolution sanctifies everything alike," Bakunin's reasoning restates the age-old extremist dictum that the ends justify the means.

Vladimir Lenin of Russia, the founder of the Soviet Union, the world's first communist state, subscribed to the same idea. In an excerpt from his essay *What Is To Be Done?* (#1), he argues that a communist uprising, traditionally viewed by Marx as an open mass movement of the working class, should be coordinated and led by a small, conspiratorial party of professional revolutionaries, operating secretly and under highly disciplined leadership. Lenin's restrictive, antidemocratic approach can be explained partially by his own temperament, but largely by his point of view: that of a leader of an illegal party in a repressive state, where the government made use of a large, powerful, and ruthless secret police force. Understandable or not, Lenin's insistence on the closed, conspiratorial approach split the Russian Communists into two movements—the Mensheviks and Lenin's Bolsheviks—and was one of the many factors that, much later, helped transform the Soviet Union from a state founded on utopian working-class ideals to a rigid dictatorship.

Almost two and a half decades after Lenin wrote *What Is To Be Done?*, Chinese Communist Mao Tse-tung pondered the question of how to apply Marxism in his own country, on the other side of the Eurasian landmass. In "The Peasant Movement in Hunan" (#7), Mao expresses his conviction that the key to successful revolution in China is to harness the radicalism of the peasantry. Events proved him correct, since it was mainly the support of the countryside that brought the Chinese Communist Party to power in 1949. Although Mao in 1926 was correct in condemning the failure of the government of 1911 to carry out land reform after toppling the imperial regime, Mao's own efforts to revolutionize the countryside in the 1950s and 1960s, culminating in the Great Leap Forward, led to famine and the mass starvation of countless millions.

Another example of the often contradictory results of Marxist revolution comes from Cuba, where Fidel Castro took power in 1959. Castro's television address of December 1961 (#10) illustrates his dogmatic, almost slavish adherence to Marxist-Leninist doctrine. To Castro, Marxism-Leninism is the most effective tool in combatting the imperial, hegemonic tendencies of the Western world, especially the United States. And yet rigid adherence to Marxist-Leninist communism, while having modernized Cuba to some extent, has also led to a high degree of dictatorship and repression.

In all these cases, it would be helpful to have statistics on how many people were imprisoned or executed by these regimes for political reasons. Also, in the case of document #7, it would be helpful to have census data related to China's peasant population.

[These paragraphs, like the ones in the previous section, provide an effective grouping. See how the transition to this part of the discussion is explicitly noted ("A third group of documents . . ."). The essay continues to provide proper attribution, an abundance of historical content and evidence, and ideas about other types of documents that would be useful. Lenin's and Bakunin's points of view are mentioned outright; point of view in other cases is implied.]

Another time-honored form of bringing about social and political change is civil disobedience, or nonviolent resistance. One of the earliest and most renowned philosophical justifications for this measure was provided during the mid-1800s by the American thinker and essayist Henry David Thoreau, in *On the Duty of Civil Disobedience* (#9). Even open and democratic governments, Thoreau argues, can do wrong. Particularly upset about the Mexican-American War, which many Americans perceived as unjust, and even more so by the institution of slavery, Thoreau asks whether a person of good conscience can justifiably violate the laws of his own society. If in a principled cause, and done without violence, Thoreau maintains that the answer is "yes."

Feminist Gloria Steinem, in the essay "Far from the Opposite Shore" (#6), motivates the women's liberation movement of the 1970s by relating how suffragettes of the late 1800s and early 1900s made spirited use of unlawful, but nonviolent, civil disobedience to fight for equal rights and the vote (the fact that Steinem is writing to a modern audience for political purposes should be taken into account when evaluating her version of history).

Perhaps the most widely admired advocate of civil disobedience is Mohandas K. Gandhi, the spiritual father of modern, independent India. In a 1909 letter (#12), Gandhi explains his philosophy of passive resistance—which combined legal principle, political action, and Hindu faith in a unique way—to the Russian novelist Leo Tolstoy, himself a well-known activist and pacifist. Over the next three and a half decades, Gandhi's method of *satyagraha* (spiritually motivated, nonviolent resistance) would prove a highly effective tool in persuading the British to leave India and set it free. As admirable and effective as civil disobedience has been, however, it does has its limits. Gandhi's confident assertion that "passive resistance will and can succeed where brute force must fail" applies only in liberal or democratic societies where law and popular opinion impose certain checks on the frequent or indiscriminate use of brute force. It is difficult to imagine *satyagraha*, or any form of civil disobedience, bringing about much change when targeted against a truly dictatorial society, such as Hitler's, Stalin's, or Mao Tse-tung's.

[These paragraphs provide a final grouping. As always, the opening of a new section is marked clearly ("Another time-honored form of bringing about social and political change . . ."). Note the historical information, as well as the balanced but critical evaluation of the concept of civil disobedience. Attribution is complete, and there are partial discussions of Thoreau's and Steinem's, and even Gandhi's, points of view.]

Of course, none of the documents provided discuss what is perhaps the most desirable and most effective means of meaningful social and political change. That is, the proper functioning of parliamentary or democratic government. As a general rule (but not always), changes wrought in this manner tend to be the most durable and the fairest for all. Conversely, although the documents provide examples of one extremist form of change—communist revolution—they make no mention of another all-too-common form of extremism: communism's polar opposite, fascism. Documents demonstrating fascist excess and the effective operation of democracy would perhaps have been useful.

[This brief conclusion helps to cap off the essay. It also raises issues not covered before, either in the essay or the documents themselves. It also makes two more suggestions about other documents that could be helpful in answering the question.]

SECTION E

Change-over-Time Essay Question Strategies

The second essay you will be asked to write on the Advanced Placement Examination in World History is the change-over-time (COT) question. The goal of this exercise is to test your ability to trace the way a broad trend or development operates over a long period of time. Topics you will be expected to write about may include cultural interchange, global trade, the movements and migrations of peoples, the role of minorities in a given society, the status of women, environmental issues, biological developments, changes in technology, artistic and cultural attitudes, and scientific innovations.

From the foregoing list, it should be clear that the COT lends itself to a topical approach. In order to be able to follow how a particular issue changed or stayed the same through long periods of time, consult the overviews that appear at the beginning of Units Two through Six. These overviews attempt to track "big-picture" issues as they played out over different historical eras.

Moreover, as you read through the material covered in Units Two through Six, try to keep in mind how long-term trends develop, not just within individual geographical areas, but overall.

APPROACHING THE CHANGE-OVER-TIME ESSAY

As with all essays, be sure to follow the General Tips for Essay Writing provided in Unit One, Section D.

You will be given 40 minutes to complete the COT. You should spend 5 or so minutes (no more than 10) looking over the question, thinking about it, then organizing and outlining your thoughts.

The COT will request that you trace and analyze the evolution of a broad historical trend or phenomenon over a long period of time. The period of time may be anywhere from a century or two to a thousand years or more. You will most likely be asked to focus on a particular nation (or nations) or geographical region (or regions). You may be given a choice as to which region you wish to write about.

Graders will judge your essay based on how well you do the following:

- *Define and support your thesis.* Your thesis should address the global issue and the time period specified, as well as the geographical area in question, if one is assigned.
- *Address all parts of the question.*
- *Substantiate your thesis with appropriate historical evidence.* Even though you are writing from a macroscopic perspective, you need to provide concrete details and facts to make your general conclusions convincing.

- *Discuss both change and continuity.* Depending on how important or interesting the balance between how much things change and how much they stay the same is, your thesis may be centered on this issue.
- *Relate your comparisons to a larger global context.* If possible, show how the trend you are discussing relates to other broad global developments. If you are writing about technological innovation in a certain society, for example, is it somehow tied with that society's move toward industrialization? Or, if you are discussing the importance of religion in a certain society, can you draw any conclusions about the religion's effect on that society's treatment of women? Be careful here, though, because you do not want to get too far off topic as you write.

SAMPLE QUESTION

2. Choose one of the following regions. Discuss the changes and continuities in how women were treated—socially, economically, and politically—from 1000 to the late 1700s. If a woman's social class factored into the way she was treated, be sure to discuss that in your answer.

Latin America
Europe
China and Japan
sub-Saharan Africa

SAMPLE ANSWER:

Throughout most of the period lasting from 1000 to the late 1700s, the status that European women were forced to occupy can best be summed up in the phrase "worst of both worlds." In other words, women had responsibilities without rights. Throughout the medieval period, the Renaissance, and the early modern era, most women, regardless of class, labored diligently, assumed many social and economic functions, and proved themselves the intellectual equal of men. And yet nowhere in Europe did women enjoy equal status with men. Inequality persisted long after the late 1700s. Only by the end of the nineteenth and the beginning of the twentieth centuries did large, determined women's movements began to make headway in reducing the inequality between the genders. Even then, it was not until after the world wars that the effects of their efforts made themselves more broadly felt. The position of women in European society has undergone many changes since the year 1000, but the most substantial of those changes were very long in coming—and they have still not succeeded in creating conditions of complete gender equality.

[This introduction takes care to mention class differences (albeit briefly) and make note of different historical time frames in European history between 1000 and the late 1700s. Note how it also places gender developments in an even wider time frame, sketching a brief outline up to the present (the conclusion does this as well; see the last three paragraphs). As well, the essay provides a clear thesis, which addresses not only the issue of women themselves, but also the question of change versus continuity.]

During the medieval period and the Renaissance, the vast majority of European women belonged to the peasant class. Their lot was difficult. The gender division of labor that had prevailed in most agricultural societies since the end of the Stone Age was very much present in medieval and Renaissance Europe. Therefore, women were expected to maintain the household, give birth, and care for children and the family. In addition, they were required to perform various farming tasks and chores. Despite her hard work and many obligations, the peasant woman was, legally and socially, very much the inferior of her male counterpart. Law codes gave her a distinctly secondary status. Although, depending on the time and place in which she lived, she might have certain inheritance and property rights, they were less extensive than those of men. Spousal abuse was common, and, due to the primitive state of medical care, many women—up to 15 percent—died in childbirth.

During the Middle Ages and Renaissance, religious and cultural prejudice played a role in keeping women of all classes in a subordinate status. Both Roman Catholicism and, in the eastern parts of Europe, Eastern Orthodoxy subscribed to the doctrine of original sin, which placed the blame for humanity's expulsion from the Garden of Eden squarely on Eve's shoulders. By extension, the established Christian churches believed that all women were more sinful than men. Not only did the Catholic and Orthodox clergy believe this, but they inculcated this view among the population at large, providing yet another "justification" for the subjugation of women.

The position of middle- and upper-class women during the Middle Ages and the Renaissance was somewhat more complex than that of lower-class women, but it was still secondary. In the small but gradually growing middle class, women had property rights, often received some kind of education, and frequently assisted their husbands in running businesses or trades. During the High Middle Ages, the Late Middle Ages, and the Renaissance, the importance of trade and money-based economic exchange increased, making the middle class—and hence the women in it—greater in number and importance.

Among the aristocracy, women were frequently well educated. Free from the hard labor of peasant women, women of the noble class played a crucial role in managing households, castles, and estates. They often had a great deal of informal influence over politics, as advisers to husbands. Women with large territorial inheritances—such as Eleanor of Aquitaine—were especially important in medieval and Renaissance political life. Some of the most dynamic and powerful rulers of this period, such as Isabella of Castile and Elizabeth I of England, were women, although they were anything but typical. Although they were relatively privileged, upper-class women were not equal to men. As did warrior elites in most feudal societies, Europe's knightly class idealized women, but condescended to them as well. The cult of chivalry placed the noble-born lady on a pedestal, but as a beautiful object that was fragile, not as an equal partner.

A number of medieval and Renaissance upper-class women (typically younger daughters, for whom it was too expensive to provide dowries for marriage) went into religious life, where they often found a cultured life and an intellectual haven. One example is the nun Hildegard von Bingen, a renowned mystic and musical composer. A few women distinguished themselves intellectually in the secular sphere. The most famous is the Renaissance author Christine de Pisan.

[The preceding five paragraphs provide a great deal of historical evidence to make points about the medieval era and the Renaissance. These include specific facts, concepts, and individuals. A good deal of attention is paid to class differences.]

Women remained subordinate to men during the 1500s, 1600s, and 1700s—or, in other words, most of the early modern period. Among the peasantry, conditions changed little. Women were still expected to work at home and on the farm, and they were still treated as second-class.

Lower-class women in the cities (or women hovering between the lower and middle classes) worked as servants, nurses, shopkeepers, artisans, and governesses. In the urban environment, many women were forced into prostitution in order to survive.

During the early modern period, the middle class was expanding, and women of this social stratum assumed an increasingly important role in economic life. They tended to be better educated, especially since the invention of the printing press led to higher literacy rates among the middle classes. Women of this class, as well as the upper class, became increasingly involved in cultural and intellectual life, such as the Italian artist Artemisia Gentileschi and the German astronomer Maria Winkelmann.

In addition, the great premium placed by the Protestant Reformation—popular among the emerging middle classes in northern and parts of western Europe—on reading the Bible for one's self contributed to the increased quality of Protestant women's education (however, just as Orthodoxy and Catholicism relegated women to a secondary, sinful status, so did the Lutheran and Calvinist forms of Protestantism).

Women of the upper classes made even greater strides forward. On the whole, their property and inheritances increased, and their legal standing improved. Like women of the middle class, they found themselves able—to a limited extent—to become involved in scientific work, philosophical debates, and arts and letters. As Enlightenment philosophy swept over the intellectual life of Europe during the 1700s, women of the aristocracy played a key role in patronizing the great thinkers of the era and organizing the famous salons at which so many new ideas were aired.

More than a few women played an even more direct role in shaping the Enlightenment, such as Catherine the Great of Russia (a woman of formidable intellect, greatly interested in philosophy) and the English writer Mary Wollstonecraft, whose *Vindication of the Rights of Women* is one of modern Europe's first, and most important, major philosophical justifications of women's equality. Along with Catherine the Great, Maria Theresa of Austria was one of the eighteenth century's "enlightened monarchs."

[These six paragraphs cover the early modern period of European history. They are rich in historical detail. They deal with several countries (even, tangentially, the United States). They continue to explore the differences that class made in how women were treated. They deal with politics, culture, economics, and social status.]

At the end of the 1700s, Europe was on the cusp of the early modern and modern eras. During this era, the entire Western world was affected by political revolution, in France, the United States, and other areas. It was also beginning to undergo the massive economic and social transformation known as the Industrial Revolution. Both political and economic revolution affected women.

Certainly, during the French Revolution, women of all classes played tremendously important roles: they helped to storm the Bastille, they marched to Versailles to bring the royal family back to Paris, they worked at home to support France's war effort, and much, much more. Despite this, however, women were not allowed to enjoy the full fruits of the freedom and justice the Revolution claimed to be about. Quite pointedly, the founding document of the Revolution, the Declaration of the Rights of Man and the Citizen, did not include women. And when actress-playwright Olympe de Gouges attempted to remedy this by proposing her own Declaration of the Rights of Woman and the Citizeness, she was rebuffed—and eventually perished in the Reign of Terror.

France, however, was not alone in depriving full rights to women. Even though political and social change had come to the entire Western world, from Boston and Philadelphia to Moscow and St. Petersburg, in no place was any revolutionary group or political party prepared to accept the notion that women should be equal to men, politically, socially, economically, or otherwise. The nineteenth-century cult of domesticity and Victorian morality suffocated women further. Voices such as John Stuart Mill's or Emmeline Pankhurst's, calling for women's suffrage and fair treatment of both genders during the 1800s, were very lonely indeed—and although more and more women were distinguishing themselves in art, literature, science, and other fields of endeavor, the majority had a long path to travel before they gained the vote and a measure of social and economic equality.

[The preceding three paragraphs form an extensive conclusion that summarizes the arguments and points made by the essay overall. It also extends its argument by looking forward to the period beyond the early 1900s. You should attempt to write a conclusion if you have time, in order to give your essay a finished feel. On the other hand, it is more important for the main body of the essay to be strong. If you are pressed for time, focus more on the points and arguments contained in the essay itself, and omit the conclusion.]

SECTION F

Comparative Essay Question Strategies

The last exercise you will complete on the Advanced Placement Examination in World History is the comparative essay. As its name suggests, the comparative essay will ask you to compare and contrast the ways in which different societies deal with major issues and phenomena. These may include technological innovation; the social and economic impact of warfare; the treatment of minorities and women; the evolution of political systems; international trade and economic exchange; and systems of labor organization.

The organizers of the Advanced Placement Examination in World History consider the comparative approach to be especially important. The overviews that precede Units Two through Six provide lists of issues that lend themselves well to comparative questions. Read them carefully. In addition, as you study the material covered in Units Two through Six, think about broad patterns of historical development and see if you can come up with examples of major developments that most, if not all, societies undergo as they evolve historically.

APPROACHING THE COMPARATIVE ESSAY

As with all essays, be sure to follow the General Tips for Essay Writing provided in Unit One, Section D.

You will be given 40 minutes to complete the comparative essay. You should spend 5 or so minutes (no more than 10) looking over the question, thinking about it, then organizing and outlining your thoughts.

The comparative essay will require you to compare and contrast how at least two (perhaps more) civilizations or nations have undergone or responded to a historical event or experience. You must be sure to give equal weight to both (or all) civilizations or nations specified in the question. You should also be sure to balance similarities and differences, although you may decide that one is more important than the other.

Graders will judge your comparative essay based on how well you do the following:

- Define and support your thesis.
- Address all parts of the question.
- Substantiate your thesis with appropriate historical evidence.
- Make relevant and direct comparisons between the societies you are discussing.
- Discuss both similarities and differences.
- Relate your comparisons to a larger global context.

Because the central task of the comparative essay is so heavily focused on comparison, rather than a specific theme, developing a strong thesis for a comparative essay may sometimes appear difficult. The question, or the way you want to answer it, may not lend itself to a clear-cut theme or argument. In that event, you can still create a thesis statement by stating that, in the case you are discussing, the likenesses outweigh the differences. Or, the differences may seem more important than the likenesses. You may argue that likenesses and differences are equally balanced. This is not the most sophisticated approach, but it will fulfill the requirement that you provide a thesis. Note that this is the approach taken in the introductory paragraph of the sample answer that follows.

SAMPLE QUESTION

3. Among the non-Western cultures that first followed the nations of Europe and North America in industrializing, Japan stands out as the most successful. In what ways did Japan adhere to the pattern of industrialization set by the West, and in what ways did Japan depart from it? How was Japan's industrializing experience similar to that of the West, and how was it different?

SAMPLE ANSWER:

Both the nations of the West and Japan spent at least part of the 1800s industrializing, although they did so half a world apart and almost a century separated in time. In many respects, Japanese industrialization proceeded along much the same lines that Western industrialization did. Industrialization altered both civilizations' economic practices beyond recognition, dramatically changed the class composition of their societies, elevated their level of scientific and technological advancement, and increased their ability (not to mention willingness) to use military force to affect world events. On the other hand, Western and Japanese industrialization began in different ways and under different circumstances. Some of industrialization's results were, in both societies, quite different as well. A detailed comparison of Western and Japanese industrialization demonstrates that the differences are as significant as the likenesses, if not more so.

[Note that a thesis is provided in the last sentence of the preceding paragraph.]

The most striking difference between Western and Japanese industrialization concerns origins. In the West, especially in late-eighteenth-century Britain, industrial practices emerged gradually (despite the somewhat misleading phrase "Industrial Revolution"). Also during the late 1700s and early 1800s, a number of people and parties were responsible for the rise of industrialization: artisans and craftsman who began using proto-industrial practices, aristocratic landowners who drove poorer farmers off their land by means of laws like the Enclosure Acts, middle-class mine owners and factory owners who saw machine power as a way to increase their profits, the engineers and scientists who built new machines and harnessed steam power, and so on.

In Japan, by contrast, industrialization was a government-sponsored policy, imposed from above after 1868. True, during the 1700s and early 1800s, a rising merchant class was gaining greater economic clout, and artisans were using proto-industrial methods. Still, the Tokugawa shoguns and the samurai class they shared power with were economically and politically conservative, and resisted change as much as possible. Until the arrival of the U.S. Navy in the 1850s, Japan's leaders also isolated Japan from the science, ideas, and technology of the outside world. Upon coming to power in 1868, the Emperor Meiji changed all this. Meiji's aim was to keep his country free of Western dominance. In particular, he sought to avoid the fate of nearby China, which had been opened up to Western trade in a humiliating fashion, both by force and intimidation. In contrast to the Qing emperors of China, Meiji decided to adopt the military and economic methods of the West. This meant industrializing Japan's economy. Although a number of non-Western parts of the world sought to industrialize and modernize in the Western style during the mid-to-late 1800s and early 1900s, Japan was by far the most successful.

[The preceding two paragraphs provide a key point of contrast. They also back up the thesis with historical evidence: the example of England, the discussion of Meiji. By mentioning China, as well as pointing to Japan's unique success, the second paragraph provides some global context.]

A second difference, therefore, is that industrialization was a "home-grown" phenomenon in the West, whereas it was imported into Japan. This was the case in many non-Western parts of the world, such as North Africa, the Ottoman Empire, and elsewhere, where industrialization practices were introduced by national rulers in a deliberate attempt to imitate the West, or transplanted into colonies by the imperial nations of the West.

A third difference is that industrialization helped to cause urbanization in the West (although a certain level of urbanization was necessary to get industrialization underway in the first place). Japan, on the other hand, was already heavily urbanized before it industrialized.

A fourth major difference between Western and Japanese industrialization involves the accelerated pace of the latter. Britain took several decades to industrialize. Even the other nations of western Europe, such as France, Prussia (later Germany), and others, took a long time to adopt industrial practices. Thanks to Meiji's efforts, Japan took much less time to industrialize. During the early 1870s, Meiji ended the last of Japan's feudal social and economic practices. By the 1880s and 1890s, Japan was well on its way to becoming a fully industrialized society.

Yet another difference involves the ways in which the industrial working class did or did not become politicized. In Europe and the United States, the industrial working class developed many means of struggling against the ways in which their employers exploited them. European and American workers formed trade unions and went on strike. They established political parties that fought for their rights in government. The more radical among them joined socialist, communist, and anarchist groups. By contrast, the Japanese government tightly restricted the working class, and trade unionism, radical movements, and the practice of going on strike were all very slow to develop in late-nineteenth- and early-twentieth century Japan.

Another difference is the degree to which industrialization led to the adoption of a capitalist style of economic organization. In the West, the move to industrialization coincided with the transition from mercantilism to capitalism. At least in countries such as France, Britain, and the United States, industrialization went hand-in-hand with the growing laissez-faire convictions that trade should be free and that governments should keep their hands off the workings of the economy. The Japanese regime, on the other hand, closely monitored and regulated the workings of the economy. In this case, Japanese industrialization was less capitalist and less laissez-faire than at least some countries in the West (it should be noted that some countries, such as Germany and Russia, industrialized in ways that were heavily state-regulated and not purely capitalist, and it is no coincidence that many of the economic and technical advisers who helped Japan industrialize were German).

Finally, because it industrialized later than the nations of western Europe and North America, Japan was able to learn from the mistakes of its predecessors. In many cases, factory owners and mine operators in nations such as Britain and France still used older methods and machines, because they were too expensive to replace, even as newer and better ones emerged. By contrast, Japan was able to take advantage of state-of-the-art machines and methods (incidentally, this was also the case with European nations that industrialized later in the 1800s, such as Germany and Russia, a factor that makes this comparison more complex).

[The preceding six paragraphs continue to contrast Western and Japanese industrialization. They also provide historical evidence, as well as a global context. They talk about the many ways

in which industrialization affected not just economics, but politics and society. Also note that, in several sentences, the essay makes the point that "the West" consists of many countries, some of which had a different approach to industrialization than others.]

Despite these many differences, there are also important similarities. In both cases, industrialization undercut the power and influence of traditional landowning aristocracies. The dukes, barons, counts, and so forth of Europe lost wealth and status, except for the few who were able to adapt to the new reality. In Japan, Meiji deprived the samurai class of its traditional rights and privileges.

In both Japan and the West, industrialization benefited the middle class and made its numbers grow. Factory owners, entrepreneurs, merchants, and bankers all profited from the new economic style. An economic system in which wealth was based on money, not land, was well suited to the middle class. Also, with wealth came increased social status and greater political power.

The effects of industrialization on the lower classes of Japan and the West were similar. In both cases, the traditional peasant class shrank. In both cases, an industrial working class sprang up quite quickly, and its numbers grew rapidly and steadily. Both in Japan and the West, the industrial working class was heavily exploited. Japanese and Western laborers experienced horrible workplace conditions, worked long hours, and received low wages. Although, in both cases, industrialization led to a general rise in national wealth and prosperity, it took a long time (decades in the Western case, years in Japan's) for that general rise to benefit the lower classes.

Another likeness is that, in both Japan and the West, industrialization increased military capacity and, just as important, the willingness of governments to use it. Starting around the 1840s, the Industrial Revolution began to have a real impact on the armies of the West, leading to the creation of modern rifles, modern artillery, steamships, and other advanced forms of weaponry. Later in the century, Japan adopted modern industrial weaponry as well. Indeed, the modernization of the military had been one of Meiji's principal reasons for industrializing in the first place.

Finally, and related to the above point, industrialization spurred the imperial ambitions of Japan and the West. The desire to gain new markets for manufactured goods, the need (and perceived right) to raw materials, and the dependence of modern steam-driven navies on coal bases around the world all stimulated the willingness of the West, then Japan, to use their modern military forces to conquer and colonize less technologically advanced parts of the world. By the end of the 1800s, Japan was targeting Manchuria, Korea, and the Chinese coast as a sphere of influence, just as Western nations had staked out empires around the globe. Famously, Japan became the first non-Western nation in the industrial era to develop a modern empire, and, during the Russo-Japanese War, the first to defeat a European power in the history of modern armed conflict.

[The preceding five paragraphs deal with likenesses. In keeping with the thesis declared at the beginning of the essay, the similarities are fewer than the differences. Nonetheless, they are important. So they must be described, backed up with historical evidence, and, when possible, placed in a global context.]

To conclude, Japan and Europe had similar experiences in terms of industrialization's undercutting the power and influence of landowning classes, bettering the lot of the middle class, expanding the number of factory workers, building up the military, and spurring imperial ambitions. However, when comparing industrialization in European countries with that in Japan, the differences appear to outweigh the likenesses. This essay has shown that industrialization markedly differed between European countries and Japan in terms of origins, how industrialization related to urbanization, how political industrialization became the extent to which a country adopted a capitalistic economic system, and when countries chose to industrialize.

[This conclusion summarizes the arguments and points made by the essay overall. You should attempt to write a conclusion if you have time, in order to give your essay a finished feel. On the other hand, it is more important for the main body of the essay to be strong. If you are pressed for time, focus more on the points and arguments contained in the essay itself, and omit the conclusion.]

UNIT TWO

Foundations of World Civilization

(ca. 4000 B.C.E.–1000 C.E.)

Unit Overview

GENERAL REMARKS

This unit is so wide-ranging in terms of time and geography that it is difficult to encapsulate in a brief overview. The purpose of this unit is to provide an understanding of the foundations of world civilization. The unit will also provide a geographical orientation, introducing the world's major landmasses and bodies of water.

Humanlike, or hominid, creatures emerged on earth approximately 3 to 4 million years ago. Modern humans (*Homo sapiens sapiens*) developed sometime between 100,000 and 250,000 years ago. According to most scholars, humanity's birthplace was Africa. From there, humans spread to the rest of the globe, starting around 100,000 years ago.

The period from approximately 5,000 or 6,000 years ago to 2.5 million years ago is referred to as the Stone Age. During this time, human communities took shape, but remained at a relatively primitive state of development, socially and technologically. After 10,000 or 12,000 years ago, however, thanks to the phenomenon generally known as the Neolithic revolution, human societies gradually became more advanced. Over time, various peoples learned how to domesticate plants and animals. They developed what are generally considered to be the basic attributes of civilized society. They practiced agriculture, invented systems of writing, and made metal (rather than stone) tools. They developed complex forms of social and political organization, and they employed sophisticated modes of economic exchange.

The first four civilized societies appeared between 4,000 and 5,500 years ago, or between 3500 and 2000 B.C.E. All four were born along the banks of major river systems. These civilizations were:

- The Sumerian-Babylonian civilization of Mesopotamia (the Tigris and Euphrates rivers)
- Egypt (the Nile River)
- The Indus valley civilization (the Indus River)
- Early China (the Yellow River, or Huang Ho)

Very quickly, other civilizations appeared throughout the world. By 1000 C.E., developed societies had emerged in Asia, Europe, North Africa, sub-Saharan Africa, North America, and Central and South America. Many of these civilizations were connected by trade, warfare, and other forms of interaction. All the major religions of the world had been born by 1000 C.E. as well.

BROAD TRENDS

GLOBAL POWER AND INTERNATIONAL RELATIONS

- Early on, the most advanced civilizations were to be found in the Middle East (especially the river valleys of Egypt and Mesopotamia) and China.
- As time passed, other developed societies emerged. Joining the Middle East and China as the most powerful and sophisticated regions was the Mediterranean world (particularly Greece and Rome).

- Cultures in North and South America were physically and culturally isolated from the rest of the continents.
- The cultures of Europe, North Africa, the Middle East, South Asia, and East Asia were all linked, directly or indirectly, by war, conquest, trade, travel, religious interaction, and cultural exchange.
- By 1000 C.E., several civilizations could claim to be among the world's most powerful and advanced, especially China and the Islamic caliphates. Europe was on the brink of joining the ranks of powerful and influential civilizations.

POLITICAL DEVELOPMENTS

- With the development of agriculture during the Neolithic revolution, advanced forms of political organization began to appear.
- Most governments were monarchies (rule by a single leader) or oligarchies (rule by a small elite). More representative forms of government, such as republics and democracies, were very rare.
- In some cases, decentralized civilizations were governed by confederations of independent city-states (such as Greece) or feudal systems (such as medieval Europe).
- Many civilizations, by means of military conquest, built empires. Among the largest and longest lasting were Assyria's, Persia's, Rome's, and China's.

ECONOMIC DEVELOPMENTS

- Until the development of agriculture during the Neolithic revolution, systems of economic exchange remained quite primitive. Most prehistoric cultures, mainly hunting and gathering societies, lived at subsistence (they gathered or grew only enough food to feed themselves) and possessed few goods. There was very little specialization of labor. Any trade tended to be limited, and based on simple barter.
- The development of agriculture allowed the accumulation of food surpluses. This enabled some members of society to make a living by means other than growing food. This led to specialization of labor.
- Specialization of labor led to social stratification and the emergence of socioeconomic classes (upper-class aristocracies, middle-class merchants and artisans, lower-class urban dwellers and peasants).
- The switch from nomadic life to sedentary, or settled, life led people to develop the concept of private property.
- As settled civilizations encountered each other, they traded with each other. Trade became one of the most important forms of interaction between civilizations. Trade networks tended to follow waterways, for ease of transport. Trade routes were especially wide-ranging in Eurasia, connecting civilizations in Europe with those as far away as East Asia.
- Systems of currency (particularly coinage) were devised.

CULTURAL DEVELOPMENTS

- Even during the Stone Age, human beings expressed themselves artistically, by means of painting and music.
- Prehistoric societies buried their dead, worshiped gods, and practiced religious rituals.
- Systems of writing emerged in most civilized societies, starting around 3000 B.C.E.
- Systematic scientific observation, experimentation, and thought emerged, especially in China, the Middle East, and the Mediterranean world.
- The world's major religions were born.

GENDER ISSUES

- The ability of humans to mate when and with whom they chose gave rise to family units during the prehistoric era.
- Basic physical differences between the sexes led to a gender division of labor in most Stone Age societies.
- The emergence of agriculture deepened the gender division of labor. In most agricultural and settled societies, gender division gave rise to gender inequality.
- Organized religions often reinforced this sense of inequality.
- In most societies up to 1000 C.E., women were relegated to a secondary, subservient role. The degree of subservience depended on the society. In some cultures, women had at least some rights (divorce, inheritance, and ownership of property, for example). They might also exercise certain forms of influence within their societies or, at least, families. In other cultures, women had almost no rights or influence. Whatever the case, in almost no society were women granted a status equal to that of men.

COMPARATIVE ISSUES TO CONSIDER

- Various religions' conceptions of good, evil, proper behavior, and the universe itself
- The rise, organization, characteristics, and collapse of different empires (for example, Rome versus Han China)
- The treatment of women in different cultures
- Differing societies' attitudes toward patriarchy and family life
- The importance of cultural interaction and diffusion versus that of independent innovation in fostering technological, scientific, or cultural advancement
- Varying views of social hierarchy or caste systems
- Patterns of social and economic organization in major societies

KEY TERMS AND CONCEPTS

Pangaea and Panthalassa
Oceania
Eurasia
the seven continents: Africa, Antarctica, Asia, Europe, North America, South America, and the Middle East
Siberia
the Sahara
the Himalayas
the four oceans: Arctic Ocean, Atlantic Ocean, Indian Ocean, Pacific Ocean
the Mediterranean Sea
the Caribbean Sea
the Panama isthmus and canal
the Suez isthmus and canal
the Nile River
the Tigris and Euphrates rivers

the Indus and Ganges rivers
the Yangtze (Yangzi) and Yellow (Huang Ho) rivers
the Volga, Danube, and Rhine rivers
the Mississippi-Missouri river system
the Amazon River
prehistory versus history
features of civilization
stages of hominid development: australopithecines, *Homo habilis*, *Homo erectus*, *Homo sapiens* (Neanderthal and Cro-Magnon), *Homo sapiens sapiens* (modern humans)
the "Out of Africa" thesis versus the multiregional thesis
the Stone Age: the Paleolithic era (ca. 10,000 to 2.5 million years ago) and the Neolithic

era (ca. 5,000 or 6,000 to 10,000 years ago);
also the Mesolithic era (10,000 to 12,000
years ago)

family units, clans, and tribes

hunting and gathering (foraging) societies

gender division of labor

the Neolithic revolution (ca. 10,000 to 12,000
years ago)

the domestication of animals and plants:
pastoralism and agriculture

herding societies

civilization

the city

specialization of labor

metallurgy and metalworking

the Bronze Age (ca. 3500–1200 B.C.E.)

writing

Mesopotamia: Sumeria and Babylon

the Fertile Crescent (the Tigris and Euphrates
rivers)

cuneiform

the Gilgamesh epic

Hammurabi's law code

Egypt (the Nile River)

the Egyptian Book of the Dead

pyramids

hieroglyphics

Indus valley civilization (the Indus River)

early China (the Yellow River)

the Celts

the Hittites and iron weapons

the Assyrians and cavalry warfare

the Persian Empire

the Hebrews and monotheism

the Phoenicians and the alphabet

the Lydians and coinage

the Greek city-states (Sparta and Athens)

democracy

the Persian Wars

the Peloponnesian War

Alexander the Great

Hellenism

Homer

Socrates and Plato

Aristotle and the foundations of Western
scientific thought

the Roman Republic

plebeians versus patricians

the Punic Wars

Julius Caesar

the Roman Empire

China's Qin (Ch'in), Han, and Tang dynasties

Shi Huangdi

the Chinese tributary system

the Silk Road

Nara and Heian Japan

the Fujiwara clan

Lady Murasaki and *The Tale of Genji*

Central Asia and Mongolia

the Aryan invasion of India

the Dravidians

the Indian caste system

Ashoka

Constantinople and the Byzantine Empire

Justinian

early medieval Europe (the "Dark Ages")

feudalism

Charlemagne

Mohammed and the foundation of Islam

the Umayyad and Abbasid caliphates

the Bantu and their migrations

Nubia

Ghana

the Olmec

the Maya

Andean societies

the Mississippian culture

the Anasazi

cultural diffusion versus independent
innovation

class distinctions, hierarchy, and social
stratification

social mobility

caste systems

patriarchies and matriarchies

aristocracy (nobility or noble class)

parliamentary bodies

oligarchy

republics and democracies

theocracy

slavery versus serfdom

war

trade and trade routes

religious interaction and missionary activity

migration

the Bantu migrations, the Polynesian
migrations, and Eurasia's great age of
migrations

polytheism

Zoroastrianism (the Avestas)

Judaism and monotheism (the Ten
 Commandments, the Torah, the Talmud)
YHWH (Yahweh or Jehovah) and the
 Messiah
Abraham
Moses and the Exodus from Egypt (Passover)
David and Solomon
the Jewish Diaspora
Vedism (the Rig-Veda)
Hinduism (the Upanishads, the Mahabharata,
 the Bhagavad-Gita)
samsara, karma, and dharma
Brahma, Vishnu, and Shiva
the caste system (the Laws of Manu)
Buddhism (the Four Noble Truths and the
 Eightfold Path)
Siddhartha Gautama (the Buddha)
nirvana
Theravada (Hinayana) and Mahayana
 Buddhism

Daoism (the Tao-te Ching and the I Ching)
Laozi (Lao-tzu)
Confucianism (the Analects)
K'ung Fu-tzu (Confucius)
the Mandate of Heaven
the Judeo-Christian tradition
Jesus of Nazareth (Jesus Christ)
the Bible (Old and New testaments)
the Crucifixion and Resurrection (Easter)
Peter and Paul
Constantine and the Edict of Milan
Saint Augustine
Eastern Orthodoxy and Roman Catholicism
 (the Great Schism of 1054)
Islam (the Qur'an)
Allah
Mohammed
Mecca (the Kaaba) and Medina (the Hegira)
Sunni versus Shiite
Sufism

CHAPTER 1

Geographical Orientation

One of the key forces that shape any human society is the physical environment in which it lives and grows. A basic knowledge of the earth's major geographical features is indispensable for any real understanding of world history. This chapter will introduce the world's seven continents, four oceans, major seas, and important river systems.

CONTINENTS

Although the earth is approximately 5 billion to 6 billion years old, the present configuration of the continents dates back to less than 60 million years ago. Scientists speculate that, originally, all the earth's landmasses were clustered into a single supercontinent called Pangaea. Around 180 million to 200 million years ago, geological forces began to separate Pangaea into two smaller masses, Gondwanaland (which split further into the continents of South America, Africa, Australia, and Antarctica) and Laurasia (which later broke apart into Europe, Asia, and North America).

Although it is very large, the island of Greenland is not a continent. The vast island chains that make up the nations of Indonesia, Malaysia, and the Philippines are considered to be part of Asia. The thousands of islands sprinkled throughout the Pacific Ocean form no continent, but are often referred to as Oceania (a term that sometimes includes Australia). The continents of Europe and Asia are joined together, forming a larger landmass commonly referred to as Eurasia.

AFRICA

Africa is the second-largest continent, at 11.7 million square miles. Most paleontologists and anthropologists believe that the human race and its immediate ancestors originated here, then spread outward to the other continents. The northern third of Africa is home to the world's largest desert, the Sahara. Southern, or sub-Saharan, Africa consists mainly of grassland (savannah), rain forest, or thick woodland. At present, Africa is the third most populous continent. The ethnic, cultural, and linguistic diversity of this large continent is considerable.

ANTARCTICA

Antarctica, the third-smallest continent (5.4 million square miles), is also the world's coldest and least inhabited. Antarctica covers the earth's southern Pole. More than 90 percent of the continent is capped by a vast ice shelf, which supports very little plant or animal life. Antarctica has no native human population and, according to international treaty, no country exercises political control over it.

ASIA

Asia is by far the largest continent on earth, measuring over 17.3 million square miles. Thanks to its size, Asia contains the world's most diverse mix of climates, geographical features, and human inhabitants. The southwestern portion of Asia, commonly known as the Middle East (sometimes called the Near East or Mideast), is largely desert. The northern half of Asia consists of the huge Siberian subcontinent, over which stretches a massive forest (taiga) and, north of that, a permanently frigid zone called the tundra. Climatic conditions in Siberia are cold and inhospitable.

South of Siberia, in the regions of Central Asia, Mongolia, and much of China, is a band of deserts (including the Gobi, the world's second largest), open grasslands (steppe), and mountains (especially the Himalayas, the highest on the planet). The climates in these areas range from harsh to moderate. The island nation of Japan lies east of this portion of Asia.

The Indian subcontinent, southern China, and Southeast Asia (including the Philippines and the islands of Malaysia and Indonesia) are warmer and more thickly forested. The climate varies from temperate to tropical. Jungle is common. Seasonal winds called monsoons regulate the weather patterns in much of this part of Asia.

The population of Asia is incredibly diverse in terms of ethnicity, language, and religion. Asia is more populous than any other continent, with almost five times as many inhabitants as second-place Europe.

AUSTRALIA

Australia, the world's smallest continent, at 2.9 million square miles, is also the only one that consists of a single nation. Home to an indigenous population, the Aborigines (generally regarded as the earth's oldest surviving ethnic group), Australia was later colonized by settlers from Great Britain. The continent's eastern coast is largely grassland, with some mountains, and can sustain dense populations and agricultural activity. The western half of Australia is largely dry plain or desert, and much of the interior (known popularly as the outback or the bush) is arid and rocky. With the exception of Antarctica, Australia has the smallest population of any continent.

EUROPE

Europe, the second-smallest continent (3.8 million square miles), is the second largest in terms of population. It occupies the western end of the Eurasian landmass. It also includes the British Isles and Iceland, which lie off the continent's northwestern shore.

Although the northernmost regions of Europe are Arctic, the greatest part of the continent enjoys a mild, temperate climate. Only a few mountain ranges, particularly the Alps, break up what is otherwise a large flatland blanketed with woodlands and open plains. Rich in resources, nourished and linked together by many rivers, and ideally suited for agricultural production, most of Europe has been able to sustain sizable, prosperous populations. Largely because of these favorable conditions, the civilizations and countries of Europe have, during many periods of history, exerted great power and influence over the world.

NORTH AMERICA

North America is the third-largest continent, an expanse of 9.5 million square miles. It is the fourth most populated continent. North America's climate ranges from severely cold in the Arctic north to tropical in the rain forests of the far south. In between these two extremes is a tremendous mix of terrain: prairie, desert, mountains (the largest range being the Rockies), forest, flatlands, and more. North America's large middle belt is criss-crossed by a number of important river systems. Its climate is extremely temperate, and it contains a great wealth of animal, plant, and mineral resources. Over time, the middle portion of the continent, which today is made up of southern

Canada and the United States, has proven capable of supporting some of the world's largest, richest, and most technologically advanced population centers. North America is joined to its neighbor, South America, by a land bridge generally known as Central America or Mesoamerica. The actual point of connection is the Isthmus of Panama, where one of the world's most important canals is located.

SOUTH AMERICA

South America, at 6.8 million square miles, occupies fourth place among the seven continents in terms of size. Its population is the world's fifth largest. One of the world's largest mountain chains, the Andes, runs along most of South America's western coast. Highlands also dominate the continent's extreme north and its large east-central region. In the southeast are flatlands and open plains (the pampas). Through the middle north flows one of the world's greatest rivers, the Amazon, which feeds and waters the largest rain forest on the planet.

The climates of South America vary greatly. The mountainous regions tend to be cool and arid. The rain forest of the Amazon basin is tropical, while the southeast plains are temperate. The southernmost tip, which is not far from the Antarctic coast, is cold and dry.

OCEANS AND SEAS

Approximately three quarters of the planet's surface are covered by water. The four largest bodies of water are known as oceans. At first, when only one supercontinent (Pangaea) existed, there was only one world ocean, Panthalassa. The oceans in their present form began to take shape 200 million to 180 million years ago, when Pangaea split into separate continents, dividing parts of Panthalassa from each other.

Large bodies of water that are contained within oceans or partly landlocked are called seas. They are smaller than oceans. There are dozens of them worldwide.

Oceans and seas have both separated human societies and brought them closer together. For civilizations without the scientific knowledge and technological ability to cross them, large bodies of water were formidable barriers. However, for centuries, water transport remained much cheaper and more efficient than overland travel for economic exchange. Therefore, once they became navigable, oceans and seas offered societies with access to them an effective means by which to communicate, trade, fight, and interact with each other.

THE ARCTIC OCEAN

The Arctic Ocean is the world's smallest (at 5.1 million square miles), least understood, and least navigable. Bounded by Canada, Alaska, Siberia, Scandinavia, and Greenland, it is located at the top of the world. Near its center is the North Pole. Most of the year round, the Arctic Ocean is covered by thick pack ice, making it extremely difficult to travel in. As late as the middle of the twentieth century, many parts of the Arctic Ocean were still uncharted. Even to this day, shipping and economic activities in the Arctic remain limited.

THE ATLANTIC OCEAN

The Atlantic Ocean (33.4 million square miles) is the world's second largest. It links together four continents: North America, South America, Europe, and Africa. In the south it also touches upon Antarctica. Before the late fifteenth century C.E., the Atlantic facilitated trade, travel, and interaction between North and South America in the west, and between Europe and Africa in the east. But, with the exception of Leif Ericsson's short-lived Viking expedition from Greenland to Canada in the eleventh century C.E., there was, as far as scholars can tell, no transatlantic exchange between the two pairs of continents.

The voyages of Christopher Columbus and other European explorers in the late fifteenth and sixteenth centuries changed all that. From 1492 C.E. onward, cross-oceanic transportation and communication between the so-called Old World (Europe and Africa) and New World (the Americas) turned the Atlantic basin into a gigantic cauldron of economic, cultural, religious, ethnic, political, and military interaction. In both positive and negative ways, and for more than five hundred years, almost all of the peoples of these four continents have been shaped by the dynamic transformations brought about by transatlantic interconnectedness.

THE INDIAN OCEAN

The Indian Ocean is the world's third largest (28.3 million square miles). It joins the eastern coast of Africa, the southern portions of Asia (including the Middle East, the Indian subcontinent, and the peninsula and islands of Southeast Asia), and western Australia. Antarctica lies far to the south.

Travel and economic exchange along the Indian Ocean's coastline and among its islands has led to an incredible mixing and mutual interchange of ethnicities, religions and philosophies, goods and resources, and scientific and technological knowledge among Africans, Middle Easterners, and other Asians. Because the Indian Ocean can also be reached from the Atlantic Ocean (via the Red Sea or the southern tip of Africa) and the Pacific (which its eastern waters flow into at several points), it plays a vital role in connecting both larger bodies of water.

THE PACIFIC OCEAN

The Pacific Ocean is the world's largest (measuring 64.1 million square miles). It is also the deepest (the lowest point known on Earth is the Mariana Trench, at 35,810 feet below sea level). The Pacific is home to several massive island chains, the largest of which are Polynesia, Melanesia, and Micronesia. Frequently, these thousands of islands are referred to collectively as Oceania.

In addition, the Pacific is bordered by Asia and Australia in the west, and North and South America in the east. For centuries, the Pacific shorelines allowed for interaction between North and South America. In the west, Pacific waterways helped to create a diverse network of exchange and trade among the islands and nations of East and Southeast Asia. However, it was not possible to bridge the enormous distances between the western and eastern ends of the Pacific until the sixteenth century C.E. Then, the expedition of Ferdinand Magellan became the first to sail across the Pacific Ocean and, with that, the first to circumnavigate the globe. This circling of the earth and the discovery of points of connection between the Atlantic and Pacific oceans (the Isthmus of Panama and the tip of South America) created, for the first time in human history, the possibility for all of the earth's peoples to be linked together, one way or another, by water transport and communication.

SEAS OF THE ATLANTIC OCEAN

In Europe, the North Sea and Baltic Sea played key roles in joining eastern Europe, Scandinavia, northern Europe, and the British Isles to each other and the rest of the continent.

The Mediterranean Sea, from the Latin phrase meaning "Inland Sea," is a central body of water in the history of several continents. Thousands of years ago, it helped give birth to some of the most important civilizations of ancient times. It has supported trade, travel, and interaction among three continents: Europe, Asia, and Africa. The Mediterranean is directly connected to a neighboring body of water, the Black Sea, which joins the Middle East with many parts of eastern Europe. The point that connects the Mediterranean and Black seas—the western tip of the Anatolian landmass (today Turkey)—has, for millennia, been one of the most economically and strategically important places in the world.

The Caribbean Sea is a point of connection and exchange between North and South America. Its many islands are resource-rich, and they were the first territories that settlers from Europe reached in the fifteenth and sixteenth centuries C.E. The Caribbean played a crucial part in building the transatlantic economy that emerged after the Europeans' encounter with the Americas. The Caribbean is also home to the place where the Atlantic and Pacific oceans most conveniently come together: the Isthmus of Panama. This land bridge fully joined the two oceans once a canal was built there in the early twentieth century C.E.

SEAS OF THE INDIAN OCEAN

The Red Sea has always been a key link between the Mediterranean world and the Indian Ocean. Even before the creation of the Suez Canal in the mid-nineteenth century C.E., the Suez isthmus joined Europe, northern Africa, and the Middle East with the Indian Ocean network of trade and travel. Similarly, the Arabian Sea has tied the Middle East together with the Indian subcontinent.

SEAS OF THE PACIFIC OCEAN

The Bering Sea, which forms the extreme north of the Pacific Ocean (and links it to the Arctic Ocean), is the narrowest point between Asia and North America. Scientists theorize that the continents of North and South America were first settled by ancient peoples who traveled over a land bridge that used to cross the Bering Sea thousands of years ago.

The eastern coastline of Asia, as well as the many islands offshore, are all bound together by a number of seas that form the western edge of the Pacific Ocean. These include the Sea of Japan, the East China Sea, and the South China Sea. All of these (and others) provide a waterway linking Asian societies from those of Indonesia and Malaysia in the south to those of Japan, China, and Korea in the north.

RIVER SYSTEMS

Throughout history, river systems have been vital to the birth, growth, and continued viability of human societies. For early settlements, rivers served as water sources. Rivers stimulated the invention of agriculture and the emergence of cities, helping to give birth to the first civilizations.

All during the preindustrial era, rivers (along with seas and oceans) proved to be the most effective mode of transportation. They made possible the large-scale movement of passengers and freight, encouraging trade and travel. Rivers linked inland communities with each other, with towns and cities on ocean coastlines, and with countries beyond those oceans. Like oceans and seas, they enabled the transfer of people, goods, ideas, technology, religious beliefs, and cultural practices.

AFRICAN RIVERS

The great rivers of Africa include the world's longest, the Nile (4,160 miles). From its source in central Africa, Lake Victoria, the Nile flows north into the Mediterranean, giving life to a vast valley that stretches from Uganda, through the Sudan, to Egypt. The Egyptian civilization, one of the world's oldest, and otherwise surrounded by desert, was born on the banks of the Nile. Other key rivers in Africa are the Niger (2,590 miles), which curves through much of West Africa; the Congo (2,900 miles), found in the central part of sub-Saharan Africa; and the Zambezi (1,700 miles), which joins south-central Africa with the Indian Ocean.

ASIAN RIVERS

As the world's largest continent, Asia contains many of the world's largest and most important rivers. The greatest rivers of the Middle East are the Tigris (1,180 miles) and Euphrates (1,700 miles), which run from what is today Turkey, through present-day Iraq, to the Persian Gulf. The Tigris and Euphrates irrigate the desert reaches of the Middle East and, thousands of years ago, allowed the emergence of the world's oldest civilizations.

The Siberian subcontinent is home to a number of long rivers that flow north to the Arctic Ocean. They include the Ob-Irtysh, the Yenisei, and the Lena. These and other rivers have proven key in the development of the Russian nation.

Flowing from the Himalayas and neighboring mountains to the Indian Ocean, a network of rivers runs through the lush forests and jungles of the Indian subcontinent and Southeast Asia. The Indus (1,800 miles), in modern Pakistan, gave birth to one of the world's first civilized societies. The Ganges (1,560 miles) is not the longest of India's many rivers, but its tremendous cultural and religious significance makes it the most famous. The largest rivers draining the peninsula of Southeast Asia are Burma's Irrawaddy and the Mekong of Vietnam, Laos, and Cambodia.

Two mighty rivers flow eastward through China, emptying into the Pacific. The northern river is the Huang Ho (3,395 miles), also known as the Yellow River. To the south is the Yangtze, or Yangzi (3,964 miles). Not far from the Pacific coast, these two waterways are joined by a human-made Grand Canal. Both rivers are crucial for the movement of people and goods through China. More than three and a half thousand years ago, the Huang Ho was where China's first civilized societies emerged.

EUROPEAN RIVERS

Europe's longest river is the Volga (2,290 miles), which flows southward through the heartland of Russia and provides the country with a central artery for water transport. Other major rivers in the eastern half of Europe are the Dnieper and the Don.

Linking the western and eastern parts of Europe is the Danube (1,776 miles), which runs from the Swiss Alps to the Black Sea and provides a key east-west waterway for the entire continent. An important north-south river is the Rhine (820 miles), which flows from southern Europe, through Germany, to the North Sea.

RIVERS OF THE AMERICAS

The major river system of the North American continent is the Mississippi-Missouri (3,710), which runs from Minnesota and North Dakota to the Gulf of Mexico, spanning almost the entire United States from north to south. The role that the Mississippi-Missouri has played in American economics, military strategy, and culture is central. Among the dozens of North America's long and important river systems are the Arkansas, the Colorado, the Columbia, the Ohio-Allegheny, and the Rio Grande (which separates the United States from Mexico).

South America is dominated by the Amazon (4,000 miles), the world's second-longest and, according to most scientists, the largest in terms of water volume. The Amazon flows eastward through northern Brazil and into the Atlantic Ocean. It provides water for the vast tropical rain forest that covers much of the northern part of the continent. Many of South America's other long and important rivers are tributaries (smaller rivers that connect to a larger one) of the Amazon.

Other major South American rivers include the Orinoco (in Colombia and Venezuela), the Rio de la Plata (in Argentina), and the Paraná (in Brazil, Paraguay, Uruguay, and Argentina).

QUICK REVIEW

1. The Arctic Ocean is bounded by all but which of the following countries?

   (A) Canada
   (B) the United States
   (C) Russia
   (D) Norway
   (E) Ireland

2. Which of the following landmasses is NOT a continent?

   (A) South America
   (B) Australia
   (C) Greenland
   (D) Antarctica
   (E) Asia

3. The place where Central America connects with South America is

   (A) the Yucatán peninsula
   (B) the Isthmus of Panama
   (C) Belize
   (D) Costa Rica
   (E) Managua

4. Who is thought to have led the first transatlantic expedition?

   (A) Eric the Red
   (B) Christopher Columbus
   (C) Vasco da Gama
   (D) Leif Ericsson
   (E) Ferdinand Magellan

5. Why has the western part of Turkey been considered one of the most strategically and economically important places in the world?

   (A) The Mediterranean and Black seas connect at this spot.
   (B) The Atlantic Ocean and Mediterranean Sea connect at this spot.
   (C) It is where the Silk Road ended.
   (D) It is a fertile area that is the world's largest fruit producer.
   (E) It is considered the birthplace of Western civilization.

6. Why are rivers considered so important to the development of the first civilizations?

   (A) They discouraged ocean travel.
   (B) They encouraged both the growth of agriculture and urban areas.
   (C) They stimulated the invention of agriculture.
   (D) They stimulated the emergence of cities.
   (E) They really were not very important to the development of early civilizations.

7. The Grand Canal joins which two major rivers in China?

   (A) the Yellow and the Yangtze
   (B) the Yellow and the Ganges
   (C) the Indus and the Mekong
   (D) the Yangtze and the Volga
   (E) the Tigris and the Nile

8. The Nile River stretches from _____ to _____.

   (A) Uganda, Egypt
   (B) Egypt, Ethiopia
   (C) Kenya, Tanzania
   (D) Egypt, Iraq
   (E) Turkmenistan, Egypt

9. Iceland is a part of which continent?

    (A) Antarctica
    (B) North America
    (C) Asia
    (D) Africa
    (E) Europe

ANSWERS:

1. **E**, p. 41	6. **B**, p. 43
2. **C**, p. 39	7. **A**, p. 44
3. **B**, p. 41	8. **A**, p. 43
4. **D**, p. 41	9. **E**, p. 40
5. **A**, p. 42	10. **D**, p. 42

10. The islands located throughout the Pacific Ocean are sometimes referred to collectively as

    (A) Micronesia
    (B) Polynesia
    (C) Melanesia
    (D) Oceania
    (E) Islandia

CHAPTER 2

Building Blocks of Civilization

Hominid, or humanlike, life has existed on earth for 3 million to 4 million years. Humans and their immediate ancestors have gathered themselves into social groups for almost as long. The history of human civilization, however, stretches back only a little more than 5,000 years. The vast expanse of time that precedes the birth of civilized societies is called prehistory. During this long prehistoric period, human beings evolved into their present biological form. It was also then that human populations developed the technological, cultural, political, and economic features that characterize civilized societies.

Much of the knowledge historians have of the prehistoric period comes from the work of other types of scholars, including paleontologists (who study the physical remains and fossils of animals and plants), anthropologists (who study the physical, social, and cultural characteristics of human beings), and archaeologists (who study the objects and buildings left behind by humans). These scientists are constantly making new discoveries and forming new theories. Therefore, the ways in which historians understand the prehistoric age often change.

What distinguishes a civilization from less advanced forms of society (those often referred to as primitive or barbaric)? Webster's Dictionary defines civilization as "social organization of a high order, marked by advancements in the arts and sciences." One distinguished historian has described civilization as a state of social and cultural development that is marked by four things:

- An economic system able to make available basic goods and services
- A form of political organization capable of governing, creating social institutions, enforcing laws, and protecting people from outside threats
- A moral code, generally in the form of a shared religion
- An intellectual tradition that includes a written language and encourages the pursuit of knowledge, science, and the arts

The purpose of this chapter is to describe how the earliest humans emerged and how their prehistoric descendants gradually developed social forms of increased sophistication, until they progressed to the point of forming the first civilizations.

HOMINID DEVELOPMENT

Scientific investigation of the origins of humanity is a relatively recent phenomenon, dating back to the nineteenth century C.E. Research on this topic continues to the present day. Theories and answers come from the work not just of historians, but also biologists, zoologists, and paleontologists. Because new information about the development of early humanity frequently comes to light, the state of knowledge about the subject regularly changes. This is especially the case when it comes to providing precise dates. Still, there is consensus among most scientists about basic facts.

EARLY HOMINIDS

The earth is estimated to be 4 billion to 5 billion years old. Living beings are said to have appeared approximately 3.5 billion years ago. Sometime around 3 million to 4 million years ago, the first hominid, or humanlike, creatures appeared. These hominids were part of the zoological order called primates: mammals that developed about 65 million years ago and include apes, monkeys, and other related animals.

The earliest hominids (known as australopithecines) emerged in southern and eastern Africa 3 to 4 million years ago. Many of the oldest hominid fossils were found in the 1950s and 1960s in the Great Rift Valley and Olduvai Gorge by Mary and Louis Leakey. Their son Richard added to their paleontological discoveries in the 1970s, as did Donald Johanson, who uncovered the famous australopithecine fossil nicknamed "Lucy" in 1974. Three features made australopithecines and their later descendants more advanced than earlier primates: bipedalism (the ability to walk upright), a sizable brain (which enabled abstract thought and fine motor control over the hand and tongue), and a larynx, or voice box, that allowed for complex speech (leading to the development of language).

Between 2 million and 3 million years ago, humanity's immediate predecessors, the early members of the genus *Homo*, were born, also in Africa. First was *Homo habilis*, or "handy human." *Homo habilis* had a larger brain than the australopithecenes and made use of crude stone tools. About 1 million years ago, *Homo habilis* died out, but an even more sophisticated hominid, *Homo erectus*, or "upright human," had already emerged, approximately 1.8 million years ago. Like previous hominids, *Homo erectus* originated in southern and eastern Africa. *Homo erectus*, however, became the first human species to spread throughout the entire continent of Africa. Moreover, it was the first to migrate to other parts of the world. Asian remains of *Homo erectus* (popularly known as "Peking Man" and "Java Man") date back to 1.6 million to 1.8 million years ago, and fossils of *Homo erectus* between 500,000 and 700,000 years old have been found in northern China and Europe. *Homo erectus* had a brain one third larger than *Homo habilis*, and the newer species manufactured stone axes and basic wooden tools. They also clothed themselves in skins and furs. *Homo erectus* survived and prospered for more than a million years, until at least 800,000 years ago, and almost certainly longer. Precisely how and when *Homo erectus* faded away and true humans developed remains poorly understood. The two species may have coexisted for a number of years.

TRUE HUMANS

At some point between 100,000 and 250,000 years ago, true humans (*Homo sapiens,* meaning "wise human") appeared. Most likely, as *Homo erectus* did, *Homo sapiens* emerged in Africa, then spread to other continents. The earliest variant of *Homo sapiens* was the Neanderthal. A more advanced form was the Cro-Magnon, appearing sometime between 60,000 and 100,000 years ago. Both used advanced tools, wore clothing, and created semipermanent or permanent dwellings. Both organized themselves into social groups. Both spread from Africa to Europe and Asia. How and when the Neanderthals and the Cro-Magnon died out, giving way to modern humans, remains uncertain, although it is thought that the Neanderthal died out approximately 30,000 years ago. Also unknown is exactly how Neanderthals and Cro-Magnon interacted, if at all.

Finally, between 100,000 and 200,000 years ago, modern humanity (*Homo sapiens sapiens*) emerged. To what degree *Homo sapiens sapiens* coexisted with Neanderthals or Cro-Magnon is unknown. Most scientists believe that *Homo sapiens sapiens*, like all other hominids, emerged in Africa, then migrated outward. This would imply that Africa is also the source of many features of modern human behavior (complex social networks, economic strategies, personal adornment, and the use of symbols and rituals in daily life). This theory is informally referred to as the "Out of Africa" thesis. An opposing model, the multiregional thesis, proposes that modern humans appeared simultaneously throughout the world, descending from earlier hominid groups that had already left Africa. However, this theory is held by a minority of scholars.

Homo sapiens sapiens continued the pattern of worldwide hominid movement, spreading to Australia, the Arctic, and the Americas, as well as Africa, Europe, and Asia. No earlier than 20,000 to 30,000 years ago (and perhaps as recently as only 5,000 to 6,000 years ago), these migrations, along with the need to adapt to different climates and environments, gave rise to minor evolutionary modifications. The most noticeable of these are skin color and racial type (African, Asian, and Caucasian). In terms of human biology, however, these racial differences are minute, and the genetic structure of all modern humans is virtually identical.

PALEOLITHIC (OLD STONE AGE) AND MESOLITHIC (MIDDLE STONE AGE) TOOL USE

THE STONE AGE

Because one of the principal characteristics separating hominids from their immediate ancestors was tool use, it has been traditional to divide human prehistory into eras based on levels of technological capability. Hominids made their tools out of many materials, such as wood, bone, and animal skins. But the most noteworthy (and the most numerous today, because they have survived best over time) were those made of stone. Consequently, the first period of prehistory is known as the Stone Age. Typically, this era is further broken down into at least two periods: the Paleolithic, or Old Stone Age (ca. 10,000 to 2.5 million years ago), and the Neolithic, or New Stone Age (ca. 5,000 or 6,000 to 10,000 years ago). The change from Paleolithic to Neolithic is associated with the end of the Great Ice Age (or Pleistocene Ice Age), which lasted from 1.5 million or 2 million to 10,000 or 12,000 years ago. Many historians propose that there was a Mesolithic era, or Middle Stone Age, from approximately 10,000 to 12,000 years ago, marking the transition from the ice age to a warmer epoch.

To generalize about Paleolithic humanity is difficult. This is due not only to a relative lack of concrete evidence, but also to the fact that different people in different parts of the world made various inventions, discoveries, and advances at different times. Nonetheless, there are common features that apply to most peoples of the Paleolithic and Mesolithic eras.

EARLY TOOLMAKING

During the Paleolithic era, *Homo habilis* and *Homo erectus* used crude tools, including clubs and choppers to crack open bones, rudimentary axes, and scrapers to prepare animal hides. The earliest humans—Neanderthal, Cro-Magnon, and *Homo sapiens sapiens*—improved upon these tools and created new ones. Tools were generally designed to provide shelter, protection and defense, and food and clothing. The last motive seems to have been most important.

The earliest hominids lived in natural shelters such as caves and canyons. As early as 1 million to 1.5 million years ago, they used fire for light and heat. During the Paleolithic era, humans developed the tools to make lean-tos, tentlike structures, and simple huts. By the end of the Paleolithic and during the Mesolithic era, they were building more advanced wooden and stone structures that demanded significant skills in carpentry and construction.

At what point organized warfare began to be practiced is unknown, but Stone Age humans had to protect themselves against dangers of many sorts. The first weapons included rocks and clubs. Certain tools meant for hunting and food preparation could also be used in combat, such as the knife, the spear, the ax, and the bow and arrow.

Perhaps the greatest concern of Stone Age humans was ensuring a steady and plentiful food supply. Clothing was important as well. Most tools of the Paleolithic and Mesolithic peoples were intended to serve these needs. Multipurpose devices like knives and axes were especially useful. Spears, bows and arrows, fishhooks, and harpoons were used for hunting and fishing. There were wooden implements to dig roots from the ground, as well as mats and baskets to carry nuts, berries, and other foodstuffs. Clay pots were used for cooking as early as 12,500 years ago. The earliest clothes had been made from furs or animal hides. As time passed, humans also began to use plant fibers. By 26,000 years ago, at least some Stone Age peoples were weaving cloth. The practice of dyeing cloth to add color started during the Paleolithic era.

HUNTING AND GATHERING: STONE AGE SOCIETY AND CULTURE

FAMILIES, CLANS, AND TRIBES

As time passed, hominids began to organize themselves into social groups. Because humans mated when they chose, rather than seasonally, they were able to select their sexual partners. Emotional bonding and the length of time (and the great effort) it took to raise human offspring to adulthood encouraged the formation of long-term sexual bonds. In turn, this gave rise to family units. Groups of extended families tended to cluster together, forming clans, bound together by ties of kinship. As clans became larger and mixed with neighboring groups, they grew into bands or tribes.

HUNTING AND GATHERING (FORAGING) SOCIETIES

Almost universally, Paleolithic and Mesolithic groups sustained themselves by hunting and gathering. This practice is also referred to as foraging. Rather than produce food themselves, hunter-gatherer societies lived off the resources they could take directly from the land. Hunter-gatherer societies killed a variety of birds and animals for food, especially mammals such as mammoths, mastodons, bison, camels, sloths, deer, and rodents. They fished lakes, rivers, and seashores. They gathered nuts, berries, and roots. If and when these resources grew scarce, hunter-gatherers moved on to another area. This made most hunter-gatherer societies mobile, or nomadic. This foraging mode of existence continued long after the Paleolithic and Mesolithic eras. But after approximately 10,000 B.C.E., it was no longer the exclusive, or even dominant, form of social organization.

Although primitive by later standards, the hunter-gatherer societies of the Stone Age developed certain social and cultural complexities. In some cases, the political and cultural organization of clans and tribes could be quite sophisticated, involving chiefs, leaders, and religious figures. Many historians speculate that the coordination and teamwork necessary to hunt large creatures facilitated the development of effective means of waging war.

Stone Age humans also worshiped deities and practiced a variety of religious rituals. It is known that Cro-Magnon humans buried their dead as early as 100,000 years ago, indicating the ability to imagine some kind of an afterlife. Ceremonial sophistication increased, and Paleolithic and Mesolithic peoples worshiped and made sacrifices to gods, goddesses, and spirits.

Paleolithic humans also expressed themselves by means of art and music. The oldest cave paintings discovered to this date are 32,000 years old. The first known musical instruments are flutes from 30,000 years ago.

A final feature of Stone Age society that should be noted is the gender division of labor. Because of basic physical differences, various food-gathering tasks and everyday activities tended to be assigned by sex. Men, who were on average stronger and larger, hunted, made war, and performed heavy labor. Women, for the most part smaller and weaker, gathered nuts, berries, and plants; prepared food; maintained the home; and tended children. Some historians theorize that during the Stone Age, division of labor did not necessarily mean that men's roles were seen as superior to those of women (although this supposition remains open to debate). Whatever the case, the division of labor by gender continued long after the Stone Age and eventually gave rise to gender inequality. Over time, especially after agriculture and city building created settled, permanent societies, the persistence of the gender division of labor led to a long-standing inequality of the sexes that most commonly favored men and greatly disadvantaged women. Regrettably, traces of this inequality can still be found today, in even the most advanced societies, despite technological advances that have made the genders' differences in physical strength much less important.

NEOLITHIC REVOLUTION: PASTORALISM AND AGRICULTURE

THE NEOLITHIC REVOLUTION

The end of the Great Ice Age around 10,000 to 12,000 years ago gradually brought about milder conditions, warmer temperatures, and higher ocean levels. These and other climate changes profoundly altered the lives of Stone Age people. To begin with, human population increased rapidly. It is estimated that fewer than 2 million humans were alive during the ice age. There were at least 10 million by 5000 B.C.E. By 1000 B.C.E., the human population had reached somewhere between 50 million and 100 million.

Just as important as the population growth (and a major cause of it) was a key transformation in how human societies provided themselves with food. Although activities such as hunting and gathering did not cease, different groups in various parts of the world, starting around 12,000 years ago, began to produce their own food. This depended on new skills: the domestication of animals and plants. These skills gave birth to the practices of pastoralism and agriculture. Both, especially the latter, allowed humans to manipulate their environment to a greater degree than ever before. Because it required great effort and organization, agriculture encouraged closer social ties and the formation of long-lasting settlements. The permanence and stability associated with agriculture proved crucial in making early societies fully civilized.

The tremendous importance of pastoralism and agriculture has made it traditional for historians to refer to their emergence as the Neolithic revolution. Recently, some scholars have questioned the validity of this label, on the grounds that this "revolution" took

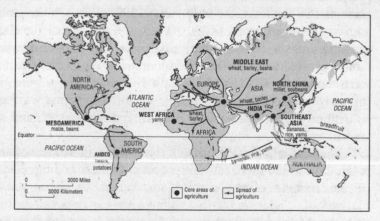

The Practice of Agriculture, ca. 8000 B.C.E.
During the transition from the Paleolithic Era to the Neolithic, communities in the Middle East and northern China began to make systematic use of agricultural practices. The concept of agriculture spread to or arose independently in other parts of the world as time passed.

place over a long period of time, and that, in some parts of the world, the changes began in the Mesolithic period. However, whether one considers them revolutionary or gradual, the changes brought about by Neolithic agriculture were immense.

PASTORALISM AND HERDING SOCIETIES

Pastoralism resulted from humankind's domestication of animals. The first to be tamed was the dog, which, as early as the Paleolithic era, provided many societies with companionship, security, and help in hunting. The goat may also have been domesticated during the Paleolithic era for meat and milk.

The Neolithic era saw the full-scale domestication of many more animals. Horses, water buffalo, oxen, and (in the Americas) llamas provided transport and labor. For groups already involved in agriculture, animal droppings were useful as fertilizer. Many animals, particularly sheep, were raised for wool or hides, in order to make clothing. Most important, animals provided a steady source of food. Sheep, goats, cattle, pigs, and poultry yielded meat, milk, eggs, and other edible products.

Pastoralism affected early social development primarily in two ways. Groups that domesticated animals, but not plants, became herding societies. Like hunter-gatherer societies, herding societies tended to be nomadic. Because the livestock these groups herded consumed great quantities of grass or other fodder, they had to move from place to place on a constant basis. Herding societies also typically migrated according to the pattern of the seasons. This wandering made it less likely for herding groups to develop quickly into civilized societies. Other pastoral societies began to mix animal husbandry with the domestication of plants. This combination of pastoralism and agriculture became a powerful engine driving forward many social advancements, leading to the emergence of the first civilizations.

AGRICULTURE

The cultivation of plants, or agriculture, began in many parts of the world about 10,000 years ago. Whether the concept of agriculture arose in one place, then spread through a process of cultural diffusion, or originated and was adopted independently by many peoples at the same time is a matter of debate among historians. The prevailing theory combines both views. In the Middle East, wheat and barley cultivation began approximately around 8000 B.C.E. From there, it spread to the Balkans (6500 B.C.E.), the Nile valley (6000 B.C.E.), other parts of northeast Africa (5500 B.C.E.), and continental Europe (4000 B.C.E.). Central Africa developed its own agricultural tradition, growing crops such as plantains, bananas, and yams. Likewise, the peoples of North and South America, isolated from the other continents, learned agriculture on their own. Their early crops were maize (corn), beans, and squash. Millet and barley were grown in India as early as 7000 B.C.E. Probably independently, the people of northern China were growing millet by 6000 B.C.E. Rice cultivation began in Southeast Asia around 5000 B.C.E., and seems to have spread from there to southern China.

After the initial emergence of agriculture in separate parts of the world, cultural diffusion entered more and more into the process. As more and more societies began to domesticate plants, certain techniques were borrowed and handed on. Seeds and crops were exchanged as well. The majority of scholars agree that women, already responsible for food collection in most Stone Age cultures, played a key part in stimulating the transition from hunting and gathering to agriculture.

The most primitive forms of agriculture included migratory farming and slash-and-burn farming. The former consisted of small-scale farming in a single area for a brief time, then moving on when the soil was exhausted. The latter, only slightly more advanced, involved burning down forestland to clear a space for cultivation. For a time, ashes from the trees kept the soil fertile. When the soil wore out, the people farming it moved on and started the cycle elsewhere. Later, a more sophisticated form of planting, shifting (or swidden) agriculture, allowed farming communities to stay in the same area for longer periods of time. Rather than cultivating all the fields in a given region, farmers using this technique planted in some fields, left others fallow (or unfarmed), then switched on a regular basis. This practice avoided using up all the nutrients in the local soil. Other advanced techniques like fertilizing, irrigation, and mixing crop types were also helpful.

As the Neolithic era continued, more societies began to combine agriculture with the domestication of animals. They also began to raise a variety of crops, including grains (such as wheat and barley), rice (especially in East and South Asia), peas, beans, corn (particularly, if not only, in the Americas), and roots (such as potatoes and yams). Near the end of the Neolithic, the fermentation of alcoholic beverages, beginning with beer, had been discovered in the Middle East.

FROM STONE AGE TO CIVILIZATION: EARLY CITIES, METALLURGY, AND WRITING

TRANSITION TO CIVILIZED SOCIETIES

As agricultural practices took root throughout the Neolithic era, so did more elaborate and cohesive types of social organization. Because agriculture required an increased commitment to a single region, more and more social groups ceased to be nomadic. When groups stopped wandering and developed a sedentary lifestyle, they tended to gather together into villages and communities with strong social ties and clear-cut rules of government and politics.

There was a corresponding increase in the complexity of religious practices. Rituals became more complicated. Stone Age peoples began to worship a greater variety of gods and goddesses, in addition to forces of nature and the spirits of departed ancestors. They also built permanent sites of worship, including shrines, temples, and megaliths (large standing stones, such as those used at Stonehenge).

CITIES AND THE SPECIALIZATION OF LABOR

In some places, the increased social sophistication of the Neolithic era led to the emergence of a key ingredient in the development of early civilizations: the city. Cities offer protection and defense for large numbers of people. They serve as points of trade and economic activity. They enable the exchange of ideas, information, religious beliefs, and cultural values. Cities also permit people with different skills and talents to gather in a single area. This concentration of skills and talents allows the specialization of labor, an important feature of civilized societies. Consequently, artisans and craftspeople joined agricultural laborers in what were becoming increasingly diverse social groups. The first cities date back to 8000 to 7000 B.C.E. They include Jericho, on the west bank of the Jordan River, and Çatal Hüyük, in what is today Turkey. An urban center, Danpo, also appeared in China, approximately 5000 to 4000 B.C.E. Rare during most of the Neolithic era, cities were becoming more common after 4000 to 3000 B.C.E.

NEW TOOLS AND THE BRONZE AGE

Advanced agricultural and social forms also necessitated advanced tool use. All during the Neolithic, the technological aptitude of Stone Age humans improved. Tools that had been invented during the Paleolithic—axes, knives, bows and arrows, for example—became more refined. Newer devices, such as plows, needles, baskets, hoes, shovels, chisels, and saws appeared. Peoples in the Middle East invented the wheel. Many groups taught themselves the multipurpose craft of pottery. Some anthropologists have argued that, in particular, the plow was a key prerequisite of civilization. Its use extended the areas of land under cultivation and increased the productivity of a society's labor force. This created surplus production, and such surpluses gave rise to the specialization of labor described previously, as well as the stratification of society.

Whatever the case, Neolithic humans were developing tools that enabled them to perform agricultural tasks more effectively, to build dwellings that were more sophisticated and more comfortable, and to invent even newer tools and devices. By the middle of the Neolithic, many societies were on the brink of discovering how to use new substances: metals.

As a material for making tools, metal is much stronger and more versatile than stone. However, metallurgy (the science of extracting and refining metal from raw ore) and metalworking (the craft of shaping refined metal into tools) are highly advanced skills that took humanity thousands of years to discover and perfect. Small objects and jewelry of relatively soft metals— gold, silver, lead, copper—date back as early as 6400 B.C.E. But not until harder metals could be produced affordably and in large quantities did societies start to make tools out of metal, and thus move out of the Stone Age.

Large-scale metallurgy first began in the Middle East and China, sometime between 4000 B.C.E. and 3000 B.C.E. In both areas, toolmakers hit upon the idea of mixing copper and tin to create a harder alloy, bronze. Bronze tools were greatly superior to stone implements in terms of quality and adaptability. Therefore, metal devices eventually replaced those of stone. It is at this point, the Bronze Age (ca. 3500–1200 B.C.E.), that the Neolithic era is considered to have come to an end. Even the Bronze Age faded away, with the development around 1200 B.C.E. of iron, a metal of even greater strength and usefulness.

A final innovation that almost always accompanies the emergence of civilization is writing. During the Stone Age (and, in the case of less sophisticated groups, even afterward), societies relied on the spoken word to preserve their knowledge and cultural heritage. Although many ancient societies developed extremely rich oral traditions, it was the written word that enabled them to keep records, pass on learning, and transfer information much more effectively than ever before. By capturing poems, stories, and folktales in permanent form, writing gave birth to literary traditions. The skill of writing also allowed societies to leave behind detailed historical accounts of themselves. Perhaps the earliest form of writing was developed in the ancient Middle East, by the Sumerians, between 3500 and 3000 B.C.E. A handful of cultures, such as the Inca, reached a civilized state without the benefit of a system of writing, but this happened very rarely.

As the next chapter will describe, the world's first civilizations emerged approximately 5,500 to 5,000 years ago, or roughly 3500 B.C.E. to 3000 B.C.E. Although these first civilizations were, in many ways, different from each other, they all shared the characteristics described previously: complex forms of social and political organization, the practice of agriculture, advanced tool use (including, in most cases, metallurgy), and the rise of cities. It was these common factors that distinguished these newer civilizations from the less developed societies around them, as well as those of the Stone Age that was, by this time, fading rapidly into the past.

QUICK REVIEW

1. Paleontologists

   (A) study the physical, cultural, and social characteristics of humans
   (B) study the physical remains and fossils of animals and plants
   (C) study the objects and buildings created by humans
   (D) study astronomy
   (E) study ancient urban centers

2. Surplus production

   (A) is caused by poor cultivation methods
   (B) prevents specialization of labor
   (C) gives rise to the specialization of labor and stratification of society
   (D) can never occur in modern societies
   (E) none of the above

3. The earliest hominids evolved in southern and eastern Africa _____ years ago.

   (A) 100,000
   (B) 10 million
   (C) 3 million to 4 million
   (D) 20 million
   (E) 10,000

4. In what ways were the earliest hominids and their descendants more advanced than earlier primates?

   I. bipedalism
   II. a large brain
   III. use of agriculture
   IV. larynx

   (A) I, II, and IV
   (B) I, III, and IV
   (C) I and III only
   (D) II and IV only
   (E) III only

5. Hunting and gathering societies were marked by

   I. widespread specialization of labor
   II. a subsistence lifestyle
   III. limited trade
   IV. little specialization of labor

   (A) I and III
   (B) II and IV
   (C) I, II, and III
   (D) II, III, and IV
   (E) IV only

6. The "Out of Africa" thesis

   (A) argues that modern humans appeared throughout the world at the same time
   (B) proposes that modern humans emerged in Africa
   (C) submits that only the Neanderthal emerged in Africa
   (D) argues that crops were first cultivated in Africa
   (E) proposes that only the most primitive human behavior originated in Africa

7. The earliest period in which humans began expressing themselves in both art and music is thought to be

   (A) the Mesolithic era
   (B) the Neolithic era
   (C) the Paleolithic era
   (D) the Bronze Age
   (E) none of the above

8. How did pastoralism affect early social development?

   (A) Herding societies tended to settle on particular lands, and thus civilization emerged relatively quickly.
   (B) Pastoralism led to the adoption of a monotheistic approach to religion.
   (C) No pastoral societies mixed animal husbandry with the domestication of plants.
   (D) Herding societies tended to migrate frequently, and thus civilization took longer to emerge.
   (E) Pastoral societies tended to be led by women.

9. Which of the following is the least advanced agricultural technique?

   (A) slash-and-burn
   (B) shifting
   (C) irrigation
   (D) fertilizing
   (E) mixing crop types

10. What development marked the end of the Bronze Age?

   (A) the first use of tools
   (B) the use of iron
   (C) the beginning of agriculture
   (D) the invention of the wheel
   (E) the adoption of the earliest form of writing

ANSWERS:

1. **B**, p. 47
2. **C**, p. 54
3. **C**, p. 48
4. **A**, p. 48
5. **D**, p. 50
6. **B**, p. 49
7. **C**, p. 50
8. **D**, p. 52
9. **A**, p. 52
10. **B**, p. 54

CHAPTER 3

Major Societies, Kingdoms, and Empires to 1000 C.E.

Although the Advanced Placement World History exam places most of its weight on the period of history following 1000 C.E., it requires some knowledge of the major civilizations that existed before that time. Of particular interest are the cultural, political, economic, and intellectual legacies that these older societies left behind to the newer ones that replaced them.

This chapter provides an overview of the principal states, kingdoms, and empires of the world before 1000 C.E. It begins with the four earliest civilizations. It then focuses on various regions of the globe, highlighting the key characteristics and achievements of the societies that rose and fell in these places.

THE RIVER VALLEY CIVILIZATIONS

MESOPOTAMIAN SOCIETIES

From around 3500 to 2000 B.C.E., river systems in the Middle East, India, and China gave birth to the world's first four civilizations. One of the two oldest—if not the oldest—was the Sumerian-Babylonian civilization that arose in the region of Mesopotamia (a Greek term meaning "land between the waters"). The rivers that gave life to this so-called Fertile Crescent were the Tigris and Euphrates. Settlement began in this area as early as 8000 B.C.E., and large-scale agriculture was being practiced by 5000 B.C.E. Between 3500 and 2350 B.C.E., the first true civilization in Mesopotamia was begun by the Sumerians. As time passed, a variety of other local ethnicities, especially the Babylonians (1900–1600 B.C.E.) achieved political dominance over the region. But the language, culture, and religious traditions of the Sumerians influenced all the peoples of Mesopotamia for centuries to come.

The peoples of Mesopotamia built many cities (including the famous urban center of Babylon). They also created a highly centralized society governed by a small ruling class of priests and a kinglike figure known as the lugal (literally, "big man"). At least in the Western tradition, if not worldwide, the Sumerians were the first to develop a written language. Around 3300 B.C.E., they created a script called cuneiform, in which wedge-shaped characters were pressed into clay tablets with a small stick. Sometime before 2000 B.C.E., one of the world's oldest literary works, the Gilgamesh epic—which tells the story of a king's quest to achieve immortality—appeared in Sumeria. One of the world's first law codes was designed in Mesopotamia, by the Babylonian king Hammurabi (1792–1750 B.C.E.). Although Hammurabi's law code was very harsh (death and mutilation were common punishments) and favored the upper classes, the idea that a systematic, consistent set of regulations, rather than the arbitrary will of a ruler, should govern society was an important innovation.

The peoples of Mesopotamia were skilled builders and crafts-people. Using clay as their primary building material, they erected dozens of large cities. To honor their many gods and goddesses, they constructed large, pyramid-like temples called ziggurats. They built canals and dams. They were accomplished at pottery and metal-working (bronzeworking began here around 3000 B.C.E.). Skilled astronomers, the Sumerians and Babylonians developed a high level of mathematical knowledge, origi-nating the base-60 number system

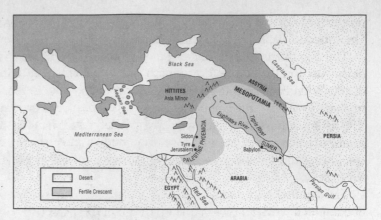

The Ancient Middle East, ca. 1200 B.C.E.
Note the importance of bodies of water in giving birth to ancient civilizations. The Fertile Crescent between the Tigris and Euphrates rivers encouraged the formation of advanced societies in Mesopotamia. The Nile did the same in Egypt. The Mediterranean Sea was crucial for the movement of people and trade goods.

that is still used today to measure time and navigational calculations. The peoples of Mesopotamia were great traders, and their economic network extended throughout the Middle East, as well as North Africa, the Indian Ocean, and perhaps the Indian subcontinent.

EGYPT

The other early civilization of the Middle East appeared in Egypt, on the banks of the Nile. Surrounded by desert, Egypt depended for survival on the Nile's waters. Agricultural settlements began to emerge along the Nile as early as 5500 B.C.E. But Egyptian history is considered to have begun in 3100 B.C.E., when the king Menes united Upper (southern) and Lower (northern) Egypt. The political history of ancient Egypt is traditionally divided into several long periods. During the Early Dynastic (ca. 3100–2575 B.C.E.) and Old Kingdom (2575–2134 B.C.E.) periods, the basic features of Egyptian society and politics took shape. Civil war tore Egypt apart during the First Intermediate Period (ca. 2134–2040 B.C.E.), but a more powerful and intellectually and culturally dynamic Middle Kingdom arose around 2040 B.C.E. The Middle Kingdom lasted until approximately 1640 B.C.E., when outside invaders called the Hyksos conquered it and ushered in a Second Intermediate Period (ca. 1640–1532 B.C.E.). Rebelling against Hyksos rule around 1532 B.C.E., the Egyptians formed a New Kingdom that lasted until 1070 B.C.E. Under vigorous leaders, New-Kingdom Egypt became extremely active militarily, conquering a great deal of territory in northern Africa and the Middle East. Eventually, the grandeur of the New Kingdom collapsed, due to internal disorder and foreign invasions. By the 900s B.C.E., most of Egypt had lost its independence.

Like the Mesopotamians, the Egyptians developed a centralized society that was presided over by a monarch and a small caste of priests. The monarch, or pharaoh, was considered to be the living incarnation of the sun god. Although their society was less urban than that of the Mesopotamians, and although they did not trade as widely, the Egyptians still erected many cities and built up a sizable economic network—particularly during the Middle and New Kingdoms.

Although Egyptian women were secondary to men in terms of power and status, they enjoyed a fair amount of privileges. Women typically managed household finances and the education of children. They had the right to divorce their husbands and could receive alimony. They could own property. Some women managed businesses, and upper-class women could become priestesses. One queen, Hatshepsut, became pharaoh of Egypt in her own right.

The Egyptians had an elaborate religion and worshiped many gods and goddesses. The chief deity was Re, the sun god. A central part of Egyptian religious practice was a belief in life after death. What happened to the soul after death and how to reach a happy afterlife were the subjects of the Egyptians' most important religious text, the Egyptian Book of the Dead. Concern about life after death gave rise to many of the most famous aspects of Egyptian life, including mummification (the art of preserving bodies after death) and the building of gigantic tombs (including the famous pyramids, which were meant to provide resting places for pharaohs after they died).

The cultural and scientific attainments of the Egyptians were many. Around 3100 B.C.E., they developed a written script made up of pictorial characters called hieroglyphics. Using the fiber of reeds called papyrus, they invented the craft of papermaking. The Egyptians were skilled engineers and architects. From the beginning, they knew how to irrigate their fields, extending the reach of the Nile's waters far from the river valley itself. They began to construct pyramids around 2630 B.C.E., and their other buildings and monuments were impressive. The Egyptians were talented makers of bronze tools and weapons. They possessed a great knowledge of medicine, mathematics, and astronomy. It was the Egyptians who devised the 365-day calendar that, with only minor modifications, is still in use today.

THE INDUS VALLEY CIVILIZATION

Farther to the east was a third civilization, which grew up on the coast of the Arabian Sea and farther inland, in what is today Pakistan and northwestern India. This was the Indus River civilization, and it arose sometime around 2600 B.C.E. Although the people of the Indus River had a written language, it has never been deciphered by modern scholars. As a result, much about the Indus River civilization remains unclear, especially their origins, their religious beliefs, their culture, and the reasons for their decline and disappearance.

What is known about the Indus River civilization is that it was quite large (about the size of present-day France) and heavily urbanized. The Indus River people built several hundred cities, the largest of which were Harappa and Mohenjo-Daro (these are the modern names, since the original names are unknown). Because the design of most of the cities is virtually identical, it is thought that the Indus River society was tightly unified and centralized politically. The Indus River civilization produced metal tools and objects of high quality, as well as precious stones. It traded not only with its neighbors, but far beyond its borders, perhaps even with the peoples of Mesopotamia.

The Indus River civilization lasted until approximately 1900 B.C.E. How it met its end is a matter of debate. It used to be thought that outside enemies invaded the region and destroyed the Indus River society. However, a majority of scientists now believe that environmental factors—most likely the drying up of local rivers or the erosion of soil—led to the downfall.

EARLY CHINA AND THE YELLOW RIVER

The fourth river valley civilization emerged in China, along the river known as the Yellow (or Huang Ho). The western reaches of China border on desert, and much of China's center is hilly or mountainous. This makes the two east-west rivers, the Yellow and the Yangtze, exceptionally important in supporting agriculture, allowing movement between communities, and fostering social and political unity. Around 8000 B.C.E., Neolithic cultures began to form small agricultural societies along the Yellow River. The Chinese grew wheat, millet, and, later, rice, a high-yield crop that required an immense amount of cooperative labor. By 2000 B.C.E., the Chinese had discovered the science of bronzeworking.

Most of China's long history as a civilization, from the 1700s B.C.E. to 1911 C.E., is measured in dynasties, or successions of emperors. Myth and tradition speak of a dynasty called the Xia aris-ing around 2000 B.C.E., but most scholars consider the Xia not to have existed. Therefore, the first historically verifiable dynasty—and the bedrock of Chinese civilization—is the Shang Dynasty, which emerged on the banks of the Yellow River around 1750 B.C.E. and ruled a gradually grow-ing state until 1027 B.C.E. Led by a warrior aristocracy, the Shang fought its northern and western neighbors (whom it considered to be barbarians) and expanded its boundaries by conquest.

The Shang traded extensively, its economic network stretching perhaps as far as the Middle East. Principal commodities include jade, ivory, and silk (on which the Chinese enjoyed an unbroken monopoly for over a thousand years). The Chinese system of writing, pictograms, origi-nated with the Shang. So did two of the most important aspects of Chinese religion: fortune-telling and ancestor worship.

The second, and longest-lasting, dynasty was the Zhou (Chou), which was founded when King Wu rebelled against the Shang and overthrew it in 1027 B.C.E. The Zhou lasted until 221 B.C.E., although it was in serious decline long before that, from around 800 B.C.E. The internal collapse and civil wars that plagued the Zhou are reflected in the name given to the last phase of the dynasty's history: the "Warring States" period (480–221 B.C.E.).

The Zhou preserved the technology and learning of the Shang, but added innovations of its own. Around 600 B.C.E., the Chinese learned how to make tools and weapons out of iron. Political sophistication increased: a central principle of the Zhou was the Mandate of Heaven, the idea that, as long as a leader governed wisely and fairly, he could claim a divine right to rule. Key religious and philosophical traditions, such as Confucianism and Daoism, emerged during these years (see Chapter 5).

THE CELTS

Their lack of a written tradition, as well as the fact that they never united into a single political unit, has led most scholars to consider the Celts to be noncivilized. However, the Celts are widely regarded as the first ethnic group to establish a widespread presence in Europe. Although they never formed an actual state, the Celts developed a society based on close-knit tribal groups. They are believed to have emerged somewhere in central Europe, north of the Danube, thousands of years ago. After approximately 500 B.C.E., the Celts began to migrate, spreading throughout Europe, especially to the west. Their remaining presence is strongest in northwestern France, parts of Spain, and the British Isles (particularly Ireland, Scotland, and Wales).

Although they had no written language, the Celts had a rich oral tradition, which survives in the form of myths, songs, and folktales. The Celts were highly skilled at crafts, especially metalwork-ing. They worshiped a variety of gods and goddesses, developing a sophisticated form of religion whose priests were known as druids.

THE ANCIENT MIDDLE EAST

THE HITTITES

From approximately 1500 B.C.E. onward, the ancient Middle East witnessed the rise and fall of a number of important civilizations besides the Egyptians and the peoples of Mesopotamia. Many of them made noteworthy contributions. Although they did not invent the science of ironworking, the Hittites, who appeared in Mesopotamia around 1700 B.C.E. and dominated the region in the 1200s B.C.E., were very likely the first group to make systematic use of iron weapons.

THE ASSYRIANS AND NEO-BABYLONIANS

Even more powerful were the Assyrians, who created the world's first true empire—a large state created by the conquest of one's neighbors—from 911 to 612 B.C.E. With an army of 500,000 troops, armed with iron weapons and making use of the new skill of cavalry (horseback) warfare, the Assyrians took over most of the Middle East, including Mesopotamia and Egypt. The Assyrians held their empire together by means of a deliberate policy of ruthlessness and cruelty. Assyrian rule over the Middle East was ended by a new conqueror, the Chaldeans, or Neo-Babylonians, who controlled the region from 626 to 539 B.C.E. Their most famous ruler was Nebuchadnezzar (ca. 605–562 B.C.E.), renowned for building the Hanging Gardens of Babylon.

THE PERSIANS

The last group to dominate the Middle East politically before Alexander the Great (discussed subsequently) was the Persians (550–331 B.C.E.), who, in an extremely short time, created one of the largest empires in world history. The Persians' first ruler, Cyrus the Great, conquered present-day Iran in 550 B.C.E. By the end of the reign of the third emperor, Darius the Great (522–486 B.C.E.), the empire stretched from Turkey and Libya in the west to the borderlands of India in the east. The empire measured more than 2 million square miles, and it was the largest ever seen in the world to that date. The Persians governed with the help of an advanced postal system, an excellent network of roads, a single currency, and a decentralized form of government, in which around twenty local officials called satraps ruled in the name of the emperor. The official religion of the Persians was Zoroastrianism (see Chapter 5), but they remained relatively tolerant of other faiths. The Persians would fight several wars with their Greek neighbors to the west during the 500s and 400s B.C.E. In 331 B.C.E., Persia fell to the Macedonian conqueror Alexander the Great.

THE HEBREWS

Other notable peoples of the ancient Middle East include the Hebrews (later known as Israelites and Jews). Sometime after 2000 B.C.E., this tribe, under the leadership of Abraham, became the first in the world to practice monotheism, or worship of only one god. The Hebrews were politically weak during most of their history. They were enslaved by the Egyptians (ca. 1400–1200 B.C.E.), conquered by the Assyrians (in 721 B.C.E.), and taken over by the Neo-Babylonians (ca. 587–539 B.C.E.). Nevertheless, the religious and cultural legacy of the Hebrews, in the form of the Judeo-Christian tradition, has shaped world history in countless ways.

THE PHOENICIANS AND LYDIANS

By about 1100 B.C.E., the Phoenicians had settled on the eastern coast of the Mediterranean, in what is today Syria and Lebanon. From their great cities of Tyre and Sidon, the Phoenicians developed an advanced economy, based on the export of timber (particularly cedar) and highly valued purple dye made from shellfish. The Phoenicians were skilled traders and sailors, and they established many colonies along the coast of North Africa. One of these, Carthage, became one of the ancient world's great cities and a serious rival to Rome (discussed subsequently). Around 1400 B.C.E., the Phoenicians devised the world's first true alphabet: a system of writing in which the signs represent sounds, rather than pictures. These twenty-two letters made writing and reading much easier. They were adapted by the Greeks, then (in modified form) by the Romans. The Latin script devised by the Romans now serves as the alphabet for most modern Western languages, including English. In this way, the cultural legacy of the Phoenicians persists to this day. A last Middle Eastern people, the Lydians (ca. 600–500 B.C.E.) are reputed to have invented metal coinage as a practical and portable form of currency.

GREECE AND ROME

Over the course of many centuries, the ancient Greeks and Romans lay the political and intellectual foundations of Western culture. Both of these Mediterranean civilizations played a central role in shaping the history of Europe, the Middle East, North Africa, and, in a sense, the entire world.

EARLY GREEK HISTORY

The earliest civilizations in what became the Greek world were the Aegean civilizations (ca. 2000–1150 B.C.E.), centered on the island of Crete (the Minoan culture, 2000–1450 B.C.E.) and the Greek mainland (the Mycenaean civilization, 1450–1150 B.C.E.). Both were trading societies, and the Mycenaeans also grew wealthy through conquest (they are best known for fighting the Trojan War, ca. 1250 B.C.E.). Around 1200 B.C.E., a series of Greek-speaking tribes invaded the southeastern tip of Europe, as well as the nearby islands. Over time, these tribes joined together into a single culture, the Greeks (or, as they called themselves, Hellenes). These years of gradual cultural union are known as the Greek Dark Ages (1150–800 B.C.E.). Although a common language and religion emerged during this period, political and social development remained at a relatively low level.

GREEK CITY-STATES

More advancement characterized the archaic period (ca. 800–500 B.C.E.). Rugged, mountainous terrain and the fact that so many of the Greeks lived on islands prevented them from creating a single nation. Instead they formed dozens of independent—and typically competing—city-states (urban centers that controlled the immediate regions surrounding them). It is from the Greek word for city-state, *polis*, that the word "politics" comes.

Key city-states included Corinth and Thebes, but even more important were Sparta and Athens. Sparta was a rigid, slave-holding dictatorship that created the Greek world's most effective and most feared army. Athens became a culturally and politically advanced city that gained wealth through trade and power thanks to its naval strength.

The Greek city-states governed themselves in a variety of ways, but most were oligarchies, in which a narrow elite made up of rich, powerful families ruled. Slavery was common in all Greek city-states, but it was most prevalent in Sparta. Greek women were treated as social and political inferiors. Ancient Greece's most significant political innovation came from the city of Athens. This was democracy, or rule by the people. Democratic government began in Athens in 508 B.C.E. It reached its peak under the leadership of the statesman Pericles (ca. 461–429 B.C.E.). As in other Greek city-states, women and slaves were excluded from Athenian political life, and did not have the right to vote. Even with these restrictions, however, Athens had the most representative government not just in the Greek world, but the entire ancient world.

THE CLASSICAL PERIOD AND THE AGE OF ALEXANDER THE GREAT

During the Greeks' classical period (ca. 500–338 B.C.E.), the Greeks fought two major wars with the Persians, in 492 to 490 B.C.E. and 480 to 479 B.C.E. In both cases, the Persians attempted to invade Greece, only to be driven back, thanks mainly to Spartan and Athenian leadership. Afterward, competition between Sparta and Athens for dominance over the Greek world led to a long and devastating civil conflict known as the Peloponnesian War (431–404 B.C.E.). Although Sparta and its allies won the war, the conflict left all of Greece's city-states weakened. That weakness left Greece open first to Persian influence, then, in 338 B.C.E., to conquest by its neighbor to the north, Macedonia (a region whose people were related to the Greeks, but not as politically or socially advanced).

It was from this Greek-Macedonian kingdom that the ancient world's most skilled general, Alexander the Great (356–323 B.C.E.), launched one of the most successful military campaigns of all time. In less than a decade, Alexander crossed into Asia, took over the Persian Empire, and conquered territory all the way to the borderlands of India. Before dying at the age of thirty-three—of exhaustion, alcoholism, and fever—he had led an army of 30,000 to 50,000 troops on a journey of more than 20,000 miles, lasting almost 3,600 days. An important effect of Alexander's conquest was to preserve Greek culture and spread it throughout a vast portion of Eurasia and northern Africa.

HELLENIC (GREEK) CULTURE

The cultural accomplishments of ancient Greece are too numerous to describe in such a short space. The Greeks' general cultural outlook is known as Hellenism (after the Greeks' own name for Greece, Hellas). Although the Greeks worshiped a number of gods, Hellenism tended to be more worldly and rational than other ancient cultural traditions. Science was extremely important. From the 600s to the 300s B.C.E., Greek thinkers (influenced somewhat by learning from Egypt) outlined many of the basic laws of geometry, physics, mathematics, and astronomy.

The celebration of life and the experience of being human (as opposed to fear of the gods and fixation on the afterlife) was a hallmark of Hellenic culture. Starting with the poet Homer (ca. 850–800 B.C.E.) and ending with the classical playwrights Aeschylus, Sophocles, and Euripedes (all during the 500s and 400s B.C.E.), Greek writers created the Western world's first literary masterpieces. Western thought rests on the intellectual foundation established by the philosophers Socrates (470–399 B.C.E.), Plato (428–347 B.C.E.), and Aristotle (384–322 B.C.E.). Aristotle's writings on logic, observation, and experimentation set into place a mode of scientific inquiry that influenced the Middle East and the Western world for centuries, and remains at the heart of the modern scientific method. Greek sculpture and architecture are still considered to be among the ancient world's finest. In countless ways, classical Greece can be considered the wellspring of much of Western culture.

EARLY ROMAN HISTORY

As the Greeks faded politically, a new power emerged in Mediterranean Europe. This was the city of Rome, traditionally considered to have been founded in 753 B.C.E. From their homeland on the Italian peninsula, the Romans gradually spread outward to dominate the entire world, creating one of the largest and longest-lasting empires in history. For several centuries, Rome was governed by a monarchy. It was also controlled for some time by foreign overlords, the Etruscans. In 509 B.C.E., the Romans rebelled against the monarchy (and the Etruscans), forming a new government called the Roman Republic (509–31 B.C.E.).

THE ROMAN REPUBLIC

During the republican period, Roman society experienced tensions between the lower (plebeian) and upper (patrician) classes. Through a long process of compromise and negotiation, the plebeians gradually gained greater, but never complete, social and political equality. It was also during the republican period that Rome began to expand into a Mediterranean power. By 270 B.C.E., the Romans had conquered almost the entire peninsula of Italy. From 264 to 146 B.C.E., Rome fought three bitter campaigns, collectively called the Punic Wars, against the powerful city of Carthage. Carthage was a former Phoenician colony on the African coast of the Mediterranean. Rome's victory in the Punic Wars made it the strongest state in the western Mediterranean, with a large amount of new territory in Europe, the Mediterranean islands, and North Africa. From 214 to 169 B.C.E., the Romans turned east, absorbing Greece, the Balkans, and parts of what is today Turkey. From that point forward, the Romans would take over even more territory, moving steadily to the east (into Asia and Egypt) and north (into Europe).

THE COLLAPSE OF THE ROMAN REPUBLIC

Such rapid territorial expansion caused a number of political, economic, and social crises throughout the first century B.C.E. Rome was shaken by a series of civil wars from 91 to 30 B.C.E. During this period of conflict, the republican form of government began to fail, and political power began to fall into the hands of a single ruler. The most famous of the late republican politicians was Julius Caesar, who assumed dictatorial powers during Rome's second civil war (49–45 B.C.E.). Julius Caesar was assassinated in 44 B.C.E. by people opposed to his growing strength. More war followed, until the republic came to an end in 31 B.C.E.

THE ROMAN EMPIRE

A new Roman regime, the Roman Empire, remained in place for approximately five centuries, from 31 B.C.E. to Rome's downfall in 476 C.E. The first emperor was Julius Caesar's grandnephew and adopted son, Octavian, who renamed himself Caesar Augustus (30 B.C.E.–14 C.E.). Over time, the emperor's powers grew, and his position became more despotic. During the first two and a half centuries C.E., Rome's economic and military might increased. Its huge territory extended from Spain in the west to Asia Minor in the east, from northern Africa in the south to the British Isles in the north.

From the early 200s C.E. onward, Rome found itself in crisis. During the 300s C.E., the eastern half of the empire broke away. It formally separated in 395 C.E., evolving into the Byzantine Empire (discussed subsequently). Overextension of military and political strength made it difficult to govern what remained of the western empire. The army gained a large degree of control over the imperial government. The economy experienced severe downturns. Perhaps worst of all, waves of Asiatic and Germanic barbarians attacked Roman lands from the east and the north for more than four centuries. By the 400s C.E., the heartland of the empire lay open to barbarian invasion. The city of Rome itself was sacked by Gothic tribes in 410 C.E. Another wave of Goths took over the city completely in 476 B.C.E., the year when Rome and the entire western empire are considered to have fallen.

ROMAN SOCIETY

Roman society was sharply divided into citizens and noncitizens, who were subject peoples with no civil rights. Within the Roman citizenry, the primary social distinction was between upper-class patricians and lower-class plebeians. As time passed, however, Roman social divisions became less rigid. Wealth, as much as one's ancestry or birth, determined one's place.

As in ancient Greece (and most ancient societies), slavery was widely practiced. Roman social and economic functions were heavily dependent on slave labor, and occasional slave revolts (such as that of Spartacus in the 70s B.C.E.) periodically disturbed the order of things. The role of women in Roman society changed over time. During the republican period, Roman society was strictly patriarchal. The family head (paterfamilias), always male, had almost absolute power over his wife and children. By the late republican period and early empire, however, this tradition was breaking down somewhat. Although males remained dominant and women could not vote, women gained more freedom to divorce, more economic rights, and greater influence over family financial affairs.

ROME'S CULTURAL LEGACY

For the Western world, the cultural heritage of Rome is incalculable. To begin with, the Romans, who were great admirers of Greek culture, preserved for generations to come the Hellenic philosophy, literature, and scientific learning of ancient Greece. The Romans were master builders and engineers. Many of the roads, fortifications, cities, and buildings they constructed were of use to the people who came after them for many centuries (in a few cases, up to the present). The ideal of Roman imperial unity was a political concept that kings and emperors in a very disunified Europe would attempt to live up to during the medieval period. Roman political thinking guided the formation of many of Europe's nations. Roman law remains one of the keystones of Western legal thought. Finally, it was at the eastern end of the Roman Empire that the religion of Christianity was born, during the first century C.E. By making Christianity legal (313 C.E.), then making it the official faith of the empire (380 C.E.), the Romans ensured that the new religion would be a major intellectual, cultural, and even political force for centuries to come, long after the empire itself had faded away.

CHINA THROUGH THE HAN AND TANG DYNASTIES

From the 200s B.C.E. to the eve of the first millennium C.E., a united and steadily growing China was ruled by four major imperial dynasties. These were the Qin, or Ch'in (221–206 B.C.E.); the Han (206 B.C.E.–220 C.E.); the Sui (589–618 C.E.); and the Tang (618–906 C.E.).

THE QIN DYNASTY

Although short-lived, the Qin dynasty was important because of its principal ruler, Shi Huangdi, which means "The First Emperor." Shi Huangdi turned the Qin state —which many historians believe gave the country its name of "China"—into a dictatorial, tightly centralized nation. He also modernized the Chinese army by introducing iron weapons, crossbows, and cavalry warfare. Shi Huangdi used forced labor to build thousands of miles of roads, as well as the first of the structures that collectively came to be known as the Great Wall of China. Many of the political features that the Qin handed down to later dynasties— among them the concept of a strong emperor and the importance of a large bureaucracy—became basic institutions of the Chinese state for centuries afterward.

The Great Wall of China.
The so-called Great Wall was, in actuality, a network of many walls. Construction on this network began as early as the 200s B.C.E., under the emperor Shi Huangdi. Construction took centuries, and thousands of the workers, many of them prisoners forced to labor on the walls, died. As impressive a feat of engineering as the Great Wall is, it failed in its main purpose of defending China from attack. Note the state of disrepair depicted in this engraving.

THE HAN DYNASTY

The Qin state survived the death of Shi Huangdi by only four years. Then, in 206 B.C.E., after a rebellion, a new dynasty, the Han, rose up to become one of China's strongest and longest lasting. Building on the foundations of Shi Huangdi's Qin state, the Han dynasty created a powerful, efficiently governed empire. Especially under the Emperor Wu (140–87 B.C.E.), Han armies expanded hundreds of miles to the west, north, and south. They took over and absorbed all of Inner China, much of Outer China, parts of Southeast Asia (including northern Vietnam), portions of Korea and Manchuria, and inner Mongolia.

Like the Qin before them, Han rulers put into place an effective administration, postal service, and tax-collecting system. They built roads, defensive fortifications (enlarging the so-called Great Wall), and canals to link the country's major rivers (particularly the Yellow and Yangtze). During most of the Han dynasty, the economy was strong, spurred by improved agricultural techniques and China's monopoly on silk production. By 200 C.E., however, the Han state was in decline. A downturn in agricultural production and an overall economic slump sapped its strength. So did governmental corruption and weak leadership. Outside invaders, bandits, and rebels on the frontiers made it difficult for the Han to protect their borders. In 220 C.E., the Han dynasty collapsed. It has become increasingly common for historians to draw parallels between the Han and Roman empires, which existed at roughly the same time, and became large and powerful by similar combinations of conquest and effective administration. Over the next three and a half centuries, several minor dynasties rose and fell, while China itself was mired in a state of chaos and anarchy. Not until 589 C.E. did a strong dynasty rise up to reestablish order.

THE SUI AND TANG DYNASTIES

This new dynasty was the Sui (589–618 C.E.). Despite its short span, it reunified China and expanded its borders in a tremendous burst of military conquest. Following the Sui was the Tang dynasty (618–906 C.E.). Under the Tang, China became larger than ever before, extending its rule westward to parts of Central Asia and southward, over the Pacific coast. Tang China also forced many of its neighbors into a tributary system, in which regions like Tibet, Korea, Vietnam, and Japan were compelled to make regular monetary payments to the Chinese. The Tang economy was immensely strong. Its strength was due partly to an advanced infrastructure (good roads, waterways, and canals). Tang economic growth was also stimulated by increased trade. One commodity in particular that made the Chinese exceptionally wealthy was silk, the production of which remained a secret known only to the Chinese for hundreds of years. Greater control over the southern coast allowed China to participate in the great trade network that flourished in the Indian Ocean, connecting East Asia with the Middle East. Just as helpful to the Chinese economy, if not more so, was the Silk Road, a very important overland trade route that stretched more than 5,000 miles from the Mediterranean and Middle East to China (see Chapter 4, Trade).

Unfortunately for the Tang rulers, a series of peasant rebellions and military disasters on the frontier caused the dynasty to fall into decay during the 800s. Finally, in 906 C.E., the Tang dynasty collapsed completely. China itself split into several independent states and empires. This disunity lasted for several centuries, so that by 1000 C.E., no single Chinese nation existed. Not until the late 1200s would the country be joined together again.

CENTRAL ASIA

Although it did not give rise to settled civilizations until comparatively late, Central Asia was the birthplace of enough important nomadic groups that it deserves mention here. The arid grasslands and deserts of Central Asia and neighboring Mongolia were home to many herding societies. They tended horses, sheep, goats, and other livestock. They lived highly mobile lifestyles. Most were extremely adept at horsemanship and cavalry warfare.

Many cultures that originated in Central Asia and Mongolia migrated westward to other parts of Eurasia, in many cases traveling thousands of miles. A number of Central Asian peoples had a tremendous impact on the development of civilizations and the movement of peoples in Europe and Asia. Central Asia may be the birthplace of the Indo-European linguistic and cultural group, although this question of ethnogenesis has never been proven conclusively. Certainly many of the ethnic groups belonging to the Indo-European tradition came from Central Asia, including the Aryas (or Aryans), who invaded India in approximately 1500 B.C.E., and perhaps the Persians. An assortment of Turkic peoples, among them the Scythians, Tatars (Tartars), Seljuks, and Ottomans, trace their origins to Central Asia. Other nomadic peoples from Central Asia who greatly affected the course of early history were the Huns (who helped bring an end to both China's Han dynasty and the Roman Empire), the Magyars (ancestors of the modern Hungarians), and the Mongols (see Chapter 10), who, during the thirteenth and fourteenth centuries, went on to carve out one of the world's largest empires ever.

NARA AND HEIAN JAPAN

ORIGINS OF THE JAPANESE STATE

The origins of civilization on the Japanese islands remain cloudy. Various communities gathered together during the Stone Age. As early as the 300s and 200s B.C.E., tightly knit societies were appearing, but the mountainous terrain of the home islands kept settlements relatively isolated. Although tradition and myth trace the ancestry of the Japanese imperial family back to the 600s B.C.E., there is no evidence of an organized Japanese government before the 300s or 400s C.E.

THE NARA STATE

The first imperial state was the Yamato regime, established during the 300s or 400s C.E. The Yamato state was headquartered at the city of Nara, which, until the late 700s, served as Japan's capital. During the Nara period (ca. 300–794 C.E.), the foundations of the Japanese nation were laid. Japan also came into contact with Korea and China. The Chinese had a tremendous influence on the development of Japanese art, architecture, literature, and religion. It was from China (and through Korea) that faiths like Confucianism and, especially, Buddhism arrived in Japan. Nara became famous throughout East Asia as a center of Buddhist scholarship.

HEIAN JAPAN

By the late 700s, the imperial family wished to escape the political influence of the Buddhist priesthood in Nara. In 794, the emperor shifted the capital to the city of Heian (present-day Kyoto). Most of the Heian period (794–1185 C.E.) was marked by peace, prosperity, and cultural splendor. Imperial politics was dominated by the Fujiwara clan. Art and culture thrived, giving birth to one of Japan's literary masterpieces, *The Tale of Genji,* by Lady Murasaki. In 1000 C.E., the Heian regime was at its high point; these years are remembered as a golden age in premodern Japanese history. However, by the late 1000s and early 1100s, the Heian state began to decline, primarily as a result of decadence and weak leadership. It would be swept away altogether in 1185.

CLASSICAL INDIA

THE ARYAN INVASION

To what degree the Indus River valley civilization, which existed until approximately 1900 B.C.E., can be considered "Indian" is unclear. Therefore, the true foundations of Indian culture remain unknown. Conventionally, Indian history is said to have begun around 1500 B.C.E., when northern

India was invaded by a nomadic group known as the Aryas (also called the Aryans). Originally from Persia and Central Asia, the Aryas are considered to be among the earliest of the Indo-Europeans, one of the principal linguistic and ethnic groups of Eurasia (famously and tragically, Adolf Hitler and the Nazis would, centuries later, misinterpret the concept of the "Aryan" race to justify their discriminatory and genocidal racial policies). The light-skinned Aryas conquered the darker-skinned natives of India (collectively known as the Dravidians), expanding steadily from north to south. At first, the Aryas established a warrior aristocracy and enslaved the Dravidians. Over time, Aryan and Dravidian elements blended to form a culture that was truly Indian. However, it should be noted that, even today, the Indian subcontinent is home to literally dozens of ethnicities, languages, and traditions.

The Aryan-Dravidian fusion gave to India several of its characteristic features. One was an elite language, Sanskrit, for religious, literary, and intellectual purposes. Another was a religious tradition, the Vedic and early Hindu faiths, that would shape India for centuries to come. In addition, a caste system emerged, dividing society into specific social and occupational classes. The original castes included the following:

- priests (brahmins)
- warriors and political rulers (kshatriyas)
- commoners (vaishyas)
- servants and peasants (shudras)
- the "untouchables"

Over time, the Indian caste system grew increasingly complex, with new groups and subgroups. People were born into their castes, and their descendants remained in the same caste permanently. Movement from one caste to another was almost impossible, and the system led to a tremendous degree of social rigidity and stratification that persisted well into the twentieth century.

THE MAURYAN EMPIRE

India is large and diverse enough that, during the ancient and classical periods of its history, it was rarely unified as a single state. The first rulers to bring most of India together politically were the Mauryas, who created an empire that lasted from 324 to 184 B.C.E. The best-known of the Mauryan emperors was Ashoka (269–232 B.C.E.). A great warrior as a youth, Ashoka converted to Buddhism and became an advocate of peace and tolerance. He was admired for his justice and wisdom, and he remains famous for his efforts to create harmony between Buddhists, Hindus, and the worshipers of India's other religious traditions.

THE GUPTA EMPIRE

In 184 B.C.E., the Mauryan Empire collapsed, because of attacks by outside enemies. For the next five hundred years, India reverted to a state of political disunity. Not until 320 B.C.E. did another large empire rise up: the Gupta Empire. It lasted until 550 C.E. and controlled most of northern and central India. Although the Gupta rulers were Hindu, they practiced religious toleration. Like the Mauryans before them, the Gupta emperors fell as a result of outside pressure, especially from the northwestern frontier. From then until after 1000 C.E., India would remain decentralized. By that point, Muslim invaders, who had appeared on the northwestern borderlands during the 700s C.E., would begin to move into the Indian subcontinent. The Muslims would do much to shape Indian politics and culture after 1000 C.E.

BYZANTIUM

When the Roman Empire split into two in 395 C.E., the eastern half continued and flourished, even after the western empire fell in 476. The eastern Roman Empire became known as Byzantium, after the original name of its capital, better known as Constantinople. The unique position of Constantinople, between the Black and Mediterranean seas, the crossroads of Europe and Asia, made it a city of remarkable economic and military importance for a millennium and a half. The Byzantine Empire played a crucial role in providing commercial and cultural connections among the Europeans, the peoples of the Middle East, and those of Asia as a whole. It also served as a cradle and preserver of Christianity in eastern Europe and the Middle East.

Byzantium was a glorious center of art and culture. It blended Greek and Roman elements into a sublime fusion. Under the emperor Justinian, who reigned during the 500s C.E., the city of Constantinople underwent a breathtaking architectural renovation. It was during this time that the Church of Hagia Sophia was built. Now an Islamic mosque, it remains one of the ancient world's finest monuments. The famous form of religious art known as the icon—painted images of Christian saints, the Virgin Mary, and Christ—originated in Byzantium and spread throughout medieval Europe, the Middle East, and eastern Europe (especially Russia).

The territorial might of the Byzantine Empire reached its peak in the 500s C.E., under the emperor Justinian. In the short term, Justinian succeeded in recapturing many of the lands that had been controlled by the western Roman Empire before its fall. From the 600s onward, the Byzantine Empire gradually lost territory in northern Africa and the Middle East, principally because of the rapid expansion of Islam (discussed subsequently). However, by 1000 C.E., Byzantium remained a regional power of great strength, both in Europe and Asia.

EARLY MEDIEVAL EUROPE

THE CONCEPT OF "MIDDLE AGES"

After the fall of the western Roman Empire, Europe entered a state of relative backwardness. In the west, the centralizing institutions of Roman rule had been rotted out by economic decay and political corruption, then shattered by the incursion of the Germanic and Asiatic barbarians that had swept into much of Europe. This thorough collapse began Europe's long medieval period, also known as the Middle Ages (the term "medieval" comes from the Latin translation of this term). Europe's Middle Ages lasted approximately from 500 to 1500 C.E. The first 500 years, or early medieval period, is commonly called the Dark Ages, although most historians consider this label to be inaccurate and judgmental.

BARBARIAN INVASIONS

During the early medieval period, Europe continued to undergo numerous invasions by barbarian tribes from the north and east. This great age of migrations was one of the principal forces shaping European culture during these years. Most of these people were Germanic (Saxons, Angles, Goths) or Asiatic (Huns, Magyars) in origin. A number of them, especially the former, settled permanently in European lands. The kingdoms they formed tended to be unsophisticated and short-lived. Nonetheless, as the barbarian tribes of the medieval era became less nomadic and more civilized, they played a crucial part in forming Europe's emerging nations.

FEUDALISM AND EARLY NATION BUILDING

In the aftermath of Rome's fall, Europe's political situation was one of extreme decentralization. No single ruler or institution was strong enough to provide Europe with unity or central authority. For most of the early medieval period, European rulers made use of a practice called feudalism. In this system, lords and monarchs awarded land to loyal followers in exchange for their promise to administer that land, ensure its economic productivity, and protect it militarily. Feudalism was also a method of harnessing peasant labor. To ensure a steady food supply, as well as to keep the lower classes under control, feudal rulers in most of Europe subjected the majority of the peasant population to the system of serfdom, a form of unfree agricultural labor not dissimilar to slavery (see Chapter 4). Feudalism, and the loose decentralization that went along with it, remained at the heart of medieval European politics for centuries.

Not until the 800s and 900s did true nations—centralized states, generally united by a common ethnic, linguistic, and cultural heritage—begin to form. One of the earliest nations in European history was the central European state, the Holy Roman Empire, created by the famous emperor Charlemagne (768–814 C.E.). Later nations included England, France, and a new Germanic Holy Roman Empire that followed Charlemagne's.

EARLY ISLAM AND THE CALIPHATES

From the 200s to the early 600s C.E., the dominant civilizations in the Middle East were the Byzantine Empire and a Persian state ruled by the Sassanid dynasty. Very suddenly, however, the political and religious landscape of the Middle East—and much of Eurasia as a whole—would be changed dramatically. This transformation was due to the appearance of a new and dynamic faith: Islam, whose founder was Mohammed (570–632 C.E.) and whose followers were known as Muslims. The religious history of Islam, as well as its doctrines and practices, are related in Chapter 5. But because it was a central belief among the Muslims for over 600 years that church and state were not separate entities, the political history of early and classical Islam is equally important.

THE ORIGINS OF ISLAM

Mohammed's religious community originally formed in Mecca, a city on the Arabian peninsula. To this day, Arabic is the holy language of Islam. In 622 C.E., Mohammed and his followers were driven out of Mecca to Medina. This flight, known as the Hegira, marks the beginning of the Islamic calendar. By the end of the 620s, the new faith had begun to spread rapidly, helped largely by aggressive conversion of the Arabians by Mohammed's followers. By Mohammed's death in 632, the Muslims had retaken Mecca and spread throughout the entire Arabian peninsula.

THE EXPANSION OF ISLAM

After Mohammed's death, the leaders of the Islamic faith were known as caliphs, or "successors." Despite a vicious civil war within the Islamic leadership from 656 to 661 C.E., Muslim armies proved incredibly successful during the 600s and 700s in spreading Islam—and political control—beyond Arabia. The Muslims destroyed the Sassanid Empire and badly weakened Byzantium by taking vast amounts of territory from it. By the early 700s, the Muslims had conquered most of the Middle East, most of North Africa, Spain, Central Asia, and the borderlands of India (the region that is today Pakistan).

THE CALIPHATES

Because Muslims considered the political community to be identical to the religious community, all Muslim lands were ruled by the caliph. Not counting the immediate successors to Mohammed, the first caliphate was the Umayyad Caliphate (661–750 C.E.). Its capital was Damascus, in present-day Syria. In 750, the Umayyad Caliphate was overthrown by a series of rebellions.

What followed was a new state, the Abbasid Caliphate (750–1258). From their capital in Baghdad (in what is today Iraq), the Abbasid rulers presided over what was essentially the golden age of classical Islamic culture. From 750 to about 900 C.E., the caliphs were strong. The most famous and best loved was Harun al-Rashid, who reigned from 776 to 809. From Spain to the frontiers of India, a single authority provided peace and stability. The scientific and mathematical aptitude of the Muslims was great, especially in contrast to their more backward European neighbors. Some of the greatest works of Islamic literature date back to the Abbasid years. Although the Abbasid dynasty lasted until 1258, it was in serious decline from 1000 C.E. onward.

BANTU AFRICA, NUBIA, AND GHANA

The incredible linguistic and ethnic diversity of Africa, especially the sub-Saharan portions, makes it difficult to generalize broadly about the appearance of early societies and civilizations.

THE BANTU

The one linguistically based group that most resembles a common cultural source in sub-Saharan Africa is the Bantu. Bantu-speaking peoples emerged in the Niger River basin of west central Africa. Around 1000 B.C.E., Bantu groups began to migrate throughout the continent. By 1000 C.E., descendents of those groups had spread to the southern and eastern ends of Africa.

It is impossible to say that the Bantu provided Africa with a single cultural heritage. It can be argued, however, that, of all the many peoples of sub-Saharan Africa, the Bantu played the greatest role in shaping the region's cultural, ethnic, and linguistic character. It is believed that Bantu-speaking tribes spread the knowledge of agriculture and ironworking to many parts of eastern and southern Africa. They transformed an area that had earlier been sparsely populated by groups of hunter-gatherers to one that was more densely populated and dominated by farming communities. All Bantu-speaking groups of southern and eastern Africa—including the Swazi, the Sotho, the Tswana, the Shona, the Ndebele, the Venda, the Xhosa, and the Zulu—came to depend on the wealth of cattle as the foundation of their economic and political systems. The amount of cattle one possessed determined one's access to land and one's political authority.

NUBIA AND GHANA

Not counting Egypt, the first major civilizations in Africa appeared in Nubia and Ghana. The former is a thousand-mile region south of Egypt that links sub-Saharan Africa with the Mediterranean coast. With the Nile running through it, Nubia became an important corridor for trade between north and south. A particularly valuable commodity was gold. Nubia was settled around 3000 B.C.E., more advanced societies appeared about 2300 B.C.E., and a powerful kingdom known as Kush emerged in approximately 1750 B.C.E. For 500 years, the Egyptian New Kingdom dominated Nubia, but its control gradually faded.

A new Nubian kingdom rose during the eighth century B.C.E. From the fourth century B.C.E. to the fourth century C.E., that kingdom was centered at the large and prosperous city of Meroë, the southernmost point of Egyptian civilization. Meroë, surrounded on three sides by rivers, offered its inhabitants sufficient rainfall for irrigated cultivation and nearby grasslands to sustain livestock herds. It also contained large deposits of iron ore and the hardwood timber needed for smelting. The scale of iron production in Nubia was once large, and various kinds of iron weapons and tools have been recovered. Meroë collapsed in the second century C.E., as a resut of changing trade patterns in the Red Sea area and, most notably, because of erosion of the topsoil, caused by heavy deforestation.

Far to the west, on the Atlantic coast, was Ghana. The first major sub-Saharan kingdom, this "land of gold" dates back to the 500s C.E. Part of the trans-Saharan trade network that extended throughout the Sahara, Ghana grew during the next 500 years, expanding throughout northwest Africa.

When Europe began minting gold coins during the 1200s C.E., Ghana's gold gained in value. During these years, Ghana was the major supplier of gold to the world economy. Koumbi Saleh, a town that once served as one of Ghana's capitals, hosted a prosperous Muslim community of merchants linked to the trans-Saharan trade route. Ironically, iron and copper were more useful, and thus more valuable, to Africans than gold was. So caravans carried iron, copper, and copper alloy across the Sahara as well as the precious metal.

Over time, Ghana's ecological and demographic conditions weakened its society. As its population grew, its food production failed to meet demand in what was by then an extremely arid environment. All of this left Ghana vulnerable to Muslim conquest, the immediate cause of Ghana's downfall.

EARLY CULTURES IN THE AMERICAS

MEXICO AND CENTRAL AMERICA

Advanced civilizations began to appear in the Americas after 1200 B.C.E. The oldest and most sophisticated were in Mexico and Central America, where a succession of cultures, each influencing the ones that followed it, emerged. The first major society in the Americas was that of the Olmec (ca. 1200–400 B.C.E.). Located in east-central Mexico, on the coast of the Gulf of Mexico, the Olmec created what is considered to be the "mother civilization" of Central America. Although their written language remains a mystery to modern scholars, it is clear that the art (consisting mainly of large heads carved from stone), architecture, and religion of the Olmec had an impact on the peoples that came after them.

The next major society in the region was centered on the vast city of Teotihuacán, founded approximately 150 to 100 B.C.E., near modern-day Mexico City. With a population greater than 200,000, Teotihuacán was one of the world's largest cities at the time. It existed until 750 C.E. By that point, it had been eclipsed, perhaps taken over, by one of the most complex societies of the ancient Americas, the Maya, who flourished from 250 to 900 C.E. Mayan territory included present-day Guatemala, Honduras,

Mayan Pyramid of Chichén Itzá.
The Maya founded the city of Chichén Itzá around 250 C.E. It remains a treasure trove of archaeological evidence about how the Maya lived. The pyramid, a major center of Mayan worship, was constructed in approximately 1100 C.E.

Belize, and southern Mexico. There was no single nation. Instead, independent city-states and rival kingdoms ruled over the Mayan lands.

The elaborate religion of the Maya, which included large-scale human sacrifice and the worship of serpent gods and jaguar deities, seems to have derived at least partly from the Olmec and Teotihuacán cultures. Like the Teotihuacán, the Maya built huge terraced pyramids, such as Chichén Itzá, primarily for religious reasons. Along with human sacrifice, the most famous feature of Mayan worship was a ritual ballgame in which players tried to hit a small ball through a hoop without using their hands. This game was played for ceremonial purposes. The Maya were excellent astronomers and mathematicians—their unusual calendar system was extremely intricate and accurate. They were also gifted architects, as their pyramids and other buildings demonstrate. A combination of disease and environmental factors brought about the decline of the Maya, and their civilization was finished off by war around 900 C.E. The last dominant social group in Central America before 1000 C.E. was the Toltec (968–1156 C.E.). Throughout central Mexico, the fierce Toltec created a large state by means of aggression—until they themselves were conquered by invaders from the north.

ANDEAN SOCIETIES IN SOUTH AMERICA

In the northwest portion of South America, several civilizations rose up in the peaks and valleys of the Andes. Recent archaeological discoveries indicate that the first city in the Americas, Caral, was founded along the Supe River, in central Peru, around 2600 B.C.E. Most Andean cultures were skilled at weaving, pottery, and metalworking. It is thought that in the Americas, metallurgy originated here, then spread northward. Andean cultures formed heavily urban societies that tended to be socially stratified. Their most important domesticated animal was the llama. The oldest of these societies was the Chavin (ca. 900–250 B.C.E.). Also prominent were the Moche (200–700 C.E.), the Tiahuanaco and Huari (both ca. 500–1000 C.E.), and the Chimu (800–1465 C.E.).

The South American plains gave rise to nomadic herders. The rain forests of the Amazon basin were home to innumerable tribes. But in neither area did settled civilizations of the complexity of the Andean cultures appear before 1000 C.E.

NORTH AMERICAN CULTURES

To North America, advanced social structures came comparatively late. A number of tribes began to form together in the river valleys and forests of the eastern part of the continent. The first was the Adena (ca. 500 B.C.E.–100 C.E.), which was followed by the Hopewell (100–400 C.E.) and Mississippian (700–1500 C.E.) cultures. All three spread out along the Ohio and Mississippi river valleys. They were loose confederations rather than actual nations, and they built few large urban centers (one exception was the Mississippian city of Cahokia, North America's largest at the time). The most famous archaeological legacy of the Adena, Hopewell, and Mississippian cultures is a large variety of giant earth mounds, built for ceremonial and religious purposes.

Around 700 B.C.E., a civilization in North America's desert Southwest began to reach its peak. This was the Anasazi (a Navajo word meaning "ancient ones," because the original name of the actual people is lost). Small settlements date back to 450 C.E., but Anasazi may have appeared in the area many years before that, and the exact date of their origins remains unknown. The Anasazi—and the Southwest Native Americans who followed them—are famous for their elaborate cliff dwellings, made of clay and rock, perched hundreds of feet above the floors of the canyons and desert below.

QUICK REVIEW

1. One of the main innovative ideas in Hammurabi's law code was that

    (A) the ruler's will is to be followed at all costs
    (B) the upper classes are to have the most rights
    (C) the lower classes were to have special privileges
    (D) a consistent set of regulations should govern society
    (E) anyone who spoke against the king would be executed

2. In 3100 B.C.E., the history of Egypt is said to have begun when

    (A) Cleopatra met Mark Antony
    (B) King Menes united Upper and Lower Egypt
    (C) the Old Kingdom began
    (D) the Egyptians rebelled against Hyksos rule
    (E) pyramids began to be constructed

3. What do many researchers now think brought about the fall of the Indus River society?

    (A) fighting between the Hindus and Sikhs
    (B) outside invasions from Mesopotamia
    (C) environmental factors
    (D) population growth
    (E) all of the above

4. Why was the Zhou dynasty in China so long-lived?

    (A) It innovated technology and increased China's political sophistication by obligating the leader to rule fairly.
    (B) Its leaders were ruthless.
    (C) It did not have to contend with the conflicting dictates of Confucianism.
    (D) It prevented average people from acquiring weapons.
    (E) It actually was very short-lived.

5. Why are the Assyrians considered to have created the world's first real empire?

    I. They had a large army that used horseback warfare.
    II. They made and used iron weapons.
    III. Their leaders were permitted to rule ruthlessly.
    IV. They conquered most of the Middle East.

    (A) I, II, and III
    (B) II, III, and IV
    (C) I and III only
    (D) II and IV only
    (E) all of the above

6. Which peoples developed the world's first true alphabet?

    (A) the Lydians
    (B) the Phoenicians
    (C) the Hebrews
    (D) the Persians
    (E) the Egyptians

7. In Greek society, women were treated as

    (A) equals to men, especially when it came to voting
    (B) gods
    (C) inferior to men in both social and political affairs
    (D) slaves in every household
    (E) none of the above

8. Which of the following was NOT one of Rome's cultural legacies?

   (A) The Romans preserved Hellenic philosophy.
   (B) The Romans built roads and fortifications that have lasted for centuries.
   (C) The Romans adopted the Islamic religion as the official faith of the empire.
   (D) The Romans made Christianity the official faith of the empire.
   (E) The Romans adopted a legal code still in some use today.

9. Which of the following is an accurate statement about the Indian caste system?

   (A) Its top stratum was the untouchables.
   (B) Its top stratum was the Sikhs.
   (C) People enjoyed social mobility.
   (D) All Aryans were in the untouchable caste.
   (E) There was virtually no social mobility.

10. What proved to be the most effective way for the Islamic faith to expand?

   (A) Muslim armies conquered large territories and spread Islam beyond Arabia.
   (B) It expanded through the publishing of the Qu'ran.
   (C) Muslim missionaries moved to foreign lands to spread the word of Mohammed.
   (D) It did not expand outside of the Arabian peninsula until after 1000 C.E.
   (E) none of the above

ANSWERS:

1. **D**, p. 57
2. **B**, p. 58
3. **C**, p. 59
4. **A**, p. 60
5. **E**, p. 61
6. **B**, p. 61
7. **C**, p. 62
8. **C**, p. 64
9. **E**, p. 68
10. **A**, p. 70

CHAPTER 4

Social Structure and Cross-Cultural Connections

To generalize about civilizations around the globe—and throughout history—is difficult, if not impossible. Human communities are diverse, and each of them possesses unique characteristics. Nonetheless, most societies have certain broad features in common. This chapter will discuss some of those features, focusing on the various ways that cultures in world history have tended to organize themselves politically, socially, and economically.

This chapter will also show how societies interacted, especially in the early eras of world history. Cross-cultural interaction can take place in a number of ways, all of which serve to bring civilizations into closer contact with each other, with both positive and negative consequences. By 1000 C.E., many civilizations had begun to interact with other groups, in some cases over considerable distances. Sometimes encounters were peaceful, often they were not.

Often, many things about individual societies—what they knew, how they lived, the material possessions they had available to them, whether or not they survived at all—were deeply affected by how they met and dealt with other civilizations. One of the most common forms of social, cultural, technological, and economic change is diffusion: the spread of inventions, foods, trade goods, concepts, and practices from one people to another. Determining to what degree a given society's basic features are shaped by cultural diffusion or independent innovation is one of the most challenging and interesting questions in the study of ancient cultures. Both cultural diffusion and independent innovation have played important roles in the evolution of civilizations.

CLASS STRUCTURES

Almost all societies have some form of class distinction, according to which people are defined by such things as wealth, ancestry, or occupational function. Differentiation by class is quite limited in pre-agricultural societies. Typically, among hunters, gatherers, and herders, all members of the group perform similar functions (although, as described in Chapter 2, labor is, in most cases, divided by gender) and have the same skills. Most possessions are shared or owned commonly. Thus, members of these societies remain more or less equal. Exceptions include chieftains and elders (who provide leadership) and priests or shamans (who provide religious guidance and, often, medical care).

True class distinction generally coincides with a society's adoption of agriculture. Agriculture encourages permanent settlement and technological advancement. Because land and the tools and livestock needed to work it are so important, agriculture makes the concept of private property meaningful. Agriculture also leads to the creation of food surpluses, meaning that, unlike in pre-agricultural societies, substantial numbers of people not directly involved in food production can be fed. These people are free to develop other skills for the benefit of their society and themselves. As noted in Chapter 2, this gives rise to the specialization of labor.

Up to 1000 C.E., the vast majority of people in almost all societies were peasants and farmers, directly engaged in agricultural work. Still, an increasing percentage of those societies' members performed other functions. Ruling classes, generally in the form of royal families, emerged to run governments that were becoming more complicated as time passed. Other examples of more specialized occupations in early societies include soldiers, priests, craftspeople, artisans, scribes, and accountants.

Certain social roles—such as political or military leadership—were inherently more powerful than others. Also, over time, some occupations came to be more valued than others. This gives rise to the phenomenon of social stratification, in which upper and lower classes emerge. A culture's system of ranking social classes is known as a hierarchy. Each society judges for itself which classes are more important and which are less so. Each society also has its own way of determining how classes interact with each other, how difficult it is for an individual to move from one class to another (the concept of social mobility), and what benefits or disadvantages each class possesses. In most societies up to 1000 C.E. (and even later), the privileged, or elite, classes were quite small. Social stratification tended to be rigid, meaning that upward social mobility was very difficult. Certain civilizations, such as India, had extremely strict arrangements, called caste systems, in which movement from one class to another was impossible. In most early civilizations, lines between classes were very sharply drawn. Upper classes typically enjoyed many legal and financial advantages, such as more lenient treatment before the law and immunity from taxation.

At most times and in most parts of the world, political power, religious leadership, and important social functions have generally been in the hands of males, especially since the rise of settled agricultural and urban cultures. Societies in which this male domination prevails are called patriarchies. A small minority of early societies gave more political, religious, and social power to women. These matriarchies, however, were rare. There are a few archaeologists and anthropologists who have tried to prove that most pre-agricultural societies were originally matriarchal, but their theories are not accepted by most scholars. In either case, from the development of agriculture onward, the gender division of labor has remained an important (and unfortunate) way, along with class, that societies differentiate certain members from others.

FORMS OF GOVERNMENT

Very few communities, no matter how primitive, fail to provide themselves with a form of leadership. Even the least advanced group will have some kind of chief or war leader. As societies grow into civilizations, they invariably develop more complex forms of government. Although details vary from society to society, most political systems fall into one of a few basic categories.

Perhaps most common before the modern era was monarchy, or government led by a single ruler—most typically a king, queen, emperor, or empress. Most monarchs govern with the assistance of a small upper class, known as the nobility (or aristocracy). This political elite assists the monarch with political administration, economic development, military defense, and other matters that he or she cannot take care of directly or alone. In cases where the monarch's powers are relatively weak, he or she often rules in tandem with a parliament (or some sort of lawmaking body), or according to the rules of a constitution, or both. Before 1000 C.E., however, such arrangements were extremely rare. In most instances, monarchical rule is hereditary (as is noble or aristocratic status). Monarchies in which the monarch possesses an unusual amount of power—or all of it—are referred to as autocratic or despotic.

Also prominent was oligarchy, or rule by the few. In oligarchic systems, political power rests in the hands of a small elite group, generally chosen from the wealthy or the aristocracy.

Two forms of government that remained fairly uncommon before 1000 C.E. were the republic and democracy. Often thought to be identical, the two can actually be substantially different. A republic (from the Latin term *res publica,* meaning "public thing") is a state in which all adult citizens (generally, until quite recently, only males) play some role in government. However, the republican form of government does not guarantee that all citizens will play an *equal* role in government. For example, the votes of a republic's upper class may count for more than those of lower classes. Or members of the lower classes may be allowed to vote, but not to run for office. Unlike a republic, a democracy grants more or less equal political rights and opportunities to all adult citizens, or, until the modern era, all adult male citizens (the word comes from the Greek phrase for "rule by the many"). It is possible for a republic to be fully democratic, but it does not have to be (the modern United States is considered to be a democratic republic). One of the very few democracies to exist before the modern age was the Greek city-state of Athens.

A government dominated by a religious elite is known as a theocracy.

Nations (also nation-states or countries) are states run by centralized governments and bounded by set borders. They are also united by more or less uniform legal systems and a sense of common national identity. Generally, a nation-state's population (or the majority of the population) is linked by a common language, ethnicity, and cultural heritage. Citizens of a nation often share a common religion as well. Not all societies are nation-states in the modern, technical sense. Especially during the ancient period, and even later, states tended to be less centralized, and they were thought of as a monarch's personal property. The concept of nationhood is a relatively modern phenomenon.

SLAVERY

One of human society's most shameful institutions is the ownership of human beings by other human beings, or slavery. Until comparatively recently (the 1800s), slavery was widespread. In some parts of the world, it still exists today. Before and around 1000 C.E. (and long afterward), most societies around the world practiced slavery or engaged in and benefited from economic activities that were dependent on it.

Slaves performed a number of functions. These were divided mainly into household tasks and hard labor (especially jobs associated with construction or agriculture). Questions such as the severity of slaves' treatment, the length of their service, and the degree to which they did or did not have legal rights or protections all depended on the laws and customs of each society.

People fell into slavery in many ways. Some were prisoners of war or captives taken during raids into enemy territory. Some were debtors who were sold—or sold themselves—into slavery. Slaves were sometimes simply kidnapped or pressed into service by force. In some societies, slave status was hereditary, passed on from parent to child.

Trade in slave labor went on in almost every major society. Regional networks grew up around the globe for the exchange of slaves. Prior to 1000 C.E., particularly important slave markets appeared in the Mediterranean, Africa, China and the Far East, and the Arab world. From the 1400s through the 1800s, Europeans and Americans transported millions of slaves from Africa to North and South America. This infamous Atlantic slave trade is discussed in further detail in Units Four and Five, Chapters 18 and 26.

A special institution similar to slavery existed in many times and places. This was serfdom. In serf-holding societies, the majority of a country's peasants would be unfree. Serfs were not technically slaves. They had more freedoms and protections than slaves (who were seen in most law codes simply as property). Still, serfs were bound to the land they lived on, unable to move or change profession without permission of the land's owner. Whether or not they had theoretical legal protections, serfs were, in real life, often vulnerable to many of the same abuses that slaves were. In some parts of Europe (especially Russia), serfdom persisted until the 1800s.

WAR

Regrettably, one of the most—if not *the* most—straightforward modes of human interconnection is war. Exactly when humans began to engage in organized violence is unknown. Most scholars speculate that combat emerged among hunter-gatherer societies during the Paleolithic era, growing out of the cooperative efforts needed to track and kill large animals.

From the beginning, wars were fought for a variety of reasons. These included competition over resources such as hunting grounds, water sources, and livestock. Fear and ethnic hatred caused conflicts, as did the desire for captives to use as slaves or for forced labor.

During the Stone Age, few, if any, societies maintained any type of professional military organization. Instead of forming armies, hunter-gatherer and herding societies assigned the responsibility for fighting to all, or most, able-bodied males. However, during the Bronze Age, the character of warfare changed. The advent of agriculture, the increased permanency of farming communities, and the rise of cities made it possible and necessary to create a specialized class of soldiers for the protection of a civilization's territory and property. Improved metallurgical techniques gave these new soldiers better weapons and armor.

Therefore, by the 3000s and 2000s B.C.E., sizable and well-organized armies, led by professional generals and officers, had begun to appear in many parts of the world, especially the ancient Middle East and China. Military skills and equipment increased in sophistication and complexity. From the Bronze Age onward, war became a driving force in world history—and one of the most striking, most important ways in which societies, over the course of centuries, have interacted.

TRADE

A powerful motivator of interaction between societies is trade, or the exchange of goods. From prehistory onward, human communities have found it mutually beneficial to buy, sell, or barter resources with each other. Trade takes place within societies, bringing cities, villages, and rural communities into closer contact. Societies also trade with other societies, creating connections and interdependencies throughout large areas of the world.

As long as the economic terms are relatively fair and equal, trade generally leads to increased prosperity or advantage for all parties. Economic relationships also stimulate the exchange of ideas, information, and cultural practices between civilizations. In many cases, healthy economic relationships between societies and states have helped to preserve peace. Conversely, disputes over trade have frequently led to hostility, even war. In times of conflict or disagreement, it is common for enemies to attempt to deprive each other of the ability to trade, either by means of blockade (physically interfering with a society's ability to move goods across its borders) or sanctions (refusing to trade with a society).

Until the industrial era and the invention of the railroad and modern roads, the movement of large amounts of goods overland was quite difficult. Water transport was much easier. Therefore, trade tended to flourish most along rivers, lakeshores, and the coastlines of oceans and seas. Before and around 1000 C.E., key international trade routes sprang up in the Mediterranean Sea, the North and Baltic seas, the Arabian Sea and Indian Ocean, the river systems of western Europe (especially the Rhine and Danube), the river basins connecting Scandinavia and Russia with the Black

Sea, and East Asia's Pacific shore. Land routes included the caravan routes of the Sahara desert, the Arabian peninsula, and the expanses of Eurasia. The longest and most important overland trade route was the Silk Road. This network stretched more than 5,000 miles, linking China with the Mediterranean coast of the Middle East—and, by extension, Europe. For years, the Silk Road was enormously important as an avenue for the exchange of wealth, ideas, cultural practices, science, technology, and religious beliefs throughout Eurasia.

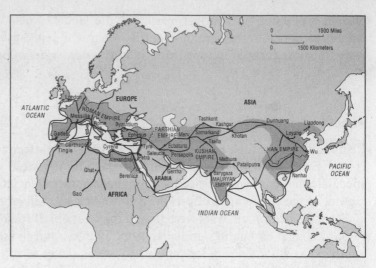

Principal African-Eurasian Trade Routes, ca. 200 B.C.E.–200 C.E.
During this time, merchants sold goods along a vast trade network that spanned from England in the northwest, to western Africa, Central Asia, and as far east as the Han Empire.

RELIGIOUS INTERACTION

Every society develops or adopts some kind of belief system in order to address questions of ethics, morality, and humanity's place in the universe. The world's major faiths are described in Chapter 5. It should be noted here, however, that religious beliefs cross borders very easily, allowing different cultures and civilizations to affect each other profoundly. Sometimes, religions spread peacefully, through simple cultural contact or deliberate proselytizing and missionary activity. In other cases, religious faiths are brought to other societies by means of aggression and war.

As societies interact, they often absorb some of the deities and basic religious concepts of their neighbors, even if specific names and details change. This took place among many of the native populations of Africa, South America, and North America. Throughout Eurasia, many elementary religious ideas are shared by the mythologies of the various descendants of the Indo-Europeans, who spread throughout Europe and Asia thousands of years ago. Famous examples of religious borrowing in the ancient Western tradition include the adoption of Sumerian gods and goddesses by the Babylonians and other Mesopotamian peoples, as well as the Romans' use of Greek deities, with slightly modified names.

All of the world's key religions had traveled far from their original birthplaces by 1000 C.E. Hinduism was prominent not only in India, but throughout Southeast Asia. Buddhism spread from India to all of East Asia, including China, Korea, and Japan. Confucianism and Daoism, which originated in China, influenced religious and philosophical thought elsewhere in East Asia. Judaism, Christianity, and Islam had all burst out of the Middle East to have huge effects on North Africa, Asia, and Europe (a few centuries later, Christianity and Judaism would be exported to South and North America as well).

THE MIGRATION OF PEOPLES

Human populations rarely develop in isolation. This is especially the case in times when communities are less settled. The mass movement, or migration, of large numbers of people in the early periods of global history has had a tremendous effect on the ethnic and cultural makeup of most of the world's major societies, even today.

As described in Chapter 2, humanity originated in Africa, then spread to all the other continents (excepting Antarctica). *Homo sapiens sapiens* moved into the Middle East and much of Asia around 100,000 years ago. Perhaps as far back as 50,000 years ago, settlers crossed from Southeast Asia to Australia. By 40,000 years ago, there were numerous human communities throughout Europe. Most scholars think that humans did not reach the Americas until comparatively late. Scientists estimate that *Homo sapiens sapiens* first came to the Americas around 15,000 years ago. At that time, peoples from Asia crossed an ice shelf or land bridge that is thought to have spanned what is now the Bering Strait, the narrow waterway that separates the tip of Russia from Alaska (however, there is recent genetic evidence to suggest that the crossings could have taken place as early as 29,000 years ago). Whatever the case, by 8000 B.C.E., humans had settled in almost all parts of the globe.

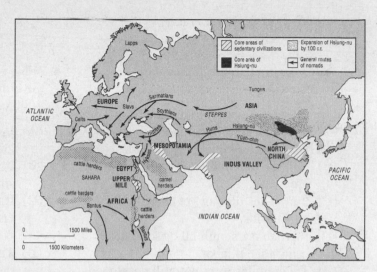

The Movement of Peoples in Eurasia and Africa After 2000 B.C.E.

Migration played a major role in the formation and development of early civilizations. Migrations often led to war and conquest, but they also facilitated cultural interaction and the spread of technology, science, languages, and religions.

After the settlement of all the continents, the regions that experienced the greatest and longest-lasting waves of mass migration were Africa, the Pacific, and Eurasia. From 2,500 to 5,000 years ago, the Bantu peoples began to spread throughout sub-Saharan Africa. Starting sometime around 2500 B.C.E., the epic migration of the Polynesians from Southeast Asia throughout the vast expanse of the Pacific Ocean began, leading to the settlement of literally thousands of islands sprinkled along an east-west axis 20,000 miles long. In Eurasia, a number of peoples, mainly from Central Asia, migrated outward, deeply affecting the ethnic and linguistic makeup of many European and Asian peoples. In particular, Europe was flooded by a tremendous influx of invaders and migrating tribes, from approximately the 200s C.E. to 1000 C.E.—a period known as the Great Age of Migrations. During this time, a variety of Germanic and Asiatic peoples moved toward and into Europe. Among the former were Goths, Angles, Saxons, Franks, Lombards, and Vikings. The latter included Avars, Bulgars, Huns, and Magyars. Although they were generally seen as a threat—and often perceived as barbarians—many of these peoples eventually settled throughout Europe and western Asia, playing an immensely important role in the development of many Eurasian ethnicities and cultures.

QUICK REVIEW

1. Why were trade routes particularly extensive in Eurasia?

   (A) Because a wide variety of communities, from Europe to East Asia, had to be linked by them.
   (B) Eurasia was where most goods were produced.
   (C) Europeans did not yet know how to build roads.
   (D) Russian tsars built all these routes using forced labor.
   (E) Trade routes were not well developed at all in Eurasia.

2. Which of the following statements about gender relations up to 1000 C.E. is most accurate?

   (A) Across all societies, women were subservient to men to the same degree.
   (B) In some societies, women enjoyed more rights than in others.
   (C) Because of the widespread worship of the mother goddess, in most societies, women were politically dominant.
   (D) Organized religions tended to strengthen gender equality.
   (E) The emergence of agriculture weakened gender division of labor.

3. What is diffusion?

   (A) the assimilation of a minority ethnic group into a larger, more homogeneous population
   (B) the splitting of the atom
   (C) the conquering of one civilization by a much more powerful one
   (D) the spread of foods, trade goods, concepts, norms, practices, and inventions among different peoples
   (E) none of the above

4. What role did the aristocracy play in governing during the period that led up to 1000 C.E.?

   (A) It usually opposed the monarchy's goals.
   (B) It worked in the interests of its constituents, the peasants.
   (C) It tended to assist monarchs with such tasks as political administration and defense.
   (D) The aristocracy is another word for the monarchy, so it acted as king.
   (E) The aristocracy was an early middle class.

5. Which of the following is an example of a democracy?

   (A) the city-state of Sparta
   (B) republican Rome
   (C) the Mauryan Empire under Ashoka's rule
   (D) Byzantium
   (E) none of the above

6. Where were there no slave markets prior to 1000 C.E.?

   (A) Antarctica
   (B) Africa
   (C) China
   (D) the Far East
   (E) the Mediterranean region

7. Why would a class of soldiers appear in a society?

   I. Because farming meant that land needed to be protected.

   II. Because the society was nomadic and thus more vulnerable to attack.

   III. Because urban areas were built up that needed to be guarded.

   IV. Because agriculture led to labor specialization.

   (A) I and II only

   (B) I, II, and III

   (C) I, III, and IV

   (D) all of the above

   (E) none of the above

8. Leading up to 1000 C.E., what was the world's most vital overland trade route?

   (A) the Silk Road

   (B) the Sahara desert

   (C) Main Street USA

   (D) the Sahel

   (E) the Trans-Siberian

9. According to scientists, modern humans reached North America by crossing a land bridge spanning the Bering Strait sometime between _____ years ago.

   (A) 500,000 and 700,000

   (B) 3,000 and 5,000

   (C) 2 million and 3 million

   (D) 15,000 and 29,000

   (E) 1 million and 2 million

10. During the so-called Great Age of Migrations,

   (A) humans moved back to Africa

   (B) many Germanic and Asiatic peoples moved into Europe

   (C) many Europeans moved to Asia to seek a more temperate climate

   (D) humans moved out of Africa into Indo-China

   (E) Polynesians moved to mainland Asia

ANSWERS:

1. **A**, p. 80	6. **A**, p. 78
2. **B**, p. 77	7. **C**, p. 79
3. **D**, p. 76	8. **A**, p. 80
4. **C**, p. 77	9. **D**, p. 81
5. **E**, p. 78	10. **B**, p. 81

CHAPTER 5

Religious Traditions and Belief Systems

Integral to the growth of any civilization is the development of a belief system providing a relatively coherent set of concepts and convictions that enable a social group to address questions of ethics, morality, spirituality, and the possibility of an afterlife. Over time, some of these belief systems grew into established religions. By 1000 C.E., all of the faiths that currently enjoy a major following worldwide had come into being. Each of these religions has become a distinguishing feature of many cultural traditions. They give the societies that adopt them a sense of unity, pride, and inspiration. Missionary activity and other proselytizing efforts have often led to dynamic and fruitful interactions across cultures. On the other hand, clashes between different faiths (or denominations within faiths) have frequently resulted in bigotry, persecution, and war. In both positive and negative ways, religion continues to be an indispensable factor in the functioning of all civilizations.

POLYTHEISM

ANCESTOR WORSHIP AND OTHER EARLY FORMS OF RELIGION

Almost without exception, the belief systems that emerged in the earliest human societies were polytheistic, meaning that they involved the worship of more than one deity. Among the oldest forms of polytheism are ancestor worship and the veneration of nature spirits and other vaguely defined supernatural beings. Examples of the latter are totemism (identification of the self with various animal symbols), shamanism (a belief in unseen spirit worlds, common in Central Asia, Siberia, and the Americas), the "dreamtime" (a spiritual concept peculiar to the aborigines of Australia), Shinto (native to Japan), and animism (a worship of life forces prevalent among tribes in Africa, the Pacific Islands, and parts of Asia).

PANTHEONS

As they grew more sophisticated, certain civilizations developed elaborate pantheons of numerous gods, each of whom had a distinct personality and specific function. Among the best-known of these are the Sumerian-Babylonian deities, shared by many peoples of the ancient Middle East; the Egyptian gods, the worship of whom was bound up with an intricate set of rituals dedicated to preparing oneself for the afterlife; the Olympian deities worshiped by the Greeks (and, in modified form, by the Romans); the Vedic gods and goddesses of ancient India; the Teutonic and Norse

Aesir and Vanir worshiped in northern Europe and Scandinavia; and the "celestial bureaucracy" of deities venerated in China.

TRANSITION TO MONOTHEISM: ZOROASTRIANISM

Most of these intricate polytheisms faded away, remaining only as bodies of myth and legend. A few, such as Hinduism and some forms of Buddhism, survive as major religions and are discussed in more detail subsequently. One faith that represents a partial commitment to monotheism (worship of a single god or goddess) is Zoroastrianism, founded in ancient Persia by the priest Zoroaster (also Zarathustra), sometime in the 500s B.C.E. Basing his teachings on a collection of texts called the Avestas, Zoroaster proposed the worship of only one god, Ahura Mazda (also Ormazd), the "wise lord." Later, Ahura Mazda's son Mithra was venerated as well. The enemy of Ahura Mazda was Ahriman, the god of darkness. Zoroaster taught that Ahura Mazda would eventually defeat Ahriman in a vast cosmic struggle. Ahura Mazda's followers would then be gathered into heaven; evil souls would be doomed to hell. Although Zoroastrianism resembles monotheistic religions, its belief that Ahriman is a god in his own right, with powers equal to those of Ahura Mazda, makes it dualistic instead. Zoroastrianism flourished in Persia until the 600s C.E., when the expansion of Islam drove it out. It lingers today mainly in India, among the small religious community known as Parsis. However, basic concepts from Zoroastrianism are thought by most religious historians to have played a crucial role in shaping later Jewish thought and, by extension, early Christianity.

JUDAISM

THE FIRST MONOTHEISTIC FAITH

Judaism emerged among the Middle Eastern people known as the Hebrews (the terms *Jews* and *Jewish* were not commonly used until the 900s B.C.E.). This religion is generally considered to have been the world's first monotheistic faith—that is, the first to devote itself exclusively to the worship of one deity alone. Along with Christianity, which grew out of it, Judaism forms a key part of the Western world's ethical, intellectual, and cultural foundation.

ABRAHAM'S COVENANT

According to the Judaic tradition, the patriarch Abraham, who lived near the Sumerian city of Ur, entered into a covenant with the god YHWH (often rendered as Yahweh or Jehovah). In exchange for their complete religious allegiance, YHWH swore to make the Hebrews his "chosen people" and to lead them to the "promised land" of Canaan (present-day Israel). Sometime between 2000 and 1850 B.C.E., the Hebrews left Ur and journeyed westward, their new faith taking shape as they went. Abraham's leadership of the Hebrews was carried on by his son Isaac and Isaac's younger son Jacob (who took the name Israel and whose twelve sons are considered to be the founders of the Twelve Tribes of Israel).

SLAVERY IN EGYPT, EXODUS, AND MOSES' LEADERSHIP

In approximately 1700 B.C.E., during a time of famine, the Hebrews migrated to Egypt. This event is narrated in the story of Jacob's son Joseph, who was sold into slavery by his brothers, but rose to glory, thanks to YHWH's favor. Over the course of several centuries, the Hebrews became the slaves of the Egyptians. However, around 1300 to 1200 B.C.E., under the great prophet and leader Moses, the Hebrews escaped from Egypt. This exodus is remembered in the celebration of Passover, the most important holiday in the Jewish faith. Moses and the young war leader Joshua took the Hebrews back to Canaan (although Moses himself was forbidden by YHWH to return). During the long journey, Moses is said to have handed down from YHWH the basic principles of Jewish law, including the Ten Commandments, revealed to him on Mount Sinai. He is also considered to be the author of the Torah ("Teaching"), the first five books in the Hebrew scriptures (the Tanakh). The books of the Torah were later incorporated by the Christian Bible as the first five books of the Old Testament.

THE HEBREW KINGDOMS: FREEDOM AND CONQUEST

Reconquest and consolidation of the homeland followed. The Hebrews were ruled at first by judges, then by kings, starting with Saul (ca. 1020–1000 B.C.E.). The Hebrew kingdom reached its zenith under its second monarch, David (ca. 1000–961 B.C.E.) and his son Solomon (ca. 961–922 B.C.E.). David, a talented military commander, united the kingdom of Israel and created a Hebrew capital at Jerusalem. He was also a skilled musician, and many of the religious songs and poems known collectively as the Psalms are attributed to him. Solomon made Israel extremely prosperous by taking advantage of its location at the crossroads of many trade routes in the Middle East. In Jerusalem, Solomon dedicated to YHWH the great Temple, which was, for centuries, at the heart of Jewish religious life.

After Solomon's death, the Hebrew kingdom split into two lands: Israel and Judah. The Hebrews were then conquered by a number of invaders, including the Assyrians (722 B.C.E.), the Babylonian Empire of Nebuchadnezzar (587 B.C.E.), the Persians (539 B.C.E.), Alexander the Great (333–331 B.C.E.), and the Romans (66–64 B.C.E.). Under Nebuchadnezzar, the Hebrews were uprooted from their lands (the "Babylonian Captivity"), and Solomon's Temple was torn down (a second temple was built during the 530s and 520s B.C.E.). In the face of their conquerors, all of whom were polytheistic, the Jews, guided by prophets and priests (rabbis, or "teachers"), remained true to their monotheistic worship of YHWH. They also clung to their faith in numerous prophecies that a savior, or Messiah ("anointed one") would someday appear to free them from oppression and exalt the name of YHWH.

ROMAN RULE AND THE JEWISH DIASPORA

During the years of Roman rule, the Judaic tradition gave birth to the new faith of Christianity, based on the teachings of Jesus of Nazareth (see the section on Christianity). Shortly thereafter, attempts to rebel against the Romans led to the permanent dissolution of the Hebrew state. During the Jewish Wars of 70 to 73 C.E., the Romans deprived the Jews of their homeland, destroyed the second Temple, and forced them into a diaspora that lasted until the middle of the twentieth century. While some Jews remained in the Middle East, others scattered throughout Europe, Asia, and the rest of the world. Until the establishment of the modern state of Israel in 1948, Jews were linked not by geography, but by shared cultural heritage, continued dedication to the monotheistic worship of YHWH, and observation of the laws and customs laid out by scripture.

JEWISH PRINCIPLES

In addition to its emphasis on the worship of a single god, the Hebrew scripture contained in the Tanakh outlines a strict code of conduct and places a high premium on righteous behavior. The same can be said about the Talmud ("Instruction"), the main collection of Jewish laws and commentaries upon them. Judaism is therefore often referred to as a system of ethical monotheism. Among the ancient Hebrews, legal practices operated on a retributive principle—an eye for an eye, a tooth for a tooth—that was common throughout the ancient Middle East. Dietary restrictions were extremely strict, as were rules governing sexual practice. Although women were respected in the home, Hebrew society as a whole was rigidly patriarchal, and the place of women in law and religious practice was decidedly lower than that of men. As did most people of the eastern Mediterranean, the Hebrews practiced slavery on at least a limited basis, but Jewish scripture also insisted on charity, social responsibility, and concern for the poor.

HINDUISM

Born in India, Hinduism is an extremely complex, polytheistic faith. Arguably, its roots extend further back in time than those of any other religion still practiced today. Rather than being a single faith in the Western sense—founded by a single individual or group, following a single god or set of gods, recognizing a single body of scripture—Hinduism is a synthesis of many religious traditions. It has been gathered together over many centuries and worshiped by many peoples, all of different ethnicities and speaking different languages. In fact, the word *Hinduism* is a foreign term, coined by Muslim invaders to describe any non-Islamic religious practices "beyond the Sindhu River." Today, the vast majority of the people of India are Hindu. Sizable Hindu minorities live in Pakistan, Bangladesh, and Sri Lanka. There are Hindu populations throughout South and Southeast Asia, as well as in emigration throughout the world.

VEDIC ROOTS OF HINDUISM

No precise date can be assigned to the birth of Hinduism. Instead, Hinduism evolved over the course of hundreds of years, from a combination of the religious practices of the people of the Indus River valley civilization (which had existed since 3000–2900 B.C.E.), other ethnic groups native to the Indian subcontinent, and Aryan invaders (who arrived from Central Asia sometime around 1500 B.C.E.). From this mixture emerged the tradition of Vedism, commonly regarded as the foundation of Hinduism. At the core of Vedism are four Aryan scriptures called Vedas, meaning "knowledge." The Vedas began to appear in written form after 1500 B.C.E., but are thought to be much older. In oral form, they may have existed as far back as 4500 B.C.E. The oldest and largest of the Vedas is the Rig-Veda, which includes over 1,000 hymns and stories about the gods.

Several dozen gods and goddesses were venerated in the Vedic texts. Chief among them was Varuna, the sky god and giver of justice, and Indra, the god of war and storms. Also important were Agni, the fire god; Mitra, the patron of humankind; and Surya, the sun god.

EARLY HINDU SCRIPTURES

Hinduism itself began gradually to take shape after 900 B.C.E., as a result of profound transformations in Vedic thought. New texts started to appear, particularly the Upanishads (written between 900 and 500 B.C.E.), essays and poems that outline the basic concepts of Hindu spirituality. Whereas the Vedas and Brahmanas focus on obedience to the gods and complex sacrifices and rituals carried out by the priestly class, the Upanishads emphasize simplicity, the inner development of the individual, and methods for spiritual self-improvement (including forms of yoga, meditative practices meant to foster physical and mental discipline).

Other scriptural literature emerged after the Upanishads, such as the Puranas (popular tales about gods and heroes). Moral teachings known as sutras became widespread. An influential work was the Laws of Manu (compiled between 200 B.C.E. and 200 C.E.), best known for its support of the caste system.

Along with new scripture, key texts that were both religious and literary in nature appeared during this time. One such story was the Ramayana (written ca. 350 B.C.E.), a tale describing the adventures of Rama, the seventh incarnation of the god Vishnu. Equally important, if not more so, is the Mahabharata (composed between 200 B.C.E. and 200 C.E.), a grand epic of 90,000 stanzas, making it perhaps the longest poem in the world. The Mahabharata depicts a great war between two royal houses. Its most famous section is the Bhagavad-Gita ("Song of the Lord"), a poetic dialogue between the young prince Arjuna and the demigod Krishna, who lectures Arjuna on the concept of moral duty.

HINDU DOCTRINE

The basic beliefs and concepts of classical Hinduism were all in place by at least the 200s B.C.E., after the Vedic and Upanishadic traditions had had time to merge with each other and spread throughout India. The major features of Hindu doctrine are outlined as follows.

At the center of all time and space is the World Soul, or the Brahman (also translated as "Ultimate Reality" or the "One"). All things that exist, human or nonhuman, are reflections of the Brahman's perfection. Every living creature has its own individual soul, known as atman. However, the material world is an illusion (maya). It causes suffering and prevents the individual soul from perceiving or being connected with the World Soul. The goal of existence is to rejoin one's atman with the Brahman, allowing oneself to be absorbed into perfection.

Union with the Brahman is accomplished by undergoing a cycle of life, death, and rebirth called the wheel of life (samsara). Hindus believe that spiritual perfection is attained by this process of incarnation and reincarnation. According to the law of deeds (karma), a person's actions—whether good or evil—in one life will have consequences in a future life. An atman's spiritual evolution therefore depends on a person's own deeds. Evil actions and spiritual laxity will increase the atman's karmic debt, keeping one trapped in the cycle of samsara. Good actions and spiritual discipline will reduce an atman's karmic debt, leading one to a greater understanding of moral duty (dharma). When a person has eliminated his or her karmic debt and achieved a sufficient understanding of dharma, his or her atman gains release (moksha) from samsara. Liberated from the cycle of life and death, the atman is free to join with the Brahman.

Moksha and union with the Brahman can be attained in a number of ways. The early Vedic scriptures placed great value on obedience to the gods and ritual practices. This meant that people were compelled to rely almost completely on the priestly class (brahmins) for their spiritual well-being. Over time, however, later scriptures, such as the Upanishads, argued that, by means of proper conduct and spiritual exercises, ordinary men and women could take greater responsibility for their own spiritual development. As Hinduism developed into a more coherent form, the majority of its followers came to recognize most paths of spiritual improvement—prayer, meditation, ritual, worship, good actions—as valid.

HINDU DEITIES

In addition to the Brahman, Hinduism recognizes literally hundreds of gods and goddesses (including the older Vedic deities, although their importance faded over time). This makes Hinduism a polytheistic religion. However, Hindus consider all deities to be avatars, or incarnations of the Brahman. By the 200s B.C.E., three gods in particular gained the largest followings, forming a trinity of sorts within the Hindu tradition: Brahma, Vishnu, and Shiva. Technically the most important (although the most poorly defined and the least popular) is Brahma the Creator, who, as his name suggests, is the masculine personification of the Brahman, or World Soul.

Vishnu the Preserver began as a minor Vedic deity associated with the sun. As Hinduism matured, he became a savior figure, a great friend to humanity. In various incarnations (avatars), he appears as a hero in classical India's greatest literary works. In his seventh incarnation, he is Rama, the protagonist of the Ramayana. His eighth incarnation is Krishna, the demigod who teaches the prince Arjuna about moral responsibility in the Bhagavad-Gita.

Shiva the Destroyer also started as a Vedic god with various functions, including healing, disease, and fertility. As a major Hindu deity, he is seen as the god of both creation and destruction.

He reflects the duality of life and death. He is also associated with sexual energy and cosmic regeneration. Shiva is frequently depicted in paintings and sculptures as a dancer.

Goddesses are important in Hinduism. All major female deities are considered to be incarnations of the great mother goddess, Mahadevi Shakti. Shakti's most famous avatars are Parvati (the wife of Shiva), Durga (a warrior goddess), Lakshmi (Vishnu's wife), and Kali (a widely venerated and feared goddess of death).

THE CASTE SYSTEM AND THE PLACE OF WOMEN

One of the best known features of Hindu belief involves the caste system of India. As much a social and political institution as it is a religious concept, the caste system was given moral justification by Vedic thought and Hindu theology as time passed. The origins of the caste system date back to the Aryan invasion of India. As the Aryans extended their hegemony over ever-greater portions of India, they established a rigid system of social stratification that relegated menial tasks and manual labor to the darker-skinned natives. From the 800s to the 600s B.C.E., this system grew into a more elaborate scheme that involved four distinct classes. At the highest level were the priests (brahmins). Near the top were the warriors and political rulers (kshatriyas). Commoners (vaishyas), such as farmers and artisans, were next. Servants, serfs, and members of the lower class (shudras) made up the lowest of the four main castes. As time went on, another major category, the "untouchables"—who performed the most degrading tasks, including the handling of human waste or burial of the dead—was formed. Over the centuries, the caste system grew increasingly more complex, with more divisions and subdivisions being devised.

In the hierarchical Hindu society, males were thought superior to women, although the Hindu code of behavior required that women be treated with respect, and women played a vital role within the family unit. Although men performed the family rituals, had a monopoly on education, and were allowed to own property, women were considered legal minors even as adults and could not own property. Many women married in childhood, and divorce was rare. The most notorious symbol of female subservience to men was the sati ritual (also known as suttee), by which wives were required to throw themselves on the funeral pyres of their dead husbands and be burned alive. This practice was discouraged by India's colonial masters, the British, during the nineteenth century. It was outlawed by the Indians themselves in the twentieth century.

The caste system and the place of women were given religious sanction by Hindu doctrine. Acceptance of one's social situation was considered to be virtuous. Performance of one's caste duties was an essential part of dharma, or moral duty. Indeed, only someone born into the highest caste—the brahmins—could hope to achieve moksha, release from the cycle of life and death. Good behavior as a member of a lower caste in one life would result in good karma, increasing the likelihood of being reborn into a higher caste, until one finally reached the level of brahmin. Ultimately, since material life was simply maya, or illusion, to begin with, the social position one occupied in one's earthly life was of secondary importance, compared to one's

The Practice of Sati.
The ritual of sati (or suttee) was a long-standing Hindu tradition. When a man of high caste died, his widow was expected to be burned to death on her husband's funeral pyre. Only in the twentieth century was this practice fully abolished.

spiritual development. The Laws of Manu is considered to be the most famous expression of Hinduism's religious argument in favor of the caste system.

BUDDHISM

Originating in India, the numerous forms and denominations of Buddhism have spread worldwide. This complex religion is followed principally in China, Japan, Sri Lanka, Tibet, Korea, and elsewhere in southern and eastern Asia. Although the foundations of Buddhism are associated with the teachings of one person, the variety of beliefs, gods, and theologies that fall into the category "Buddhist" is staggering. Broadly speaking, there are two major schools of Buddhist doctrine: Theravada (also known as Hinayana) and Mahayana. Both will be detailed subsequently, after a discussion of the Buddha himself and the movement he started.

RELIGIOUS TRANSITION IN INDIA

Buddhism was one of several religious movements born in India during the 500s B.C.E., as the long transition from Vedism to classical Hinduism stirred up religious debate and doctrinal controversy. This century was one of great spiritual ferment, and many teachers, hermits, and philosophers experimented with various means by which they could achieve understanding of and union with the World Soul. One religious path that emerged during this time—and might possibly have grown into a larger faith, if not for the simultaneous appearance of Buddhism—was Jainism, established by Mahavira (ca. 540–468 B.C.E.), who preached a doctrine of nonviolence and asceticism (self-denial).

SIDDHARTHA GAUTAMA AND THE BIRTH OF BUDDHISM

The individual who founded Buddhism was Siddhartha Gautama (ca. 563–483 B.C.E.). Gautama was born into a noble family from northern India, near the foothills of the Himalayas. At the age of twenty-nine, he ventured outside his palace, only to be appalled by the pain and poverty experienced by the common people of his land. In shock, he abandoned his aristocratic life to seek an answer to the question of human suffering. Having been born into one spiritual extreme— sensuality and an obsession with worldly matters—Gautama sought his answers in the opposite extreme: fasting and asceticism. After six years of self-deprivation, he decided that neither extreme led to salvation or gave true answers about life and suffering. He therefore chose to follow a "middle way" of moderation, peace, and contentment.

While following this middle way, Gautama is said to have achieved enlightenment, after spending a night meditating under a tree. It was at this point that he took the name Buddha, "the enlightened one" (or "awakened one"). The Buddha began to preach what he had learned from his enlightenment. A community of followers spread his teachings, and, after his death, the Buddha's creed was reaching beyond the borders of India to the rest of Asia.

BUDDHIST DOCTRINE

In its earliest form, Buddhism was less a religion than a philosophy. At no time did the Buddha make claim to divinity or godhood. Instead, his goal was to correct what he saw as the worst features of Vedism and Hinduism, as well as to modify some basic points of Vedic-Hindu doctrine. He also intended to purify concepts such as karma and reincarnation by reducing the role that complicated rituals, ceremonies, and the priestly brahmins played in spiritual life. As a result, the truths that the Buddha claimed were revealed to him in his moment of enlightenment either draw on or depart from the fundamental ideas contained in Hindu theology.

Like Hinduism, Buddhism postulates that individual souls evolve toward spiritual perfection by means of samsara, the wheel of life, death, and reincarnation. However, the Buddha rejected the caste system, and with it the notion that only a brahmin could be freed from samsara. Any person could achieve liberation from the wheel of life, without the aid of priests, rituals, or ceremonies. Instead, liberation resulted from enlightenment. All that was necessary to attain enlightenment was to realize the Four Noble Truths and to follow the Eightfold Path of good conduct (as well as the Five Moral Rules).

The Four Noble Truths, revealed to the Buddha in his moment of enlightenment, are as follows:

- Human existence is inseparable from suffering.
- The cause of suffering is desire.
- Suffering is extinguished by extinguishing desire.
- Desire may be extinguished by following the Eightfold Path.

The Eightfold Path of good conduct involves the following practices:

- Know the truth.
- Resist evil.
- Do nothing to hurt others.
- Respect all forms of life.
- Work for the well-being of others before that of yourself.
- Free your mind of evil.
- Control your thoughts.
- Practice meditation.

In addition to the Eightfold Path, the Buddha described Five Moral Rules (do not kill any living being; do not take what is not given to you; do not speak falsely; do not drink intoxicating drinks; do not be unchaste).

By coming to these realizations and by following this moral code, any person can reach enlightenment and thereby free himself or herself from samsara. In Buddhist terms, this liberation is called nirvana, the literal meaning of which is "to extinguish." According to the original teachings of the Buddha, the result of nirvana is not a union of the individual soul with the World Soul. Instead, nirvana leads to a state of superconsciousness, in which one's self is dissolved into the all-encompassing life spirit that transcends place and time, animating all creatures in all eras.

THERAVADA BUDDHISM

After the Buddha's death in 483 B.C.E., the tradition he founded not only spread throughout Asia, it also split into various denominations, roughly divided into two large movements. The older movement is Theravada Buddhism ("Way of the Elders"), also referred to as Hinayana ("Lesser Vehicle") Buddhism. Prominent in South and Southeast Asia (although certain forms are followed in the north), Theravada Buddhism remains closer in spirit to the Buddha's actual teachings. It emphasizes simplicity, meditation, and an interpretation of nirvana as the renunciation of the self and of human consciousness. Gods and goddesses have very little place in Theravada Buddhism, and the Buddha himself is not considered to be a deity.

MAHAYANA BUDDHISM

The second and newer movement, Mahayana ("Greater Vehicle") Buddhism, is widespread in northern and northeastern Asia, especially in Japan, Korea, Tibet, and parts of China. Mahayana forms of Buddhism tend to be more elaborate and complicated than Theravada forms, involving much more ritual and symbology than the Buddha himself had intended. Part of this change resulted from the fact that Buddhism, upon reaching new lands, often blended with indigenous religions, absorbing elements of local belief. Moreover, many later Buddhists found the austerity and spareness of the original teachings to be of little spiritual comfort, and they began to argue that means of salvation that the Buddha himself had not spoken of were possible. In some Mahayana denominations, the concept of nirvana came to resemble traditional ideas of heaven, rather than the suppression of desire or the self. Concepts of hell, or some kind of punishment in the afterlife, appeared. Whereas the Buddha had made little or no mention of gods or goddesses, many Mahayana forms developed complex pantheons of deities, and the Buddha himself became god-like in nature. Veneration of these deities became just as important as meditation, if not more so, in the quest for nirvana. Adherents of Mahayana also prayed to bodhisattvas (souls who had achieved nirvana, but chose to remain in the earthly realm, in order to help living humans reach salvation). Worshipers came to rely more and more heavily on priests, ceremonies, and new scriptures, all of which sprang up in great profusion. The obvious irony is that many of these additions and accretions were very much like those aspects of Hinduism of which the Buddha himself had disapproved. Nonetheless, Mahayana traditions flourished and developed into a respected, highly popular branch of Buddhist theology.

DAOISM (TAOISM)

Like Buddhism, Daoism appeared during the 500s B.C.E. Also like Buddhism (at least in its original form), Daoism was less a religion and more a philosophical system, whose founding figure made no claim to divinity. However, Daoism did have a mystical strain that grew increasingly pronounced as time passed.

THE FOUNDERS OF DAOISM

Traditionally, the founder of Daoism is considered to be Laozi (Lao-tzu), the "Old Master" (born ca. 604 B.C.E.). Laozi may or may not be an actual historical figure. He is also said to have written Daoism's central text, the Tao-te Ching, although most scholars believe that this collection of writings was compiled sometime in the 300s and 200s B.C.E. Another figure associated with the development of Daoism is Zhuangzi (Chuang-tzu), who is known to have lived approximately from 369 to 286 B.C.E.

FOLLOWING THE DAO

To follow Daoism is simply to follow "the way," or "the path," the two most common translations of dao (therefore, the Tao-te Ching is the "Book of the Way"). Daoist belief is metaphysical and instinctual. It maintains that the universe is governed by a natural force that is invisible yet irresistible, divine yet impersonal. This force cannot be understood intellectually, but it can be felt or sensed intuitively. Daoist thought is deliberately antirational, using parables and paradox to train the worshiper to perceive the world in nonlogical ways.

A Daoist attains wisdom and happiness by seeking the dao in all things. He or she is not concerned with worldly things, such as politics, money, or material possessions, because all of these are illusory and meaningless. The dao can be found in nature, in poetry, and in spontaneous behavior. The wise man or woman does not resist the dao, but, recognizing that he or she has little or no control over the course of events in the physical world, seeks to be in harmony with the deeper truth of the dao. Daoism places a great deal of emphasis on individuality, since each person pursues the dao in his or her own unique way.

DAOIST RITUAL

After a time, Daoism became associated with mystical and magical practices, such as charm making, alchemy, and fortune-telling. The I-Ching, or "Book of Changes," is a Daoist text used in reading the future. The most famous symbol associated with Daoism is the yin-yang, a circle whose black and white halves are divided by a double-curved line, serving to illustrate that nothing is absolute, and that even opposites flow into each other.

Perhaps the most flexible of the world's major religions, Daoism has traditionally coexisted with other faiths. It is not at all uncommon for a worshiper to blend elements of Daoist worship with practices from other religions, particularly Buddhism and Confucianism. Since Daoism and Confucianism arose in China at approximately the same time, the relationship between the two has generally been quite a tight one—often uncomfortably so, since their philosophical outlooks are, for the most part, diametrically opposed.

Daoism spread throughout its native China. Certain of its elements were transported to those parts of Asia where China had a strong cultural influence, especially Japan and Korea.

CONFUCIANISM

CONFUCIANISM: RELIGION OR PHILOSOPHY?

Of the world's major belief systems, Confucianism, which was developed in China during the 500s B.C.E., is the least religious in nature. In fact, lacking any objects of worship, any clergy, or any ritual practices, Confucianism cannot be defined as a religion at all. It is instead an ethical code based almost completely on secular principles. Confucianism's founders believed in the existence of gods, spirits, and heaven, but gave little place to them in the philosophical system they articulated. They argued that a morally concerned person should most properly be interested in how he or she acted here and now, in the material world. What happened beyond one's physical life was of less importance, or at least could not be written or theorized about in any meaningful way.

CONFUCIAN TEXTS

Confucianism grew out of the teachings of the sage K'ung Fu-tzu, better known by the Latinized version of his name, Confucius (ca. 551–479 B.C.E.). K'ung Fu-tzu lived during the politically chaotic Zhou (Chou) dynasty. A minor aristocrat, he served as a government official in the court of the Prince of Lu. Upon retiring from state service, K'ung Fu-tzu began to ponder the nature of the relationship between the individual and society at large. He gathered a group of disciples who shared his ideas. It is these followers who captured K'ung Fu-tzu's thoughts and words on paper. Although K'ung Fu-tzu is traditionally considered to have authored the Confucian classics (books on history, divination, ritual, and poetry), in actuality he left behind no works of his own. His *Analects* ("Selected Sayings") are recordings of his conversations with his students, written in dialogue form.

A second Confucian theorist was Meng-tzu, or Mencius (371–289 B.C.E.). His commentaries on the *Analects* and early Confucian thought helped the movement reach its highest level of sophistication.

CONFUCIAN PRINCIPLES

Confucianism proposes that a happy, harmonious society can be created by a combination of benevolent rulership from above and good behavior from below. The well-being of the group comes before that of the individual. Order and hierarchy are paramount, so long as the government is good. Good government is the responsibility of the ruler, and as long as the ruler performs his duties well, his people have an obligation to obey him (Confucianism, a very patriarchal philosophy, made no provision for the possibility of female rulers). Meng-tzu proposed that a good and just ruler possesses the Mandate of Heaven, a moral justification for his authority. Unjust rulers who abuse their power lose the Mandate of Heaven, and can therefore be removed by their people.

Ideally, society operates in much the same way as a model Chinese family does, with all junior members paying respect to their elders. Confucianism regards the family unit as the most important institution in any civilization; if the home is blessed by filial piety, society at large is healthy. This vision is reflected in the five relationships K'ung Fu-tzu described as most important to social tranquility: the ruler should be just, those who are ruled should be loyal; the father should be loving, the son respectful; the husband should be righteous, the wife obedient; the older brother should be genteel, the younger brother humble; the older friend should be considerate, the younger friend deferent.

Confucian thought also established the female as the subservient sex. Men ruled society, fought wars, and acted as scholars and ministers. They could keep more than one wife and divorce any wife who failed to produce a male heir. Women were exclusively homemakers and mothers. Laws prohibited women from owning property, and they were not provided financial security through a dowry system. However, Confucianism allowed women to have a limited education.

Implicit in all these relationships are the concepts of reciprocity and mutual respect. Those who are superior may expect deference from those below them, but only if they themselves treat those below them well. Likewise, those who are inferior may expect good treatment from those above, but only if they are properly deferent. Central to Confucian thought is a "golden rule" which is practically identical to the one found in Christianity: in the *Analects*, K'ung Fu-tzu declares, "Never do to others what you would not like them to do to you."

Honorable behavior (*li*) consists of etiquette, grace, virtue, and courtesy. Anyone who practices *li*, no matter what class he comes from, is considered "gentlemanly." Those who occupy high stations in society are further expected to exhibit sympathy or "human-heartedness" (*jen*).

CONFUCIANISM, NEO-CONFUCIANISM, AND CHINESE POLITICAL LIFE

By 1000 C.E., Confucianism had coexisted with and, at times, competed with Daoism and Buddhism. Several times, it gained, lost, and regained its status as a code of conduct officially sponsored by China's imperial regime. By the 600s C.E., a newer variation of the creed, called Neo-Confucianism, appeared. Even during those years when it was not in official favor, Confucianism continued to be tremendously influential. China's traditional emphasis on filial piety, social hierarchy, and respect for authority stems in large part from Confucianism and has persisted into the modern era, even under the Communist regime.

CHRISTIANITY

THE JUDEO-CHRISTIAN TRADITION

Doctrinally, historically, and philosophically, Christianity is a child of Judaism. The relationship between the two faiths has often been a troubled one, but it has always been intimate. Both religions, in the form of what is known as the Judeo-Christian tradition, have formed the bedrock of Western thought and culture for two millennia.

THE LIFE AND MINISTRY OF JESUS

The founder of Christianity was Jesus of Nazareth (ca. 4 B.C.E.–29 C.E.), later known as the Christ (from the Greek translation of the Hebrew term *mashiah*, or "anointed one"). Details about Jesus come from the Gospels, the four books of the Christian Bible that describe his life and ministry. Jesus was born into a Jewish family of humble background. Upon reaching adulthood, he began to attract a following as a wandering teacher. He gathered an inner circle of disciples, but also preached throughout the countryside and in the major cities of Judaea.

Jesus maintained that his purpose was to uphold Jewish laws and traditions, but he also sought to reform them. He insisted that obeying the rabbis and observing customs and rituals were not enough to please YHWH (in later Christian usage, God). Jesus taught that the sincerity of one's belief mattered more than symbolic professions of that belief, such as giving large offerings of money to the rabbis, wearing proper dress, or following strict dietary guidelines. He maintained that charity, compassion, and forgiveness were of paramount importance in living a truly religious life. He reinforced this message in the Sermon on the Mount ("Blessed are the poor in spirit . . .") and in what came to be known as the Golden Rule ("Do unto others as you would have them do unto you").

During his three-year ministry, Jesus claimed to be the Christ, or the Messiah: the "anointed one" that Hebrew prophecy had foretold would appear to fulfill YHWH's promise to them as His chosen people. Although many Jews expected that the Messiah would be a political ruler who would restore the might of the Hebrew kingdom, Jesus had a heavenly kingdom in mind instead. He spoke of himself as the "Son of God," whose teachings would redeem and lead to God all those who followed his words.

The teachings of Jesus proved immensely popular, especially among the common people and the poor. On the other hand, his claims to be the Messiah and his questioning of traditional custom and practice angered conservatives within the Jewish religious establishment. At the same time, rumors that Jesus had assumed the title "King of the Jews" (a misinterpretation of what he meant by being the Messiah) made Roman authorities extremely suspicious. When Jesus came to preach in Jerusalem during the Passover season, Jewish religious authorities demanded that the Roman procurator, Pontius Pilate, arrest him. Pilate, fearing the political repercussions of Jesus' ministry, agreed. Jesus was tried for blasphemy (a charge brought against him by the Jewish authorities) and treason (of which he was accused by the Romans). Found guilty, Jesus was put to death by the Romans. The method of execution was crucifixion, and the instrument of Jesus' death—the cross—is the most important symbol in the Christian faith.

THE EARLY CHRISTIAN CHURCH

Before his arrest, Jesus had claimed that he would return from the dead before returning to God, his Father, in heaven. After his crucifixion, Jesus' closest followers began to preach that he had indeed been resurrected (an event celebrated during Easter, the holiday most central to the Christian faith). This veneration of the risen Jesus, which soon came to be known as Christianity, was carried on at first by his closest disciples, such as Peter (generally considered to be the first pope) and the authors of the four Gospels (Matthew, Mark, Luke, and John). Other adherents of the new faith began to spread the words and teachings of Christ as well. These figures, instrumental in establishing the early Christian church, are known as the apostles. The apostles perpetuated the teachings of Christ and told the story of his Crucifixion and Resurrection. They also foretold the Second Coming of Christ, when the physical world would come to an end, the Kingdom of Heaven would be established, and all souls would be subjected to a Day of Judgment. Good Christians would live with God and Christ in heaven; evildoers and nonbelievers would be damned to hell.

Early Christianity began as an obscure Jewish heresy. Its practice was also made illegal by Roman law. Despite those obstacles, Christianity gained an increasingly larger following over the next three centuries, not just in Judaea, but throughout the Middle East and the entire Roman Empire. One individual who played a crucial role in organizing the early church was the apostle

Paul. Born Saul of Tarsus, Paul, originally a persecutor of Christianity, changed his name after a sudden conversion to the new faith. With Peter, Paul worked tirelessly from approximately 45 to 64 C.E. to establish new centers of worship. Perhaps his greatest contribution was to widen the appeal of Christianity beyond the circle of its original Jewish worshipers. By decreeing that Christians did not have to observe Jewish law (including dietary restrictions and the circumcision of male adherents), Paul made it much easier to convert Greeks, non-Jewish Middle Easterners, and other peoples in the Roman Empire to Christianity. This flexibility allowed the expansion of the new religion to proceed with even greater rapidity. With Peter, Paul traveled to Rome in 64 C.E. There, both men were put to death by the Emperor Nero.

Christianity caught on in many communities and among many groups. It was especially popular among those who felt a sense of powerlessness in Roman society: noncitizens, slaves, the poor, commoners, and women. The new religion was open to all, and it held out the hope of a happy afterlife to those whose lives in the present were drab, miserable, or wretched. Although organized Christianity later became highly male-dominated, the early Christian church gave women a sense of belonging and, within certain limits, influential roles within apostolic communities. As time passed, however, a strict interpretation of the story of Adam and Eve assigned the blame for humanity's "original sin" to women as a whole. Paul's writings on women clearly put them in a secondary position. Women were to obey men, and they were not allowed to occupy the positions of highest leadership within the church (including priesthood). All cultures that adopted Christianity would be affected by this worldview for centuries to come.

ROMAN PERSECUTION OF CHRISTIANITY

In spite of Christianity's great appeal and organizational success, to worship as a Christian remained dangerous for more than three hundred years. Christians devised secret codes and signals, and practiced their services and ceremonies in hidden places, often in underground chambers called catacombs. Roman persecution was a constant peril, and many Christians were arrested and executed. Worshipers who died for their faith were known as martyrs. Ironically, the campaigns of persecution, rather than destroying the new religion, only strengthened the resolve of the followers. Moreover, the bravery and dignity with which many of the martyrs perished often attracted new converts.

LEGALIZATION AND THE FORMAL ORGANIZATION OF CHRISTIANITY

In 313 C.E., legal status was granted to Christianity by the Edict of Milan, handed down by the emperor Constantine. In 380 C.E., Christianity was made the official religion of the Roman Empire, and in 392 C.E., it was proclaimed to be the empire's only legal faith. Free from persecution, the church turned to questions of ecclesiastical organization, setting up a formal hierarchy of priests and bishops (by the fifth century C.E., the bishop of Rome, a position traditionally said to have been held by the apostle Peter, was becoming known as the pope). Only men could serve as clergy. The newly legalized church also found it necessary to establish a body of dogma, an officially agreed-upon set of beliefs. Important issues included the nature of Christ (considered to be both fully human and fully divine) and the doctrine of the Trinity (the belief that God has a triune nature, existing in the three persons of God the Father, Jesus Christ the Son, and the Holy Spirit). Beliefs that were not declared to be part of dogma were condemned as heresy.

Another task was to decide which religious texts would be considered sacred. In this way, the books of the Christian Bible were compiled. The Bible consisted of two main parts: the Old Testament (containing the Hebrew Torah, stories from Jewish history, and the writings of Hebrew prophets) and the New Testament (comprised of the four Gospels, episodes from the history of the early Christian church, and letters written by the Apostles). Decisions about dogma and the Bible were made at a series of councils held during the 300s C.E. and afterward. The first of these was the Council of Nicaea, called by the emperor Constantine in the 320s C.E. and resulting in the Nicene Creed, a declaration of fundamental Christian beliefs. The priests and scholars who attended the councils or helped to clarify and defend the councils' decisions are often referred to collectively as the church fathers. Among the most famous are Jerome (347–420 C.E.), whose Vulgate Bible was the first Latin translation of the holy book, and Augustine (354–430 C.E.), whose *City of God* is considered to have laid the intellectual foundation for the further development of Christian doctrine.

CHRISTIANITY AFTER THE FALL OF THE ROMAN EMPIRE

With the collapse of the Roman Empire during the 400s C.E. came a new era for the Christian church. In Asia Minor, the Middle East, and North Africa, where the Roman legacy was carried on by the Byzantine Empire, metropolitan centers such as Antioch, Alexandria, and especially Constantinople were the great centers of Christian worship. In the west, where Europe was collapsing into political confusion and social breakdown, the headquarters of the Christian church was Rome.

Although the Christian church called itself catholic, or universal, it was, in reality, deeply divided. Doctrinal disagreements, geographical separation, and the simple passage of time all caused the western and eastern churches to grow apart after the 500s C.E. By 1000 C.E., a rupture was imminent, and, in the Great Schism of 1054 C.E., the western and eastern churches broke with each other formally and permanently. Eastern Orthodoxy remained the faith of the Byzantine Empire, and it was the form of worship adopted by most Christians in the Middle East, the Russian lands, and much of eastern Europe. Roman Catholicism remained the favored form of Christianity in western Europe. During the Middle Ages, the Roman Catholic Church became one of the most important institutions in Europe, providing Europeans with a sense of religious unity, preserving Latin manuscripts and texts from the Roman era, and exerting a tremendous sway over secular and political affairs. Further splits within the western Christian church would come later, during the 1500s and 1600s C.E. But, during the medieval era, its power and influence remained paramount.

ISLAM

THE ORIGINS OF ISLAM

The youngest of the world's major religions, Islam transformed itself with amazing speed from a local faith into a cultural, social, and political force of global dimensions. Islam is a monotheistic form of worship that originated in the Middle East. It is linked with Judaism and Christianity in many ways, although the relationships that have prevailed among the three of them have frequently been stormy, even tragic. Nonetheless, the three faiths contain many similarities and possess an eventful shared history.

Islam arose in the Arabian peninsula during the 600s C.E. At the time, Arabia was a relatively backward part of the Middle East, whose desert interior remained largely unexplored. Arabia's few major settlements were built up around oases and, on the coast, port towns that served as centers of the caravan trade that linked the region with the rest of the Middle East. From Arabia, the new religion spread rapidly throughout the eastern Mediterranean. By 1000 C.E., its influence stretched from Spain and the Atlantic coast of Africa in the west to the borderlands of India in the east.

MOHAMMED AND HIS TEACHINGS

The founder of Islam was Mohammed (also Muhammad), a prosperous merchant from the trading center of Mecca, on the southwestern coast of Arabia. Born in 570 C.E., Mohammed began to meditate in the mountains near Mecca when he turned forty. In 610 C.E., during what Muslims call the "Night of Power and Excellence," he experienced a profound vision. According to Mohammed, the archangel Gabriel, the divine messenger, appeared to him, delivering the word of Allah (Arabic for "God").

For the next twenty-two years, Mohammed dedicated his life to spreading the teachings that had been revealed to him by Allah. With the help of family members such as Ali (his cousin and son-in-law), Aisha (his favorite wife), and Abu Bakr (Aisha's father and his father-in-law), Mohammed began to preach and gather a religious community around him. In 622, however, Mohammed and his followers were forced out of Mecca by local religious authorities. They fled to the city of Medina, about two hundred miles to the north. The flight of Mohammed—the Hegira—remains a key event in the early history of Islam, and it is this moment that marks the beginning of the Islamic calendar. Mohammed's religious community flourished in Medina, and by 630, he and his followers were able to return to Mecca and convert the city to his new faith. In 632, Mohammed himself died, but the religion he had founded survived and grew.

THE PRINCIPLES OF ISLAMIC FAITH

The faith that Mohammed established, like Judaism and Christianity, recognized only a single deity. From the beginning, it drew upon Judeo-Christian images and concepts. Mohammed taught that there is one god, Allah. Like the Christians, he believed that there is an afterlife in which believers go to heaven and nonbelievers to hell. A final judgment will end the world and weigh all souls, good and evil, in the balance. Islam also pays respect to many figures from Jewish and Christian faith. Muslim Arabs, like the Hebrews, consider Abraham to be their patriarch and Abraham's son Ismail (Ishmael) to be their direct ancestor. Prophets of Allah include Adam, Noah, Moses, David, Solomon, John the Baptist, and Jesus. Islamic teaching instructs Muslims to respect Jews and Christians as "people of the book."

These similarities notwithstanding, Mohammed went on to formulate a religious tradition that was unique. His principal claim was that he was the last of twenty-eight prophets sent by Allah to reveal His teachings to humankind. As the "Seal of the Prophets," he was therefore the only teacher privileged to have received the full and perfect message of Allah. To enter into the community of true believers, it is necessary to submit to the will of Allah. The name of the religion itself, *Islam*, comes from the Arabic phrase "to submit to God." Likewise, the term *Muslim*, which describes a follower of Islam, means "servant of God," or "one who has submitted to the will of God."

Submission to Allah involves living by the five Pillars of Faith described by Mohammed. These are

- To declare that "There is no god but Allah, and Mohammed is his prophet"
- To pray five times a day, facing in the direction of the holy city of Mecca
- To fast during the holiday of Ramadan, which commemorates the month in which Mohammed received his vision
- To give alms to the poor
- To make a pilgrimage (hajj) to Mecca at least once during one's lifetime

Other Islamic beliefs and traditions include abstinence from alcohol and pork; avoiding the portrayal of human or animal figures in art; and polygamy (Muslim men are allowed to take up to four wives). There are also tight restrictions on how women are allowed to dress or appear in public. Most famously, a strictly observant Muslim woman is to guard her modesty and veil herself when in public. In modern life, these traditions have been loosened or abandoned by many Islamic communities. A number of Muslim nations have become more secular and allow a less stringent observance of these practices. Even in earlier times, male domination of women in Islamic societies was offset by the Qur'an's command that men treat women with respect. Women also enjoyed the right to inherit, have dowries, and own property.

The teachings of Mohammed are contained in the holy scripture of Islam, the Qur'an (Koran), or the "Recitation," which contains 114 chapters, or suras. Muslims consider the Qur'an to be the word of Allah, transmitted directly by Mohammed, so every word is considered sacred. The Arabic that Mohammed spoke is the holy language of Islam. Other important texts in the Islamic tradition are the Hadith, a collection of the sayings and proverbs of Mohammed, and the Sharia, a codification of traditional Islamic law.

THE EXPANSION OF ISLAM

The expansion of Islam during the 600s, 700s, and 800s C.E. went hand-in-hand with military conquest and political domination. Early Islam made no distinction between political allegiance and religious affiliation; to be a Muslim meant also to belong to a political and social community (*umma*) linked by religious belief. After Mohammed's death in 632, it was decided that the umma was to be governed by a caliph (*khalifa*), or "successor," who was both a religious and political leader. The first caliph was Mohammed's father-in-law, Abu Bakr.

Before the death of Mohammed, most of the Arabian peninsula had converted to Islam. It was up to the first three caliphs—Abu Bakr, Umar (Omar), and Uthman—to break out of Arabia and bring Islam not only to the rest of the Middle East, but beyond. By the end of the 700s C.E., Muslim forces had swept through the Middle East, destroying the Persian Empire, threatening the Byzantine Empire, and bringing under Islamic rule territories such as Iraq, Syria, Palestine, Egypt, most of north Africa, parts of the Caucasus Mountains, the region that is today Pakistan, Spain, and parts of the Italian peninsula. From the 600s to the 1200s C.E., this vast territory was ruled over by two Islamic states, or caliphates: the Umayyad Caliphate (661–750 C.E.), centered at Damascus, and the Abbasid Caliphate (750–1258 C.E.), whose capital was Baghdad. The zenith of Islamic civilization, as a single political and religious entity, came during the first 300 years of the Abbasid Caliphate, roughly the years between 750 and 1050 C.E.

ISLAMIC DENOMINATIONS

Triumph and expansion did not prevent major splits within the Islamic faith. After the death of the caliph Uthman in 656 C.E., a dispute over who should succeed to the caliphate led to civil war between various members of Mohammed's family, particularly Mohammed's son-in-law Ali and Mohammed's wife Aisha. Although Ali's forces defeated Aisha's, he himself was killed during the fighting. In 661 C.E., another leader, Muawiyah (661–680 C.E.), proclaimed himself caliph and established his clan, the Umayyad, as the political and religious rulers of the Islamic community for the next century. The vast majority of Muslims accepted Muawiyah and his successors as legitimate caliphs. These Muslims refer to themselves as Sunni Muslims, the "People of Tradition and Community." To this day, more than 80 percent of all Muslims are Sunni. The followers of Ali, however, considered Muawiyah and the Umayyads to be usurpers. They formed a minority denomination that still exists today, known as the Shiites, from *Shi'at Ali*, or "Party of Ali." The Shiites maintain that Ali was Mohammed's rightful successor.

Another movement that appeared within the Islamic faith was Sufism, a mystical tradition that appeared during the 700s and 800s C.E. Sufism places a premium on fasting, prayer, and meditation as means by which a worshiper can grow closer to Allah.

THE GEOGRAPHY OF ISLAM

Several holy places are connected to Islamic worship. One of them, Jerusalem, is also shared by Judaism and Christianity, a fact that has led to considerable friction. According to Islamic tradition, Mohammed ascended to heaven from Jerusalem. The mosque known as the Dome of the Rock (al-Buraq) is built on the spot from which he and the horse that carried him are said to have risen. The holiest site in the Islamic faith is Mecca: Mohammed's birthplace and home to the shrine known as the Kaaba, or Black Rock. Making a pilgrimage, or hajj, to Mecca is one of Islam's five Pillars of Faith. Observant Muslims also pray to Mecca five times a day. Mediná, to which Mohammed fled during the Hegira, is also a key center of faith.

Islam is most famously associated with the Middle East, and the vast majority of the people who live there are Muslim. As a legacy of Islam's rapid and extensive spread during its first three centuries of existence, however, there are Muslim communities worldwide. Countries with Islamic majorities include most of the nations of North Africa, Pakistan, Indonesia (the country with the largest Muslim population), and others. Sizable Islamic minorities can be found around the globe.

QUICK REVIEW

1. Which of the following is an example of a pantheon?

   (A) the 12 apostles of the New Testament
   (B) the first five American presidents
   (C) a winning sports team
   (D) the Vedic gods and goddesses of ancient India
   (E) nature according to Zen worshipers

2. The Christians incorporated the Jewish books of the Torah as

   (A) the first five books of the New Testament
   (B) the first five books of the Old Testament
   (C) the first half of the Qu'ran
   (D) their official prayer book
   (E) none of the above

3. Which of the following is NOT related to the Jewish faith?

   (A) a belief that a Messiah would appear and free them from oppression
   (B) the Torah
   (C) monotheism
   (D) the Eightfold Path
   (E) the Tanakh

4. Which of the following is an accurate statement about Hinduism?

   (A) It draws from many different religious traditions.
   (B) It was founded in isolation from other religions.
   (C) It originated in China.
   (D) It was founded in 1500 B.C.E.
   (E) It is monotheistic.

5. What is a major similarity between Hinduism and Buddhism?

   (A) Both religions support a caste system.
   (B) Both religions accept that souls reach spiritual perfection through a cycle of life, death, and reincarnation.
   (C) Both embrace the Four Noble Truths.
   (D) Both follow the Eightfold Path.
   (E) These two religions are diametrically opposed.

6. Daoist thought is

   (A) based on reason
   (B) only proclaimed by the one god, Dao
   (C) based exclusively on Confucianism
   (D) largely antirational
   (E) intrinsically linked to Islam

7. Scholars largely learn about Jesus from

(A) Roman archives
(B) oral histories
(C) books written by the ancient Egyptians
(D) the Gospels
(E) Greek myths

8. How did the early Christians gain adherents?

(A) They offered new adherents free trips to Roman spas and other such enticements.
(B) They decreed that new followers did not have to observe Jewish law.
(C) They befriended Emperor Nero, who proclaimed Christianity a state religion.
(D) Their armies swept across Europe and forced the captured people to accept Christianity.
(E) They found adherents in the upper classes of Roman society.

9. According to Muslims, how did Mohammed receive the word of Allah?

(A) He was born speaking God's wisdom.
(B) He was on his deathbed.
(C) An archangel delivered him the word through a vision.
(D) His mother told him.
(E) He received Allah's words when he was lost in the Saharan desert.

10. After Mohammed's death, the Muslim community began to be ruled by a caliph, who was

(A) a religious leader
(B) a political leader
(C) thought to be the reincarnation of Mohammed
(D) both a political and religious leader
(E) none of the above

ANSWERS:

1. **D**, p. 84
2. **B**, p. 86
3. **D**, p. 86
4. **A**, p. 87
5. **B**, p. 91
6. **D**, p. 92
7. **D**, p. 95
8. **B**, p. 96
9. **C**, p. 98
10. **D**, p. 99

Unit Two: Review Questions

SAMPLE ESSAY QUESTIONS

1. Compare the rise, organization, characteristics, and collapse of two of the following empires: Rome, Han China, Byzantium, Ghana, the Maya.

2. How did patterns of social and economic organization change in China during this period?

3. Compare and contrast the ways in which the following civilizations took shape, despite political decentralization: sub-Saharan Africa, classical India, and medieval Europe.

MULTIPLE-CHOICE QUESTIONS

1. Which statement about early humans do most scholars today agree is accurate?

   (A) Humans originated in Asia, then spread to Africa.
   (B) Humans originated in Africa, then migrated to other continents.
   (C) Antarctica was inhabited by early hominids.
   (D) Humans appeared simultaneously throughout the world.
   (E) none of the above

2. The Indian Ocean

   I. is the world's second-largest ocean
   II. is the site of thousands of years of travel and economic exchange
   III. can be reached from the Atlantic and the Pacific Oceans
   IV. extends only as far south as the eastern coast of Africa

   Which are correct?

   (A) I, III, and IV
   (B) I, II, and IV
   (C) II, III, and IV
   (D) II and III
   (E) all of the above

3. The largest continent on Earth is

   (A) Africa
   (B) Asia
   (C) Australia
   (D) Europe
   (E) South America

4. Which of the following is an incorrect description of agricultural societies?

(A) Agriculture allowed humans to manipulate their environment as never before.

(B) Women probably played a key role in promoting the transition from hunting and gathering to agricultural societies.

(C) Agriculture promoted permanent settlements.

(D) People began producing their own food nearly 12,000 years ago.

(E) Agricultural societies were less organized than hunter-gatherer societies.

5. Civilization is marked by

  I. an intellectual tradition, including a written language
 II. an economic system that makes available basic goods and services
III. a tendency to use violence to resolve conflict
 IV. a moral code
  V. a form of political organization

(A) I, II, III, and IV

(B) II, III, IV, and V

(C) I, II, IV, and V

(D) I, III, IV, and V

(E) all of the above

6. What developments in classical China (before 1000 C.E.) had long-lasting implications for Chinese civilization?

  I. The supreme ruler was an emperor.
 II. Han rulers installed an effective bureaucracy, postal service, and tax-collecting system.
III. An improved infrastructure and fortifications helped defend China from invasion.
 IV. Trade expanded greatly during the Tang dynasty.

(A) I, II, and III

(B) II, III, and IV

(C) I, III, and IV

(D) II and III

(E) all of the above

7. Where was the capital of the Abbasid Caliphate?

(A) Babylon

(B) Jerusalem

(C) Delhi

(D) Baghdad

(E) Constantinople

8. Which sub-Saharan kingdom was a major center of trade before 1000 B.C.E.?

(A) Zulu

(B) Bantu

(C) Ghana

(D) Nigeria

(E) Swahili

9. The longest and most vital overland trade route before 1000 C.E. was

(A) the Silk Road

(B) the Trans-Siberian

(C) the Appalachian Trail

(D) the Sahara

(E) the Appian Way

10. How did serfdom differ from slavery?

(A) Serfs were not bound to the land, whereas slaves were.

(B) Serfdom was given religious sanction, whereas slavery was not.

(C) Technically, slaves had more freedoms than serfs.

(D) Technically, serfs had more freedoms than slaves.

(E) Serfdom ended long before slavery did, in the 1600s.

11. Which of the following is NOT a reason why the adoption of agriculture tends to lead to class distinction?

(A) Most members of society stay involved in food production.

(B) It promotes technological advancement.

(C) People are free to develop other skills beside food production.

(D) It encourages permanent settlement.

(E) none of the above

12. Why are the Bantus important to African culture?

(A) They ruled Egypt for thousands of years.

(B) They built the major cities in Tunisia.

(C) They come the closest to resembling a common cultural source in sub-Saharan Africa.

(D) They were the first civilization to use numerals.

(E) all of the above

13. In an oligarchy

(A) one ruler, an olig, controls an entire nation

(B) a small elite group holds political power

(C) the people elect representatives to vote on their behalf in a national legislature

(D) the aristocracy governs along with a monarch

(E) military rule is the dominant form of government

14. In what city-state did democratic government emerge?

(A) Athens

(B) Sparta

(C) Rome

(D) Venice

(E) Thebes

15. Why is the period between 200 and 1000 C.E. known as the "Great Age of Migrations"?

(A) Millions of barbarian tribes migrated to China.

(B) Bantus migrated to northern Africa.

(C) Peoples from Asia crossed a land bridge to North America.

(D) A large number of Germanic and Asiatic peoples moved toward and into Europe.

(E) all of the above

16. According to the map on page 80, to which of the following areas did the main African-Eurasian trade routes NOT extend?

(A) Central Asia

(B) Siberia

(C) China

(D) North Africa

(E) Spain

17. The truths that the Buddha claimed either draw on or depart from the fundamental principles of which belief system?

(A) Christianity

(B) Hinduism

(C) Islam

(D) Judaism

(E) Hellenism

18. Which of the following is the correct chronology for the development of these major belief systems?

(A) Judaism, Hinduism, Daoism, Buddhism, Islam, Christianity

(B) Hinduism, Buddhism, Judaism, Christianity, Buddhism, Islam

(C) Islam, Judaism, Hinduism, Daoism, Buddhism, Christianity

(D) Hinduism, Judaism, Buddhism, Daoism, Islam, Christianity

(E) Judaism, Hinduism, Buddhism, Daoism, Christianity, Islam

19. Which answer places events from Islamic history in the correct order?

(A) Gabriel's revelation to Mohammed; the Hegira; the establishment of the Abbasid Caliphate; the split between Sunni and Shiite Muslims

(B) the Hegira; the establishment of the Abbasid Caliphate; Gabriel's revelation to Mohammed; the split between Sunni and Shiite Muslims

(C) the Hegira; the split between Sunni and Shiite Muslims; Gabriel's revelation to Mohammed; the establishment of the Abbasid Caliphate

(D) Gabriel's revelation to Mohammed; the Hegira; the split between Sunni and Shiite Muslims; the establishment of the Abbasid Caliphate

(E) the establishment of the Abbasid Caliphate; the Hegira; the split between Sunni and Shiite Muslims; Gabriel's revelation to Mohammed

20. Which of the following could NOT be a feature of polytheistic worship?

(A) a willingness to blend practices and rituals from more than one religion

(B) a belief that all living beings are animated by divine energy

(C) a rigid insistence on the worship of one deity

(D) the veneration of a wide variety of nature spirits

(E) the identification of each member of a clan with a different totemic animal symbol

ANSWERS:

1. **B**, p. 34	11. **A**, p. 76
2. **D**, p. 42	12. **C**, p. 71
3. **B**, p. 40	13. **B**, p. 78
4. **E**, p. 52	14. **A**, p. 78
5. **C**, p. 47	15. **D**, p. 81
6. **E**, p. 59	16. **B**, p. 80
7. **D**, p. 70	17. **B**, p. 90
8. **C**, p. 71	18. **E**, p. 85
9. **A**, p. 80	19. **D**, p. 97
10. **D**, p. 78	20. **C**, p. 84

UNIT THREE

World Cultures Maturing

(1000–1450)

Unit Overview

GENERAL REMARKS

Broadly speaking, the period between 1000 and 1450 was an era during which newer world civilizations matured, largely on the foundations of older civilizations that had collapsed or faded away. It was also an age during which world civilizations came into ever-increasing contact with each other.

From approximately the 200s through 1000 C.E., many of the world's ancient civilizations failed altogether or were falling into decline. These include a large number of the cultures described in Unit Two, Chapter 3, such as the Roman Empire (with the Greek influence it had kept alive), Han and Tang China, Heian Japan, India's Mauryan and Gupta Empires, the great civilizations of the Middle East, and others. Most of these ancient cultures are referred to as classical. The term "classical" has many meanings. In this case, it defines an older civilization that attains a high level of advancement, then, after falling, leaves behind its cultural legacy for new states and nations that rise up in its place in the same part of the world. Frequently, classical periods are looked back upon as "golden ages."

By 1000 C.E., the classical period had ended, or was in the process of ending, in almost all areas of the world. New civilizations were created on the foundations of the great classical cultures. In some cases, as in medieval Europe after the fall of Rome, a lengthy period of backwardness, decentralization, and chaos followed the collapse of a classical civilization. In others, as in China, the transition was less traumatic, or at least lasted a shorter time. Whatever the case, mature, sophisticated, advanced cultures were appearing throughout the world during the period between 1000 and 1450. And most of them were building on the legacy left behind by their classical predecessors.

Another general trend of the period was increased connection and communication between world cultures. Although the Americas remained isolated from the rest of the world, vibrant and stimulating systems of interaction and exchange appeared among the civilizations of Africa, Europe, the Middle East, Central Asia, Southeast Asia, and the Far East. Trade, religious influence, technological exchange, and cultural and artistic interaction all marked this era. Even though the world was not yet as joined together as it would later become—with the Europeans' encounter with the Americas and, more generally, greater improvements in communications and transport technology—it is safe to say that extensive systems of global interaction were emerging between 1000 and 1450.

BROAD TRENDS

GLOBAL POWER AND INTERNATIONAL RELATIONS

- With the exception of the Americas, the major civilizations of the world were coming into increased contact with each other.
- The most advanced and politically influential civilizations during these years were China (especially during the Yuan and Ming periods) and the Ottoman Empire.

- The nations of medieval Europe, particularly in the west, were gaining in power and sophistication.
- Major states and empires—such as Mali, Ghana, Great Zimbabwe, the Delhi Sultanate, the Aztecs, and the Incas—flourished, but only for a comparatively short time.
- During the 1200s and 1300s, the Mongols radically altered the balance of power in Eurasia. The vast empire they created, one of the largest in world history, brought together vast portions of Europe and Asia. For a time, a single authority imposed not just political unity, but a measure of economic and cultural connectedness that had not been seen since the days of ancient Rome.
- The invention of gunpowder weaponry would gradually start to change the equation of world power.

POLITICAL DEVELOPMENTS

- Most forms of government remained nonrepresentative. Monarchies and oligarchies were most common.
- In a few cases, nations managed to place formal restrictions on the power of the monarch—such as concrete legal systems or lawmaking bodies that shared governmental authority—and still remain centralized. England, with its Magna Carta and Parliament, is a classic example.
- Most states were not nations in the modern sense of the word. Many were decentralized. Others were multicultural empires joined together only by the fact that a single civilization had conquered them all.
- Feudalism became a common form of political (as well as economic) organization in areas that were decentralized. The best-known examples of feudal systems are medieval Europe and Japan under the shoguns.

ECONOMIC DEVELOPMENTS

- Most societies remained fundamentally agricultural, meaning that the vast majority of people resided in the countryside and made their living by farming.
- However, artisanry and craftsmanship were becoming increasingly important.
- This helped give rise to a slow (but steady) trend: urbanization, or the growth of cities.
- In addition, trade and commerce—and even banking—were becoming a basic part of economic life in most developed societies.
- The growing importance of trade and commerce made merchant classes larger and more influential in most societies.
- Trade and commerce also led to the creation of intercultural and international trade networks. Among the most important were the Silk Road, the Indian Ocean trade network, the Mediterranean trade network, caravan routes in the Sahara desert, and the gold trade along the Niger River in sub-Saharan Africa.
- Certain cities became exceptionally important centers for intercultural and international trade. They include Venice, Cairo, Mombasa, Zanzibar, Samarkand, Canton (Guangzhou), Malacca (Melaka), and Timbuktu.

CULTURAL DEVELOPMENTS

- Distinct artistic and cultural traditions were developing in each major region of the world.
- The civilizations that possessed the greatest degree of scientific knowledge and cultural sophistication were China, the Middle East, Japan, and Muslim Spain.

- European nations underwent significant cultural development, especially during the Renaissance.
- China and India had a tremendous cultural and religious influence on their neighbors. Buddhism, Hinduism, art forms, and architectural styles spread from these countries to Southeast Asia, Korea, Japan, Tibet, and elsewhere.
- The Middle East played a large role in spreading knowledge, scholarship, music, art, and architecture to North Africa and Europe. The Middle Eastern influence on culture in medieval and Renaissance Europe was considerable.
- Travelers and explorers were creating links between societies or increasing their own nations' geographical and cultural knowledge. Examples include Zheng He (Cheng Ho), Marco Polo, and Ibn Battuta.
- The invention of block printing in China (perhaps Korea) began to alter cultural life not only in Asia, but elsewhere, as this new innovation spread.
- Even more dramatically, the invention of the movable-type printing press in Europe, during the 1430s, led to an information explosion, the rapid spread of knowledge and ideas, and a revolution in intellectual life.

GENDER ISSUES

- As in earlier times, women continued to occupy a secondary role in most societies. In most societies, women's political rights were minimal or nonexistent.
- Women had sharply defined occupational roles. They were largely assigned to the domestic sphere: they were seen primarily as childbearers and homemakers. Most work women did outside the home—such as weaving, food gathering, or farm chores—was seen as low status.
- However, in the majority of world civilizations, women possessed at least some freedoms, including legal and economic rights: the right to divorce abusive husbands, the right to a dowry, the right to inherit and own property.
- In many societies, women played certain informal, but important, roles. They managed households and family finances, supervised the education of children, and influenced their husbands.
- Being in certain occupations or social classes allowed women some respect or escape from male domination. Noblewomen played influential roles in most societies, often as cultural patrons, sometimes as political advisers to their husbands. Priestesses and nuns often enjoyed high status, as well as an intellectual life, although their conduct was strictly regulated.
- In some African societies, women enjoyed a great deal of respect, and family trees were matrilinear (traced through the mother), rather than patrilinear.
- In most societies, upper-class women lived easier lives, but found themselves more constrained by religious and cultural restrictions on their behavior. Lower-class women, whose lives were much harder, were often less bound by those restrictions, because the niceties of "proper" behavior applied less to them.
- Societies that feared magic or witchery tended to blame women (especially elderly ones) disproportionately for such things.

COMPARATIVE ISSUES TO CONSIDER

- Differences and likenesses of various world trading systems
- Intellectual and cultural developments in different societies, and the ways in which societies influence each other (for example, the Middle Eastern influence on medieval European

culture, or India's influence on the development of Southeast Asian religion, art, and architecture)

- Comparisons and contrasts between European and Japanese feudalism
- Comparisons and contrasts between one of the major European states (or western Europe as a whole) and one of the major African states
- The differences and likenesses between the Mongol Empire and earlier conquest states, such as Rome or Han China
- The successes and failures of (1) the Roman Catholic Church and (2) the Islamic caliphates in their attempts to create a large, multinational civilization united by religion
- The economic, social, and political roles of major cosmopolitan cities such as Constantinople, Samarkand, Canton (Guangzhou), Timbuktu, Venice, Córdoba, Malacca (Melaka), and Calicut

KEY TERMS AND CONCEPTS

classical civilizations
Europe's medieval era (the Middle Ages)
feudalism and chivalry
the manor
serfdom
the Roman Catholic Church, the medieval popes, and the ideal of Christendom
the Holy Inquisition
the Vikings
William the Conqueror and the Norman invasion of England
the Magna Carta
Parliament
the Capetian dynasty and the centralization of France
the Hundred Years' War
the Habsburgs
Florence and Venice
the Reconquista
Córdoba
the fall of Constantinople
the Crusades
trade, commerce, and urbanization in medieval Europe
the Hanseatic League
the Medicis and the Fuggers
social uprisings in late medieval Europe
the Black Death
Romanesque versus Gothic architecture
Scholasticism
Dante Alighieri, Geoffrey Chaucer, and vernacular languages
Johannes Gutenberg and the printing press
the Renaissance

humanism
Leonardo da Vinci and Michelangelo
the disintegration of the Abbasid Caliphate
the Berber states
Mali
Timbuktu
Mansa Musa
the *Son-Jara* (*Sundiata*) epic
the Mamluks and the Seljuk Turks
Saladin
the Ottoman Turks
Osman I
Mehmed II
Avicenna, *Canon of Medicine*
Averroës
Maimonides, *Guide to the Perplexed*
Omar Khayyám, *The Rubaiyat*
Ibn Battuta
the Song Empire and its scientific-technological achievements
the Chinese invention of gunpowder
Canton (Guangzhou)
the Silk Road
Neo-Confucianism
Chan (Zen) Buddhism
the Yuan Empire
Zhu Yuanzhang (Emperor Hung-wu)
the Ming dynasty
Emperor Yongle (Yung-lo)
the tributary system
the voyages of Zheng He (Cheng Ho)
development of the Chinese novel
silk, porcelain, and "china"
Heian Japan and the Fujiwara clan

Lady Murasaki, *The Tale of Genji*
the Taira-Minamoto war and the fall of the
  Fujiwara
Japanese feudalism
the shogun
the daimyo and the samurai
the code of Bushido
the Kamakura shogunate
the Ashikaga shogunate
Zen and Pure Land Buddhism
haiku poetry
Noh drama
the Delhi Sultanate
the Indian Ocean trade network
Calicut
the Khmer Empire
Angkor Wat
the Srivijayan Empire
Borobudur
Malacca (Melaka)
the Polynesian migrations
the Mongols and Tatars
Genghis Khan and the Mongol army
Ögödei (Ugedei)
Batu, Subudei (Subutai), and the invasion of
  Russia and eastern Europe
the Pax Mongolica

the Silk Road
the breakdown of the Mongol Empire
the Golden Horde
Khubilai Khan
Timur (Tamerlane)
the Bantu
Saharan trade networks
the Arab slave trade in Africa
the African gold trade
Mali
Ghana
Great Zimbabwe
East Africa and the Indian Ocean trade
  network
Mombasa and Zanzibar
the Anasazi
the Mississippian culture
Cahokia
the Toltec
the Aztecs
Tenochtitlán
Aztec pyramids, the sun god, and human
  sacrifice
the quipu "writing" system
the Incas
Machu Picchu and Cuzco
the Temple of the Sun and the *acllas*

CHAPTER 6

Europe During the Middle Ages and the Renaissance

The medieval period of European history, also known as the Middle Ages, is considered to have lasted from approximately 500 to 1500. Traditionally, the medieval era is broken down into three phases: the Early Middle Ages (ca. 500–1000), the High Middle Ages (ca. 1000–1300), and the Late Middle Ages (ca. 1300–1500). Not all historians, however, use these labels. Also, the question of periodization is complicated by the fact that during the Late Middle Ages, certain parts of Europe—particularly Italy—began to experience the famous cultural rebirth known as the Renaissance.

Whatever one calls the various periods of the medieval era, certain trends are clear. As discussed in Chapter 3, the years from 500 to 1000 were a time of extreme political decentralization and overall backwardness.

From 1000 to 1300, Europe enjoyed a general revival. Nations became stronger, the economy grew healthier, and the level of technological and cultural knowledge improved. The concept of Europe as a single civilization, joined together by a common cultural heritage and the Christian religion, took greater shape during these years.

The period between 1300 and 1500 was a complex one, marked both by crisis and advancement. On one hand, Europe was struck by social unrest, constant warfare, and, in the form of the so-called Black Death, one of the worst medical disasters in world history. On the other hand, these were the years when the Renaissance began, ushering in a period of tremendous artistic and intellectual achievement.

FEUDALISM AND THE MANOR SYSTEM

THE CONCEPT AND ORIGINS OF FEUDALISM

As described in Chapter 3, the primary method of political, social, and economic organization was feudalism. After the fall of Rome, Europe was decentralized to such an extent that monarchs typically found themselves without the power, money, or military strength to govern their lands effectively. For help in controlling their lands, monarchs began to enfeoff their territory, giving control over portions of their land to trustworthy retainers. In exchange, the retainers guaranteed that these smaller pieces of territory would be governed, that law and justice would be dispensed, that crops would be grown, and that the land itself would be protected. Feudal retainers often divided the territories they received into smaller parcels, granting those pieces of land to people they could rely on. This process was called subinfeudation.

European feudalism began to emerge during the 700s, in what is today France and western Germany. From there, it spread throughout the continent. By the eleventh century, most countries in Europe, especially in the western and central parts of the continent, had adopted some form of feudal practice.

MILITARY SERVICE, KNIGHTHOOD, AND THE EMERGENCE OF THE NOBLE CLASS

Over time, the retainers to whom monarchs gave large land grants developed into Europe's noble (or aristocratic) class: dukes, counts, earls, barons, and so on. In conjunction with the monarch, the noble class provided political leadership. Structurally, the feudal nobility resembled a pyramid. At the top was the monarch. Below him (or her) were powerful nobles, who had been granted control over large portions of the country's land. Below them were lesser nobles, to whom the more powerful nobles had given smaller pieces of their land. All members of the feudal nobility were, in theory, tied to the king by bonds of loyalty and landownership.

The feudal nobility also served a crucial military function. One of feudalism's main goals was to provide an army of foot soldiers (recruited by individual nobles) and an elite force of armored cavalrymen (knights) formed by the nobles themselves. Horses, weapons, and equipment were so costly, and the training so specialized, that only members of the upper classes could afford to become knights.

In theory, the knight was supposed to be a virtuous warrior who served his lord loyally, fought fairly, treated the lower classes with justice, and acted gentlemanly toward women. A formal code of behavior for knights, inspired by Christian principles, developed during the High Middle Ages. It was called chivalry. Songs and legends, such as those of the knights of King Arthur's Round Table, provided examples of how real-life knights were supposed to conduct themselves. Some knights did, in fact, guide themselves according to the code of chivalry, and chivalry did play a certain role in restraining the most violent behavior of knights. However, in actuality, the rules were often broken, and chivalry tended to be more myth than reality.

A Medieval Tournament.
The military and political backbone of medieval Europe's feudal system was the knight. High-born and trained from youth in cavalry warfare, the knight was the state-of-the-art warrior of his era. Knights also made up Europe's noble class. Knights honed their military skills—and cultivated the arts of chivalry—at tournaments such as the one portrayed here.

THE MANOR SYSTEM, PEASANT LABOR, AND SERFDOM

The feudal system involved more than the ruling class. The vast majority of people in medieval Europe were peasants who farmed lands under the control of the feudal nobility. The basic unit of feudal landholding was the manor, a parcel of land small enough for one nobleman or knight to supervise closely. At the heart of the typical manor was the lord's residence (an estate house or castle). Nearby was a village, home to the peasants who worked on the manor. Surrounding the lord's residence and the village would be fields for farming, as well as woodland, where food would be gathered and animals hunted (generally a privilege reserved for the lord).

Economically, the feudal system relied on the labor of the peasants. Most peasants in Europe during the Middle Ages were serfs (from the Latin term *servus*, or "slave"). Although serfs were not technically slaves, they were legally unfree. They were not allowed to change residence or profession without permission. Most of the fruits of their work benefited not themselves, but the lord. A certain portion of their own crops and livestock had to be given over to the lord. In addition, serfs had to spend a certain number of days per month fulfilling various labor obligations: building roads, clearing forests, gathering firewood, or, most commonly, farming the lord's private fields. Serfs had to pay fees to use any of the manor's facilities that were owned by the lord, such as the water mill, the bread oven, the cider press, or the smithy. In times of war, serfs also had to fight: lords would recruit foot soldiers from among them. Overall, living conditions were harsh.

THE TIME LINE OF FEUDALISM

Feudalism persisted throughout the medieval period, and its effects were felt long afterward. Ironically, it outlasted its original purpose. Even after political units in medieval Europe began to centralize and resemble nations in the modern sense, many feudal practices remained in place. Serfdom took many centuries to disappear, especially in central and eastern Europe. The knightly class transformed into an aristocratic nobility that remained a permanent part of European politics and society until the 1800s (in some countries, the 1900s). The class differences that feudalism set into place also survived as tensions between the poor and powerless on one hand and the rich and powerful on the other.

THE IDEAL OF CHRISTENDOM

THE UNIFYING INFLUENCE OF CHRISTIANITY

One of the few institutions binding European nations and communities together in the first four or five centuries following the fall of Rome was the Christian faith. Large numbers of people in Europe and the Mediterranean world had converted to the new religion before Rome's collapse. After the Roman Empire faded away, Christianity survived, spread to even more parts of Europe, and, during the Middle Ages, became an important unifying force throughout the continent, both culturally and politically.

Rome itself continued to be one of the two major headquarters of the network that organized and formalized Christian worship. The other was Constantinople, capital of the Byzantine Empire. By 1054, doctrinal differences and geographical distance led to the Great Schism, which separated the Christian community into two large churches: the Roman Catholic Church and the Eastern Orthodox Church. The former became dominant in central and western Europe, whereas the latter was prominent not only in the Middle East, but in the Greek and Slavic parts of eastern Europe.

The Catholic Church played a key role in the development of most of medieval Europe. From 500 to 1000, its monasteries preserved many of the Latin and Greek manuscripts left over from the

Roman era. These included scientific ideas, philosophical essays, literary works, and a tremendous wealth of learning that otherwise would have been lost. The church also provided the people of Europe with a sense that, despite national and linguistic differences, they were linked by a single faith. This gave a much-needed feeling of cultural cohesion to Europe at a time of extreme decentralization.

CATHOLIC HIERARCHY

The leader of the Catholic Church was the pope, technically the bishop of Rome. At the lowest level of Church organization was the priest, who served the needs of an individual community. Only men could become priests. Above the priest was the bishop, who presided over a large territory and supervised many priests. Archbishops and cardinals were extremely powerful Church officials. The latter were the pope's closest advisers. Also part of the Church hierarchy were monks and nuns (described subsequently).

THE MEDIEVAL PAPACY AND THE POLITICAL POWER OF THE CATHOLIC CHURCH

After 1000, the Catholic Church became immensely powerful in a political sense. This is in contrast with the Eastern Orthodox Church, which, in general, viewed itself, a spiritual institution, as subservient to worldly authority. The pope came to govern a sizable territory in central Italy, the Papal States. During the eleventh through thirteenth centuries, many popes, especially Gregory VII (1073–1085) and Innocent III (1198–1216), went to great lengths to assert that the spiritual authority of the papacy should be considered superior to that of kings and emperors. Using not only their position's moral authority, but also their privilege to determine what was heresy, to exclude worshipers from the Catholic Church (excommunication), and to issue calls for holy wars (crusades), medieval popes were able to gather a tremendous amount of political power. The ultimate goal of medieval popes was to join all the nations of Europe together into a single Christian community. Referred to as Christendom, this community was to be governed first and foremost by the pope, with kings and emperors subject to his rule. In the end, the Catholic Church never realized this ideal. Still, for several hundred years, it exerted a weighty influence on how the monarchs of Europe ruled their countries.

The Catholic Church also became the owner of vast amounts of land throughout Europe. Combined with its right to collect tithes from the general population, this made the Church very wealthy. Another way in which the Church exercised worldly power was its high degree of control over education, thought, and culture. Most institutions of learning were connected in one way or another with the Catholic Church. More broadly, it was dangerous for any scholar or artist to write, say, or produce anything that ran counter to Catholic doctrine. In 1231, the Holy Inquisition, a set of special courts with wide-ranging powers, was established to hunt out and harshly punish heresy and religious nonconformity.

MONASTICISM

A prominent feature of medieval Christianity (both Catholic and Orthodox) was monasticism, the formation of religious communities whose members are not ordained as priests. Men who took monastic orders were monks, whereas women became nuns. The first European monasteries were modeled on the example of the Benedictine order, which stressed contemplation and seclusion from worldly affairs. This approach remained dominant from the 500s through the late 1100s. In the early 1200s, new orders, such as the Dominicans and Franciscans, were established to work actively outside the monastery and carry on the work of the Catholic Church in the wider world.

THE WESTERN MONARCHIES AND THE EASTERN FRONTIER

The first European nations began to take embryonic shape during the 700s through the 900s. By 1000 and afterward, an even greater number of relatively centralized states had emerged.

THE VIKINGS

One group that played an important role in shaping the development of European nations before and after 1000 C.E. was the Vikings. The Vikings were expert sailors and fierce warriors from Scandinavia. Mainly as a result of overcrowding in their homelands, large numbers of Vikings poured out of Denmark, Sweden, and Norway from the 800s through the 1100s. One of the few peoples of this era who could navigate on the open ocean, without needing to stay within sight of land, the Vikings roamed far and wide. They raided and conquered throughout almost all of coastal Europe, as far south as the Mediterranean.

The Vikings settled Iceland and Greenland. Under Leif Ericsson, a small group even reached what is today Canada, around 1000 C.E. The Vikings also settled in parts of England, Scotland, and Ireland. They created long-lasting kingdoms in northwestern France and Sicily. A group of Vikings established a trade route from Scandinavia to Byzantium, through Russia. In the process, they created the first Russian state. By forcing nations such as England, France, and the Holy Roman Empire to defend against their attacks, the Vikings (albeit inadvertently) prompted those nations to centralize to a greater degree than they had during the early medieval period.

ENGLAND

In the west, the most stable states were England and France. During the High and Late Middle Ages, the political fortunes of both countries were intertwined. In 1066, French-speaking Normans (descendants of Vikings who had settled in northwestern France) led by William the Conqueror, invaded England, defeated its Saxon king, and established their rule there. William and his successors were connected to the French royal family by blood ties and feudal obligations. For the next 400 years, there was a great deal of confusion and competition between the two over land and political legitimacy.

Over time, England developed into a monarchy that was, by the standards of the day, quite centralized. William the Conqueror brought French-style feudalism to England. Despite civil war and chaos after his death, England's government began to take more solid shape during the 1100s. During the late 1100s, Henry II moved beyond simple feudalism by creating a single law code for the entire country (common law), a unified court system, and the concept of jury trials. In England, significant checks were placed on the power of the king, without reversing the trend toward centralization. In 1215, the Magna Carta, imposed upon King John by his barons, guaranteed the nobility certain rights and privileges, thereby legally restricting the king's might. Later in the 1200s, the English nobility won the right to form a parliament. Gradually, this nobles' council became a representative lawmaking body that governed in conjunction with the king and assumed an increasingly important position in English politics. Another major development during these years was expansion. During the late 1200s and 1300s, under Edward I and Edward III, the English conquered Wales and Scotland. Ireland would follow later. As described presently, wars with France over territory were frequent.

FRANCE

In France, the Capetian dynasty that emerged in the 900s controlled only a small area around Paris. During the High and Late Middle Ages, however, the Capetian kings would prove extremely effective in extending their rule to most of what is today France, despite interference from England (which controlled large territories such as Aquitaine and parts of Brittany) and the independent spirit of large and wealthy regions (such as Burgundy and Flanders). One of the earliest centralizers, Philip II Augustus (1180–1223), tripled the size of the French kingdom, thanks to political skill and military victories over King John of England. Another wave of consolidation followed in the 1400s. Not only did France defeat England in the Hundred Years' War, centralizing further in the process, but kings like Charles VII (1429–1461) and Louis XI (1461–1483) gained control over stubborn regions that had managed to stay autonomous, such as Flanders and Burgundy. By the late 1400s, France was a large, centralized nation, ruled over firmly by a monarch with considerable powers.

THE HUNDRED YEARS' WAR

The political event that most affected England and France during the fourteenth and fifteenth centuries was the Hundred Years' War (1337–1453). The war's first years coincided with the onset of other European crises, including several major uprisings and the Black Death. The war had several causes:

- The political entanglement of the English and French royal families
- France's attempts to regain continental territories controlled by the English
- Competition over the lucrative wool trade that centered on southeastern England and, across the English Channel, Flanders

Until the early 1400s, the English won a number of key victories. In these, the military obsolescence of the medieval knight was proven several times by the success of English archers. The English invaders established control over more than half of France. Only after the 1420s did the *dauphin* (crown prince) Charles, later Charles VII, begin to turn the tide. Helped greatly by the warrior maid Joan of Arc, Charles VII managed to drive the English out of France (with the exception of a few port cities, such as Calais). The war ended in 1453. For the most part, the awkward connections between the English and French royal dynasties did as well.

THE HOLY ROMAN EMPIRE

Important states formed in the central and southern parts of Europe, but they were less centralized than England and France. Dominating the middle of Europe was the Holy Roman Empire. The Empire was a multicultural monarchy in which the crown passed back and forth among a group of various German noble families. Founded in the 900s, the Empire was seen as the heir to the great state founded by Charlemagne in the eighth and ninth centuries. Although the rulers were Germanic, the population consisted not just of Germans, but also Italians, French, Hungarians, Slavs of different types, and others. As its name suggests, the Holy Roman Empire was, at least at the start, defined not so much by common nationality or language, but by a shared (and largely imagined) memory of the bygone Roman era, as well as religion—specifically, Roman Catholicism. In theory, the emperor was supposed to work in partnership with the Pope to achieve the ideal of Christendom: a single Catholic community extending throughout Europe. In reality, the emperor's relationship with the Pope was more often competitive than cooperative.

The Holy Roman Empire was one of the largest states in medieval Europe. However, the emperor's position was elective, not hereditary: he was chosen from among one of a number of powerful noble clans. Also, because the empire's population was so ethnically diverse, and because it consisted of literally dozens of separate duchies, principalities, kingdoms, and counties (approximately two hundred before the mid-1300s)—most of which carefully guarded their local privileges and autonomy—the empire was not a highly centralized state. This changed somewhat after the mid-1300s. Although the Golden Bull of 1356 affirmed the rights and powers of the various dukes, princes, and counts who ruled under the emperor, the number of states that could take part in elect-ing the emperor was radically reduced (from almost two hundred to seven). Another trend that con-tributed to a greater degree of centralization was the emergence of the Habsburg family as a force in imperial politics. From Austria, the Habsburgs became one of the powerful families competing for the position of emperor as early as 1273. In 1438, the Habsburgs succeeded in gaining perma-nent control over the imperial throne. They would rule the Holy Roman Empire (later the Austrian Empire) until 1918. The greater centralization brought about by the Habsburgs' assump-tion of power came just as the empire began to perform an extremely important function for the rest of Europe: serving as the military bulwark against the encroachments of the Turks. Starting in the late 1300s, the Turks proved remarkably successful in threatening, then breaking into, the borderlands of Europe.

THE ITALIAN STATES

Even more decentralized than the Holy Roman Empire was Italy—a term that, at the time, referred not to an actual country, but to the various states of the Italian peninsula. Many parts of northern Italy were under the control of the Holy Roman Empire. Some areas in the south passed in and out of the hands of other foreigners, such as the French, Spanish, Muslims, and Byzantines. The parts of Italy that remained free were governed by dozens of city-states: independent, small, and often very quarrelsome with each other. Italy was one of the most urbanized parts of Europe. Its cul-tural level was high as well (as discussed later in this chapter, it would be the birthplace of the Renaissance). Its position in the Mediterranean made it very active in trade, and most of its cities developed strong commercial economies. By means of the Mediterranean, Italian cities were able to trade with the Middle East (and, by extension, the Silk Road network that led to the Far East and China) and Egypt (whose Suez isthmus connected to the Red Sea and the Indian Ocean trade network).

By the 1300s and 1400s, the Italian states were still disunified, but centralization took place to the extent that the number of independent city-states shrank, as larger ones conquered and absorbed smaller ones. The chief city-states of fourteenth- and fifteenth-century Italy were Florence, Milan, and Venice in the north, and Naples in the south. Also important was Rome, heart of the Papal States that lay in Italy's center. In particular, Venice—which called itself "the most serene"—created one of this era's richest and most powerful maritime and commercial empires.

SPAIN AND PORTUGAL

During the Middle Ages, the national development of Spain and Portugal was shaped above all by the fact that they had been taken over by Muslim invaders, known as the Moors, during the 700s. For the next seven and a half centuries, the people of Spain and Portugal fought the Moors in a long, intense war of resistance known as the Reconquista. The legend of El Cid, an eleventh-century general and one of Spain's great medieval heroes, grew out of this reconquest. By the end of the 1200s, the Spanish had managed to push the Moors into the southernmost part of the country, the province of Granada. For the next 200 years, the Moors held out in Granada, until they were expelled completely in 1492, by the armies of King Ferdinand and Queen Isabella.

The effects of the Moors and the war against them were many. Because Spanish territory was liberated gradually, region by region, it did not centralize quickly. Each newly freed area remained independent and kept its own unique identity. By the 1400s, there were about half a dozen Spanish kingdoms, not counting Portugal. Only late in the 1400s, when the rulers of the two largest kingdoms, Ferdinand of Aragón and Isabella of Castile, married and joined their lands together, did Spain begin to take shape as a single country. Another result of the Reconquista was intense religious intolerance. The war caused Catholic authorities in Spain to be extremely rigid in terms of doctrine and practice, and made them hostile to nonbelievers. Muslims and Jews (whom the Moors had welcomed to Spain) were persecuted, and, by the end of the 1400s, forced to convert to Catholicism or leave the country.

There were, however, benefits to be had from the Moorish presence as well. Because Islamic culture was much more advanced than that of the Europeans during most of the medieval era, Spain was able to take advantage of the medical, scientific, and technological knowledge brought there by the Muslim conquerors (as well as the Jewish scholars and professionals who came with them). For example, the Spanish city of Córdoba was one of Europe's greatest centers of learning and science, thanks to the long-standing Muslim presence there. Spanish art and architecture were also profoundly affected by the Moorish style, elements of which still persist today.

Portugal, an independent principality, began its tradition of world exploration during the 1400s, starting a trend that would sweep the globe over the next centuries. (For more on this, see Chapter 14.)

BYZANTIUM AND EASTERN EUROPE

The farther east, the less centralized European nations became, with the exception of the Byzantine Empire, the crossroads between Christian Europe and the Islamic Middle East. Constantinople was a tremendously important trading center, linking the commercial activity of Mediterranean Europe with that of the Middle East and, by extension, the overland routes (such as the Silk Road) and sea lanes that joined the Middle East with China, India, and the East Indies.

Although Byzantium was far superior to the rest of Europe in terms of economic and cultural advancement, it was, after the eleventh century, in a long period of political and military decline. A new enemy, the Seljuk Turks, had appeared on its eastern frontier and defeated its armies decisively at the Battle of Manzikert (1071). From that point forward, the Seljuk Turks, then their even more dangerous successors, the Ottoman Turks, slowly—but unceasingly—stripped territory away from Byzantium. By the 1400s, the empire had shrunk to such a degree that the capital itself was under threat. Finally, in 1453, Constantinople was captured by the Ottoman Turks. The Byzantine Empire was destroyed, its capital became the Turkish city of Istanbul, and—for the next several hundred years—the Ottoman Empire would go on to conquer and rule over large parts of southeastern Europe, clashing for years with the Holy Roman (Austrian) Empire.

Territories on the eastern and northern fringe of Europe tended to be more poorly defined, politically speaking. Much of this had to do with the stress of invasions from the east. Mongol attacks in the mid-1200s and the constant pressure of the Ottoman Turks during and after the 1400s took their toll and, in many ways, helped to hold back the political development of nations in this area. Countries like Hungary, Sweden, and Poland (united during much of the medieval era with a large and powerful Lithuania) were exceptions: they became stable and sophisticated, at least for the time being. More typical were the Russian lands, farther to the east. During most of the medieval era, "Russia" was a loose confederation of city-states, governed by constantly feuding princes. The Mongol invasions of the 1240s placed the Russians under the domination of the Golden Horde, and not until the mid-1400s did Russia become free. Only after that point did a Russian nation begin to take shape, under the rulership of the city of Moscow.

THE CRUSADES

THE CONCEPT AND ORIGIN OF CRUSADING

Among the powers of the medieval popes was the ability to request kings and emperors to provide troops and money for holy wars known as crusades. Crusades were fought for a number of reasons: to convert nonbelievers to Catholicism, to crush Christian movements the Church considered heretical (the most famous crusades of this type were fought in southern France during the early 1200s), and to protect against attacks by foreigners who were not Christian (especially Muslims).

The best-known crusades, and the ones generally referred to when the term "the Crusades" is used, are those fought by European Catholics against the Muslims of the Middle East and North Africa from 1095 to 1291. Many underlying factors motivated the Crusades:

- Genuine religious fervor on the part of both Muslims and Christians
- Geopolitical conflict between Europe and the Middle East
- The Europeans' desire to become more involved in the international trade network stretching from the Mediterranean to China
- The personal ambitions of many Europeans, hoping to gain wealth and land in the Middle East
- Racial and religious prejudice

THE FIRST CRUSADE

The spark of the First Crusade (1096–1099) came in 1095, when the Byzantine Empire asked Christian Europe for military assistance against the wave of attacks launched by the Seljuk Turks after 1071. The Byzantine plea was strengthened by the fact that the Turks had recently captured Jerusalem and other sites in the Holy Land sacred to all Christians. To increase his chances of receiving aid from European Catholics, the Byzantine emperor exaggerated the rumors of atrocities that the Turks were supposedly committing in the Holy Land. Pope Urban II responded by summoning the Council of Clermont and calling upon the leading nobles of Catholic Europe to travel to the Holy Land, recapture Jerusalem, and liberate the Holy Land from the Turks. In 1096, a massive Catholic army—the Crusaders—traveled overland to Constantinople, then through the Middle East, fighting Muslim forces along the way. By the summer of 1099, the Crusaders had reached Jerusalem and placed it under siege. Within weeks, they took the city and, in one of the bloodiest episodes in military history, butchered almost every Muslim and Jew within its walls (as well as a number of native Christians whom they mistook for Muslims).

THE LATIN KINGDOMS AND THE LATER CRUSADES

The Crusaders then went on to establish four Christian states known as the Latin Kingdoms. While they lasted, the Latin Kingdoms served as a military and political foothold in the Middle East. They also enabled European knights and nobles to become involved in the lucrative commercial economy that made the region so wealthy.

The Christians were able to maintain their presence in the Middle East for two centuries. However, the Turks, Arabs, and other Muslims were eager to expel the Europeans, and they gradually did so. The many crusades that followed the first were generally responses to successful Muslim campaigns. The Second Crusade (1146–1149) followed the fall of one of the Latin Kingdoms in the 1140s. The Third Crusade (1189–1192) resulted from the capture of Jerusalem in 1187 by Saladin, one of the most skilled military leaders in the history of the Muslim world. The Third Crusade united the efforts of Richard I the Lion-Hearted of England, Philip II Augustus of France, and Frederick I Barbarossa of the Holy Roman Empire. The rivalry between Richard and Saladin became legendary, and their war ended in stalemate: Jerusalem remained in Muslim hands, but Christian pilgrims were free to visit the city.

From 1200 onward, many more crusades were launched against the Middle East, but most were unsuccessful or lost their focus. The Fourth Crusade (1202–1204) ended up targeting the Christian city of Constantinople instead of the Muslims. The infamous Childrens' Crusades of the early 1200s resulted in the death or enslavement of tens of thousands of boys and girls. Other crusading forces attacked Egypt and North Africa, but to no avail. In the meantime, the Turks made steady progress in driving the Christians out of the Latin Kingdoms, which grew smaller every year. Finally, in 1291, the Crusaders' last major outpost, the fortress of Acre, fell to the Muslims (the last remnant of the Christian presence in the Middle East, the port of Gibelet, was abandoned in 1302).

EFFECTS OF THE CRUSADES

Long-term effects of the Crusades include the worsening of the relationship between the Muslim and Christian worlds. Also important was the greater awareness of the wider world, especially the lands of the east, that the Crusades stimulated among the Europeans. Along with this came an increased knowledge of—and desire for—the economic wealth to be gained by greater interaction with the Near and Far East. Moreover, the crusading ideal—the notion that Christian warriors were fighting a holy war on behalf of a sacred cause—contributed to the powerful myth of knighthood and chivalry that emerged in European culture during the Middle Ages.

URBANIZATION, TRADE, AND SOCIETY

If the Early Middle Ages had been a time of social and economic backwardness for Europe, significant gains were made during the High and Late Middle Ages, although the latter period was a time of great social crisis as well.

POPULATION GROWTH, TRADE, AND COMMERCE

From approximately 1000 to 1300, population growth in Europe was considerable. Advanced agricultural techniques—such as the three-field system of crop rotation, the use of the horse collar, and the invention of better plows—caused the food supply to increase.

Trade and commerce became a larger part of the European economy during these years. Great political centralization and stability made banking and the movement of goods safer and more convenient. The number of fairs (special gatherings held several times a year to encourage trade) and permanent markets grew substantially. Because the movement of goods was easier by water than by land, trade tended to follow river systems and coastlines. One major trade network, centered on Italy, sprang up throughout the Mediterranean, and did much to connect Europe with the commerce of the Near and Far East (as described previously, the Crusades did much to stimulate this). Other

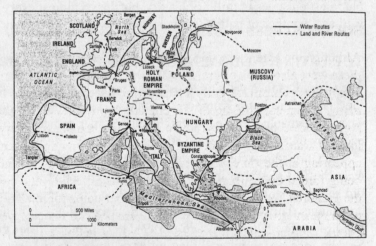

European Trade Routes During the Late Medieval Period and the Renaissance.
As the Middle Ages came to an end, the nations of Europe were basing an increasing proportion of their economic activity on trade. The Europeans became more economically connected with Africa and the Middle East. By extension, they became linked with India, China, and Southeast Asia. The Europeans' desire for more direct access to the goods of East and South Asia prompted the great wave of exploration that began during the 1400s and continued during the 1500s and 1600s.

important networks formed along the Rhine River, in the North Sea and English Channel (especially between England and Flanders), and throughout the Baltic Sea. Trade in the Baltic region was dominated by the Hanseatic League, a trading group whose influence stretched from England in the west to Russia in the east. The relatively new practice of banking made trade more feasible and dependable as well. Powerful banking houses were run by the Medicis in Italy and the Fuggers in central Europe.

URBANIZATION

Along with the greater volume of trade, another social trend was urbanization. Although the vast majority of people in medieval Europe remained in the countryside, working as peasants and serfs, an increasingly large number were moving to cities. Existing cities grew larger, and new cities were founded at a great rate. Some parts of Europe, particularly Italy and Flanders, urbanized more quickly than others.

Cities were excellent sites for trade. They attracted artists, writers, and scholars. They also contributed to social diversity: because urban populations included shopkeepers, artisans, tradespeople, and laborers of all sorts, the growth of cities encouraged specialization of labor and the development of new skills. Most trades in medieval cities were organized according to the guild system. Guilds were labor groups that maintained a monopoly on their respective trades. They restricted membership, established prices, set standards of quality and fair practice, and provided pensions. Only members of skilled trades belonged to guilds.

Cities were often overcrowded and polluted, and many people lived in abject poverty. There were many advantages to city life, however, including increased cultural opportunities and the chance to gain greater wealth. One of the most important advantages was immunity from feudal obligations, especially serfdom. Typically, if a person left the countryside and lived in a city for a year and a day, he or she was released from his or her status as a serf. This was reflected in the popular saying, "city air makes you free."

SOCIAL STRESS IN THE LATE MEDIEVAL PERIOD

Although the extent of trade and urbanization continued to increase during the Late Middle Ages, these were also years of great social stress in Europe. To begin with, a wave of uprisings and revolts swept Europe from the early 1300s through the early 1500s. The causes of these disturbances were many. A general cooling of the climate, referred to by environmental historians as the Little Ice Age, affected harvests and made life in the countryside very difficult. Not only were more (and longer) wars being fought, but armies were growing larger, and the new gunpowder weaponry appearing at the time was extremely expensive. This meant that more and more peasants were being forced into military service (this was especially the case for the English and French during the Hundred Years' War). The taxes of common people also increased. In the cities, rapid growth often meant greater numbers of impoverished and unemployed citizens. During the last half of the 1400s, religious disagreements and dissatisfaction with the Church sometimes led to rebellion. Famous examples of late-medieval social strife include

- The peasant Jacquerie, or uprising, in France (1358)
- The revolt of the wool carders (*ciompi*) of Florence (1378)
- The English Peasants' Revolt, also known as Wat Tyler's Rebellion (1381)
- The Hussite rebellions against the Catholic Church and the Holy Roman Empire (1419–1436)
- The German Peasants' War (1524)

Another manifestation of social stress was a sharp rise in the persecution of people thought to be witches. Catholic authorities sought to root out suspected witchcraft. By the late 1400s, the Church issued a manual, *The Hammer of Witchcraft*, to help in spotting and trying witches. Ordinary people were caught up in the hysteria as well. Most of the victims of witch hunts were women.

THE BLACK DEATH

Social trauma also came in the form of the Black Death, the popular name for the bubonic plague. The arrival of bubonic plague in the middle of the fourteenth century ranks as one of the greatest medical disasters in European history. After killing millions of people in China, the disease traveled westward to the Middle East. It reached Europe in 1347, on a ship landing in Sicily.

In 1347 and 1348, the plague ravaged southern Europe. By 1349 and 1350, it spread to central Europe and the British Isles; it was felt in Russia and Scandinavia from 1351 to 1353. The disease's deadliness and the speed with which it spread caused tremendous panic throughout Europe. This initial bout of the plague also killed 25 to 30 million people, roughly one third the population of Europe. In addition, for centuries afterward, the bubonic plague persisted in Europe, recurring periodically (although no attack was ever again as bad as the first).

WOMEN IN MEDIEVAL EUROPE

As a general rule, women were subservient to men in all parts of Europe during these years. How much freedom or how many rights a woman enjoyed depended mainly on her social status and where in Europe she lived.

Women of lower classes performed domestic labor, caring for the household and assisting in farmwork. They bore children and raised them. In this era of poor hygiene and limited medical knowledge, many women—as many as 10 to 15 percent—died in childbirth.

In most parts of medieval Europe, women did have property rights. They could own and inherit land and property. The often received dowries (although in some places and times, it was the woman's family that had to provide a dowry to the husband-to-be). Women could separate from their husbands, although obtaining divorces and annulments was difficult, especially for women of the upper classes. Women had protection, although not always equality, before the law.

Except in Orthodox Byzantium, women could enter religious life. Women could not become clergy (especially priests) in either the Catholic or Orthodox church. They could, however, join religious communities (convents) and become nuns. During the High Middle Ages, the majority of nuns were from the upper classes, drawn from the families of the landed aristocracy. To marry off daughters, noble families often had to provide potential husbands with land, money, or a title. This meant that an aristocratic family with a large number of daughters often found itself unable to pay for all of them to get married. The most common solution was to place younger daughters in convents. Women who preferred intellectual pursuits sometimes found a safe haven in nunneries. For example, Hildegard of Bingen (1098–1179), celebrated for her mystical writings and songs, became an abbess of a German convent in the twelfth century.

Aristocratic women, while not legally the equal of men, could exert a great deal of political and cultural influence. If an aristocratic woman was heir to rich property or even a kingdom, she was an extremely desirable match. Noblewomen often managed their husbands' estates and financial accounts in their absence. Not infrequently, the mothers of young kings whose fathers had died early served as regents and advisers until their sons came of age.

Some women ruled in their own right, as queens. This was not common, and countries whose legal systems were based on tribal Germanic (Salic) law, such as France and the Holy Roman Empire, did not allow women to inherit thrones. But women would come to rule England, parts of Spain, Russia, and elsewhere. Perhaps the most famous example of a politically important woman during the High Middle Ages was Eleanor of Aquitaine (ca. 1122–1204), one of the richest heiresses of France. A dynamic, intelligent woman, Eleanor was married to Louis VII of

France, then, more famously, Henry II, the great centralizer of medieval England. She had a great deal of influence over politics in both countries. She was also a great patron of art and music.

MEDIEVAL CULTURE

THE MYTH OF THE "DARK AGES"

For many years, it was traditional to consider the Middle Ages a dark era almost completely devoid of cultural attainment or intellectual sophistication. More recently, it has become standard to recognize the richness of medieval culture. Both the High and Late Middle Ages saw Europe make great strides forward in the fields of art, thought, and literature. On the other hand, the culture of the Europeans lagged behind that of neighbors such as Byzantium and the Islamic world for most of this time.

CATHOLICISM AND CLASSICISM AS INFLUENCES ON MEDIEVAL CULTURE

The most important single factor shaping medieval culture was the Catholic Church. Most institutions of learning—monastery schools and, later, universities—were wholly or partly administered by the Church. The Church was the largest employer of artists, musicians, and architects. Art, literature, music, or poetry that was not in line with Church doctrine could be banned and the people who produced it punished severely.

Another key influence on medieval culture was the learning and literature preserved from the Roman and Greek, or classical, eras (mainly by the Church, another measure of its cultural importance). For several centuries, the Latin manuscripts left by the Romans were more familiar to the Europeans, and during the Middle Ages (and long afterward), Latin was the language of learning, culture, and intellectual life. The Europeans had much less knowledge of Greek until later, when interaction with Arab and Jewish translators made materials in that language (such as the writings of Aristotle) more accessible. Eventually, the increased familiarity of European artists and scholars with Greek and Roman texts led to the great classical revival that helped bring about the Renaissance (discussed subsequently). Scientific thought was dominated by the theories of the ancient Greeks, especially Aristotle (who was overwhelmingly important to the medieval Europeans), Ptolemy (whose geocentric, or earth-centered, view of astronomy argued that the sun revolves around the earth), and the physician Galen (whose writings on anatomy, though somewhat flawed, remained standard wisdom in Europe for centuries).

MEDIEVAL ARCHITECTURE

Some of the most distinctive products of medieval culture were architectural. Starting in the tenth and eleventh centuries, and largely

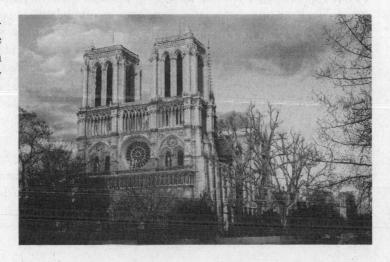

Cathedral of Notre Dame, Paris, France.
One of the best-known landmarks of Paris, the Cathedral of Notre Dame is perhaps the quintessential example of the Gothic style that prevailed in the construction of cathedrals in high medieval Europe.

inspired by Byzantine and Middle Eastern methods, the Europeans became adept at castle building. By the end of the Middle Ages, military architecture was a well-developed art in Europe. Even more impressive were Europe's cathedrals, which demanded a high degree of skill, immense amounts of money, and decades (sometimes more than a century) to build. The prevailing styles were Romanesque (which featured thick walls, small windows, and a square, blocky build) and the technically more advanced Gothic (characterized by tall, slender spires, ornate carvings, large stained-glass windows, and flying buttresses to support the weight of the walls).

SCHOLASTICISM AND MEDIEVAL PHILOSOPHY

The principal school of philosophy in medieval Europe was Scholasticism, which attempted to reconcile reason (logic, the senses, and the scientific learning of Greek and Roman authorities such as Aristotle) with faith in God and Christianity. The greatest of the Scholastics was the Italian monk Saint Thomas Aquinas (1225–1274), whose *Summa Theologica* is considered the most brilliant attempt to integrate logic with Christian belief. An earlier philosopher, Peter Abelard (1079–1142) of France, placed more emphasis on nonconformity and independent thinking in his *Sic et Non* (*Yes and No*).

The Jewish and Muslim thinkers of the Middle East and Moorish Spain, such as Maimonides, Avicenna, and Averroës, had much influence over the development of medieval European philosophy and intellectual life in general (see Chapter 7).

MUSIC AND LITERATURE

At first, religious music consisted mainly of Gregorian chant (also known as plainsong): simple chant unaccompanied by musical instruments. As time passed, arrangements grew more complex, and instruments began to be used by the end of the Middle Ages. Secular music dwelled on themes of love and adventure. The troubadours and minstrels who made this sort of music popular appeared in the eleventh and twelfth centuries (an important sponsor was Eleanor of Aquitaine, queen of France, then England). Their favorite subjects were the heroic legends of King Arthur and his knights, Roland (one of Charlemagne's warriors), and the Spanish general El Cid.

Trends in literature paralleled those in nonreligious music. Although Latin remained the language of the educated elite, an increasing number of poetic and literary works were being written in native tongues, or vernacular languages. The lyrics of the troubadours and minstrels are one example. But literature of high quality—previously written only in Latin—was appearing in French, Spanish, Italian, German, English, and other languages. One effect of this trend was to make literature more available to a greater number of people. It also stimulated a growth in literacy. Pioneers of vernacular writing include the Italian poet Dante Alighieri (1265–1321), author of the *Divine Comedy*; the poet Geoffrey Chaucer (1340–1401), whose *The Canterbury Tales* is a classic of English literature; and Christine de Pisan (1364–1410), whose French and Italian works made her one of Europe's first female writers.

UNIVERSITIES

The overall level of learning in medieval Europe was boosted by the appearance of a steadily growing number of universities. The first universities emerged in Italy during the 900s (according to tradition, the first was at Salerno). During the eleventh, twelfth, and thirteenth centuries, more and more universities were founded: Bologna, Paris, Oxford, Cambridge, and many others. Although most were at least partially under Church influence, they provided Europe with havens of learning, discussion, and the exchange of ideas.

THE PRINTING PRESS

Near the end of the Middle Ages, a single invention appeared that would revolutionize not only European culture, but the intellectual life of the entire world. This was the printing press developed by the German inventor Johannes Gutenberg (ca. 1397–1468) in 1436 to 1437. The concept of printing by means of carving images and words into blocks of wood had originated in China (perhaps Korea) centuries before, and was known to the Europeans. But this system was costly and unwieldy. Gutenberg's innovation was to create a movable-type printing press, in which individual metal characters could be placed in a frame to form pages, used, taken out, rearranged, and used again to create an entirely different page. Almost single-handedly, the printing press, which spread throughout Europe, was responsible for raising literacy rates, spreading information, increasing the impact of new ideas and scientific theories, and encouraging the expansion of libraries and universities. It is no exaggeration to say that the printing press played an indispensable role in the Renaissance, the Protestant Reformation, and, in general, an explosion of knowledge that would transform Europe and the West for centuries to come.

THE RENAISSANCE

THE CONCEPT OF THE RENAISSANCE

At some point during the early 1300s, an important cultural and intellectual revival began in parts of southern Europe, especially the city-states of the Italian peninsula. Over time, this revival became known as the Renaissance, or "rebirth." By the end of the 1400s, it had begun to spread from Italy to the rest of Europe. It is considered to have lasted until approximately 1600.

As noted previously, it was common until recently to think of the entire medieval era as a time of minimal cultural advancement. Consequently, the Renaissance was commonly viewed as a revolution, a sudden explosion of new ideas and learning. Because historians now have a better understanding of the richness of medieval culture, it has become standard to see the Renaissance less as a revolution, and more as a gradual change, an outgrowth of cultural and intellectual trends that were already under way. Nonetheless, it did represent a change, and a significant one at that.

THE CULTURAL OUTLOOK OF THE RENAISSANCE

One of the hallmarks of Renaissance culture (as distinct from medieval culture) was classicism: a greater understanding of and admiration for the literature and learning of the Greek and Roman eras. Of course, medieval Europeans were familiar with the Latin heritage of the Romans, as well as the legacy of the Greeks (although to a much lesser extent). What changed during the Renaissance was that a greater number of people probed more deeply into Latin sources and, thanks largely to translations provided by Jews and Arabs (who were more fluent in the Greek language), the learning of the Greeks.

Renaissance thought also differed from that of the medieval era in its secular nature. Whereas most of medieval art, literature, and philosophy was oriented toward religious concerns, Renaissance thought and culture placed a greater emphasis on the natural world. The authors, thinkers, and artists of the Renaissance did not ignore religion. Even if they had wanted to, doing so would have been dangerous, thanks to the Catholic Church's influence over culture. Still, many of their writings, paintings, and artworks were worldly in nature. And when Renaissance scientists and thinkers attempted to solve problems, they were just as likely to seek natural causes or turn to the learning of the Greeks and Romans as they were to turn to Christianity to explain the world around them.

A final feature of Renaissance culture was humanism, a concept pioneered by the Greeks and Romans, and one that went hand-in-hand with the classical revival and the secular nature of Renaissance thought. Simply put, humanism is a conviction that to be human is, in and of itself, worthwhile—that to be alive as a human being is something to celebrate and in which to rejoice. This attitude ran counter to the prevailing Church-dominated medieval view that to be human was to be tainted with sin, and, therefore, that the worldly life was less important than the heavenly afterlife.

CAUSES OF THE RENAISSANCE

Why did the ideals of classicism, secularism, and humanism arise first in Italy? One cause was the urban sophistication of the Italian city-states. Another was the strength of the Italian cities' commercial economies. Italian cities generated an amount of excess wealth sufficient to support a sustained cultural revival. Italy's success in trade and commerce also gave birth to a new class of patrons who, although not of noble blood, were rich, educated, and eager to increase their social standing by sponsoring artists and writers (the most famous example is the Medici family of Florence). Also, Italy's position as a naval and economic crossroads in the Mediterranean caused it to come into contact with new ideas and advanced knowledge from the outside world more quickly than the rest of Europe.

MAJOR FIGURES AND TRENDS OF THE RENAISSANCE

Important figures in the early stages of the Italian Renaissance were the writer and poet Petrarch (1304–1374), the author Giovanni Boccaccio (1313–1375), and the painter Giotto (ca. 1267–1337). As the Renaissance continued and matured, key individuals included the architect Filippo Brunelleschi (1377–1446), the political philosopher Niccolò Machiavelli (1469–1527), the artist and scientist Leonardo da Vinci (1452–1519), the painter and sculptor Michelangelo (1472–1564), and the painters Raphael (1483–1520) and Titian (1477–1576).

In keeping with its humanistic and secular nature, Renaissance poetry and literature addressed worldly concerns, political issues, human emotions (especially love), and earthy subjects (including sex). In many cases, Renaissance authors found themselves at odds with Catholic authorities, and many of their works were banned by the Church. Renaissance architects attained a high degree of engineering skill, boosted by a better understanding of mathematics and a deeper knowledge of the techniques of the Greeks and the Romans, who had been master builders. The painters of the Renaissance achieved a level of realism in their work that was astonishing, compared to the art of the medieval era. As in architecture, this was due partly to an increased familiarity with mathematics. This enabled painters to work out the laws of perspective necessary to depict a three-dimensional subject on a two-dimensional surface convincingly. Better paints and equipment, the technique of foreshortening, and the effective use of light and shadowing also increased the quality of Renaissance paintings.

THE SPREAD OF RENAISSANCE CULTURE

By the 1400s, the Italian Renaissance was exerting its influence on the rest of Europe. Travelers, especially northern students attending Italian universities, carried with them tales of and techniques drawn from the art and literature of the south. As noted previously, the invention of the movable-type printing press in the 1430s dramatically increased the speed and scope by which information could be produced and transmitted throughout Europe. The printing press deserves much of the credit for spreading the ideals of the Renaissance far beyond Italy. The Renaissance took hold in southern France, then all of France, as well as England, Spain, the Holy Roman

Empire, Poland, Hungary, and elsewhere. By the late 1400s, it was possible to speak of a "Northern Renaissance." This Northern Renaissance had a profound impact on the rest of Europe, especially with regard to the vast religious controversies of the 1500s that led to the Protestant Reformation.

QUICK REVIEW

1. Why were knights drawn principally from the nobility?

   (A) Nobles were smarter than commoners.
   (B) Monarchs did not believe that commoners could think strategically.
   (C) The weapons and equipment required for the knighthood were too costly for anyone but members of the nobility.
   (D) Only noblemen could serve as foot soldiers (knights-in-training).
   (E) none of the above

2. Which of the following is an accurate statement about feudalism in Europe?

   (A) It was discontinued by the 700s C.E.
   (B) Serfs were allowed to own land.
   (C) The basic unit of feudal landholding was the village.
   (D) Feudalism led to major class differences in society.
   (E) Feudalism embraced the practice of chivalry.

3. In what area did the Vikings NOT settle?

   (A) England
   (B) the Arabian Peninsula
   (C) Sicily
   (D) France
   (E) Greenland

4. In 1215, the Magna Carta

   (A) was the most complex world map of its kind
   (B) sailed to India with a crew of only seven and a cat
   (C) granted English nobles certain rights and privileges
   (D) granted English commoners voting rights
   (E) none of the above

5. Which of the following was NOT a cause of the Hundred Years' War?

   (A) political entanglement of the English and French royal families
   (B) competition over the wool trade
   (C) France's wish to gain additional English lands
   (D) Mongol invasions
   (E) All of the above were causes.

6. Which of the following is NOT a reason for the Crusades?

   (A) racial and religious prejudice
   (B) geopolitical conflict between Europe and the Middle East
   (C) the Black Death
   (D) religious fervor
   (E) the personal greed of many Europeans to gain wealth and land

7. The Hanseatic League

   (A) was a trade union based in the Mediterranean region
   (B) fought in the Middle East during the Crusades
   (C) was a powerful banking house in Italy
   (D) dominated trade in the Baltic region
   (E) traded in diamonds

8. Women in medieval Europe

   (A) all lacked property rights
   (B) had equality before the law, especially in matters of reproductive rights
   (C) had some legal protections, but their rights often depended on where they lived and which class they belonged to
   (D) could become members of the clergy
   (E) could enter religious life only in Orthodox Byzantium

9. Flying buttresses and slender spires are characteristics of _____ architecture.

(A) Gothic
(B) Romanesque
(C) modern
(D) Moorish
(E) Art Nouveau

10. Today, many historians view the Renaissance as

(A) a revolution
(B) a gradual but significant change in cultural and intellectual ideas and trends
(C) a sudden explosion of new ideas in the arts, sciences, and scholarly pursuits
(D) a radical shift in what was once practiced in the arts
(E) none of the above

ANSWERS:

1. **C**, p. 114
2. **D**, p. 115
3. **B**, p. 117
4. **C**, p. 117
5. **D**, p. 118
6. **C**, p. 121
7. **D**, p. 123
8. **C**, p. 124
9. **A**, p. 126
10. **B**, p. 127

CHAPTER 7

Islam in the Middle East and Africa

Before 1000, the Islamic world had been united religiously and politically by the Abbasid Caliphate, based in its glorious capital, Baghdad. From 750 onward, the Abbasids ruled a massive territory that stretched from Spain and Morocco in the west to the borderlands of India in the east. Relatively quickly, however, the caliphs fell victim to overextension and gradual breakdown. Although the Abbasids retained theoretical control over the Islamic world until 1258, their power had started to wane as early as 850. While Islamic culture remained quite advanced during this era, the years after 1000 were a period of steady decline, politically speaking.

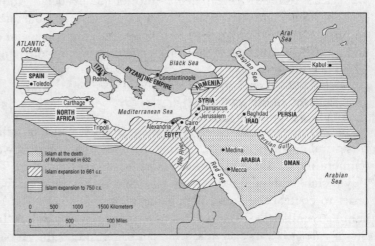

The Birth and Expansion of Islam, 632–750.
Born in Arabia, the dynamic new faith of Islam triumphed throughout the Middle East, where it is still dominant. It then continued to expand, both eastward and westward.

By the same token, a chief characteristic of these years was political confusion. From 1000 to the 1400s, many Islamic states rose and fell. Other Middle Eastern peoples, such as the Persians and Turks, began to rival the Arabs as major forces in the Islamic community. Outside enemies and invaders added to the chaos. Finally, by the end of the fifteenth century and the beginning of the sixteenth, the Islamic world—at least in the Middle East and North Africa—would be more or less reconsolidated under Turkish groups, specifically the Ottoman Turks. However, if the Ottomans recentralized the Islamic world, they would also recast it in a somewhat different mold. And, even under the Ottomans, Islam was never again united to the extent it had been under the Abbasids.

On the treatment of women in early Islamic cultures, see Chapter 5.

DISINTEGRATION OF ABBASID RULE

OVEREXTENSION OF THE ABBASID CALIPHATE

Technically, the Abbasid Caliphate was in power from 750 to 1258. However, long before 1258, the caliphate began to disintegrate in several ways. Overextension was a serious problem. The territory ruled by the Abbasids—extending thousands of miles from east to west, and home to millions of people of different ethnicities and languages—was exceptionally difficult to govern. Another factor contributing to disunity was the existence of a religious minority within Islam: Shiite Islam, which differed in several respects from the Sunni majority (see Chapter 5).

As a result, certain regions began to break away by the 900s. As early as 875, Persia and Central Asia came under the control of the Samanid dynasty. This marked the first time that a major non-Arabic entity wielded significant political power in the Islamic world. For more than two hundred years, a Shiite caliphate, the Fatimids (909–1171), rebelled and ruled over Egypt. In faraway Spain, a new Umayyad Caliphate, named after the earlier caliphate that had ruled from Damascus from 661 to 750, achieved brief independence from 929 to 976.

Abbasid decline also resulted from a huge wave of nomadic movements in North Africa, Syria, and Iraq. The mass movement of peoples caused much social disruption, economic displacement, and political confusion. All of this instability made it difficult to maintain solid political control over these regions.

MILITARY THREATS TO BAGHDAD

To make things worse, Baghdad itself was under constant military threat, then fell into the hands of several enemies in a row. During the 800s, the Abbasids were compelled to move their capital temporarily to Samarra, sixty-five miles to the north. In 945, Baghdad was captured by the Buyid clan. Although the Buyids were Shiite, they retained the Abbasid caliph as a figurehead, in order to control the Sunni population more effectively. The Buyids controlled Baghdad and the caliphate until 1055. That year, a new conqueror, the Seljuk Turks, captured the city and restored Sunni rule. Like the Buyids, the Seljuks permitted the Abbasid caliph to retain his position as nominal ruler.

Military stress continued, finally tearing the Abbasid Caliphate apart. The Abbasids' weakness largely accounts for the European Crusaders' success in seizing territory in the Middle East from 1095 to 1291. An even deadlier foe appeared in the mid-1200s. In 1258, Mongol invaders captured Baghdad and killed the last Abbasid caliph (because Mongol tradition forbade the shedding of royal blood, the Mongols wrapped the caliph in a carpet and trampled him with horses). After the destruction of the Abbasid Caliphate, the Middle East was split into many separate states. Later, it would be reunited, but only partially, by the Turks.

ISLAM IN SAHARAN AND SUB-SAHARAN AFRICA

THE SPREAD OF ISLAM TO AFRICA

Islam reached the eastern parts of North Africa (especially Egypt) very quickly, during the new religion's initial wave of expansion in the 600s and 700s. It spread more gradually through the Sahara, and even to sub-Saharan Africa, over the next few hundred years. A few nations and communities of northeastern Africa remained Christian: the Nubian kingdoms of Kush and Axum (at least until the 1300s and 1400s), Ethiopia, and the Coptic Christians of Egypt. But the majority of the population converted to Islam.

Islam was brought to Africa by Arabs engaged in trade—either by overland caravan or by sea, along the continent's Indian Ocean coastline. In most cases, conversion was a peaceful process, although it was sometimes done by force. In addition, much of the commercial activity that brought Islam to southern Africa was connected with the extensive slave trade carried on by Arabs there. Trade northward largely consisted of slaves, salt, ivory, and animal skins. Trade southward generally included such manufactured goods as glass, metalwork, and pottery.

Many of the Swahili city-states of Africa's east coast were home to large Muslim communities. In general, after the 1100s, Middle Eastern culture was one of the many elements that contributed to the incredible diversity of East African civilizations.

THE BERBER STATES

The first state in the western part of sub-Saharan Africa to adopt Islam was Takrur, in 1030. An even larger and more powerful state that extended into the sub-Saharan parts of Africa was established by the Berbers, desert nomads of the western Sahara. The Berbers were converts to Islam; they were also hardened warriors. The strongest Berber clan, the Almoravids, was based in the city of Marrakesh, in present-day Morocco. In 1076, the Almoravids drove to the south, conquering the great state of Ghana and forming a large kingdom that stretched from Morocco to Mali. Berber domination of this region continued into the twelfth century and afterward, although the leadership changed. A fundamentalist clan, the Almohads, displaced the Almoravids. After 1130, the Almohads formed an even larger Islamic empire that ruled Africa from Tunisia to the Atlantic and included parts of Spain.

MALI

By the 1300s and 1400s, Islamic states in western sub-Saharan Africa included Songhai, Kanem-Bornu, and many Hausa city-states. The biggest and most powerful at the time was Mali (ca. 1250–1460), along the Niger River basin, which has been a main north-south transportation route for thousands of years. Founded in the mid-1200s by the conqueror Sundiata, and blessed with sizable deposits of gold and metal ore, Mali became a key center for trade in western and northern Africa. It also controlled a major communications network, encompassing the upper Niger River and its territories.

The fact that Mali was led by Muslims proved beneficial. First, it helped politically. It allowed Mali to cultivate good trade relations with Arab states north of the Sahara. It also created a group of educated scholars who acted as public servants. Gold and salt were the kingdom's main mediums of exchange. Merchants used a central currency system and systems of weights and measures in their daily business. Mali's products were highly valued. They included gold, ivory, animal skins, and slaves.

Mali's chief commercial outpost (although not its capital) was the famous city of Timbuktu, stopping point for caravans and trade expeditions traveling to and from all directions. Its growth and importance was almost wholly attributable to the vast amount of salt sold in its markets. The salt was then shipped hundreds of miles to various points along the Niger River system. Timbuktu was also a renowned center of religious studies and Islamic scholarship. Mali's most powerful ruler was Mansa Musa (1312–1337), famous throughout Europe and Africa as one of the world's wealthiest monarchs (a Spanish map of 1375 referred to Mali as home to the "richest and noblest king in all lands"). Mansa Musa more fully systematized government, including appointing members of the royal family to governorships. By the early 1400s, Mali was under foreign attack, and its territory was steadily shrinking. Mali's might collapsed by the end of the century.

Culturally speaking, Mali (like most parts of Africa) was home to a strong tradition of oral storytelling and songmaking. One of Africa's most famous epic poems from this period comes from Mali. This is the *Son-Jara* (also known as the *Sundiata*). It dates from the 1200s, and it tells of the many exploits of the chieftain Son-Jara (Sundiata, 1230–1255), founder of the Mali state.

THE RISE OF THE TURKS

THE ORIGINS OF THE TURKS

The steppes and open plains of Central Asia served as the original homeland of many peoples who later spread throughout Eurasia. Among them were the various nomadic tribes known collectively as the Turks. After 1000, various Turkic groups (especially the Mamluks, the Seljuks, and the Ottomans) would exert a profound influence on the Middle East. By the end of the 1400s, the Ottoman Turks would be the dominant political force there.

THE MAMLUKS

Most Turkish tribes were extremely adept at horseback riding and cavalry warfare. As a result, many Turks were brought to the Middle East by the Arabs to serve in their armies. By the eleventh century, there were a great number of these cavalry warriors. They were called Mamluks. Over time, they became dedicated converts to Islam, and they were among the best soldiers in the Middle East. Many of these Mamluks gravitated toward Asia Minor, or what is today called Turkey. Later, in the 1200s, a large group of Mamluks would migrate to Egypt.

THE SELJUKS

Meanwhile, in the early eleventh century, another Turkish group moved from the east into Iraq, then Asia Minor. These were the Seljuk Turks, who founded a state during the 1030s. As described above, they captured Baghdad in 1055, deposing the Buyid clan but, like the Buyids, supporting the Abbasid caliph as a figurehead ruler.

Soon after, the Seljuks expanded even farther to the west, moving into territory controlled by the Byzantine Empire. In 1071, Byzantine and Seljuk forces clashed at the Battle of Manzikert. The Seljuks won a resounding victory. They then went on to capture most of Asia Minor, along with the eastern coast of the Mediterranean, including Syria, Lebanon, and Palestine (including Jerusalem). These Turkish successes crippled the Byzantine Empire and ushered in its long period of decline. However, the victories also helped to prompt the Christians of Europe to embark upon the Crusades, which, as described in Chapter 6, began in 1095 and continued until 1291.

THE CRUSADES

For a time, European successes during the crusading period, especially the First Crusade (1095–1099) and the establishment of the Latin Kingdoms in 1099, threw the Middle East into political confusion. Initially, the Abbasid Caliphate was incapable of providing leadership, as were the Fatimids in Egypt, the Seljuks, and the Arabs. Not until the mid-1100s was there any effective resistance to the Crusaders (the Second Crusade, from 1146 to 1149, was a failure for the Christians). By the end of the 1100s, the great leader Saladin (ca. 1137–1193), a Kurdish general, overthrew the Fatimid dynasty in Egypt and united Egypt with Syria. Saladin inflicted a major defeat upon the Crusaders by capturing Jerusalem in 1187 and fighting the leaders of the Third Crusade (1189–1192) to a stalemate (thereby gaining a favorable treaty settlement).

Saladin's dynasty came to a quick end, as Mamluks seized control of Egypt in 1250. By this point, the Mamluks, Arabs, and Seljuks had become better at fighting the European Crusaders, whose foothold in the Middle East was disappearing. Before the end of the 1200s, the last of the major outposts held by the Christians (Acre) would fall to the Muslims, and the Crusades would be over.

THE MONGOL INVASIONS

However, a new—and, by now, even more dangerous—enemy had already appeared. As described previously (and in Chapter 10), Mongol attackers appeared during the middle of the 1200s. In the process of conquering the vast empire they carved out for themselves during the thirteenth century, the Mongols, in 1258, took Baghdad and destroyed the Abbasid Caliphate by putting the last caliph to death. The Mongols' advance through the Middle East was stopped only in 1260, at the Battle of Ain Jalut (the Springs of Goliath) in Syria. Here, a Mamluk army defeated the Mongols and halted their progress.

Still, the Mongols established a state in the Middle East, the Il-Khan Empire, which lasted until 1349. The presence of a Mongol state in the region created political disarray. For a long time, no single unit was strong or powerful enough to centralize the Middle East. Major states included the Il-Khan Empire, Mamluk Egypt, and the Seljuk kingdom of Rum, but none of them was dominant.

THE RISE OF THE OTTOMAN TURKS

The group that would eventually dominate the Middle East began to do so in the 1300s and 1400s. These were the Ottoman Turks. The Ottomans had begun to settle in the northwestern part of Asia Minor during the 1200s, serving as vassals of the Seljuks. By the end of the 1200s, they had formed their own independent state. Their ruling dynasty was founded by the sultan Osman I (r. 1280–1326), from whose name the word "Ottoman" derives. Throughout the 1300s and 1400s, the Ottomans absorbed the territory of the Seljuks, the Il-Khan Mongols, the Egyptian Mamluks, and other Middle Eastern states. By the early 1500s, almost all of the Middle East was firmly under their control.

The Ottomans also attacked southeastern Europe and what remained of the Byzantine Empire. By the late 1300s, the Ottomans were moving into the Balkans (a key victory came at Kosovo, over the Serbs, in 1389). They continued to pressure the Byzantines. Their navies gained control over many of the islands and ports of the eastern Mediterranean. Finally, in 1453, Ottoman armies, led by the sultan Mehmed II, captured Constantinople after a long siege and heavy bombardments with what was, at the time, the world's largest and most advanced gunpowder artillery. The Ottomans' victory at Constantinople brought the 1,100-year history of the Byzantine Empire to an end. It also set the stage for what would be an intense, protracted struggle against Christian Europe during the late 1400s, the 1500s, and beyond.

ISLAMIC CULTURE

THE GOLDEN AGE OF ISLAMIC CULTURE

For all its political failures, the Abbasid caliphate presided over the golden era of Islamic culture. Compared with most of its neighbors—medieval Europe, sub-Saharan Africa, the steppes of Central Asia—the Islamic world was far more culturally advanced during the 700s through the 1200s. In Eurasia, the Islamic world's only rivals in terms of cultural and intellectual attainment during these years were India and China.

MATHEMATICS AND SCIENCE

The mathematical and scientific aptitude of the Muslims was great. It was under the Abbasids that the use of so-called Arabic numerals (which are generally thought to have originated in India) became widespread. The term *algebra* comes directly from Arabic, and the Muslims were expert at trigonometry as well. Medicine was another area in which Islamic scholars were adept. During the 900s, the physician Razi compiled the *Hawi*, the most thorough medical encyclopedia of its time. Even more famous was the Persian doctor and scientist Ibn Sina, known to the West as Avicenna (980–1037). His *Canon of Medicine* remained in wide use until the 1600s, both in Europe and the Middle East. The fact that many of the stars in the night sky bear Arabic names attests to the skill of Muslim astronomers during these years. One of the reasons for the great military successes of the Ottomans was a high degree of expertise with gunpowder weaponry, which required a good working knowledge of metallurgy and chemistry.

PHILOSOPHY

The Islamic world produced a number of great philosophers: some Muslim, some Jewish (but fully accepted as citizens and recognized for their intellectual accomplishments). Like the Scholastics of medieval Europe, Islamic philosophers expended much effort in investigating the relationship between human reason and religious faith.

The two most famous thinkers came from Muslim Spain. Ibn Rushd, better known as Averroës (1126–1198), played an indispensable role in Islamic *and* European cultural life. A celebrated doctor, Averroës also translated and analyzed the works of the Greek philosopher Aristotle. Almost single-handedly, he reintroduced Aristotle's philosophical and scientific ideas to Europe, where they played an important role in shaping thought and culture during the Middle Ages. A second philosopher was Moses ben Maimon, or Maimonides (1135–1204), a Spanish Jew. A rabbi, Maimonides wrote many commentaries on Jewish scripture and law. Like Averroës, he did much to encourage the dissemination of Aristotle's ideas throughout Europe. His most famous work, *Guide to the Perplexed*, was an attempt to reconcile the rationality of Greco-Roman thought with Jewish theology (in an effort similar to that of Thomas Aquinas with regard to Christian thought).

ISLAM'S INFLUENCE OVER CULTURE

As in Christian Europe, religion played a large role in cultural activity. Muslim authorities had a certain degree of control over what was or was not acceptable art or literature. Because the Qur'an forbids the worship of graven images, Islamic art during these years tended to feature geometric patterns and shapes rather than human or animal figures (although this was not a hard-and-fast rule). Religious colleges, or madrasas, were major centers of learning and education. Much intellectual activity in the Islamic world revolved around debates and commentaries on the Qur'an, the sayings of Mohammed (Hadith), and Islamic law (Sharia).

ISLAMIC LITERATURE

Among the classics of Islamic literature from the Abbasid years is the collection of stories known as *The Thousand Nights and a Night*, commonly referred to in the West as *The Arabian Nights*. These stories of genies, heroes, and monsters, set in various places throughout the Muslim world, include the tales of Sindbad the Sailor, Ali Baba and the Seven Thieves, and Aladdin. Also important is the *Rubaiyat* of Omar Khayyám (ca. 1038–1131). Famous as a mathematician and astronomer, Khayyám also composed this collection of seventy-five quatrains (four-line verses), sometime in the early 1100s. Bittersweet and meditative, the *Rubaiyat* is considered to be one of the masterpieces of world literature.

Another important written work was the journal of Ibn Battuta (1304–1368), the greatest explorer and traveler of the Islamic world. Born in Morocco, Ibn Battuta spent 30 years visiting almost every Muslim country in the world. He traveled to Mecca, Persia, Mesopotamia, Turkey, Central Asia, Spain, Timbuktu, India, China, and Sumatra. His journey covered more than 75,000 miles. Ibn Battuta told of his adventures in his book *Travels*.

Arabic was the holy language of Islam: Mohammed had spoken it, the Qur'an was written in it. Because of this, Arabic was also the principal language of Islamic cultural and intellectual life, just as Latin was for the Christians of medieval Europe. However, starting in the 800s and 900s, with the rise of the Samanid dynasty in Persia, another language joined Arabic as a major element in Islamic thought and literature. This was Persian. Although it was written in Arabic characters, it became important in its own right as an elegant and refined language in which a sizable and significant body of poetry, religious commentary, and scientific work was written.

Also from Persia came an important aspect of Islamic culture: Sufism, a mystical strain within the Muslim faith. The origins of Sufism date back to the 700s and 800s, when it began to appear in Persia. It places a strong emphasis on attaining union with Allah by means of ritual disciplines and spiritual exercises (chanting and dancing are among the best known). By the 1100s and 1200s, Sufism was becoming popular outside of Persia and reaching other parts of the Muslim world. The best example of Sufi thought and belief can be found in the eight books of verse contained in the *Mathnawi*, by the Persian poet Jalal al-Din Rumi (1207–1273).

QUICK REVIEW

1. A chief characteristic of Islamic states from 1000 to 1400 was

   (A) political unity
   (B) the consolidation of democracy
   (C) political chaos
   (D) steady strengthening of political power
   (E) the weakening of Turkish control over Islamic lands

2. How did the Abbasids "overextend" themselves as rulers?

   (A) They failed to govern vast and ethnically diverse lands effectively.
   (B) They sold off too many parcels of land to feed their financial reserves.
   (C) They became a caliphate.
   (D) They forced Christianity on their occupied territories.
   (E) They lost great numbers of men in the Crusades.

3. Which of the following places in Africa remained Christian despite the spread of Islam on the continent?

   (A) Marrakesh
   (B) Swahili city-states
   (C) Mali
   (D) Ethiopia
   (E) Tunisia

4. After the mid-1200s, Mali

   I. was soon conquered by Arabs, who installed an administration that was controlled from Turkey
   II. stopped acting as a trade center
   III. became a key trade center and controlled a major communications network
   IV. was led by Christians

   (A) III only
   (B) IV only
   (C) I, II, and III
   (D) III, and IV
   (E) I and II only

5. Timbuktu was renowned for its

   (A) gold and its role in opposing the slave trade
   (B) salt reserves and Islamic scholarship
   (C) large harbor
   (D) glass and ceramic architecture
   (E) many Gothic churches

6. The Turkish military campaigns

   (A) crippled the Holy Roman Empire
   (B) crushed the Mongols
   (C) introduced Islam to the Middle East
   (D) weakened the Byzantine Empire
   (E) none of the above

7. During the 700s through the 1200s, which of the following was the most culturally advanced civilization?

(A) medieval Europe
(B) sub-Saharan Africa
(C) the Islamic world
(D) Central Asia
(E) Southeast Asia

8. Which of the following is a factor that made the Ottomans so militarily successful?

(A) They practiced guerrilla warfare.
(B) They used radio communications.
(C) They used the stars to guide them.
(D) They stopped using horses in invasions.
(E) They had well-made gunpowder weaponry.

9. In what way were scholars in medieval Europe and the Islamic world similar?

(A) They both believed in Christianity.
(B) They both studied the relationship between reason and faith.
(C) They both introduced astrology into their studies of metaphysics.
(D) They were both persecuted by their rulers.
(E) They were required to be members of the clergy.

10. Why did Islamic art during this period usually feature geometric patterns and shapes rather than depictions of living things?

(A) The Qu'ran forbids the worship of graven images.
(B) The Bible forbids the worship of graven images.
(C) Artists were not yet properly skilled to draw human figures.
(D) Geometric shapes were seen to be more godlike.
(E) none of the above

ANSWERS:

1. **C**, p. 131
2. **A**, p. 132
3. **D**, p. 132
4. **A**, p. 133
5. **B**, p. 133
6. **D**, p. 135
7. **C**, p. 135
8. **E**, p. 135
9. **B**, p. 136
10. **A**, p. 136

CHAPTER 8

China, Japan, and East Asia

When the eleventh century began, there was no single China. The collapse of the Tang dynasty in 906 had thrown all of East Asia into political turmoil. China itself split into various empires and states. This disunity lasted for several centuries. Not until the late 1200s would the country be joined together again.

During the 1200s, China, like the rest of Eurasia, would be rocked by the explosive military expansion of the Mongols. China was conquered by the Mongols—indeed, Mongol rule played a significant part in the country's reunification. After the mid-1300s, China underwent even greater centralization under the Ming dynasty.

Other countries of East Asia, especially Japan, Korea, and Vietnam, passed in and out of the Chinese political orbit, but they were constantly being influenced by their larger neighbor. At times they were under China's direct control, at others they were free. China also exerted a strong artistic, literary, and religious pull on them. As time passed, all three became more independent politically and culturally.

LIAO AND SONG (SUNG) CHINA

THE SONG EMPIRE AND ITS RIVALS

Following the breakdown of the Tang dynasty in 906, China fragmented into separate states until the late 1200s. The largest and longest lasting was the Song (Sung) Empire, which, at first, ruled east central China, from the Yellow River in the north to the Vietnamese border in the south. The Song Empire lasted until 1279, but its territory shrank considerably, as a result of war with its neighbors, the Liao and Jin empires.

The Liao Empire, in Mongolia and northern China, was the first Chinese nation to make Beijing its capital. It lasted from 916 to 1121. Its people were skilled at ceramics and painting. The Liao armies were especially adept at cavalry warfare and siegecraft, making the empire a serious military threat to the Song. For many years, the Song paid a large annual tribute of silk and cash to the Liao. Then, in the 1110s, the Song made an alliance with the Liao's northern neighbors, the Jurchens. Trapped between the Song and the Jurchens, the Liao Empire was conquered and destroyed by 1121.

However, victory over the Liao backfired on the Song. The Jurchens proclaimed their own empire, the Jin. They also renounced their alliance with the Song and attacked it. By 1127, the Jin Empire had expanded greatly at the expense of their former partners. The Song withdrew to the south, past the Yellow River. This reduced state is referred to as the Southern Song. It paid tribute to the Jin Empire and went on to survive from 1127 to 1279. The Song would finally fall to the Mongols (discussed presently).

SONG SOCIETY AND ECONOMICS

Despite its political misfortunes, the Song Empire was culturally and economically impressive. Song China enjoyed steady population growth. It was also the world's most heavily urbanized society, home to the largest cities on earth, several of them with a million or more inhabitants. Although its economic ties with Central Asia and the Middle East lessened during these years, Song China was still connected with the lengthy trade routes that extended to those regions. China still maintained contact with Silk Road cities in Central Asia, such as Bukhara and Samarkand, the greatest caravan stopping-place and commercial center between China and the Middle East.

If their contacts with the Middle East lessened, the Song became increasingly involved with the elaborate commercial network along the Pacific coast and in Southeast Asia. The port of Canton (now Guangzhou) became one of the world's busiest and most cosmopolitan trading centers. Goods, merchants, ideas, and money from all of China, Japan, Korea, Southeast Asia, Malaysia, India, and Central Asia flowed through Canton. Song China's large trading vessels, known as junks, cruised the eastern seas, carrying silk and manufactured goods. The Song's ties with Japan and Korea were especially tight, religiously as well as economically.

SONG CULTURE AND RELIGION

Song China was perhaps the most scientifically and technologically advanced society of its time, with the possible exception of the Abbasid Caliphate. The Song experienced an avalanche of knowledge and innovation. Excellent mathematicians and astronomers, the Song Chinese greatly expanded their understanding of the stars' movements. Song scientists developed accurate clocks, as well as a working compass (first used for navigation at sea in 1090). Perhaps the most unusual example of Song China's aptitude in combining scientific knowledge with technological expertise was the celestial clock of Su Song, built in 1088. Su Song's clock was an 80-foot-tall structure that told the time of day, the day of the month, and the positions of the sun, moon, planets, and major stars. It was the first device in world history to use a chain-driven mechanism (which was powered by flowing water). Also during the Song period, the Chinese invented gunpowder (sometime during the late 1000s or 1100s), pioneered the use of paper currency (which they called "flying money"), and made use of block printing (a practice they may have adopted from the Koreans).

Religious and cultural practices evolved in Song China, and the resulting changes went on to affect China's neighbors as well. A great revival of Confucius's teachings—Neo-Confucianism—got under way during the Song period. Both during the Song period and later, Neo-Confucianism proved to be an important unifying factor for a China that was politically diffracted. It cemented into Chinese culture a strong tendency for hierarchy, social stratification, and obedience. It put a premium on education and cultured behavior. Most governmental officials gained their posts by scoring well on complex and rigorous civil-service examinations, a very Confucian practice. Another religious development of the period was the emergence of a new form of Buddhism: Chan, known as Son in Korea and Zen in Japan. Chan was a simplified form of worship, stressing the importance of meditation. It became very popular, not just in China, but far abroad. Both Neo-Confucianism and Chan spread beyond China's borders, influencing Japan, Korea, and other parts of East Asia.

WOMEN IN CHINESE SOCIETY

Unfortunately, Neo-Confucianism, along with Chinese tradition, was used as a justification for the greater subordination of women. Upper-class women, whose families were most likely to follow Confucian dictates, were especially subject to restrictions. Whereas earlier, a husband's family needed to produce a dowry for a new bride, now the reverse became the norm. Marriages were arranged, mainly to the benefit of the groom.

The best-known feature of the subjugation of women that Neo-Confucianism inspired was foot-binding. This painful practice, which kept women's feet tiny and dainty but in the process crippled them, was firmly established by 1200, and it continued into the early 1900s.

Women of the lower classes were generally freer from the strictures that applied to those in the upper classes, but they still occupied a secondary status in comparison to men. On the other hand, women of all classes had inheritance and property rights, and retained control over their dowries after divorce or a husband's death. Still, the position of women in Chinese society was decidedly second-class.

THE MONGOLS AND CHINA

MONGOL ATTACKS ON SONG CHINA

As discussed in Chapter 10, almost all of Eurasia was affected during the 1200s by the sudden and astonishingly successful military campaigns of the Mongols. As Genghis Khan and his sons began to expand outward from their Mongolian homeland, the Chinese states were among their earliest targets.

In 1211, Genghis Khan's horsemen attacked the Jin Empire. By 1215, the Mongols had captured Beijing, the Jin capital. Throughout the 1220s, the Mongols assaulted the Jin Empire and the Tanggut Empire of western China, eventually subduing and absorbing them. Genghis Khan died in 1227, but his sons continued the wars of conquest. The campaign against China fell to Genghis Khan's son and heir, Ögödei, the new Great Khan. By 1234, the Mongols controlled almost all of western and northern China, and were threatening the Southern Song. This state of affairs—in which the Mongols expanded their territory in all directions, grew stronger, and put ever-greater pressure on Song China—continued throughout the 1240s and 1250s.

KHUBILAI KHAN AND THE CONQUEST OF CHINA

During the 1260s, things changed dramatically. Even beforehand, the Mongol Empire, which was too large and unwieldy to rule as a single state, had been breaking apart into separate units. In 1260s, this gradual disintegration turned into rapid breakup. That year, Genghis Khan's grandsons warred among themselves and took over various parts of the empire that had been left to them. One of them, Khubilai (Kublai) Khan, chose to stake his claim to China and Southeast Asia. He moved his capital from Mongolia to the Chinese city of Beijing. Although he continued to refer to himself as the Great Khan of the Mongols, Khubilai Khan also established a new state: the Yuan Empire (1271–1368). It was this Yuan Empire that would conquer most of China and reunify it as a single country.

YUAN CHINA AND THE ESTABLISHMENT OF THE MING

KHUBILAI KHAN AND THE YUAN EMPIRE

An adept general, Khubilai Khan, soon after proclaiming his Yuan Empire in 1271, lost no time in conquering China and unifying it under his rule. The Southern Song fell in 1279. The Jin, Tanggut, and Nanzhao states came under Khubilai's control soon after.

Although the Yuan Empire was a multiethnic state ruled by a Mongol emperor, it developed into a truly Chinese nation. Khubilai Khan and the Mongol leadership became Sinified, or acculturated in the Chinese style. The Mongol rulers adopted Buddhism (although not Confucianism). Mandarin Chinese, the dialect of the Beijing region, became the official language of Yuan China, and remains China's official dialect to this day.

Khubilai Khan reigned until 1294. During his lifetime, Yuan China was rich and powerful. Most of Khubilai's military campaigns—both in China and beyond its borders—were successful, although he was unable to conquer countries like Japan (which he tried to take in 1274 and 1281) and Java (which he fought in 1293). When he did not conquer them directly, Khubilai Khan forced most of China's neighbors to pay tribute. The Yuan Empire also resisted attacks from other Mongol states in Central Asia.

Khubilai Khan also proved effective in rebuilding China's bureaucracy and economy. He created a governmental administration that helped run the entire country. He repaired roads and canals (including the Grand Canal linking the Yellow and Yangtze rivers). He built new cities (including the resort of Shangdu, famous in the West as the pleasure garden of Xanadu). Khubilai Khan also restored trade with the west. The Silk Road, which had fallen into inactivity, once again became a vital trade route under the Mongols. In general, the level of Chinese trade grew under the Yuan rulers, making the merchant class increasingly important. It was Khubilai Khan's China that the famous Venetian merchant Marco Polo visited in the 1270s. The colorful stories that Marco Polo told about Khubilai Khan's realm when he returned to Italy did much to create an image in Europe of China as a fabulously rich and glorious land. Marco Polo's tales also did much to stimulate the desire of Europeans to trade with the Far East.

THE DECLINE OF THE YUAN EMPIRE

The Yuan state was not so fortunate after Khubilai Khan's death. During the early 1300s, China suffered a tremendous population loss (estimated at 30 to 40 percent). Much of this loss was due to the appearance of bubonic plague (which traveled westward to affect Europe during the 1340s, as the Black Death). Severe economic decline accompanied the population loss. By the 1340s, a series of civil wars broke out, challenging the ability of the Yuan rulers to hold their state together. Finally, in 1368, a rebellion led by a warlord named Zhu Yuanzhang brought an end to the Yuan Empire. Zhu Yuanzhang would go on to establish one of the longest-lasting and most famous dynasties in Chinese history: the Ming (1368–1644).

THE ESTABLISHMENT OF THE MING

Before becoming a rebel leader, Zhu Yuanzhang had been a soldier, a thief, and a priest. After his victory in 1368, he renamed himself Hung-wu. He ruled until 1403, then his son, Yongle (Yung-lo, 1403–1424) took the throne. These were the first two Ming rulers, and they both proved remarkably effective at rebuilding China and repairing the damage done by the stress and warfare of the early 1300s.

THE MING, MILITARY STRENGTH, AND THE OUTSIDE WORLD

Abroad, Ming China expanded its borders. It also forged alliances with the Vietnamese states of Annam and Champa, as well as the Yi kingdom in Korea. The Ming retained and expanded the tributary system that Khubilai Khan had created. Under this system, many states in East and Southeast Asia were forced to pay tribute to the Ming. When the Mongol warlord Timur attacked China in the late 1300s, he was decisively repelled.

Not only was the Ming army large and effective, the Ming navy was too. During the late 1300s and early 1400s, the Ming emperors used the navy as an instrument of diplomacy and intimidation. From 1405 to 1433, the Chinese admiral Zheng He (Cheng Ho) made seven long voyages to

Southeast Asia, Indonesia, and India, then as far west as the Persian Gulf, the Red Sea, and the East African coast. Zheng He forced fifty nations and city-states to pay tribute to China, established trade relations with many others, and gained a large amount of knowledge about the outside world. Had the Ming chosen to continue this tradition of naval excellence, China might well have initiated a wave of exploration and colonization similar to the one that made the Europeans so wealthy and powerful in the late 1400s, 1500s, and onward. After the reign of Yongle, however, the Ming rulers lost interest in the outside world, and expeditions such as Zheng He's ceased.

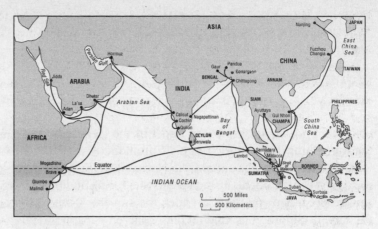

The Voyages of Zheng He, 1405–1433.
China's greatest mariner, Zheng He, sailed several times from China to Arabia and East Africa, as well as points in between, along the coastlines of the Indian Ocean. He explored, established diplomatic relations, and exacted monetary tribute from weaker states nearby. If the Ming emperors had continued their interest in exploration and navigation, China, like—or, perhaps, instead of—the nations of Europe, might have become a global colonizing power.

THE MING AT HOME

At home, the Ming dynasty recentralized the country. Hung-wu and Yongle were able to rebuild the economy and restore trade relations with China's neighbors and even countries farther afield. During their reigns, the Chinese population rebounded, reaching—then surpassing—its pre-1300 level of approximately 100 million. Although few of the Ming emperors were as politically or militarily active as Hung-wu or Yongle, the Ming state remained in place for centuries, until 1644. By 1450, its might was at a peak.

MING ART AND CULTURE

Culturally, the Ming years remain famous as a time of artistic grandeur and intellectual dynamism. This was not just the case in China itself, but throughout East Asia. Chinese artistic forms, religious ideas, and literature continued to exert an influence on the cultures of countries such as Korea, Vietnam, and Japan (although China's cultural sway over Japan had lessened since the eleventh century).

Confucianism was restored to its place of prominence, rejoining Buddhism as a guiding force in Chinese philosophy and religion. Some of the greatest works of classical Chinese literature appeared, including a new form of writing, the novel (one example is *The Golden Lotus*, a story about a wicked landowner who mistreats those around him). Ming artisans produced some of the most exquisite glassware, pottery, ceramics, and, especially, porcelain that the world has ever seen (it is no accident that the word *china* is synonymous with fine dishware). Another major art form was scroll painting. Chinese painters depicted landscapes, historical scenes, and human and animal figures in exquisite fashion on long, vertical scrolls of silk and paper.

It was also under the Ming that Beijing was transformed into a breathtakingly magnificent capital for the imperial family. Although a southern capital was established in Nanjing, Beijing remained paramount. Yongle began the construction of what is still called the Forbidden City: an imperial residence, fortress, and government complex at the heart of Beijing. Surrounded by moats and great vermilion walls, the Forbidden City houses acres of courtyards, gardens, and palaces. It still serves as an important seat of Chinese government.

THE DECLINE OF HEIAN JAPAN

THE POLITICAL SYSTEM OF HEIAN JAPAN

In 1000 C.E., Japan was in the midst of the Heian period (794–1185), a classical period regarded as something of a golden age in premodern Japanese history. In 794, the Japanese imperial family had moved its capital from Nara to the city of Heian (modern-day Kyoto), in order to escape the growing political influence of the local Buddhist clergy. Over time, a complex form of government had emerged, in which the emperor—who was considered to be the direct descendant of Japan's Shinto gods, and therefore sacred—lost political power, but remained extremely important as a symbolic figurehead. Real power rested with whatever noble clan assumed the position of chancellor (*kwampaku*) and, with it, the duty of "protecting" the emperor and his family. Whichever clan did so was able to keep the emperor in seclusion and rule in his name.

THE FUJIWARA CLAN AND THE HIGH POINT OF HEIAN CULTURE

From 858 onward, the ruling family in Heian Japan was the Fujiwara clan, which managed to gain permanent custody over the chancellorship and the imperial family. During the 1000s and early 1100s, the Fujiwara presided over a Japan that was peaceful, prosperous, and culturally brilliant. Japanese painting reached a high level of skill, and one of the classics of Japanese (and world) literature, Lady Murasaki's *The Tale of Genji*, an epic about love and Japanese court life, dates to this period. Many of Japan's classical prose writers were women. Men considered poetry to be a more elevated art form.

During the Heian period, Japanese culture was influenced in countless ways by Tang, then Song, China. Japanese religious development was fundamentally altered by the importation of Buddhism, as well as some elements of Confucianism and Daoism. All of these coexisted alongside Japan's native faith, Shinto. The written forms of the Japanese language owed much to the Chinese system of ideograms. Chinese poetry, painting, and architecture did much to shape Japanese styles, especially during China's Tang dynasty.

After about 1000 C.E., however, the Japanese began to develop a cultural tradition that was more independent of China's. The culture of the late Heian, therefore, although by no means completely free from Chinese influence, was definitely less derivative and more uniquely Japanese.

Heian Jingu Shrine, Kyoto, Japan.
The modern city of Kyoto, the old capital of Japan, still contains many of the architectural masterpieces from the Heian era (794–1185), when the city bore that same name. Heian became a major center of Buddhist worship and scholarship, and hundreds of shrines and temples were built there during these years. This photograph is one of many examples of the religious architecture of the period.

HEIAN DISINTEGRATION AND THE TAIRA-MINAMOTO WAR

Unfortunately for the Fujiwara, their pursuit of cultural refinement and their preoccupation with the details of political and aristocratic intrigue at court led them to neglect fundamental military questions. For many decades, the Fujiwara had delegated military responsibilities to various warrior clans (it was from these families that the famous samurai class was emerging). By the early 1100s, these warrior clans were beginning to quarrel among themselves and, at the same time, with the Fujiwara clan.

In 1156, two rival claimants to the emperor's throne appeared. A civil war erupted, with two warrior clans, the Taira and Minamoto, backing the two candidates. At first, the Taira gained the upper hand. By 1160, they had beaten the Minamoto, taken control of the government, and displaced the Fujiwara, whose power faded forever. Two decades later, however, in 1180, the Minamoto rose up from their previous defeat, beginning a five-year civil war. This conflict inspired one of Japan's great epic works of literature, *Tales of the Heike*. It also ended the Heian period. By 1185, the Minamoto had seized the reins of power, eliminated the Taira (along with the boy emperor they supported), and changed the Japanese political system forever. The victorious Minamoto established a new government in the port city of Kamakura, far from Heian. This new government became known as the shogunate.

FEUDAL JAPAN UNDER THE KAMAKURA AND ASHIKAGA SHOGUNATES

JAPANESE FEUDALISM, THE SHOGUN, AND THE SAMURAI CLASS

With the Minamoto victory in 1185, Japan entered a centuries-long feudal period, in which political power was, to a large extent, decentralized. As before, a figurehead emperor was the symbolic head of the country. But real rulership now rested in the hands of the shogun ("great general"), among whose duties was to keep the emperor under his care. The Kamakura shogunate (1185–1333) established by the Minamoto clan was a military government. Below the shoguns were warlords called daimyo, landed aristocracy who developed into a new noble class, much as the knights of feudal Europe did during the Middle Ages.

The daimyo and their followers came from the warrior elite called the samurai, meaning "one who serves." To belong to the samurai class was a great privilege. Just as European knights (in theory) lived by the ideals of chivalry, the samurai followed a strict code of loyalty and proper conduct called Bushido, or "way of the warrior." On the whole, Bushido was even more stringent than European chivalry. It tended to be taken more seriously. Famously, the most extreme penalty for violating the rules of Bushido was seppuku, or ritual suicide (popularly known as hara-kiri).

THE KAMAKURA SHOGUNATE

During the 1200s and early 1300s, the Kamakura shoguns kept order in Japan. They even repelled two attempts (in 1279 and 1281) on the part of Khubilai Khan's Yuan China to invade. The second invasion force—a massive navy ferrying 140,000 troops to the Japanese islands—was destroyed by a sudden storm that the Japanese called *kamikaze*, or "divine wind."

GO-DAIGO'S REBELLION

By the 1330s, however, decentralization proved too much for the Kamakura shoguns. In 1333, the emperor of Japan, Go-Daigo, attempted to throw off shogun "protection" and rule in his own right.

This action started a civil war called Go-Daigo's Rebellion (1333–1336). Although Go-Daigo failed to win his fight, the effect of the war was also to sweep away the Kamakura shoguns. In their place, a new feudal clan, the Ashikaga, sprang up.

THE ASHIKAGA SHOGUNATE

The Ashikaga Shogunate (1336–1573) moved the seat of government back to Kyoto, where it would stay until the 1600s.

Under the Ashikaga Shogunate, trade and commerce flourished, and a wealthy merchant class emerged.

Chan Buddhism, known as Zen in Japan, arrived from China and became popular among the samurai class. Another widespread form of Buddhism was Pure Land (*Jo Do*) Buddhism. This promised a heaven to those who led moral lives during their worldly existence. Pure Land gained a great following among those of the lower classes.

Rather than leaning so heavily on China for cultural inspiration, the Japanese now developed painting and musical styles that were uniquely their own, even more so than during the late Heian and Kamakura periods. The ritualized form of theater known as Noh drama was born during these years. Many Japanese cultural forms were influenced by the growing popularity of Zen Buddhism. These included the famous tea ceremony (*cha-no-yu*), which placed emphasis on tranquility and intricate ritual. Landscape gardening, closely related to philosophical and religious principles, became an important art form in Japan. The cultivation of bonsai (trees shaped in such a way as to miniaturize them) and the arrangement of rock gardens were standard features of Japanese landscaping. Haiku verses—composed of triple lines, measured in 17 syllables—dominated Japanese poetry. Haiku's simplicity, peacefulness, and emphasis on insight and enlightenment blend well with Zen Buddhism.

Politically, however, the Ashikaga shoguns were unable to maintain any real degree of centralization, especially after the mid-1400s. Although the Ashikaga were nominally in charge of Japan until 1573, many daimyo and warlords were already ruling their lands semi-independently by 1400. They defied the shoguns and, frequently, fought each other. Starting in 1467, Japan would be shaken by civil war after civil war. Over the next century, the Ashikaga Shogunate would become more and more meaningless, while Japan became more and more divided. Not until the end of the 1500s and early 1600s would unity be restored.

KOREA AND VIETNAM

CHINA'S INFLUENCE ON KOREA AND VIETNAM

Like Japan, Korea and Vietnam fell under the cultural and religious (and, at times, political) influence of China. As in China, agricultural production in Korea and Vietnam revolved mainly around rice cultivation. As with the Japanese, Korean and Vietnamese art, music, literature, and architecture were all shaped at least partly by those countries' relationships with China. Even the writing systems of all three countries—*hiragana* and *kanji* in Japan, *hangul* in Korea, and *chu nom* in Vietnam—were based at least somewhat on Chinese ideograms. From China came Confucianism and various forms of Buddhism.

KOREA

The early Korean states had a long, tangled relationship with the Chinese. The first united Korean nation, Silla, which formed during the 500s C.E., was a close ally of Tang China. When the Tang collapsed, Silla did as well. The second state, Koryo (from which the present-day name *Korea* derives), had relations with the Song. Koryo was invaded by the Mongols in the 1230s. Although it won its freedom by the mid-1300s, it collapsed soon after. The third Korean nation, the Yi kingdom (1392–1910), enjoyed close ties with Ming China. Some scholars speculate that block printing was invented in Korea during the Koryo period, then passed on to the Chinese. It was also through Korea that much of the Chinese influence on Japanese culture was transmitted.

VIETNAMESE STATES

The Vietnamese had contact with the Chinese as early as the 200s B.C.E. Close ties formed between Tang China and the Vietnamese states of Annam and Champa. At various points after 1000, Annam and Champa were under Chinese rule, paid tribute to the Chinese, or formed alliances with China.

The widespread practice of rice-paddy farming, or growing rice by means of wet cultivation, originated in Southeast Asia—most likely in the Vietnamese states—around 500 B.C.E. Before this time, rice had been grown dry, like most other crops. Wet cultivation suited rice much better and led to increased crop yields. The rice-paddy method spread to other parts of Asia, including China and Japan. In this way, the Vietnamese kingdoms had a profound agricultural and environmental impact on a vast portion of Asia.

QUICK REVIEW

1. On which countries did China exert the strongest cultural and political influence?

   (A) Burma, Japan, and Korea
   (B) Vietnam, Cambodia, and India
   (C) Japan, Korea, and Vietnam
   (D) Pakistan, India, and Japan
   (E) the Philippines, Thailand, and Bangladesh

2. During the 1100s, _____ was the world's most urbanized society.

   (A) the Tang dynasty
   (B) the Song Empire
   (C) the Liao Empire
   (D) the Jin Empire
   (E) the Mongol Empire

3. Neo-Confucianism

   (A) encouraged average Chinese to exert their individualism
   (B) is another term for Daoism
   (C) is a monotheistic religion
   (D) did not spread beyond China's borders
   (E) reinforced hierarchy and social stratification

4. Which of the following is an accurate statement about women in China in this period?

   (A) The position of women was equal to that of men.
   (B) Neo-Confucianism promoted women's equality.
   (C) Upper-class women enjoyed more rights than lower-class women.
   (D) Women of the lower classes tended to be freer from restrictions than those of the upper classes.
   (E) The practice of foot-binding was outlawed.

5. How was Khubilai Khan an effective ruler of China?

   (A) He rebuilt its bureaucracy and economy.
   (B) He killed all of its former bureaucrats.
   (C) He outlawed Buddhism.
   (D) He forced all bureaucrats to speak Mongolian.
   (E) He installed only Mongolians in administrative positions.

6. Under the shogunates of Japan

(A) real power still rested with the emperor
(B) power rested with Buddhist monks
(C) the emperor's power was largely symbolic
(D) the shoguns were the religious priests
(E) none of the above

7. During the Ashikaga Shogunate

(A) trade and commerce were sharply curtailed
(B) the Japanese developed their own painting and musical styles
(C) Chan Buddhism was outlawed
(D) Japan became highly centralized after the 1400s
(E) Japan did not experience civil war

8. Haiku

(A) is a martial art that originated in Japan during the Ashikaga shogunate
(B) was Japan's emperor in the mid-1400s who promoted trade with China
(C) is a form of poetry emphasizing enlightenment
(D) is a form of Noh drama popularized in the 1300s
(E) was outlawed as a practice that discriminated against women

9. The first united Korean nation, 500s C.E., was

(A) Koryo
(B) Yi
(C) Nara
(D) Silla
(E) Jomon

10. Some scholars speculate that block printing was invented in

(A) Korea
(B) Thailand
(C) Japan
(D) Vietnam
(E) Cambodia

ANSWERS:

1. **C**, p. 139	6. **C**, p. 145
2. **B**, p. 140	7. **B**, p. 146
3. **E**, p. 140	8. **C**, p. 146
4. **D**, p. 141	9. **D**, p. 146
5. **A**, p. 141	10. **A**, p. 147

CHAPTER 9

South and Southeast Asia

South and Southeast Asia are regions of remarkable ethnic and cultural diversity. Even the Indian subcontinent—the largest portion of South Asia—is home to people of several races, dozens of different languages, and many minor and major religions.

Both India and the lands that surround it are environmentally and geographically diverse as well. India itself measures 2,000 miles east to west and 2,000 miles north to south. In the north are mountains and forest. The center is cut by the Ganges and Indus river basins. The southernmost third is more tropical. The entire climate of the Indian Ocean region is affected twice per year by huge seasonal rainstorms called monsoons (which occur in June–July and December–January). The majority of Southeast Asia is tropical in climate.

Until the modern era, both Southeast and South Asia experienced tremendous political fragmentation. India in particular was seldom unified as a single state. More often, it was divided into many nations and societies. Even in other parts of South Asia, kingdoms and states tended to rise very rapidly. Culture, tradition, language, and religion served as unifying factors more than politics did.

INDIA AND THE DELHI SULTANATE

INDIAN DISUNITY BEFORE 1000 C.E.

Just before 1000 C.E., India had been in a state of disunification for quite some time. The last major nation to have joined most of India together, the Gupta Empire, collapsed around 550 C.E. The next group to unite a large part of India were Muslim invaders. Starting in the early 700s, Muslim forces had reached India's borderlands: they had moved into the Indus valley and Pakistan (on India's northwest frontier), then converted the region to Islam. By the 900s, Muslims were escalating their attacks on the Indian border. By 1000, they were poised to break into India itself.

MUSLIM INVASIONS AND THE DELHI SULTANATE

In 1022, Muslim armies, led by Afghan warlords, seized and annexed the Indian province of Punjab. This began the conquest of northern India by the Muslims, a process that would continue for the next two hundred years. By 1206, the Muslims had captured the important city of Delhi, and most of northern India was in their hands. Muslim generals established the Delhi Sultanate (1206–1520s), ruled at first by Muhammad Ghuri (assassinated in 1206) and later by the sultan Iltutmish (1211–1236). Technically, the Delhi Sultanate was part of the Abbasid Caliphate (see Chapter 7). But this subordination lasted only until the caliphate's destruction in 1258.

The major effect of the Muslim invasions and the establishment of the Delhi Sultanate was to introduce a new religion—Islam—into India. Islam did not displace earlier faiths such as

Hinduism and Buddhism, but joined them as one of the country's most important religions (one interesting development is that, in India, Muslim women tended to enjoy more property rights than Hindu women, especially those of low caste; it was also possible for Muslim women in India to divorce and remarry after their husbands died).

There were religious conflicts under the Delhi Sultanate. At first, the sultans were quite harsh about imposing their new religion on the areas they ruled. They became less severe over time. Still, Hindu and Muslim populations did not tend to mix, and tensions—sometimes outright violence and persecution—characterized the relationship between the two.

THE PEAK AND DECLINE OF THE DELHI SULTANATE

Politically, the Delhi Sultanate grew from the middle of the 1200s to the middle of the 1300s. Under the reign of Muhammad ibn Tughluq (1325–1351), the sultanate reached its territorial peak: it controlled most of India. After the mid-1300s, however, the Delhi Sultanate began to shrink. Many regions in the south (described presently) began to break away and become independent. In addition, the Central Asian warlord Timur (see Chapter 10) attacked and captured the sultanate's capital, Delhi, in 1398. When Timur left Delhi in 1399, after a year of plundering, the city was left in ruins. The Delhi Sultanate survived, but barely. It was crippled and growing steadily smaller. It finally collapsed in the 1520s, succumbing to new invaders from the north.

OTHER INDIAN STATES

Although India's ethnic complexity defies generalization, it was mainly the case for many years that the northern parts of the country were populated by Indo-Europeans (largely descended from the Aryas who invaded ca. 1500 B.C.E.), while the south was inhabited by darker-skinned peoples of Dravidian origin.

INDEPENDENT SOUTHERN STATES

There was also a tendency in the south of India for various states and kingdoms to emerge, independent of the larger governments that formed in the north. Among them were the Tamil kingdoms of Chola, Pandya, and Chera, on the Indian Ocean coast. The Tamil kingdoms formed around the 100s B.C.E. and survived for approximately 2,000 years.

The 1300s saw the emergence of even more states in the south, most of them breakaways from the Delhi Sultanate. Bengal became an independent Muslim state in 1338. The Bahmani kingdom (1347–1482), also Muslim, appeared in the center of the subcontinent. Gujarat, a Muslim city on the western coast, flourished as a trading center after declaring independence from the Delhi Sultanate in 1390. It played a large role in the Indian Ocean trading network. The Vijayanagara Empire (1336–1565) and the city-states of the Malibar both formed free Hindu enclaves on the Indian coast. The former controlled many southern ports, as well as the island of Sri Lanka. The latter ruled much of the southwestern coast. The most important of the Malibar cities was Calicut.

INDIAN OCEAN TRADE

One of the most vibrant trading networks in the world was the one that sprang up along almost the entire coastline of the Indian Ocean. This network tied together East Africa, the Arabian peninsula, the Persian Gulf, India, the Malay peninsula, the vast archipelago of Indonesia, China, and Japan. From west to east, the expanse covered by this exchange network was greater than 6,000 miles.

In the west, a zone controlled largely by Arab traders, goods came from Africa and the Middle East. From Africa, they included ivory, animal hides, forest-related goods (such as timber), gold, and slaves. From the Middle East came textiles, carpets, glass, and Arabian horses, praised the world over for their beauty and speed. The middle zone was dominated by various Indian cities and kingdoms, such as Gujarat, Malaba, and Chola. India offered precious gems, elephants, salt, and cotton cloth. From Sri Lanka (Ceylon) came cinnamon. Other spices, as well as exotic woods, came from the Indonesian islands. In the east, there was a Chinese zone. China traded silk, porcelain, and paper. Japan was a major source of silver.

Major ports in the Indian Ocean network included Sofala, Mombasa, and Mogadishu in East Africa; Jidda, Mecca, and Ormuz in Arabia and Persia; the Gujarati port of Cambay and the great Malibar metropolis of Calicut, both in western India; and Canton (Guangzhou) and Hangzhou in China. By means of the Red Sea and Suez isthmus, the Indian Ocean trade network could be connected to the Mediterranean Sea and the trade networks flourishing there.

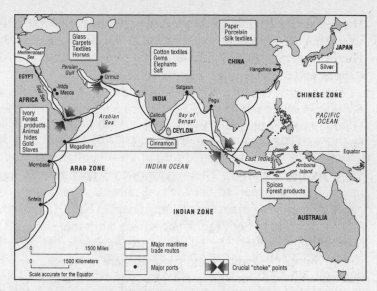

The Indian Ocean Trade Network before 1500 C.E.
The flow of ships, people, and goods among East Africa, the Middle East, India, Southeast Asia, and China is clearly marked out in this map. The arrival of Portuguese traders just before 1500, then the massive influx of other Europeans, changed the economic patterns of this region forever.

SOUTHEAST ASIA

THE GEOGRAPHY OF SOUTHEAST ASIA

Geographically, Southeast Asia consists of three zones: the mainland, through which the large river basins of the Mekong and Irrawaddy flow; the Malay Peninsula; and the islands and archipelagoes of the Indian Ocean and South China Sea, many of which are volcanic. The climate is tropical, and most of the terrain is mountainous or blanketed by rain forest.

Between 3000 B.C.E. and 2000 B.C.E., Malays and settlers of other ethnicities arrived, both from China and India, as well as other areas. Local inhabitants were practicing agriculture by around 2000 B.C.E. The early peoples of Southeast Asia were also skilled bronzeworkers and navigators (the peoples of the islands traveled great distances in outrigger canoes of sophisticated make).

SOUTHEAST ASIAN STATES

Major states began to emerge in Southeast Asia before and around 500 C.E. These included Funan (200–500) on the Malay Peninsula; Chenla in Cambodia; Mon in lower Burma; Burma itself (500 onward); the Thai kingdom (ca. 500 onward); and the Vietnamese states of Champa and Annam (see Chapter 8). Most of these states were culturally and economically influenced by China, India, or both. They traded spices (cinnamon, nutmeg, cloves, and pepper), especially for silk from China. Most Southeast Asian states were key players in the vast and complex trade networks in the Indian Ocean and along the Pacific coast. Thanks to their contacts with India and China, most

Southeast Asian states tended to adopt Hinduism or Buddhism, and sometimes both. Before 1000 C.E., Islam also appeared in Southeast Asia, brought mainly from the west by sea.

THE KHMER EMPIRE OF CAMBODIA

For many years, the two most developed states in Southeast Asia were the Khmer Empire (500s–1454 C.E) in Cambodia and the Srivijayan Empire (500s–1100s C.E) of Sumatra. The Khmer civilization emerged in Cambodia and Laos by the 500s C.E. It reached its peak during the Angkor period (889–1454), so named for the great capitals the Khmer built at Angkor Wat and Angkor Thom during the 1100s. The Angkor rulers were militarily aggressive, expanding the Khmer state into parts of Burma and the Malay Peninsula. Culturally and religiously, the Khmer were influenced primarily by India. The Khmer adopted both Hinduism and Buddhism. They were serious in their dedication to both faiths: the Khmer built more than 21,000 temples, which were staffed by over 300,000 priests. The fabulous city complex of Angkor Wat and Angkor Thom covers forty square miles. The palaces and pagodas there are ornate and complex. Until 1861, when they were rediscovered by French archaeologists, Angkor Wat and Angkor Thom were lost to the jungle after the fall of the Khmer. The Khmer state collapsed in the 1400s, after Cambodia was conquered by neighboring Thailand.

THE SRIVIJAYAN EMPIRE OF SUMATRA

The mighty Srivijayan Empire took shape in the islands of the south. The name comes from the Sanskrit for "Great Conquest." From their capital on the southeastern coast of the Indonesian island of Sumatra, the Srivijayans spread their political and economic influence outward. By the end of the 600s C.E., they had gained control of the maritime trade routes that led through the waters of Indonesia and the Malay Peninsula. The Srivijayans then took over parts of the Malay Peninsula, as well as the large Indonesian island of Java. Like Khmer Cambodia, the Srivijayan Empire was influenced by India and accepted both Hinduism and Buddhism (although Buddhism was dominant). The greatest architectural legacy of the Srivijayan Empire is the Buddhist temple complex of Borobudor, built on the island of Java from 770 to 825. Borobudor is in the shape of a mountain, over 100 feet high. Visitors ascend a winding walkway more than three miles long. Every level they pass represents a stage on the path to spiritual enlightenment. By the 1000s and 1100s, the Srivijayan Empire was declining. Attacks by Chola, one of the Tamil kingdoms of southeast India, weakened the Srivijayans. They were then displaced by the Kertanagara Empire, which took over Sumatra and Java during the 1200s. It was also during the 1200s that Islam arrived in the Indonesian islands. It remains a dominant faith there to this day.

POLITICAL CHANGES, 1200s–1400s

More political change came to Southeast Asia from the 1200s through the 1400s. The Chinese and Mongols made repeated attacks from the north. Thailand expanded substantially, conquering the Khmer state in Cambodia. The Vietnamese state of Annam became a great military power after the early 1400s. By the 1500s, Burma emerged as another great power, with an army of more than half a million.

After 1400, the economic powerhouse of Southeast Asia was the city of Malacca (Melaka), located on the narrow waterway separating the Malay Peninsula from the island of Sumatra. It connected the Indian Ocean with the South China Sea and was, therefore, a crucial nexus in the Indian Ocean trade network. Established in 1400, Malacca was controlled by China, then the Thais. It next enjoyed a brief period of freedom before being conquered by European colonists—the Portuguese—in 1511.

THE POLYNESIAN MIGRATIONS

One of history's most epic journeys was that made by the Polynesians across the Pacific Ocean from approximately 2500 B.C.E. to 900 C.E. Originally from Southeast Asia, the Polynesians left their homes in the Philippine and Indonesian islands around 4,500 years ago. After a process lasting well over three millennia, the Polynesians had spread eastward across a 20,000-mile expanse, settling literally thousands of islands throughout the Pacific Ocean. The region known as Oceania is populated mainly by their descendants.

EARLY POLYNESIAN CULTURE

The original Polynesians were root farmers, growing taro and sweet potatoes and supplementing their diet with domesticated pigs and chickens. The Polynesians were also skilled fishers. Linguistically, they belonged to the Austronesian language group, common to Indonesia, the Philippines, and other parts of Southeast Asia. Their social organization was quite hierarchical. Tribes were led by powerful chiefs. Polynesian religion was animistic. It was very concerned with avoiding improper behavior, or taboo (known as *tabu* or *kapu* to the Polynesians).

Because so much of their life was based on the sea, the Polynesians were expert sailors and navigators. Their outrigger canoes allowed them to travel vast distances over open water. Ocean-going outriggers were constructed from hollowed-out tree trunks, joined together by a large platform. Large sails could be attached, or the canoe could be paddled. Outrigger canoes could sail more than 120 miles per day. The Polynesians were also greatly skilled at maritime navigation. Not only could they find their way over open water by the sun, moon, and stars, but they possessed an intimate knowledge of tides, currents, and patterns of oceanic waves and swells. The Polynesians even created woven maps, in which twigs and grasses represented various currents and wave patterns.

THE MIGRATIONS

Precisely why the Polynesians began their long migrations is unknown. Most scholars speculate that some kind of ecological crisis drove them from their homes. Certainly environmental necessity kept them going once they started. When the Polynesians settled an island, the population would grow to such a point that part of the tribe (sometimes all of it) would have to move onward in order to keep from depleting all the resources.

The first wave of migration took the Polynesians to the island chain of Micronesia, directly east of the Philippines. Not long afterward, around 2000 to 1300 B.C.E., some Polynesians moved on to Melanesia, east of New Guinea and Australia and including Fiji.

Another major wave of migration took the Polynesians to the vast oceanic expanse that now bears the name Polynesia. Polynesia proper is bounded by an imaginary triangle, with Hawaii at the north, New Zealand to the southwest, and Easter Island to the southeast. Among the best-known Polynesian islands are the Hawaiian chain, Tonga, Samoa, the Marquesas, and Tahiti. By 300 to 400 C.E., Polynesians had settled Easter Island, building the famous black stone statues of huge heads that still remain. Deforestation, environmental stress, and tribal war destroyed the Easter Island civilization. More successful was the Polynesian settlement of New Zealand. The Maori culture, a Polynesian society established around 800 to 900 C.E., survived and prospered. A warrior society, the Maori were the largest single subculture in the Polynesian world by the 1700s C.E.

QUICK REVIEW

1. Until the modern era, India

   (A) enjoyed relative political unity
   (B) was not often united into a single state
   (C) experienced cultural homogeneity
   (D) was dominated by a single religion
   (E) was highly urbanized

2. Over two hundred years, between the 1000s and 1200s, the _____ seized parts of northern India.

   (A) Muslims
   (B) British
   (C) Mongolians
   (D) Chinese
   (E) Pakistanis

3. For centuries, the northern sections of India were populated by _____ and the southern parts by _____.

   (A) peoples of Dravidian ancestry, Indo-Europeans
   (B) Pakistanis, Africans
   (C) Tibetans, Chinese
   (D) the British, the French
   (E) Indo-Europeans, peoples of Dravidian ancestry

4. Indian Ocean trade tied together all of the following areas EXCEPT

   (A) East Africa
   (B) the Arabian peninsula
   (C) the Persian Gulf
   (D) Russia
   (E) India

5. Southeast Asia states

   I. included Funan, Chenla, and the Thai kingdom
   II. adopted Hinduism or Buddhism, and sometimes both
   III. traded spices for silk from China
   IV. took part in Indian Ocean trade

   (A) I, II, and III
   (B) II and IV only
   (C) III and IV only
   (D) III only
   (E) all of the above

6. Angkor rulers of Cambodia

   (A) were not motivated to expand their borders
   (B) focused on internal economic development
   (C) were militarily aggressive
   (D) encouraged the spread of Christianity
   (E) ruled well into the nineteenth century

7. The following religion arrived in Indonesia by the 1200s and soon became the dominant religion there:

   (A) Daoism
   (B) Zen Buddhism
   (C) Islam
   (D) Hinduism
   (E) none of the above

8. Ancestors of the Polynesians largely came from

   (A) China and Japan
   (B) the Philippine and Indonesian islands
   (C) Portugal
   (D) Scandinavia
   (E) Australia and New Zealand

9. According to most scholars, why might the Polynesians have migrated so often?

(A) They were constantly invaded by Muslims.

(B) They were belligerent by nature and so sought out other lands to conquer.

(C) They were cannibals.

(D) They wanted to avoid depleting their resources.

(E) none of the above

10. Which people settled Easter Island by 300 to 400 C.E.?

(A) Christian missionaries

(B) Colombians

(C) the Incas

(D) the Maya

(E) Polynesians

ANSWERS:

1. **B**, p. 149	6. **C**, p. 152
2. **A**, p. 149	7. **C**, p. 152
3. **E**, p. 150	8. **B**, p. 153
4. **D**, p. 150	9. **D**, p. 153
5. **E**, p. 151	10. **E**, p. 153

CHAPTER 10

The Mongol Empires

During the course of the 1200s, almost all of Eurasia was swept over by a whirlwind from Central Asia: the Mongols. United for the first time in their history by the warlord Genghis Khan, the Mongols burst out of their homeland in the 1210s, beginning one of the most successful and most extensive campaigns of conquest of all time. They defeated enemy after enemy, adding territory after territory to their growing empire. At its peak, the Mongol Empire was the largest conquest state that has ever existed. It stretched over almost all of Asia, as well as parts of the Middle East and Europe.

Eventually, by the late 1200s and early 1300s, the Mongol state broke apart into smaller units. The nomadic Mongols were adept at warfare, but less so at nation building. This makes for an interesting contrast between their empire and those created by states such as Rome and Han China.

Nonetheless, the rapid expansion of the Mongols, along with their equally rapid absorption of so much territory, had a tremendous effect on many parts of Eurasia during the 1200s and 1300s. Nations were formed and destroyed by the Mongols. Many countries had important cultural, social, and political characteristics shaped by decades, even centuries, of living under Mongol rule. Also, for a while, the presence of Mongol states stretching east to west, across most of the Eurasian landmass, meant that much of the continent was united—or at least connected—by political authority, economic networks, and cultural links that were created or encouraged by the Mongols. It is increasingly common for historians to speak of the thirteenth century as a period of Pax Mongolica (or Pax Tatarica): the "Mongol (or Tatar) Peace." Although the notion of peacefulness implicit in such a phrase may be somewhat exaggerated, there is no denying that the Mongols, for a time, tamed the wild spaces of Eurasia, joining together many of the great civilizations in and around those spaces.

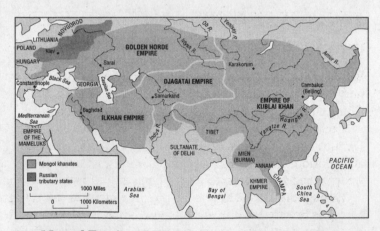

The Mongol Empires, 1294 C.E.
By this time, the Mongols, a nomadic people, had conquered most of Asia and key portions of Europe and the Middle East. Mongol control over these territories had a major and lasting effect on many parts of Eurasia.

GENGHIS KHAN AND THE RISE OF THE MONGOLS

ORIGINS OF THE MONGOLS

The Mongols (also known commonly as Tartars or Tatars) were a group of tribes of mixed Turkic-Paleoasiatic heritage. They emerged in the steppes, or open plains, of Central Asia and the area that now bears their name, Mongolia. Originally, the Mongols' lifestyle was nomadic. They herded livestock. They were excellent horsemen and archers.

The Mongols are frequently perceived as having been primitive and barbaric, even bloodthirsty. This is a stereotype. While the Mongols did not have large fixed communities or a sophisticated society—especially before their great wave of expansion—they proved very adept at cultural borrowing. As they became more settled, the Mongols developed a law code, a written language, new religious practices, better technology, and other social and cultural advancements by adopting them partially, even completely, from their neighbors and the people they conquered.

GENGHIS KHAN AND THE UNIFICATION OF THE MONGOLS

Before 1200, the Mongols were not joined together in a single social group. By the end of the 1100s, the Mongol population was somewhere between 1.5 million and 3 million, and that population was divided into more than thirty tribes. It was normal for these tribes to war against each other as often as they did non-Mongol enemies.

This disunity came to an end after 1200, due to the rise of a warlord named Temujin, better known by his adopted name, Genghis Khan (also Chingiz Khan, Jenghiz Khan, or Chinggis Khan). Born between 1155 and 1162, Temujin was born into a family that had been disgraced during a clan dispute. Despite this unfavorable beginning and a difficult childhood, Temujin became an important tribal leader as an adult.

In 1206, Temujin did what no other Mongol chieftain had ever been able to do: he united the dozens of Mongol tribes under one authority. He proclaimed himself *khan*, or "ruler," and took the name Genghis, meaning "limitless strength." Not only did Genghis Khan unify the Mongols, he completely reorganized the Mongols' armies. Only a few years after coming to power, he began to lead the Mongols on their great campaign of conquest—one of the most successful such campaigns in world history.

THE FIRST WAVE OF CONQUEST

GENGHIS KHAN AND EARLY MONGOL CONQUESTS

In 1211, Mongol armies attacked the state of Xi Xia. That same year, they launched an assault on northern China, which was nearby. By 1214 to 1215, the Mongols had breached the Great Wall of China and seized the Jin (Jurchen) capital of Beijing.

Genghis Khan then turned briefly to the west. In 1218, he conquered the land of Kara-Khitai. He then moved against a powerful Central Asian state, the Khwarazm Empire (home to the rich and glorious Silk Road trading center, Samarkand). After defeating Khwarazm and seizing its wealth, the Mongols captured the large city of Herat, in Afghanistan.

Throughout the 1220s, the Mongols fought in the east and scouted the west. In the east, the Mongols battered the Jin and Tanggut empires of western China, finally absorbing them. Genghis Khan also sent large forces westward, to investigate the possibility of further invasions in that direction (it was during these raids that the Russians and their neighbors first encountered the Mongols, in 1223).

Genghis Khan died in 1227. This ended the first wave of Mongol conquest, as his sons settled questions of inheritance and power among themselves. Already by this point, the Mongols controlled a large empire. But the expansion had only just begun. A second—and greater—wave of conquest would begin immediately after Genghis Khan's heirs put their political affairs in order.

REASONS FOR MONGOL SUCCESS

What accounted for the Mongols' tremendous success? It used to be thought that the secret lay in great numbers, but it is known now that this was not the case. The early Mongol armies were large—about 80,000 to 100,000 men—but not so large that they could easily have overwhelmed such a large territory. Mongol warriors were extremely talented cavalrymen, and they were gifted at archery (in fact, they were able to combine these skills by firing from horseback, galloping at full speed, forward or backward). The Mongols (and their horses) were possessed of great endurance and hardiness. In contrast to the popular image of the Mongols as primitive barbarians, they organized their armies extremely efficiently, into tightly knit military units based on groups of ten. The Mongols were also quick to adopt advanced military technology and techniques from their more advanced neighbors. This was especially the case with equipment and methods pertaining to siege warfare—which the Mongols learned from the Chinese and the Central Asian Khwarazm Empire, then mastered very quickly in order to be able to capture walled cities and fortresses.

THE SECOND WAVE OF CONQUEST AND THE PAX MONGOLICA

ÖGÖDEI'S NEW CONQUESTS

Soon after Genghis Khan's death in 1227, his sons continued the wars of conquest. The new Great Khan was Genghis's third son Ögödei (Ugedei), who ruled the Mongols until his death in 1241. Under Ögödei, the Mongol Empire reached tremendous proportions. Ögödei also built a capital, Karakorum, for that empire.

In the east, Ögödei's armies moved into almost all of northern and western China. By 1234, they had taken over those territories and were also encroaching on the boundaries of the Southern Song (which the Mongols would take in the 1260s). In 1231, Ögödei also forced Koryo, or Korea, into tributary status.

THE MONGOL DRIVE INTO EUROPE

Ögödei had even more ambitious goals in the west. In 1236, he gave command of a large invasion force (approximately 150,000–200,000 troops) to his nephew Batu and the general Subudei (Subutai). This army's goal was to conquer as much of Europe as possible. From 1237 to 1240, Batu's army conquered most of Russia and Ukraine. From 1240 to 1242, the Mongols pushed onward to eastern Europe—Bulgaria, Romania, Hungary, and Poland—where their appearance caused tremendous panic and hysteria. By now, however, the Mongols were overextended, too far from home to continue. They were also fighting on unfamiliar terrain—forests and mountains instead of flat, open grassland—and the fortresses and castles of East Central Europe slowed their advance. Moreover, Ögödei died in 1241, and during the brief political chaos that followed (and forced Batu to return to the Mongol homeland), the assault on Europe ground to a halt.

Despite their failure to move more deeply into Europe, Batu and the Mongols still managed to gain an immense amount of land in the west: almost all of Russia and Ukraine, as well as parts of Bulgaria, Hungary, and Romania. This territory was ruled over by Batu and his descendants, who called their government the Golden Horde (from the Mongol word *orda*, or "camp"). The Mongols would rule over the Russians for two centuries.

PAX MONGOLICA: THE MONGOL EMPIRE AT ITS PEAK

During the 1240s and 1250s, under the next two khans, Guyuk and Mongke, the Mongol Empire grew even larger. The Mongols moved further into China. They also took over eastern Tibet in 1252. Also in the 1250s, the Mongols moved into the Middle East, destroying the Abbasid Caliphate. The commander Hulegu captured the Caucasus, most of Mesopotamia, much of Turkey, Persia, and Syria. Only in 1260 was he halted, by Mamluk cavalrymen, at the Battle of Ain Jalut.

By the end of the 1250s, therefore, the Mongols ruled over an empire that stretched from Poland in the west to Korea in the east, and from Siberia in the north to Southeast Asia in the south. Over this massive expanse, the Mongols imposed a single political authority, encouraged economic exchange, made conditions for travel and movement safer, and imposed legal order. The Silk Road—Eurasia's major overland trade route from the Middle East to the Far East—flourished. Silk Road cities such as Samarkand, with its oases, bazaars, and markets, became crucial commercial gathering points. Merchants, travelers, religious pilgrims and missionaries, and people of all professions and many ethnicities passed through Samarkand.

As was noted previously, many historians refer to this brief joining of most of Eurasia—a semi-unification of sorts–as the Pax Mongolica (sometimes Pax Tatarica), or "Mongol Peace." This term is reminiscent of the Pax Romana that was said to have prevailed when ancient Rome controlled most of the world known to the peoples of the Mediterranean.

The Mongols created and maintained this Pax Mongolica not just by means of force, but also by a level of administrative skill that was surprisingly high for a people which had, comparatively recently, been quite unsophisticated. Using the Turkic language of Uighur as their written script, the Mongols created a law code (the *yasa*), borrowed from several cultures, including the Chinese. They used paper currency, another innovation that came from China. The Mongols tended to adopt the religions of the people they conquered, most often Buddhism or Islam. The Mongols also put their skill with horses to good use in creating a postal system. This was the *yam*, an elaborate network of couriers who carried messages on horseback, rapidly covering vast distances.

BREAKUP OF THE MONGOL EMPIRE

OVEREXTENSION AND BREAKDOWN OF THE MONGOL EMPIRE

A Chinese proverb is often quoted in connection with the Mongol Empire: "One can conquer an empire on horseback, but one cannot govern that empire from horseback." Notwithstanding the might of the Mongols' forces—or their often underestimated ability to administer such a huge territory in an age without modern transport or communications technology—the Mongol Empire began to break apart soon after its size and power peaked.

The last khan who truly ruled over a united Mongol Empire was Mongke. With his death in 1260, civil war broke out among the leading nephews and grandsons of Genghis Khan. In the process, the empire's four largest units became independent states. The homeland, or Domain of the Great Khan, included Mongolia and the conquered territories to the east and southeast. The Golden Horde (also known as the Kipchak Khanate) ruled over Russia and other east European territories. The Jagadai (Chaghadai) Khanate consisted of the Central Asian lands to the west of the Domain of the Great Khan. The Il-Khan Domain controlled the Middle Eastern conquests gained by Hulegu.

THE DOMAIN OF THE GREAT KHAN AND YUAN CHINA

The civil war of 1260 destroyed the unity of these four lands, as well as the Mongol capital of Karakorum. When the fighting ended in 1265, the Domain of the Great Khan—and the title of Great Khan—went to Khubilai, grandson of Genghis. As described in Chapter 8, Khubilai Khan shifted his political focus away from the Domain of the Great Khan to the Yuan Empire he created in China.

THE GOLDEN HORDE

The Golden Horde retained control over Russia until the mid-1400s, when their rule was ended by the rising city-state of Moscow. After that, many Mongols (or, as the Russians refer to them, Tatars) left. But many others remained in what was becoming a large and powerful Russian state. Over time, the Mongols became inhabitants of Russia, in many cases intermarrying and assimilating.

THE IL-KHANS

The Il-Khan rulers of the Middle East converted to Islam. Their reign lasted into the 1300s. During the 1370s, however, the Il-Khans were weakened by attacks from their fellow Mongols: armies of the Jagadai Khanate. At the same time, and shortly afterward, the Mongols were displaced by the Ottoman Turks, whose rapid expansion during the 1370s onward made them the new masters of the Middle East.

THE JAGADAI KHANATE AND TIMUR'S CONQUESTS

For two and a half centuries, the Jagadai Khanate held sway over the realms of Central Asia. Like the Il-Khans, the Jagadai converted to Islam. From 1370 to 1405, the Jagadai warlord Timur (also known as Tamerlane) rose up and attempted to repeat the military triumph of his ancestor, Genghis Khan. In a short time, he conquered Central Asia, the Crimea, Persia, parts of northern India, sections of southern Russia, and parts of the Il-Khan Domain in the Middle East. The expansion ended with his death in 1405, however, and the Jagadai Khanate's boundaries shrank. Still, Timur's descendants ruled over Central Asia—and the Silk Road cities of Samarkand and Bukhara—until the early 1500s.

QUICK REVIEW

1. The Mongols were descended from

   (A) Russian tribesmen who had wandered eastward
   (B) Inuit wanderers who had come from the north
   (C) a mixture of Central Asian, Turkic, and Paleoasiatic peoples
   (D) the Han Chinese
   (E) Dravidian peoples who had intermarried with indigenous shamanic peoples of Central Asia

2. The Mongols were skilled in _____, but not in _____.

   (A) warfare, nation building
   (B) administration, warfare
   (C) archery, horsemanship
   (D) nation building, cultural borrowing
   (E) architecture, painting

3. The most effective Mongol troops were

   (A) light cavalry archers
   (B) heavy cavalry lancers
   (C) light infantry javelin throwers
   (D) heavy infantry pikesmen
   (E) heavy infantry armed with muskets

4. Why were the Mongols successful at conquest?

   I.   They had the largest army of all time.
   II. They adopted advanced technology quickly.
   III. They organized their armies efficiently.
   IV. They were talented cavalrymen.

   (A) I, II, and III
   (B) II, III, and IV
   (C) I and III only
   (D) I only
   (E) all of the above

5. Which of the following territories did the Mongols NOT conquer?

   (A) Russia
   (B) Ukraine
   (C) Bulgaria
   (D) Romania
   (E) France

6. What is the popular name of the Mongol khanate that ruled Russia from the 1200s to the 1400s?

   (A) the Jagadai Khanate
   (B) the Il-Khan Kingdom
   (C) the Golden Horde
   (D) Huun-Huur-Tu
   (E) the Khazar Realm

7. Which of the following is an accurate statement about Mongols' cultural adaptation?

   (A) They tended to adopt the religions of the people they had defeated.
   (B) They learned equestrian skills from the Europeans.
   (C) They adopted the Persian language as their written script.
   (D) They borrowed portions of a law code from the French.
   (E) They began dressing like Russians.

8. Which Mongol leader first declared himself Great Khan of all the Mongol tribes?

   (A) Ögödei
   (B) Batu
   (C) Subudei
   (D) Genghis
   (E) Khubilai

9. Which Mongol leader won the civil war of the 1260s and went on to conquer China?

   (A) Ögödei
   (B) Batu
   (C) Subudei
   (D) Genghis
   (E) Khubilai

10. Why did the Mongol Empire break up?

   (A) The Mongols wanted to revert to pastoralism again.
   (B) They failed to administer such a large territory effectively.
   (C) After Genghis Khan died, his successors were too incompetent to rule.
   (D) Russia conquered Mongolia.
   (E) none of the above

ANSWERS:

1. **C**, p. 157	6. **C**, p. 158
2. **A**, p. 159	7. **A**, p. 159
3. **A**, p. 158	8. **D**, p. 157
4. **B**, p. 158	9. **E**, p. 160
5. **E**, p. 159	10. **B**, p. 159

CHAPTER 11

Sub-Saharan Africa

Not just physically, but also culturally and politically, Africa is divided by the Sahara desert. As described in Chapter 7, almost all of Saharan Africa and the northern continent had fallen into the orbit of the Islamic world. The story of sub-Saharan Africa is much more complex.

INTRODUCTION TO SUB-SAHARAN AFRICA

FACTORS RESTRICTING THE GROWTH OF MAJOR SUB-SAHARAN STATES

In sub-Saharan Africa, the development of strong, sizable political units occurred later and more slowly than in many other parts of the world. Much of this had to do with the tremendous varieties of ethnicity and language in sub-Saharan Africa. For example, more than 2,000 languages and dialects are spoken there.

One of the few common threads shared by many—but not all—peoples of sub-Saharan Africa is descent from the Bantu tribes. Around 1000 B.C.E., the Bantu began to move out of their homeland in west central Africa. By 1000 C.E., descendants of the Bantu tribes had settled in almost all parts of the continent south of the Sahara. With the passage of time, however, each smaller group developed its own distinct language and cultural tradition.

Another factor limiting the growth of major states was environmental. The fluctuating climate of sub-Saharan Africa and human susceptibility to various insect- and animal-borne diseases in sub-Saharan regions were both obstacles to increasing the size of local populations and the number of workers available to cultivate the land.

BASIC FEATURES OF SUB-SAHARAN SOCIETIES

Most sub-Saharan communities were small. Social life revolved around the village. Food was provided by means of a combination of hunting, herding, and limited agriculture. It appears that most African societies gained the skill of metalworking on their own, rather than having it taught to them by outsiders, as was commonly thought until recently.

As in most early civilizations, women in sub-Saharan Africa tended to be treated as subservient to men. Women were often valued, though, for their labor as fieldworkers (while men tended cattle) and for producing heirs. Women also were respected for their storytelling abilities and their role in educating young people about moral values and religious beliefs. Interestingly, unlike in most other societies, in Africa, lineage was sometimes matrilinear, rather than patrilinear. Women often inherited property, and the husband was required to move into his wife's house. Rules of behavior between the sexes tended to be more informal than in the Middle East, China, or India.

ART AND CULTURE

African tribes possessed a high degree of skill in carving and sculpture, especially in wood and ivory. Metal sculpture became more common over time. By the thirteenth and fourteenth centuries, West African artists were creating masterpieces out of bronze and iron. In Ife, in present-day Nigeria, metalworkers formed bronze and iron statues by first designing molds with melted wax. These sculptures may have influenced the work of metalworkers from the West African state of Benin. Such artists are famous for their sophisticated and detailed bronze, brass, and copper sculptures of heads, ornaments, animal figures, and reliefs depicting court life.

Architecture in Africa varied across regions due to diverse cultural influences. In sub-Saharan Africa, Greater Zimbabwe stood out for its impressive stone buildings and walls. The stones had been carefully cut and then set in place without mortar. In Mali, fourteenth-century builders used timber as skeletons in reinforcing mud mosques that still stand today. In Zanzibar, architecture is distinguished by the use of coral for decoration on buildings.

African literature of this period was preserved less by the written language than by oral tradition. In their narratives, professional storytellers, called bards, chronicled history and social custom. They also acted as entertainers and served as advisers to kings. The most famous epic of sub-Saharan Africa from these years is *Son-Jara* (or *Sundiata*), from Mali (see Chapter 7).

Most native African religions were animistic faiths (see Chapter 5), based on the worship of the spirits of animals and ancestors.

ISLAM AND CONTACTS WITH NORTH AFRICA

As time passed, there was increased interaction between North Africa and the sub-Saharan part of the continent. This included trade. Unfortunately, it also included slavery: for hundreds of years, Arab slavers from the Middle East penetrated to the south, capturing Africans and forcing them into bondage. By the eleventh century, some traders in the Sahara and Sahel regions owned more than 1,000 slaves apiece.

To a good extent, Islam became part of sub-Saharan life. In West Africa, the state of Mali (see Chapter 7), with its great city of Timbuktu, was an important part of the Islamic world. Muslims also brought their religion to the cities of the eastern coast. The spread of Islam brought trade to previously isolated parts of southern Africa. Still, in comparison to North Africa, which became almost completely Muslim, Islam's presence in sub-Saharan Africa was not as extensive.

WEST AND CENTRAL AFRICA

GHANA

In West Africa, the state of Ghana (see Chapter 3) continued to be strong and prosperous for a time. When Europe began minting gold coins during the 1200s C.E., Ghana's gold gained in value. During these years, Ghana was the major supplier of gold to the world economy. Koumbi Saleh, a town that once served as one of Ghana's capitals, hosted a prosperous Muslim community of merchants linked to the trans-Saharan trade route. Ironically, iron and copper were more useful, and thus more valuable, to Africans than gold was. So caravans carried iron, copper, and copper alloy across the Sahara as well as the precious metal.

Over time, Ghana's ecological and demographic conditions weakened its society. As its population grew, its food production failed to meet demand in what was by then an extremely arid environment. All of this left Ghana vulnerable to Muslim conquest, the immediate cause of Ghana's downfall.

CENTRAL AFRICAN STATES AND GREAT ZIMBABWE

In Central Africa, a few large city-states became home to advanced civilizations. Among them were Kongo and Benin.

From the 1250s to the 1450s, the most powerful of the central African states was the one that emerged around the cities of Mutapa and Great Zimbabwe. Politically linked, Mutapa and Great Zimbabwe controlled seven hundred miles of the Zambezi river basin.

The larger and more important of the two cities was Great Zimbabwe (ca. 1000–1400). Its name means "sacred graves of the chiefs," and it was crucial as both a political and religious center. Zimbabwe was a great walled city, encircling 193 acres. It was home to approximately 20,000 people. It is clear that the people of Great Zimbabwe were skilled builders.

Great Zimbabwe was reputed to be immensely wealthy, thanks to large deposits of gold and diamonds. The city gained its wealth from the gold trade. Gold was shipped east to Sofala, where it became part of the East African–Indian Ocean coastal trade complex (see Chapter 9). Archaeologists have since found in the ruins of the city gold, jewelry, copper ornaments, birds carved out of soapstone, iron tools, Chinese ceramics, and Persian artworks. This assortment of artifacts is a testament to how extensive trading patterns were in the area at the time.

Rumors of Great Zimbabwe's wealth—and of lost treasures and hidden mines—persisted for hundreds of years, long after the city itself collapsed in the mid-to-late 1400s.

THE EASTERN COAST

EAST AFRICA AND THE INDIAN OCEAN TRADE NETWORK

As part of the large Indian Ocean trade network, the East African coast was open to a remarkable variety of outside influences, culturally and economically. East Africa gained its wealth from the sale of a diverse selection of desirable goods like ivory. Slaves were already a part of the economic equation at this time. Through trade, African societies also had an impact on the outside world. As early as during the Roman era, East Africa already had commercial ties with India and the Mediterranean region. Later, African-made goods were reaching China by the tenth and eleventh centuries, by way of the Indian Ocean trade network. Chinese maritime trade expanded during the early part of the Ming dynasty (see Chapter 8), and many Chinese vessels made their way to the East African coast.

THE DIVERSITY OF EAST AFRICAN CITY-STATES

Many city-states flourished on the East African shores between 1000 and 1500. Nearly forty large urban centers were sprinkled along the 1,500-mile stretch of coast running from Mogadishu (in what is today Somalia) to the south. They were all multiethnic. Beginning in the twelfth century, Persians and Arabs immigrated to Mogadishu and started to press southward, mixing with the local Africans. The East African city-states were politically independent. Many of them were ruled by Arab sheiks, who were the leaders of rich mercantile families. Key cities included Malindi, Mombasa, Sofala, and Zanzibar.

East African cities were also diverse in terms of their populations. They contained native Africans of many types; Arabs, Turks, and other Middle Easterners; and Indians and others from South and Southeast Asia. There was a tremendous amount of ethnic, religious, cultural, and linguistic mixing along the East African coast. Muslims migrated in increasing numbers to the area, starting in the mid-to-late 600s. Islam became important, but did not displace local religions. The most widespread language in the region was Swahili, which became the lingua franca, or common tongue, for much of the entire coast. The Arab culture also penetrated the region's poetry and lexicon. East Africa was a vibrant area with a booming economy from approximately 1200 to 1500. Even Indonesians, in search of better economic opportunities, crossed the Indian Ocean to settle on Madagascar, an island off the southeast coast of Africa.

By the early 1500s, however, the arrival of European colonists and explorers would change everything, not just for East Africa, but the entire Indian Ocean basin.

CHRISTIANITY IN EAST AFRICA

It should be noted that Christianity existed as a dominant, even official, religion in two parts of northeastern Africa. The Copts, a Christian minority, formed communities in predominantly Islamic Egypt and Sudan.

Ethiopia (also known then as Abyssinia), on the cusp between Saharan and sub-Saharan Africa, was not only the oldest African state, but, for many centuries, a Christian kingdom. Ethiopians explored parts of Europe as early as the twelfth century. In 1306, Ethiopians had visited Italy, whereas the first European to visit Ethiopia, an Italian, came in 1407. By the early 1500s, Ethiopia was a Christian autocracy whose rulers aimed to adapt certain aspects of European civilization to Ethiopia. Before and during Europe's great Age of Exploration, rumors about the wealth and Christianity of the Ethiopian monarchs gave rise in Europe to the famous legends of "Prester John"—a mythical Christian king in Africa who possessed fabulous wealth. These legends were among the many factors that helped to spur on the Europeans' exploring efforts.

QUICK REVIEW

1. Which of the following is a viable reason why the development of strong and sizable political units occurred later and more slowly in sub-Saharan Africa than in many other regions of the world?

    (A) Language was not yet developed.
    (B) People in Africa had not yet evolved sufficiently to develop political units.
    (C) There were many cannibals in this part of Africa.
    (D) There was a vast array of languages and dialects spoken.
    (E) none of the above

2. How did women in the small communities of sub-Saharan Africa tend to be treated?

    (A) They were seen as political equals.
    (B) They were valued as fieldworkers and for educating children.
    (C) They were treated as goddesses.
    (D) More women served as chiefs than men.
    (E) Women tended the cattle and so had a lot of power.

3. African literature of this period was preserved through

    (A) oral tradition
    (B) scroll painting
    (C) writings on large slabs of stone
    (D) stories written on bronze statues
    (E) manuscripts kept in pyramid-shaped archives

4. The immediate cause of Ghana's downfall was

    (A) environmental calamity
    (B) the Crusades
    (C) its takeover by the Portuguese
    (D) Muslim conquest
    (E) the slave trade

5. How do researchers know that Great Zimbabwe was so wealthy at one time?

   (A) It left behind written accounts of its history.
   (B) Explorers testified to its great wealth.
   (C) Gold, jewelry, and other valuable items were found in its ruins.
   (D) It still exists, and has remained wealthy for hundreds of years.
   (E) none of the above

6. As far back as what era did East Africa already have commercial ties with India and the Mediterranean region?

   (A) the 1700s
   (B) the 1400s
   (C) the Sumerian era
   (D) the Egyptian Old Kingdom
   (E) the Roman era

7. Which of the following is an accurate statement about East African cities during this period?

   (A) The area was not ethnically diverse.
   (B) The most widely used language was Swahili.
   (C) The area unfortunately never enjoyed a booming economy.
   (D) Islam had not reached the shores of East Africa yet.
   (E) East African city-states were all under the rule of a single Arab sheik.

8. The Copts were and still are a _____ minority in predominantly Islamic Egypt.

   (A) Jewish
   (B) Buddhist
   (C) Christian
   (D) Muslim
   (E) agnostic

9. Which of the following is an accurate statement about slavery at the time in sub-Saharan Africa?

   (A) By the 1200s, some traders owned more than 1,000 slaves apiece.
   (B) Slavery was confined to Timbuktu, at least until the 1400s.
   (C) Only Muslims could own and sell slaves.
   (D) The people who were enslaved tended to live in East Africa.
   (E) Slavery had not arrived to this region of the world yet.

10. How did African societies gain the skill of metalworking?

   (A) The Muslims taught Africans the skill.
   (B) Western Europeans taught Africans this skill.
   (C) African societies only learned this skill after they were enslaved.
   (D) They gained it on their own, without outside help.
   (E) none of the above

ANSWERS:

1. **D**, p. 162	6. **E**, p. 164
2. **B**, p. 162	7. **B**, p. 164
3. **A**, p. 163	8. **C**, p. 165
4. **D**, p. 163	9. **A**, p. 163
5. **C**, p. 164	10. **D**, p. 162

CHAPTER 12

The Americas

Unlike the peoples of the three continents of Eurasia and Africa, who came to interact with and influence each other over time, the early societies of North and South America developed in isolation. Settled by the descendants of Stone Age travelers who, 15,000 to 30,000 years ago, crossed from Asia over a land bridge that joined Alaska with northeastern Siberia—then disappeared with the rising of ocean levels—North and South America remained geographically separated from other continents for thousands of years.

By approximately 9000 B.C.E., the entire length of the Americas, north to south, had been settled. The passage of time, geographical spread, and the environmental diversity of the Americas all caused the social groups scattered throughout the Americas to develop unique cultural, social, and linguistic characteristics.

Major areas of settlement in the Americas included the eastern woodlands of North America, North America's desert Southwest, the open plains of North America, the deserts and jungles of Mexico and Central America, and the Andes Mountains of South America. Before 1000 C.E., as discussed in Chapter 3, advanced civilizations emerged in all these areas. Many of these groups are unusual in that they are among the few societies that reached an advanced state of civilization without developing systems of writing (such as the Inca and Mississippians) or inventing the wheel.

The geographical isolation of the Americas continued until the end of the fifteenth century. Only with the voyages of Christopher Columbus in 1492 did the societies of North and South America come into any sustained contact with outsiders. The arrival of the Europeans would change the Americas beyond recognition beginning in the 1500s. In the meantime, between 1000 and 1450, several major civilizations emerged in the Americas or reached their peak of development.

NORTH AMERICA

HUNTER-GATHERER CULTURES IN NORTH AMERICA

In North America, most Native Americans (known popularly by the erroneous term "Indians") were hunter-gatherers. Their lifestyles tended to be nomadic or seminomadic. Native American groups were divided into tribes. Around 1000 C.E., the number of tribes—and the differences between them—increased dramatically. Most of the tribes that are well known today appeared during the years after 1000, and the variety and quantity of tribes grew until about the 1500s.

The role of women in most North American tribes seems to have been defined relatively loosely. Since most of these groups were not yet settled and fully agricultural, the gender division of labor was not as sharply formed as in the more developed empires of Central and South

America. Women tended to gather berries and roots, weave, make pottery, and raise children. But their status was not necessarily secondary to that of men, at least not in a formal sense.

SOCIETIES OF THE SOUTHWEST

Not counting what is today Mexico, two regions of North America became home to more advanced Native American societies. One was the desert Southwest, especially in what is presently Arizona and New Mexico. Settlement here seems to have begun during the 300s B.C.E. By the 800s C.E., advanced cultures such as the Mogollon and Hohokam had appeared. They most likely learned agricultural techniques from even more sophisticated groups to the south, in Mexico.

Along with the Mogollon and Hohokam, there were the Anasazi, who lived in the region from approximately 300 to 1300. The peoples of the Southwest lived in complex dwellings known generally as pueblos—sometimes built on the open flatland, sometimes high up in the caves of canyons like Chaco Canyon, Mesa Verde, and Canyon de Chelly. The Anasazi believed that humans had emerged from the earth, so they held religious ceremonies in underground chambers called kivas. This practice was passed on to tribes that later settled in the Southwest.

Women in Anasazi communities may have had the right to own property. How important women may have been is hinted at in the practices of the present-day Pueblo, the Anasazis' descendants. Among the Pueblo, women are often the principal owners and heads of households, where extended families live. This may also have been the case with the Anasazi.

OHIO AND MISSISSIPPI VALLEY CIVILIZATIONS

To the north and east, sophisticated native American societies emerged in the Ohio and Mississippi river valleys. These groups built large mounds, presumably for religious and ceremonial purposes. The first was the Adena culture (ca. 500 B.C.E.–100 C.E.). This was followed by the larger Hopewell culture (ca. 100–400), which spread far beyond the Ohio valley.

Between 1000 and 1500, the most advanced culture in what are now the United States and Canada was the Mississippian civilization (ca. 700–1500). Like their predecessors, the Mississippians built great mounds. They also built cities. The largest of these was Cahokia, located in what is now western Illinois. By 1200, Cahokia had a population of over 30,000. It was also home to the largest mound in North America—well over a hundred feet high. For reasons that remain unclear, Cahokia was abandoned sometime around 1250.

THE EMERGENCE OF NEWER TRIBES IN NORTH AMERICA

Between 1250 and 1500, the Mississippian culture was in decline. At the same time, the Native Americans of North America began to organize themselves into smaller hunter-gatherer groups. These evolved into the large number of major Native American tribes that were in existence when the Europeans first started to arrive, at the end of the 1400s and the early 1500s. With the appearance of European settlers and colonizers, of course, the lives of all Native American tribes would be forever changed.

MEXICO AND CENTRAL AMERICA

BASIC FEATURES OF CENTRAL AMERICAN SOCIETIES

Archaeological evidence suggests that it was in Mexico and Central America that major civilizations first developed in the Americas. Agriculture—in the form of the cultivation of maize (corn) and the potato—was first practiced here somewhere between 5000 and 3000 B.C.E. As described in Chapter 3, several important civilizations rose and fell in this area, including the Olmecs (ca.

1200–400 B.C.E.) and the Maya (250–900 C.E.). In general, there was a remarkable degree of cultural and religious continuity among the peoples of Central America, from the Olmecs onward, all the way through the Aztecs (described presently).

Most of the Central American societies tended to be despotic: they were rigid dictatorships ruled by kings and priests. Despite their cultural and religious commonalities, they were often politically disunited, with city-state warring against city-state. On the other hand, there was a high level of trade and economic interaction among the peoples of the region.

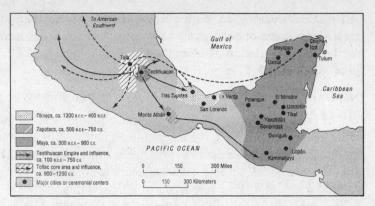

States in Pre-Columbian Central America, ca. 1200 B.C.E.–1200 C.E.
This map demonstrates that, in Central America, many civilizations developed, rose, and fell in succession. The Olmec set the pattern for cultural development here, followed by the Teotihuacán, Maya, Toltec, and Aztecs.

Women in Central American empires were subject to rigidly defined gender roles. A few upper-class women were able to gain influence as priestesses. They also exerted informal influence by means of their noble standing. In the Aztec culture, women could own property and sign business contracts, independently of their husbands. Still, most women were restricted to those roles traditionally assigned to females.

Many of the peoples of Central America—most famously the Mayans and the Aztecs—built large pyramids, mainly for religious purposes. In general, the art and architecture of the indigenous peoples of Latin America existed largely for religious purposes. Temples were built on top of pyramids to honor the gods. The main Aztec pyramid in Tenochtitlán was dedicated to Huitzilopochtli (the sun god) and Tlaloc (the rain god), and priests carried out human sacrifices to appease them. Aztec pyramids were once covered with brightly colored sculptures and paintings. Aztec artisans worked with stone as well as gold and silver in creating their depictions of gods and religious ceremonies. One of the most famous stoneworks is the Aztec calendar, which was created with the help of skilled builders and scientists.

THE TOLTEC

Around 1000 C.E., the dominant civilization in Mexico and Central America was that of the Toltec (ca. 968–1156). The Toltecs were very aggressive. From their capital, Tula, their fierce warriors spread out to conquer most of central Mexico. After the Toltecs reached the peak of their strength, however, they tore their society apart in a series of civil wars over religion. This left them weak enough that invaders from the north were able to destroy them in the 1160s.

THE AZTECS

The next major group to rise up in Central America—and the last before the arrival of the Europeans—were the Mexica, better known as the Aztecs (ca. 1300–1520). The chief city of the Aztecs was the twin metropolis of Tenochtitlán (on the site of what is today Mexico City) and Tlatelco. At the height of Aztec power, Tenochtitlán-Tlatelco had a population of half a million. Its marketplace could hold more than 60,000 people. The palace of the king covered two acres and contained 300 rooms.

The Aztecs were even more warlike than the Toltecs before them. During the 1300s, the Aztecs began the process of conquering an empire that would cover more than 125,000 square miles. They ruled over a population of 10 million.

AZTEC RELIGION

One of the most famous aspects of Aztec culture was religion. As noted previously, the Aztecs built great pyramids to serve as temples. They worshiped many of the same gods as the Central American peoples who came before them, especially the Mayans. Key deities included the jaguar god, the feathered serpent (Quetzalcoátl, who also appeared in the guise of a light-skinned, bearded man), and, most important of all, the sun god.

The sun god was Huitzilopochtli, who took the form of a giant hummingbird. The Aztecs believed that the reappearance of the sun every morning—and how much warmth it gave—depended on how devoted their worship of Huitzilopochtli was. The Aztecs also believed that the sun drew its energy from human blood. This meant that they practiced human sacrifice on an extremely large scale (earlier Central American societies had included human sacrifice as part of their worship, but in a much more limited way). Victims included prisoners of war, but ordinary Aztec citizens as well. Historians estimate that, by the end of the 1400s, over 20,000 people per year were being slain as a part of religious ritual.

THE SPANISH CONQUEST

The Aztec thrived in Central America until the early 1500s, when Spanish conquistadors (conquerors), led by Hernan Cortés, arrived. The last ruler of the Aztecs was Moctezuma II (1502–1520), popularly known as Montezuma. The defeat of the Aztecs would lead to Spanish domination of Mexico and Central America until the 1800s. The Spanish conquest of the region is described in Chapter 19.

SOUTH AMERICA

The ecological diversity of South America is staggering. Climates range from tropical to cool and arid. Terrain types include jungle, desert, mountains, grassland, and more.

EARLY ANDEAN CIVILIZATIONS

The environment in which complex societies first developed in South America was mountainous. It was on the west coast of the continent, in the Andes Mountains—one of the longest mountain chains in the world—that civilizations first took shape. At first glance, the harsh, rugged nature of the terrain might seem inhospitable enough to discourage the full-scale growth of settlements into advanced societies. But that very harshness and ruggedness demanded of the local inhabitants a high degree of cooperation and efficient coordination of human labor. That cooperation and efficiency gave rise to a number of major South American cultures, both before and after 1000 C.E.

Most of these societies appeared in the northwestern Andes, in the region that today makes up Ecuador, Bolivia, and Peru. Among the earliest of these societies were the Chavín (ca. 900–200 B.C.E.). A second and later set of civilizations include the Nazca (100–800 C.E.) and the Moche (200–700 C.E.). A third group of culture began to emerge after approximately 500 C.E.: the Huari (ca. 500–1000), the Tiahuanaco (ca. 500–1000), and the Chimu (ca. 800–1465).

FEATURES OF ANDEAN CIVILIZATIONS

Most of these societies had certain features in common. Most Andean peoples were organized into clans called *ayllu*. Within each clan, smaller groups cooperated by taking on rotational labor obligations for the entire clan. These obligations were referred to as *mit'a*. The peoples of the Andes practiced animal husbandry. The primary animals they bred and used were llamas, alpacas, and vicuñas. These were all used for transport, as well as food products, but their wool was also used to make clothing and other woven products.

Women in these Andean societies tended to be greatly constrained in their rights and freedoms. Wives were considered to be little more than domestic servants to their husbands. Lower-class and common women typically worked as weavers, farmers, and child rearers. One alternative was to become involved in religious life. Especially in Incan society, many young girls were chosen to serve in the temples of the gods.

The Andean cultures grew crops as well, but cultivating land was difficult in such a mountainous region. To overcome this difficulty, Andean peoples devised a method of terrace farming, in which flat surfaces were carved, in staircase fashion, out of the sloped sides of the mountains. Terrace farming was tremendously labor-intensive, but it allowed farmers to gain a substantial yield from environments not naturally favorable for agriculture.

Another noteworthy feature of Andean societies is that most of them accomplished such a high level of cultural sophistication without developing an alphabet or any written form of language. In order to keep financial records and

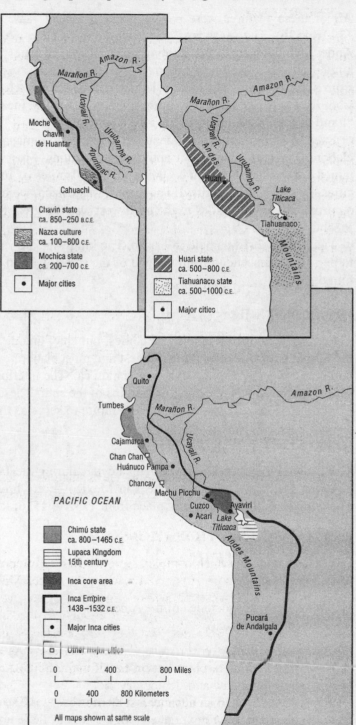

Andean Civilizations, ca. 850 B.C.E.–1532 C.E.
The earliest major civilizations of South America emerged in the Andes Mountains, on the continent's western coast. The last and greatest was the Inca Empire.

accounts, Andean civilizations used an elaborate system of knots tied in cords and strings. It was called *quipo* (quipn).

THE INCAS

All of these features were passed on to the most famous Andean civilization, the Incas (ca. 1300s–1536). The Incas rose very quickly during the late 1300s to build a huge empire in the Andes, subduing and incorporating many of the other peoples mentioned previously. In less than a hundred years, the Incan Empire grew into a massive expanse of land that covered 3,000 miles from north to south. The Incas ruled a territory that stretched from Chile to northern Ecuador and from the Pacific coast to the upper Amazon basin. The Incas called their empire Tawantinsuyu, or "Land of the Four Corners."

Even in such rough, mountainous terrain, the Incas managed to link their lands together with an elaborate system of transport and communications. Most impressively, the Incas built or maintained somewhere between 13,000 and 19,000 miles of roads. The Incas also constructed large cities, from which they ruled. The capital was Cuzco, which rested in a valley of the same name. Approximately fifty miles to the northwest was the great fortress and temple complex of Machu Picchu.

The royal court was held in Cuzco. The king was known as the Great Inca. He was considered to be sacred, descended from the god of the sun. It was an offense punishable by death to look at him directly.

INCAN WORSHIP

The Incas worshiped a number of deities, but chief among them was the sun god. The Temple of the Sun in Cuzco was by far the largest and most elaborate of the Incas' places of worship. It was laid out in the shape of a puma, a mountain cat. The interior was lined with gold. The temple was staffed by thousands of *acllas*, or "virgins of the sun." These were young women chosen each year from the various villages of the Incan Empire to serve as the temple's acolytes.

ARRIVAL OF THE SPANISH

The Incan civilization would enjoy its heyday during the 1400s and early 1500s. After that point, however, the Incas—like the Aztecs in Mexico—were brought down by Spanish conquistadors. The conquest of the Incas took place from 1532 to 1536; it is detailed in Chapter 19.

QUICK REVIEW

1. Why are many societies of the Americas considered unusual?

   (A) Their form of governance was not based on hierarchies but on equality before the law and democracy.
   (B) They reached an advanced state of civilization without developing systems of writing.
   (C) Women acted as the warriors.
   (D) They were more brutal to outsiders.
   (E) They all spoke the same language, Spanish.

2. The peoples of the Southwest lived in complex dwellings called

   (A) tipis
   (B) yurts
   (C) cliff homes
   (D) pueblos
   (E) totem poles

3. Which of the following Native American societies built large mounds and are thought to have used them for religious purposes?

(A) Pueblos
(B) Hopewells
(C) Inca
(D) Maya
(E) Hopi

4. Most of the Central American societies

I. tended to be despotic
II. were often politically fractured
III. had a low level of trade with other peoples of the region
IV. had a high level of trade with other peoples of the region

(A) I, II, and III
(B) I, II, and IV
(C) I and III only
(D) II and IV only
(E) I and IV only

5. Toltec warriors conquered parts of

(A) Mexico
(B) North America
(C) Central America
(D) South America
(E) Easter Island

6. Which of the following was the Aztecs' principal god?

(A) the lion god
(B) the jaguar god
(C) the sun god
(D) the feathered serpent god
(E) the moon god

7. In South America, where did the first complex societies develop?

(A) on offshore islands
(B) along the east coast
(C) along the west coast
(D) along the north coast
(E) in the Andes Mountains

8. What major features did Andean civilizations have in common?

I. They developed written forms of language.
II. They were organized into clans.
III. They practiced animal husbandry.
IV. Women tended to have equal rights with men.

(A) I, II, and III
(B) II, III, and IV
(C) I and IV only
(D) II and III only
(E) I only

9. At its height, how large was the Incan Empire?

(A) It stretched from Chile to what is today Panama.
(B) It stretched from Argentina to Brazil.
(C) It stretched from Chile to northern Ecuador.
(D) It stretched from Colombia to Peru.
(E) It stretched from Mexico to Costa Rica.

10. The Incas and Aztecs were conquered by the

(A) Maya
(B) Spanish
(C) French
(D) Russians
(E) Mexicans

ANSWERS:

1. **B**, p. 167   6. **C**, p. 170
2. **D**, p. 168   7. **E**, p. 170
3. **B**, p. 168   8. **D**, p. 171
4. **B**, p. 168   9. **C**, p. 172
5. **A**, p. 169   10. **B**, p. 172

Unit Three: Review Questions

SAMPLE ESSAY QUESTIONS

1. With the exception of the Americas, the major world civilizations were encountering each other more often. Choose one of the pairs below and describe in what ways they interacted and to what extent each benefited from such contacts.

   Mongols and Russians
   Chinese and Japanese
   East African city-states and Muslims

2. This era was marked by different forms of treatment of women and the different roles they played in society. Choose two different cultures below and compare and contrast the role and treatment of women in them.

   China
   Japan
   Central America
   Anasazi
   western Europe
   sub-Saharan Africa

3. Discuss the way in which forms of international and interregional economic exchange took shape during these years.

MULTIPLE-CHOICE QUESTIONS

1. Why did the Catholic Church play a key role in the development of a large part of medieval Europe?

   (A) It controlled the Eastern Orthodox Church.
   (B) Its monasteries preserved ancient manuscripts, and the Church provided cultural cohesion.
   (C) It was led by Protestant reformers.
   (D) Catholics joined with Jews in developing cities.
   (E) none of the above

2. Which of the following is an accurate statement of the status of women in medieval Europe?

   (A) It differed according to social class and geographical location.
   (B) It tended to be the same across Europe, despite class differences.
   (C) Women could serve as leaders in both the Catholic and Orthodox Christian churches.
   (D) Aristrocratic women all held some kind of political power.
   (E) Women enjoyed the right to vote.

3. The population of the Holy Roman Empire consisted of which ethnic groups?

   (A) English, Irish, Italians, Scandinavians
   (B) Moors, Italians, German, Greeks
   (C) English, Irish, Italians, Greeks
   (D) Germans, Italians, French, Hungarians, and Slavs
   (E) Italians only

4. Which of the following was NOT a major benefit of Moorish occupation of Spain in the Middle Ages?

   (A) The Moors brought with them advanced knowledge of medicine and science.
   (B) The Moors brought with them advanced knowledge of technology.
   (C) The Moors Christianized Spain.
   (D) The Moors provided a haven for Jewish scholars and professionals.
   (E) The Moors profoundly affected Spanish art and architecture.

5. How did urbanization contribute to social diversity in Europe during the Middle Ages?

   (A) The city offered increased cultural opportunities.
   (B) Cities allocated more benefits to workers than rural areas.
   (C) Guilds practiced affirmative action.
   (D) City governments tended to be more tolerant.
   (E) The growth of cities called for specialization of labor and the development of new skills.

6. What is meant by humanism?

   (A) a belief that humans are sinful and should be forced to comply with Church dictates
   (B) a type of atheism
   (C) a belief that humans came to the earth from spaceships millions of years ago
   (D) a conviction that humans descended from apes
   (E) a conviction that being human is something to celebrate

7. Which ethnic group came to dominate most of the Middle East and North Africa by the end of the fifteenth century?

   (A) Turks
   (B) Germans
   (C) French
   (D) Spanish
   (E) Egyptians

8. Which do historians consider the major achievements during the golden era of Islamic culture?

   I.   They invented the wheel at this time.
   II. The use of Arabic numerals became widespread.
   III. Muslims contributed to human understanding of astronomy and mathematics.
   IV. Several pieces of Islamic literature, including the *Rubaiyat*, are considered world masterpieces.

   (A) I, II, III
   (B) II, III, IV
   (C) I and III only
   (D) II and IV only
   (E) all of the above

9. Which of the following is an example of Song China's capacity to combine scientific knowledge with technological expertise?

   (A) the world's first telescope
   (B) a celestial clock that used a chain-driven mechanism
   (C) foot-binding
   (D) Zen
   (E) fireworks

10. The reign of Khubilai Khan in China was marked by all but one of the following:

    (A) economic strength
    (B) effective bureaucracy
    (C) economic malaise
    (D) renewed trade with the West
    (E) the repairing of roads and canals

11. During the Heian period in Japan, with whom did real power rest?

    (A) the emperor
    (B) the samurai
    (C) the head of the Buddhist faith
    (D) the shogun
    (E) whichever noble clan assumed the position of chancellor

12. At periods after 1000, the Vietnamese states of Annam and Champa were under which country's rule?

    (A) Korea
    (B) Japan
    (C) Thailand
    (D) China
    (E) Cambodia

13. What was the major effect of the Muslim invasions and the founding of the Delhi Sultanate in India?

    (A) peace for many hundreds of years
    (B) the introduction of Islam
    (C) the introduction of a caste system
    (D) all of the above
    (E) none of the above

14. What were some examples of the Mongols' cultural borrowing during the Pax Mongolica?

    I.   the adoption of advanced law codes
    II. the adoption of a written language
    III. the adoption of new religious practices
    IV. the adoption of nomadism

    (A) I and II only
    (B) II and III only
    (C) I, II, and III
    (D) II, III, and IV
    (E) none of the above

15. Why did strong, large political units develop in sub-Saharan Africa later and more slowly than they did in other parts of the world?

    (A) Other parts of the world were more democratic.
    (B) Other parts of the world were more technologically advanced.
    (C) This part of Africa was very ethnically and linguistically diverse, so there was little political interaction.
    (D) There was little interaction among people in sub-Saharan Africa because there was nothing to trade.
    (E) all of the above

16. Why did the city of Zimbabwe become both a political and religious center between the 1250s and 1450s?

    (A) Zimbabwe dominated the East African slave trade.
    (B) Zimbabwe's vast army gave it control over Central Africa.
    (C) Zimbabwe was the first African state to trade with European merchants.
    (D) Zimbabwe made great advantage of its wealth in gold and diamonds.
    (E) Zimbabwe's library attracted a number of Muslim scholars.

17. According to the map on page 156, the Golden Horde empire encompassed what country?

    (A) Mongolia
    (B) Russia
    (C) India
    (D) Germany
    (E) Turkey

18. In what kind of dwellings did the peoples of the Southwest in North America tend to live?

    (A) huts
    (B) pyramids
    (C) yurts
    (D) pueblos
    (E) tipis

19. Which of the following statements about Central American societies in the period between 1000 and 1450 are accurate?

I. Many of them built pyramids for religious rituals.
II. There was a significant degree of cultural and religious continuity among them.
III. They often were politically disunited.
IV. There was a high level of trade and economic interaction among the various peoples.

(A) I, II, and III
(B) II, III, and IV
(C) II and III only
(D) all of the above
(E) none of the above

20. Which of the following was NOT a characteristic of Andean societies?

(A) highly developed written languages
(B) clan organization
(C) the practice of animal husbandry
(D) use of wool to make clothing and other woven goods
(E) the keeping of financial records

ANSWERS:

1. **B**, p. 115
2. **A**, p. 124
3. **D**, p. 118
4. **C**, p. 119
5. **E**, p. 123
6. **E**, p. 128
7. **A**, p. 131
8. **B**, p. 135
9. **B**, p. 140
10. **C**, p. 141
11. **E**, p. 144
12. **D**, p. 147
13. **B**, p. 149
14. **C**, p. 159
15. **C**, p. 162
16. **D**, p. 164
17. **B**, p. 156
18. **D**, p. 168
19. **D**, p. 168
20. **A**, p. 171

UNIT FOUR

World Cultures Interacting

(1450–1750)

Unit Overview

GENERAL REMARKS

During the years from 1450 to 1750, the civilizations of the world became truly connected for the first time in history. Without a doubt, the most significant trend of this era was the emergence of a fully global system of exchange and interaction. Regrettably, much of this interaction consisted of warfare, exploitation, and slavery. Nonetheless, trade, discovery, cultural interchange, and the faster and easier movement of peoples all did much to bring the various societies of the world into greater proximity. One can accurately speak of world cultures interacting, for good and for bad, during the period from 1450 to 1750.

One of the primary causes of this greater degree of interaction was the massive and sustained effort of the Europeans to explore the rest of the world, starting in the 1400s. Driven by scientific curiosity, the quest for power, the hope of spreading Christianity, and, above all, a burning desire for wealth, European sailors began seeking out oceanic trade routes that would link them directly with China, India, Japan, and elsewhere in the Far East. During the 1400s and 1500s, European explorers reached all these areas. In the meantime, they also encountered the Americas: a "New World" that had, for thousands of years, lain outside the bounds of knowledge of the peoples of Asia, Africa, and Europe.

Within decades, European traders, missionaries, and conquerors had spread throughout the world. It was a European mariner whose expedition, from 1519 to 1521, became the first in history to sail around the world. The Europeans established a presence in many parts of coastal Africa, Southeast Asia, and parts of the Far East. Most dramatically, European colonizers conquered and transformed the Americas. The opening of the Americas to the rest of the world was done brutally and out of greed. But it also played a tremendous role in shifting the world's economic, linguistic, religious, and cultural patterns. It also changed forever the environments of the Americas, Africa, and Europe, as new animals, new foods, and new diseases were brought back and forth in a development known as the Columbian Exchange.

Another major trend of this era (1450–1750) was the rise of Europe. Until the 1400s, Europe had been relatively weak and backward, compared with civilizations such as China and the Ottoman Empire. During the 1500s and 1600s, however, Europe began to pull even with China and the "gunpowder empires" of the Islamic east (Ottoman Turkey, Safavid Persia, and Mughal India) in terms of scientific advancement, global power, and overall wealth. During the 1700s, Europe overtook these other civilizations, becoming the militarily strongest, most technologically adept, and economically mightiest civilization in the world. By the middle of the 1700s, Europe would be well situated to do what it went on to do in the 1800s: dominate the vast majority of the globe, militarily and economically.

Technological development intensified in many parts of the world during this time. The degree of scientific knowledge increased. Economic and technological practices that can be referred to as proto-industrial were appearing in such places as Europe, China, and elsewhere. The foundations for the rapid and thorough industrialization and mechanization of many societies during the late 1700s and 1800s were laid during the 1600s and early-to-mid 1700s.

On a more traditional note, agricultural techniques in most societies improved dramatically during these years. In Europe, it is common to speak of an "Agricultural Revolution" during this era. Worldwide, the improvement of agricultural technique helped lead to a significant increase in world population. The rate of growth was the fastest ever seen to that date, as the world population rose from 350 million in 1400 to 610 million in 1700.

BROAD TRENDS

GLOBAL POWER AND INTERNATIONAL RELATIONS

- During the first centuries of this era (the 1500s and 1600s), global might was concentrated in China and the Islamic world's "gunpowder empires" (Ottoman Turkey, Safavid Persia, and Mughal India).
- All during this period, the nations of Europe, especially in the west and north, were growing steadily more powerful. By the early 1700s, they were overtaking the civilizations listed previously in terms of military, scientific, and technological aptitude.
- The most dramatic and global development of the era was the campaign of the nations of Europe to explore (and, where possible, conquer and colonize) the rest of the world. In particular, the Europeans' encounter with the Americas—and their incorporation of the Americas into the world economic system—transformed the world forever.
- European colonization of the Americas, the African coast, and parts of Southeast Asia set the stage for their massive burst of imperial activity during the 1800s. During the 1700s, European colonization led to the emergence of a truly global economic system. It also created a worldwide system of military competition among European powers for global dominance. Some of the European wars of the 1700s—especially the Seven Years' War (1756–1763), which raged not only in Europe, but also North America and India—can, in a way, be considered the first "world wars" in history.
- The increased importance of gunpowder weaponry in the warfare of this period meant that, from this time forward, technological aptitude and military strength would be intimately connected.

POLITICAL DEVELOPMENTS

- In many parts of the world, political organization became more centralized and sophisticated. Many of the features of modern government, such as bureaucracies, agencies, admiralties, treasuries, general staffs, state banks, and other institutions, began to appear.
- Nation-states in the contemporary sense of the word began to emerge. Nation-states were solid political units with relatively fixed borders, a sense of national unity, and populations that were mostly (though never completely) homogenous in terms of language and ethnicity.
- Europe began to experiment with new forms of monarchy: absolutism and parliamentarism.

ECONOMIC DEVELOPMENTS

- Social diversification resulted from the growing importance of nonagricultural ways of making a living. Banking, commerce, trade, shopkeeping, artisanry, and craftsmanship all led to the creation of a middle class (often referred to as the bourgeoisie, or bourgeois class) in many societies, but especially in Europe. This middle class was small to begin with, but steadily grew in numbers and importance.
- In general, more and more economic importance began to be placed on trade, commerce, and money, rather than land (which had been the traditional source and measure of wealth).

- In several civilizations, but primarily Europe, proto-industrial modes of production began to appear, especially during the 1700s. By the late 1700s, the concept of capitalism was beginning to emerge as well. Both of these trends would have a profound impact on the 1800s.
- Europe's exploration and colonization of the Americas created a new major trade network in the Atlantic. This economic system linked Europe, Africa, North America, and South America. Indirectly, it was connected by trade with the Middle East and Asia.
- During the 1500s and 1600s, Spanish and Portuguese extraction of precious metals (especially silver) from the Americas affected economies around the world. Over time, this huge and relatively sudden influx of gold and silver coinage into the economies of so many societies created a glut of precious metals. Many civilizations, from Europe to China, experienced severe inflation as a result of this trend during the 1600s.
- By far the most unfortunate by-product of this era's economic trends was the birth and growth of the Atlantic slave trade, which, from the late 1400s to the late 1800s, resulted in the capture and forced deportation to the Americas of perhaps 12 million Africans.

CULTURAL DEVELOPMENTS

- Most major societies had by now developed well-defined artistic and literary traditions. Increased technological aptitude in most of these societies enabled the production of arts and crafts of very high quality.
- The level of scientific knowledge and technological achievement was especially high in civilizations such as China, Ottoman Turkey, Mughal India, and Safavid Persia.
- Europe made exceptional strides in terms of scientific knowledge and technological achievement. The Renaissance, the Scientific Revolution, and the Enlightenment all furthered the intellectual growth of Europe, up to the point that, during the late 1600s and 1700s, it overtook the civilizations listed previously.
- The steadily increasing influence of the printing press led to the rapid spread of information, scientific knowledge, religious debates, and new ideas. By creating more materials to read—and therefore more incentive to read—the printing press also helped to boost literacy rates in the parts of the world that used it.
- Europe experienced a religious earthquake, the Protestant Reformation, that had a profound impact not just on matters of faith, but also cultural life in general, military affairs, politics, and economics. The split between Protestants and Catholics also affected the ways in which Europeans spread Christianity to other parts of the world.
- In addition to the cultural, religious, and artistic interchange that had gone on among the societies of Africa, Europe, and Asia, the European encounter with the Americas led to even greater cultural interaction. The movement of Europeans and Africans (mainly slaves) forever altered the patterns of North and South American ethnicity, religion, language, art, and music. The changes were both positive and negative. In all cases, they were extensive.
- As a result of their Age of Discovery, the Europeans established a presence in almost all parts of the world during this era. Consequently, European colonies and trading missions spread European culture to Africa and the Far East, as well as to the Americas.
- The Columbian Exchange brought new foods, plants, and animals from North and South America to Africa and Europe. In particular, the importation of corn and potatoes dramatically altered the diets and agricultural practices of Europe. To North and South America, the Europeans brought new technology, the horse, and Christianity. By bringing African slaves to the New World, the Europeans also imported foods, cultural practices, and religious beliefs from Africa. The Europeans also brought diseases, such as smallpox and measles, to which the peoples of the Americas had no immunity. It is estimated that up to 25 percent of the pre-

Columbian population of the Americas perished within decades of the diseases brought to the New World by European conquerors and colonizers.
- World population growth was considerable during these years. From 1400 to 1700, the world's population increased from 350 million to 610 million. Up to that point, this was the longest period of uninterrupted and rapid population growth. The increase was due mainly to improvements in agricultural technique in most world cultures, as well as a general warming of the global climate. The parts of the world that grew the most were Asia and Europe. Africa's population grew more slowly, primarily because of hostile environmental factors.

GENDER ISSUES

- Throughout most parts of the world, women continued to occupy a secondary status, in terms of social roles, economic opportunities, and political influence.
- In most societies, marriage remained a primarily economic arrangement. Marriage ties were often a way to gain or transfer wealth and property. Marriage also ensured the inheritance of one's goods and assets by legitimate heirs.
- In a limited, gradual sense, parts of Europe began to develop a greater awareness of the injustice of the position of women.
- Also in Europe, individual women or women of various small but important segments of society (noble and aristocratic women, or women of the emerging middle class, for example) managed to gain educations, become active in business, make scientific discoveries, or become artists and writers.
- In most societies, women discovered or developed ways in which they could gain influence or advance their desires in informal, often subtle ways (advising husbands and sons, educating children, running or helping to run businesses, managing household finances, and so on).

COMPARATIVE ISSUES TO CONSIDER

- Compare a major European monarchy of this period (such as England under Elizabeth I, Spain during the 1500s and early 1600s, or France under Louis XIV) with an Asian empire (such as Ottoman Turkey, Ming China, or Mughal India).
- Contrast Russia's relationship with western Europe with the interaction of one of the following with the West: Mughal India, the Ottoman Empire, Tokugawa Japan, or China.
- Consider various forms of monarchy during this era.
- Compare the growing Atlantic slave trade with other systems of unfree labor (such as serfdom in medieval Europe, serfdom in Russia, or the Arab slave network in North and East Africa, for example).
- Examine the likenesses and differences between the global economy that emerged after European exploration and the international trading networks that had existed beforehand (also compare and contrast both with the globalization of the world economy during the late twentieth and early twenty-first centuries).
- Compare the European Age of Discovery with other and earlier efforts at exploration, such as Zheng He's or Ibn Battuta's.
- What features distinguish the kingdoms and empires of Africa or the Americas from those in Europe and Asia? What features did they have in common?
- Compare the different approaches of the various European nations to colonization (both in the Americas and worldwide).

KEY TERMS AND CONCEPTS

the Protestant Reformation

Martin Luther and the Lutheran Church

John Calvin and Calvinist movements

Henry VIII and the Anglican Church

Protestant doctrines

the Catholic Counter-Reformation

Saint Ignatius Loyola and the Jesuits

European religious wars

the Thirty Years' War and the Treaty of Westphalia

the emergence of the nation-state

absolute monarchy versus parliamentary monarchy

Louis XIV

Maria Theresa and Joseph II

Frederick the Great and the Seven Years' War

Peter the Great and Catherine the Great

the English Civil War (Charles I versus Oliver Cromwell)

the Glorious Revolution (William I) and the English Bill of Rights

the Northern Renaissance

the Baroque

Nikolai Copernicus and the heliocentric theory

the Scientific Revolution

Galileo

Sir Isaac Newton

the Enlightenment (also the Age of Reason)

Voltaire and Jean-Jacques Rousseau

class diversification in Europe

population growth and the Agricultural Revolution

mercantilism versus capitalism

Adam Smith, *The Wealth of Nations*

proto-industrialization

the lodestone and compass

the Iberian wave of exploration

Prince Henry the Navigator and Sagres

Christopher Columbus

Ferdinand Magellan and the circumnavigation of the globe

colonization

the northern wave of exploration

Jacques Cartier

the North American fur trade

the Dutch East India Company

Henry Hudson

New Amsterdam (New York)

the British East India Company

Osman I and the Ottoman Turks

the sultan and his viziers

Istanbul (formerly Constantinople)

Mehmet II and the conquest of Constantinople

Suleiman the Magnificent

the janissaries

the millet system

the harem

the Siege of Vienna

the Safavid Empire

Abbas the Great

Isfahan

the Ming dynasty

Francis Xavier and Matteo Ricci

the Qing (Ch'ing) Empire

tea and Chinese trade with Europe

Kangxi

the Ashikaga Shogunate

the Onin War, the Era of Independent Lords, and Japanese disunity

the reunification of Japan

Oda Nobunaga and Toyotomi Hideyoshi

Tokugawa Ieyasu

the Tokugawa Shogunate and the Great Peace

the Delhi Sultanate

Babur the Tiger

the Mughal Empire

the Taj Mahal

Akbar the Great

Aurangzeb

the Sikhs

Askia Mohammed and the Songhai state

the gold trade in West and Central Africa

Osei Tutu and the Asante (Ashanti) kingdom

the Boers

apartheid

the Zulu

European and Arab domination of the East African–Indian Ocean trade network

the Atlantic slave trade

sugar production and the slave trade

the Middle Passage

the triangular trade

the "Columbian Exchange"

Hernán Cortés and the conquest of the Aztecs

Francisco Pizarro and the conquest of the
Incas

New Spain and Mexico City (formerly
Tenochtitlán)

the Spanish importation of smallpox and
measles to the Americas

the encomienda system

Bartolomé de Las Casas, *The Tears of the
Indians*

silver mining and sugar production in the
Americas

Portuguese sugar production in Brazil and the
beginning of the Atlantic slave trade

the Dutch West India Company

Peter Stuyvesant

Jamestown, John Smith, and Pocahontas

Plymouth Rock and the *Mayflower* Pilgrims

the Massachusetts Bay Colony

the French and Indian Wars

the Russian-American Company

CHAPTER 13

Europe: Reformation, Absolutism, and Enlightenment

The years between the mid-1400s and the late 1700s—often referred to as the early modern period of European history—were years of political, religious, intellectual, and socioeconomic transformation. European nations grew stronger and more stable as political units. A new variant of the Christian faith, Protestantism, was born. Until approximately 1600, the Renaissance spread northward from Italy, affecting all of Europe. Afterward, the scientific awareness and intellectual sophistication of Europe (at least its upper classes) increased by leaps and bounds. The continent's population grew and diversified. Europeans improved their agricultural techniques. Their technological aptitude increased, and they took the first steps in building the industrial and commercial economies that would make their civilization so wealthy in the future.

In addition to this, Europe's global power skyrocketed during the early modern period. The Europeans did not invent gunpowder weaponry, nor were they the first to use it successfully. In the long term, however, the Europeans proved to be the most efficient in incorporating gunpowder weapons into their armies and navies and using this new technology to their benefit. Also, as described in Chapter 14, it was during these years that Europe, unlike any other major civilization, explored most of the globe, then conquered and colonized a vast portion of it. In the 1400s, Europe was simply one of many major civilizations, and a relatively small, weak one at that. By the end of the 1700s, it was among the most powerful of the world's civilizations, if not *the* most powerful. And its leaders had positioned themselves well to achieve what they set out to achieve during most of the 1800s: military, diplomatic, and economic dominance over most of the rest of the world.

THE PROTESTANT REFORMATION AND ITS AFTERMATH

THE POWER OF THE MEDIEVAL CATHOLIC CHURCH

For more than one thousand years, there had been only one major denomination of the Christian church in most of Europe: Roman Catholicism. The Byzantine Empire had subscribed to the Eastern Orthodox version of Christianity, and the two Christian churches had broken apart in 1054. But with the fall of Constantinople, Byzantium's capital, in 1453, Orthodoxy was the official church only for Russia and the easternmost parts of Europe (many of which fell under Turkish rule during the late 1400s and early 1500s).

In the meantime, the Catholic Church had become a tremendously powerful institution, both religiously and politically, in western and central Europe. As described in Chapter 6, the Catholic popes enjoyed an immense amount of influence and might during the medieval period.

CRISIS WITHIN THE CATHOLIC CHURCH

However, crisis began to strike the Catholic Church during the 1400s, and things would only get worse during the 1500s. Already during the 1300s and the early 1400s, the Church's prestige had declined sharply, as a result of France's 7-decade transfer of the papacy to Avignon, then the 40-year Great Schism. During this time, there were two popes claiming allegiance from all Catholics (see Chapter 6). In general, many worshipers—even priests and religious scholars—were becoming dissatisfied with what they saw as the Church's too-great concern with wealth and power. With every passing year, more people saw the Catholic Church as hypocritical and spiritually bankrupt.

FAILED ATTEMPTS AT CATHOLIC REFORM

Even before the actual Protestant Reformation, there were a number of churchmen who attempted to reform the Church radically or restore purity to it, but failed. The English theologian John Wycliffe, of Oxford University, argued that the Church should return to spiritual values. Although the Church did not retaliate against him while he was alive, it had his body burned, then persecuted his followers, the Lollards. The Bohemian clergyman Jan Hus, who, like Wycliffe, called for reform, was burned at the stake in 1415. In revenge, his followers rose up in a decades-long war that raged throughout the Holy Roman Empire. Most dramatic of all was Savonarola, a Dominican friar who used violence to rid Florence of what he thought of as wordly vanity and sin. He also condemned the Church as corrupt, and was executed in 1498.

MARTIN LUTHER AND THE BEGINNING OF THE PROTESTANT REFORMATION

The Protestant Reformation itself began in 1517, when a German monk named Martin Luther protested the sale of indulgences in his hometown. Luther regarded the sale of indulgences—certificates of forgiveness that could be purchased for money—as symbolic of the Church's spiritual emptiness and monetary greed. When the Church ordered him to recant, or retract, his criticisms, Luther refused and was excommunicated.

In a short time, what had started as a simple doctrinal dispute grew into a complete rupture of the Catholic Church. Even though he was a fugitive and his life was in danger, Luther founded a new church, the Lutheran Church, that became the first of what would eventually be known as the Protestant denominations.

CALVINISM AND ANGLICANISM

Other Protestant groups emerged during the mid-1500s. The French scholar John Calvin established a Protestant community in the Swiss city of Geneva that became a model for so-called Calvinist styles of Protestantism in areas like France (the Huguenots), the Dutch Republic (the Reformed Church), parts of England (the Puritans), and Scotland (the Presbyterians). In England, Henry VIII (previously a staunch defender of the Catholic Church) declared his country to be Protestant—mainly for political and marital reasons, not religious ones—forming the Church of England, also known as the Anglican Church.

PROTESTANT DOCTRINE

The beliefs and practices that separated Protestants from Catholics were many. At least in the beginning, most Protestant churches favored institutional simplicity. One of the reasons Protestant parishioners had left the Catholic Church was that they felt it had become too involved with politics, bureaucracy, and organizational matters (of course, once Protestant churches became larger and more established, they themselves experienced much the same problems).

Protestant churches put much less emphasis on rituals and sacraments than the Catholics. Many opposed the Catholics' veneration of saints and the Virgin Mary, considering such practice to interfere with a pure, sincere relationship with God. Central to Lutheran and Calvinist belief was the conviction that only the grace of God could save a sinful man or woman—not the pope (or any church official), a priest, or any sort of ritual. Protestants were in favor of reading the Bible and (within limits) interpreting it for themselves. This caused most Protestant denominations to place heavy emphasis on education and literacy. Protestants were more lenient about divorce, allowed clergy to marry, and rejected the Catholic doctrine of transubstantiation (the belief that, during the rite of Communion, the bread and wine are actually transformed into the body and blood of Christ, rather than simply representing them).

Not all Protestant denominations were in complete agreement with each other in terms of doctrine. Calvinist churches, for example, tended to be more severe and puritanical than other Protestant groups. By contrast, England's Anglican Church was, in many ways, not far removed from the Catholic Church. This meant that sometimes Protestant quarreled with Protestant. The most famous example is the struggle between the Anglican majority in England and the Puritan (Calvinist) minority, who were heavily persecuted, almost as heavily as English Catholics.

THE CATHOLIC COUNTER-REFORMATION

One effect of the Protestant Reformation was to compel the Catholic Church to reorganize itself and reform some of its practices. This change is typically called the Catholic Counter-Reformation (sometimes simply the Catholic Reformation). During the mid-to-late 1500s—especially at the Council of Trent, which lasted from 1545 to 1563—the Catholic Church worked to eliminate the worst of its financially and spiritually corrupt practices.

The Catholic Church also took measures to improve its ability to compete against the Protestant churches for worshipers. To increase its appeal, the Church sponsored the creation of highly impressive religious art and architecture (this was one of the factors that gave birth to the Baroque movement). To stiffen religious discipline, the Church established an Index of Forbidden Books, reaffirmed the authority of the pope, and gave new powers to the Holy Inquisition. The Church also approved the formation of a new religious order, the Society of Jesus, better known as the Jesuits. Founded between 1534 and 1540 by Saint Ignatius of Loyola, the Society of Jesus called itself the "Church Militant," and the Jesuits worked tirelessly as missionaries, educators, diplomats, and confessors to kings and queens to keep Catholic parts of Europe from slipping into the Protestant orbit. The Jesuits played an active role in European political life well into the 1700s.

RELIGIOUS WARS IN EUROPE

By the middle of the 1500s, the Protestant Reformation had become as much a political and military issue as it was a religious one. Along with the pope, Catholic monarchs of countries such as Spain and the Holy Roman Empire (as well as France and parts of Italy) were determined to force Protestant countries to return to the Catholic fold. The first serious religious wars began in Switzerland (where civil war broke out during the 1520s) and the German states of the Holy Roman Empire, during the 1540s. In the German states, the Catholic forces of the Holy Roman Empire won, but the resulting Treaty of Augsburg, which allowed some German states to remain Protestant, required both sides to compromise.

Persecution and religious war plagued England and Scotland from the 1530s to the beginning of the 1600s. The Dutch war of independence from Spain, which began in the 1560s and lasted eighty years, was motivated largely by the determination of the Dutch majority to remain

Calvinist, even in the face of Spanish religious oppression. All during the last half of the 1500s, France tore itself apart in a series of bloody civil wars between the Catholic majority and the Calvinist (Huguenot) minority. The famous—and failed—attack of the Spanish Armada in 1588 was part of Spain's attempt to defeat the England of Elizabeth I and destroy English Protestantism.

These religious wars were particularly brutal. Each combatant felt justified by religious beliefs in committing horrible atrocities. Religious wars tended to last a long time. They generally involved women, children, and other civilians, not just soldiers. Another reason these wars were so awful was that they took place at the time when European armies were starting to use gunpowder weaponry in a large-scale fashion.

THE THIRTY YEARS' WAR

Religious wars between Catholic and Protestant continued into the 1600s. They climaxed with the long, brutal Thirty Years' War (1618–1648). The war was a huge cataclysm that began as a religious dispute between Protestant Bohemians in the Holy Roman Empire and the Catholic authorities. Eventually, it drew in most of Europe's major nations. On the Catholic side were Spain, the Austrians of the Holy Roman Empire, and those German states of the Holy Roman Empire that had remained with the old church. Fighting for the Protestants were the Dutch, the Danes, the Swedes, and the German states that had adopted Lutheranism and Calvinism. Financial and diplomatic support came from other Protestant nations and regions, such as England and Transylvania.

As time passed, the Thirty Years' War became less about religion and more about straightforward political interests. As a sign of this dynamic, the Catholic nation of France joined the war during the 1630s, but on the side of the Protestants, not the Catholics. Its purpose was to weaken Spain and the Holy Roman Empire, which it considered threats to its power, despite their common religion. By the end of the 1640s, the French had succeeded: they and the Protestant powers defeated Spain and the Holy Roman Empire. Their victory was sealed by the Peace of Westphalia in 1648. The French intervention on the side of the Protestants was a sign of a growing secular spirit in Europe.

The end of the Thirty Years' War marked the end to the great wave of religious wars that had shaken Europe since the 1520s. Religious rivalries, persecution, and strife did not disappear, but—after more than a century—the age in which warfare in Europe had been driven primarily by religious debate was finally over.

Religious Divisions in Europe, ca. 1600.
For centuries, Christianity had been divided into two large denominations, Eastern Orthodoxy and Roman Catholicism. In most of Europe, the latter had been predominant. Starting with the Protestant Reformation in 1517, however, new religious rifts began to appear. By the end of the sixteenth century, western and northern Europe were divided into Catholic and Protestant camps, as shown in this map.

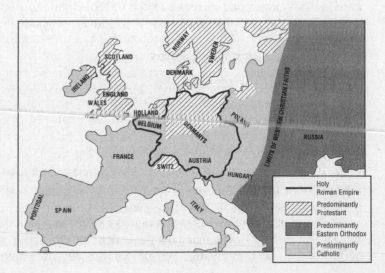

ABSOLUTE AND PARLIAMENTARY MONARCHIES

THE FADING OF FEUDALISM AND THE EMERGENCE OF EUROPEAN NATION-STATES

Although vestiges of feudalism survived into Europe's early modern period, countries during these years were becoming much more like nation-states in the contemporary sense: solid political units with relatively fixed borders, a sense of national unity, and populations that were mostly (though never completely) homogenous in terms of language and ethnicity.

Much of this development had to do with the strengthening of state institutions. During the Middle Ages, central state institutions had been weak (if not nonexistent), forcing kings and monarchs to resort to the feudal system. By the 1500s onward, however, this power structure was changing. Especially during the 1600s and 1700s, major European states were developing bureaucracies and agencies, such as tax-collecting bodies, central banks, general staffs (for the army), admiralties (for the navy), and ministries and cabinets of various types. Although monarchs and aristocrats still controlled most positions of power, governments were starting to become more rational and bureaucratic. Combined with advancements in communications and transport, the development of stronger state institutions allowed monarchs to centralize in a way they had not been able to during the Middle Ages.

CENTRALIZING RULERS

During the late 1400s and all during the 1500s, many rulers went to great lengths to centralize political power and place it in their own hands. Frequently, this effort meant competing with the noble (aristocratic) class, which was anxious to keep for itself the privileges it had been granted under the feudal system of the medieval era. Monarchs who were especially successful in building strong states during these years include

- Henry VIII and Elizabeth I of England
- Louis XI and Henry IV of France
- Charles V, the Habsburg ruler who governed both Spain and the Holy Roman Empire (he was more successful with the former than with the latter)
- Philip II of Spain (colonization and economic dominance of the Americas before and during his reign made Spain immensely powerful and wealthy)
- Ivan IV of Russia (known as "the Terrible" for the extreme violence he used to gain control over his nobles)

Not coincidentally, many of these rulers also emerged as strong—if not always successful—military leaders during the wars of religion. The Protestant Reformation played a large role in how states took shape during the sixteenth century.

By the 1600s and 1700s, as centralization continued, two major forms of monarchy emerged, one more centralized than the other. The more centralized form was absolutism, the less centralized was parliamentarism.

ABSOLUTE MONARCHY

In absolutist systems, the monarch is, at least in theory, all-powerful. There are no legal limitations to his or her power (although, in real life, even absolute monarchs were restricted in their actions by informal factors, such as a weak personality, uncooperative nobles, or an unreliable army).

The European ruler considered to have been the archetypal absolute monarch was Louis XIV of France, the "Sun King" who ruled from 1661 to 1715 (technically, Louis ascended the throne in 1638, but he was only a five-year-old boy at the time). Louis XIV used his government to create a highly centralized bureaucracy and national economy. He broke the power of his aristocracy and made it obey him. He built up the largest army and navy that Europe had seen in centuries. He turned Paris and his palace of Versailles into grand, impressive centers of power. In many ways, Louis illustrated the strengths and weaknesses of absolute monarchy. He was an intelligent, forceful man who used his extensive powers to change France into a better-organized, better-run country that was among the mightiest in the world. On the other hand, he involved France in too many wars, damaging the economy he had worked so hard to improve. Near the end of his reign, he also began to persecute the French Huguenots, or Protestants, to whom his grandfather had guaranteed religious freedom.

France remained an absolute monarchy all during the 1700s, until the French Revolution of 1789. Other countries attempted to create absolute monarchies, largely in imitation of what Louis had done in France. Starting in the late 1600s, the Austrian Habsburgs tried to turn their Holy Roman Empire into an absolutist monarchy. The Emperor Leopold I built great palaces around Vienna, centralized his government and economy, and fought wars against the Turks (in 1683, the Turks almost captured Vienna, but were turned back; afterward, the Austrians and their allies pushed the Turks steadily to the east). The constant military pressure caused by the Turkish presence on Austria's eastern frontier provided a good excuse for greater imperial control. In the eighteenth century, empresses and emperors such as Maria Theresa and Joseph II carried on the tradition of absolutism in Austria.

The small but militarily powerful German state of Prussia also became an absolute monarchy during the late 1600s and 1700s. Its king during the middle of the 1700s, Frederick the Great—a great general as well as a skilled ruler—was one of the most effective absolute monarchs of his time. His victory over Austria, France, and Russia during the Seven Years' War (1756–1763) is considered to be one of the greatest military triumphs in European history. As with all absolute monarchs, however, the price Prussia paid for Frederick's skill was greater dictatorship and decreased freedoms.

The largest nation in the world, Russia, also emerged as an absolute monarchy during these years. Russia already possessed a tradition of strong central authority. But during the late 1600s and early 1700s, Peter the Great modernized Russia, centralized it, and made the tsar more powerful than ever before. Peter the Great also changed Russia's fundamental geopolitical orientation. Before, Russia had been a country mainly cut off from Europe and concerned with events in Asia. By fighting and winning a long, hard war with Sweden, however, Peter gained a place for Russia in European diplomatic politics. From 1700 onward, Russia would be Europe's great power of the east. During and after Peter's reign, Russia would become more European in nature, although never completely so. The other great absolute ruler of Russia during the eighteenth century was Catherine the Great, who gained an international reputation for her intellectual achievements and her military conquests.

PARLIAMENTARY MONARCHY

Other governments, such as those in England and the Dutch Republic, took another direction. Even as these states centralized and became more modern, the rulers became less powerful, at least technically. These monarchies were known as parliamentary monarchies, because the ruler governed in conjunction with some kind of lawmaking body that was appointed by the aristocracy, elected by some or all of the people, or some combination of both.

During and after their war of independence from Spain, the Dutch wavered back and forth between centralized and decentralized rule. No matter what, however, the *stadholder*—an executive leader who was not quite a king—had to share power with a larger council called the States General.

Even more famous was the system that emerged in England (which joined with its neighbors,

Wales, Scotland, and Ireland, to form Great Britain in the early 1700s). Ever since the 1200s, the monarch of England had been compelled to share power first with his or her nobles, then with the legislative body known as Parliament. Gradually, Parliament assumed increasingly greater powers, although the monarch tended to remain paramount. This balance of power shifted during the 1600s. The English Civil War (1640–1649) was partly about religion (Anglican versus Puritan), but even more about power (king versus Parliament). The forces of Parliament won the civil war, killed the king (Charles I), and, for over a decade, established a Commonwealth ruled by the Parliament (then by the lord protector, Oliver Cromwell, the general who had won the civil war).

Even when the royal family was allowed to return to England in the Restoration of 1660, the rivalry between monarch and Parliament remained (the three-way religious struggle between Catholic, Puritan, and Anglican caused problems as well). Another disturbance—the "Glorious Revolution" of 1688—followed, and another king (William I, who was also the ruler of the Dutch Republic) was invited to take the throne. In this case, however, the invitation was conditional: William I had to agree not only to an act of religious toleration, but also a Bill of Rights that, among other things, curtailed the powers of the monarch and made Parliament the dominant partner in English politics. From 1688 onward, Parliament grew steadily stronger, while the kings and queens grew steadily weaker and more symbolic.

The advantages of parliamentary monarchy are clear from the examples of the English and the Dutch. Both nations developed strong economies, powerful navies, urbanized societies (especially in the case of the Dutch), and intellectual and cultural outlooks that were relatively open and free from religious persecution (again, in the case of the Dutch). Although poverty and inequality existed in both countries, society was more flexible, and social advancement was more feasible, than in most absolute monarchies.

THE PRINTING PRESS, THE SCIENTIFIC REVOLUTION, AND ENLIGHTENMENT PHILOSOPHY

THE NORTHERN RENAISSANCE AND THE BAROQUE

The level of intellectual sophistication rose constantly in Europe during these years. The Renaissance, which had begun in Italy during the 1300s, spread to the rest of Europe and continued till approximately 1600. Important figures in this later, Northern Renaissance included the Dutch philosopher Desiderius Erasmus, the Spanish novelist Miguel de Cervantes, and the English poet and playwright William Shakespeare.

The cultural style that followed the Renaissance was the Baroque. The Baroque style dominated painting and architecture from the early 1600s through the early 1700s. In music, it lasted longer, until the mid-to-late 1700s. Baroque culture placed a large emphasis on the bold, the dynamic, the colorful, and the impressive. Another major trend of this era was the birth of opera.

THE MOVABLE-TYPE PRINTING PRESS AND ITS EFFECT ON EUROPEAN CULTURE

Another element in Europe's remarkable cultural development during the early modern period was the invention of the movable-type printing press by the German printer Johannes Gutenberg in the 1430s (see also Chapter 6).

Almost single-handedly, the printing press—which spread throughout Europe, then elsewhere—was responsible for raising literacy rates, spreading information, increasing the impact of new ideas and scientific theories, and encouraging the expansion of libraries and universities. The spread of Renaissance ideas from Italy to the rest of Europe was due largely to the printing press.

The printing press had even more of an impact on the religious debates that preceded, then caused, the Protestant Reformation: because an increasing number of people could read the Bible itself, not to mention the hundreds of essays and articles written for and against church reform, religious ideas had a much wider effect than they could ever have had before.

RENAISSANCE SCIENCE AND THE HELIOCENTRIC THEORY

Europe's scientific and technological aptitude increased during the early modern period. During the late Renaissance, certain thinkers and scholars were already moving away from the intellectual orthodoxy of the Middle Ages, in which a fixed set of ideas from the age of ancient Greece and Rome (especially selected theories from the writings of Aristotle, Ptolemy, and Galen) were combined with Catholic doctrine.

During the mid-1500s, despite the continued power and willingness of the Catholic Church to control European intellectual life, individuals like the Flemish doctor Andreas Vesalius and the Polish astronomer Nikolai Copernicus began to cross important scientific boundaries. Vesalius did pioneering work in the field of human anatomy. Even more famously, Copernicus provided astronomical and mathematical proof for the heliocentric theory, or the theory that the earth and other planets revolve around the sun. The Catholic Church favored the geocentric theory, in which the earth—home to what the Church considered God's greatest creation, human beings—was at the center of the universe. Because of this, it took more than another century before the heliocentric theory was accepted as fact throughout Europe.

THE SCIENTIFIC REVOLUTION

The pace of scientific discovery accelerated during the 1600s and early 1700s. Consequently, it is common to speak of these years as a period of scientific revolution in Europe. During this time, thinkers like René Descartes of France and Roger Bacon of England laid the groundwork for modern formal logic and revitalized the ancient concept of the scientific method.

Also during these years, astronomers such as the German Johannes Kepler and the Italian Galileo reconfirmed and popularized Copernicus's theories (Kepler also proved that the planets move in elliptical, not circular, orbits).

Many of the ideas that make up our basic understanding of science were discovered or proven during the Scientific Revolution. They include the states of matter (liquid, gas, or solid), the question of whether light is made up of waves or particles, the fact that living creatures are made up of cells, the existence of small blood vessels called capillaries, the concept of the vacuum, and the science of statistics. Among the basic scientific instruments invented or perfected during these years were the telescope, the microscope, the pendulum clock, the thermometer, and the barometer.

The single person who most represents the Scientific Revolution at its peak was Sir Isaac Newton (1642–1727) of England. Newton is famous for a number of ideas and discoveries, including his laws of motion, his laws of thermodynamics, his thoughts on the concept of gravity, and his role in inventing the mathematical system of calculus. The publication of his mathematical work *Principia* (1687) is considered one of the most important moments in European intellectual history. Just as important as all of these accomplishments, however, is the fact that Newton, more than any other figure of the Scientific Revolution, understood scientific thought as a totality. Newton was able to take all the discoveries and theories of his day, and tie them together into a single system of thought—Newtonian physics—backed up by mathematical proof. Not until Einstein's development of the theory of relativity at the beginning of the twentieth century would Newton's fundamental conception of how scientific principles operated be seriously challenged or altered.

THE AGE OF REASON (THE ENLIGHTENMENT)

During the 1700s, even more so than during the years of the Scientific Revolution, the educated public of Europe (still a very small segment of society, although it was growing) felt that it was living in a culturally and intellectually advanced era. Europeans—at least the middle and upper classes—considered themselves to have left behind what they thought of as the intellectual crudeness and superstitious darkness of the Middle Ages and even the 1500s and 1600s, with their wars over religion. The Europeans of this era put a great deal of faith in the power of human logic and rationality, as well as the recent discoveries of the Scientific Revolution, to solve problems and understand the world around them. Accordingly, it was common to refer to the 1700s as the Age of Reason or the Age of Enlightenment.

In addition to placing a heavy emphasis on science, Enlightenment culture also valued philosophy and ideas about how to make human society and government more just, more efficient, and more humane. Philosophical societies, salons, and literary circles appeared in all the major cities of the Western world during the 1700s, from Boston and Philadelphia in the United States to St. Petersburg and Moscow in Russia. Among the most important centers of Enlightenment thought were Edinburgh, London, and, most famously, Paris.

Women played a significant role in the Enlightenment. More women from the upper (and even middle) classes were gaining educations and proving that they were intellectually equal to men. A number of women became renowned for important Enlightenment writings and activities, including, late in the century, Mary Wollstonecraft of England (author of *A Vindication of the Rights of Women*) and Catherine the Great, Empress of Russia. Upper-class women, particularly in France, also played a key part in organizing and hosting the salons and gatherings at which much Enlightenment discussion and debate took place.

Among the most prominent Enlightenment philosophers were John Locke of England (a very early figure), Voltaire, Denis Diderot, and Baron Charles de Montesquieu (the latter three were from France). A later Enlightenment figure was Jean-Jacques Rousseau, also of France. All of these figures, as well as many other important thinkers, shared a faith in order and logic. Beyond that, however, not all of them had the same ideas about politics and society. All believed that government should be rationally organized and fairly regulated. Most believed in freedom of expression, opinion, and religion. Some, however, were monarchists (they simply felt that the monarch should govern according to law, not tyranny). Others, such as Rousseau, believed in granting more political power to ordinary people, although Rousseau viewed women as naturally inferior to men.

Some Enlightenment philosophers remained Christian (although they opposed religious war), others—especially Voltaire—opposed organized religion as a flawed human institution, and some became atheists altogether. Nonetheless, their common emphasis on reason and progress bound Enlightenment thinkers together. As described in Chapter 20, Enlightenment ideas played a crucial role in motivating several revolutions at the end of the 1700s, including those in America and France.

AGRICULTURAL REVOLUTION, POPULATION GROWTH, AND PROTO-INDUSTRIALIZATION

SOCIAL TRANSFORMATION DURING THE EARLY MODERN PERIOD

Europe experienced considerable social and economic change during the early modern period. From the late 1400s to the late 1700s, most European societies remained highly stratified, with a small upper class and large lower class. Societies were overwhelmingly rural, and agriculture was at the heart of most European economies.

However, more and more people began to move out of the lower classes into the slowly emerging middle class. More and more people left the countryside for the city. And, although agriculture remained extremely important, commerce and industry started to become key components in European economic systems. Another socioeconomic trend was population growth, at least during the 1700s.

CRISES OF THE SIXTEENTH AND SEVENTEENTH CENTURIES

The first two centuries of the early modern period—the 1500s and 1600s—were generally a time of social and economic crisis. Ecologically, Europe was still suffering from the "Little Ice Age" that had begun during the Late Middle Ages (see Chapter 6). Agricultural techniques, left over from the medieval era, were primitive. Crop failures and famines were common. As described previously, warfare, especially over religious disputes, was almost constant. Not only did combat kill people directly, but long, drawn-out wars interfered with agricultural production, spread disease, and caused mass starvation. The fledgling commercial, financial, and banking system that was being born in Europe during these years was highly susceptible to busts, bubbles, and periods of depression. Overall, populations declined or barely maintained their replacement level, depending on the part of Europe under consideration.

CLASS DIVERSIFICATION IN EIGHTEENTH-CENTURY EUROPE

European society began to change during the eighteenth century. The vast majority of people in Europe were still peasants. The royal families and noble classes of Europe made up a very small aristocracy. However, a steadily increasing percentage of people in most European societies began to make their living by some means other than agriculture. They became craftsmen, artisans, shopkeepers, or servants. They entered the world of banking and finance. They became merchants, or even professionals, such as doctors or lawyers. These people began to make up what is now referred to as the middle class. A larger proportion of people from the middle class—and even the lower classes—came to live in cities.

POPULATION GROWTH AND THE AGRICULTURAL REVOLUTION

The population of Europe began to grow considerably during the 1700s. Much of this growth had to do with what is known as the Agricultural Revolution—a great array of improvements in agricultural technology and technique. Thanks to pioneering work by scientists such as Charles Townshend and Jethro Tull (both from England), new ideas and methods for effective food growth began to appear. They included the aeration of soil, the use of iron plows rather than wooden ones, the rotation of crops (to avoid wearing out the nutrients in soil), the planting of seeds in rows (rather than scattering them by hand), and the systematic use of manure. As a result of the Agricultural Revolution, the number and severity of famines declined, the size and quality of crop yields increased, and the food supply of Europe was able to support much larger populations than ever before.

Another reason for the improved state of agriculture is that the Little Ice Age seems to have come to an end during the early 1700s. Also, new foods from North and South America—especially the potato and corn—revitalized European agriculture (see Chapters 14 and 19). Both corn and the potato were high-yield crops: even with a small amount of land and seed, one could gather a sizable harvest.

CAPITALISM AND PROTO-INDUSTRIALIZATION

Another important socioeconomic change for early modern Europe involved the birth of capitalism and proto-industrial economic production. Starting in the 1700s, a new theory of economics, based on the ideas of free trade, competition, and the market forces of supply and demand, began to take shape. This was capitalism, and it was in complete opposition to the standard economic approach of the Middle Ages and Renaissance: mercantilism, in which the state controlled economic activity as much as possible. Capitalist theories emerged in many parts of Europe, and even America, but the economist most associated with early capitalist thought is Adam Smith of Scotland. Smith's book, *The Wealth of Nations* (1776), is among the most influential economic treatises in modern history. Capitalism would become the Western world's dominant approach to economics during the 1800s.

Capitalism went hand-in-hand with the other emerging economic trend of the day: early industrialization, also known as proto-industrialization. Industrialization—the manufacture of items in a systematic, large-scale, and mechanized fashion—would not begin full-scale until the very end of the 1700s, then, especially, all during the 1800s. However, already during the early and middle 1700s, an increasingly large number of people would make their living—or at least part of their living—by producing goods, rather than working as peasants. Cottage industry (in which large manufacturers parceled work out to peasants or small shops), the "putting-out" system (in which textile mills hired women, often peasants, to do piecework at home), and large-scale craftsmanship were all part of what economic historians call proto-industrialization, the immediate precursor to the actual industrialization of Europe during the late 1700s and early 1800s.

WOMEN IN EARLY MODERN EUROPE

The status and rights of women changed considerably in early modern Europe. The degree of change depended mainly on class and geography. On the whole, women of the upper class gained much greater access to education and participated more actively in intellectual life than before. Many women in the gradually emerging middle class also tended to gain a growing amount of education. They assumed a greater economic role as business partners, bookkeepers, and operators of various enterprises (often, but not always, with their husbands). Generally women of all classes were gaining more control over when and whom they married, as well as matters such as divorce, childbirth, inheritance, and similar issues.

In no sense, however, were women considered equal to men, intellectually or economically. Nor did they have equal status or rights. The rates of death during childbirth were still high. Women made up the majority of victims—approximately 75 percent—in the witch hunts of the 1500s and 1600s. Both Catholicism and the new Protestant faiths maintained that women were inferior to and more sinful than men, and both used arguments based on scripture to reinforce these notions.

One area in which a select group of European women made significant progress was cultural and intellectual life. Many Catholic nuns maintained a high level of education. Protestantism's emphasis on literacy led great numbers of upper-class and middle-class women to gain at least some degree of learning.

A number of Renaissance, Baroque, and eighteenth-century painters were women. They included Artemesia Gentileschi of Italy and Elisabeth Vigée-Lebrun of France. Women took part in scientific life, although they were not allowed to become members of university faculties (except on extremely rare occasions) or join scientific societies. England's Margaret Cavendish wrote many scientific treatises during the 1600s. Also during the seventeenth century, German astronomer Maria Winkelmann became famous for discovering a comet.

Women also turned to writing and philosophy, especially during the eighteenth century. A key writer of the late 1700s was Mary Wollstonecraft, described previously. The role of women in the Enlightenment was also detailed previously.

Some of the most important monarchs of Europe's early modern period were women. Among them were Isabella of the Spanish kingdom of Castile, Elizabeth I of England, Maria Theresa of Austria, and Catherine the Great of Russia.

QUICK REVIEW

1. Which of the following best describes the general European sentiment toward religious affairs just before the 1500s?

   (A) Most people felt a devout, unquestioning allegiance to the Catholic Church.

   (B) Many people were turning toward Calvinist forms of worship.

   (C) Most people had become altogether apathetic about religion.

   (D) Many people doubted the Catholic Church's ability to provide spiritual leadership.

   (E) Most people were turning toward the teachings of Martin Luther.

2. France's role in the Thirty Years' War illustrates which of the following?

   (A) an emphasis on one's own geopolitical interests, rather than religious belief

   (B) a sincere commitment to pacifistic principles

   (C) the influence of religious faith on military decision making

   (D) a relentless pursuit of harsh military treatment of civilians

   (E) strict neutrality

3. What European country below did NOT develop an absolute form of monarchy during the 1600s and 1700s?

   (A) the Austrian Empire

   (B) the Netherlands

   (C) Spain

   (D) France

   (E) Russia

4. Which of the following is most likely to be a feature of parliamentary systems of monarchy?

   (A) higher levels of political repression

   (B) greater degree of religious intolerance

   (C) rigid class structures

   (D) elimination of poverty

   (E) flexible social systems

5. Europe's so-called Scientific Revolution accomplished which of the following?

   (A) led to the triumph of the geocentric theory

   (B) promoted the scientific theories of Aristotle and Galen

   (C) built on Descartes's and Bacon's revival of the scientific method

   (D) immediately swept away Catholicism's authority over intellectual affairs

   (E) provided universal education for the population of Europe

6. What grand and dynamic artistic and musical movement was largely associated with the Catholic Counter-Reformation?

   (A) the Renaissance

   (B) the Baroque

   (C) Rococo

   (D) Romanticism

   (E) Surrealism

7. Which of the following is NOT true about the emergence of capitalism in Europe?

   (A) One of the earliest advocates of capitalism was Adam Smith.

   (B) The rise of capitalism paralleled the rapid growth of Europe's middle class.

   (C) Capitalism operated according to the principle of economic competition.

   (D) Capitalist theory favored the lessening of governmental control over economic activity.

   (E) Capitalism involved greater governmental control over economic activity.

8. Which of the following applies to the early development of industrialization in Europe?

(A) A period of proto-industrialization during the 1600s and 1700s preceded the Industrial Revolution.

(B) The steam engine fueled industrial development during the late 1600s.

(C) There was almost no industrial or proto-industrial activity in Europe before the end of the 1700s.

(D) European industrialization was hindered by the rise of capitalism.

(E) Initiative on the part of the aristocracy was chiefly responsible for Europe's early industrialization.

9. Enlightenment thought is best characterized by which of the following?

(A) a complete rejection of religious faith

(B) a conviction that logic and reason were capable of solving social and political problems

(C) active advocacy of the rights of women to vote

(D) support of the established political order

(E) a deep faith in religious principles

10. Who among the following was associated with Enlightenment philosophy?

(A) Thomas Hobbes
(B) Voltaire
(C) Erasmus
(D) all of the above
(E) none of the above

ANSWERS:

1. **D**, p. 187	6. **B**, p. 192
2. **A**, p. 189	7. **E**, p. 196
3. **B**, p. 191	8. **A**, p. 196
4. **E**, p. 192	9. **B**, p. 194
5. **C**, p. 193	10. **B**, p. 194

CHAPTER 14

Age of Discovery, Age of Imperialism: The Western Campaign of Exploration and Colonization

Between the early-to-mid 1400s and the mid-to-late 1700s, the nations of Europe accomplished something that no other civilization had ever done: they explored the wider world around them, discovered how to sail around the globe, and mapped all the planet's major oceans and landmasses.

With this knowledge came might and wealth. From the very beginning of their campaign of world exploration, the nations of Europe began to establish control over the territories they encountered. They conquered and colonized. They forced open foreign markets. European explorers and generals were aided by superior technology, the fact that many of the peoples they conquered were vulnerable to European diseases, and, in many cases, sheer ruthlessness.

The legacy of Europe's age of exploration is mixed. On one hand, exploration gave the nations of Europe an unprecedented amount of geographical, navigational, and scientific knowledge. Colonization made Europe incredibly rich and powerful. It was during the years of exploration— and largely *because* of exploration—that Europe ceased to be one of the smallest and weakest of the world's important civilizations, and started to become the dominant culture on the planet.

On the other hand, there was a great moral and ethical price to pay for the knowledge and power Europe gained from exploration and colonization. Exploration and colonization went hand-in-hand with war, greed, prejudice, religious intolerance, and slavery. Many parts of the world remained under European rule for hundreds of years. Even now, long afterward, the long-standing tensions left over between Western nations and their former colonies continue to have an impact on international relations.

In general, the environments, populations, economies, and political systems of many peoples of the world were altered enormously by the Europeans' outward expansion. The effects of the Europeans' sudden incursion into other parts of the globe are detailed in other chapters in this unit.

ECONOMIC MOTIVATIONS AND TECHNOLOGICAL CAPABILITIES

EUROPE'S RELATIVE BACKWARDNESS BEFORE THE 1400s

Why and how did the Europeans become the first to explore the entire world? As noted in previous chapters, the peoples of Europe were, for many centuries, much less technologically and scientifically advanced than their neighbors in the Middle East or faraway cultures such as China. During the Middle Ages, any observer would have considered it unlikely that Europe would emerge as the leader in world exploration only a short time later.

Until the 1400s, the Europeans' geographical understanding of the world around them was limited. They knew the Mediterranean well. They were also familiar with the Baltic and North seas. Africa, the Middle East, Asia, and even Russia were unknown, inaccessible, or impassable. For the time being, the only outlet was the Atlantic Ocean—but this was frighteningly unfamiliar.

ECONOMIC MOTIVES FOR EXPLORATION

The Europeans' primary motivation for exploring further was economic. During the Middle Ages, the nations of Europe had become aware of the fabulous wealth of other parts of the world, especially to the east. The Europeans were also aware of how sophisticated and desirable many eastern goods were. Mediterranean trade, greater knowledge about the Middle East gained during the Crusades, and the tales of Marco Polo all whetted the Europeans' appetites for the wealth of far-off places such as China, the Indies, and Japan.

By the 1400s, the Europeans were dreaming of silk, metal goods, spices, fruit, jewels and precious metals, and other items unknown or in short supply in their own lands. If they could reach the Far East directly, rather than trading with middlemen in the Middle East, they would be able to gain access to these goods and make tremendous profits.

NEW NAVIGATIONAL AND MARITIME TECHNOLOGY

If the Europeans had become interested in traveling beyond their immediate locale by the 1400s, they were also developing the technology and knowledge to do so. Already by the 1300s, Europeans had learned the secret of the lodestone from the Chinese. Magnetized, and therefore always pointing north and south, the lodestone allowed the Europeans to create working compasses. Better knowledge of the stars (gained largely from the Arabs) and better navigational tools, such as the astrolabe and sextant, made it possible for European sailors to venture farther from shore without getting lost.

Naval technology improved as well. It was during the 1300s and 1400s that the Europeans began to build large, long ships. Large ships can carry large food supplies, and ships with longer hulls are able to sail faster. Both meant that Europeans were able to sail longer distances than ever before. Larger ships were also able to crest the huge waves of the open ocean without capsizing or breaking apart. Finally, more advanced systems of sails and rigging allowed ships to travel in almost any direction their captains wanted to go, even if the wind was not favorable.

Finally, European nations were beginning to incorporate gunpowder weapons into their armies and navies during the 1300s, 1400s, and onward. Although it was not until the 1500s and 1600s that the Europeans invented the huge gunships that eventually allowed them to carry massive firepower to every part of the globe, European sailors and soldiers came equipped with muskets, pistols, and small artillery pieces. Not only could they use gunpowder weapons at sea, but, perhaps more importantly, European explorers and conquerors would be able to use them against less technologically advanced native populations when they reached new lands.

THE IBERIAN WAVE OF EXPLORATION: SPAIN AND PORTUGAL

SPAIN AND PORTUGAL BEGIN TO EXPLORE

The first European nations to explore the wider Atlantic world were Portugal and Spain. As a result, the first expeditions of the age of exploration are sometimes referred to as the Iberian wave. Both the Portuguese and Spanish were on Europe's Atlantic frontier. They were close to Africa and the islands off Africa's coast. They had also gained a great deal of maritime experience in the Mediterranean, thanks to trade and a long series of naval wars against the Ottoman Turks.

Broadly speaking, Portuguese and Spanish exploration during the 1400s and early 1500s proceeded in two ways. First, the Portuguese attempted to reach the lands of the Far East by inching their way down the coast of Africa, rounding the continent, then sailing across the Indian Ocean to India and Southeast Asia. Second, and in the meantime, the Spanish—competing with the Portuguese—attempted to find their own route to China and the Indies by sailing west, around the world. Famously, the Spanish found the continents of North and South America instead, as well as an ocean previously unknown to them: the Pacific. Quickly, the Spanish and Portuguese figured out the relationship between the Atlantic and Pacific oceans. That understanding gave them a basic knowledge of the world's major landmasses and bodies of water. By the 1520s, they had succeeded in sailing around the globe for the first time in human history.

HENRY THE NAVIGATOR AND PORTUGAL'S EXPLORATION OF WEST AFRICA

The Portuguese began Europe's age of exploration. This achievement was due mainly to the efforts of Prince Henry (1394–1460), known popularly as Henry the Navigator. Henry created a maritime center and navigation school at the port of Sagres. From there, he and the princes who followed him sent out many voyages to the west and south, attempting to find a sea route to India and the Far East that would enable them to bypass the traders of the Middle East. The Portuguese claimed several Atlantic island groups, including the Madeiras and Azores. They also traveled down the western coast of Africa, conquering as well as exploring. They seized the Moroccan port of Ceuta in 1411. Soon afterward, they took the Cape Verde Islands. The Portuguese continued to expand along Africa's western shore until 1488. That year, Bartolomeu Diaz reached the southernmost tip of Africa. This completed the first leg of the journey to India, and, in honor of this, the Portuguese named the tip of Africa the Cape of Good Hope.

SPAIN, CHRISTOPHER COLUMBUS, AND THE "NEW WORLD"

In the meantime, the Spanish, distracted by the Reconquista, their war against the Moors (see Chapter 6), had not been as quick as their Portuguese neighbors to start exploring. Falling behind meant that, if the Spanish wanted their own sea route to the Far East, they would have to try something completely different. The result was the famous voyage of the Italian captain Christopher Columbus in 1492, sponsored by King Ferdinand and Queen Isabella.

What Columbus proposed to the Spanish government was to sail west in order to reach China and India. The boldness of his idea lay not in the idea that the world was round, because that was well known to most educated Europeans. What made his proposal striking were his beliefs that the world was small enough and that the Atlantic was open enough that an expedition would be able to sail from Spain to China or India without getting lost or running out of food and water.

Columbus set sail in August 1492, and his ships reached the islands of the Caribbean on October 12, 1492. This European encounter with the "New World"—the continents of North and South America—changed forever the history of the entire globe.

Despite the fact that Columbus remained convinced all his life that he had found the Indies (hence the mistaken term "Indians" for the Native Americans), the Spanish and Portuguese realized almost immediately that what Columbus had found were lands completely unknown to them. (Columbus's mistake is the main reason that the American continents are not named after him, but after Amerigo Vespucci, who consciously mapped the American coasts as new land-masses). The two countries turned to the pope to determine which of them would be allowed to claim which parts of the New World. In

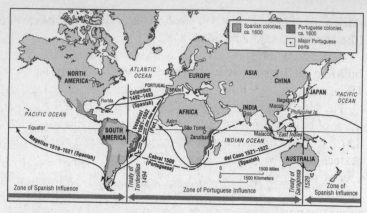

Spanish and Portuguese Exploration, 1492–1529.
The first European nations to explore and colonize the wider world were Spain and Portugal. Their successes are attested to in this map. The north-south lines of demarcation were established by the Papacy, to whose authority both nations, being Catholic, submitted.

lines of demarcation agreed to in 1493 and 1494, the pope gave jurisdiction of most of South America and all of North America to the Spanish. The Portuguese received only Brazil.

THE PORTUGUESE REACH INDIA

By the end of the 1490s, then, the Spanish and the Portuguese had two worlds to explore and conquer. The Portuguese continued to sail eastward to India, from the southern tip of Africa. In 1498, Vasco da Gama became the first European to reach India by sea. He returned in 1499 with his ships full of cargo. The profit from the voyage equaled sixty times the original investment, indicating how lucrative the business of exploration would eventually become.

MAGELLAN AND THE CIRCUMNAVIGATION OF THE GLOBE

Shortly thereafter, the Portuguese captain Ferdinand Magellan (sailing for Spain) led an expedition that tied together all of the efforts the Spanish and Portuguese had been making from the early 1400s onward. Magellan was inspired by the 1513 discovery of Panama by the Spanish explorer Vasco de Balboa. In the process, Balboa had become the first European to sight the Pacific Ocean from the New World. Hoping to cross both oceans, Magellan's ships left Europe in 1519 and traversed the Atlantic. They then rounded the tip of South America and made their way through the Pacific. Although Magellan himself died in the Philippine Islands, his ships reached India, sailed to Africa, then returned to Europe in 1522. This made Magellan's expedition the first ever to circumnavigate the globe.

SPANISH AND PORTUGUESE COLONIZATION

Having reached Africa, Southeast Asia, and the Far East on one hand, and the New World on the other, the Spanish and Portuguese also began to establish a colonial presence in all of these areas. In the Far East and Southeast Asia, there were many countries and regions that were too strong or too advanced for the Portuguese to conquer. For the most part, the Portuguese settled for trade. Still, there were areas they were able to seize, including the Indian port of Goa (1510), the thriving commercial center of Malacca (1511), and the island of Sri Lanka. Just as they had in western

Africa, the Portuguese took over much of the coast in east Africa, setting up strongholds in cities like Mombasa and Zanzibar.

In the New World, the Portuguese moved into Brazil during the early 1500s. The Spanish began building up their American empire in the Caribbean, using islands such as Cuba, Puerto Rico, and Hispaniola (today Haiti and the Dominican Republic) as bases.

The North and South American mainland fell to the conquistadors—generals who brought huge parts of both continents under Spanish control. Florida fell to Juan Ponce de León after 1513. From 1519 to 1521, Hernán Cortés waged a remarkably effective and brutal campaign against the Aztecs, ruled by Moctezuma II. The Aztec capital, Tenochtitlán, became Mexico City, the chief city of what the Spanish were now calling "New Spain." Later, the areas that are today California, Arizona, New Mexico, Colorado, Texas, Missouri, Louisiana, and Alabama were taken over by other conquistadors, such as Hernando de Soto, Francisco de Coronado, and Álvar Cabeza de Vaca. Farther to the south, Francisco Pizarro destroyed the mighty Incan Empire during the 1530s.

Both in Africa and the New World, Portuguese and Spanish colonies were originally intended to boost their home countries' power and wealth. Exploitation and extraction of raw materials were central to the Spanish and Portuguese colonial experience. Over time, the spread of Roman Catholicism became important as well. From the start, the Spanish and Portuguese attempted to use native Americans as slaves. When that failed, they began to bring slaves to the New World from Africa. More details on how the Spanish and Portuguese treated their new colonies are contained in future chapters, especially Chapters 18 and 19.

THE NORTHERN WAVE: FRANCE, THE DUTCH REPUBLIC, AND ENGLAND

THE NORTHERN WAVE OF EXPLORATION

During the 1500s, other European nations began to explore and colonize. The most important were France, the Dutch Republic, and England. These countries' involvement in European expansion is often called the northern wave.

For decades, the Spanish and Portuguese jealously guarded their geographical knowledge and their navigational techniques. They were especially anxious to lock the countries of northern Europe out of Atlantic exploration. At stake were military power, immense wealth, and religious rivalry (as described in Chapter 13, the Protestant Reformation divided Europe's Christian community into two bitterly feuding halves during the 1500s). During the early 1500s, the only area that countries like France, the Dutch Republic, and England were able to explore and settle was the northern coast of North America, which was seen as less desirable by the Spanish. One of the reasons these countries began to explore the northern parts of North America is that they were hoping to find an alternate route (a "Northwest Passage") to China and India through the Arctic.

Only after the middle of the sixteenth century were the French, the Dutch, and the English able to steal enough information, shadow enough Spanish and Portuguese ships, and gain enough independent knowledge about sea routes to begin their own campaigns of exploring and colonizing. All during the 1500s and 1600s, for the French, English, and Dutch to explore and colonize typically meant also fighting the Spanish and Portuguese—either at sea, or on land, as the new arrivals tried to take colonial territories away from the older powers.

FRENCH EXPLORATION AND COLONIZATION

France's first major encounter with the New World came in the 1520s, when the Italian captain Giovanni da Verrazano (commissioned by the French) surveyed the Atlantic coast from what is now North Carolina to Newfoundland. From 1534 to 1541, Jacques Cartier traced the course of the St. Lawrence River, taking the first step in France's settlement of Canada. France established its first cities in Canada in the early 1600s: Port Royal in Nova Scotia (1605) and Quebec, founded by Samuel Champlain (1608). The principal reason for colonizing Canada was to take advantage of the rich supply of animal furs there.

Later in the 1600s, the French also moved southward, exploring the Great Lakes and major rivers. In 1673, Louis Joliet and Father Jacques Marquette, traveling westward from the Great Lakes, discovered the Mississippi River and did much to map its northern reaches. In 1682, René Robert de la

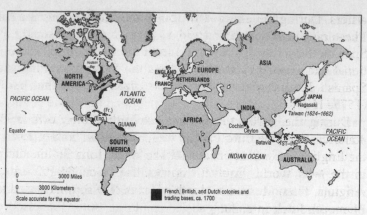

French, English, and Dutch Colonization by 1700.
During the late 1500s and 1600s, France, England, and the Netherlands began to compete with the Spanish and Portuguese for overseas possessions. Over time, the northern countries broke the Iberian nations' monopoly on trade routes and navigational knowledge. By 1700, France, England, and the Netherlands had gained many imperial footholds in North America, South America, the Caribbean, Africa, and Asia.

Salle sailed down the entire length of the Mississippi, claiming land for France, even though much of this territory was already under Spanish control. During the late 1600s and 1700s, the French would take much of the Mississippi basin and some of the coast of the Gulf of Mexico away from the Spanish. This large French holding in what is today the United States was called Louisiana (different from the state that currently bears the name).

DUTCH EXPLORATION AND COLONIZATION

Dutch exploration was, at first, closely tied to the war of independence the Dutch Republic fought against Spain, starting in the 1560s. An important part of the Dutch strategy was to fight the Spanish at sea and, if possible, disrupt their connections with their colonies. Soon, the Dutch began to do the same to the Portuguese. By the 1590s, the Dutch were actually seizing colonies from the Portuguese: the Spice Islands in 1595, the Southeast Asian port of Malacca in 1641, the island of Sri Lanka, much of west Africa, and a number of Caribbean islands. To manage their colonies in Asia, the Dutch formed the Dutch East India Company (1602). The Dutch also began to invade many islands of Indonesia, where they would maintain a colonial presence for hundreds of years. They ran pepper and spice plantations on the island of Sumatra. On Java, they established the colonial capital of Batavia (1619), now the Indonesian capital Jakarta.

The Dutch became involved in North American colonization as well. In 1609, they commissioned the English sailor Henry Hudson to explore the bay and river that now bear his name. In 1624, Dutch settlers purchased the island of Manhattan from the local Native Americans. There they built a sizable city called New Amsterdam. That city would eventually become New York, after the English took it from the Dutch in the mid-1600s.

ENGLISH EXPLORATION AND COLONIZATION

Although England did not begin a major campaign of exploration until after the mid-1500s, it did establish legal claim to parts of North America as early as the 1490s, thanks to the voyages of John Cabot, who attempted to find an Arctic passage to India, Japan, and China through Canadian waters. During the mid-to-late 1500s, the English fought a series of naval wars with the Spanish. These ranged all over the world, as English captains sought to harass Spanish colonies or capture Spanish treasure ships returning from the New World. The English gained a great deal of navigational and geographical knowledge from these wars. For example, in the process of fighting the Spanish, English mariner Sir Francis Drake became the first Englishman to sail around the world (1577–1580).

During the 1600s, the English established their own colonies on the eastern coast of North America, from the Carolinas up to the Canadian border. Two colonies failed during the 1580s. But the English settlement of Jamestown, led by John Smith, survived and gave the English a foothold in the New World. English Puritans, the so-called Pilgrims, came to America as well, seeking religious freedom. Famously, the first such Pilgrims sailed across on the *Mayflower*, landing at Plymouth Rock in 1620.

The English made incursions into South Asia as well. Their first expedition to the Indies came in 1591. Shortly afterward, the English founded the British East India Company (1600), to manage economic—and, later, military—relations with South and Southeast Asia. The English landed at Surat, in northwestern India, in 1608, and would gradually take over more and more of India. The English seized the Southeast Asian port of Malacca from the Dutch in 1795.

As with the Spanish and Portuguese, the countries of the northern wave were eager to gain military strength and, especially, economic wealth from their colonies. The English were also eager to turn their colonies into genuinely permanent settlements (something other colonizing powers were, for a long time, not interested in doing). Exploitation of natural resources—and of the native populations—was the norm. Like the Spanish and Portuguese, the French and English brought slaves to the New World from Africa (see Chapters 18 and 19 for more on this).

QUICK REVIEW

1. Which European nation first began a sustained campaign of exploration?

   (A) France
   (B) Portugal
   (C) the Netherlands
   (D) England
   (E) Austria

2. What made Christopher Columbus's proposed voyage in 1492 unusual was

   (A) his new theory that the world was round
   (B) that his recent invention, the compass, would shorten sailing times across the Atlantic
   (C) that the world was small enough that a ship could sail from Europe to the Far East by going westward
   (D) his hope that an undiscovered continent lay to the west of Europe
   (E) his intention to circumnavigate the globe

3. Which of the following helped to encourage the Europeans to explore the wider world?

   (A) Marco Polo's reports of the riches found in China
   (B) exposure to Middle Eastern trade during the Crusades
   (C) a desire for foodstuffs, especially spices, not available in Europe
   (D) all of the above
   (E) none of the above

4. What was Portugal's principal colony in Latin America?

   (A) Chile
   (B) Ecuador
   (C) Mexico
   (D) Belize
   (E) Brazil

5. Whose authority arbitrated Spain's and Portugal's rival claims in the New World?

(A) the pope
(B) the Holy Roman emperor
(C) the prince of Portugal
(D) the United Nations
(E) the king of Spain

6. Which parts of the New World did the French colonize during the 1500s and 1600s?

(A) Mexico and Brazil
(B) Massachusetts and New York
(C) Canada and the Mississippi Valley
(D) the mid-Atlantic coast
(E) Canada and Cuba

7. Primarily from which country did the Dutch seize colonies in Southeast Asia?

(A) Spain
(B) Portugal
(C) England
(D) France
(E) none of the above

8. Which Spanish conquistador conquered the Aztecs and took Mexico for Spain?

(A) Cortés
(B) Pizarro
(C) Coronado
(D) Ponce de León
(E) Cabeza de Vaca

9. Which of the following became England's first successful colony in North America?

(A) Plymouth Rock
(B) Charleston
(C) Pennsylvania
(D) Jamestown
(E) New York

10. Early on, what factor played the greatest role in determining where France, England, and the Netherlands were able to explore and colonize?

(A) their climatic preference for cooler environments
(B) their relative technological backwardness in comparison to Spain and Portugal
(C) their peace treaties with Spain and Portugal
(D) the authority of the pope
(E) Spain's and Portugal's temporary monopolies on navigational knowledge

ANSWERS:

1. **B**, p. 201	6. **C**, p. 203
2. **C**, p. 201	7. **B**, p. 204
3. **D**, p. 200	8. **A**, p. 203
4. **E**, p. 203	9. **D**, p. 205
5. **A**, p. 202	10. **E**, p. 201

CHAPTER 15

Islamic Empires in the Middle East and Africa

The unity of the single Islamic state, the Abbasid Caliphate, stretching from Spain to India, had vanished during the 1200s. Decades of chaos and confusion followed, as Mongol warriors invaded and the Seljuk and Ottoman Turks rose up as regional powers.

Afterward, however, strong Islamic empires emerged in place of the fallen caliphate: the Ottoman Empire, the Safavid Empire in Persia, and the Mughal Empire in India (the last is described in Chapter 17). All three were extremely centralized, technologically advanced, and militarily powerful. They are commonly referred to as the "gunpowder empires," because of their mastery of new weaponry and their effective use of it in accumulating regional might.

The grandest and most influential of the Islamic states was the Ottoman Empire. It was also the longest lasting, with a geopolitical role to play on three continents: Africa, Asia, and Europe. Its neighbor to the east, Persia's Safavid Empire, was also impressive. But it was clearly not as strong as the Ottoman state, and it did not survive nearly as long.

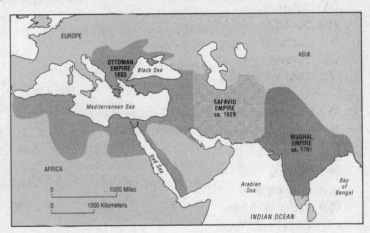

The Islamic World's Gunpowder Empires, ca. 1629–1707.
So named because of their effective and innovative use of new military technology, the gunpowder empires of the Islamic world included Ottoman Turkey, Safavid Persia, and Mughal India. All were significant Eurasian powers during the sixteenth and seventeenth centuries, but declined during the eighteenth and nineteenth.

THE OTTOMAN EMPIRE

ORIGINS OF THE OTTOMAN TURKS

Like all Turkic tribes, the Ottomans originated in the steppes of Central Asia. They migrated westward, to Asia Minor (now Turkey) during the 1200s. They were vassals of the Seljuk Turks, but established their own state, under Osman I, in 1280. They gained power and territory during the 1300s and early 1400s.

THE OTTOMAN STATE

The Ottoman sovereign was the sultan. His ministers were *wazirs*, or viziers (their head was the grand vizier). The sultan ruled with the help of provincial governors called *beys* (or "knights"). Other local officials, especially in the Ottomans' African possessions, were *pashas*. As time passed, the Ottoman sultans centralized their empire more tightly, controlling affairs of state from the Topkapi ("Cannon Gate") Palace in the capital, Istanbul. In the early 1500s, the sultan claimed the status of caliph, giving himself religious as well as political authority.

OTTOMAN MILITARY CONQUESTS

The Ottoman Empire was a mighty conquest state. Under a series of aggressive sultans, it had moved into the Balkans by the late 1300s, and its navies gained hegemony over the eastern Mediterranean. One of the great military triumphs of the Ottoman Empire was the destruction of the Byzantine Empire in 1453. That year, the 80,000-strong army of Sultan Mehmed II (1451–1481) captured the city of Constantinople, after besieging and bombarding it with 26-foot-long cannon that fired ammunition weighing 1,200 pounds. After seizing Constantinople, Mehmed turned it into his new capital of Istanbul.

Further conquests followed during the late 1400s and early 1500s. Selim I moved into North Africa (see subsequent discussion). Ottoman forces pushed farther into Europe, moving along the valley of the Danube River. They seized the Romanian province of Wallachia in 1476, then paused for the next four and a half decades (this time was spent fighting in the Middle East and Africa, as well as consolidating domestic affairs).

Another huge—and much more successful—thrust into Europe came under Suleiman I the Magnificent (1520–1566); the greatest of the Ottoman sultans. Suleiman resumed the Ottoman assault on the Danube Valley and the territories of Romania, Hungary, and Austria's Holy Roman Empire. In 1521, the Ottomans took Belgrade. In 1526, they shattered the Kingdom of Hungary at the battle of Mohács. By 1529, they had reached the outskirts of Vienna. The Austrians pushed the Turks back somewhat, but the Ottomans now controlled a vast part of southeastern Europe. Moreover, the Turkish fleet enjoyed almost complete superiority in the Mediterranean until the end of the 1500s—and remained a deadly enemy even afterward. The Ottoman presence in Europe would linger until after World War I, in the twentieth century.

The Blue Mosque, Istanbul, Turkey.
Officially known as the Sultan Ahmed Mosque, this seventeenth-century masterpiece is popularly known as the Blue Mosque. One of the great landmarks of Istanbul, the Blue Mosque is one of the many places of Islamic worship the Ottoman sultans constructed there after Mehmed II took the city, formerly Constantinople, from the Byzantine Empire. The Blue Mosque is unusual in having six minarets, rather than the usual four.

THE OTTOMAN MILITARY

During the 1500s and first two thirds of the 1600s, the Ottoman Empire was at its military and organizational peak. As one of the Islamic world's three "gunpowder empires," Ottoman Turkey was, at least in the beginning, innovative in its adoption of military technology and capable in the administration of its armies and navies. During the 1400s, the sultans had begun to incorporate gunpowder artillery, or cannon, into their armies. Later the Ottoman navy placed cannon on its ships.

The sultans also supplemented the traditional cavalry (who were not only outdated, but more loyal to local beys than to the sultan) with elite soldiers called janissaries (from *yeni cheri*, or "new troops"). Janissaries were specifically recruited, at childhood, from conquered Christian communities. They were converted to Islam and raised to be loyal to the sultan. Although they were essentially slaves, they were given many privileges. They received advanced training as modern infantry, and they were equipped with new gunpowder weapons. For many years, the janissary system, although harsh, kept Ottoman Turkey at the forefront of world military affairs.

RELIGIOUS POLICY AND THE OTTOMAN POLITICAL SYSTEM

Also during the 1500s and early 1600s, the Ottomans proved efficient in governing their large territory, as well as the diverse population that lived there. The Ottomans did not just rule over Sunni Muslims, but also members of the Shiite minority. They governed Jews, in addition to several types of Christians: Orthodox, Nestorian, Coptic, Catholic, and Protestant. Many tongues—especially Turkish, Arabic (Islam's holy language), and Persian—were spoken in the empire. Both for political and economic reasons, the sultans practiced relative religious tolerance: non-Muslims were allowed to convert to Islam if they wished, but were not forced to do so. They did not have completely equal rights, they were not permitted to serve in the military, and they had to pay a special head tax. Still, non-Muslims were, on the whole, not treated badly. This policy kept the peace, and the extra tax revenue was economically beneficial. Each religious group (Muslims included) was grouped into an administrative unit called a *millet* ("nation"): there was a Jewish millet, an Orthodox Christian millet, and so on.

The sultan's position was hereditary, although the eldest son did not always inherit. This practice was largely due to the fact that the sultan typically did not marry, but fathered his heirs with a number of enslaved concubines. Concubines lived in the harem ("sacred place"). A concubine whose son was chosen to become the sultan's heir was known as the queen mother, and generally enjoyed a great deal of influence as an adviser to the sultan and her son. When a new sultan came to power, he often killed his brothers to eliminate potential competition. The preferred method of execution was strangling.

WOMEN IN THE OTTOMAN EMPIRE

Among the Ottoman elite, women played several influential, albeit informal, roles. The sultan's mother, or queen mother, ran the household and could be involved in diplomatic relations with foreign officials. Queen mothers controlled marriage alliances.

Despite its popular reputation, the harem was not simply a collection of concubines for the sultan's pleasure. The harem was a complex elite social network. Many of its members were originally slaves (slaves could not be Islamic) or prisoners. Male members of the harem were trained for military or administrative positions, while concubines were educated to read the Qu'ran, to sew, and to perform music. Members of the harem were ranked by status, and some could leave the harem to marry officials. Few of the women in the imperial harem were used for sexual purposes. In fact, most of them were members of the sultan's extended family. These women also gained influence over male rulers by raising them as boys and training them to respect their guidance.

Outside the imperial family, women on the whole were not seen in public in Istanbul or other major cities. However, women had the right to own property and retain property after marriage. According to court records, women took part in the urban real estate market through male agents. They sold inherited shares in their fathers' estate, bought and sold real estate, and founded religious endowments. Women could even testify for themselves in court.

THE LONG DECLINE OF THE OTTOMAN EMPIRE

The last truly gifted Ottoman sultan was Suleiman the Magnificent. In addition to being a talented commander, he was an excellent domestic ruler. Because of his gift for governance, he is often referred to as Suleiman the Lawgiver. Few of the sultans who followed had Suleiman's qualities, and many were mediocre or worse.

In Europe, the Ottomans made one last attempt at a major offensive, during the late 1600s. The attack almost succeeded, but was turned back in 1683. That year, the Turks placed Vienna, capital of the Holy Roman Empire, under siege. At the last minute, Vienna was saved by a massive Austrian counteroffensive (greatly assisted by other Catholic allies, especially the Poles, whose cavalry, led by King Jan Sobieski, played a key role in the battle). Afterward, the Europeans pushed the Ottomans back to the east. The Turks were not expelled from Europe, but they lost much territory from 1683 to 1718.

During the 1700s, the Ottomans fought the Europeans—especially the Austrians and Russians—frequently. But they never again succeeded in launching a substantial attack against Europe. The Turks' power declined steadily during the 1700s and 1800s. By the 1800s, the Ottoman Empire was, in a bit of black humor, being routinely referred to as the "sick man of Europe."

OTTOMAN CULTURE

The culture of the Ottoman Empire was sophisticated. Its level of intellectual advancement was high. However, after the 1500s and early 1600s, the Ottomans lost the huge scientific and technological advantages they had enjoyed over their European neighbors. Partly because of Europe's Scientific Revolution (see Chapter 13), partly because of the Turks' own complacency, the Ottoman Empire started to fall behind the nations of Europe in terms of learning and innovation.

Nonetheless, the Ottomans were skilled at art, literature, and music. Perhaps the field at which they excelled the most was architecture. The best-known of the Ottoman architects is Sinan: during the mid-1500s, he designed eighty-one mosques (Islamic places of worship) with large domes and tall, thin minarets. The Turks were also renowned for their mosaics.

NORTH AFRICA UNDER THE OTTOMAN EMPIRE

Just as North Africa had converted to Islam from the late 600s onward, much of the region fell to the Ottomans. During the early 1500s, Selim I (1512–1520) conquered Egypt. He also declared himself caliph; as described previously, this (at least in theory) gave the sultan religious authority over all Sunni Muslims, including those in North Africa.

Moving westward from Egypt, the Ottomans took most of Africa's northern coast. They captured the ports of Tripoli, Tunis, and Algiers, as well as many other cities.

The Turkish presence in North Africa was mainly restricted to the coast. Further to the south, the Ottomans made sure to establish their control over the trade routes that crossed the Sahara. They also supervised the trading towns along the Niger River and other waterways. Beyond that, the Turks ruled relatively lightly, leaving day-to-day administration to local officials and appointed governors called pashas.

THE SAFAVID EMPIRE IN PERSIA

PERSIA UNDER ISLAMIC INFLUENCE

Since Islam's early days, the land of Persia (now Iran) had been an important part of the Muslim world. It had been absorbed by the Umayyad and Abbasid caliphates, then, during the 1200s to 1400s, controlled by various Mongol and Turkic warlords. By the end of the 1400s, however, a power struggle began that would gain Persia its independence and give birth to a new Islamic empire there.

ESTABLISHMENT OF THE SAFAVID EMPIRE

In 1501, a fifteen-year-old boy named Ismail gained control of Persia (as well as much of Iraq), took the ancient title of shah, and established the Safavid Empire. The name came from the Islamic sect to which Ismail belonged. The Safavids were strict Shiite Muslims (see Chapter 5), and Ismail's main priority as shah of Persia was to convert the population to the Shiite denomination. Ismail died in 1526, and his descendants continued the conversion.

ABBAS THE GREAT AND THE SAFAVID ARMY

The Safavid rulers also fought their neighbors. In the west, the Ottomans were a constant threat. Conflict between the Persians and the Central Asians (especially the Uzbeks) to the east was frequent. Military strength was crucial to Safavid Persia's survival. Consequently, it (like Ottoman Turkey and Mughal India) built itself up into a gunpowder empire.

The most famous Safavid shah, Abbas I the Great (1587–1628), created a new, highly effective army. He combined traditional cavalry (aristocratic troops armed with bows) with modern infantry troops, equipped with gunpowder weapons (like the Ottoman janissaries, these soldiers were slaves). In addition to being a good military organizer, Abbas was an excellent administrator and a culturally and intellectually tolerant ruler.

ISFAHAN AND SAFAVID TRADE

The original capital of Safavid Persia had been Tabriz. Abbas moved the government to Isfahan, Persia's grandest metropolis (and still one of the jewels of Iran today). An architecturally magnificent city, Isfahan also became Persia's most important trading center. Safavid Persia was famous for its silk (for years, Persia, like China in past centuries, maintained a monopoly on silk production), as well as ceramic tiles, glassware, and metalwork. It was even better known for the carpets it produced, and Persian rugs are still highly valued today.

THE DECLINE OF SAFAVID PERSIA

Like the Ottoman Empire, Safavid Persia declined during the late 1600s and 1700s. Unlike the Ottomans, the Safavid Empire collapsed altogether during the early 1700s. Persia was not completely landlocked, but it lacked major ports and never built a navy of any size. This circumstance made the Safavids militarily weak. It also put them at a distinct disadvantage when it came to trade. Persia's economy began to slump during the 1600s. The Safavids also came under constant attack from the east. In 1722, Isfahan was sacked by Afghan raiders. It was a crippling blow, and, in 1723, the Safavid dynasty fell altogether.

QUICK REVIEW

1. What group rose to dominate the Middle East during the 1400s and afterward?

    (A) the Safavid Persians
    (B) the Egyptian Mamluks
    (C) the Berbers
    (D) the Ottoman Turks
    (E) the Kurds

2. What was the greatest military triumph of the Ottoman Empire during the 1400s?

    (A) the invasion of Albania
    (B) the capture of Constantinople
    (C) the siege of Vienna
    (D) the battle of Mohács
    (E) the annexation of Moldavia

3. The janissaries were

    (A) elite gunpowder troops recruited from Christian communities
    (B) aristocratic cavalry units from the Egyptian provinces
    (C) mercenary crossbowmen from East Asia
    (D) artillery specialists
    (E) skilled naval commanders

4. Which of the following applies to Suleiman I?

    (A) he was known as the "Magnificent"
    (B) he led a highly successful campaign of conquest in southeastern Europe
    (C) he was a wise and skilled domestic ruler
    (D) all of the above
    (E) none of the above

5. What best describes the religious policy of the Ottoman rulers?

    (A) ruthless suppression of non-Islamic faiths
    (B) relative tolerance of religious minorities
    (C) complete acceptance of non-Islamic faiths
    (D) expulsion of non-Islamic minorities
    (E) gradual conversion from Islam to Christianity

6. The basic unit of religious categorization in the Ottoman Empire was

    (A) the exarchy
    (B) the parish
    (C) the umma
    (D) the caste
    (E) the millet

7. Which of the following are among the areas that fell under Ottoman rule?

    (A) Egypt, Hungary, Turkey
    (B) Persia, Egypt, Serbia
    (C) Tunisia, Spain, Hungary
    (D) Greece, Austria, Egypt
    (E) Egypt, Persia, Spain

8. What moment marked the high point— and the end—of the Ottoman advance into Europe?

    (A) the 1476 capture of Wallachia
    (B) the 1521 seizure of Belgrade
    (C) the 1529 siege of Vienna
    (D) the 1683 siege of Vienna
    (E) the 1718 treaty of Passarowitz

9. The official religion of the Safavid Empire was

    (A) Sunni Islam
    (B) Orthodox Christianity
    (C) Shiite Islam
    (D) Judaism
    (E) Hinduism

10. The most successful and militarily adept of the Safavid rulers was

(A) Akbar the Great
(B) Abbas the Great
(C) Babur the Tiger
(D) Ismail
(E) Muhammad Ali

ANSWERS:

1. **D**, p. 207
2. **B**, p. 208
3. **A**, p. 209
4. **D**, p. 208
5. **B**, p. 209
6. **E**, p. 209
7. **A**, p. 208
8. **D**, p. 210
9. **C**, p. 211
10. **B**, p. 211

CHAPTER 16

China, Japan, and East Asia

Between the 1400s and 1700s, China and Japan consolidated their position as the dominant powers of East Asia. Under the Ming dynasty, which had been established in 1368, China reached a peak of cultural grandeur and elegance. Even after 1644, when a younger dynasty, the Qing (Manchu), arose, the Chinese enjoyed a tremendous level of artistic and intellectual sophistication, as well as significant military and political prominence in East Asia.

As for Japan, it began this period disunited and divided. For more than two centuries—the mid-1300s through the late 1500s—Japan tore itself apart in countless feudal wars and civil conflicts. During the late 1500s and early 1600s, however, Japan finally reunified, becoming a single country for the first time in hundreds of years. The government that completed the reunification, the Tokugawa Shogunate, established strict control over Japanese politics and society. It would rule until after the mid-1800s. Like China, Japan was a considerable local power in East Asia.

In terms of global politics, however, a major change was taking place that not even the Chinese or Japanese were aware of. Despite their cultural advancement and their tightly-knit societies, China and Japan were beginning to slip in terms of the international balance of power. Both countries were losing the scientific and technological advantages they had possessed during the period between 1000 and 1450. This power shift, which resulted from a certain stagnation on the part of China and Japan, would leave both countries—especially the former—vulnerable to foreign influence and domination during the 1800s.

MING CHINA

In 1450, the Ming dynasty was almost a century old. From its foundation in 1368 to the early 1400s, Ming China had been a politically dynamic and militarily active state, conquering neighbors and exploring faraway lands. Ming China was economically prosperous. Its population grew steadily during the late 1300s and 1400s, recovering from the wars and diseases of the late Yuan period.

MING CULTURE

Although Ming China remained powerful during the 1500s and early 1600s, its principal strengths during these years were cultural. As described in Chapter 8, the artistic and intellectual achievements of the Ming were impressive: literary masterpieces, fine porcelain ("china"), architecture, and the revival of Confucianism.

THE ARRIVAL OF THE EUROPEANS

It was also during the Ming period that the first European explorers began to arrive. As Portuguese traders and captains arrived in Southeast Asia and colonized parts of it, they established commercial ties with the Ming. The Spanish arrived later. China was too large and powerful for the Portuguese or Spanish to conquer, but both nations established embassies and trading houses there.

Catholic missionaries were important as well. Among the most famous were Francis Xavier, who worked in China during the 1540s and 1550s, and Matteo Ricci, who was there in the 1590s and early 1600s.

THE DECLINE AND COLLAPSE OF THE MING

The 1600s were a time of rapid decline for the Ming. The late Ming rulers were weak and allowed the government to decentralize, then unravel. The Portuguese and Spanish traded with silver from North and South America, and the sudden, massive influx of precious metal triggered inflation, then economic breakdown. At the same time, agricultural yields shrank (perhaps because of a worsening of soil quality or a general cooling of the climate). The population was growing more quickly than the land's ability to support it.

Finally, revolution and war drove the Ming to collapse. Serious military threats came from Central Asia, Mongolia, and Manchuria. The huge cost of defending China's long borders drained the economy, leaving the country open to attack. A massive peasant revolt, which lasted from 1636 to 1644, toppled the Ming dynasty. The last Ming emperor, Chung-cheng, committed suicide, after first having tried to kill his family.

The victory of the peasant rebellion was short-lived, however. Within a few weeks of Chung-cheng's death, enemies from the north, the Manchus, swept into northern China, took Beijing, and established a new dynasty.

THE QING (MANCHU) CONQUEST OF CHINA

THE MANCHUS AND THE ESTABLISHMENT OF THE QING EMPIRE

The Manchus were from Manchuria, the large region to the north and east of China itself. Although they were related to the Chinese, the Manchus were ethnically distinct. For many years, the Manchu rulers created an ethnically based system of social stratification, in which the Chinese, as a subject people, were forced to wear certain clothing and to wear their hair in long braids, or queues. Males had to shave their foreheads, as reflected in a Chinese proverb of the time: "lose your hair or lose your head."

The empire established by the Manchus was called the Qing (or Ch'ing, 1644–1911). It included Manchuria, then, after 1644, northern China. Skilled warlords, the Manchus continued their conquests. By 1683, they had absorbed southern China into their empire, as well as the large island of Formosa (now Taiwan).

The Manchus also controlled or added to their tributary system areas such as Mongolia, Tibet, Nepal, Burma, and much of Central Asia. Qing expansion to the north and west also brought the Chinese into contact with Russia, which was moving into Siberia and East Asia by the 1600s and 1700s. It took much negotiation for the Chinese and Russians to arrive at a mutually acceptable boundary.

QING ECONOMICS

Full-scale trade with European nations began under the Qing, during the 1690s. Foreign trade was closely regulated by the state, and by the 1750s, it was directed exclusively through the port of Canton. Along with silk and porcelain, China's most important commodity was tea. While the Qing Empire sent a high volume of exports to other nations, it allowed few imports, giving it a highly favorable balance of trade.

EMPERORS KANGXI AND QIANLONG

During the late 1600s and early 1700s, the Qing emperors were capable rulers, good administrators, and strong centralizers. The emperor Kangxi (1662–1722) is widely considered to be one of the greatest monarchs in Chinese history: a skilled general, a just lawgiver, and a sponsor of culture and learning. Kangxi bolstered the imperial authority of the Qing by patronizing Confucianism, with its emphasis on respect for authority. Another eighteenth-century ruler, Qianlong (1736–1795), was the last intelligent, dynamic ruler the Qing had. He strengthened China's borders, fostered economic growth, and promoted scholarship.

THE FIRST STAGES OF QING DECLINE

After Qianlong, however, the quality of the Qing rulers declined. They grew softer and less active. Also, as during the late Ming period, the Chinese population grew steadily—and much faster than the economy (population surpassed 300 million by 1799). Over time, national wealth was barely sufficient to support the population. For all but the upper classes, poverty worsened.

Overall, despite its strength as a regional power, Qing China was slipping backward in terms of technological innovation, scientific advancement, and global power. By the early-to-mid 1800s, China would be increasingly open to European and American influence, then domination.

FEUDAL WAR AND REUNIFICATION IN JAPAN

JAPANESE FEUDALISM AND THE SHOGUNATES

As discussed in Chapter 8, Japan had been governed by a series of military governments called shogunates since 1185. During the 1200s and most of the 1300s, the shogunates—the Kamakura (1185–1333) and Ashikaga (1336–1573)—preserved order and kept Japan relatively unified.

However, decentralization became an increasingly serious problem during the late 1300s and early 1400s. Although, in theory, the Ashikaga Shogunate ruled the entirety of Japan, the country was, in reality, breaking down into a patchwork of independent or semi-independent feudal states. The rulers of these small states were nobles called daimyo. Just as most medieval European nobles had been knights, most Japanese daimyo belonged to the warrior elite called samurai.

THE ONIN WAR AND JAPANESE DISUNITY

In 1467, the gradual breakdown of Japan suddenly turned into a condition of anarchy and collapse. A civil conflict called the Onin War broke out that year and lasted till 1477. Even its conclusion did not heal the country's political wounds. For the next hundred years, Japan slipped into a state of chaos and disunity known as the "Era of Independent Lords." Daimyo fought daimyo constantly, and each treated his own territory as if it were an autonomous state. Samurai troops, loyal to their daimyo masters, followed the code of Bushido, or "way of the warrior." Samurai who left their masters or whose masters were killed were known as *ronin*. They often served as mercenaries or became bandits.

THE REUNIFICATION OF JAPAN

The reunification of Japan was a five-and-a-half decade process that lasted from 1560 to 1615. Three men brought about the unification; all of them were politician-warlords who used both force and diplomacy to bring their country together.

First was the general Oda Nobunaga, one of the first military leaders to use gunpowder weapons in Japan (especially at the battle of Nagashino in 1573). Nobunaga fought from 1560 onward, establishing his rule over eastern and central Japan. In 1582, before he could complete full unification, he was assassinated by one of his followers.

The second of Japan's unifiers, Toyotomi Hideyoshi, brought almost all of the country back together again as a single nation. However, he failed to create a political system that could survive his death. A man of humble origins (and therefore never able to assume the title of shogun, even after he became ruler), Hideyoshi became Nobunaga's successor in 1582. By 1590, he had united most of Japan, and he ruled the country from his own capital, Osaka, until his death in 1598. A good general and clever politician, Hideyoshi did much to centralize Japan and tame the power of the previously independent daimyo. Unfortunately for him, he died before his son reached adulthood. Soon after 1598, the five men Hideyoshi had appointed as regents for his son began to fight each other—and rebel against their boy ruler.

TOKUGAWA IEYASU

The victor—and ultimate unifier of Japan—was Tokugawa Ieyasu, a brilliant, ruthless commander. In 1600, Ieyasu defeated his fellow regents at the battle of Sekigahara, a pivotal moment in Japanese military history. In 1603, he appointed himself shogun. By 1615, Ieyasu had captured Osaka, defeated Hideyoshi's son, and forced him to kill himself. From that moment forward, Ieyasu and his descendants would be the masters of Japan. Of course, as all shoguns did, they technically ruled in the name of the emperor, who was cloistered and powerless in the ancient city of Kyoto (formerly Heian).

THE TOKUGAWA SHOGUNATE AND THE CONSOLIDATION OF JAPAN

THE TOKUGAWA SHOGUNATE AND THE GREAT PEACE

The new government Ieyasu created was known as the Tokugawa Shogunate, and it lasted from 1603 to 1868. There were fifteen Tokugawa shoguns, and until near the end, their grasp on power and control over the nation were unassailable. After so many years of war and chaos, stability, law, and order were the shogunate's chief priorities. Accordingly, the Tokugawa years are also known as the Great Peace.

CENTRALIZATION, DICTATORSHIP, AND SOCIAL STRATIFICATION

Much as Hideyoshi had done before him, but even more so, Ieyasu centralized the country. He established a new capital in his home province, at the city of Edo (which is now the modern capital, Tokyo). Peace came at the price of dictatorship, as well as increased social stratification. Japan's class system became more rigid than ever before, and until the mid-1700s, it was almost impossible for a person to move from one class or profession to another. The power of the daimyo was reduced, and ordinary citizens were forbidden to own weapons. The Tokugawa rulers also maintained a monopoly on gunpowder technology, and kept the number of guns in Japan as small as possible.

WOMEN IN TOKUGAWA JAPAN

In Tokugawa Japan, women lived under increased restrictions, particularly in the samurai class, which was guided by Confucian teachings. Wives had to obey their husbands or face death. They had little authority over property. Females were educated at home, whereas their brothers studied in schools. In upper-class families, however, women expressed their literacy through creative pursuits and displayed social graces as a reflection of their husbands' rank and status.

In the lower classes, gender relations were more egalitarian. Both men and women worked in the fields, and women were given respect as homemakers and mothers. Some peasant women during the Tokugawa era became active in social protests and demonstrated against government officials, landlords, and merchants who had mistreated them. However, as in previous eras, girl children were less valued, and sometimes either put to death or sold into prostitution.

JAPANESE ISOLATIONISM

The Tokugawa shoguns also sealed Japan off from the rest of the world as much as they could. They were especially concerned to restrict the access of Europeans. There had been Spanish, Portuguese, and Dutch in Japan during the 1500s: they traded and converted many Japanese to Christianity. Distrusting the new religion, Japan's rulers (including Hideyoshi) had struck out against Christianity several times, persecuting and even crucifying believers. Hostility to Christianity and fear of foreign political and economic influence were behind the Tokugawas' decision to close off the country in 1649. From then until the 1720s, foreign merchants were allowed entry only into one city, the port of Nagasaki. A brief period of openness followed, and then Japan sealed itself off again until the 1850s.

ECONOMIC AND SOCIAL GROWTH

Despite the oppressive nature of the Tokugawa regime, it had many accomplishments to its credit. It restored and kept the peace. The population grew rapidly. Rice and grain production more than doubled between 1600 and 1720. Tokugawa Japan became highly urbanized (Edo was one of the world's largest cities), and the shogunate built an elaborate network of roads and canals. Economic growth was impressive: the Japanese became great producers of lacquerware, pottery, steel, and quality weapons. During the 1600s and especially the 1700s, one class that became increasingly wealthy and powerful was the merchant class (an exception to the general rule of social rigidity under the Tokugawa).

TOKUGAWA CULTURE

In Japan, castle architecture partly imitated that of Europe. As in Europe, Japanese castles were strategically built on hilltops, constructed of stone, and featured small windows, watchtowers, and massive walls. Himeji Castle, one of the most famous of its kind in Japan, has decorated gables and roofs that once underscored the importance of its noble inhabitants.

In the field of drama, the formerly dominant, more restrained, and classically styled Noh play was now being eclipsed by kabuki. Kabuki theater emphasized violence, physical action (acrobats and swordplay), and music. It often depicted urban life in brothels and dance halls, and shogunate officials criticized it for its potentially corrupting effect on their subjects' morals.

During the Tokugawa era, wood-block print came into its own as an artform. In addition, whereas Chinese artists turned inward, Japanese art was more and more influenced by the outside world. For example, Japanese potters fashioned their ceramics out of Korean techniques and designs. Some artists experimented with Western styles in oil painting, including perspective and the interplay of light. Major reasons for this difference between Japan and China include the fact that Japanese urban areas were developing rapidly, along with their merchant and artisan classes, and Confucian values carried less weight there than in China.

THE TOKUGAWA SHOGUNATE DURING THE LATE 1700s AND EARLY 1800s

The Tokugawa shoguns remained strong and dynamic through the mid-1700s. Afterward, although the Tokugawa still kept a tight grip over Japan, age and inflexibility began to take their toll on the system. Gradual decentralization began to set in. Political troubles were brewing by the early-to-mid 1800s. Then, the forcing open of Japan by foreign powers (specifically the United States) in the 1850s would finally end Tokugawa rule.

QUICK REVIEW

1. Who was Francis Xavier?

   (A) a Portuguese warlord who conquered Macao
   (B) a Jesuit missionary who traveled widely in China
   (C) a Spanish colonial administrator in Asia
   (D) a Dominican priest who advocated equal rights for all Asians
   (E) an Italian composer influenced by Asian music

2. Which of the following adversely affected Ming economics during the first half of the 1600s?

   (A) inflation caused by the glut of silver coming from Spanish and Portuguese colonies in the New World
   (B) the financial strain caused by the need to defend China's long frontiers
   (C) the decline of agricultural yields and disturbances in the countryside
   (D) all of the above
   (E) none of the above

3. Which of the following is true about the Qing dynasty?

   I. The Qing rulers were ethnically distinct from most of China's inhabitants.
   II. The Qing came to power in China by peaceful means.
   III. The Qing forced ordinary male citizens to wear their hair in queues.
   IV. The early Qing rulers were militarily active.

   (A) I and II only
   (B) I and III only
   (C) I, III, and IV
   (D) II, III, and IV
   (E) all of the above

4. Upon what religious-philosophical tradition did Qing rulers rely to strengthen their imperial authority in China?

   (A) Confucianism
   (B) Daoism
   (C) Pure Land Buddhism
   (D) Hinduism
   (E) shamanism

5. Who is considered to be the most successful Qing ruler?

   (A) Wu
   (B) Yongle
   (C) Kangxi
   (D) Chung-cheng
   (E) Cixi

6. How would one best characterize Japan's political situation during the 1400s and 1500s?

   (A) a condition of peace and prosperity
   (B) a state of disunity and civil war
   (C) a time of tight political cohesion
   (D) a division of the country between two warring factions
   (E) a dominance of politics by religious authorities

7. Which of the following is NOT true of Japan's samurai class?

   (A) Samurai developed into a military aristocracy.
   (B) Samurai followed a rigid code of behavior called Bushido.
   (C) Samurai were philosophically attracted to the simplicity of Zen Buddhism.
   (D) Samurai without masters to serve were known as ronin.
   (E) Samurai were governed by principles of nonviolence.

8. What best describes the political legacy of Toyotomi Hideyoshi?

(A) He unified Japan as a single state and established a solid government that survived after his death.

(B) He unified Japan as a single state, but his government collapsed after his death.

(C) He plunged Japan into a permanent state of civil war.

(D) He attempted to unify Japan, but failed.

(E) He left Japan less unified than it had been before his rule.

9. Which of the following characterized the politics of the Tokugawa shogunate?

(A) rigid social stratification backed by a dictatorial government

(B) a gradual opening of Japanese economic and intellectual life to the outside world

(C) ruthless extermination of political enemies and racial minorities

(D) a high degree of social mobility

(E) a move toward limited forms of participatory democracy

10. Which social class began to gain a substantial amount of new social and economic influence in seventeenth-century Japan?

(A) the peasantry

(B) the industrial working class

(C) the merchant class

(D) the urban poor

(E) artisans and craftspeople

ANSWERS:

1. **B**, p. 215
2. **D**, p. 215
3. **C**, p. 215
4. **A**, p. 216
5. **C**, p. 216

6. **B**, p. 216
7. **E**, p. 216
8. **B**, p. 217
9. **A**, p. 217
10. **C**, p. 218

CHAPTER 17

South and Southeast Asia

During the period between 1450 and 1750, South and Southeast Asia experienced, on the whole, greater political centralization. These regions were also confronted by the sudden appearance of European explorers and merchants at the end of the 1400s and the beginning of the 1500s. Both developments changed South and Southeast Asia considerably.

The largest and most powerful states in the region were in India. In 1450, India was ruled by the Delhi Sultanate, which was declining rapidly. During the 1520s, invaders from the north destroyed the Delhi Sultanate and established in its place an even stronger state: the Mughal Empire, which survived into the mid-1700s.

As before, India and the rest of South and Southeast Asia were characterized by an incredible diversity of ethnicity, language, and religion (major faiths included Hinduism, several forms of Buddhism, Islam, and more). In many ways, this diversity enriched India and its neighbors. However, it also created deep social and cultural divisions, which often caused conflict and strife.

MUGHAL INDIA

THE COLLAPSE OF THE DELHI SULTANATE

The origins and history of the Delhi Sultanate are discussed in more detail in Chapter 9. As noted there, the sultanate began to lose territory during the 1300s. Delhi itself was taken and ransacked by the Mongol commander Timur in 1398 and 1399, then weakened steadily during the 1400s. The final blows against the sultanate came in the 1520s.

BABUR THE TIGER

Starting around 1520, Babur—a Mongol warlord in the tradition of Genghis Khan and, more recently, Timur—launched a full-scale invasion of India from the north. Known as the Tiger, Babur was a talented general and quickly defeated the Delhi Sultanate. With an army of only 12,000, he defeated a force more than ten times the size of his own. In 1526, after the battle of Panipat, Babur founded his own government in India. He died in 1530.

THE MUGHAL EMPIRE

Babur's government became known as the Mughal Empire, from the Persian word for "Mongol" (the word *mughal* is often spelled *mogul*, which, even in English, now refers to any rich or powerful individual). Babur ruled until his death in 1530. His descendants conquered most of the rest of India, and the empire continued for the next 200 years.

Like the Delhi sultans, the Mughal rulers were Muslims. This made the Mughal state one of the three great Islamic empires of the period, the other two being the Ottoman Empire and Safavid

Persia (see Chapter 15). Just as the Ottoman and Safavid states were, Mughal India was a "gunpowder empire," using military force and advanced weapons technology to maintain power, both at home and abroad.

Another similarity to the other Islamic empires is that, although Mughal India was more technologically and scientifically advanced than most parts of the world during the 1500s and first half of the 1600s, it lost ground, especially to the nations of Europe, during the late 1600s and afterward. But in its prime, Mughal India was mighty.

Mughal India expanded steadily southward. The Mughals ruled India from their famous Peacock Throne. At first, the Mughals' capital was Agra. Agra is still the site of one of India's greatest landmarks: the Taj Mahal. The Taj Mahal, a gorgeous mausoleum of white marble, was built in 1648 by Shah Jahan, in memory of his wife (the original plans called for a twin mausoleum, made of black marble, to be erected nearby, but it was never built). Later, the Peacock Throne was moved to Delhi, which had been rebuilt and restored to its former glory.

The Mughal rulers centralized India. The economy thrived, thanks largely to a boom in the Indian cotton trade. With some exceptions, the Mughals were religiously flexible, allowing Hindus and Buddhists to practice their own faiths, even under Muslim rule. Only during the last years of the empire did this approach change.

WOMEN IN MUGHAL INDIA

The question of how much effect Mughal rule had on women remains unsolved. On the one hand, the Mughals allowed women certain rights. Female aristocrats were awarded titles, earned salaries, owned land, and ran businesses. Some of them received an education and were allowed to express their creative talents openly. Women of all castes were permitted to augment their family's income by selling their woven products. In Indian society, women could inherit land and sometimes played an active part in running businesses.

However, the Mughals restricted women's rights through Islamic law. These practices tended to coincide with restrictions that Indian society had already placed on women, such as cloistering women inside the home, as in the case of Hindu upper-class women. Under Mughal rule, the Hindu practice of sati remained legal, and women were instructed to serve under their husbands.

MUGHAL ARTS AND CULTURE

During the Mughal period, the most visible artistic achievement was in architecture. The principal example is the Taj Mahal, mentioned previously. A new style of painting during this period resulted from a blending of two cultures, the Persian with the Indian. It was characterized by the use of extended space and a depiction of human physical activity, once thought sacrilegious by orthodox Muslims at court. European influences also appeared. Christian subjects were sometimes portrayed, and artists in India experimented with the use of perspective, color shadings featured in Renaissance painting, and realistic portraits. Poetry, much of which was written in Persian, grew in stature during the Mughal era. Lastly, there was a revival of devotional literature to Hindu gods such as Krishna and Rama.

AKBAR THE GREAT

Mughal rule reached its peak under Akbar the Great (1556–1605), the grandson of Babur. It was Akbar who completed the conquest of India. A great commander, Akbar used heavy artillery to gain control over almost all the subcontinent.

Akbar also created the bureaucratic machinery and administrative structure that allowed the Mughals to govern the country efficiently. The tax codes and legal system operated fairly. Akbar's reign was, overall, one of prosperity.

Akbar was also famed for his religious tolerance. Not only did he allow non-Muslims to worship as they wished, but he worked actively to encourage friendly relations among Muslims, Buddhists, and Hindus. He even sought advice from the Catholic priests who accompanied the European traders who had established themselves in Indian ports. Akbar made sure that a specific percentage of government officials were Hindu, and he himself married a Hindu princess. Near the end of his life, Akbar attempted to create a new, inclusive religion called the Divine Faith, but it did not survive his death.

DECLINE OF THE MUGHAL EMPIRE

The Mughals' fortunes took a downward turn during the late 1600s and early 1700s. Akbar's great-grandson, Aurangzeb (1658–1707), was a militant Muslim and abandoned his predecessors' policy of religious tolerance. He forced thousands of people to convert to Islam against their will. His policy caused tremendous civil strife within India. This, in turn, had an adverse effect on the economy. Aurangzeb's intolerance also had the effect of turning one religious minority, the Sikhs, into a rebellious and warlike group. The Sikhs' religion, which stressed the power of prayer and meditation to achieve holy enlightenment, had been founded in the late 1400s by the teacher Nanak. During the 1500s and most of the 1600s, the Sikhs had been peaceful. In 1675, however, their leader was killed by Aurangzeb. The Sikhs rebelled, founded their own state in Punjab, and developed a strong warrior tradition.

Overall, the Mughal state declined during the 1700s. The social and economic effects of religious struggle continued. With every year, more provinces broke away and became independent. In 1739, an Iranian marauder sacked Delhi and carried away the Peacock Throne, the symbol of Mughal glory and power.

ARRIVAL OF THE EUROPEANS

In addition, European interference in Indian affairs steadily increased. The Portuguese trader Vasco da Gama arrived in 1498 (see Chapter 14). More Portuguese, then Spanish, came to South Asia. They were followed by the Dutch, then the French and English, who arrived in the 1600s. During the 1500s and early 1600s, the gunpowder empire of the Mughals was strong and technologically advanced enough to keep the Europeans in their place.

During the 1600s, however, the balance of power was shifting. During the 1600s, the English established textile factories at Fort William (near Calcutta, in the northeast) and Madras. The western gateway port of Bombay (now Mumbai) was ceded to the English in 1661. The Dutch established bases in Colombo, the chief city of Ceylon (now Sri Lanka). The Portuguese established themselves at Calcutta and the western port of Diu. The French created a great garrison and trading center at Pondicherry, on the east coast. The Europeans profited by gaining control over the trade of Indian cotton for spices from the East Indies.

European, particularly English, control over India increased during the 1700s. Starting in the 1740s, large numbers of French and British troops were fighting each other in India, for the "right" to colonize the entire subcontinent. By the 1750s, the English had expelled the French. They then turned to the conquest of India itself. They defeated the Mughal state easily, although they kept Mughal rulers in charge of certain parts of India as puppets. In a short time, one of the world's mightiest empires had been transformed into a weak colonial possession.

SOUTHEAST ASIA

KINGDOMS OF SOUTHEAST ASIA

Like India, the nations of Southeast Asia solidified politically. They also had to face the arrival and constant encroachments of European explorers and colonizers.

Strong states in the region during these years included Thailand (which conquered the neighboring Khmer state in Cambodia), the Vietnamese nation of Annam, and Burma (which maintained the largest army in Southeast Asia). The islands of Indonesia—Sumatra, Java, and hundreds of others—were politically and economically important.

Buddhism and Hinduism were dominant religions. Islam was important as well, especially in Indonesia, where it became the majority faith.

THE EUROPEAN PRESENCE IN SOUTHEAST ASIA

Europeans began to come to Southeast Asia after 1498, when Vasco da Gama reached India. The Portuguese quickly took over whatever parts of Southeast Asia they could: Malacca, Goa, Sri Lanka, and more. Where they could not conquer, they traded. The same was true for the Europeans who followed: the Spanish, Dutch, French, and English. Because they were smaller and less advanced than India, it was harder for the nations of Southeast Asia to remain free from European colonization—although many managed to, at least until the 1800s, when European imperialism became even harder to resist.

AUSTRALIA AND ITS NEIGHBORS

Much farther to the south, the English encountered the continent of Australia. In 1770, British mariner and explorer James Cook charted the east coast of Australia and claimed the continent for his country. The nearby islands of New Zealand, home to the Polynesian Maori, and Tasmania, came under English control as well.

Full-scale settlement of Australia began in 1788. For years, the population consisted mainly of soldiers, government officials, and criminals deported ("transported") to the colony as punishment. In 1830, Britain claimed the entire continent of Australia. The rate of settlement increased, as free settlers joined the colony, seeking their fortunes. Mainly sheep farmers, Australians pushed into the interior, displacing the original inhabitants, the Aborigines who had lived there for tens of thousands of years. The confrontations between colonists and Aborigines were often violent and one-sided, ending with the dispossession and ill treatment of the natives.

QUICK REVIEW

1. In sixteenth-century India, the Delhi Sultanate gave way to which government?

   (A) the Gupta Empire
   (B) the Srivijayan Kingdom
   (C) French rule
   (D) the Mughal Empire
   (E) British rule

2. The founder of the Mughal Empire was

   (A) Aurangzeb
   (B) Babur
   (C) Akbar
   (D) Jahan
   (E) Nanak

3. What major faiths were most prominent in South Asia's religious landscape during the sixteenth and seventeenth centuries?

   (A) Hinduism, Islam, and Buddhism
   (B) Christianity and Buddhism
   (C) animism, Buddhism, and Zoroastrianism
   (D) animism, Hinduism, and Zoroastrianism
   (E) Islam, Christianity, and animism

4. A boom in what commodity led to increased prosperity in the Mughal Empire during the 1600s and 1700s?

(A) nutmeg
(B) coffee
(C) cotton
(D) wool
(E) cloves

5. The most famous architectural legacy of the Mughal Empire is

(A) the Red Fortress of Gwalior
(B) the temple of Borobudor
(C) the Great Gate of Mumbai
(D) the Taj Mahal
(E) Gandhi's tomb

6. Which of the following is true of Akbar's reign in India?

I. He completed the Mughal conquest of India.
II. He improved India's tax code and legal system.
III. He pursued a policy of religious tolerance.
IV. He promoted a new religion known as the Divine Faith.

(A) I, II, and III
(B) II, III, and IV
(C) I and IV only
(D) II and III only
(E) all of the above

7. The most striking aspect of Aurangzeb's reign was

(A) his continuation of Akbar's policy of religious tolerance
(B) his ruthless suppression of Muslim beliefs
(C) his ruthless suppression of non-Muslim beliefs
(D) his democratization of the political system
(E) his abolition of the caste system

8. How did the Mughal Empire come to an end?

(A) It was subdued by the British, who retained some Mughal rulers in place for political purposes.
(B) It collapsed as a result of a global shift in the cotton trade during the 1700s.
(C) It was completely eradicated by French colonists.
(D) Outside invaders from the Himalayas sacked the capital and destroyed the empire.
(E) none of the above

9. The majority religion in Indonesia is

(A) Christianity
(B) Islam
(C) Hinduism
(D) Buddhism
(E) Sikhism

10. Australia's colonial population was made up largely of what group during the 1700s and early 1800s?

(A) religious dissidents
(B) gold miners
(C) Scottish refugees
(D) convicts
(E) Irish peasants

ANSWERS:

1. **D**, p. 221   6. **E**, pp. 222–23
2. **B**, p. 221   7. **C**, p. 223
3. **A**, p. 221   8. **A**, p. 223
4. **C**, p. 222   9. **B**, p. 224
5. **D**, p. 222   10. **D**, p. 224

CHAPTER 18

Sub-Saharan Africa

Africa's population had expanded from an estimated 20 million in 200 C.E. to 47 million by 1500. Yet the population outside Africa—made up of the descendants of those humans who had left Africa nearly 100,000 years before—had reached more than 300 million by that year. During the period between 1450 and 1750, African population growth would be similarly slow in comparison with the rest of the world. And this outside population would have an increasingly greater impact on Africa itself.

Starting in the early 1400s, Africa came under the increased influence of the exploring powers of Europe. All along the western and eastern coasts, Portugal, then other European nations, seized cities, built fortresses, and established permanent colonies. For centuries, Europeans exploited Africa economically, taking gold, spices, ivory, and other resources both through trade and by force. Most shameful was the Atlantic slave trade. It began in the 1400s, when Portugal started transporting Africans overseas for use as slave labor. Quickly, more nations became involved, and the size and number of slave shipments grew astronomically, with the slave trade persisting well into the 1800s. Its effect on Africa and the Americas—not to mention the economies of Europe—was profound.

For the time being, however, the interior of Africa remained largely free from European control. Not until after the mid-1800s would Europeans penetrate far beyond the coasts. Certain African nations grew strong and thrived. At times, Africans were able to defeat European forces and stop colonists and slavers from moving deeper into the continent. Nonetheless, the economic impact of European imperialism was felt even in the interior, as were the effects of the slave trade.

WEST AND CENTRAL AFRICA

ASKIA MOHAMMED AND THE SONGHAI STATE

By the mid-1400s, the previously dominant power in West Africa, Mali, was fading. For a short time, another strong state, the Muslim kingdom of Songhai, rose up. Songhai's most famous ruler was Askia Mohammed (1493–1528), who came to the throne by killing his uncle. A devout Muslim and skilled general, Askia Mohammed sponsored art and scholarship. He also expanded Songhai's boundaries greatly. A fictionalized account of his reign, *The Epic of Askia Mohammed*, is one of the classics of the African oral tradition. Songhai prospered during most of the 1500s, until its conquest in 1590 by Morocco.

Farther to the south, many states lined the coast of West Africa. Among the largest was Kongo, in west central Africa (during the 1600s and 1700s, Kongo would split into a number of smaller states). West and west central Africa were rich in gold, ivory, foodstuffs, and animal hides. In particular, the trade in gold had always been brisk and active.

THE EUROPEANS AND WEST AND CENTRAL AFRICA

All of West Africa was affected by the arrival of the Europeans in the 1400s. First the Portuguese, then the Dutch, English, and French, landed on the African coast, began trading, and built permanent outposts. The original purpose of the Portuguese had been to find their way south and east to India. As they became more interested in Africa for its own sake, the Portuguese and other Europeans sought to gain control over the gold and ivory trade networks that extended throughout West and Central Africa. For example, the Portuguese conquered the Shona people's Mwene Metapa dynasty during the 1500s, in order to dominate the gold trade along the upper Zambezi River.

WOMEN IN WEST AND CENTRAL AFRICA

As mentioned earlier in the text, several African groups, particularly in West Africa, were organized along matrilineal lines. In these cases, there often existed a hierarchy of women who served in leadership positions that paralleled those of men. The mother, wife, and sisters of the chief, as well as a council of matrons, would play an influential role in each group. In some instances, women were involved in corulerships or even became chiefs themselves. For example, a woman named Queen Nzinga (1582–1663) ruled the Mbundu peoples in what is now Angola. She became much respected for successfully defending her people against the Portuguese.

In West African trading villages, women were known to have sold surplus produce from their land, and some administered the market system on a larger scale. Women's councils formed to administer the markets.

In North African urban cultures where Islam dominated, upper-class women were more likely to be cloistered and made to wear veils. However, economic necessity compelled lower-class women to work outside the home.

THE EMERGENCE OF THE SLAVE TRADE

From the late 1400s onward, the development of African nations, the patterns of African trade, and the histories of entire tribes were all shaped by the growing European presence. The strongest states in West Africa—Oyo, Benin, Dahomey, Kongo, and the Asante (Ashanti) kingdom—were those that cooperated with the European slave trade, warring on and imprisoning other African tribes, then selling the captives to European slavers.

In particular, Asante, founded by Osei Tutu in 1680, became immensely strong because its leaders sold gold and slaves to Europeans in exchange for muskets and gunpowder. The nickname of West Africa became the "Gold Coast" in recognition of the lucrative exchange of gold for slaves. Asante, in fact, was one of the very few parts of Africa where both minerals and agricultural resources were found in abundance.

Even states and tribes in Central Africa, beyond the direct impact of the Europeans on the coast, were affected. The trade networks that connected Central Africa with the west coast were redirected or dried up by the Europeans. Some West African peoples began to raid Central Africa for goods to trade with Europeans. Worst of all, the Europeans' desire for slaves frequently led West Africans to fight neighboring states and tribes in Central Africa.

SOUTH AFRICA

THE PORTUGUESE IN SOUTH AFRICA

Before the arrival of the Europeans, the southern tip of Africa had been settled by various tribes, mainly descended from the Bantu (see Chapter 3). The Portuguese had rounded the tip of Africa in 1488, establishing an outpost on what they called the Cape of Good Hope.

THE BOERS

During the 1600s, control of the region passed from the Portuguese to the Dutch. Dutch settlers arrived in 1652, both to farm and to trade with ships sailing around Africa, between Europe and the East Indies. The chief city of the Dutch was Cape Town. The Dutch settlers, known as Boers (also Afrikaners), became firmly established in Africa. Their language evolved, becoming known as Afrikaans. Even more so than most white Europeans, the Boers possessed an extremely strong sense of racial superiority. They looked upon Africans and other peoples of color as inferior. Over the centuries, the Boers' harsh treatment of native Africans developed into the infamous system of apartheid.

Very quickly, the Boers enslaved the nearest African tribe, the Xhosa, a peaceful herding people. As the Boers expanded to the north, they would encounter a stronger and more warlike people, the Zulu. Many wars broke out between the Boers and the Zulu. By the early 1800s, the entire region came under British control, although the Boers continued to live there. This awkward, three-way situation would cause much conflict during the 1800s.

EAST AFRICA

As discussed in Chapter 11, the towns and states of East Africa were part of the vibrant, cosmopolitan system of economic and cultural exchange that had formed around the Indian Ocean. From the 1400s onward, this system continued to exist, although the arrival of European merchants and conquerors changed conditions considerably.

THE PORTUGUESE IN EAST AFRICA

The Portuguese, the first to arrive, originally viewed East Africa simply as a platform for reaching the Indies. For example, in 1498, the East African port of Malindi had been Vasco da Gama's jumping-off point to Calicut, in India. Quickly, however, the Portuguese realized the advantages of having permanent bases in East Africa. Not only would this allow them to reach India more efficiently, but it would allow them to gain even tighter control over trade in the Indian Ocean basin, especially in spices.

During the early 1500s, the Portuguese conquered a chain of cities along the East African coast, turning them into colonies and garrisons. These included Malindi, Kilwa, Sofala, Mozambique, and Mombasa. Although Arabs expelled the Portuguese from Mombasa in 1728, Portugal's presence in the region remained strong for hundreds of years. Other Europeans, including the English, later colonized East Africa as well.

AFRICAN CULTURE

Africa was not a place that had a unified or monolithic approach to art, although it is possible to make some generalizations. First of all, sculpture was its most dominant medium. Secondly, African art was concerned with human adornment, as in masks and elaborate beadwork. Notably, much of African art has been abstract, or not made to recreate visual reality. Thus, African artists were creating abstract art long before it became a popular concept in the West in the twentieth century.

During the period between 1450 and 1750, artists continued to produce wood carving, sculpture, metalwork, and painting in their traditional forms, although they introduced innovations as prompted by local art patrons and leaders. European traders brought home with them carved ivory pieces and textiles that ended up in the homes of distinguished art patrons. Textile arts were prevalent among the Kuba people of the West Congo basin. Although textiles were considered prestige objects, owned by the elite, they were also sold to people in lower classes. The oldest types were made from the beaten inner bark of certain trees.

Finely woven basketry, often done in intersecting geometric patterns, was treasured by royal families in East Africa. Basketry of high value was once produced in Rwanda and Burundi. Although most African groups typically used gold only for trade purposes, some, such as the Asante, melded gold into elaborate swords of state, which often were adorned with symbolic emblems. In the seventeenth and eighteenth centuries in Christian Ethiopia, kings commissioned artists to produce churches with brightly colored wall paintings of holy events. One of the most famous of these churches, and one which still stands today, is the Church of Debre Berhan Selassie in Gondar, Ethiopia.

The first written literature in the form of novels, poetry, or plays was not conceived in African or European languages until the nineteenth century. However, architecture became increasingly influenced by Arabs and European colonists who built fortresses and residents in East and West Africa.

THE ATLANTIC SLAVE TRADE

SLAVERY IN AFRICA BEFORE THE EUROPEANS

As in most parts of the world, slavery had existed in Africa for many years. African tribes often enslaved members of other tribes in a quest for more workers, wives, and children, as well as for reasons of greed and conquest.

In addition, Arab traders had created a large and long-lasting slave trade that extended throughout the Sahara and southward.

THE ORIGINS OF THE ATLANTIC SLAVE TRADE

The arrival of the Europeans, however, changed forever the character of slave trading in Africa. The Portuguese began this process, but other European nations followed suit. Over time, the Atlantic slave trade became a central part of the European economy and a primary factor in Europe's ability to generate such great wealth from the 1500s onward.

Starting in 1441, the Portuguese began to enslave Africans, taking them to Portugal and selling them in Europe. The number of slaves brought directly to Europe was relatively small: approximately 1,000 per year. During the early 1500s, however, slaves began to be taken to the Americas, and the numbers grew tremendously.

REASONS FOR THE EXPANSION OF THE ATLANTIC SLAVE TRADE

Several factors increased the demand for African slaves. One was the labor-intensive nature of planting, harvesting, and refining sugar. As sugar cultivation became more important to European colonial economies, the need for labor became more urgent. In 1490, the Portuguese began using slaves on the sugar plantations of São Tomé, an island off the West African coast. During the 1500s, Portuguese and Spanish colonies in Brazil and the Caribbean became major centers of sugar production, and the desire for slave labor there became more intense.

Also during the early 1500s, it became clear to the Spanish and Portuguese that, in the New World, Native Americans were not well suited as slaves. In addition, the Catholic Church had managed by 1542 to abolish the encomienda system that had allowed the Spanish to place Native Americans in servitude (see Chapter 19). If the Spanish and Portuguese wanted a source of slave labor—not just for sugar cultivation, but also mining, agricultural work of all kinds, and menial labor in general—they had to turn elsewhere. Africa seemed to them to be the ideal source.

THE GROWING SCOPE OF THE ATLANTIC SLAVE TRADE

A small trickle of slaves had already been brought from Portugal and Europe to the Americas during the late 1400s. It was in 1518, however, that the Portuguese brought the first recorded shipment of slaves directly from Africa to the New World. If almost 1,000 slaves per year had been taken from Africa to Europe during the last half of the 1400s, the number of slaves taken from Africa—now to the Americas—more than doubled during the 1500s, to more than 2,000 per year. At least 275,000 slaves were brought to the New World over the course of the century.

The slave trade mushroomed in scale during the 1600s and 1700s. First, the Spanish and Portuguese appetite for slaves increased dramatically. Roughly 37 percent of all slaves ever brought to the New World went to Brazil, while 15 percent went to Spanish America. Second, as other European nations founded colonies in the Caribbean and North America, they wanted slaves as well. The non-Spanish Caribbean was the destination for fully 41 percent of all slaves taken from Africa. The southern colonies of British North America, where slaves were used to grow crops such as cotton and tobacco, became home to approximately 5 percent. More than a million slaves were transported from Africa during the 1600s. At least 6 million were shipped during the 1700s, the Atlantic slave trade's peak century. All told, perhaps 12 million Africans were enslaved from the late 1400s through the late 1800s.

THE MIDDLE PASSAGE

The conditions under which slaves were captured and shipped to the Americas were notoriously appalling. Many slaves were captives or prisoners of war, herded like animals to the coast and sold to European slavers by other Africans. Most slaves were separated from their families; many were mixed in with members of other tribes, who spoke different languages and followed different customs.

At ports on the West African shoreline, slaves were loaded onto ships to make the infamous "Middle Passage" across the Atlantic. The more slaves a ship could carry, the greater its profits, so slaves were packed into boats as tightly as possible. Typically chained, lying on their backs, surrounded by hundreds of other bodies, all in darkness, slaves endured a nightmarish sea journey for weeks. Upon arrival in the New World, they would be taken to slave markets and sold to their new masters. During the early years of the slave trade, up to 25 percent of slaves perished during the Middle Passage. By the 1700s, slavers had become more efficient at keeping slaves alive during the journey (not for humane reasons, but to cut down on the financial loss that every dead slave represented). During the 1700s and 1800s, the average death rate had been reduced to 10 percent or under.

ATLANTIC SLAVERY, THE TRIANGULAR TRADE, AND THE WORLD ECONOMY

By the 1700s, African slavery had become a crucial element in European economic life and global trade. Until the early 1800s, not a single major nation made slavery or the trade in slaves illegal. Not only was slavery open and legal, but the slave trade was an integral part of the pattern of economic exchange known as triangular trade. Although European home countries also traded directly with their New World colonies, exchanging colonial raw materials for European manufactured goods, triangular trade was most common during the 1600s and 1700s. Typically, European manufactured goods (metalware, cotton textiles, processed alcohol such as gin and rum, firearms) would be brought to Africa and exchanged for gold, ivory, timber, and slaves. While the gold, ivory, and timber would eventually be brought back to Europe, the slaves were taken to the Americas and sold for hard cash or traded for goods.

The Middle Passage was, therefore, the second leg of the triangular trade. In the Americas, slaves would be traded for raw materials, such as furs, tobacco, raw cotton, sugar products, and silver. These raw materials would be brought back to Europe. Overall, the slave-based triangular trade—in other words, the ruthless exploitation of Africa—was paramount in the growth and expansion of European wealth during these years.

QUICK REVIEW

1. In the late 1400s, which state succeeded Mali as the primary power in West Africa?

   (A) Zimbabwe
   (B) Songhai
   (C) Kongo
   (D) Benin
   (E) Dahomey

2. What goods did European traders primarily seek in West Africa?

   (A) gold and ivory
   (B) bananas and mahogany
   (C) oranges and ivory
   (D) coffee and gemstones
   (E) ivory and gemstones

3. Which of the following best characterizes Africa's relations with Europe between 1450 and 1700?

   (A) European powers controlled the entire continent.
   (B) The European impact on Africa remained minimal during these years.
   (C) The effects of the Atlantic slave trade were felt only in West Africa.
   (D) The Europeans' direct influence was felt mainly on the coasts, while the African interior remained largely free.
   (E) Only North Africa fell under European influence.

4. In what part of Africa did women enjoy the most amount of prestige and influence?

   (A) North Africa
   (B) South Africa
   (C) West Africa
   (D) East Africa
   (E) Central Africa

5. The Asante kingdom grew strong by which of the following means?

   (A) cooperating with Europeans who were engaged in the Atlantic slave trade
   (B) purchasing and making use of gunpowder weaponry
   (C) increased involvement in the West African gold trade
   (D) all of the above
   (E) none of the above

6. Which European power first colonized parts of East Africa?

   (A) Portugal
   (B) Spain
   (C) England
   (D) France
   (E) the Netherlands

7. What art forms were most prominent in sub-Saharan Africa?

   (A) painting and composed music
   (B) sculpture and textiles
   (C) written literature and painting
   (D) textiles and written literature
   (E) sculpture and composed music

8. Which of the following is true of the Boers?

   (A) They were English settlers in South Africa.
   (B) They were Arab merchants in East Africa.
   (C) They were Dutch settlers in South Africa.
   (D) They were French settlers in East Africa.
   (E) They were Spanish colonists in North Africa.

9. Besides the Europeans, which other group ran a major slave trade in Africa?

(A) the Turks
(B) the Persians
(C) the Sri Lankans
(D) the Syrians
(E) the Arabs

10. The largest percentage of Africans captured in the Atlantic slave trade were taken to

(A) Brazil
(B) Virginia
(C) Canada
(D) Cuba
(E) Haiti

ANSWERS:

1. **B**, p. 226   6. **A**, p. 228
2. **A**, p. 227   7. **B**, p. 228
3. **D**, p. 227   8. **C**, p. 228
4. **C**, p. 227   9. **E**, p. 229
5. **D**, p. 227   10. **A**, p. 230

CHAPTER 19

The Americas as "New World"

As described in Chapter 14, North and South America, which had existed in a state of isolation for thousands of years, came into contact with the rest of the world after the middle of the fifteenth century. European explorers arrived in the 1400s, considering themselves to have discovered what they thought of as the New World. Of course, both the concepts of "discovery" and "New World" were meaningless to the Americas' original inhabitants. Equally meaningless was the name given by the Europeans to the indigenous peoples of the Americas: "Indians," reflecting Christopher Columbus's mistaken belief that he had reached China and the Indies during his voyages of the 1490s.

All during the 1500s and afterward, the Spanish and Portuguese, then other Europeans, turned North and South America into their own spheres of influence. The Europeans also brought the Americas into contact with the rest of the world, economically, culturally, ecologically, and politically.

Most notably, the Europeans made North and South America part of a developing network of trade and exchange that was beginning to expand literally around the world. Traders, settlers, explorers, and slaves came to the Americas, as did new technology, new knowledge, and new cultural traditions. The environment of the Americas changed forever, thanks to the Europeans' exploitation of the continents' resources—and their introduction of new diseases, new plants, and new animals. Conversely, the new foods and natural resources (especially precious metals) extracted from the New World had a significant impact on civilization worldwide—not just in Europe, but also Asia and Africa. This so-called Columbian Exchange proved to be one of the most significant global developments during the period of 1450 to 1750.

NEW SPAIN

THE ESTABLISHMENT OF NEW SPAIN

From the voyages of Columbus in 1492 onward, the Spanish began to build up a large presence in North and South America. As far as European claims on the two continents were concerned, the pope, in 1494, had granted jurisdiction over all the Americas to Spain. The exception was Brazil, which went to Portugal.

At first, the Spanish moved into the islands of the Caribbean. One of their most important outposts in the New World was Havana, in Cuba. As described in Chapter 14, the Spanish then conquered, during the early-to-mid 1500s, Florida, Mexico (the Aztecs there were defeated by Hernán Cortés, from 1519 to 1522), much of what is now the southwestern and southern United States, and the northern Andes (the Incas were toppled by Francisco Pizarro from 1531 to 1536). The Spanish called this domain New Spain, and the principal headquarters there was Mexico City, built on the Aztec capital of Tenochtitlán.

Over time, Spain's system of governing this constantly expanding territory became more complex. Spain established viceroyalties (from the word "viceroy," meaning "in place of the king"): the Viceroyalty of New Spain (the oldest and most important, created in 1535), the Viceroyalty of Peru (founded in the 1590s), the Viceroyalty of New Granada (formed in 1730 to control what are today Ecuador, Colombia, Venezuela, and Panama), and the Viceroyalty of La Plata (which administered Bolivia, Paraguay, Argentina, and Uruguay after 1776).

REASONS FOR THE SUCCESS OF THE SPANISH CONQUEST

Why were the Spanish, with such small forces, able to conquer large and powerful Native American civilizations so quickly and decisively? The Spaniards' advantage in military technology, including gunpowder weapons, played a key part. The Spanish also proved adept at "divide-and-conquer" tactics: stirring up rivalries among various native tribes and allying with some against others.

First and foremost, however, was disease. Unwittingly, Spanish (and Portuguese) explorers and colonizers brought with them diseases, such as smallpox and measles, to which the Native Americans had never been exposed. Having no immunity to these new illnesses, Native Americans sickened and died in massive numbers. Such a major population loss had the obvious effect of weakening the natives' ability to resist Spanish invasion. Estimates of how many Native Americans perished as a result of European-borne diseases vary greatly, from one quarter of the original population to almost one half. Whatever the case, the death toll was hideously high.

ECONOMIC EXPLOITATION OF NEW SPAIN

What did the Spanish do with their new lands? The explorer and conquistador ("conqueror") Cortés famously remarked that he had come to the Americas for "God, gold, and glory." On the whole, the Spanish felt the second to be most important. Spain was in the New World mainly for profit. True, the Catholic Church, which was losing thousands of believers in Europe to Protestantism, saw the conversion of Native Americans to Catholic Christianity as a major priority. Still, Spain's principal motivation for exploration and colonization was the extraction of natural resources from the Americas. At first, the conquistadors simply sent *la quinta*, or one fifth, of whatever they gained from their conquests back to Spain, keeping the rest as profit.

FORCED LABOR AND SLAVERY

The conquistadors also benefited from a system known as the encomienda, which made all Native Americans subjects of the Spanish crown. Spanish generals and explorers were allowed to use the "Indians" as a source of labor. Although it was not technically meant to do so, the encomienda effectively enslaved the Native Americans for a number of decades.

The character of Spanish rule changed during the 1530s and 1540s. The viceregal system placed New Spain under the control of the government in Madrid, rather than the conquistadors themselves. The House of Trade was established to direct all trade and shipping from the New World through the Spanish port of Seville. As a local labor force, the Native Americans proved unwilling and unable to work in the manner the Spanish had wanted. In addition, many Catholic clergy, especially the Dominican monk Bartolomé de Las Casas, protested the cruel treatment of the Indians under the encomienda system. De Las Casas's book *The Tears of the Indians*, written after 1514, did much to sway opinion about the plight of Native Americans. Thanks to the New Laws, a set of labor regulations sponsored by de Las Casas, the encomienda system was abolished in 1542.

Harsh treatment of Native Americans continued, however. Also, the effect of freeing the Indians from forced labor was to encourage the Spanish to bring black slaves from Africa to the New World (in this, they imitated the Portuguese, who had already started the practice).

MINING AND PRECIOUS METALS

Whatever their labor force, the central purpose of the Spanish in the Americas remained the exploitation of natural resources. By far the most important was precious metals: the Spanish, along with the Portuguese, took 185,000 kilograms of gold from the Americas between 1503 and 1650. Even more astounding was the amount of silver mined: 16 million kilograms. The largest silver mines were located north of Mexico City and in Bolivia (at Potosí, the so-called "mountain of silver").

AGRICULTURE AND SUGAR PRODUCTION

Agricultural production was also important. The Spanish organized agriculture according to the plantation system: huge estates known as *haciendas*, *estancias*, and *latifundias* (the names depended on the part of Latin America in question) allowed European settlers to grow large quantities of a single crop very cheaply. This practice is also commonly known as monoculture. The labor was provided either by Native Americans, who worked very cheaply, or by slaves, so the plantation system was doubly profitable for Spanish landowners. Besides encouraging slavery or unfair labor practices, plantation monoculture, by placing so much emphasis on farming one crop or a small number of crops, tended to be environmentally damaging. Plantation agriculture also fails to diversify a country's resource base. It has generally led to long-term economic backwardness in Latin America.

The agricultural products the Spanish took from or harvested in the New World included coffee, bananas, tomatoes, corn, and potatoes. The last two had a profound influence on European diets, because they provide a high calorie yield per acre grown—meaning more food for less work. For the Spanish (and Portuguese), however, the most crucial cash crop was sugarcane. Especially on their Caribbean islands, the Spanish set up many sugar plantations, where sugarcane was grown, processed, and refined into sugar, as well as other products, such as molasses and rum. Sugarcane production is exceptionally labor-intensive, and it further stimulated the growth of the African slave trade (see Chapter 18).

ETHNIC DIVERSITY AND SOCIAL STRATIFICATION

Another effect of the arrival of the Spanish was to increase the racial diversity of the Americas. Pure-bred Spanish who arrived in the New World were known as *peninsulares*. Those of Spanish descent born in the colonies were *criollos* (better-known as creoles). When Spanish and Native Americans intermarried, their families were known as *mestizos*, or "mixed." Other mixed races were *mulattos* (Europeans and African blacks) and *zambos* (Native Americans and African blacks). The intermixing of so many ethnicities and traditions has made the culture of Latin America very rich.

Unfortunately, during the centuries of Spanish rule, all these groups were organized into a rigid social hierarchy, with European Spaniards at the top and those of mixed blood and native ancestry near the bottom. Slaves, of which there were many, were on the lowest rung of the social ladder.

PORTUGUESE BRAZIL

THE PORTUGUESE COLONIZATION OF BRAZIL

Brazil was the one major territory in the New World allotted to Portugal rather than Spain. It was discovered by accident in 1500 by Pedro Cabral, whose ship was blown off course in a storm. At first, the Portuguese did not consider Brazil important. They established an outpost there only in 1532. By 1549, however, Brazil was upgraded to a governor-generalship, indicating that the home government recognized its economic potential. Brazil became a viceroyalty in 1720.

Many of the same trends found in New Spain applied to Brazil. Native populations were decimated by Portuguese conquerors, falling victim to both superior technology and the new diseases brought by the Europeans. Portugal's treatment of the natives, a mixture of labor exploitation and mass conversion to Catholicism, was similar to Spain's. Various ethnic mixes of European, Native American, and African emerged. Plantation agriculture was dominant.

SUGARCANE AND SLAVERY

Mining was important in Portuguese Brazil, as were the forest industries of the Amazon basin (although this region was extremely difficult for colonizers to master). For years, however, the most important resource the Portuguese concentrated on was sugar. Sugarcane plantations proliferated.

As in the Caribbean, sugar production and slavery were intimately connected. Indeed, it was in connection with Brazil's sugar economy that the full-scale exchange of slaves between Africa and the New World began. The labor-intensive nature of sugarcane agriculture persuaded the Portuguese, who had already started taking slaves from Africa during the last half of the 1400s, to bring slaves to Brazil. At first, the number of slaves was fairly small, and the slaves had already been captured from Africa and taken to Portugal or its island colonies off the African coast.

The first boatload of slaves to be shipped directly from Africa to the New World arrived in Brazil in 1518. This single event set into motion one of the ugliest, longest-lasting, and, sadly, most profitable enterprises in human history: the Atlantic slave trade, which lasted well into the 1800s. Brazil, even after independence from Portugal, continued to use slaves until 1888. It was the last country in the Americas to outlaw slavery.

DUTCH AND ENGLISH NORTH AMERICA

THE DUTCH IN THE AMERICAS

As noted in Chapter 14, Protestant nations such as the Netherlands and England started attempting to break the Portuguese and Spanish monopoly on navigational know-how, global trade routes, and overseas colonization by the late 1500s. They also began to settle in North America. The Dutch began in the late 1500s and early 1600s.

As part of their rivalry with the Portuguese, as well as of their war of independence with the Spanish, the Dutch took over a number of islands in the Caribbean. They presented a challenge to Spanish power in the region. The Dutch also seized part of northwestern Brazil from the Portuguese. In 1621, the Netherlands established the Dutch West India Company, a twin to the older Dutch East India Company, to administer Dutch holdings in the Americas.

NEW NETHERLANDS AND NEW AMSTERDAM

The largest and most famous—but not longest-lasting—Dutch colony in the New World was New Netherlands, founded in what is now New York in the early 1600s. This region had been explored and claimed by Henry Hudson, on behalf of the Dutch, in 1609.

Dutch settler Peter Minuit purchased the island of Manhattan from a local Native American tribe in 1624. On that site, the Dutch constructed the city of New Amsterdam, which grew into a thriving commercial center.

The most able and dynamic leader of New Amsterdam was Peter Stuyvesant, under whom the colony grew and prospered. The Dutch lost New Netherlands and New Amsterdam after only a few decades. In 1664, after defeating the Dutch in a naval war back in Europe, the English insisted on the surrender of New Amsterdam. That year, the English took possession of the colony, renaming it New York. Reminders of the Dutch presence remained in local place names and the influence of aristocratic Dutch families (known as knickerbockers).

ENGLISH COLONIES IN THE AMERICAS

English attempts to colonize the New World dated back to the 1500s. Like the Dutch, the English took islands in the Caribbean, sometimes from the Portuguese and Spanish. Important bases there were Barbados, Trinidad, and Jamaica. But it was the North American mainland that most interested Queen Elizabeth I and the monarchs who followed her. Two failed colonies, including Sir Walter Raleigh's Roanoke settlement, were founded during the 1580s.

Not until 1606 did the English establish their first successful colony in North America: Jamestown, Virginia, led by Captain John Smith and greatly assisted by the Indian woman Pocahontas. Colonies in the Carolinas followed later in the 1600s.

Other English colonies appeared farther to the north. Fleeing religious persecution at home, for their Puritan beliefs, the *Mayflower* pilgrims landed at Plymouth, Massachusetts, in 1620. Nearby, the Massachusetts Bay Colony was founded in 1628; the city of Boston was established in 1630. As outlined above, the Dutch colony of New Amsterdam fell to the English and became New York in 1664. Another major colony, Pennsylvania, was organized in 1682 by the Quaker William Penn. Its chief city, Philadelphia, became the largest city in the English New World. Later expansion would come during the 1700s, largely as a result of war with French colonists.

THE ENGLISH AND PERMANENT SETTLEMENT IN THE NEW WORLD

English colonies in the Americas were distinguished by their high proportions of permanent settlers. More than any other European nation, England viewed its colonies as more than areas from which to extract resources (although profit was important). The population of English colonies grew quickly; for example, the population of Massachusetts grew from 4,000 in the 1620s to 40,000 by 1660. As English settlements expanded, they became more sophisticated politically, developing strong systems of local government. By the 1700s, this trend resulted in a constantly deepening sense of local identity, even independence.

The economic resources England took from the colonies were mainly raw materials. Timber was important, as were corn and potatoes (which became a staple foodstuff in the closest of England's possessions, Ireland). From Virginia and the Carolinas came tobacco, an immensely profitable crop. Sugar was grown in the Caribbean, and rum and molasses were refined from it.

FRENCH CANADA AND LOUISIANA

FRENCH SETTLEMENT OF CANADA

French colonization followed the exploring efforts during the late 1500s and 1600s of Champlain, Joliet, Marquette, and others (see Chapter 14). The French first moved down the St. Lawrence River into Canada, establishing settlements at Quebec and Montreal. Traveling across the Great Lakes and down the Mississippi River, the French seized the vast territory they called Louisiana, which became the property of the French crown in 1663. By the end of the 1600s, therefore, the French had laid claim to a huge part of North America: all of eastern Canada and much of the interior of what is now the United States.

FRANCE IN THE CARIBBEAN

The French also had island bases in the Caribbean, including Martinique, Guadeloupe, and Saint Domingue (today Haiti). As elsewhere in the region, sugarcane production was the economic mainstay of French colonies here.

THE FRENCH AND THE NORTH AMERICAN FUR TRADE

Like the Spanish, but unlike the English (both of whom split North America with them), the French were primarily interested in economic extraction. The asset they treasured above all was fur: the majority of French in North America were hunters and trappers harvesting skins and pelts for the European market.

ANGLO-FRENCH COMPETITION IN THE NEW WORLD

During the 1700s, France lost control over most of its territory in the New World. Its principal enemy was England, although Spain was a foe as well. Despite having allied with a number of Native American tribes, French colonists lost a series of conflicts with English settlers, including Queen Anne's War (1701–1714), King George's War (1740–1748), and the French and Indian Wars (1756–1763).

As a result of the third conflict, the English took over Canada (the province of Quebec stubbornly retained its French heritage). The large region of Louisiana was handed over to Spain, although the French would get it back again briefly during the late 1700s. French culture remains important in eastern Canada, the northern fringe of the United States, and the state of Louisiana. The Cajuns of Louisiana are descendants of the Acadians of Canada, who were expelled and forced southward by the English after their victory in the French and Indian Wars.

THE RUSSIAN-AMERICAN COMPANY

RUSSIAN SETTLEMENT OF THE ALEUTIAN ISLANDS AND ALASKA

The least famous case of European colonization of North America is that of the Russians. After conquering Siberia in the 1500s and reaching the Pacific coast during the 1600s, the Russians set their sights on areas like Alaska. During the 1730s and 1740s, the Bering Expedition, organized by the Russian government, surveyed the waterways separating Siberia from North America. Afterward, Russian hunters and soldiers moved into the Aleutian Islands. Alaska itself was next. At least 80 percent of the Aleutians' native population is said to have perished over the next half-century, thanks to violence, the spread of disease, and alcoholism.

THE FUR TRADE AND THE RUSSIAN-AMERICAN COMPANY

What stimulated Russian settlement of North America was fur. Pursuit of the fur trade led the Russians to establish their first permanent colony in Alaska in 1784. In 1799, hunters and merchants created the Russian-American Company to regulate trade. Not only did the Russians take over Alaska, they moved southward along the Pacific coast, until they reached northern California, where they built fortresses. The Russian presence in the New World continued until 1867. In the meantime, it caused friction with England, which claimed the Canadian coast, Spain, which feared Russian encroachments in California, and the United States, which had designs on what are now Oregon and Washington.

DIVERGENT APPROACHES TO COLONIZATION

Different European powers approached North American colonization in different ways. The same applies to their relationships with the Native Americans they encountered. There are, of course, commonalities. All European powers hoped to benefit economically from their colonies. All were guilty of mistreating the Native Americans. All imported slaves from Africa and perpetuated the Atlantic slave trade for centuries.

SPANISH AND PORTUGUESE APPROACHES TO COLONIZATION

For the Spanish and Portuguese, resource extraction, especially of silver and sugar, was of paramount importance. Their treatment of the Native Americans, whether in Mexico, South America, or what is now the southern and western United States, tended to be harsh. Until relatively recently, the Spanish and Portuguese were saddled with a reputation as the cruelest of European colonizers. However, recent scholarship has shown that other nations were little better. Still, the Spanish and Portuguese at first used Indians as slaves, then exploited them as cheap labor and kept them near the bottom of the Latin American social scale.

The importation of African slaves, particularly into Brazil (the last country in the Americas to abolish slavery) was massive. Many more slaves were brought from Africa to Latin America and the Caribbean than to the United States. Even though exploitation, not settlement, was the primary goal of the Spanish and Portuguese, the Spanish and Portuguese population of Brazil and New Spain grew steadily. For missionaries and priests, the conversion of Native Americans to Catholicism became a high priority. The settled presence of Spaniards and Portuguese, complete with major cities, was extensive enough to create permanent colonies.

FRENCH APPROACHES TO COLONIZATION

Like the Spanish and Portuguese, the French focused on economic exploitation. Their concern was mainly with the fur trade. Unlike the Spanish and Portuguese, the French made little effort to create long-term settlements. For example, from 1608 to 1763, only 11,000 French came to live permanently in North America. Combined with English military successes against them during the 1700s, a smaller population meant that the French would be less able to maintain a viable colonial presence in North America (the same had been the case with the Dutch during the 1600s).

On the other hand, while the French remained in the New World, their hunters, trappers, and soldiers proved remarkably adept, more so than the people of any other European country, at adapting themselves to local customs and environment. They came to know the woods and rivers of North America well. They learned the languages of Native American tribes and even allied with several of them, especially the Huron and Algonquin, who joined the French in fighting English soldiers and settlers.

ENGLAND AND NEW WORLD COLONIZATION

Of all the major European powers, the one that most encouraged long-term settlement in the New World was England. Economic extraction was important, but the formation of viable, long-lasting colonies was also seen as desirable. Despite initial difficulties during the early 1600s, English colonies thrived in North America. They grew rapidly, becoming full-fledged communities, if not major cities, whose men, women, and children were in the Americas to stay. England's American colonies developed strong systems of local government.

Many English colonists went to the New World to escape religious persecution at home, some for new opportunities. A number were convicts sentenced to exile in the Americas. Perhaps the greatest number of English settlers, at least during the 1600s, were indentured servants, who agreed to work for their masters a set number of years to pay for their passage across the Atlantic. Like other colonizing powers, the English used African slaves, especially in the tobacco- and cotton-growing southern settlements. In the beginning, the relationship between English colonists and Native Americans had been relatively peaceful. During the French and Indian Wars of the 1700s, however, that relationship soured. From that point onward, relations between English colonists and the Indians tended to be tense, if not hostile.

THE COLUMBIAN EXCHANGE

No matter how a European nation approached the colonization of the New World, it both affected the Americas and was affected by them. This impact went beyond military conquest and political control. The environmental effects that Europe and the Americas, as well as Africa, had on each other during the 1500s and 1600s rank among the most rapid and profound ecological transformations in world history. This transfer of plants, animals, foods, and diseases is typically referred to as the Columbian Exchange.

The exchange of foods, plants, and animals was considerable. From Europe came horses, sheep, goats, cattle, and pigs. The importation of these animals vastly increased the meat and milk supply of the peoples of North and South America. The horse provided labor and transport, and particularly changed the lifestyles of Native Americans, especially on the North American plains. Wheat, olive trees, and grapevines were brought to the Americas as well. Coffee, which had come from Arabia and Turkey, then had been transported to Africa, was found to flourish in the highlands of South America.

A vast array of foods came back to Europe from the Americas. They included manioc (which caught on in Africa, where it broadened the dietary base of many peoples there), squash, sweet potatoes, beans, peppers, peanuts, and vitamin-rich tomatoes. The southeastern part of North America was an excellent source of cotton (cotton was grown in many other parts of the world, such as Egypt and India, but North America became equally important).

Sugarcane from the Caribbean became exceptionally important to the European economy (as did, as noted previously, the growth of slavery). Tobacco and cacao (for the making of chocolate) were new discoveries, and both became eagerly sought luxury goods in

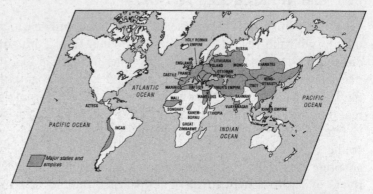

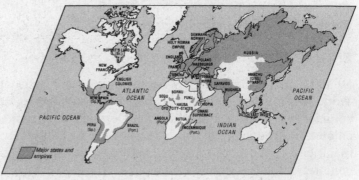

World Boundaries in 1453 and 1700.

In 1453, major states and empires were concentrated in Eurasia and small territories in Africa and the Americas. By 1700, large civilizations had spread into Russia, more portions of the Americas, and deeper into Africa.

Europe. Perhaps the most important New World crops for the Europeans were corn (maize) and potatoes. Both were easy to grow and had extremely high calorie yields per acre.

As detailed previously, disease was an unfortunate part of the Columbian Exchange. The transfer of diseases was almost completely one-sided. Because the Americas had been environmentally isolated from Eurasia and Africa for so many centuries, its peoples had never had the opportunity to build up an immunity to common diseases such as smallpox and measles.

When the Europeans arrived, carrying these and other germs, the effects were devastating. The death rate may have run as high as 25 percent of the original native population of North and South America. The only disease that Europeans are thought to have brought back from the natives of the New World is the debilitating, eventually fatal sexually transmitted disease syphilis (although not all scholars are completely agreed upon the origins of this disease).

QUICK REVIEW

1. Spain's principal reason for colonization in the New World was

   (A) economic profit
   (B) conversion of Native Americans to Catholicism
   (C) scientific curiosity
   (D) strategic advantage
   (E) the desire of ordinary Spanish to settle elsewhere

2. The main accomplishment of Bartolomé de Las Casas was

   (A) to develop a new method of silver mining
   (B) to discover the fabled Fountain of Youth
   (C) to help end the harsh treatment of Indians by Spanish conquistadors
   (D) to revolutionize agricultural technique in the New World
   (E) to conquer the Incas

3. The precious metal most sought by the Spanish and Portuguese in the Americas was

   (A) gold
   (B) copper
   (C) tin
   (D) silver
   (E) nickel

4. Which of the following best describes the Spanish and Portuguese approach to agriculture in the Americas?

   (A) The Spanish and Portuguese encouraged a balanced cultivation of a variety of crops.
   (B) The Spanish and Portuguese relied on large-scale plantation monoculture.
   (C) The Spanish and Portuguese experimented with a variety of agricultural methods.
   (D) The Spanish and Portuguese were mainly unconcerned with agriculture.
   (E) The Spanish and Portuguese made agriculture their highest priority in the Americas.

5. Which is an example of changes brought about by the Columbian Exchange?

   (A) the exportation of horses from North America to Europe
   (B) the extraction of silver from South America by the Spanish
   (C) the importation of coffee to the Americas from Europe
   (D) the spread of smallpox to Europe from North America
   (E) the arrival of corn and potatoes from the Americas to Europe

6. Native American victims of the Spanish conquest perished primarily by what means?

(A) gunpowder weapons
(B) starvation and famine
(C) diseases such as smallpox and measles
(D) mass execution by hanging
(E) mass execution by burning

7. Peter Stuyvesant was the leader of which colony?

(A) Hudson Bay
(B) New Amsterdam
(C) Pennsylvania
(D) Quebec
(E) Roanoke

8. What was the sole European nation to be concerned with the long-term settlement of large numbers of its people in the New World?

(A) England
(B) Portugal
(C) France
(D) the Netherlands
(E) Spain

9. What commodity were the French most interested in finding or harvesting in the New World?

(A) coffee
(B) tobacco
(C) sugar
(D) fur
(E) rum

10. What European power colonized Alaska and the Aleutian Islands?

(A) Great Britain
(B) Russia
(C) Spain
(D) Portugal
(E) Belgium

ANSWERS:

1. **A**, p. 234	6. **C**, p. 234
2. **C**, p. 234	7. **B**, p. 237
3. **D**, p. 235	8. **A**, p. 237
4. **B**, p. 235	9. **D**, p. 238
5. **E**, p. 240	10. **B**, p. 238

Unit Four: Review Questions

SAMPLE ESSAY QUESTIONS:

1. Compare and contrast the various approaches that Europe's major exploring powers took toward colonization. What motivated the nations of Europe to explore? How did they treat native peoples? For what purposes did they use their colonies?

2. Examine the likenesses and differences between the Ottoman Empire and Ming China. Pay special attention to the question of how such grand and powerful civilizations could, by the 1700s, have fallen so far from the position of global might and technological leadership they had enjoyed in the 1400s and 1500s.

3. How did the rise of the Atlantic slave trade affect Africa, economically, politically, and otherwise?

MULTIPLE-CHOICE QUESTIONS

1. Which of the following is NOT a reason why Europeans joined Protestant churches during the Reformation?

   (A) Many felt that the Catholic Church was too concerned with wealth and power.
   (B) Roman Catholic priests stopped performing rituals.
   (C) Many people saw the Catholic Church as hypocritical and corrupt.
   (D) Many people saw the Catholic Church as too bureaucratic.
   (E) none of the above

2. What was the purpose of the Counter-Reformation?

   (A) to reorganize and reform the Catholic Church and increase its public appeal
   (B) to avoid reforming the Catholic Church
   (C) to force individuals to adopt Catholicism
   (D) to colonize Africa
   (E) to outlaw abortion

3. Which of the following countries did NOT fight in major religious wars during the 1500s and 1600s?

   (A) Spain
   (B) Switzerland
   (C) Holland
   (D) England
   (E) Greece

4. Why did an increasing number of countries in Europe function more like nation-states beginning in the 1600s?

   (A) Feudalism became more widespread.
   (B) Politics began to decentralize.
   (C) State institutions, especially bureaucracies, central banks, and armed forces, strengthened.
   (D) Populations became more heterogeneous.
   (E) none of the above

5. How did Peter the Great change Russia's geopolitical orientation?

   (A) by focusing its foreign affairs more on Europe than Asia
   (B) by focusing its foreign affairs more on Asia than on Europe
   (C) by making it a democracy
   (D) by creating a parliament with control over the direction of foreign policy
   (E) by colonizing parts of Africa

6. In the 1700s,

   (A) most Europeans were merchants or involved in global trade in some way
   (B) the aristocracy grew in numbers
   (C) the majority of Europeans were peasants
   (D) the population began to shrink
   (E) the feminist movement gained momentum in France

7. How is capitalism different from mercantilism?

   (A) Capitalism focuses on state-controlled wealth accumulation, while mercantilism gives all commercial power to the merchants.
   (B) Capitalism arose earlier than mercantilism.
   (C) Capitalism is a socialist theory, whereas mercantilism is not.
   (D) Capitalism focuses on free trade and the market forces of supply and demand, while mercantilism features state-controlled economic activity.
   (E) Capitalism involves trade on land, whereas mercantilism involves maritime trade.

8. How did Ottoman leaders rule their empire during the 1500s?

   (A) They were religiously intolerant and failed to gain bureaucratic control over their subjects.
   (B) They were fairly religiously tolerant and efficient in governing their territory.
   (C) They allowed local people to vote for their own leaders, as long as they did not oppose Ottoman dominance.
   (D) They carried out a policy to exterminate non-Muslims.
   (E) The Ottoman Empire did not exist in the 1500s.

9. Why did China become more open to foreign influence after the end of the 1700s?

   (A) Its national wealth had declined, and it slipped backward in technological innovation and scientific advancement.
   (B) Its leaders encouraged more imports.
   (C) England promised the Chinese military support.
   (D) The Chinese economy was booming, and China's leaders wanted to increase trade with the West.
   (E) China welcomed Christian missionaries as modernizers.

10. How was Japan reunified by 1615?

   (A) The emperor reasserted his power.
   (B) It was forced to unify against outside invaders from Europe.
   (C) Its politicians settled their disputes for largely economic reasons.
   (D) Three politician-warlords used both force and diplomacy to reunite the country.
   (E) none of the above

11. The Mughal rulers

    I.   were Muslims

    II. ruled Thailand

    III. used military force and advanced weapons technology to maintain power

    IV. harmed the economy with their corruption

    (A) I, II, and III

    (B) II, III, and IV

    (C) I and III only

    (D) II and IV only

    (E) all of the above

12. In the early 1400s, what was the main result of Portuguese exploration of West and Central Africa?

    (A) The Portuguese gained control over the gold and ivory trade networks.

    (B) The Portuguese found a route to the West Indies.

    (C) The Portuguese established a position from which to conquer Egypt.

    (D) The Portuguese gained control over the iron trade.

    (E) none of the above

13. Which country did the Boers come from and in which African region did they settle?

    (A) Tunisia and Central Africa

    (B) the Netherlands and South Africa

    (C) Scotland and Kenya

    (D) France and Algeria

    (E) none of the above

14. In the 1400s, what was the trading system in the region of the Indian Ocean like?

    (A) Trade and development were in decline.

    (B) The Indian ocean was swarming with pirates, who prevented trade from taking place.

    (C) There was no trading system in this area at the time.

    (D) The area was a vibrant and cosmopolitan system of economic and cultural exchange.

    (E) none of the above

15. Why was there such a strong demand for African slaves among the Europeans?

    (A) Sugar cultivation in Brazil and the Caribbean became an increasingly important part of the Europeans' colonial economies.

    (B) European settlers in the New World became convinced that Native Americans were not suited for slavery.

    (C) Slaves were central to the triangular trade system in the 1600s and 1700s.

    (D) The encomienda system was abolished soon after the Spanish established their rule over most of the New World.

    (E) all of the above

16. Which of the following was NOT a part of the triangular trade system?

    (A) the so-called Middle Passage that brought slaves to the Americas

    (B) colonial raw materials that went to Africa

    (C) European manufactured goods that went to Africa

    (D) slaves traded for raw materials in the Americas

    (E) raw materials sent back to Europe from the Americas

17. Why were the Spanish able to conquer large and powerful Native American societies so quickly and decisively?

    I.   The Spanish had more sophisticated military technology.

    II. Native Americans tended to be pacifists and did not put up a fight.

    III. Native Americans died in great numbers from European diseases.

    IV. The Spanish used effective divide-and-conquer tactics.

    (A) I, II, and III

    (B) II, III, and IV

    (C) I, III, and IV

    (D) I and III only

    (E) II and IV only

18. According to the two maps on page 240,

(A) the size of Russia had contracted greatly between the 1450s and the early 1700s

(B) the Incas still controlled the west coast of South America even in the 1700s

(C) Great Zimbabwe still existed by 1700

(D) the same dynasty led China in the early 1700s as did in the 1450s

(E) both the Holy Roman and the Ottoman empires existed in some form between the years 1453 and 1700

19. What was a major consequence of plantation monoculture?

(A) the underuse of slaves

(B) low profits

(C) many different crops were harvested on the same plot of land

(D) environmental degradation

(E) farmers became more susceptible to disease

20. Which set of the following colonies is in the correct chronological order according to date of founding?

(A) Jamestown, Plymouth, Massachusetts Bay Colony, Pennsylvannia

(B) Plymouth, Jamestown, Pennsylvannia, Massachusetts Bay Colony

(C) Plymouth, Massachusetts Bay Colony, Pennsylvannia, Jamestown

(D) Jamestown, Pennsylvannia, Plymouth, Massachusetts Bay Colony

(E) none of the above

ANSWERS:

1. **B**, p. 187	11. **C**, p. 221
2. **A**, p. 188	12. **A**, p. 227
3. **E**, p. 188	13. **B**, p. 228
4. **C**, p. 190	14. **D**, p. 228
5. **A**, p. 191	15. **E**, p. 229
6. **C**, p. 195	16. **B**, p. 230
7. **D**, p. 196	17. **C**, p. 234
8. **B**, p. 209	18. **E**, p. 240
9. **A**, p. 214	19. **D**, p. 235
10. **D**, p. 217	20. **A**, p. 205

UNIT FIVE

World Cultures in the Modern Era

(1750–1914)

Unit Overview

GENERAL REMARKS

During the period from 1750 to 1914, the world entered the modern age. In this, it was led by the nations of the West, consisting of Europe and the United States.

Exactly what defines the modern age is a question of great debate among historians. In popular terms, the word *modern* is used simply as a synonym for "contemporary," or as a way to describe one's own times. In historical terms, the term *modern* is used to describe an era that is characterized by certain features. Although different scholars outline modernity's features in different ways, almost all are agreed that they include the following:

- In politics, there is a move away from traditional monarchy and toward greater political representation. The end result in most societies is some form of democracy, or at least the appearance of democracy.
- In economics, mechanization and industrialization become driving forces. There is a shift from feudalism and mercantilism to capitalism. Rather than being based primarily on agriculture, economies are based increasingly on industry and commerce.
- In society, there is class transformation, as old aristocracies (whose status derives from noble birth) gradually fade away, in favor of new elites whose status derives from wealth. New classes expand or emerge, especially the middle class and industrial working class. As agriculture gives way to industry, modern societies become urbanized. Population growth accelerates in the modern era.
- In culture, a scientific, secular worldview becomes dominant. In arts and letters, styles change more rapidly and radically than ever before.

In all these things, Europe, along with the young United States, moved forward first. Great political upheavals such as the American Revolution and the French Revolution began the long process of expanding political representation and giving greater numbers of people a greater voice in politics. It was in Europe that the Industrial Revolution began, and it was there that capitalism emerged. Both transformed the economies of the world irrevocably. Population growth, class diversification, and urbanization were hallmarks of Western social development during the late 1700s and throughout the 1800s. As for modern culture and intellectual life, the foundations for that had already been laid in Europe during the 1700s, during the Scientific Revolution and the Enlightenment.

To varying degrees, modernization reached the rest of the world during the nineteenth and early twentieth centuries. A few non-Western nations adapted well and quickly, such as Japan. Some modernized slowly or half-heartedly, such as the Ottoman Empire, China, or the nations of Latin America. Other civilizations, most notably those of Africa and Southeast Asia, lagged farther behind. No matter the pace, however, change eventually came to all these regions.

Another overarching development of the era of 1750 to 1914 was the rise of the West as the world's dominant civilization. Not only did the West's rapid industrialization and modernization make it prosperous and technologically advanced, they made it powerful as well. European (and

American) imperialism gave control over most of the world's habitable territory to the nations of the West. Many of the areas of the world that had originally been colonized during the Age of Exploration—such as North and South America—became free during the late 1700s and early 1800s. However, a new wave of imperialism, referred to by many historians as the new imperialism, swept over East Asia, Southeast Asia, Central Asia, the Middle East, the Pacific, and Africa during the 1800s and early 1900s. Seeking markets and raw materials, armed with industrial-era weaponry, the nations of the West established control over a vast portion of the globe. Never before in history had a single civilization become so powerful. As impressive as imperialism was as a practical accomplishment, however, it carried with it a steep moral and ethical price. Imperialism was inextricably bound up with warfare, racial prejudice, economic rapacity, and slavery. Many of the harmful effects of Western imperialism are still felt in regions such as Africa, Latin America, and Asia to this day.

By the end of the nineteenth century, Europe—wealthy, sophisticated, militarily dominant—was at the peak of its power. Unbeknownst to them, however, the nations of Europe were about to fall from that pinnacle. The young United States was overtaking Europe in economic and military strength. New philosophies, scientific theories, and cultural movements were calling into question the traditional certainties and values of the Western world. Most important, diplomatic trends were inclining the nations of Europe toward war. The conflict that resulted from the diplomatic tensions of the late 1800s and early 1900s—World War I—would be the worst war ever fought to that date. Although no one could have guessed it before its starting date of 1914, World War I would do much to start, then speed up, the process of European decline.

BROAD TRENDS

GLOBAL POWER AND INTERNATIONAL RELATIONS

- The technological, economic, and military rise of the West—Europe and the United States—completely altered the balance of global power. World affairs were increasingly determined by foreign-policy and military developments in Europe, especially during the 1800s.
- The United States broke away from English rule during the late 1700s. During the 1800s, it went on to dominate the North American continent and become a world power.
- The Spanish and Portuguese colonies of Central and South America freed themselves from European rule during the early 1800s.
- In North Africa, the eastern Mediterranean, and the Middle East, the gradual collapse of the Ottoman Empire presented the nations of Europe with a troubling and destabilizing diplomatic issue that became known as the Eastern Question.
- European (and U.S.) imperialism—the "new imperialism" of the mid-to-late 1800s—gave the nations of the West unprecedented global dominance. In 1815, the nations of the West controlled 35 percent of the world's habitable territory. In 1914, they controlled 85 percent.
- The one non-Western nation that developed an effective, modern, colonial empire was Japan, in the late nineteenth and early twentieth centuries.
- In Europe, the new nations of Germany and Italy appeared.
- By the end of the nineteenth century, diplomatic tensions, nationalism, and competition over overseas imperial possessions made it increasingly likely that the nations of Europe would go to war. An alliance system formed. The level of aggression rose steadily. In 1914, the war that resulted was World War I.

POLITICAL DEVELOPMENTS

- The hallmark of modern political life is greater popular representation in government and politics.
- This trend first got underway in the West. It began in the late 1700s, primarily with the American Revolution and the French Revolution.
- During the 1800s, especially after the 1848 Revolution, politics in Europe and the West became increasingly representative. By the end of the century, Great Britain, France, and the United States, along with a few smaller countries, had become democracies (although women could not yet vote). Even in nondemocratic states, bureaucracies and parliamentary bodies were becoming an increasingly important part of government, even more so than the will of individual rulers and monarchs.
- Other parts of the world tended to be slower in moving away from traditional autocracies or monarchies. A few, however, such as Japan and the Ottoman Empire, did so, developing parliamentary forms of monarchy by the start of the twentieth century. The nations of Latin America developed parliamentary governments in theory, but many of those slipped into dictatorship or military rule.
- Much of the non-Western world spent most of the nineteenth century under European (in some cases, U.S.) colonial domination.

ECONOMIC DEVELOPMENTS

- Economic life was transformed by the phenomenon of industrialization, which displaced agriculture as the largest and most important sector of the economy. Industrialization swept Europe in the late 1700s and early 1800s, then spread to the rest of the world. The Industrial Revolution began in England.
- The dominant mode of economic organization in the West became free-market, laissez-faire capitalism. Along with industry, commerce and banking—the foundations of a money-based economy (as opposed to a land-based one)—grew in importance.
- Industrialization transformed class structures. The traditional aristocracy, with its status based on land and family prestige, faded. Among the lower classes, the proportion of people who remained employed in agriculture shrank. The middle class grew tremendously, gained great wealth, and diversified. A new lower class, the industrial working class, was born.
- Industrialization led to urbanization, as industry and commerce grew, relative to agriculture, as sectors of national economies. Cities grew in size, and more cities were established.
- For any society, the first decades of industrialization were typically painful for the lower classes. Working conditions were generally poor, and wages were low. Over time, however, industrialization greatly raised the average prosperity of a society's population, and even the lower classes began to benefit after some time.
- The non-Western world adopted industrialization at varying speeds and in varying ways. Sometimes, European imperial powers introduced industrial practices into their colonies. In other cases, rulers of free non-Western nations would try to impose industrialization from above.
- One of the bedrocks of the world economy during the late 1700s and most of the 1800s was slavery. Africa was the primary victim of slave trading. The East African and Atlantic slave trades continued into the 1870s and 1880s, respectively.

CULTURAL DEVELOPMENTS

- Starting in the West, a scientific, secular worldview became paramount. The technological and scientific advancements of the Industrial Revolution, as well as the theories of scholars such as Charles Darwin, accelerated this process.

- Greater access to public education became a normal part of life in western Europe, northern Europe, Canada, and the United States throughout the 1800s. Literacy rates rose as a result. The same is true for many other parts of the world during the late 1800s.
- There was a tremendous movement of peoples during this period. In particular, there were massive waves of emigration from Europe and China to North and South America during the mid-to-late 1800s and early 1900s. The United States was the preferred destination, but Canada, Argentina, and Chile took in many immigrants as well.
- Nationalism became an incredibly powerful cultural attitude in Europe, then elsewhere. By the end of the 1800s, nationalist movements were becoming prevalent in non-Western parts of the world that were dominated by foreign colonial rule. Both in Europe and elsewhere, nationalism became a strong and volatile political force.
- The non-Western world began to adopt many of the artistic and literary forms of the West, especially print culture and writing styles, as well as architecture. Conversely, styles from Asia, Africa, and the Middle East had an influence on Western culture, particularly in painting, sculpture, and décor.
- In Europe and the Americas, the pace of cultural change sped up considerably. By the end of the 1800s and the beginning of the 1900s, new artistic and literary trends were emerging at a rapid rate. Increasingly, new artistic and literary trends were about breaking rules and defying conventions.

GENDER ISSUES

- Although in most societies the status of women remained secondary, the period of 1750 to 1914 saw great changes in gender relations.
- In the West, a greater awareness of the unfair and unequal treatment of women began to spread, starting around the late 1700s. This was stimulated largely by the theories of Enlightenment philosophy, as well as by the active role played by women in the American and, especially, French revolutions.
- During the late 1700s and early 1800s, the Industrial Revolution profoundly altered the conditions under which women worked. The Industrial Revolution shifted the workplace away from the farm, where men and women both lived and worked, to mines, factories, and other spaces away from the home. This shift created a domestic sphere and a separate working sphere away from the home.
- In Europe and the United States, women of the lower classes were generally compelled to enter the workplace (most frequently textile factories). These women also bore the double burden of serving as the primary homemakers and caregivers for their families.
- After the mid-1800s, the number of working women in Europe and the United States declined. Women of the middle and upper classes had rarely worked to begin with. As wages for industrial workers rose (making those jobs more desirable to men), and as laws restricting the number of hours women and children could work were passed, the number of lower-class working women fell. A cult of domesticity, stressing that women's place was in the home, whereas men's was in the workplace, dominated Western culture—especially among the middle and upper classes—during the mid-to-late nineteenth century.
- Certain occupations were open to women, such as child care (governesses), teaching, domestic household work (servants and maids), nursing, and artisanry.
- Strong and vigorous women's movements appeared in Europe, Canada, and the United States. They agitated for suffrage (the right to vote), equal opportunity to work, equal pay, temperance, and other causes.
- A handful of European nations—but no major ones—gave women the right to vote before World War I.

- The move toward women's equality tended to be slower in non-Western societies. In some, however, the educational level of women rose, as did the extent of property rights. As in the West, women worked especially in certain occupations, such as agricultural laborers, artisans, teachers, nurses, and so on. As non-Western parts of the world industrialized, lower-class women tended to enter the workplace, as they did in the industrial West.

COMPARATIVE ISSUES TO CONSIDER

- Discuss the response of various non-Western parts of the world to the imperial encroachments of Europe and the United States during the nineteenth century.
- Compare the status of women in the West and that of women in other parts of the world. Alternatively, how were women of various classes within a given society affected by industrialization?
- Describe the various approaches taken by various Western powers to colonization.
- How does the late-nineteenth-century wave of imperialism (the "new" imperialism) compare to earlier waves of colonization?
- Discuss the various ways in which non-Western states attempted to modernize and adopt industrial practices. How important is the question of whether industrialization was imposed on a society from above, by the ruler, or emerged from below?
- Take a close look at Japanese industrialization and European industrialization. How were they alike and how did they differ?
- How did Western intervention in Latin America differ from Western intervention in Africa during the period from 1750 to 1914?
- Examine the emergence of various nationalist and anticolonial movements in non-Western parts of the world. Compare and contrast their methods and their successes or failures.

KEY TERMS AND CONCEPTS

Louis XVI and Marie Antoinette
the Estates General and the Tennis-Court
   Oath
the French Revolution
Bastille Day
Declaration of the Rights of Man and the
   Citizen
the Jacobins, the Committee of Public Safety,
   and the Reign of Terror
Thermidor
the Directory
Napoleon Bonaparte
the Congress of Vienna and the Congress
   System
Klemens von Metternich
reaction
serfdom in Russia
the Revolution of 1848
the Third Reform Act
Napoleon III (Louis Napoleon)

the Dreyfus Affair
nationalism
the unification of Italy
the unification of Germany
Otto von Bismarck
the *Augsleich*
Alexander II and the emancipation of Russian
   serfs
Mary Wollstonecraft, *A Vindication of the
   Rights of Woman*
women's movements and women's suffrage
Romanticism
Realism
Charles Darwin, *On the Origin of Species*
Impressionism
Friedrich Nietzsche, Albert Einstein, Sigmund
   Freud
imperialism and "new" imperialism
Cecil Rhodes
social Darwinism

Rudyard Kipling and the "White Man's Burden"

la mission civilisatrice

manifest destiny

the Balkans

Wilhelm II

the Triple Alliance

the Anglo-German naval race

the Triple Entente

the Schlieffen Plan

proto-industrialization

the Enclosure Acts

the English textile trade

the steam engine

James Watt

the Industrial Revolution

the steamship

the railroad

the telegraph

vulcanization (rubber)

the Bessemer process (steel)

electricity and petroleum as new power sources

industrial war

the internal combustion engine

the decline of the aristocracy

the rise of the middle class

the birth of the working class

population growth in Europe and North America

urbanization

capitalism and laissez-faire economics

Adam Smith, *The Wealth of Nations*

Thomas Malthus, *Essay on Populations*

David Ricardo and the iron law of wages

socialism

the utopian socialists

Karl Marx, Friedrich Engels, and communism

trade unions

the global spread of industrialization

monoculture

the Ottoman Empire

the janissaries

the reforms of Mehmed III

the Tanzimat reforms

the Eastern Question

the Greek War of Independence

the revolt of Muhammad Ali

the Crimean War

the Balkan crisis of 1876–1878 and the Congress of Berlin

Enver Pasha and the Young Turks

the Balkan Wars

the Suez Canal

Isma'il

the Anglo-Egyptian Administration

Charles Gordon, the Mahdi, and the battle of Khartoum

the partition of Persia

the Russian conquest of Central Asia

the Great Game

Kangxi and Qianlong

Cao Xueqin, *Dream of the Red Chamber*

tea as China's leading economic commodity

the opium trade

the Opium Wars and the Treaty of Nanking

Hong Xiuquan and the Taiping Rebellion

the Empress Dowager Cixi

the Sino-Japanese War

the Open Door Policy

missionaries in China

the Boxer Rebellion

Sun Yat-sen, the People's Principles, and the Nationalist (Kuomintang) Party

the Chinese Republic

the Tokugawa Shogunate

Commodore Matthew Perry

Emperor Meiji and the Meiji Restoration

the abolition of Japanese feudalism

Japanese industrialization and the *zaibatsu*

the annexation of Korea

the Russo-Japanese War

the Mughal Empire

the British East India Company

Sir Robert Clive and the battle of Plassey

Indian cotton and the East Indian spice trade

the zamindar system

the Raj

sati (suttee), thuggee, and the untouchables

sepoys

the Indian Mutiny (Sepoy Rebellion)

the Indian National Congress (Congress Party)

Mohandas K. (Mahatma) Gandhi

the British establishment of Singapore

the French conquest of Indochina

Thailand's modernization and independence

the Spanish-American War and the annexation of the Philippines

Emilio Aguinaldo

the Atlantic slave trade
the scramble for Africa
Asante (Ashanti)
the Boers (Afrikaners)
the Zulu
Shaka Zulu
the diamond and gold industries of South
   Africa
Zanzibar and the Arab influence in East Africa
the East African slave trade
the outlawing of the Atlantic slave trade
David Livingston
Leopold II and the Belgian Congo
Menelik II and the battle of Adowa
the Herero Wars
Otto von Bismarck and the Berlin Conference
the American Revolution
George Washington
the Declaration of Independence and the
   United States Constitution
the Monroe Doctrine

the Louisiana Purchase
slavery in the United States
immigration to the United States
Canada and the British North America Act
John Macdonald
François Toussaint L'Ouverture and the Haitian
   Rebellion
the Latin American wars of independence
Simón Bolívar
Pedro I of Brazil
Miguel Hidalgo and José Maria Morelos
Agustín Iturbide
caudillos
Benito Juárez
monoculture, plantation agriculture, and
   foreign economic dominance of Latin
   America
the Mexican-American War
Maximilian
U.S. "dollar diplomacy" in Latin America
José Martí

CHAPTER 20

The Europeans at Home: Revolution, Reaction, and Reform

During the century and a half that lasted from 1750 to 1914, the European political order changed dramatically. In the mid-1700s, all of Europe's major nations were ruled by monarchies. Although a handful of these monarchies were parliamentary in nature, allowing for some level of popular representation, most were absolute—meaning that, in theory, the monarch had few, if any, restrictions on his or her power. In general, governments in Europe were dominated by kings, queens, and emperors, who shared power only with aristocratic noble classes. In any given country, the nobility made up an extremely small proportion of the overall population, but controlled most of the country's wealth, owned most of the nation's land, and enjoyed virtually all influence over politics.

From the 1770s through the 1810s, this state of affairs was shaken apart by a wave of revolutions that swept the Atlantic world. The most famous of these uprisings took place in Britain's North American colonies (see Chapter 27) and France, but there were others as well. Although not all of these revolutions accomplished their goals, they dealt a death blow to absolute monarchy in most parts of Europe. Another effect was to cement in place among the peoples of Europe a set of political ideals and to inspire a hope that those ideals could be met in the future. From the early 1810s onward, an ever-increasing number of people in Europe began to dream of—and fight for—social and political systems that treated people more fairly and gave them more of a voice in government. Another factor that played a role in changing ordinary Europeans' aspirations was the huge social and economic change brought about by the Industrial Revolution, which took place roughly at the same time as the political revolutions in America, France, and elsewhere, and is described in Chapter 21.

Although a conservative backlash, known as reaction, settled over Europe during the three decades that followed the French Revolution and its Napoleonic aftermath, the desire for more equitable and more representative government never died. In every European country, rulers and the people they ruled struggled over this question. Each nation dealt with this issue in different ways and at different paces. The general trend, however, was for most European governments to liberalize and democratize over time. This was especially the case after 1848, another year of revolutions and great uprisings. During the second half of the century, reform movements helped to accelerate political change—as well as social and economic progress—in most European nations.

By the end of the 1800s and the beginning of the 1900s, most countries in Europe were more or less representative, and at least a few were, by the standards of the day, democratic. Most European economies were fully or partially industrialized. As described in Chapter 22, European powers, thanks to their imperial successes, dominated a vast amount of the rest of the world, politically, militarily, and economically. These years were Europe's peak period of global might. Underlying diplomatic and strategic tensions, however, would give rise to World War I (1914–1918): the huge cataclysm that started the process of toppling Europe from its position of world power.

THE FRENCH REVOLUTION AND OTHER ATLANTIC REVOLUTIONS

LONG-TERM CAUSES OF THE FRENCH REVOLUTION

The causes of the French Revolution (1789–1799) are many and complex. Deep, long-term factors included

- The wide social and economic gap between ordinary citizens (known as the Third Estate) and the country's elite, the Catholic clergy (First Estate) and aristocracy (Second Estate)
- The unfairness of the tax system, from which the wealthy First and Second Estates were exempt
- The frustrated ambitions of the growing middle class, who possessed wealth and education but, because they belonged to the Third Estate, like the lower classes, were barred from social advancement
- The influence of the ideas of the Enlightenment (see Chapter 13), whose philosophers, many of whom were French, made powerful arguments in favor of fair government, equal treatment of all citizens, the separation of governmental powers, and civil rights of various types

Added to this list were the political ineptitude of the last two absolute monarchs of France, Louis XV and Louis XVI (1774–1792), and a serious, long-standing financial crisis in France. Another ingredient was the example of the American Revolution of 1775 to 1783 (see Chapter 27), which France supported economically (adding to its financial troubles) and militarily, and which the French people admired. Little did the French government realize that by helping the American Revolution succeed, it would be encouraging revolution in its own country shortly afterward.

FINANCIAL CRISIS IN FRANCE

The immediate cause of the French Revolution was the impending bankruptcy of the French government in the mid-to-late 1780s. Saddled with debts piled up by the previous king, having spent even more money on America's revolution, unable to tax the rich First and Second Estates, and burdened with a wife, Marie Antoinette, who spent lavishly, Louis XVI could not solve France's financial crisis. By 1787 and 1788, inflation, unemployment, poor harvests, food shortages, and rising prices were tormenting the entire country.

THE ESTATES GENERAL AND THE BEGINNING OF THE FRENCH REVOLUTION

In 1789, desperate for a solution, Louis XVI summoned the Estates General: a national assembly composed of delegates from each of the three estates. In May 1789, these delegates, approximately half of them from the Third Estate, met with the king at his palace of Versailles. The delegates of the Third Estate—mainly middle-class lawyers and civil servants—fully expected to negotiate seriously about changing the tax system and granting middle- and lower-class French citizens basic civil rights. By June, however, it was clear that neither Louis XVI nor the First and Second Estates were prepared to reach any kind of useful compromise. This clash of wills sparked ten years of revolution that changed France, Europe, and the world forever.

On June 20, 1789, the delegates of the Third Estate, joined now by a few liberal members of the First and Second Estates, withdrew from the Estates General to an indoor tennis court at Versailles, calling themselves the National Assembly. With its so-called Tennis-Court Oath, the National Assembly swore not to disband or leave Versailles until Louis XVI agreed to grant France a constitution.

In the beginning, Louis pretended to cooperate, but in secret, he summoned troops to come to Versailles to arrest the National Assembly. When word of this leaked out, the National Assembly called upon the people of nearby Paris to rise up in support. The people of Paris, especially lower-class radicals called *sans-culottes*, already weary of rising prices and food shortages, stormed the city streets and rioted for several days. The climax of the Paris revolt was July 14, 1789, or Bastille Day, when crowds seized the dreaded fortress where political prisoners were kept. Bastille Day is still considered to be the French day of independence.

Throughout the summer and fall of 1789, the revolution spread. Other large cities rose up in imitation of Paris. In the countryside, peasants revolted. They burned noblemen's estates and seized aristocrats' lands. By October, Louis XVI and Marie Antoinette had been taken into custody and brought from Versailles to Paris.

PHASES OF THE FRENCH REVOLUTION

In the meantime, the National Assembly, the first of many revolutionary governments, had assumed political leadership in France. Most historians divide the ten years that followed into three phases:

- A moderate period (1789–1791)
- A radical period (1792–1794)
- A period of mildly conservative backlash (1794–1799)

The general pattern was that political power at first rested with the middle class and liberal members of the nobility. As time passed and France's various problems worsened, power shifted more and more to the lower classes (especially in the cities) and the politicians who represented them. This stance was much more left leaning. For a time, this extreme radicalism prevailed. Afterward, however, there was a move back toward the middle. By 1799, the French Revolution had exhausted itself. It would end with the rise of Napoleon.

THE MODERATE PHASE OF THE FRENCH REVOLUTION

During the first phase, the goal of the National Assembly was to create a constitutional monarchy, based somewhat on Britain's parliamentary system and inspired by the ideals of the Enlightenment and the recent American Revolution. For example, a major figure in the National Assembly was the Marquis de Lafayette, a liberal nobleman who had fought on the side of George Washington's troops. In August 1789, the National Assembly issued the Declaration of the Rights of Man and the Citizen. This document guaranteed basic civil rights and liberties; it was based solidly on America's Declaration of Independence, and Thomas Jefferson himself assisted in drafting it.

Over the next two years, the National Assembly, then the Legislative Assembly (which replaced it after elections in 1791), liberalized France greatly. They abolished noble privileges (including tax exemption), nationalized lands belonging to the Catholic Church, and separated state and religion. The Legislative Assembly was elected by adult male citizens. Almost all power rested with the assembly. The king was allowed to stay on the throne, but his constitutional role was extremely limited. Louis XVI and Marie Antoinette, therefore, were reduced to the status of figureheads.

Overall, the guiding principle of the National and Legislative Assemblies was the famous motto, "Liberty, Fraternity, and Equality."

There were, however, problems. For one thing, the rights and ideals proclaimed by the revolutionary regime applied at first only to white, Catholic, adult males. It took many months for full privileges and the right to vote to be extended to Jews, Protestants, and the blacks of France's Caribbean possessions. Legally, the principles of liberty, fraternity, and equality—especially the right to vote—were never extended to women, even though female intellectuals, peasants, and workers had played a major role in toppling Louis XVI's absolutist regime.

More practically, the National and Legislative Assemblies proved unable to solve the many problems France suffered in 1790 and 1791. The economy worsened. Other countries, hostile to the concept of revolution and fearful for the safety of the royal family, threatened war (in particular, Austria, Marie Antoinette's original home, warned the French that harm to the royal family would result in war). The Legislative Assembly, elected in September 1791, was significantly more radical than the original National Assembly, and more willing to fight other countries in order to spread the revolution beyond France's borders.

Other problems were stirred up by France's former aristocrats, as well as Louis XVI and Marie Antoinette. Many French nobles fled the country during the revolution's moderate phase, and plotted across the border in countries like Austria and the German states to overthrow the new government in a counterrevolution. The royal family, while pretending to cooperate with the revolutionary government and fulfill its constitutional role, secretly plotted with counterrevolutionary nobles (this was especially due to the prompting of Marie Antoinette, who was more conservative than Louis). In June 1791, the royal family attempted to escape from France; their failure caused a scandal and made it increasingly difficult for the National and Legislative Assemblies to trust the king and queen. All of these tensions would soon burst out of control.

THE RADICAL PHASE OF THE FRENCH REVOLUTION AND THE REIGN OF TERROR

In 1792, French politics took a sharp leftward turn, and the Revolution entered its second, radical phase. In April 1792, France went to war with Austria and Prussia. For the next two decades, France would be fighting constantly with its neighbors. From 1792 through the summer of 1794, wartime hysteria and the paranoia caused by early defeats quickly radicalized the entire country.

Throughout 1792, the economy continued to worsen. The mood of the general population darkened, and fewer and fewer people had patience for the moderate constitutional monarchy. In September 1792, rioting and street fighting in Paris led to the fall of the Legislative Assembly and the original constitutional arrangement. A new constitution was written, the king was stripped of all power, and the French Republic was proclaimed. A new legislature, the National Convention, was elected, and it was dominated by radical parties, the most important of which was the Jacobins. Louis and Marie Antoinette had survived the first two years as figurehead monarchs. They were now private citizens, and they were placed under house arrest.

Although the National Convention was elected by universal male suffrage in 1792, it became increasingly dictatorial under radical leadership. The chief party, the Jacobins, led by Maximilien Robespierre, created a small executive body called the Committee of Public Safety, which quickly seized all control. The radical government continued and expanded the war effort against the rest of Europe. It put the king on trial for treason in December 1792 and put him to death in January 1793 (Marie Antoinette was executed in October 1793). Caught up in a full-scale war effort, the Jacobin-led Committee of Public Safety mobilized the entire economy for combat and instituted the modern world's first national draft.

Robespierre and the Committee of Public Safety carried out a massive Reign of Terror (summer 1793–summer 1794), searching for spies, traitors, and counterrevolutionaries. Even other radical parties fell victim to the Terror. Civil liberties and due process were completely ignored, as more than 300,000 people were arrested without warrant and tried without jury or appeal. During the Reign of Terror, 30,000 to 50,000 of these people were put to death, mostly by guillotine.

THERMIDOR AND THE THIRD PHASE OF THE FRENCH REVOLUTION

This second phase of the Revolution came to an end in July 1794, when Robespierre himself was arrested and executed by fellow members of the Committee of Public Safety. This moment is known as the Thermidorian reaction, and it began the third phase of the Revolution: the antiradical backlash that attempted to restore order and normality to France. This third phase lasted from 1794 to 1799. A new constitution was written, and it gave most political power to a governmental body known as the Directory. The new constitution was less democratic than that of 1792, and the Directory ranged from moderate to mildly conservative in its politics. It tried to heal the wounds caused by the Reign of Terror, but its middle-of-the-road politics made it quite unpopular. The Directory would be overthrown in November 1799, bringing an end to the French Revolution.

OTHER ATLANTIC REVOLUTIONS

Before going on to the French Revolution's aftermath, it should be noted that other political upheavals were taking place during the 1790s. A number of other "Atlantic revolutions" occurred during these years, most of them inspired by the American and French revolutions. European countries that rose up against absolute monarchy or foreign domination included Ireland, Belgium, the Netherlands, and Poland. All of these uprisings failed, but they were serious blows to the governments against which they were staged.

As described in Chapter 27, the French Revolution, in conjunction with the earlier American Revolution, sparked successful uprisings in Haiti and Latin America.

NAPOLEON BONAPARTE

As for France, following the Revolution was the reign of Napoleon Bonaparte (1799–1815). An exceptionally talented general, Napoleon served in the armies of the French Revolution and gained a reputation as a national hero during the mid-1790s. He joined the coup that overthrew the Directory in 1799. His tremendous popularity and political skills allowed him to become the sole leader of France. Napoleon claimed to follow the ideals of the French Revolution. In reality, he created a dictatorship that was stronger and more efficient than the absolute monarchy of the French kings had been. Indeed, in 1804, Napoleon had himself crowned emperor of France.

Evaluating Napoleon's reign is difficult. He was arrogant and autocratic, with very little respect for democracy or constitutional rule. His wars lasted for years, cost untold amounts of money, and killed millions of people. On the other hand, he modernized France in many ways, creating institutions that still exist today, such as the Bank of France and the Civil Law Code (known then as the Napoleonic Code, and still the foundation of modern French law). Until his wars began to go badly in 1812, his military skills made France immensely rich and powerful.

Napoleon is best known for his military career. He gained national fame during the mid-1790s with flamboyantly successful campaigns in Italy and Egypt. After coming to power, he continued the wars France had started fighting during the Revolution. His chief enemies were Great Britain, Austria, Prussia, and Russia. From 1805 through 1811, he won a series of wars that made France the most powerful nation in Europe, if not the world: the only major nations not under his influence by this point were Britain and Russia.

Several factors brought about Napoleon's downfall: his inability to counter Britain's naval power, a long and painful guerrilla war in Spain and Portugal, and finally, an overambitious invasion of Russia in 1812. From 1812 to 1814, Napoleon's military fortunes declined. He was defeated and captured in 1814. However, he escaped in 1815 and made an attempt to return to power. This was foiled by the British and Prussians, led by the Duke of Wellington, an English general, at the Battle of Waterloo. After his second defeat, Napoleon was exiled to the island of St. Helena, where he spent the rest of his life in captivity. He died in 1821.

SUCCESSES, FAILURES, AND LONG-TERM EFFECTS OF THE FRENCH REVOLUTION

What made the French Revolution and its Napoleonic aftermath so important? After all, in many ways, the Revolution failed. The dream of a popular government, run by elected officials of the people, faded, only to be replaced by the harsh Committee of Public Safety, the semidictatorial Directory, and the unmistakably dictatorial Napoleon. Then, after Napoleon's defeat, the old royal family was actually restored to power. Moreover, it is hard to argue that liberty, fraternity, and equality were achieved by means of Jacobin terror and the guillotine.

On the other hand, the French Revolution, along with the other Atlantic revolutions, did away with absolute monarchy during the 1790s and early 1800s. Kings, queens, and emperors continued to sit on European thrones after these revolutions. But in no major country—with the possible exception of Russia—were monarchs all-powerful. As time passed, they had to yield more and more of their power to ministries, parliaments, legislatures, and other governmental bodies. Even more important, governments during the nineteenth century and afterward had to be more attentive to their peoples' desires and demands. Perhaps the greatest legacy of the Atlantic revolutions—especially the American and French ones—was to start a trend that remains the hallmark of modern politics: greater popular participation in government. The rulers of the 1800s might not give into all of their subjects' demands. But they could no longer ignore them as they had before. And, as time passed, ordinary people became more and more successful in getting their voices heard and their demands met. The story of European politics during the nineteenth and early twentieth centuries is primarily *this* story.

REACTION AND RETRENCHMENT: POLITICS IN EUROPE, 1815–1848

THE CONGRESS OF VIENNA

After the defeat of Napoleon, a distinctly conservative political order settled over Europe. This was largely due to the peace settlement that followed the Napoleonic Wars, the Congress of Vienna (1814–1815). Although delegates from all European nations were present, the countries that dominated the Congress of Vienna were Austria, Russia, Prussia, and Great Britain. France, although the defeated power, was allowed to take a substantial part in discussions. At Vienna, the great powers redrew the map of Europe. They shrank France to its prerevolutionary borders. They each took territory for themselves, especially in Poland, eastern Europe, and the Italian peninsula. It was decided not to allow the German states or Italian states to unify.

Greed and self-interest were part of these decisions, but the great powers were also concerned with strategy and long-term peace. Hoping to prevent another large, long-lasting, and costly set of conflicts such as the Revolutionary and Napoleonic wars had been, the great powers sought to achieve a balance of power in Europe. Peace, it was felt, could be preserved if all major countries agreed to maintain a rough equilibrium of geographical advantage and military forces. This idea came mainly from the Austrian politician Klemens von Metternich. In a military sense, Metternich's balance of power, the so-called Congress System, or Concert of Europe, kept the peace. Not until the 1850s did the nations of Europe go to war with each other. Even then, and for the rest of the 1800s, wars tended to be small in scale and short in duration.

REACTION IN EARLY NINETEENTH-CENTURY EUROPE

The Congress of Vienna also acted out of conservative principle. Convinced that revolution caused war, and that any kind of liberalism automatically led to revolution, politicians such as Metternich believed that the best way to preserve peace and stability was to oppose any widening of governmental representation and any kind of liberal or democratic concessions. Most rulers, frightened by the excesses of the French Revolution, agreed.

This conservative backlash was known as reaction. For the next three decades, political controls tightened in most European nations. Where kings had been toppled, they were brought back—this included France, where Louis XVI's brother, Louis XVIII, ascended the throne (Louis XVIII was not, however, an *absolute* monarch). Freedom of expression and freedom of the press were curtailed, and censorship was heavy, especially in central and eastern Europe. Secret police forces, which watched over their nations' populations, became commonplace in most countries. Civil liberties of all types suffered.

GREAT BRITAIN

Each nation worked its social tensions out in different ways. Britain, with its parliamentary system and, among Europe's major nations, the longest tradition of recognizing civil liberties, inched toward a more participatory form of government. Progress was slow. Even though the monarch had very few powers compared to Parliament, the number of people who could vote for or be in Parliament was quite small. Political participation was restricted mainly to the aristocratic and upper middle class, less than 5 percent of the population. During the first half of the 1800s, almost no one among the national leadership had an interest in widening political participation. However, Britain's lower classes—especially the growing industrial working class—agitated for greater political rights, as well as greater economic protections. Over time, the government, in order to avoid revolt, gradually gave into such demands. This took a long time, and it was done not by means of revolution or violence, but by means of reform. Three major Reform Acts would change Britain's electoral laws throughout the century. The First Reform Act was passed in 1832. It widened suffrage only slightly, but did much to improve districting and the general operation of the voting system. The First Reform Act was the first step on Britain's long road toward democratization.

FRANCE

Another country that made some progress toward greater liberalization during these years was France. However, whereas Britain did so by means of reform, France did so by means of occasional revolutions. After Napoleon's defeat in 1815, France was placed under a parliamentary monarchy, with the family of Louis XVI back on the throne. But, remembering the rights and privileges they had gained during the years of the revolution, the French were restless under royal rule, and overthrew the monarchy in 1830. A new king came to the throne, but the fact that he felt compelled to nickname himself the "Citizen-King" shows how important public opinion was becoming in France. From 1830 to 1848, a little progress was made toward making the French legislature more representative, but not enough. As a result, it was in France that the great revolutionary wave of 1848 (described presently) began.

CENTRAL AND EASTERN EUROPE

The nations of central and eastern Europe tended to remain more repressive. During the first part of the century, there was little, if any, widening of political representation. Austria's emperor was advised by Metternich, the architect of reaction and the Congress System. Although Prussia developed a law-based state, in which the crown shared power with a legislature and was subject to constitutional guidelines, the king exercised great authority. Prussia remained militaristic and authoritarian for years. In Russia, the tsar continued to be all-powerful, at least in theory. There were no meaningful legal checks on the tsar's authority, and Russia's rulers between 1815 and 1855 were exceptionally conservative. Russia was also home to one of Europe's most oppressive institutions: serfdom, the system of unfree agricultural labor that had died away in most parts of Europe decades, if not centuries, before. In addition to being immoral, serfdom was inefficient and caused Russian society and the Russian economy to remain backward.

THE REVOLUTION OF 1848

The great dividing point in nineteenth-century European political history is the 1848 Revolution. This was a massive disturbance that shook almost every country of Europe to its political roots. Underlying causes of the revolution include

- Popular impatience with over three decades of reactionary rule
- The social and economic effects of the Industrial Revolution (see Chapter 21)
- The growing strength of nationalism (discussed presently)
- A long series of economic downturns and bad harvests that had caused much distress during the 1840s (the decade was popularly known as the "Hungry Forties." The Irish Potato Famine, for example, was the best-known and most deadly example of the agricultural problems of the time)

The events that set off the Revolution of 1848 took place in France. In the spring, the king, Louis-Philippe (the "Citizen-King" who had come to power in 1830), refused demands for electoral reform. Riots began, and, by the summer, the king had been deposed. Over the next few months, a heated political struggle was waged throughout France. In the end, Napoleon Bonaparte's nephew, Louis Napoleon, became France's president.

In the meantime, revolution spread from France to the rest of Europe (referring to the contagious nature of French revolutionary sentiments, Metternich was fond of commenting that every time France sneezed, all of Europe caught cold). The only nations that remained immune during 1848 and 1849 were Britain, which was flexible and liberal enough to keep its people from feeling the need to revolt, and Russia, which punished liberals and radicals so harshly that revolution was too dangerous to consider. In Prussia, Austria, most of the German states, and a good number of the Italian states (many of which were under Austrian control), revolution broke out, lasting sometime for months. In areas ruled by Austria, such as Czech Bohemia, Croatia, and Hungary, nationalist sentiment combined with political activism to cause further revolts.

In the end, except in France, all of the revolutions were crushed or faded away. Russia lent troops and arms to Austria and several German states to assist in quashing revolt. By late 1848 or early 1849, rulers who had been toppled briefly came back to power. One historian has described 1848 as "the turning point that did not quite turn." However, the revolutions of 1848 did have their effects. They compelled the king of Prussia and the emperor of Austria to grant certain constitutional reforms. They demonstrated the increasing importance of nationalism in European politics. They laid the groundwork for the unifications of Germany and Italy later in the century. Most of all, the revolutions demonstrated once and for all to rulers throughout Europe that at least some of the political, economic, and social demands of ordinary people had to be met, or at least listened to and taken seriously.

REFORM EFFORTS AND REPRESENTATIVE GOVERNMENTS: POLITICS IN EUROPE, 1848–1914

THE GRADUAL MOVE TOWARD REPRESENTATIVE GOVERNMENT

Most European countries moved closer to representative, in some cases democratic, forms of government during the second half of the century. Part of this trend was due to the fact that industrialization, modernization, urbanization, and population growth had made government too difficult a task for one person or a small group of people to manage. Even in less democratic nations, political power began to spread outward to larger numbers of governmental advisers, agencies, ministries, and institutions.

REFORM AND DEMOCRACY IN GREAT BRITAIN

The two major nations that developed democratic forms of government—defined in nineteenth-century terms as a meaningful vote for all adult males—during these years were Great Britain and France. In Britain, during the reign of Queen Victoria, the two major parties in Parliament—the Conservatives, led by Benjamin Disraeli, and the Liberals, led by William Gladstone—became more willing to extend the vote to the middle and lower classes. This process took many years, and it was accomplished by means of the Second (1867) and Third (1885) Reform Acts. As a result of the latter, virtually all adult males could vote in parliamentary elections. The few remaining restrictions on male suffrage were removed over the next two decades.

However, reform did not remove all problems from British life. There were economic tensions among the aristocracy, still trying to retain its privileges from previous centuries; the growing middle class, with ambitions and pretensions to respectability; and the enormous working class, which, after the painful early days of the Industrial Revolution, was constantly striving for political equality and economic justice. The growing political clout of the lower classes was demonstrated by the fact that, during the early 1900s, a new political party, Labour, displaced the older, more middle-class Liberals as the primary anti-Conservative party.

Another problem that plagued Britain during the late 1800s and early 1900s was the question of Irish home rule: should Ireland be set free, and if so, should the north, bitterly divided between Catholic and Protestant, remain in British or Irish hands?

DEMOCRACY IN FRANCE

France's progress toward democracy was less consistent and less gentle than Britain's. After the 1848 Revolution, France briefly had a republic in which all adult males could vote. However, the president, Louis Napoleon, was not satisfied with his office. In 1851, he staged a coup and made himself Napoleon III, emperor of France. He was not as dictatorial as his more famous uncle, and during his twenty-year reign, he helped to industrialize and modernize France. Paris in its modern form took shape under his rule. Still, Napoleon III did curtail civil liberties and political rights. In 1870 to 1871, after losing the bitter Franco-Prussian War against the neighboring Germans, Napoleon III was deposed.

From 1871 onward, France was a democratic republic, with universal male suffrage. As in Britain, democracy did not solve all of France's problems. The Fourth Republic was rocked many times by corruption and financial scandal. The national controversy sparked by the Dreyfus Affair (1894–1906)—in which a Jewish officer was wrongly accused of selling military secrets to Germany—exposed not only an ugly streak of anti-Semitism within French society, but also deep divisions between the left (which maintained Dreyfus's innocence) and the right (which remained convinced of his guilt).

THE UNIFICATIONS OF ITALY AND GERMANY

Among the most dramatic developments of late nineteenth-century politics were the unification of Italy and the unification of Germany, both during the 1860s and early 1870s. Both were examples of the growing power of the popular will, guided in this case by nationalism rather than the desire for greater democracy. In both cases, unification was brought about by a complicated combination of war and diplomatic intrigue. The prime movers of Italian unification were the statesman Camillo Cavour and the general Giuseppe Garibaldi. The country was partially united in 1861, then fully united in 1870. Under Victor Emmanuel II, Italy became a constitutional monarchy.

Germany's unification was spearheaded by Prussia, which defeated Austria in 1864 in a war for leadership of the German states. The mastermind of unification was the Prussian statesman Otto von Bismarck. Germany joined together in 1871, following its decisive victory over France in the Franco-Prussian War (see Chapter 22). Prussia's king became Kaiser (emperor) Wilhelm I, of the new German Reich (empire).

AUSTRIA-HUNGARY

The empires of central and eastern Europe—Austria, the new Germany, and Russia—were more conservative than the nations of the west. But even they moved away from traditional autocracy, at least somewhat. In Austria, the 1848 Revolution had driven out the archconservative Metternich. In 1861, the emperor, Franz Josef, agreed to the creation of an elected parliament, with which he shared power.

Austria, a multinational empire, also had to make certain concessions to the dozens of ethnic minorities—Czechs, Poles, Slovaks, Croats, Serbs, Italians, Hungarians, and others—it ruled. The pressures of nationalism were particularly strong here, and Austria had an increasingly difficult time containing the desire of many minorities for greater autonomy, if not complete freedom. In 1867, the largest and most powerful minority, the Hungarians, forced the Austrian government to grant them equal status within the empire. This *Augsleich* ("compromise") turned Austria into the Austro-Hungarian Empire.

GERMANY

Even the German government, ruled by the emperor and administered until 1890 by the highly conservative Bismarck, had to make concessions to its people. As Germany became an industrial powerhouse, its working class grew larger, and the appeal of trade unionism and socialism grew stronger. To prevent ordinary Germans from becoming attracted to left-wing ideologies, Bismarck allowed all adult males to vote in elections to the German parliament, or Reichstag (this universal male suffrage, however, was compromised by the fact that the voting system weighed the ballots of upper-class voters more heavily than those of the lower class). Bismarck also passed a generous set of laws that granted workers many economic benefits: unemployment insurance, disability insurance, pensions, a shorter workday, and so on. Ironically, for a time, workers in late nineteenth-century Germany were better off than in more liberal nations such as France, Britain, or the United States. Nonetheless, the government, even after Bismarck's dismissal by Kaiser Wilhelm II in 1890, continued to be quite conservative.

RUSSIA

Of all Europe's major nations, Russia remained the most autocratic. It had no constitution and, until 1905, no elected body with which the tsar shared power. At least for a time, however, sweeping change came to Russia. Shocked by its embarrassing defeat in the Crimean War (1853–1856), Tsar Alexander II, a moderate liberal, attempted to modernize Russia with a series of Great Reforms. By far the most important of these was the emancipation of the serfs in 1861: that year,

Alexander ended one of the most morally reprehensible and economically damaging institutions in Russian history. Alexander II also lightened censorship, reformed the legal system, widened the powers of local government, and seems to have been considering granting Russia a constitution. Unfortunately, Alexander II was assassinated in 1881 by radical terrorists. The tsars that followed him, including Russia's last tsar, Nicholas II (1894–1917), were extremely conservative. Not only did they abandon Alexander's reforms, they did their best to undo as many of them as possible. A serious uprising in 1905 forced Nicholas II to create and share power with an elected, semiparliamentary body, the Duma. But the Duma was weak, and the tsar took every opportunity to avoid cooperating with it.

WOMEN'S MOVEMENTS

Mary Wollstonecraft, an English writer, is considered the founder of modern European feminism. In her treatise *A Vindication of the Rights of Women* (1792), she argued that Enlightenment thinking took into account the ideal that reason was an innate feature of all human beings, including women. She maintained that women therefore should be entitled to equal rights with men in education, as well as political and economic pursuits. During the French Revolution, Olympe de Gouges, a female playwright, argued in her Declaration of the Rights of Woman and the Female Citizen that women be granted the same rights as men. The National Assembly, which had approved the Declaration of the Rights of Man and the Citizen, dismissed de Gouges's proposal.

The "woman question" was the term used to describe the debate over the status of women. In nineteenth century society, women continued to remain in an inferior position to men inside and outside of the family. The "cult of true womanhood," anchored in the middle classes of the Victorian era in England, posited that the idea woman reflected the "virtues" of submissiveness, piety, domesticity, modesty, and femininity. Early feminists argued that women, like men, were individuals who had different strengths and abilities and should be permitted to develop them without social restrictions.

The early women's rights movement emerged in the 1830s among groups of women in Europe and the United States. Early on, women focused on reforming family and divorce laws to allow women to own property and file for divorce. This initial effort did not reap quick results, as women did not gain full property rights in Britain until 1870, in Germany until 1900, and in France until 1907. Moreover, many women were also frustrated that, because they as females lacked civic rights, they were unable to campaign fully for other cherished causes, such as temperance, slavery abolition, improving schools, and helping the poor.

Soon, feminists were seeking better access for women to higher education and jobs. The first professions open to women (beyond domestic servitude, which was dominated by women already) were teaching and nursing. Women also led the way toward building social welfare institutions, particularly in providing aid to orphaned children and the poor.

By the middle of the nineteenth century, women began advocating equal political rights, most notably, the right to vote (suffrage). They saw suffrage as the initial step toward political equality and full citizenship. As a general rule, women's movements in Europe and America were led by women of the upper classes. The women's movement in Britain, led by Emmeline Pankhurst, was most vocal, although it suffered from disagreement over tactics for achieving equality. In 1848, in Seneca Falls, New York, a group of women met to organize the Women's Rights Convention. They agreed there that, "We hold these truths to be self-evident: that all men and women are equal." Major figures in the U.S. movement were Susan B. Anthony and Elizabeth Cady Stanton. In the United States, suffragettes called for the right to vote and better working conditions for women in textile factories. In Canada, like the United States, women played leadership roles in movements to outlaw the sale and distribution of alcohol and institute child welfare and labor reform. However, on the whole, women were not granted the right to vote in high numbers in Western countries until after World War I. The exceptions included Norway, Finland, and a handful of U.S. states.

INTELLECTUAL AND CULTURAL CURRENTS IN EUROPE

If cultural and intellectual life in eighteenth-century Europe had for decades been dominated by one major movement, the Enlightenment, nineteenth-century Europe (and America) experienced constant change and development in this area. One of the hallmarks of modern culture in the West has been the ever-increasing speed with which artistic styles and scientific theories shift and evolve.

ROMANTICISM

The principal cultural movement of the late 1700s and early 1800s was Romanticism. Originating in the poetry and drama of German authors, as well as the writings of French philosopher Jean-Jacques Rousseau, Romanticism represented a backlash against the logic- and reason-oriented outlook of the Enlightenment. Romanticism placed a premium on emotion and passion, the self-realization of the individual, heroism, and a love of the natural world. Among the many famous Romantics are the writers and poets William Blake, Lord Byron, J. W. von Goethe, and Victor Hugo; the artists J. M. W. Turner and Eugene Delacroix; and the musicians Ludwig van Beethoven (generally considered to be the first major Romantic composer), Richard Wagner, and Pyotr Tchaikovsky.

REALISM

Although Romanticism did not die out, it yielded its place of prominence around the 1840s and 1850s. As its name suggests, Realism rejected Romanticism's idealized, dramatic outlook in favor of a more sober, critical view of life. Realist artists and writers concerned themselves with the details of everyday existence. They were interested in commenting on social problems such as poverty, social hypocrisy, and class injustice. Many sought to represent the psychological workings of their characters' minds. Well-known realist authors include Charles Dickens, George Eliot (the pen name of Mary Ann Evans), Gustave Flaubert, Emile Zola, Leo Tolstoy, and Fyodor Dostoevsky. Realism's peak lasted from the 1840s through the 1870s.

CHARLES DARWIN AND THE THEORIES OF EVOLUTION AND NATURAL SELECTION

Also around mid-century came scientific discoveries that changed the Western world's entire outlook forever. The most important was the work of English naturalist Charles Darwin. Based on field research conducted around the world on a British naval expedition, Darwin explained the biological process of evolution with his theory of natural selection. In his 1859 book *On the Origin of Species*, Darwin caused a scientific and cultural storm by arguing that evolution is a random process in which physical changes that increase an animal's chance for survival are passed on to that animal's offspring. Darwin stirred up an even greater controversy in 1871, when, in *The Descent of Man*, he applied the principles of natural selection to human beings and postulated that humans and apes share a common evolutionary ancestry. Darwin's ideas went hand-in-hand with other materialist trends brought about by an ever-greater scientific awareness of how the world works. His theory of evolution did much to erode faith in traditional religion and encourage a more secular worldview in the West.

MODERNIST THOUGHT AND CULTURE DURING THE LATE 1800s AND EARLY 1900s

The culture of the late nineteenth and early twentieth centuries was characterized by diversity and innovation. Turning away from Realism in the 1870s and beyond, artists and writers began to break the rules of traditional culture and experiment with a dazzling array of new styles: Symbolism, Impressionism, Post-Impressionism, and, on the eve of World War I, Expressionism, Cubism, and even abstraction.

Most of the nineteenth century had been a time when Western culture was characterized by faith in progress, as well as excitement about new technological and scientific developments. For the most part, especially among the general public, this sense of optimism continued until the eve of World War I. However, in some ways, the late 1800s and early 1900s were becoming a time of crisis and uncertainty in intellectual life. The German philosopher Friedrich Nietzsche not only proclaimed famously that "God is dead," but argued that all systems of morality were valueless in the materialistic modern age. The theory of relativity, elaborated shortly before World War I by Albert Einstein, opened up disturbing new questions in the field of physics for the first time since the days of Isaac Newton. The early theories of the Austrian doctor Sigmund Freud about dreams and the subconscious probed the secrets of the human mind, laying the foundation of the new science of psychology. Freud's insights made many people feel uneasy, both before and after World War I.

Aristide Bruant at Les Ambassadeurs **(1892), by Henri de Toulouse-Lautrec.**
French painter and poster artist Henri de Toulouse-Lautrec (1864–1901) was one of many artists who, during the late 1800s, departed from the strictly realist styles of the early and middle nineteenth century. Like many of France's Impressionist and Post-Impressionist painters, Toulouse-Lautrec was influenced by foreign art, most particularly Japanese prints.

QUICK REVIEW

1. Which social class(es) in France did NOT pay taxes before the Revolution of 1789?

   (A) the First Estate
   (B) the Second Estate
   (C) the First and Second Estates
   (D) the First and Third Estates
   (E) the Third Estate

2. During the French Revolution, the *sans-culottes* were

   (A) radical revolutionaries who came from the urban mob
   (B) liberal aristocrats who sided with the Third Estate
   (C) peasant counterrevolutionaries who led the first stage of the Revolution
   (D) middle-class lawyers and merchants who led the first stage of the Revolution
   (E) an elite force of bodyguards attempting to protect the royal family

3. Which of the following remain(s) a part of Napoleon's legacy as ruler of France?

   I. the Bank of France
   II. the Academie Française
   III. the University System
   IV. the Civil Law Code

   (A) I and III only
   (B) II and III only
   (C) I, II, and IV
   (D) I, III, and IV
   (E) II, III, and IV

4. The principal architect of the "Congress System" that prevailed in Europe during the first half of the 1800s was

   (A) Metternich
   (B) Cavour
   (C) Bismarck
   (D) Gladstone
   (E) Castlereagh

5. Great Britain's First Reform Act did which of the following?

   (A) It gave all adult males the vote.
   (B) It improved districting and the operation of the voting system.
   (C) It granted women the right to vote.
   (D) It abolished the House of Lords.
   (E) It provided for voting by secret ballot.

6. The Dreyfus Affair

   (A) was a scandal that rocked the British financial world
   (B) was a diplomatic crisis that nearly spoiled Germany's relationship with Austria
   (C) was a miscarriage of justice that split French society and demonstrated a spirit of anti-Semitism there
   (D) was a court case in Russia involving a serial murderer
   (E) was a love triangle that embarrassed the Hungarian aristocracy

7. According to the terms of the 1867 *Augsleich*, the Austrians agreed to rule their empire jointly with

   (A) the Hungarians
   (B) the Croats
   (C) the Czechs
   (D) the Serbs
   (E) the Slovenes

8. The hallmark of Alexander II's reign in Russia was

   (A) his victory in the Crimean War
   (B) his suppression of peasant revolts in Siberia
   (C) his creation of Russia's first constitution
   (D) his establishment of Russia's first university
   (E) his emancipation of Russia's serfs

9. Which of the following best describes the struggle of nineteenth-century feminists in Europe and the United States?

(A) Feminists were concerned only with gaining the right to vote.

(B) Feminists struggled for the vote, but also for social reform in areas such as education and temperance.

(C) Feminists chose to focus mainly on social reform, ignoring the struggle for the vote.

(D) Feminists gained the vote in several major nations just before World War I.

(E) Feminists failed to gain the vote anywhere until after World War I.

10. Charles Darwin's accomplishments can best be summed up as follows:

(A) He was the first to propose the theory of evolution.

(B) He single-handedly caused Western civilization to experience widespread doubt regarding the Christian faith.

(C) He successfully argued against the theory of evolution.

(D) He was the first satisfactorily to explain the concept of evolution, by means of the theory of natural selection.

(E) He was the first satisfactorily to explain the concept of evolution, by means of genetic theory.

ANSWERS:

1. **C**, p. 256
2. **A**, p. 257
3. **D**, p. 259
4. **A**, p. 260
5. **B**, p. 261
6. **C**, p. 263
7. **A**, p. 264
8. **E**, pp. 264–65
9. **B**, pp. 265–66
10. **D**, pp. 266–67

CHAPTER 21

Industrialization and Worldwide Economic Trends

Until the end of the 1700s, the economies of all the world's major civilizations were principally agricultural, and their societies were rural. Most people in most nations lived in the countryside and worked at growing food and tending livestock. Over the course of centuries, trade and commerce, as well as arts and crafts, had become increasingly important as sectors of economies throughout the world. Compared to agriculture, however, they remained relatively minor.

In Europe, as well as the United States, this state of affairs changed dramatically during the end of the 1700s and the first half of the 1800s. The mass production of goods by means of machine power—industrialization—became a key part of Western economies. The importance of trade and commerce skyrocketed, and a growing number of people moved from rural areas to the city. The economic system known as capitalism was born. Taken together, these phenomena are part of what is commonly known as the Industrial Revolution. The first stage of the Industrial Revolution coincided roughly with the political revolutions that took place in America, France, and the Atlantic world (see Chapters 20 and 27). Although industrialization was a "revolution" only in a metaphorical sense—it was a decades-long process with no clear-cut beginning and no real end—it changed life in Europe, then the rest of the world, more thoroughly than the political revolutions did. The Industrial Revolution placed new machines and inventions at the disposal of ordinary people. It affected old social classes and created new ones. It changed the way millions of people worked, where they lived, how they viewed political problems, and how they viewed themselves.

By the end of the 1800s and the beginning of 1900s, the United States and most nations in Europe—especially in the north and west—were industrialized, modernized, and urbanized. By that time, industrialization had also become important in other parts of the world, as the nations of the West both spread industrial practices to their colonies and exploited those colonies economically in order to foster industrial growth at home.

PROTO-INDUSTRIALIZATION AND THE ORIGINS OF INDUSTRIALIZATION

PROTO-INDUSTRIALIZATION

As noted in Chapter 13, the manufacture of goods was becoming an increasingly important part of the European economy during the 1700s. The level of production went beyond the scale of simple arts and crafts, but did not become fully industrialized until near the end of the century.

Economists refer to this early or primitive phase as proto-industrialization. It served as one of the preconditions for genuine industrialization.

PRECONDITIONS FOR INDUSTRIALIZATION IN ENGLAND

Proto-industrialization was especially pervasive in England, which is generally considered to be the epicenter of the Industrial Revolution. Other factors led to the development of industrial production in England. The country was small enough that it could be blanketed with a network of roads, canals, and, after the 1820s, railways, in order to facilitate transportation and efficient economic exchange. England was already heavily urbanized, by eighteenth-century European standards. Trade and commerce, which, like industry, favored money over land, had been a crucial part of Britain's economy for many years. Agricultural laws passed by wealthy landowners in Parliament—the Enclosure Acts—privatized and fenced off a large amount of farmland that had once been common property. Small farmers either had to pay rent to large landowners or forfeit their farms. The displacement of so many farmers sent great numbers of people to the city. It also created a large pool of available labor once industrialization got under way.

Technological and environmental change played a key role as well. The depletion of timber—stripped from the forests of England and Ireland for hundreds of years, not only for fuel, but also to build ships for the Royal Navy—caused Britain to rely more heavily on coal for fuel. Coal mining required machine power, especially to pump water out of mine shafts.

Another sector of the economy that lent itself to mechanization was the English textile trade. Inventions such as the flying shuttle (1733) and spinning jenny (1764) allowed cotton to be spun into thread and woven into cloth faster than ever before.

MACHINE POWER AND THE STEAM ENGINE

The major limitation on the use of machines was the source of power. Until the development of truly powerful steam engines near the end of the 1700s, machines were driven mainly by wind, water, or animal (sometimes human) power. These were relatively weak power sources, as were the few existing steam engines (used since 1702 to drain coal mines), which remained quite primitive. It was the better-developed steam engine of the late 1700s that would fully unlock the potential of the machine and, in so doing, give birth to the Industrial Revolution.

THE INDUSTRIAL REVOLUTION

PUTTING THE STEAM ENGINE TO WORK: THE INDUSTRIAL REVOLUTION

If the Industrial Revolution can be said to have had a beginning, it was the 1780s, when the steam engine was used to power machines in the English textile industry. Coal mining was another field in which the steam engine was put to early use. Several versions of the steam engine had been invented earlier in the 1700s, but they were too expensive and too weak to be economically useful. The person who first developed a powerful and cost-effective steam engine was the Scottish mechanic James Watt, who patented his designs in 1782. The application of Watt's steam engine to the textile and coal-mining trades marked the big bang of the Industrial Revolution.

THE SECOND STAGE OF THE INDUSTRIAL REVOLUTION

The steam engine proved to be useful in practically every economic field. As Watt's business partner remarked, "We sell what everyone desires, and that is power." The second stage of the Industrial Revolution, which lasted roughly from the early 1800s until the middle of the century, involved the almost universal adaptation of steam—and, more slowly, electricity—in almost all areas of economic activity. Another result of the Industrial Revolution's second stage was to stimulate a huge wave of invention and technological innovation. Transport was modernized: steamships (1807) began to appear on rivers and seas along with sailing ships, and railroads (starting in 1825) started to replace animal-drawn transport. Electricity, in the form of the telegraph (1837), brought communications into the modern age.

THE INDUSTRIAL STYLE OF PRODUCTION

Industrialization changed forever the way everything was made. It systematized, or better organized, production. It mechanized production. It brought about large-scale production, increasing the availability of consumer goods for people of all classes. As more goods were produced more easily and more quickly, they became cheaper. The concept of interchangeable parts, pioneered by American inventor Eli Whitney, as well as American gunsmith Samuel Colt, allowed for faster production and the manufacture of spare parts, making the maintenance and repair of machines much easier.

THE WIDESPREAD INFLUENCE OF INDUSTRIALIZATION AND NEW INVENTIONS

By the middle of the 1800s, industrialization had come to affect many spheres of life. At least in major cities in western Europe and the United States, many features of modern life were appearing: bus service, sidewalks, streetlights (gas at first, then electric), steam heating of homes, icebox refrigeration, indoor plumbing, sewing machines, canned food, urban sewage systems, and many advances in medicine (such as vaccination, germ theory, and the practice of antisepsis, or maintaining a clean environment). In the countryside, machinery, such as the tractor, and more advanced planting and harvesting techniques led to an agricultural boom.

Although the Industrial Revolution can be considered to have ended around the mid-nineteenth century, the industrial era continued throughout the rest of the century. After the 1840s and 1850s, new energy sources, new raw materials, and new inventions continued to pour forth. The vulcanization of rubber began in 1840. The Bessemer process, perfected in the 1850s, created a cheap and easy way to make steel, which was stronger and more useful than iron. Electric generators, which had been invented in 1834, would later overtake steam and coal in importance as an energy source by the end of the century (Thomas Edison's electric light first appeared in 1879). The first commercial uses of petroleum began after 1859, making oil just as crucial as electricity. Chemical industries took off during the late 1800s.

On the high seas and on battlefields, the Industrial Revolution affected navies and armies of all countries. After the 1840s, modern militaries developed steam-powered (later oil-powered) battleships, modern rifles, modern artillery, and eventually the machine gun. The Western world's first "industrial" wars were the United States Civil War (1861–1865) and the Franco-Prussian War (1870–1871).

Transport and communications continued to be shaped by the steamship, railroad, and telegraph, but new devices appeared during the late 1800s and early 1900s: the internal combustion engine (1860s–1870s), which eventually led to the automobile; the telephone (1876–1879); the radio (1895–1901); and the airplane (1903).

INDUSTRIALIZATION AND ITS EFFECTS ON SOCIAL CLASSES

The social effects of the Industrial Revolution were far-reaching and complex. Trade, commerce, and manufacturing had been important during Europe's early-modern period, but now they far surpassed landownership as ways of generating wealth. This transformation diminished the economic clout of the traditional aristocracy, which was also steadily losing its political importance during the 1800s. The social stratum that benefited most readily from the Industrial Revolution was the middle class, or bourgeoisie. They were the merchants, bankers, factory owners, and industrialists who stood most to profit from the new economic changes.

The Industrial Revolution gave birth to a new class as well: the working class, or proletariat. This class was made up of the masses who worked in factories, mines, and other industrial enterprises. Early on, most of the working class was made up of peasants and farmers who had abandoned agriculture or been forced out of it as a result of economic pressure or laws such as England's Enclosure Acts.

During the first decades of the Industrial Revolution, the working class bore the heaviest economic burden. It was thanks to their labor that the Industrial Revolution took place, but until the second half of the 1800s, they were poorly treated and barely compensated for their work. During the first decades of the industrial era, the working class received low wages, worked long hours (14 hours a day, six days a week, was not unusual), lived in squalid and crowded housing, and dealt with unsafe working conditions of all kinds (the risk of fire, dangerous machines, exposure to poisonous or harmful materials). Child labor was common.

After the 1830s and 1840s, the condition of the working class gradually improved, as various laws and measures were passed to prevent the worst of the exploitation. But fair treatment, social equality, and full political rights were distant goals, and the working class would achieve them only after much effort, and not until the end of the 1800s, or even the early 1900s.

It should be noted that, despite industrialization and urbanization (discussed presently), many people remained in the countryside, employed as farmers and agricultural workers, during the nineteenth century. Social divisions in the countryside during the 1800s, however, were still largely affected by industrialization. More and more land was owned by independent, well-off farmers and homesteaders who were, essentially, middle class. Under them, renting land and performing heavy agricultural work, were poor laborers. In essence, these agricultural laborers formed a second working class in the countryside, alongside the growing industrial working class in the cities. In Russia, most agricultural labor was, until 1861, performed by serfs. In the southern United States, slavery continued until 1865.

POPULATION GROWTH, URBANIZATION, AND THE GRADUAL RISE IN LEVELS OF PROSPERITY

Broad trends affected by the Industrial Revolution included population growth, urbanization, and an overall increase in prosperity throughout the Western world. Partly as a result of greater agricultural efficiency, partly as a result of medical advances, and partly as a result of gradually rising levels of prosperity, the population of Europe grew tremendously: from 175 million to 187 million in 1800 to 266 million in 1850, and again to 423 million by 1900. Similar growth took place in the United States.

Since most of the new jobs created by the Industrial Revolution were in or near cities, most of the Western world's population growth spurred the second trend: urbanization. Cities that already existed grew much larger. In 1800, London became the first European city since the days of ancient Rome to reach a population of 1 million; it was home to 2.2 million by 1856. Paris reached the 1 million mark in the 1830s. Berlin, New York, and other cities in Europe and the United States grew similarly. Moreover, new cities appeared throughout industrialized Europe. The English cities of Manchester and Liverpool are examples of large metropolises that emerged with lightning speed, thanks to the Industrial Revolution. By mid-century, England and Wales were urban societies, meaning that more than half the population lived in cities. In France and the German states, the level of urbanization had reached 25 percent by 1850, and it continued to grow.

Conditions in these rapidly growing cities could often be dismal, especially in poorer neighborhoods, which were often little more than slums or shantytowns. Cities became extremely crowded. Overcrowding increased the ease with which disease could spread, and illnesses such as cholera and tuberculosis caused many deaths in European cities during these years, especially among the lower classes. In an era when modern sewage systems were rare and homes were heated by burning wood and coal, water and air pollution were horrific problems.

If industrialization urbanized the Western world and boosted its population growth, it also, over time, increased the general level of prosperity. This was a slow trend, long in coming. The Industrial Revolution generated immense wealth quite quickly. For example, Great Britain's national wealth more than doubled between 1790 and 1840. However, that wealth was distributed very unevenly. During the first decades, the late 1700s and early 1800s, only a comparatively small segment of society—mainly the middle class—benefited from the riches brought about by industrialization. As noted previously, the Industrial Revolution tended to be a painful, traumatic time for most working-class men and women. Most economic historians calculate that not until after the 1840s did industrialization bring about any meaningful material improvements for a wide cross section of the European population. In other words, not until the Industrial Revolution was almost over did industrialization begin to benefit large numbers of people. Once the economic improvements caused by industrialization started to widen out during the 1850s onward, they had a powerful effect on European society, and the overall standard of living in the Western world improved dramatically as time passed.

WOMEN AND INDUSTRIALIZATION

Before the Industrial Revolution, European women of the lower (and sometimes middle) class worked alongside men on the farm or in the family business, so motherhood and homemaking were not full-time pursuits. The Industrial Revolution altered that reality. It turned the husband into the wage earner outside the home and the wife the homemaker. Thus, the Industrial Revolution gradually created a sharply defined domestic sphere for women, separate from the workplace, which, by the mid-to-late 1800s, would be dominated by men.

However, early in the nineteenth century, for couples in the lower classes, often both husband and wife (and increasingly, their children) were forced to work in factories to make ends meet. Before 1870, women made up 50 percent of the workforce in textile factories. Ironically, this meant that lower-class women had more opportunity to work than those of the middle and upper classes. In this case, however, "opportunity" was not a matter of privilege or right, but economic necessity. Also, women who did work were paid a good deal less than men.

Throughout the nineteenth century, most working women remained in traditional types of female labor, that is, as domestic servants or agricultural workers. Most working women were single, not married. Some single women, desperate for jobs, left Europe for Australia or the United States. By the end of the nineteenth century, large numbers of poor women were working outside the home, in factories, mines, markets, and on farms.

Increasingly, though, as salaries improved in heavy industry (making these jobs more desirable to men) and laws restricted the number of hours women were allowed to work, more women in working-class families stayed at home. Fewer middle-class (and almost no upper-class) women worked. In such a way, a new social pattern emerged that separated work from the home. Men were the primary breadwinners, whereas women became the homemakers who dabbled in low-paying, part-time work to supplement income. Families started to have fewer children, partly as a result of the adoption of child-labor laws and a decline in infant mortality rates. Children were beginning to be perceived more as dependents than family wage earners.

Around the turn of the century, a mass consumer society began to emerge along with a higher standard of living. Such consumer products as sewing machines, clocks, and cast-iron stoves focused families on obtaining higher levels of consumption and freed up time for women of all classes to pursue activities outside the home.

THE GEOGRAPHY OF INDUSTRIALIZATION

What countries industrialized most quickly and thoroughly? Measuring industrial growth by major indicators such as iron, coal, steel, and cotton production, as well as railroad building, Britain, the first country to industrialize, led the way for most of the 1800s. Only near the end of the century did it start to lose ground to countries such as Germany and the United States. Belgium industrialized heavily, as did France, the Netherlands, the western German states (then Germany as a whole after 1871), and the northern parts of the Italian peninsula. The nations of Scandinavia industrialized somewhat as well. Near the end of the century, Germany in particular became an industrial powerhouse, overtaking Britain in several areas. Across the Atlantic, the United States became the world's fastest-growing and largest industrial power during the late 1800s and, especially, the early 1900s.

The parts of Europe that lagged behind were generally in the south and east. Spain, Portugal, and southern Italy tended to remain agricultural. Likewise, the Austrian Empire was slow to industrialize. Even more backward was Russia, which remained overwhelmingly agricultural—and, until 1861, economically stagnant, thanks to its reliance on the old-fashioned practice of serfdom. Southeastern Europe and the Balkans remained the most economically outdated region on the continent.

ECONOMIC THEORIES AND MOVEMENTS

Industrialization and modernization stimulated new thinking about economics, as well as new ways of reacting to economic pressures.

CAPITALISM AND THE CLASSICAL ECONOMISTS

The Industrial Revolution coincided with—and mutually affected—the fall of mercantilism and the rise of capitalism. As discussed in Chapter 13, the central feature of mercantilism was strict governmental control over the economy. By the end of the 1700s, however, a number of economic thinkers began to argue that economies were more likely to flourish when they were left alone to function freely. These classical, or laissez-faire, economists theorized that competition, free trade, and the laws of supply and demand, operating by themselves, created greater wealth for all nations and all people. These became the key principles of capitalism. The first major capitalist thinker was the Scottish philosopher Adam Smith. Smith's *The Wealth of Nations* (1776) used the elegant metaphor of the "invisible hand" to describe how the laws of supply and demand naturally increased prosperity.

Other classical economists accepted Smith's principles and approved of capitalism, but were not so optimistic that the new economic approach would benefit all people, especially the working masses. One of these was England's Thomas Malthus, whose *Essay on Population* (1799) argued that population growth caused poverty. His reasoning was that, while population growth grew at a geometric rate, food supply grew at an arithmetic rate. Malthus saw war, disease, and starvation as natural mechanisms by which population growth was regulated. David Ricardo created the theory known as the "iron law of wages." Ricardo stated that an employer will naturally pay his workers no more than whatever it takes to keep them at a subsistence level. If population growth expands more quickly than the economy, too many workers will compete for too few jobs. Wages will decline and those without jobs will starve. However, according to Ricardo, to interfere with this "iron law" will only lead to economic ruin. The pessimism of thinkers like Malthus and Ricardo caused classical economics to be nicknamed the "dismal science." Nonetheless, classical capitalist thought became the dominant economic approach of the nineteenth and early twentieth century.

SOCIALISM, MARXISM, AND COMMUNISM

Another economic approach, socialism, remained in the minority—and, in some times and places, it became illegal. Socialism's basic principle is that economic competition is inherently unfair and leads to injustice and inequality. There were many different forms of socialist thought. The earliest socialists, who appeared between the 1810s and 1840s, were known as the utopian socialists. These included the Scottish industrialist Robert Owen, as well as the French thinkers Charles Fourier and Comte de Saint-Simon. Rejecting capitalism and Ricardo's "iron law," utopian socialists felt that, by means of good planning and judicious regulation, economies could be made to prosper without exploiting the working class.

A more radical form of socialism appeared later, during the 1840s. This was Marxism (also known as communism). It was originated by the German philosophers and radicals Karl Marx and Friedrich Engels. The movement's fundamental principles came from *The Communist Manifesto* (1848) and *Das Kapital* (1867–1894). Based heavily on the philosophy of G. W. F. Hegel, Marxism condemned capitalism and economic competition. Marx and Engels argued that, since ancient times, social and historical development have always been driven by the class struggle between the upper classes (who control capital, or the means of economic production) and the lower classes (who are forced to labor for the upper classes). They felt that their own age—the capitalist era, during which the class struggle pitted the bourgeoisie (factory owners, businessmen, the middle class) against the proletariat (the industrial working class)—was the final stage of human history before the achievement of socialism. From socialism, human society would pass to communism: an economic state of perfect justice, social equality, and plenty. In order to bring about socialism, however, revolution was necessary. Marx and Engels therefore advocated, and fought for, the overthrow of the capitalist order. Much more so than utopian socialism, Marxism captured the imagination of hundreds of thousands of intellectuals and workers, and it would go on to become one of the most influential doctrines of the modern era.

POLITICAL REPRESENTATION FOR THE MIDDLE CLASS

The rapid expansion of the middle class and the birth of the industrial working class affected politics in many ways. The gradual widening of political representation described in Chapter 20 was due largely to agitation and ambition on the part of both these classes. Early in the 1800s, the middle class, which favored liberalization, won greater political rights and economic privileges for itself, both by means of reform (in countries like Britain) and more drastic political action like opposition or revolt (as in France).

WORKING-CLASS RADICALISM

What options were open for the working class? The most desperate tended to turn to radical forms of agitation: socialism, communism, even anarchism (developed as a political movement by the Russian revolutionaries Mikhail Bakunin and Prince Pyotr Kropotkin). Marxism drew most of its strength from disgruntled workers. But as a movement, it was often led by radicalized intellectuals who promoted communism as the way toward social equality and economic justice.

TRADE UNIONS AND THE LOWER CLASSES

Most workers turned to trade unions rather than radicalism. At first, unions were illegal in Europe, as well as the United States, and joining one could be very risky: union members were often in danger of arrest, even injury, especially if they went on strike. Over time, however, trade unionism became a less extreme way of carrying on the struggle for greater political rights and fairer treatment in the workplace (higher wages, shorter workday, shorter work week, safety regulations, pensions, employee insurance). Workers' parties also emerged; one of the most famous was the Labour

Party, which became (and remains) a major force in British politics. Unions and workers' parties tended to be left leaning, but not as far to the left as socialist and communist groups.

THE GLOBAL IMPACT OF INDUSTRIALIZATION

THE UNITED STATES AS AN INDUSTRIAL POWER

If Europe was the first major civilization to develop a modern, industrialized, capitalist economy, the effects of this new economy spread quickly to the rest of the world. As stated previously, the United States also industrialized—and by the late 1800s and early 1900s, was doing so more successfully and more quickly than the nations of Europe.

INDUSTRIALIZATION AND IMPERIALISM

Western industrialization and imperialism (see Chapter 22) were also intimately connected, in several ways. First, industrialization made Western nations, particularly Britain and France, more able to conquer and colonize other parts of the world during the 1800s. Industrialization made European nations richer, it made them more technologically adept, and it boosted the scientific knowledge needed to explore or know better parts of the world that were not yet under Western control. Perhaps most important, industry placed new weaponry in the hands of the Westerners: gunboats, artillery, quick-firing and accurate rifles, and machine guns, all of which made Western armies extremely difficult for poorly armed native warriors to resist.

Second, if industrialization gave Europeans a greater capacity to conquer and colonize, it also gave them a greater variety of motives. Industrialization required ever-greater amounts of raw materials: iron ore, coal, rubber, metals, timber, and chemicals, all of which could be stripped from other parts of the world. The growing importance of steamships made it necessary for Western nations to maintain naval bases and refueling stations around the globe. Moreover, as Europe and America produced increasingly large amounts of manufactured goods, they had to have markets overseas to sell them to. All of these needs combined to spur the Western nations' intense burst of imperial activity during the 1800s, especially the second half.

THE INFLUENCE OF INDUSTRIAL NATIONS OVER NONINDUSTRIAL NATIONS

Even in non-Western parts of the world that Europe and America did not conquer or colonize, industrialization's economic clout often had a profound effect. In many parts of Africa, Asia, and Latin America, Western businessmen and industrialists struck deals with aristocrats or the political elite to exploit local resources. These bargains typically involved the large-scale growth or extraction of a small set of crops or natural resources. This practice, known as monoculture, generally damages the environment and retards the development of a healthy, diverse economy (in the tropics, the derogatory slang term for a country with this type of economy is "banana republic"). It also exploits these countries' native workers: Western payments or investments end up in the pockets of a small number of local aristocrats or politicians, rather than adding to the national well-being.

THE NON-WESTERN WORLD'S ADOPTION OF INDUSTRIALIZATION

In the long term, most non-Western parts of the world would come to imitate industrial methods of economic production. To begin with, Western colonizing powers typically exported these practices to their imperial possessions. In addition, many non-Western nations would later come to see industrialization as the means by which they could gain wealth and power. This adoption of industrialization worldwide would continue throughout the twentieth century, and continues even today, into the twenty-first.

INDUSTRIALIZATION AND THE ATLANTIC SLAVE TRADE

One other worldwide effect of early industrialization concerned the Atlantic slave trade. The 1793 invention of the cotton gin by American engineer Eli Whitney transformed the international textile trade. One of the factors that limited the ability of steam-driven machines such as the spinning jenny, the flying shuttle, and the power loom to speed up the textile industry was the fact that cleaning raw cotton balls by hand took a long time. The cotton gin changed this, enabling enough clean cotton to be produced to keep pace with the machines that turned clean cotton into thread and the thread into whole cloth. The effect of this change was to give a phenomenal boost to the English textile trade's demand for raw cotton. Although one major source for cotton was Egypt, a chief supplier was the American South, where cotton was grown and harvested primarily by slaves. Most economic historians argue that, before the 1790s, slavery was becoming less profitable in the American South, and might therefore have died away relatively quickly and easily. The advent of the cotton gin, however, as well as England's increased demand for cotton, made slave-based cotton production extremely profitable. Therefore, slavery in America was prolonged for decades— necessitating civil war to end it—largely because of the industrialization of the textile trade.

QUICK REVIEW

1. The Industrial Revolution is generally considered to have begun in

   (A) France
   (B) Germany
   (C) England
   (D) Belgium
   (E) the United States

2. The widespread application of what device played the largest part in beginning the Industrial Revolution?

   (A) the electric turbine
   (B) the water wheel
   (C) the internal-combustion engine
   (D) the windmill
   (E) the steam engine

3. The Enclosure Acts affected the Industrial Revolution by

   (A) driving peasants off their land and thereby creating the workforce needed for factories and mines
   (B) bankrupting wealthy landowners, convincing them to turn to manufacturing
   (C) increasing the land under cultivation, destroying trees, and increasing reliance on coal for fuel
   (D) educating peasants and turning them into skilled workers
   (E) setting more land aside for new factories and mines

4. What was the first major trade to be fully power-driven and industrialized?

   (A) the canning of food
   (B) the textile industry
   (C) the production of rubber
   (D) the manufacture of glass
   (E) the leatherworking trade

5. The Bessemer process allowed the cost-effective and reliable production of

(A) steel
(B) fine cotton
(C) rubber
(D) aluminum
(E) concrete

6. What effect did nineteenth-century industrialization have on Europe's aristocratic class?

(A) Industrialization made the aristocratic class more powerful.
(B) Industrialization had very little effect on the aristocratic class.
(C) Industrialization gradually weakened the power and prestige of the aristocratic class.
(D) Industrialization suddenly weakened the power and prestige of the aristocratic class.
(E) Industrialization had no effect at all on the aristocratic class.

7. Which of the following was NOT among the Western world's industrial leaders during most of the nineteenth century?

(A) Austria
(B) England
(C) Belgium
(D) the United States
(E) the western German states

8. Who was the originator of the "iron law of wages"?

(A) Adam Smith
(B) Thomas Malthus
(C) Robert Owen
(D) David Ricardo
(E) Karl Marx

9. Which of the following best characterizes standard Marxist doctrine?

(A) Economic competition leads to the highest possible level of prosperity for all.
(B) The struggle between propertied classes and laboring classes is the determining force in all human affairs.
(C) Any interference with the natural operation of supply and demand is harmful.
(D) It is possible to achieve social justice and economic equality within the capitalist framework.
(E) There is no avoiding the fact that there will always be impoverished classes in every society.

10. How did industrialization affect the Atlantic slave trade?

(A) Reliance on machines caused the slave trade to end somewhat earlier than it would have otherwise
(B) Industrialization had little or no effect on the slave trade
(C) Industrialization of the textile trade increased the demand for U.S. cotton and revived slavery for several decades
(D) Industrialization quickly ended the slave trade
(E) Steam power allowed the British and U.S. navies to stop the slave trade altogether before the 1850s

ANSWERS:

1. **C**, p. 271
2. **E**, p. 271
3. **A**, p. 271
4. **B**, p. 271
5. **A**, p. 272

6. **C**, pp. 272–73
7. **A**, p. 275
8. **D**, p. 275
9. **B**, p. 276
10. **C**, p. 278

CHAPTER 22

The Europeans Abroad: Imperialism, Nationalism, and Foreign Policy

One of the most astounding political facts of the nineteenth century is that, whereas in 1815 the nations of the West—Europe and America—controlled 35 percent of the world's habitable territory, they controlled 85 percent by 1914. The nineteenth century was truly an age of empire, in which the West came to achieve greater dominance over a larger portion of the globe than any civilization ever had before.

Western imperialism was nothing new. European powers had been influencing or conquering other parts of the world since the 1400s. From the 1700s onward, the United States grew "from sea to shining sea" by means of warfare and subjugation of the native population. What happened during the 1800s, however, was that imperialism took on a much more aggressive and systematic character. Many historians have come to refer to the imperial activity of the mid-1800s through the early 1900s as the new imperialism. This change was due to a variety of reasons, described in detail presently.

Whatever caused it, imperialism remains one of the Western world's longest-lasting and most controversial legacies. As a practical undertaking and as a military enterprise, the West's domination of the world was impressive, and it made Europe and America immensely powerful and rich. On the other hand, imperialism was inseparable from bloodshed, racial prejudice, slavery, and violence. As English-Polish author Joseph Conrad wrote in the novel *Heart of Darkness*—one of the classic literary depictions of European imperialism—"The conquest of the earth, which mostly means the taking it away from those who have a different complexion or slightly flatter noses than ourselves, is not a pretty thing when you look into it too much." Moreover, Europe's and America's massive campaigns of colonization and efforts to influence other parts of the world left deep political scars around the globe, many of which have not yet healed even in the new twenty-first century.

Both abroad and at home, European foreign policy in general became increasingly aggressive as the century wore on. During the first half of the 1800s, the balance of power achieved by the Congress of Vienna had largely kept the peace. During and after the 1850s, however, war broke out among the European powers several times: the Crimean War (1853–1856), in which Russia fought France and Britain; the wars of Italian unification, which entangled France, Austria, and several Italian states; and the three wars Prussia fought to unify the German states, especially the Franco-Prussian War (1870–1871).

Much of this aggression was caused by the growing intensity of nationalism, a relatively new cultural movement that placed a premium on patriotic sentiment. Much of it was also caused by competition over imperial possessions overseas, especially as the century drew to a close and the amount of desirable territory left to be conquered grew ever smaller. On the surface, relative stability was maintained from 1871 to 1914, a period in European history known as the Long Peace. Underneath, however, the potential for conflict grew with every passing year. The conflict that ultimately broke out, of course, was the Great War, known now as World War I. The European alliance system that emerged during the 1890s and early 1900s resulted from this growing sense of foreign-policy crisis. It was also a principal factor in the complex background of World War I.

CAUSES OF IMPERIALISM

A variety of interrelated factors enabled and motivated the nations of the West to engage in imperial conquest during the 1800s, especially during the second half of the century, when the "new" imperialism became prevalent. All of these trends apply mainly to the nations of Europe, but also, to a degree, the United States.

ECONOMIC FACTORS

One set of factors was economic. As discussed in Chapter 21, industrialization gave the West not just the ability to conquer other parts of the world, but also more reasons to do so. Large-scale industrial production made Western economies hungry for raw materials, many of which could be seized from less powerful nations by force.

Conversely, Western nations needed markets for the goods that their industrial economies produced. Colonies, they thought, would serve well as potential markets (in retrospect, economic historians have determined that this was a mistaken belief and that colonies were less suitable as markets than other industrialized countries).

Another economic factor was simply the Western world's immense wealth, which enabled it to afford the military, transportation, and communications tools with which to conquer far-off territories.

MILITARY FACTORS

Military issues were obviously important. Industrialization had bestowed new weaponry of all types upon the armies and navies of the West: ocean-going fleets powered by steam (and, later, petroleum), modern rifles, machine guns, rapid-fire and long-range artillery, and more. Only on rare occasions could native populations resist Western military forces, thanks to overwhelming numbers, miscalculation on the part of the invaders, or simple good fortune.

Another military factor was the growing need of Western nations to maintain bases and coal (or oil) stations around the world, both for their navies and civilian fleets. Steam- and petroleum-driven ships required elaborate repair and fueling facilities, so, for strategic purposes, Western nations seized islands and ports around the world.

SOCIAL FACTORS

A social factor—Europe's rapid population growth during the 1800s—played a role in prompting imperial activity. One outlet for excess population growth was emigration to the Americas, and, as discussed in Chapter 27, millions of Europeans made that choice. Another outlet, however, was to leave the homeland and go to the colonies. Ambitious (or sometimes desperate) families or individuals decided to make their fortunes abroad in this way.

THE ROLE OF SCIENCE AND TECHNOLOGY

Scientific knowledge and technological aptitude were instrumental in allowing the West to conquer and colonize. In this case, knowledge was power. As already noted, the advances in transportation, communications, and warfare brought about by the Industrial Revolution enabled Western nations to build empires. A new wave of exploration during the 1700s and early 1800s had added considerably to Western nations' knowledge of Africa, Asia, the Arctic, Antarctica, and, in South America, the Amazon basin. Better maps and greater familiarity with local environments made it easier for Westerners to conquer them.

In addition, medical advances made it possible for Europeans and Americans to penetrate the tropical regions more deeply. Previously, diseases such as sleeping sickness, yellow fever, and especially malaria had prevented Westerners from gaining control over the interior of places like Africa and Southeast Asia. In other words, these illnesses worked as a natural guard against invaders. The development of effective treatments for these illnesses (especially quinine, which relieved the symptoms of malaria) changed this.

CULTURAL FACTORS

Finally, a complex set of cultural factors motivated Americans and Europeans to build empires and spheres of influence. A sense of racial superiority was widespread among white Europeans and Americans at the time, and created a sense that Western nations were entitled to conquer and colonize areas that seemed "backward" or "primitive." Cecil Rhodes, who did much to colonize Africa for Britain, said famously of his Anglo-Saxon homeland, "I contend that we are the finest race in the world, and the more of it we inhabit, the better it is."

In some cases, this belief was "justified" in crude and prejudiced terms. In others, the doctrine of social Darwinism was used to argue in favor of imperialism. This was a misguided application of Darwin's theories of natural selection, postulating that the biological principle of "survival of the fittest" should apply to humanity—meaning that peoples who were technologically and culturally advanced were permitted to conquer those who were less so (it should be noted that Darwin himself denounced this idea as a perversion of his scientific work).

Yet another cultural impulse behind imperialism was a genuine conviction that it was the duty of white Westerners to teach and modernize the darker-skinned, supposedly "primitive" peoples of Africa and Asia. The English poet Rudyard Kipling gave this sentiment its most famous label: the "White Man's Burden." The French spoke of their civilizing mission (*la mission civilisatrice*). This attitude was well meaning and heartfelt, but also condescending. European and American missionaries, doctors, scientists, and colonial officials sometimes did much good in the places they visited. But they did so out of at least a subconscious sense of racial superiority, and they typically trampled on or eradicated native cultural practices and beliefs.

EUROPE'S OVERSEAS EMPIRES

WESTERN APPROACHES TO IMPERIALISM

Almost the entire non-Western world was either colonized during the nineteenth century or fell under the influence of Western nations. By far the largest and most widespread set of colonial possessions was Britain's. As a famous adage put it, "The sun never sets on the British Empire." France had a sizable empire, as did Belgium and the Netherlands. Although Austria is not commonly thought of as a colonizing power, its empire was in eastern and southeastern Europe. Russia conquered all of Siberia, much of the territory to its south, and, for a time, parts of North America. After 1870, new countries such as Germany and Italy also began to build overseas empires, in an attempt to catch up with older imperial powers like Britain and France.

Different powers treated their empires differently. The British are considered to have taken the most enlightened approach to colonization. Although they took their colonies by force and exploited them economically—and were prone to the same sense of racial superiority as other Westerners—they interfered as little as possible with local customs. In keeping with their sense of the "white man's burden," they also introduced positive social reforms and useful scientific and technological knowledge. Likewise, the French subscribed to the notion of *la mission civilisatrice*, but were less consistent about it. The Portuguese and Belgians were known to be especially harsh, even cruel, masters, particularly in Africa. Germany and Italy were also brutal. The latter used poison gas in conquering parts of North Africa.

THE AMERICAS

North America fell mainly under the sway of the United States, which conquered the entire western frontier during the nineteenth century. Motivated by the doctrine of "manifest destiny"—the belief that it was entitled to the entire center of the continent between Atlantic and Pacific—the United States fought Mexico, negotiated borders with British Canada, and warred on Native Americans, driving them to defeat and onto reservations. In its way, this was no less an imperial campaign than what European nations did in Africa or Asia. The Spanish lost their empire in North America when Mexico launched a revolution in the 1810s and 1820s. The Russians gave up their North American possession, Alaska, to the United States in 1867.

Latin America set itself free from Spanish and Portuguese domination during the early 1800s, in a great wave of revolutions (see Chapter 27). However, much of Latin America came under the sway of the United States. Although the United States did not conquer Latin America, it considered the region to be part of its sphere of influence. The Monroe Doctrine, issued in 1823, declared this assumption formally by stating that the United States would not permit European nations to interfere in matters pertaining to the Western Hemisphere. The United States's economic and political influence over Central and South America would increase throughout the 1800s. At the end of the century, in 1898, the Spanish-American War would give the United States control over areas such as Cuba, Puerto Rico, the Virgin Islands, and elsewhere, making it, in a sense, a colonizing power in Latin America.

SOUTHEAST ASIA

The vast expanse of Asia was colonized and influenced by a variety of powers. The region that had been longest under European control was Southeast Asia. The Dutch tightened their grasp over Indonesia. Under Napoleon III, France took over Indochina, the area that is today Laos, Cambodia, and Vietnam. By the mid-1880s, the British controlled Burma, the Malay Peninsula (with the great trading center of Singapore), and northern Borneo. Farther to the south, Britain reigned over the continent of Australia. The Philippines had belonged to Spain since Magellan's voyage of 1521, but the United States took them in 1898, following the Spanish-American War. Later in the century, Germany seized a number of small Pacific islands for use as naval posts.

INDIA

Also in South Asia, the heart of the British Empire was India. Britain and France had quarreled with each other over hegemony in India during the 1700s. At the Battle of Plassey, in 1757, the British won a major victory over the Mughal Empire. This victory enabled the British to consolidate their military presence in India, leading to a rapid decline of French influence. Over the next few decades, as French power in India dwindled, the British went on to conquer most of the subcontinent. Until the late 1850s, India was not administered directly by the British government, but by the semiprivate British East India Company, one of the richest and most powerful business ventures in world history. In 1857, however, the Indian Mutiny (also known as the Sepoy Rebellion)—which failed, but shocked the British badly—convinced the government to assume full control over the colony. India was exceptionally important to Britain, in terms of national pride, strategic position, and economic benefit. During the late 1800s, one-quarter of the wealth generated by the entire British Empire came from India.

CHINA

China, despite its vast size and immense population, fell victim to almost every European nation, as well as the United States. China was not technically colonized. However, thanks to military defeat at the hands of the British and other foreigners during the middle of the 1800s, it was compelled to open its borders and its trade to other countries at highly disadvantageous terms (see Chapter 24). It gave up pieces of territory such as Hong Kong (a British colony from 1842 until 1997, when it returned to Chinese rule as a Special Administration Region), as well as Manchuria and Korea. The British, French, Americans, Germans, Russians, and others were allowed to establish concessions on the Chinese coast. These were large districts where Western, not Chinese law, prevailed. Foreign ships were allowed to sail as far up Chinese rivers as they pleased. The balance of trade was lopsidedly in favor of the foreigners. In 1900, the Chinese rose up to resist foreign domination, in the failed Boxer Rebellion. In 1911, the Manchu dynasty, its weakness due in large part to foreign meddling, collapsed.

JAPAN RESISTS WESTERN IMPERIALISM

The one major Asian nation to resist Western imperialism was Japan. Indeed, Japan became an imperial power itself. Isolated until 1853, when the United States Navy forced it to resume diplomatic and economic relations with the wider world, Japan chose to adopt the science, technology, and military know-how of the West. Not only did Japan resist foreign takeover, it began to build its own Asian empire. It defeated China in 1894 to 1895, taking the island of Taiwan and increasing its dominance over Korea. More shockingly, Japan dealt Russia a humiliating defeat in the Russo-Japanese War of 1904 to 1905. This victory gained Japan control over more of the Asian mainland, as well as a number of islands (see Chapter 24).

CENTRAL ASIA AND THE GREAT GAME

Much of Central Asia—the wide expanse of desert and mountains through which the Silk Road had run centuries before—fell to Russia, which felt the need to protect its southern frontier. From Central Asia, Russia hoped to move west and south into the Middle East. Because Russia lacked warm-water ports, it also desired to drive to the Indian Ocean coast and gain an outlet to the sea. The Islamic khanates and cities of Turkestan, Bukhara, Khiva, Khokand, and the Afghan border were taken by the Russians between the 1820s and 1880s. Russian imperialism in this region greatly disturbed Britain, because it placed the Russians within striking distance of the Middle East, much of which was in the British sphere of influence. More important, the Russians' encroachments on Central Asia brought them closer to India, or at least threatened the lines of communication between Europe and India, which the British were determined to protect at all costs.

During most of the 1800s, until 1907, the British and Russia were locked in an intense campaign of espionage and diplomatic intrigue that was known as the Great Game (the Russians referred to it as the Tournament of Shadows). Although the Great Game never resulted in outright war, it created a deep sense of rivalry between Britain and Russia that lasted until shortly before World War I.

THE MIDDLE EAST AND THE EASTERN QUESTION

For centuries, the Middle East and most of North Africa had been in the hands of the Ottoman Empire. However, the Ottoman Empire was collapsing, and the "Eastern Question"—how to fill in the power vacuum left behind by the Ottomans' decline—became a central question in global politics (see Chapter 23). During the last half of the 1800s, large portions of this region were seized by Europeans, especially the French and British. Algeria, Tunisia, and most of Morocco became French. Part of Morocco fell to Spain, whereas Italy captured Libya.

Perhaps the most important territory was Egypt, which became a British protectorate in the 1880s. During the 1870s, Egypt, an autonomous part of the Ottoman Empire, had fallen under French and British influence. The reason was that both of these Western countries had financed the construction of the Suez Canal, which opened in 1869. Control over the canal—a vital link between Europe and the Mediterranean on one hand, and the Red Sea and the Indian Ocean on the other—was crucial, and the British used economic pressure to gain more and more political control over Egypt. They also struck to the south, establishing control over the Sudan. Both Egypt and the Sudan became part of the so-called Anglo-Egyptian Administration. Further to the east, Persia, which had remained independent of Ottoman rule, was divided into two spheres of influence by Russia and Britain. The global importance of the Middle East—based largely on its geographic position between Europe and Asia—increased dramatically with the discovery of large petroleum deposits in 1908. Middle Eastern oil still plays a key role in modern geopolitics.

THE SCRAMBLE FOR AFRICA

The part of the world that experienced the most intense burst of European imperialism near the end of the century was Africa (see also Chapter 26). Until the 1880s, only Africa's coastlines had been directly colonized or exploited, although the exploitation had been heavy. Gold, ivory, foodstuffs, and especially slaves had been wrested from Africa, either by military force or economic pressure. Although slavery and the slave trade had been made illegal by most Western nations following the French Revolution and Napoleonic Wars, both institutions continued throughout the 1800s. Slavery was practiced in the United States until the Civil War of the 1860s, and even afterward, it was still practiced in parts of the Caribbean and South America. Not until Brazil outlawed slavery in 1888 did the Atlantic slave trade end completely. More than 2 million slaves were transported from Africa during the 1800s, bringing the likely total of African slaves captured from the late 1400s to the late 1800s to at least 12 million.

The character of African colonization changed considerably after 1880. From then until the 1910s, European nations raced madly to take over territory in Africa. And by now, thanks to better maps, industrial-era weapons, and medicines that were effective against tropical diseases like malaria, European armies and colonizers were able to penetrate every part of what the West thought of prejudicially as the "Dark Continent." The "Scramble for Africa" grew so intense that it almost sparked war in Europe several times. The Berlin Conference of 1884 to 1885, presided over by Otto von Bismarck, laid down guidelines for African expansion and played a certain role in keeping the peace. Still, competition over African territory caused a number of diplomatic crises among the European powers during the early 1900s, especially the Boer War (1899–1902). For the Africans, of course, the sudden and overwhelming influx of Europeans spelled disaster. Tribe after tribe, country after country, fell to the Germans, Italians, British, French, Belgians, and others. By 1914, only two nations in Africa remained free: Liberia, whose independence was guaranteed by the United States, because it had been founded by freed American slaves, and Abyssinia (Ethiopia), which had armed itself with modern weapons and driven off Italian efforts to conquer it. Within a matter of three decades, the rest of the continent had been brought under Europe's imperial sway.

THE BALKANS

Even parts of Europe were, in a way, vulnerable to imperial tendencies. Southeastern Europe—especially the Balkans—lay at the crossroads of several empires. Although this area was the most economically and culturally backward of Europe, the imperial ambitions of Russia, Austria, the newly formed Italy, and the rapidly deteriorating Ottoman Empire were all centered on it. The level of competition among these powers increased as the 1800s ended and the 1900s began. Complicating the situation was the intense wave of nationalism that swept most of southeastern Europe during the nineteenth century. Starting with the Greek war of independence against the Ottomans in the 1820s, the various Slavic peoples and other ethnic minorities ruled by the Ottomans, the Austrians, and the Russians had constantly striven for greater independence—or, if they had independence, they craved more territory. To realize their goals, many of these peoples were willing to risk war. By the early 1900s, the nationalist ambitions of many of the Balkan peoples—especially the Serbs—had become an incredibly destabilizing force in European politics. Not only were two Balkan wars fought in 1912 to 1913, but it was in the Balkans that the events that started World War I took place.

AGGRESSION AT HOME: NATIONALISM, WARFARE, AND ALLIANCE SYSTEMS

Because European foreign policy played such a strong role in shaping world events during the imperial nineteenth century, and because World War I had such a global impact on the twentieth century, the workings of European diplomacy are worth knowing in some detail.

THE BALANCE OF POWER IN NINETEENTH-CENTURY EUROPE

As noted previously, the European balance of power had maintained peace during the first half of the 1800s. Even afterward, the wars that broke out among the European powers—the Crimean War, the wars of Italian and German unification, and the Franco-Prussian War—were short and limited in intensity. Ironically, the "Long Peace" that followed between 1871 and 1914 was a period of steadily worsening tensions. Despite the fact that this era gave birth to the modern Olympic Games (starting in 1896) and the Nobel Peace Prize (first awarded in 1901), the late 1800s and early 1900s were marked by saber rattling, jingoism (a British nickname for belligerent patriotism), and brinksmanship (a diplomatic term referring to a country's willingness to risk war in order to get its way).

FACTORS DESTABILIZING THE EUROPEAN BALANCE OF POWER

Several factors upset the diplomatic stability of Europe during the late 1800s and early 1900s. One was the force of nationalism, which, in most countries, transformed patriotic sentiment into aggressive tendencies. Another was competition over empire: as the 1800s came to an end, there were fewer places for European nations to expand. Especially in Africa, the jostling for new conquests came close to starting war several times in the early 1900s. A third destabilizing force was the ambitious nature of German foreign policy. An economic and military powerhouse, despite the fact that it had been united only in 1871, Germany came to believe that it deserved what it called "a place in the sun"—in other words, equal military and imperial status with older nations such as Britain and France. This was the case especially under Kaiser Wilhelm II, who came to the throne in 1888 and dismissed the skilled and cautious diplomat Otto von Bismarck in 1890. Under Wilhelm II, Germany became openly aggressive and forceful in pursuing its military and imperial goals, making the rest of Europe extremely nervous.

THE CREATION OF EUROPE'S TURN-OF-THE-CENTURY ALLIANCE SYSTEM

In the midst of all this, an alliance system gradually began to take shape during the 1880s through the 1910s. The end result was to divide the European powers into two armed camps. Rather than preserving the peace, the alliance system, by guaranteeing that a conflict between two nations would draw in all European countries, made war more likely. Previous to Bismarck's dismissal in 1890, a rough balance of power, created largely by him, had created a certain stability. Germany and Austria had allied in 1879, then were joined by Italy in 1881. This created the Triple Alliance. Germany was also on good terms with Russia. It also maintained a friendly neutrality with Britain. Because of the Great Game, Britain viewed Russia as its most serious rival in Europe. France, isolated, with no firm allies, bitterly resented Germany because of its defeat in the Franco-Prussian War.

Bismarck's dismissal in 1890 and Wilhelm II's aggressive behavior afterward did much to bring about a major diplomatic realignment in Europe. Furthermore, this realignment would do much to create the conditions for the outbreak of World War I. First, Wilhelm II ignored Bismarck's policy of maintaining friendly relations with Russia. Since Russia was already rivals with Germany's ally Austria in the Balkans, being dropped by Germany convinced the Russians to form an alliance with France in 1894 to 1895. France and Russia now had Austria, Germany, and Italy surrounded.

For the next ten years, Britain remained unaligned. It still disliked Russia, and it had little affection for France. However, Britain felt increasingly threatened by Wilhelm II's Germany. Germany's sudden pushiness in building an overseas empire, especially in Africa, greatly angered Britain (see Chapter 26). Even worse was Germany's military buildup, particularly at sea. The main thing Britain relied upon for its global power—and its ability to maintain its empire—was the Royal Navy. British strategic policy called for the Royal Navy to be as large as the next two biggest navies combined (not counting that of the United States). During the 1890s, Wilhelm II became obsessed with the goal of building a huge navy. Wilhelm's behavior forced Britain to enlarge its navy, and a massive arms buildup—the Anglo-German naval race—resulted. The naval race did much to sour relations between the two countries. In 1904, the British decided to conclude an informal agreement with France. In 1907, the British went a step further. Deciding that the Germans were a greater threat than the Russians, the British informally joined the Franco-Russian alliance, forming the Triple Entente.

At this point, the European powers were divided into two evenly matched and highly antagonistic sides. All were pledged to go to war if two countries quarreled. All that was needed was a single crisis to set the alliance system into motion. Increasing the tension was the fact that Germany was surrounded by France and Russia. The only way it could hope to win this two-front war was to come up with an attack plan that would knock one of its enemies out of the conflict quickly. Any such plan would have to be carried out with lightning speed. This meant that, in the event of any serious disturbance in Europe, the Germans would have to make their decision about whether or not to go to war rapidly, if not rashly. By 1906, the Germans had devised such a plan, the Schlieffen Plan. The fact that it would have to be carried out with great speed became an important element in the immediate background to World War I. As described in Chapter 28, its failure in 1914 ensured that World War I would be a long, painful conflict.

QUICK REVIEW

1. Which of the following best describes the broad trends in European foreign policy during the period of 1815 to 1914?

   (A) European nations were highly warlike in the aftermath of the Napoleonic conflicts, but became more peaceful after midcentury.
   (B) The post-Napoleonic treaties kept the peace until the 1850s, then a series of short but important wars broke out until 1871, followed by a four-decade period of peace.
   (C) There was constant war in Europe from the 1850s until the end of the century.
   (D) There were no major wars on the European continent between the defeat of Napoleon and the beginning of World War I.
   (E) none of the above

2. Which of the following did NOT encourage or enable the "new" imperialism of the late 1800s?

   (A) a sense of racial and cultural superiority
   (B) industrial-era military technology
   (C) the need to maintain far-off naval bases and refueling stations
   (D) the essays of Charles Darwin
   (E) new medical treatments for tropical diseases such as malaria

3. Which of the following nations is considered to have treated its colonies most poorly?

   (A) Belgium
   (B) Great Britain
   (C) France
   (D) the Netherlands
   (E) Austria

4. The role that the United States played in Latin America during the 1800s and early 1900s can best be described as

   (A) colonial overlord
   (B) strictly hands-off
   (C) encouraging and nurturing
   (D) warlike and aggressive
   (E) economically and politically interventionist

5. Which European power colonized Indochina?

   (A) Great Britain
   (B) Germany
   (C) Italy
   (D) the Netherlands
   (E) France

6. During the first half of the 1800s, which institution administered Great Britain's colony in India?

   (A) the British East India Company
   (B) the British crown
   (C) the British army
   (D) Lloyd's of London
   (E) the Bank of England

7. Which Asian nation proved most successful at resisting foreign domination?

   (A) China
   (B) Laos
   (C) Japan
   (D) Burma
   (E) Malaysia

8. Which European powers were enmeshed in the so-called Great Game?

   (A) Great Britain and Russia
   (B) Russia and France
   (C) Italy and Germany
   (D) Austria and Italy
   (E) Austria and Russia

9. Which country's collapse was at the heart of the Eastern Question?

(A) Persia's
(B) the Ottoman Empire's
(C) India's
(D) Afghanistan's
(E) China's

10. The number of slaves taken from Africa to the Americas between the late 1400s and late 1800s is most likely somewhere around

(A) 1 million
(B) 28 million
(C) 12 million
(D) 19 million
(E) 6 million

ANSWERS:

1. **B**, p. 280
2. **D**, pp. 281–82
3. **A**, p. 283
4. **E**, p. 283
5. **E**, p. 283
6. **A**, pp. 283–84
7. **C**, p. 284
8. **A**, p. 284
9. **B**, p. 285
10. **C**, p. 285

CHAPTER 23

The Middle East

The Middle East, along with Islamic North Africa and Central Asia, underwent a fundamental transformation between the early 1700s and early 1900s. Before 1700, the Ottoman Empire, feared and respected throughout Eurasia as a great power, reigned supreme over most of this region. Where it did not, states like Persia and the khanates of Central Asia stood strong and free.

After 1700, military setbacks at the hands of European enemies—most notably Austria and Russia—weakened the Ottoman Empire considerably. Its European possessions gradually slipped away throughout the eighteenth and nineteenth centuries. The internal decay of the Ottoman government allowed outlying territories in North Africa to gain a high degree of autonomy. An additional problem was British, French, and Italian imperialism in North Africa, which further eroded Ottoman power. By the nineteenth century, the failing Ottoman Empire had earned an unflattering nickname: the "sick man of Europe." Periodic reform efforts kept the state alive during the 1800s, but did not stave off decline. More reform would come at the beginning of the 1900s, but World War I would destroy the Ottoman Empire, which was transformed into the modern Turkish state afterward.

In the meantime, how to deal with the steady collapse of the Ottoman state—and still maintain the European balance of power—became one of the crucial foreign-policy issues of the 1800s. This "Eastern Question" puzzled and perplexed diplomats for decades.

European imperialism also dealt blows to other states in the Middle East and neighboring regions. Areas such as Egypt, the Caucasus, Persia, and Central Asia came under European—mainly British and Russian—control during the 1800s.

THE DECLINE OF THE OTTOMAN EMPIRE

THE OTTOMANS' MILITARY DEFEATS DURING THE 1700s

The Ottoman Empire sustained a heavy set of blows at the end of the 1600s and during the early 1700s. In 1683, the Turks nearly succeeded in capturing Vienna, the capital of the Austrian Habsburgs. The attempt failed, however, and an allied Christian force counterattacked. In the three and a half decades of fighting that ensued, the Turks lost battle after battle, and the Austrians stripped much territory, including Hungary and Transylvania, from the Ottomans. The treaties of Karlowitz (1699) and Passarowitz (1718) left the Turks greatly diminished in Europe.

Occasional conflicts with Austria tended to sap the Ottomans' strength. Even worse were the periodic wars the Turks fought with Russia, especially against Peter the Great in the 1710s and Catherine the Great in the late 1700s. With each new struggle, the Turks lost territory along the Black Sea coast, as well as naval superiority in the region.

INTERNAL DECAY WITHIN THE OTTOMAN EMPIRE

Internal troubles also damaged the Ottoman state. Mediocre rulers and governmental corruption had weakened the political system during the 1600s and continued to do so during the 1700s. The Ottomans' dilemma was that sultans who wished to improve or modernize the system met with opposition from influential groups and officials with vested interests in the old, traditional way of doing things.

This was especially the case with the armed forces. The janissary-led military, which had been so innovative and effective during the 1500s and 1600s, became backward and complacent. All during the 1700s and early 1800s, the janissaries refused to adapt to the new technology and tactics of the modern, increasingly industrialized military age. Unfortunately for the empire, the janissaries were, until the late 1820s, powerful enough to prevent any governmental or military change for the better. For example, when Sultan Selim III tried to reform the bureaucracy and modernize the army and navy during the 1790s and early 1800s, the janissaries, fearing to lose their privileged position, assassinated him in 1807.

OTTOMAN ATTEMPTS AT REFORM

Later sultans were more effective at changing the system. From the 1820s onward, the Ottoman leadership made some gains in modernizing the political system, the economy, and the military along Western lines. To a degree, the Ottoman Empire also secularized. The sultans boosted Western educational principles, scientific knowledge, and technological expertise, generally against the protests of the traditional Islamic clergy. During the late 1820s, Mehmed III created a professional army trained in the European style, then subdued the janissaries. He also built a modern navy.

From 1839 through 1876, the Ottoman government introduced a wide-ranging set of changes known as the Tanzimat reforms. These emphasized greater religious tolerance for the many non-Muslims living in the empire, reform of the legal system, the creation of schools that would teach Western science and technology, the establishment of national telegraph and postal systems, and more. The Tanzimat reforms even included discussing the possibility of a constitution.

Another effect of the Tanzimat reforms was to give women greater access to education. Public schools were founded for women. In addition, more women (although still a small number) began to enter public life in various capacities during the late 1800s.

None of these measures, however, was enough to solve the Ottoman Empire's deep-seated internal and external problems. Changes like the Tanzimat reforms alienated conservatives and traditionalists who found them too extreme. Conversely, they did not do enough to satisfy the growing numbers of forward-looking and innovative politicians and military officers who favored even more change than the sultan was willing to make. By the early 1900s, this generation of modernizers, known as the Young Turks, would, from within the regime, play a decisive role in ending the sultan's rule.

REVOLTS, REBELLIONS, AND THE GRADUAL DISINTEGRATION OF THE OTTOMAN EMPIRE

But long beforehand, external problems such as rebellion and war were already disintegrating the Ottoman Empire. During the first decades of the 1800s, an upsurge of nationalism, combined with the general political turmoil caused by the Napoleonic Wars, led to many uprisings in Turkish-controlled Europe. Serbia revolted in 1807, and even though the revolt failed, the Serbs remained restless.

More seriously, the Greeks began a war of independence in 1821. By 1827, France and Britain, responding to Christian Europe's popular outpouring of sympathy for the Greeks, aided the rebels (the romantic poet Lord Byron, for example, had helped turn the Greek war into an international cause by leaving England to fight and die on the side of the Greeks). The next year, Russia, which shared Greece's Eastern Orthodox faith, joined the war. Defeated by this coalition, the Ottomans were forced to recognize Greek independence in 1829 to 1832. At the same time the Greeks were breaking away, the Ottoman government had to cope with the rebellion of Muhammad Ali in Egypt (discussed subsequently). Over the next decades, local officials in the western parts of North Africa also began to agitate for—and gain—greater autonomy (also discussed subsequently).

THE EASTERN QUESTION

From the 1820s onward, the steady collapse of the Ottoman state presented the nations of Europe with a geopolitical challenge that became known as the Eastern Question. Although the Turks had been enemies of the European powers since the late 1300s, the Ottoman Empire was now seen as a satisfactory government to have in place in the Middle East. It was no longer a real threat, it was predictable, and, for the time being, it held together under one regime many volatile parts of Asia and Europe. To destroy it or allow it to fall apart quickly might cause chaos or give birth to a new state that was strong and hostile.

Another aspect of the Eastern Question was that the nations of Europe did not wholly trust each other. The Ottoman Empire sat at a geographically crucial juncture: the crossroads of Europe and Asia, the joining of the Black and Mediterranean seas, and the Suez isthmus, which linked the Mediterranean with the Indian Ocean and Asia. If one European country were to take too much advantage of the Ottomans and seize too much territory from it at one time, it would upset Europe's fragile balance of power. Informally, the nations of Europe agreed to solve this part of the Eastern Question by not acting too suddenly or decisively in the Middle East or the Mediterranean. The Ottomans' decline was to be managed carefully and slowly. If necessary, the European powers would prop the empire up if it seemed in danger of immediate collapse. This, at least, was the theory. As things turned out, Britain and France, nervous about Austrian and Russian ambitions in the Balkans and Mediterranean, tended to safeguard the Turks against the east European empires. Of course, this strategy did not stop the British and French from taking what they wanted from the Ottomans.

The complicated nature of the Eastern Question was illustrated many times. It took so long for the Europeans to decide to aid Greece during the 1820s because they were afraid of causing too much damage to the Ottoman Empire at once. Shortly after helping the Greeks against the Turks, Britain and France assisted the Turks in settling the revolt of Muhammad Ali in Egypt. The European powers feared that Muhammad Ali would be too formidable an enemy if he toppled the Ottoman sultan. The dangers of competing over the spoils of Ottoman decay were also made clear on several occasions. The Crimean War, the first major conflict among the European powers since the defeat of Napoleon in 1815, was touched off in 1853 when Tsar Nicholas I of Russia invaded the Danubian principalities of Wallachia and Moldavia, which were part of the Ottomans' European territory. In 1854, France and Britain joined the Turks in fighting Russia. The allies attacked Russia's Black Sea naval headquarters at Sevastopol, on the Crimean peninsula, and after a costly struggle that killed at least 250,000 troops, the French, British, and Turks defeated Russia by 1856.

The tensions surrounding the Eastern Question worsened after 1870. The construction of the Suez Canal in 1869 increased the geographical importance of Egypt and North Africa, as well as France's and Britain's interest in the region (discussed subsequently). The unification of Italy in the 1860s added another European power that had ambitions in the eastern Mediterranean. Moreover, Balkan nationalism was making it harder for the Turks to hold on to their European possessions. For example, Serbia gained autonomy in 1867 and thirsted for complete freedom, as well as more land. Montenegro, Romania, and Bulgaria also wanted greater autonomy from Turkish control.

THE BALKAN CRISIS OF 1876–1878

Like the Crimean War, the Balkan crisis of 1876 to 1878 further demonstrated the delicacy that the Eastern Question called for. In 1876, Montenegro, Romania, Bulgaria, and Serbia rose up against Ottoman rule. The Turks suppressed the rebellion ruthlessly. In 1877, Russia went to war against the Ottomans, defeated them in 1878, and imposed a harsh treaty. At this juncture, the rest of Europe intervened, not wishing Russia to achieve too decisive a victory. At the Congress of Berlin (1878), over which German chancellor Otto von Bismarck presided, Montenegro, Romania, Bulgaria, and Serbia gained their independence. But the powers of Europe forced Russia to grant the Turks a more generous set of peace terms. This combination of opportunistic land grabbing and balanced management remained the basic posture of Europe toward the Ottoman Empire for the rest of the century and the early 1900s, up to the beginning of World War I.

THE YOUNG TURKS

Domestically, the Ottoman Empire, steadily losing territory and constantly being interfered with by the powers of Europe, was suffering great difficulties as the 1800s came to an end. As the twentieth century began, the sultan's days were numbered. A group of pro-Western army officers, with a modern, secular outlook, began to form. They called themselves the Young Turks, and they were deeply dissatisfied with the sultan's failures to reform and strengthen the Ottoman Empire. Led by Enver Pasha, the Young Turks seized control of the empire in 1908. They deposed the last sultan, Abdulhamid II, and established a parliamentary government. The Young Turks modernized the military, aligned themselves with Germany, and began a series of social, economic, and political reforms.

THE BALKAN WARS, WORLD WAR I, AND THE FALL OF THE OTTOMAN EMPIRE

However, the Young Turks were unable to save the Ottoman Empire. When, in 1911 to 1912, Italy attacked the Ottomans' last remaining provinces in North Africa, the Turks lost. In the First Balkan War of 1912, the Ottomans were defeated by a Balkan coalition of Serbia, Greece, and Bulgaria. Although the Turks gained some of their losses back during the Second Balkan War of 1913, neither Balkan war was a triumph for the Ottoman Empire. Finally, after World War I broke out, the Young Turk government joined in on the side of the Germans and Austrians. Defeated by the Allies in 1918, the Ottoman Empire collapsed altogether, and its Middle Eastern possessions would rebel or be stripped away by the French and British. The empire would be replaced by the modern Turkish state during the 1920s.

EGYPT AND NORTH AFRICA

NORTH AFRICA UNDER OTTOMAN RULE

When the Ottoman Empire was at its peak, it ruled almost the entire expanse of Islamic North Africa. Even before the late 1700s, the empire's grip on this region was weakening, as a result of distance and the desire of local officials for greater autonomy. Over time, it was difficult for the central authorities in Istanbul to ensure that their orders were followed so far away, in great cities such as Tripoli, Algiers, and Tunis.

Things worsened with the Napoleonic Wars. In 1798, France, in an effort to cut its enemy England off from India, sent Napoleon to capture Egypt and the Suez isthmus. In a series of colorful battles, Napoleon easily defeated a number of Egyptian and Turkish armies, temporarily deposing the Mamluks who ruled Egypt on the Ottomans' behalf. Although the English restored the regime in the early 1800s, the political chaos and instability caused by the fighting had already taken their toll on the Turks' ability to maintain order in Egypt.

THE REVOLT OF MUHAMMAD ALI

Therefore, the 1805 rebellion of Muhammad Ali effectively removed Egypt from Ottoman rule. An officer of Turkish or Albanian descent, Muhammad Ali took over Egypt and began to modernize it until his death in 1839. He created a Western-style military, modernized agricultural production (especially cotton), boosted industrialization, and recruited large numbers of European professionals to serve his state and teach his people new skills. Muhammad Ali transformed Egypt into one of the world's greatest suppliers of cotton, although it should be noted that he worked his peasants oppressively to do so.

Muhammad Ali became an even more serious threat to the Ottoman Empire when he tried to expand his borders. Very quickly, he struck southward, taking the Sudan. He then went east, capturing the Sinai, Syria, parts of Arabia, and northern Iraq. Muhammad Ali threatened the capital, Istanbul, itself. Afraid that he would topple the Ottomans completely, France and Britain intervened. Recognizing Muhammad Ali as the hereditary prince (khedive) of an autonomous Egypt, the Europeans convinced the rebel not to expand further. In so doing, the French and British saved the Ottoman Empire. At the same time, however, the empire had been badly injured.

EUROPEAN IMPERIALISM IN NORTH AFRICA

As the 1800s passed, the western portions of North Africa, now cut off from the Ottoman Empire by Egypt, became more and more detached from the Turks. They also fell to European imperialists. The French seized Algeria in 1830 and turned it into the most precious of their colonies. More than 150,000 Frenchmen and Frenchwomen settled there by the mid-1850s, and the French considered Algeria to be as important to them as India was to the British. Later, the French established a protectorate over neighboring Tunisia. Morocco fell to the French and Spanish late in the century. Finally, Libya was conquered by Italy during the Italo-Turkish War of 1911 to 1912. Incidentally, this was the first war in which airplanes were used in combat.

THE SUEZ CANAL AND ENGLISH DOMINANCE OVER EGYPT

Egypt fell out of the Ottoman orbit only to be sucked into the European sphere of influence. Muhammad Ali's grandson Isma'il, also a reformer, decided to build a canal across the Suez land bridge that linked the Mediterranean with the Red Sea and, by extension, with the Indian Ocean and Asia. Isma'il's other modernizing efforts, which included building schools and hospitals, were helpful to Egypt. Building the Suez Canal was not, at least during the nineteenth century. The French engineer Ferdinand de Lesseps designed the canal, and British and French companies supervised the construction, which lasted from 1854 to 1869. When it was completed, the Suez Canal was a marvel of modern construction, and it revolutionized international shipping. However, thousands of Egyptians died during the construction, and most of the shares in the company that owned the canal were in French and British hands. Quickly, the British bought up many French shares and, in 1875, all of Egypt's. Its control over a majority of these shares gave Britain an excuse to interfere more and more in local politics. Finally, in 1881, the Egyptian military revolted against the khedive. Under the pretext of protecting their investment in the canal, the British assumed control over the region. They established a protectorate called the Anglo-Egyptian Administration. Although the khedive was technically the ruler of Egypt, the British controlled the government.

The British extended the Anglo-Egyptian Administration southward, bringing the Sudan under its control. The British war in the Sudan was a long one. In 1881, British authority was opposed by a religious leader and Islamic rebel known as the Mahdi (Arabic for "one who is rightly guided"). A British army under Charles Gordon, a great military hero, was massacred by the Mahdi and his followers in 1885, at the siege of Khartoum. This was one of Britain's most stunning imperial defeats. By 1898, however, the British general Horatio Kitchener (later a key figure in the Boer War and World War I) avenged Gordon's death by defeating the Mahdi at the battle of Omdurman. Using machine guns and modern rifles, Kitchener's tiny army mowed down thousands of poorly armed Egyptians and Sudanese. This defeat brought the Sudan, like Egypt, firmly under English control.

From the late 1800s until after the end of World War II, Egypt and North Africa would remain in European hands.

PERSIA, THE CAUCASUS, AND CENTRAL ASIA

Much the same pattern that applied to the Ottoman Empire and North Africa applied to the rest of the Middle East.

THE DECLINE AND PARTITION OF PERSIA

Like the Ottomans, the Persians had created a mighty gunpowder empire, the Safavid state (see Chapter 15), in the 1500s. It remained strong through the early 1700s, but found itself increasingly at the mercy of outside powers afterward. Persia's great enemy to the north was Russia, which, as it modernized and Westernized, was able to seize territory in a number of wars. During the late 1700s and 1800s, the Russians seized piece after piece of the Caucasus Mountains, which lay between the two countries. By the early 1800s, Russia had absorbed the Caucasian states of Armenia, Georgia, and Azerbaijan. The first two, Christian peoples living under Persia's Islamic rule, had asked Russia for assistance, but had not necessarily intended to become part of the Russian Empire. However, they did.

The Qajar dynasty, which ruled Persia from 1794 to 1925, was not able to resist foreign control, although affairs of government technically remained in its hands. During the 1800s, Britain and Russia cynically agreed to partition Persia into two spheres of influence. Partitioning Persia allowed Britain and Russia to balance their rivalry in the region, as well as to outflank the Ottoman Turks. The northern zone went to Russia, the southern zone to Britain. This partition lasted until the 1940s, after World War II. British financial investment in Persia was heavy, especially after 1908, when oil reserves were discovered there.

THE RUSSIAN CONQUEST OF CENTRAL ASIA

From the 1820s through the 1880s, the Russians waged a long, intense campaign of conquest and colonization in Central Asia. This vast expanse of khanates and city-states lined what, centuries before, had been the Silk Road connecting the Middle East with China and India. The Russians conquered these regions for several reasons: nationalistic pride, natural resources (Central Asia is a great cotton-growing region), strategic policy (the Russians feared having a long, open southern frontier), and the hope, never realized, of driving all the way to the Indian Ocean coastline to establish warm-water ports. In long, bloody wars of pacification, the Russians took Tashkent (1865), Samarkand (1868), Bukhara (1868), Khiva, and Khokand, driving all the way to the Afghan border.

As discussed in Chapter 22, Russian ambitions in this region deeply distressed the British, because the Russians not only threatened Britain's lines of communication and transport, but also drew near to India itself. The "Great Game" of espionage and diplomatic intrigue that the British and Russians waged for decades made them view each other as chief rivals until shortly before World War I.

QUICK REVIEW

1. Which part of the Ottoman Empire's European territory successfully gained its freedom in the early 1800s?

   (A) Serbia
   (B) Romania
   (C) Greece
   (D) Bulgaria
   (E) Albania

2. Until the 1820s, what institution or group stood in the way of the Ottoman sultans' efforts to reform?

   (A) the janissary corps
   (B) the admiralty
   (C) the Young Turks
   (D) the grand vizier's chancellery
   (E) the grenadiers

3. The actions of Muhammad Ali had what effect on the Ottoman Empire?

   (A) He conquered North Africa for the sultan.
   (B) He kept North Africa from breaking away from the empire.
   (C) He assassinated the sultan and assumed control over the empire.
   (D) He revolted against the empire, gaining freedom for Egypt.
   (E) He gained freedom for Tunisia and Algeria.

4. What part of North Africa became France's most prized colony?

   (A) Morocco
   (B) Algeria
   (C) Tunisia
   (D) Libya
   (E) Egypt

5. Which of the following did most to start the Crimean War?

   (A) an Ottoman massacre of Orthodox Christians on the Black Sea coast
   (B) the French naval blockade of Malta
   (C) Great Britain's assault on Damascus
   (D) Austria's annexation of Herzegovina
   (E) Russia's occupation of Moldavia and Wallachia

6. The 1869 completion of which of the following vastly increased the geopolitical importance of Egypt?

   (A) the Suez Canal
   (B) the Aswan Dam
   (C) the Giza Canal
   (D) the Luxor Bridge
   (E) the Alexandria Dockyards

7. Which group deposed the Ottoman sultan in 1908?

   (A) British commandos
   (B) Sufi assassins
   (C) the Young Turks
   (D) the janissary corps
   (E) Russian spies

8. Who led a large, religiously motivated army against the British in the Sudan during the late 1800s?

   (A) Muhammad Ali
   (B) the Mahdi
   (C) Enver Pasha
   (D) Isma'il
   (E) Rumi

9. Which European power conquered Central Asian city-states such as Bukhara and Samarkand?

   (A) France
   (B) Italy
   (C) Great Britain
   (D) Germany
   (E) Russia

10. What Middle Eastern state did the British and Russians cynically divide into two spheres of influence during the 1800s?

(A) the Ottoman Empire
(B) Persia
(C) Egypt
(D) Syria
(E) Lebanon

ANSWERS:

1. **C**, pp. 291–92
2. **A**, p. 291
3. **D**, p. 294
4. **B**, p. 294
5. **E**, p. 292
6. **A**, p. 294
7. **C**, p. 293
8. **B**, pp. 294–95
9. **E**, p. 295
10. **B**, p. 295

CHAPTER 24

China and Japan

As with the rest of the globe, the European presence in East Asia increased dramatically from the late 1700s through the early 1900s. The major states of East Asia, China and Japan, reacted to this development in two very different ways.

Famously, Napoleon Bonaparte referred to China as a sleeping dragon. By that, he meant that with its huge population, vast size, and rich resources, China had the potential to become one of the world's mightiest nations. However, under the rule of the late Qing (Manchu) emperors, China continued to slumber, and not long after Napoleon made his remark, its power decreased rather than increased. Deluded by a sense of its own grandeur, based on past accomplishments and old traditions, the Qing leadership did little to modernize and industrialize. This backwardness left it vulnerable, and during the 1800s, China suffered repeated defeats at the hands of Western powers. Although China was not actually conquered and colonized, it was forced to grant so many privileges and economic concessions to outside powers that its integrity as an independent nation was severely compromised. The Qing state also weakened internally during the 1800s. It collapsed in 1911.

By contrast, Japan responded effectively to the challenge posed by the West. When the United States and the nations of Europe forced its markets open to the world in the 1850s, Japan chose to learn from the West. From 1868 onward, under new leadership, the Japanese modernized, industrialized, and militarized. They preserved their independence. By the 1890s and early 1900s, Japan was an imperial power, expanding its sphere of influence in East Asia. As several wars during these years proved, Japan became the first non-Western nation in the modern era capable of rivaling Europe and America in military ability and strength.

QING (MANCHU) CHINA IN DECLINE

THE PEAK OF THE QING DYNASTY

The Qing, or Manchu, rulers who had conquered China from the north in 1644 had been mighty, ruthless leaders. The dynasty's peak, however, had been the long reign of Kangxi (1662–1722), and the emperor Qianlong (1736–1795) was the Qing's last strong, competent ruler.

During the last half of the 1700s, Qianlong defended China's long borders, kept the empire's far-flung regions under control, improved economic growth, and sponsored art and learning. For example, it was during the reign of Qianlong that one of the greatest novels in Chinese literary history appeared. This was Cao Xueqin's *Dream of the Red Chamber* (1791). This novel, which depicted upper-class family life in eighteenth-century China, narrated the tragedy of two young lovers caught up in the decline of a wealthy and powerful clan.

INTERNAL DECLINE OF THE QING

Unfortunately for the Qing, several negative trends began to weaken China simultaneously, almost immediately after Qianlong's death. The quality of leadership declined steeply, as weak, incompetent emperors took the throne.

More widely, the government as a whole became riddled with corruption. The cost of maintaining border defenses along the northern and western frontiers became increasingly burdensome. The economy worsened, and population growth became too rapid (China had 300 million people at the beginning of the century, and would have 400 million by the end). Popular discontent with the Qing government and bad economic conditions broke out into open revolt on a number of occasions. The most famous early revolt was the White Lotus Rebellion (1796–1804), which took years for the authorities to suppress.

CHINESE FOREIGN TRADE BEFORE THE 1830s

At the same time, an external problem began to make itself felt: increased economic and diplomatic pressure from the West, particularly from Britain. As late as the 1810s, the Chinese had the upper hand in their relationship with the West. China was too strong to conquer, and it enjoyed an enormous advantage in its balance of trade.

Aside from Macao, which had been colonized hundreds of years before by Portugal, the Europeans could trade with China only in a small number of designated ports and cities (including Kiakhta in the north and Canton on the southern coast). The Chinese accepted only a tiny selection of Western goods in trade.

Conversely, the Chinese sold the nations of the West silks and porcelain ware. The most profitable commodity was tea, which the Chinese sold in immense quantities to the outside world, especially Russia and Britain. In exchange, the West paid China vast amounts of silver bullion.

For years, Westerners complained about these conditions and requested the Chinese to allow them to sell more goods in China. In 1793, a British delegation led by Lord Macartney made such

Tea Harvesting in China.
For hundreds of years, silk, then porcelain, had been China's chief commodities in trade. During the 1600s and 1700s, however, tea began to overtake both in importance. The tea trade played a great role in global economics during the 1700s and 1800s. During those centuries, "all the tea in China" became the most popular slang phrase to describe unimaginable wealth. Shown here is the traditional method of harvesting and processing tea in China.

a request, but it was denied. Famously, Macartney, in order to meet the emperor Qianlong, was compelled to lower himself onto one knee, and he was referred to by the Chinese not as an ambassador, but as a tribute bearer. When Macartney asked that the British be allowed to sell more of their goods to China, Qianlong replied, "Your country has nothing we need." In 1816, a similar mission under Lord Amherst received much the same response.

Much of the Qing's refusal to bargain had to do with a tough business sense. Part of it also had to do with feelings of superiority: the Qing leadership sincerely believed that the emperor was the Son of Heaven, that China was the Middle Kingdom and the center of the universe, and that all outsiders were barbarians. What the Qing failed to realize, however, was that the Western "barbarians" were, by this point, much more scientifically and technologically advanced than the Chinese. Consequently, the Westerners had stronger navies, better weapons, and better-equipped armies. The days when the Chinese could intimidate foreigners into accepting such an embarrassing and unprofitable imbalance of trade were about to end quickly.

THE OPIUM TRADE

Meanwhile, the British, followed by other Europeans, found a clever, if unethical, way to break into Chinese markets: opium. This drug had been known in China since the early 1700s, but it was not yet available enough for its use to have become widespread. The British changed all this. A prime source of opium was northeast India, part of Britain's empire. In the 1820s and 1830s, the British began to flood China with opium. With lightning speed, it became the drug of choice among Chinese of all classes, and addiction became widespread. The British made fantastic profits from the opium trade, and the balance of trade, previously so heavily advantageous to China, swung suddenly in Britain's favor. Over time, other countries—such as France, Portugal, and the United States—also sold the drug to China, but Britain dominated the business, controlling 80 percent of the opium trade.

The Chinese government was outraged. The trade was illegal. It reversed the balance of trade, meaning that silver bullion, instead of flowing into China, was flowing out, and at an alarming rate. Moreover, addiction to opium was so widespread that it affected the economic productivity of the Chinese population: on any given day, millions of Chinese farmers and workers would be so incapacitated by the drug that they could not work. The Chinese protested to the West. As one official wrote, "The foreigners have brought us a disease which will dry up our bones, a worm that gnaws at our hearts, a ruin to our families and persons. It means the destruction of the soul of our nation."

THE OPIUM WARS AND FOREIGN DOMINATION OF QING CHINA

The Qing government tried to strike back by arresting dealers, seizing opium supplies, and intercepting boats carrying the drug. The problem for the Chinese was that any aggressive action might give the foreigners an excuse for war. This is what happened in 1839, when the Chinese navy blockaded Canton, one of the few ports where foreigners were allowed to trade. This action sparked the first Opium War (1839–1842), between Britain and China. The British won easily, then forced the humiliating Treaty of Nanking on the Chinese. The Qing government was required to open five more ports to foreign trade, lower tariffs on British goods, and grant extraterritorial rights to areas in China where the British lived and worked (this meant that British, not Chinese, law prevailed in these areas). In addition, China had to surrender Hong Kong to Britain.

The conflicts over opium and trade in general did not end in 1842. More fighting, including a second Opium War, the so-called Arrow War, and a Franco-British expedition to Beijing, took place between 1856 and 1860. Treaties arrived at from 1858 to 1860 made the opium trade legal, opened more ports to foreign trade, and granted greater powers to the Portuguese, French, British, Americans, and Russians who set up economic concessions on Chinese territory. During the last decades of the 1800s, China grew increasingly weaker and was steadily forced to give more and more privileges to foreign traders. Late in the century, Japan, Germany, and Italy gained concessions as well. Substantial pieces of territory along the Chinese coast were extraterritorial, meaning that they were legally under foreign, not Chinese, control. By 1898, foreign vessels were allowed unrestricted travel up the rivers of China.

THE TAIPING REBELLION

Serious internal problems dogged the Qing at the same time foreign pressure increased. The worst was the Taiping Rebellion (1850–1864), the costliest and most devastating civil war in world history. The Taiping Rebellion lasted almost a decade and a half. It claimed somewhere between 20 million and 30 million lives, making it the second deadliest war in history, next to World War II.

The uprising was started by Hong Xiuquan, a Cantonese clerk educated partly by Protestant missionaries. An aspiring government official, Hong failed his civil-service examination. The shock seems to have caused him to have visions, in which he became convinced that he was Jesus Christ's younger brother, destined to establish a "Heavenly Kingdom of Supreme Peace"—the meaning of the word *taiping*—in China.

Hong's rebellion began in 1850. An extraordinarily magnetic leader, Hong attracted many followers who were able to organize an effective, modern army. Hong's vision of a new China also proved appealing to millions of ordinary Chinese who resented the Qing's high taxes, arbitrary and oppressive rule, and the fact that the Manchu emperors were, essentially, foreign rulers dominating their Chinese subjects. In 1853, the Taiping rebels captured the major city of Nanjing; in 1860, they came close to taking the great port of Shanghai. At their peak, Hong and the Taiping leaders controlled one third of China.

The Taiping Rebellion began to wane after 1860. Competent generals took over the Qing war effort, and the government was assisted by a foreign force—the Ever-Victorious Army—commanded by an American soldier of fortune, Frederick Townsend Ward, then the English general Charles "Chinese" Gordon. Quarrels among the Taiping leadership hurt the movement as well. By the early 1860s, the Taiping forces were in retreat. Hong committed suicide by taking poison in 1864, and the remaining Taiping leaders were captured and executed.

THE LEADERSHIP OF DOWAGER EMPRESS CIXI

Nonetheless, the Taiping Rebellion left China in ruins, and the Qing government was thrown into complete chaos. Not until 1878 did a strong leader emerge—and unfortunately, this leader was adamantly opposed to modernizing reform. This leader was the Empress Dowager Cixi, who "ruled" China from 1878 to her death in 1908. A concubine to the emperor in the 1850s, Cixi became a major figure at the Qing court. In 1878, she managed to place her nephew Guangxu on the imperial throne and gain for herself the position of regent. As regent, she controlled her nephew—and the government—long after Guangxu became an adult.

Under Cixi's influence, Qing rule became more oppressive. China's outlying possessions—Tibet, the Gobi Desert and Mongolia, Chinese Turkestan—began to slip away, gain greater autonomy, or fall into foreign hands. At home, Cixi opposed all reform, which she regarded as pro-Western treason. In 1898, when her nephew, the emperor Guangxu, allowed himself to be persuaded by reform-minded advisers, she acted harshly. When Guangxu's short-lived "Hundred Days' Reform" got under way, Cixi struck back by placing her nephew under house arrest and executing the reformers.

THE SINO-JAPANESE WAR AND THE OPEN DOOR POLICY

All this time, foreign domination of China increased, especially as the new nations of Germany and Italy began to push for a greater share of Chinese trade. Germany carved out territory for itself on the Shantung Peninsula, taking the major port of Tsingtao. Japan defeated China in the Sino-Japanese War of 1894 to 1895 (discussed subsequently). In 1898, the United States, with its Open Door Policy, arranged for all Western nations to have equal access to Chinese markets. Such a policy served the purpose of reducing much of the pressure that European nations were placing on China to open up further. But it also meant that foreign control continued.

Western Spheres of Influence in China, 1910.

Starting in the early-to-mid 1800s, Great Britain, then other Western nations, pressured China into opening its markets and yielding up economic and political control over much of its coast. These concessions grew in size and number during the 1800s and early 1900s, reaching their peak just before the collapse of the Qing dynasty in 1911.

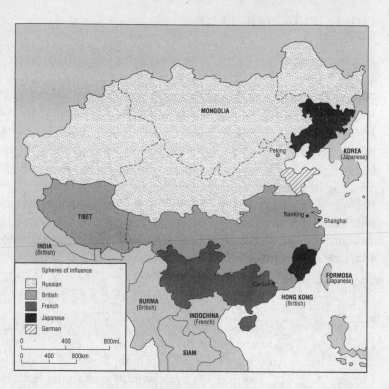

MISSIONARIES IN CHINA

Another result of the increased foreign influence in China was a steep rise in the level of missionary activity there. From the late 1800s through the mid-1900s, it became more and more common for Protestant and Catholic clergy and volunteers to travel from Europe and the United States to China in order to spread Christianity and teach Western languages. In this way, they interfered with, and even eroded, traditional Chinese culture.

But missionaries also brought scientific and technological knowledge, treated diseases and ailments with modern medicine, and helped eliminate oppressive cultural practices such as the binding of young women's feet. Missionary activity proved to be an illustration of imperialism's mixed legacy of positive and negative impact.

THE BOXER REBELLION

Finally, in 1900, Chinese anger at foreign influence burst out of control. Making things worse were a severe drought, which damaged agriculture and hurt farmers, and widespread unemployment in the cities. What followed during the summer was the Boxer Rebellion, so called because many of the rebels were Chinese "boxers," or martial-arts experts.

Most of the rebels' rage was directed at foreigners, especially in the capital, Beijing, where rebels attacked foreign residents and besieged foreign legations. In the end, the rebellion was put down, mainly by foreign troops. In revenge, the foreign communities in China burned a number of temples. They also forced the Qing government to pay a heavy financial penalty.

THE QING'S LAST-DITCH ATTEMPTS AT REFORM

Too little, too late, even Cixi recognized the need for at least some reform. In 1905, she formed a committee to investigate the possibility of writing a constitution. She and Guangxu both died in 1908, but the reform effort continued under China's last emperor, Henry Puyi. Local assemblies were formed, and elections for a national assembly were planned for 1910.

SUN YAT-SEN

However, reform came too late to save the Qing dynasty. Efforts to change were too weak and feeble. Opposition groups of many types had formed in China, especially among younger Chinese who opposed Manchu domination of their race and favored Western-style modernization. The most important of these revolutionaries was Sun Yat-sen (1866–1925), the father of modern China. During the early 1900s, Sun Yat-sen united a number of opposition groups into a movement called the Revolutionary Alliance. Sun hoped to carry out a government takeover that would progress from military revolt to the formation of a constitutional democracy. His movement was founded on three ideas, which he called the People's Principles: Nationalism (which primarily meant opposition to Manchu rule), Democracy, and People's Livelihood.

THE COLLAPSE OF THE QING AND THE ESTABLISHMENT OF THE CHINESE REPUBLIC

The Qing regime collapsed in 1911. In the fall, a major uprising began in the central Chinese industrial region of Wuhan. Although Sun Yat-sen was actually in the United States at the time, his movement was at the forefront of the rebellion. The uprising spread, and Sun returned from America. A Chinese Republic was founded by the beginning of 1912, with Sun as its president. His party was now called the Nationalist Party, or Kuomintang. For the first time in recorded Chinese history, the country was ruled not by an imperial dynasty or foreign conqueror, but by a politician brought to office by popular action.

The Chinese Republic, however, was destined to have a short and stormy history. Sun would be forced to step aside as president shortly after coming to power. Confusion, decentralization, political breakdown, and civil war would characterize the 1910s through the 1940s. In 1949, the republic would be destroyed, and a communist government would take its place.

ISOLATION AND PARTIAL MODERNIZATION IN TOKUGAWA JAPAN

THE TOKUGAWA SHOGUNATE IN THE EIGHTEENTH CENTURY

In the 1750s, Japan was ruled by the Tokugawa clan, which had seized control of the country at the beginning of the 1600s. The form of government was still the shogunate. Although, technically, supreme authority rested with the emperor, real power belonged to the shogun, who ran the country in the emperor's name. At the top of Japanese society was the samurai class, the warrior aristocracy from Japan's feudal era.

During the 1600s and early 1700s, the Tokugawa shoguns had been strong, dynamic rulers. They had centralized Japan and transformed it from a constantly warring collection of disunified states into a single country at peace. But the Tokugawa shoguns were also highly dictatorial, creating a rigidly stratified society that restricted social mobility, kept ordinary citizens out of politics, and allowed few personal freedoms. Tokugawa Japan also isolated itself from the rest of the world. By the 1720s, the only country with which Japan maintained formal relations was Korea. Informal ties were maintained with China, and the government allowed the Chinese and the Dutch to trade at the port of Nagasaki.

PARTIAL MODERNIZATION IN TOKUGAWA JAPAN

Over the course of the late 1700s and early 1800s, Tokugawa Japan partially modernized, both economically and socially. Population growth was steady. Japan, already a society of cities, experienced even more urban growth. Kyoto and Osaka were major centers, and the capital, Edo (present-day Tokyo) had a population of well over a million. Agriculture practice was rationalized, allowing fewer people to grow more food. This reform had the effect of boosting urbanization. It also created the labor force needed to accelerate yet another trend: proto-industrialization.

Trade, commerce, and manufacturing became increasingly important. A national infrastructure—more roads, canals, and ports—began to emerge. The merchant class grew in number, wealth, and influence, becoming the middle class that any society needs to modernize. Despite the country's international isolation, some Japanese gained an awareness of scientific and technological knowledge from the West.

THE DILEMMA OF PARTIAL MODERNIZATION

This partial modernization placed the shogun and the samurai class in a curious dilemma. On one hand, such developments benefited Japan, making it a more prosperous and more advanced nation. On the other hand, the spread of new foreign learning, the movement of people from countryside to city, and the increased social and economic clout of the merchant class all undermined the power of the 5 to 8 percent of the population that made up the traditional aristocracy.

Therefore, the regime allowed some modernization, but not as much as the country was capable of achieving. In particular, members of the samurai class—whose military prowess was based on skill with traditional weapons such as swords—were anxious to preserve the state's monopoly on the ownership of and ability to make gunpowder weaponry. How long the Tokugawa leadership would have persisted in this approach is impossible to say. But by the early 1850s, outside forces would change Japan forever.

COMMODORE PERRY AND THE OPENING OF JAPAN

In 1853, American gunships appeared off the Japanese coast. Their commander, Commodore Matthew Perry, bore a request from U.S. President Millard Fillmore, asking Japan to open its economy to foreign trade. Although the Americans' words were friendly, the threat of naval bombardment lay behind them. After some debate, the shogun agreed to end his country's decades-long isolation. Over the next five years, other nations, principally the powers of Europe, compelled the Japanese to open up to them as well. For a time, it appeared that Japan might fall victim to the same kind of Western economic pressure that was crippling China.

THE OVERTHROW OF THE TOKUGAWA SHOGUNATE

Painfully aware of what was happening to China, certain samurai leaders, particularly from the southern provinces of Satsuma and Choshu, urged the shogun to take a hard line with the foreigners and stand up to their intimidation. This "Sat-Cho Alliance" gained a substantial following at the Edo court and pressed for the severance of all ties with the West. It also took matters into its own hands. In 1867, a coastal fortress in Choshu fired on Western ships offshore, and the ships fired back. The resulting scandal gave the Sat-Cho Alliance the pretext it needed to move against the last shogun, Tokugawa Yoshinobu, who had just come to power.

Late in the year, antishogun forces asked Yoshinobu to resign and restore the emperor to full authority. In January 1868, these forces, led by the Sat-Cho, staged a military uprising and overthrew Yoshinobu. The young emperor, Meiji, who had just ascended to the throne in 1867, became the first emperor in nearly a thousand years to enjoy full imperial powers.

THE MEIJI RESTORATION AND JAPANESE ASCENDANCY

THE MEIJI RESTORATION AND THE MOVE TOWARD MODERNIZATION

The Meiji Restoration of 1868 began Japan's modern age. Although the rebellion that had brought the emperor to power had been largely anti-Western in nature, even the most xenophobic members of the new Japanese government realized that, in order to avoid being dominated by the West, Japan would have to adopt Western learning, economics, and military methods. In addition, the emperor himself was personally inclined toward Westernization. What followed was a revolution from above, in which Meiji's government would radically alter Japanese politics, economics, and social organization.

FROM FEUDALISM TO CONSTITUTIONAL MONARCHY

One of the first things Meiji did, in 1871, was to abolish feudalism. Although individual samurai continued to serve in positions of power, hereditary privileges were done away with. Government stipends to the samurai, a privilege of the past, were eliminated. Former samurai were forbidden to wear swords, their traditional symbols of authority, in public.

The rigid social hierarchy of the Tokugawa regime was ended legally. A formal law code, the Civil Code of 1898, was drawn up. The Constitution of 1890 provided for the creation of an elected parliament, the Diet. Due to property qualifications and other voting restrictions, suffrage was quite low, around 5 percent, and the emperor had a great deal of power over the Diet. The civil code and constitution also made little room for the rights of women, who were largely confined to a secondary status (although Japan's wave of industrialization gave many lower-class women jobs, these were low-paying, low-status positions). In effect, Meiji and his successors created an oligarchy, or rule by the few, that was less repressive and restrictive than the Tokugawa regime, but hardly representative.

INDUSTRIALIZATION AND ECONOMIC MODERNIZATION

Meiji and the emperors who followed him also altered the economy beyond recognition. As during the late Tokugawa era, agricultural productivity increased at the same time the numbers of peasants decreased, thanks to modern efficiency. The major change, however, involved industrialization. Meiji sent many young members of the upper class to visit or study in Europe and America, to learn engineering, economics, and military science. He created a Ministry of Industry in 1870, as well as state banks to give financial backing to his industrialization campaign. New railroads, steamships, ports, and canals were constructed every year. Huge corporations called *zaibatsu*, sponsored largely by the state, came to dominate much of the economic landscape. The government encouraged not just large-scale industry, but also private enterprise, spurring the growth of a larger middle class. Among the goods the Japanese became famous for were tea, silk, weaponry, ships, and sake (rice wine).

Economic growth did not come without its price. For farmers, taxes increased. As for industrialization, working conditions for the lower classes were often oppressive, just as they had been during the first decades of Europe's Industrial Revolution. Sweatshop environments, low wages, and unsafe labor practices prevailed, especially in textile mills and coal mines. In one mine near Nagasaki, workers toiled in temperatures of up to 130 degrees Fahrenheit, and were shot if they tried to escape. It was forbidden to form unions of any type.

SOCIAL AND CLASS TRANSFORMATION IN JAPAN

Social transformation was a major part of the Meiji Restoration. As described previously, the traditional privileges of the samurai class were taken away. Although the old elite still had power, access to political positions was increasingly dependent on merit and competence. The civil service, based on an examination system, grew from 29,000 in 1890 to 72,000 in 1908. Regional government, previously the privilege of the samurai daimyo, or nobles, was now handed over to prefects appointed by the imperial government in the capital (given the modern name Tokyo by Meiji).

Meiji's reforms and Japanese industrialization increased the size and power of the merchant and middle classes, much as industrialization did in the West. The feudal prejudice against trade and artisanship faded away.

Things changed for the lower classes as well. The farming population decreased, but taxes on them increased considerably. The industrial working class grew steadily. On one hand, their working conditions could be dreadful, as noted previously. The lower classes were also barred from full political participation by the Constitution of 1890. But the lower classes also benefited in many ways from the Meiji reforms. The new tax system of 1872 funded a national educational system. Commoners, who previously had not been allowed to handle or learn how to use weapons, were now allowed to serve in the military. Overall, Japanese society adopted Western dress, fashions and manners, the Western calendar, and the metric system. The population skyrocketed, growing from 35 million in 1873 to 55 million in 1918.

JAPANESE MILITARISM AND IMPERIALISM

Meiji Japan also became increasingly militaristic. Nationalist sentiment ran high during the late 1800s and 1900s, helping spur the desire for empire building. The state-sponsored religion of State Shintoism, a modern revival of Japan's ancient faith, placed great emphasis on a sense of Japanese superiority and veneration of the emperor as a descendant of the gods. Practical considerations included Japan's desire for markets for its industrial goods. Also, as a comparatively resource-poor island nation, Japan badly needed raw materials if it wished to continue its industrial growth.

Japanese expansion began in the 1870s. In 1876, Japan forced Korean ports open to trade, much as the West had done with China and Japan itself. In 1879, Japan took the Ryukyu island chain from China. This archipelago extended southwest from Japan and included the Okinawan islands, one of Japan's most prized overseas possessions. Throughout the 1880s and early 1890s, Japan intensified its military buildup, constructing a steamship navy and drafting a well-equipped and well-trained army.

Even greater military and imperial successes followed in the 1890s and early 1900s. In 1894, China and Japan went to war. Along with Japan's imperial aspirations, the cause of this Sino-Japanese War (1894–1895) was a large peasant uprising in Korea. China and Japan supported opposing sides and were drawn into conflict with each other. Although much smaller, Japan was politically determined and heavily industrialized, fighting a country that, while larger, was politically fragmented and militarily backward. The result was a resounding victory for Japan. Afterward, Japan occupied Korea and seized Taiwan. Later, in 1908, Japan would annex Korea outright.

THE RUSSO-JAPANESE WAR

An even more impressive triumph for Japan was the Russo-Japanese War (1904–1905). Competition over influence in Manchuria caused great tension between the two countries. Russia's rapid expansion in this area, and its construction of the Trans-Siberian Railroad, the longest in the world, through this territory, interfered with Japanese ambitions in the region. The Japanese opened the war with a surprise attack on Russia's Pacific naval base at Port Arthur. Tiny compared to Russia, Japan was nonetheless better prepared for war and had the advantage of fighting close to home. Russia's soldiers and supplies had to be transported more than 4,000 miles along the slender thread of the Trans-Siberian Railroad. When the war ended in 1905, Japan was victorious. It annexed the Liaotung Peninsula (the small spur of land directly west of Korea), the southern half of Sakhalin Island, and the Kurile Islands. Russia also agreed to recognize Japan's sphere of influence in southern Manchuria.

The Russo-Japanese War marked the first time in the modern era that a non-Western nation had defeated a European power in a full-scale military conflict. In a way, it was an early warning signal that, later in the twentieth century, Europe's peak as the world's dominant civilization would eventually pass—and that its empires would,·over the next few decades, slip away. As for Japan, it entered the new twentieth century as a modern industrial nation and a regional power with a growing empire. Japan would continue to modernize. Unfortunately, its militaristic, nationalistic streak would continue to widen as well, and its imperial ambitions would spin out of control.

QUICK REVIEW

1. The last truly competent ruler of Qing China is considered to be

    (A) Kangxi
    (B) Qianlong
    (C) Cixi
    (D) Guangxu
    (E) Puyi

2. Western nations were most upset with Qing China about what aspect of their trading relations?

    (A) the high price of Chinese rice
    (B) China's refusal to allow large amounts of foreign goods to be sold there
    (C) China's sponsorship of the illegal heroin trade
    (D) China's use of slave labor to manufacture its products
    (E) China's reluctance to sell silk and porcelain

3. What was the commodity that Western powers most sought from China during the late 1700s and 1800s?

    (A) rice
    (B) soy sauce
    (C) wine
    (D) tea
    (E) coffee

4. Which of the following resulted from the Opium Wars?

    I. China granted outside powers greater access to its port cities.
    II. China agreed to outlaw opium consumption.
    III. China ceded Hong Kong to Great Britain.
    IV. China allowed Germany to annex Taiwan.

    (A) I only
    (B) I and II only
    (C) I and III only
    (D) I, II, and IV
    (E) I, III, and IV

5. The Taiping Rebellion

    (A) was led by a former clerk who believed he was Jesus Christ's younger brother
    (B) overthrew the Qing dynasty
    (C) lasted only a short time and did little damage to China
    (D) was supported by Great Britain and the United States
    (E) started because of the secret work of Russian spies in China

6. Which of the following describes the Tokugawa shogunate during the late 1700s and early 1800s?

   (A) moving steadily toward economic modernization and greater democratization
   (B) isolated from the wider world and clinging to old samurai traditions
   (C) anarchic and plagued by civil war
   (D) benefiting intellectually and culturally from friendly ties with several Western powers
   (E) extremely warlike, perpetually in conflict with its neighbors

7. Who compelled the Japanese government to establish diplomatic and economic relations with the United States?

   (A) Douglas MacArthur
   (B) George Dewey
   (C) Robert Peary
   (D) Ulysses S. Grant
   (E) Matthew Perry

8. The emperor Meiji was

   (A) largely a figurehead, controlled by the shogun
   (B) a ruthless dictator
   (C) the great modernizer who overthrew the Tokugawa Shogunate
   (D) the founder of the Tokugawa Shogunate
   (E) an extreme traditionalist who opposed most forms of change

9. What were the *zaibatsu*?

   (A) huge industrial conglomerates
   (B) the most advanced battleships of their day
   (C) elite military units
   (D) large plantations that dominated Japanese agriculture
   (E) the oldest Buddhist temples in Japan

10. The Russo-Japanese War

   (A) marked the first time in the modern era that a non-Western nation had defeated a Western power
   (B) resulted from the clash of Russian and Japanese imperial ambitions in Manchuria
   (C) began with a Japanese surprise attack on the Russian-held base of Port Arthur
   (D) all of the above
   (E) none of the above

ANSWERS:

1. **B**, p. 298	6. **B**, pp. 303–4
2. **B**, p. 299	7. **E**, p. 304
3. **D**, p. 299	8. **C**, pp. 305–6
4. **C**, pp. 300–1	9. **A**, p. 305
5. **A**, p. 301	10. **D**, pp. 306–7

CHAPTER 25

India and Southeast Asia

The proverbial jewel in the crown of the British Empire was India. The conquest and ownership of this, one of the largest and most populous regions on earth, by a small group of islands 5,000 miles away was one of the central facts of nineteenth- and early twentieth-century life. All throughout the 1800s, British control over India affected global economics, the movement of navies, international relations, and the balance of world power. It gave Britain immense wealth and prestige. And, of course, it affected the course of Indian history—changing politics, economic development, social practices, language, and virtually every aspect of Indian culture—forever.

Likewise, the great arc of Southeast Asian nations and islands that stretched between British India and China came under European control throughout the 1800s. By the end of the century, only a tiny portion of Southeast Asia remained free of foreign domination.

On the other hand, it was also by the end of the 1800s that national resistance movements were beginning to form, both in India and the rest of Southeast Asia. Although, for the time being, they were unable to dislodge their foreign masters, they did lay the foundation for the freedom movements that would successfully expel European colonists after World War II.

FROM FOOTHOLD TO MASTERY: THE BRITISH IN LATE EIGHTEENTH-CENTURY INDIA

DECLINE OF THE MUGHAL EMPIRE

During the last half of the eighteenth century, most of India was technically ruled by the once-mighty Mughal Empire. But the Mughals' political fortunes had declined badly since the glory days of the 1500s and 1600s. Many parts of the subcontinent had already slipped out from under Mughal rule, becoming independent kingdoms or city-states. Also by the 1700s, increased pressure from European outsiders was destabilizing what was left of Mughal power.

ANGLO-FRENCH COMPETITION OVER INDIA

As late as the early 1700s, the Portuguese and Dutch still maintained small settlements along India's coasts. But the Europeans most intent on gaining control over India were Britain and France. For the time being, Britain's interests were represented by the British East India Company, which, on its own, financed the military takeover and economic development of British India.

From the southeast ports of Pondicherry and Madras (which they captured temporarily from the British in 1746), the French tried until the late 1750s to grapple with the British East India Company for hegemony over India. The colonial administrator Joseph François Dupleix led this effort. However, Dupleix did not receive adequate support from his home government in France.

Also, at the end of the decade, the British East India Company, under Sir Robert Clive, enlarged its power in the region by scoring key military successes against the Mughals. When Indian officials attacked the British population of Bengal and jailed many of them, officers and civilians alike, in a horrible underground prison known as the Black Hole of Calcutta, the British seized upon this action as a pretext for decisive military action. In 1757, at the crucial Battle of Plassey, Clive defeated a Mughal force more than ten times the size of his own. The Mughal government was compelled to grant the British such extensive military and economic concessions that the latter's military superiority on the subcontinent was permanently ensured. The French had no more hope of rivaling the British in India, and their zone of control quickly shrank to no more than the port of Pondicherry.

BRITAIN'S GRADUAL CONQUEST OF INDIA

The British did not yet control all of India. But the amount of territory under the company's authority would grow throughout the late 1700s, to just under one quarter of all India by 1805. Major centers of British control were Bombay, the great gateway port of the west coast; Madras, a cloth-making center on the southwest shore; and Fort William, near Calcutta, in the Bengal region of the northeast.

The British East India Company gained control over India by a combination of military and economic power. Naval might allowed the company to maintain armies in India. The skill of those armies compelled the Mughals to grant the company tax-collecting rights and administrative powers over an ever-widening area. Whereas the British at first had footholds only on the coasts, they gradually extended their reach into the interior, especially up the Ganges River in the north. In certain regions, the company governed directly. In others, it ruled through the authority of local Mughal officials or friendly natives. British expansion into India was a combination of deliberate effort and random circumstance. In many cases, local rulers, especially those not under Mughal authority, would rise up against the British or, from their own lands, threaten parts of India under British control. The British would crush these enemies, then pacify their territories. In many cases, this strategy meant conquering lands that the British might not have originally intended to take over.

Between the 1760s and 1810s, the British East India Company fought a number of campaigns. Major enemies included Haidar Ali, who led guerrilla armies in the south; Tipu Sultan, who fought on the Deccan Plateau in central India; and the Mahratta princes. Many British generals who became famous in other conflicts—such as Cornwallis, the commander-in-chief, who lost to the Americans at Yorktown, and Wellington, who defeated Napoleon at Waterloo—saw service in these wars.

By the first decade of the 1800s, the British East India Company controlled almost one fourth of India, as well as most of the island of Ceylon (now Sri Lanka). In British hands were Bombay and most of the southwest coast. All of India's east coast (except for the French enclave of Pondicherry) belonged to the British, as did Calcutta and the large region of Bengal. From Calcutta on the northeast coast, the British had also moved westward, taking over a long corridor along the Ganges River valley, stretching all the way to Delhi and beyond.

THE BRITISH EAST INDIA COMPANY'S ADMINISTRATION OF INDIA BEFORE 1800

During the late 1700s, the British East India Company's administration of British India was heavy-handed, even clumsy. The company's main goal in the beginning was to create a local textile industry. The British would process locally grown cotton into light cloth, then sell it to markets in the East Indies in exchange for spices. These, in turn, would be brought back to Great Britain.

In the beginning, British rule was harmful to the local population in several ways. First, the profits generated by Indian raw materials were sent back to Britain, rather than benefiting the local economy. Second, the size and efficiency of the British-built textile mills overwhelmed and drove out of business the local textile trade, made up of small proto-industrial enterprises, often run by women. Also, British tax law applied to the British zone of control. Unlike Indian custom, British law allowed the authorities to confiscate land from peasants unable to pay their taxes. The British thought they had created a fair taxation system by leaving tax collection to local native officials called zamindars. These zamindars, however, lost no time in overtaxing their countrymen, then making themselves rich by using British law to seize land from peasants. Such confiscations became so common in the 1770s that a severe agricultural crisis struck the countryside. Mass famines killed approximately one third of the Indian population—mainly peasants—living in land under British control.

As time passed, British economic goals in India became more diverse. British rulership became more adept and, in many ways, more enlightened. On the other hand, British rule was still imposed by military force and motivated mainly by economic exploitation and strategic concerns. And, all during the 1800s, the British masters tightened their grip on India.

INDIA UNDER BRITISH RULE: THE 1800s

THE EXPANSION OF BRITISH CONTROL

During the first half of the 1800s, the British extended their control over India. They moved from the coastline and the Ganges River valley into the interior, gaining authority—whether direct or indirect—over the entire country. The British also took outlying areas such as Punjab and parts of Afghanistan, both in the northwest, after a series of conflicts with the Sikhs and mountain peoples like the Pathans.

METHODS OF BRITISH CONTROL

British colonial authority—referred to popularly as the Raj—was complex. Although the British crown was becoming increasingly involved, the British East India Company still assumed primary responsibility for administering and exploiting the ever-expanding colony. Major cities such as Bombay and Calcutta were directly governed by the Raj, as were the coasts and large swathes of the interior. In certain parts of the interior, the British ruled indirectly, allowing certain rajas and maharajas to stay on their thrones, as long as they remained loyal and obedient. In this way, the British ruled some areas at less cost and effort to themselves.

POSITIVE AND NEGATIVE EFFECTS OF BRITISH COLONIAL RULE

The British became much better at colonial administration than they had been during the 1700s. They were guided by a combination of selfishness, a desire for efficiency, and the well-meaning but condescending sense of cultural and racial superiority that Rudyard Kipling later called the White Man's Burden. British economic interests in India, formerly restricted to cotton, now became many-faceted. A wide variety of resources was now sought and exploited. Both to make their own lives in India more comfortable, and because they genuinely felt that it would be better for the native Indians, British colonizers modernized the country in many ways. They created roads, railroads, a telegraph system, and a postal service.

The British also affected India's cultural life in many ways. They put into place a quality educational system. Its goal was partly to raise the level of scientific and technological advancement in India. It was also meant to create a group of Western-educated natives who would be more loyal to Britain and assist in governing a pro-British India. In the words of the historian Thomas

Macauley, who helped create this educational system, his intention was to educate a native elite that was "Indian in blood and color, but English in taste, in opinion, in morals, and in intellect." For the same reasons, the British created a civil-service examination system for those Indians who wished to work in the government. The Raj did not officially attempt to convert Indians to Christianity, even though a few British officials and officers sometimes violated this policy on an individual basis. Still, the British did eliminate certain cultural and religious (particularly Hindu) practices they felt were inhumane. These included sati, or suttee, the practice of burning widows alive at their husbands' funerals; thuggee, or ritual assassination of travelers in the name of the goddess Kali; and the caste system's harsh treatment of so-called untouchables. To a certain degree, the English, simply for the sake of keeping order, reduced the level of sectarian strife between Muslims and Hindus.

NATIVE OFFICIALS AND SEPOY TROOPS

In many ways, the British took great pains to instill loyalty within their native subjects. Their comparatively light touch in religious and cultural practices helped greatly. Whenever possible, the British delegated local political authority to Indians. The British East India Company also trained large numbers of native troops called sepoys. Using native troops made it somewhat easier for Indians to accept foreign rule. Also, reliance on the sepoys saved the British a great deal of money and kept them from having to draft large numbers of their own citizens to serve far from home for long periods of time. Indeed, the number of actual British soldiers and officers in India was quite low.

THE BRITISH APPROACH TO COLONIAL RULE

The British method of imperialism in India—which they tended to follow in other colonies throughout Asia and Africa—is difficult to evaluate. It is unquestionable that British rule brought many benefits and new learning to the non-Western world. It is also true that, compared to other imperial nations, the British were relatively humane in their colonial practices. Certainly the British themselves believed that they were doing their colonial subjects good. However, the undeniable truth is that British rule had been established by conquest, was supported by military might, was preserved by divide-and-conquer politics, and was done for the purpose of economic exploitation. Even the benefits of British rule were bestowed because of the Britons' conviction that they were "civilizing" a "lesser" race.

THE INDIAN MUTINY (THE SEPOY REBELLION)

Whatever the case, tensions between the British and the Indians they ruled were present throughout the 1800s. On one occasion, those tensions exploded suddenly and violently. This was the Indian Mutiny (1857–1858), also known as the Sepoy Rebellion. The mutiny ranks as one of the most traumatic events in modern Indian and British history.

Within many sepoy regiments, underlying resentment of British rule broke out into open revolt, as a result of rumors that British officers were deliberately trying to undermine Hindu and Muslim religious practices. Legally, the Raj was allowed to require sepoys to serve overseas. In the case of Hindus, crossing large bodies of water would break their caste. Hindu sepoys were not, in fact, sent overseas, but fear that they might be stirred up trouble. It was the perceived violation of Muslim and Hindu dietary restrictions, however, that actually triggered the rebellion. New rifles with greased cartridges were issued to sepoys in 1857. The false rumor that the grease was made from pig or cow fat—unclean to devout Muslims and Hindus, respectively—caused great outrage.

With lightning speed, the initial series of military disturbances became a massive wave of nationwide revolt. Tens of thousands of people were killed: British soldiers, British civilians, loyal Indian troops, rebels, and Indian civilians. Massacres and atrocities were committed by both sides. The British were fortunate that the rebels had no clear plan or single leader. Moreover, Hindu and Muslim rebels often failed to cooperate with each other—and sometimes fought each other.

By 1858, after great effort and a tremendous amount of anxiety that India would be lost altogether, British troops, along with natives who continued to serve the Raj, put down the rebellion.

THE BRITISH CROWN ASSUMES CONTROL

For the rest of the century, British rule over India remained strong and solid. One important change was that the British crown took from the British East India Company all authority over the subcontinent. It was now the British government that oversaw government, ran the army, and supervised the colonial economy. Victoria, the queen of England, took for herself the title Empress of India.

NATIONALIST MOVEMENTS IN TURN-OF-THE-CENTURY INDIA

Nonetheless, even though British control over India grew more secure, problems still simmered under the surface. The British strategy of educating a native elite in the Western style was generally successful, but in some cases, it also backfired. As time passed, larger and larger numbers of these educated young people used their knowledge to agitate for freedom. In many cases, their education exposed them to liberal or radical ideas and convinced them that it was hypocritical of the British—with their long tradition of civil liberties and representative government—not to apply those liberties to nonwhite races.

The most important of the new nationalist groups was the Indian National Congress, formed in 1885. Most members were English-speaking, educated members of the native upper classes. Eventually, the most famous and most influential member of the congress was Mohandas K. Gandhi, born in 1869. Trained as a lawyer in London, he lived in South Africa from 1893 to 1915, defending the rights of Indian workers living under the system of apartheid there. After his return to India in 1915, he started to preach nonviolent resistance to British rule. Over the next three decades, Gandhi was a central figure in India's quest for freedom.

SOUTHEAST ASIA

SOUTHEAST ASIA BEFORE 1800

Like India, Southeast Asia found itself increasingly in foreign hands throughout the late 1700s and especially the 1800s. Before 1800, the only large areas firmly under European control were Indonesia, or the Dutch East Indies, and the Philippines, which belonged to Spain. By 1786, the British also had a presence in the Malay Peninsula. The Portuguese retained parts of the island of Timor, a tiny remnant of the Indonesian empire the Dutch had taken from them centuries before. Dutch rule over Indonesia continued to be the responsibility of the centuries-old Dutch East India Company, which handed much responsibility over to upper-class natives, trained and educated in the Western style.

MALAYA AND SINGAPORE

As the British tightened their grip on India during the early 1800s, they made parallel advances into nearby Southeast Asia. In exchange for giving up their claims on territory in the Indonesian archipelago, the British were allowed by the Dutch to absorb the Malay Peninsula, which was rich in rubber, tin, oil, copper, iron, and aluminum ore (bauxite). In 1819, British colonial official

Stamford Raffles established a British outpost on Singapore, an island at the peninsula's tip. Quickly, Singapore became an extremely important trading center and fortress; with the advent of steamships, it also became a key naval base. Along with India itself and, after 1842, Hong Kong, Singapore was one of Britain's most prized possessions in Asia.

THE FRENCH CONQUEST OF INDOCHINA

For the rest of the century, the European incursion into Southeast Asia never ceased. Britain took over Burma, formerly a major military power, in 1826. In order to prevent the British from having an unbroken chain of territorial possessions stretching from India to the South China coast, France responded by moving into Indochina, the territory that now encompasses Vietnam, Cambodia, and Laos.

From 1857 to 1859, France pressured Vietnam's Nguyen dynasty into accepting foreign rule. Cambodia followed in 1863, and Laos came under French control in 1893. Indochina was the source of many valuable raw materials, but most profitable to the French were chrome, oil, bauxite, tin, and rubber, which were becoming increasingly important to new industrial processes developed at the end of the century.

The French model of imperialism in this area was similar, but not identical, to that of Britain's in India and Southeast Asia. The French placed more emphasis on religious conversion than the British did. The French exploited the economy, but in accordance with their ideal of *la mission civilisatrice,* they also brought modern science and technology to their colonies in Southeast Asia. They educated and often converted to Catholicism a local elite of upper-class, Westernized natives. In contrast to the British, however, the French were more willing to resort to repression and violence to maintain order and carry out policy.

MODERNIZATION AND FREEDOM IN THAILAND

The only state on the Southeast Asian mainland that remained independent throughout the nineteenth century was Thailand. This was due both to good leadership and good luck. Much like Emperor Meiji in Japan, King Mongkut and his successor, King Chulalongkorn (both made famous in Anna Leonowens's memoir, *Anna and the King of Siam,* which has been grossly distorted by Broadway and Hollywood), were modernizing monarchs, introducing industrialization and Western-style reform into their country. Thailand's geographic setting was also fortunate. The country lay between British-controlled Burma and French-dominated Indochina, and both European powers agreed informally that it would be mutually convenient to let it serve as an independent buffer zone between their colonies.

THE U.S. ANNEXATION OF THE PHILIPPINES

The last major colonial takeover in Southeast Asia was the annexation of the Philippines by the United States, in 1898. Annexation was the result of U.S. victory in the Spanish-American War. Although the conflict centered on Cuba, the United States sent a fleet under Commodore George Dewey to neutralize the Spanish naval forces based at Manila Bay. Dewey easily decimated the Spanish at sea. Then, with the assistance of native Filipinos (who, at first, regarded the Americans as liberators), U.S. troops landed, defeated Spanish ground forces, and occupied the islands.

American victory resulted in Spain's being stripped of all its colonies. This action raised the question of what was to be done with the Philippines. After a great deal of debate, the American government chose to turn the islands into a U.S. colony. The United States wished to keep the Philippines from falling into the hands of the Japanese. Possession of the Philippines also provided the United States with a superb naval base in the Pacific, as well as a way station for trade with China. Moreover, the Americans felt a "moral" obligation, similar to the "white man's burden," to civilize the Filipinos (indeed, the English poet Rudyard Kipling wrote the poem of that name to commemorate the American victory over the Spanish).

Thus, as with European colonizers, imperialism in this case was a mixture of practical selfishness and condescending idealism. The great tragedy of America's colonization of the Philippines was that it had to be carried out by means of a savage war in the islands' jungles. Native Filipinos, having first thought the Americans had come to free them, now fought their new masters-to-be. A guerrilla force led by Emilio Aguinaldo resisted the American takeover until 1901, and U.S. suppression of Aguinaldo's forces proved to be exceptionally bloody.

QUICK REVIEW

1. Which 1757 battle confirmed Great Britain's military superiority in India?

   (A) Chillianwallah
   (B) Mysore
   (C) Plassey
   (D) Lucknow
   (E) the Sutlej

2. Who were the zamindars?

   (A) native officials who administered parts of India for the British
   (B) freedom fighters who resisted British colonization of India
   (C) Hindu priests who called for a holy war against the British
   (D) Muslim troops who allied with the British against Hindu communities in India
   (E) the pro-British merchant class of eastern India

3. During the late 1700s and the first decade of the 1800s, British control over India was restricted to

   (A) Sri Lanka (Ceylon)
   (B) the Ganges valley
   (C) the eastern coast
   (D) the coastlines and the Ganges valley
   (E) the Brahmaputra valley

4. Among the benefits of British rule in India was/were

   I. an educated native elite
   II. the abolition of sati
   III. the construction of telegraphs and railroads
   IV. universal male suffrage

   (A) I and II only
   (B) I and III only
   (C) II and III only
   (D) I, II, and III
   (E) all of the above

5. What were native troops who served under the British authorities in India called?

   (A) brahmins
   (B) sepoys
   (C) thugs
   (D) coolies
   (E) gurkhas

6. The most effective nationalist group to oppose British rule in India, starting in the 1800s, was

   (A) the Tamil Tigers
   (B) the Muslim League
   (C) the Indian National Congress
   (D) the Independence Party
   (E) the Indian Liberation Army

7. What was the Netherlands' chief colony in Southeast Asia?

(A) Singapore
(B) Burma
(C) Macao
(D) Goa
(E) Indonesia

8. What key city and naval base was founded by Stamford Raffles for the British at the tip of the Malay Peninsula?

(A) Hong Kong
(B) Singapore
(C) Macao
(D) Goa
(E) Malacca

9. Which Southeast Asian nation managed, through Westernized leadership and good luck, to stay free of foreign domination?

(A) Laos
(B) Cambodia
(C) Vietnam
(D) Thailand
(E) Burma

10. Which Filipino guerrilla leader fought the Spanish, then the United States, late in the 1800s?

(A) Emilio Aguinaldo
(B) Ferdinand Marcos
(C) Thomas Aquino
(D) Mateo Buenviaje
(E) Edward Ramos

ANSWERS:

1. **C**, p. 310	6. **C**, p. 313
2. **A**, p. 311	7. **E**, p. 313
3. **D**, p. 310	8. **B**, pp. 313–14
4. **D**, pp. 311–12	9. **D**, p. 314
5. **B**, p. 312	10. **A**, p. 315

CHAPTER 26

Sub-Saharan Africa

Like most of the non-Western world, sub-Saharan Africa fell under the increased sway of European imperialism from 1750 to 1914. For several centuries, Africa had already been victimized by the Atlantic slave trade. Millions of Africans had been forcibly transported to the Americas. African political systems and economic patterns, even in parts of the continent not directly under foreign control, had been shaped by the slave trade. From the 1400s onward, Europeans had plundered gold, ivory, and other resources from Africa. They had also established outposts, naval bases, and small colonies on the east and west coasts of the continent.

Nonetheless, European influence over Africa, especially south of the Sahara, was comparatively limited until late in the 1800s. After the Napoleonic Wars, the slave trade was made illegal in most Western countries. Although it continued for decades unlawfully, the Atlantic traffic in slaves tapered off and faded away. Moreover, strong African states resisted foreign domination for much of this period (in a somewhat sad irony, much of this strength was due to the profits these states had made by cooperating with the Atlantic slave trade). Although the Europeans found it relatively easy to take control of North Africa (see Chapter 23) and parts of the coastline, the central and southern interior remained, for a long time, difficult to penetrate.

Great changes came after 1880. Before then, outside powers controlled approximately 10 percent of Africa. Less than three and a half decades later, in 1914, foreigners controlled the entire continent, with the exception of two small countries. By the middle of the 1800s, explorers and missionaries had gained precise geographical knowledge of the African interior. Better medicines enabled larger numbers of soldiers and settlers to travel to and live in Africa's tropical zones. Industrial-era weaponry increased the Europeans' military superiority over the Africans.

During the 1880s and 1890s, the ever-greater intensity of the Western world's competitiveness over empire drove the nations of Europe to carve up African territory while there was still room to expand. This "Scramble for Africa" subjugated virtually the entire continent. White settlers soon expropriated African grazing lands, and white traders stole the Africans' cattle and other possessions.

The Scramble for Africa also stirred up the combative passions of the Europeans and therefore contributed to the diplomatic tensions that helped cause World War I. The long-term political and economic effects of Europe's colonization of Africa still reverberate in the twenty-first century, long after the continent's decolonization.

FREEDOM'S TWILIGHT: AFRICAN STATES FROM THE LATE 1700s TO THE MID-1800s

AFRICAN STATES DURING THE LATE 1700s AND EARLY 1800s

European hegemony over Africa was a long time in coming. During the late 1700s and early 1800s, there were a number of states strong enough to resist foreign domination. Others were useful and cooperative enough economically that it was worthwhile for the Europeans to work with, rather than fight them. Some of these states, such as Benin, Oyo, Dahomey, Kongo and Asante (Ashanti), played large roles in the Atlantic slave trade. They helped European traders and slavers capture and transport their fellow Africans.

In the west, a number of states remained independent well into the 1800s. These included the various Hausa, Fulani, and Yoruba states. They formed, broke apart, and reformed, constantly fighting each other in costly civil wars. Among them were the Fulani Empire, Masina, and the Tukolor Empire. All three were Muslim theocracies. The previously great kingdom of Kongo disintegrated into a variety of smaller states.

THE ASANTE (ASHANTI) KINGDOM

The strongest and most unified of the West African states was the Asante (Ashanti) kingdom. Asante was also among those that survived the longest as independent states. Founded late in the 1600s by Osei Tutu, the Asante state took part in the flourishing trade in gold and slaves on Africa's west coast. Using their profits to buy guns, Asante became a strong military power.

Asante's might increased dramatically during the late 1700s and early 1800s, especially as its African neighbors fought each other or came under foreign control. A large military buildup began under Osei Kojo (1764–1777). During the early 1800s, the Asante were in a position to threaten European outposts and trade routes along the Gold Coast. The Asante also resisted British, French, and American attempts to destroy the slave trade in the 1820s (see subsequent discussion). Starting in 1821, when the British occupied a chain of forts on the African coast, the Asante began to skirmish with them. By 1823, Britain found itself locked in a series of Asante wars that lasted until the end of the century. Not until 1900 were the British able to subdue the Asante. Next to the Zulu of South Africa, the Asante were the most challenging of the Europeans' military foes in Africa.

SOUTH AFRICA, THE BOERS, AND THE ZULU

South Africa had been colonized by the Dutch in the mid-1600s. For a century and a half, these Afrikaner Boers, as they called themselves, displaced or conquered native Africans. When the British assumed control over South Africa during the Napoleonic Wars, the Boers were themselves displaced. In the 1830s, the Boers made their Great Trek to the north and east, eventually founding the Orange Free State and the South African Republic (Transvaal), both of which bordered British South Africa, in the early 1850s. In the meantime, the Boers and the recently arrived British came into contact with a new native power: the Zulu tribe, the most fearsome of the Europeans' African enemies.

The Zulu, a Bantu-speaking people, had been relatively quiet and peaceful before 1800. Around 1816, however, a new chieftain, Shaka, seized power and united the various Zulu clans into a single tribe. A military leader of tremendous skill, Shaka would later be thought of by many Europeans as the "Black Napoleon." He taught the Zulu how to fight in an organized, efficient fashion. Under Shaka, the Zulu became a warlike, conquering tribe. Even after his death in 1828, the Zulu remained a deadly force.

During the first half of the 1800s, the Zulu defeated neighbor after neighbor, scattering African tribes throughout the southern part of the continent. A significant wave of migration, including the movement of major groups like the Swazi, Ngoni, Gaza, and Ndebele, was caused partly by Zulu aggression. A parallel factor was the persistence of slave-trading from Delagoa Bay. White settlers made several slave raids on refugees in order to collect more labor for their farms. Recently, some historians have pointed out that the Zulus, though militaristic, were only one of several groups that were consolidating their lands at the time. Moreover, these historians argue, the large population upheavals during that time were more a result of foreign trade, drought, and the advancement of white settlers from the West and slavers from the East than purely a result of Zulu aggression.

The Zulu also fought the Boers and the British. It took several wars for the Europeans to pacify the Zulu. The last major conflict, in 1879, was provoked by British officials who hoped to move into the Zulu lands, because diamonds had recently been found there. The Zulu armies, led by their chief, Cetewayo, eventually lost the Zulu War of 1879. But it took eight months for the British to win. And one of the early battles, Isandlwana, in which a British force was massacred to the last soldier, was one of the worst military defeats suffered by a European force in Africa.

THE DISCOVERY OF DIAMONDS

Some historians argue that the modern era of African history began with the discovery of one of the world's largest deposits of diamonds at Kimberly, South Africa. Gold was also found in the region, in the 1870s.

The sudden emergence of such great potential wealth was highly destabilizing. The mines themselves would lead to increased exploitation of African labor. White control over the diamond industry also sharpened racial attitudes that were already intensely bigoted.

Located in a heavily contested area that was peopled by several ethnic groups and staked out by white farmers, the diamond fields were annexed by Britain in 1871. By the 1880s, the British had instituted racial segregation in the mines in the form of labor compounds and pass laws, among other restrictions on African workers. Along with preexisting Boer-Afrikaner prejudices, these rules set a precedent for the apartheid laws the white South African government adopted in the 1960s.

INDEPENDENT STATES IN EAST AFRICA

The East African coast, which had come under Portuguese domination between the late 1400s and late 1600s, enjoyed a period of strength and independence—at least from European control—during the late 1700s and early-to-mid 1800s. For the time being, areas like the large island of Madagascar remained free, as did the Batutsi state in what is today Rwanda.

The Coptic Christian kingdom of Ethiopia, which earlier had allied with Portugal against Muslim conquerors, expelled the Portuguese, largely over questions of religious doctrine, in 1632. For the next two and a half centuries, Ethiopia went into isolation, then modernized under Theodore II, who came to the throne in 1855. As for most of the rest of the coast, the new power was not European, but Arab. In 1728, Arabs drove the Portuguese from the port of Mombasa. After that, Portugal's strength in the region gradually waned, although it retained footholds along the coast.

ARAB INFLUENCE OVER ZANZIBAR

By the early 1800s, Omani Arabs had gained a tremendous amount of political influence in East Africa. They also controlled the flourishing trade between the East African coast and India. By far the most important East African port was Zanzibar, on a small island off the coast of Tanganyika. Its role as an economic powerhouse was demonstrated by the fact that the Omani sultan, Sa'id ibn Sultan, made it his capital in 1840. Zanzibar's primary trading partner was Bombay.

This fusion of Arab, African, and Indian stimulated not just economic interaction, but a vibrant cultural interchange as well. Zanzibar's Arab masters also extended their economic influence into Africa's interior, to the west and north.

ZANZIBAR AND THE EAST AFRICAN SLAVE TRADE

Among the principal resources that flowed through Zanzibar were cloves, spices, sugar, and ivory. Unfortunately, an even more important part of Zanzibar's economy was slavery. Ironically, just as the demand for slaves in the Atlantic was finally withering away (discussed presently), there was a major resurgence in the Arab–East African slave market. This resurgence had much to do with the growth of plantation agriculture in the area, fueled by the increased demand for sugar and spices. Between 1875 and 1884, the peak of the East African plantation economy, 44 percent of the total population was made up of slaves.

It took decades for the Western powers to eliminate the East African slave trade. Abolition came about as a result of popular outrage, missionary activity (a key figure here was the Scottish explorer and humanitarian David Livingstone), and military action. The great slave market in the center of Zanzibar was finally shut down in 1873. The British would take control of the city itself later in the century.

EUROPEAN CONQUEST

In the end, all the states described here—and many others—fell prey to European conquest. As described subsequently, many factors played a role in Africa's fall. Among the internal reasons were technological backwardness, the persistence in most regions of economies based on herding and small-scale agriculture (hence the failure to develop industrial economies), and frequent intertribal or interkingdom warfare. Whatever the case, after 1880, it became increasingly difficult, then impossible, for African states, no matter how strong they had been previously, to remain free.

THE END OF THE ATLANTIC SLAVE TRADE

THE ATLANTIC SLAVE TRADE BECOMES ILLEGAL

One of the great changes to come to Africa during the 1800s was the gradual ending of the Atlantic slave trade. Its demise resulted partly from economic and practical considerations. It was becoming more difficult, and therefore more expensive, to obtain slaves.

Equally important was the growing revulsion that slavery caused among the populations of a number of Western countries. For moral, ethical, and religious reasons, an ever-greater number of citizens and politicians alike were unwilling to continue allowing their nations' economic activities to be based so squarely on an institution such as slavery. As early as the 1790s and the first decade of the 1800s, countries such as the Netherlands (1795) and Denmark (1803) were making slavery illegal.

A great turning point came when Great Britain, in 1807 and 1808, resolved to make slavery illegal (slavery was banned in all parts of the British Empire in 1834). The British did not just ban slavery, but took it upon themselves to act as the Western world's champions of the antislavery cause. During the peace settlements of 1814 and 1815 that followed the Napoleonic Wars, the British prevailed upon almost all the nations of Europe and the Americas to outlaw slavery and the slave trade. With the exception of Spain and Portugal, all of Europe agreed (Russia continued to rely on its system of serfdom, but this was an entirely different question). For the most part, the Americas went along as well. Canada (still part of the British Empire) and most of Latin America outlawed slavery. The holdouts were Cuba and Brazil, which did not end slavery until 1883 and

1888. The United States, split between the slaveholding South and the nonslave North, agreed to make the slave *trade* illegal. The government also worked to restrict the spread of slavery within the United States as the country expanded. But not until after the U.S. Civil War (1861–1865) was slavery itself made completely illegal throughout the country.

THE ATLANTIC SLAVE TRADE CONTINUES ILLEGALLY

The continued survival of slavery in the Americas meant that the Atlantic slave trade, illegal or not, went on during a good part of the 1800s. It has been calculated that 2 million Africans were transported to Brazil, Cuba, and the Caribbean during the 1800s. A small percentage of these were smuggled into the United States as well. The best estimate of the total number of Africans enslaved by the Atlantic slave trade between the late 1400s and early 1800s is approximately 12 million.

As noted previously, a market in African slaves flourished in Zanzibar during the 1800s, not ending until 1873. According to some sources, at the end of the nineteenth century, the total number of slaves in the Islamic states of West Africa stood at nearly 5 million. Slavery therefore continued to be a painful problem for Africa throughout most of the nineteenth century—in spite of European and American efforts to the contrary.

FOREIGN EFFORTS TO END THE SLAVE TRADE

Still, foreign powers did much to end the slave trade, in addition to legislation. Abolition movements, especially in Britain and the northern United States, pressured their governments to fight slavery actively. Canada served as a haven for slaves escaping from the southern United States. Missionaries in Africa, especially those from Britain, campaigned tirelessly against slave raids and slave markets—both on the Atlantic coast and in East Africa and Zanzibar. A great crusader here was David Livingstone of Scotland.

The British founded special colonies in Sierra Leone and the Gold Coast for freed blacks. Similarly, the American Colonization Society, a group of American blacks and freed slaves, settled the nation of Liberia, on the West African coast, with sponsorship from the U.S. government.

All during the early 1800s, the British government dispatched the Royal Navy to blockade the West African shoreline, hunt down slave ships, and bombard the coastal fortresses of African states that continued to support the slave trade. Somewhat less enthusiastically, France and the United States joined in these anti-slave trade naval expeditions.

EFFECTS OF THE SLAVE TRADE ON AFRICA

The slave trade took a strong toll on Africa, but academics are in some disagreement on just how much. According to some, the slave trade led Africans themselves to rely more heavily on slavery than they had before the external slave trade began.

These scholars also point to the loss of population growth over time and the marked changes in culture and settlement patterns that were caused by the external slave trade. After the onset of the external slave trade, internal trade in Africa came more and more to rely on the importation of foreign goods, such as guns, textiles, and alcohol, rather than the production of indigenous goods by Africans themselves.

Other scholars argue that the impact of the slave trade was spread thinly and did not transform African society much, particularly because a relatively small proportion of the total population was taken from Africa. However, in a number of areas, West and Central Africa especially, the external slave trade transformed economic and political relations. For example, in this part of Africa, political economics had, before the 1800s, consisted of chiefs and other community leaders receiving occasional material tributes. By the 1800s, these economies were controlled by warlords and merchants who pressured chiefs into enslaving their subjects and using them as payments against forced loans. Moreover, slavers brought to Africa thousands of guns to exchange for slaves—and the slavers stirred up the appetite for even more guns. The greater number of guns increased the likelihood of intertribal war in Africa. The guns also made those wars more lethal.

Overall, the ending of the slave trade did enormous good for Africa, even if many of the benefits took a long time to be felt. There were, however, some unforeseen economic and political consequences. Heinous as it had been, the slave trade had been tremendously lucrative for the African states that had taken part in it. Shifting to trade in less profitable goods such as palm oil, peanuts, animal hides, and timber led to an economic slump in late nineteenth-century Africa. This slump helped to leave independent states open to foreign takeover later in the 1800s.

Moreover, the antislavery military and political intervention of nations like Great Britain, however

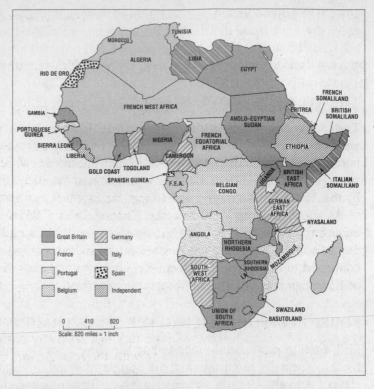

European Imperialism in Africa, 1914.
Until the 1880s, European powers had taken over only 10 percent of Africa. However, by 1914, the "Scramble for Africa" had ended with almost total European control over the entire continent. It would take until the last half of the twentieth century for African nations to gain their independence.

well-intentioned, gave Europeans a further pretext for involving themselves in African affairs. It led European powers into various armed conflicts with African states. It also accustomed Europeans to thinking of military action in Africa as legitimate. This helped pave the way for the great rush to conquer all of Africa at the end of the century.

EUROPEAN IMPERIALISM AND THE "SCRAMBLE FOR AFRICA"

EUROPE'S LIMITED CONTROL OVER AFRICA BEFORE THE LATE 1800s

As noted previously, approximately 10 percent of Africa was under foreign control before 1880. Much of that territory lay north of the Sahara, in what had been part of the Islamic caliphates, then the Ottoman Empire. As described in Chapter 23, areas such as Morocco, Algeria, Tunis, Libya, Egypt, and the Sudan fell into French, British, Italian, and Spanish hands during the mid-to-late 1800s.

By contrast, most of sub-Saharan Africa remained free of outside political domination, even if the slave trade and European and American economic influence had made their effects felt for centuries. Only on the coasts did the European powers maintain colonies or permanent outposts. All of this changed, however, after 1880. From then until the beginning of World War I in 1914, the states of Europe became caught up in a breathlessly rapid "Scramble for Africa." Nation after nation fell, until, on the eve of World War I, only two countries—Ethiopia and Liberia—remained free.

REASONS FOR EUROPE'S LATE NINETEENTH-CENTURY DOMINATION OF AFRICA

The factors that motivated and enabled the Scramble for Africa are many. First, a sustained series of geographic expeditions from the 1770s through the 1860s gave the Western world an unprecedented amount of information about the African interior. English explorer James Bruce located the source of the Blue Nile in 1770; Mungo Park of Scotland traced the entire Niger River from 1795 to 1805. The indefatigable missionary David Livingstone, who arrived from Scotland in 1841, spread Christianity, and fought the East African slave trade, also found time to explore the Zambezi Falls and discover the Victoria Falls (1855). Anglo-American adventurer Henry Stanley explored the Congo, while Englishman John Speke unraveled one of Africa's greatest geographical mysteries by locating the source of the Nile in 1863.

The development of effective medicines to treat tropical diseases—such as quinine for malaria—enabled large numbers of Westerners to move into the interior after the 1840s. Armed with industrial-era weapons such as modern rifles and machine guns, relatively small numbers of European soldiers were generally able to inflict horrible damage on native warriors, even when they were greatly outnumbered. The fact that so many African states were torn apart by civil war or locked into bloody conflicts with their neighbors made them vulnerable to European takeover. African economies—based either on commerce, as in East Africa, or a combination of pastoral herding and simple agriculture—were backward in comparison to the industrialized economies of the West. Finally, the late nineteenth century, as noted in Chapter 22, was simply an era of nationalism, aggression, and imperial competition in Europe.

THE EUROPEANS' SCRAMBLE FOR AFRICA BEGINS

From 1880 to 1914, Britain, France, and Portugal added to their preexisting territories in Africa. Belgium colonized as well. The newly united countries of Italy and Germany also saw Africa as the perfect place to gain a large number of colonies quickly, in order to build empires that would rival those of older imperial powers such as Britain and France.

BRITAIN'S AFRICAN COLONIES

Britain's zone of control in Africa included the Gold Coast, Sierra Leone, and Nigeria in the west. Even more extensive was its chain of colonies in northeast and East Africa, stretching almost, but not quite, from "Cape to Cairo," as the imperialist Cecil Rhodes described it. This almost unbroken collection of colonies included South Africa, Bechuanaland (now Botswana), Rhodesia (now Zimbabwe), Kenya, Uganda, the Sudan, and Egypt.

Late in the century, Britain also gained influence over the rich port of Zanzibar, partly in connection with its efforts to end slavery there. Zanzibar had been claimed by Germany, but Britain received control over it as part of a swap of colonial territories by Germany and Britain.

Britain's method of African colonial administration was similar to the one it followed in India: a comparatively enlightened "white man's burden" approach that made use of an educated native elite, deployed native troops trained in the Western style, and brought new science and industrial technology to the colonies.

THE FRENCH IN AFRICA

France's African empire was restricted mainly to the Saharan north: Morocco, Algeria, Tunisia, West Africa, and Equatorial Africa. But it had territories elsewhere, such as Djibouti, part of the

Somali coast, and the vast island of Madagascar. As in its Southeast Asian colonies, France acted in accordance with its "civilizing mission" and, for the most part, acted reasonably responsibly with its colonial subjects.

THE PORTUGUESE

Portugal retained control over its longtime possession in West Africa, Angola. On the eastern coast, where it had once reigned supreme, it took Mozambique. Unlike the French and British, the Portuguese were quite harsh with their African colonies.

BELGIUM AND THE CONGO

Tiny Belgium gained control over one of the largest African colonies: the vast Congo basin. Starting in 1876, King Leopold II of Belgium, working with the Anglo-American explorer Henry Stanley as his manager, established the International Association of the Congo. This was a private company formed in Leopold's name for the economic development of the Congo. By 1884, the Congo was fully under the association's control. In his will, Leopold bequeathed the colony to Belgium.

Leopold's exploitation of the Congo was brutal, and Belgium's record as a colonizing power was among the worst in Africa. The Belgium occupiers overexploited rubber trees and vines throughout the region. Belgian-owned rubber plantations brutally forced Congolese villagers to meet their quotas. A particularly vile practice was the policy of some Belgian overseers to chop off the right hands of Congolese workers who did not harvest enough rubber. Even worse were the massacres of Congolese rubber workers that Belgian colonists sometimes carried out. The Belgian occupation led to massive depopulation. Before the Belgians arrived, the area's population was around 20 million. By 1911, only about 8.5 million people remained.

ITALIAN COLONIZATION OF AFRICA

The new nation of Italy had generally poor luck in Africa. In 1911 to 1912, just before World War I, it seized Libya from the Ottoman Empire, in a short war that involved the use of aircraft and poison gas. Before that, in 1896, the Italians had attempted to conquer Ethiopia. King Menelik II, however, had prepared well by purchasing modern rifles for his army and hiring Western mercenaries to train his troops. The Italians were prevented from taking Ethiopia by their humiliating defeat at the Battle of Adowa, which ranks as one of the most embarrassing setbacks in the entire history of European imperialism.

GERMAN COLONIZATION OF AFRICA

Also new to the world stage was Germany. In keeping with the military prowess they had recently shown in Europe, the Germans quickly assembled a sizable empire in Africa. Their possessions included Togoland, the Cameroons, Southwest Africa, and German East Africa (which consisted mainly of Tanganyika, off of which the island and port of Zanzibar was located).

Unfortunately, the colonies left for the Germans to capture were those that no one else had wanted. They were hardly desirable possessions, and rather than turning a profit, they actually lost money for Germany. The Germans also had to deal with several major uprisings, including the Maji Maji revolt in Tanganyika (1905–1907) and the infamous Herero Wars in Southwest Africa (1904–1908). The latter were especially savage, and the Germans showed themselves capable of a suppression that was nothing short of genocidal. Historians estimate that the Germans killed almost 80 percent of the Herero—64,000 of 80,000—by the time they quelled the rebellion.

AFRICAN WOMEN AND EUROPEAN IMPERIALISM

One of the major consequences of colonial rule was that many African families were broken up. Husbands often went to work in mines or on plantations, while wives and children stayed behind in villages and on reserves. Women were left to grow food for their families for mere survival and to care for the sick and aged. Such long separations between spouses often led to a rise in the level of prostitution and the spread of sexually transmitted diseases.

In general, African men benefited more from the economic changes brought by colonial rule than African women did. In regions where colonial officials introduced private property rights, property was given to male heads of households, not women. Most jobs, even those in teaching, were reserved for men, and women were soon discouraged from running family businesses or selling goods in markets.

IMPERIALISM IN AFRICA AND ITS EFFECTS ON EUROPEAN DIPLOMACY

If the Scramble for Africa had been motivated partly by a general spirit of aggression among the Europeans, it had the effect of stirring up even more aggression. It did not take long for competition over African territory to bring European powers to the brink of conflict.

In 1884 and 1885, the influential diplomat Otto von Bismarck presided over the Berlin Conference, which resulted from tension caused by conflicting claims over pieces of Africa. The Berlin Conference set down rules by which the powers of Europe agreed to expand further into Africa. It was decided that no European nation could make new claims in Africa without demonstrating "effective occupation." Claimants also had to make their intentions clear to all other nations who had signed the agreement. Needless to say, the boundaries European leaders agreed on failed to take local conditions into much account. The boundaries intersected with the traditional borders of more than 177 ethnic groups, compromising the natural economic and social development of dozens of areas.

THE FASHODA INCIDENT

Although the Berlin Conference helped to prevent a European war over Africa, it did not keep general tensions from rising steadily. In 1896, France and Britain almost came to blows as a result of the Fashoda Incident, in which French troops moving eastward into the Nile Valley encountered British soldiers who regarded the whole region as belonging to them. The French eventually withdrew, but not before a short war scare.

THE MOROCCO CRISES AND THE BOER WAR

During the early 1900s, Germany's naked ambitions in Africa began to cause even more tension. German interference with French and Spanish plans for northwest Africa led to a Morocco Crisis in 1906 and another one shortly afterward, in 1911.

Even worse was Germany's public support of the Dutch Afrikaners in the Boer War (1899–1902). Here, fighting had broken out between the British and Boers in South Africa. Although the British had a larger, better-equipped army, the Boers were skilled guerrilla soldiers and excellent sharpshooters, fighting on their home territory.

The war was a painful one, with the British forced to pacify the Boer civilian population. More than 120,000 women, children, and male noncombatants (many of whom were black Africans) were placed in concentration camps by the British commander Horatio Kitchener. Between 26,000 and 28,000 died, causing an international outcry. The Germans made no secret of their sympathy for the Dutch-descended Boers. This public favoritism had the result of worsening Anglo-German relations, which were already strained because of the two countries' naval race and Britain's fears of Germany's imperial ambitions elsewhere in Africa. As noted in Chapter 22, these tensions had profound effects on the alliance system that emerged in the years before World War I.

THE SCRAMBLE FOR AFRICA AS ONE OF THE CAUSES OF WORLD WAR I

In many ways, therefore, the Scramble for Africa backfired on the Europeans. Their imperial successes there led to diplomatic problems. Taken all together, those diplomatic problems helped to feed the flames that eventually broke out into the firestorm of World War I. And it was World War I, of course, that would start the breakdown of European world power and the eventual loss of Europe's empires—including those in Africa.

QUICK REVIEW

1. Which group in South Africa embarked on the "Great Trek" during the early 1800s?

   (A) the Zulu
   (B) the Swazi
   (C) the Xhosa
   (D) the Boers
   (E) the Ngoni

2. Which leader transformed the Zulu into an extremely militarily effective tribe?

   (A) Cetewayo I
   (B) Shaka
   (C) Cetewayo II
   (D) Ingono
   (E) Mwaza

3. The discovery of what resource in South Africa during the last half of the 1800s greatly altered political and economic life there?

   (A) diamonds
   (B) bauxite
   (C) oil
   (D) silver
   (E) copper

4. Which African nation survived the entire nineteenth century as an independent Christian kingdom?

   (A) Somalia
   (B) the Sudan
   (C) Djibouti
   (D) Mali
   (E) Ethopia

5. Which East African city was the center of the slave trade in this part of the continent?

   (A) Mombasa
   (B) Zanzibar
   (C) Malindi
   (D) Sofala
   (E) Nairobi

6. Which of the following best describes the results of the outlawing of the Atlantic slave trade?

   (A) The slave trade was hindered by the ban, but approximately 2 million Africans were still taken illegally to the Americas.
   (B) No European nations made any real effort to enforce the ban on the slave trade.
   (C) Spain and Portugal took the lead in combating the slave trade once it was illegal.
   (D) The slave trade dried up almost completely within a decade of being outlawed.
   (E) The United States and France almost went to war over the continuation of slavery in North America.

7. Which is the most accurate statement about European colonization in Africa during the 1800s?

(A) European powers began the century largely in control of Africa, but were pushed out of all but 10 percent by the 1890s.

(B) Industrial-era weaponry allowed the European powers to conquer all but two countries in Africa by 1880.

(C) European control over Africa was at roughly the same level in 1900 as it had been in 1820.

(D) Despite controlling only 10 percent of Africa as late as 1880, European powers had conquered almost the entire continent shortly after the new century began.

(E) European powers failed to penetrate the interior of Africa, and they took over only 25 percent of the continent by 1900.

8. Which European nation, by exploiting the Congo horribly, gained a reputation as one of the cruelest colonial powers of the imperial era?

(A) Belgium
(B) Italy
(C) Germany
(D) Great Britain
(E) the Netherlands

9. The Germans came close to exterminating which African tribe?

(A) the Fulani
(B) the Herero
(C) the Batutsi
(D) the Hutus
(E) the Hausa

10. The twentieth century's first concentration camps were used by whom in what conflict?

(A) the French during the Fashoda Incident
(B) the Germans during the First Moroccan Crisis
(C) the Italians during their takeover of Libya
(D) the Spanish during the Second Moroccan Crisis
(E) the British during the Boer War

ANSWERS:

1. **D**, p. 318	6. **A**, pp. 320–21
2. **B**, p. 318	7. **D**, pp. 322–23
3. **A**, p. 319	8. **A**, p. 324
4. **E**, p. 319	9. **B**, p. 324
5. **B**, p. 320	10. **E**, p. 325

CHAPTER 27

Revolution and Consolidation in North and South America

During the late 1700s and early 1800s, the colonies of the New World—which had been the possessions of European powers for three centuries—threw off the ties that bound them politically and economically to their home countries. The American Revolution, the Haitian Rebellion, and the Latin American wars of independence were all part of the great wave of revolutions—including the French Revolution—that struck the Atlantic world during this era. All of these revolutions shook the political and economic foundations of the Western world. Moreover, all of them were interrelated, both in terms of intellectual influence and political effect.

However, the overall results of the various New World revolutions differed greatly. In the north, the American Revolution created an economic and political powerhouse. The United States, the modern world's first major nation to become a democracy, would steadily expand across the continent. Despite internal troubles, even wars, concerning slavery and the suppression of Native Americans, the United States would grow in size and might. Like the nations of Europe, it would industrialize. Already by the early 1800s, the United States was becoming the dominant power in the Western Hemisphere. By the end of the 1800s, it had acquired overseas territories of its own and was on the threshold of becoming a world power. During the 1900s, the United States became not only a world power, but eventually one of the strongest nations on earth, with a military reach and political influence that was truly global.

As for Latin America, revolution brought about freedom. But it did not create nations that were as well equipped to deal with freedom as the United States was. Despite high ideals and good intentions, most of the new Latin American nations were plagued by dictatorial politics, economic backwardness, poverty, racial prejudice, and frequent revolutions and civil conflicts. In addition, the great power to the north, the United States, became increasingly involved in Latin American economics and politics, and not always for the better.

THE AMERICAN REVOLUTION AND THE BIRTH OF THE UNITED STATES

CAUSES OF THE AMERICAN REVOLUTION

The American Revolution (1775–1783) resulted from the combination of several trends in the thirteen British colonies in New England and the mid-Atlantic coast:

- A growing sense of patriotism and national identity. In this sense, the "Revolution" was less a revolution and more a war of independence.
- Increased resentment of Great Britain's economic mastery over the colonies. In particular, the taxes Britain levied to pay for the army it maintained in North America angered many colonists, especially in light of the fact that they lacked representation in the British Parliament.
- The desire of the colonial merchant (that is, middle) class to better itself. Economic freedom from Britain would allow American merchants to become wealthier, thanks to free trade and the new spirit of capitalism.
- The influence of Enlightenment philosophy (see Chapter 13). Most of the political and military figures who carried out the American Revolution and shaped the government afterward had read the works of Enlightenment thinkers such as John Locke, Baron Charles de Montesquieu, Voltaire, and others.

THE AMERICAN REVOLUTION

Whatever the causes, the American Revolution broke out in 1775, with the twin battles of Lexington and Concord. At first, the poorly trained and poorly armed American forces, led by George Washington, struggled against the professional armies of Britain. By 1777, however, the tide was turning. Although some colonists, nicknamed "Tories," remained loyal to the British, popular support for the revolution was high. Another social factor that helped the Americans was that most members of all classes—lower, middle, and upper—united behind the independence movement. The Americans were fighting on their home territory. Not only did European freedom fighters with military experience arrive to train American troops, the Americans also used unconventional tactics and guerrilla warfare to counter the British soldiers' training and experience. The British were fighting far from home, at the end of extremely long supply lines.

After America's victory at Saratoga in late 1777, France, Britain's mortal enemy, began to lend military and naval assistance to the American colonists. The assistance of the French fleet against the Royal Navy, Britain's chief strength, was particularly useful to the Americans.

By 1781, the British war effort was failing, and the commander-in-chief, Lord Cornwallis, was trapped at Yorktown. When Cornwallis surrendered there, the war was effectively over, although peace talks dragged on until 1783. The Americans were victorious—and had won themselves a new country.

THE U.S. CONSTITUTION AND THE FORMATION OF
THE AMERICAN GOVERNMENT

The next step was to determine a form of government. There was much disagreement over how closely bound together the thirteen colonies would be. Also, who should have power? Should the government be elected? If so, who should be allowed to vote? What should be done about slavery? These questions and others were decided at the Constitutional Convention of 1787. By 1789, the United States Constitution had been written and accepted by all thirteen states.

The system that resulted was a democratic republic, in which a federal government shared powers with governments in each state. To prevent a dictatorship, power at the federal level was shared among three branches: executive (president), legislative (Congress), and judicial (Supreme Court). State governments, as well as the president and members of Congress, were to be elected. It should be noted, however, that "democracy" in this case—as in all cases before the twentieth century—was by no means all-inclusive. Women and Native Americans could not vote. Men who failed to fulfill certain property requirements could not vote. Moreover, the U.S. Constitution did not outlaw slavery.

Despite its initial flaws, the U.S. Constitution has remained one of the most successful political documents in world history. It is also the product and cause of a great deal of intellectual and philosophical exchange. Most of the Constitution's general ideals, and many of the specific political principles, came from England and France, thanks to the influence of Locke, Voltaire, Montesquieu, Rousseau, and others. In turn, the Constitution (along with the Declaration of Independence that the colonists wrote in 1776) had an enormous impact on the Atlantic revolutions that followed in the 1780s, 1790s, and early 1800s. France's Declaration of the Rights of Man and the Citizen drew heavily upon America's Declaration of Independence and Constitution. The failed Dutch rebellion of the 1780s did likewise. In the early nineteenth century, the revolutionaries of Latin America did their best to adapt the Americans' political methods and ideals. Therefore, the American Revolution, and the political documents at the heart of it, had a tremendous impact on the rest of the world.

THE GROWING GLOBAL IMPORTANCE OF THE UNITED STATES

The domestic history of the United States is beyond the scope of the Advanced Placement World History examination. A few points, however, should be made about the new country's effect on global affairs during the 1800s and early 1900s:

- *Inspiring freedom:* America's example of representative government and respect for civil liberties (in spite of obvious flaws such as slavery) stood out as an example to people in countries throughout the rest of the world who wished to bring about similar changes in their own nations.
- *Sphere of influence:* The Monroe Doctrine (1823), in which the U.S. government warned the nations of Europe against intervening in the Western Hemisphere's political affairs, was the first step in the United States' creation of a sphere of influence in the Americas. The United States quickly became the dominant power in the Americas. By the end of the 1800s, especially after the Spanish-American War (1898), the United States' economic and political influence over Latin America was considerable—and, in some cases, almost imperial.
- *Expansion:* The rapid and massive growth of the United States, from a collection of small colonies on North America's east coast to a vast land sprawling from Atlantic to Pacific, greatly altered the balance of world power. This growth began with the Louisiana Purchase of 1803 (discussed presently) and continued with the Mexican-American War (1846–1848), along with other events. The United States became a huge nation, incredibly rich in natural resources. In the process of growing, the United States also displaced other powers with imperial interests in North America, such as France, Spain, Mexico, Britain, and Russia.
- *Slavery:* The persistence of slavery in the American South was a key factor in allowing the Atlantic slave trade to continue for so long, even after it had been made illegal in the 1810s.
- *Industrial growth:* During the last two thirds of the 1800s, the United States not only followed Europe in industrializing, but surpassed it. Many of the key innovations and inventions of the industrial era came from the United States. Also, by the end of the 1800s and 1900s, America was poised to become the strongest economic power in the world. It was already overtaking Europe's strongest industrial powers, Britain and Germany, in many areas.
- *Immigration:* America's reputation as a land of freedom and economic opportunity drew millions of immigrants from Europe and Asia during the 1800s. It has been estimated that, between the 1830s and 1890s, more than 17 million people came to settle in the United States. Immigrants continued to arrive during the early 1900s. Combined with the large numbers of Europeans and Asians who emigrated to Latin America during these years, this development had a tremendous demographic effect on the geographical balance of world population.

DEVELOPMENTS IN CANADA

Canada, the other British colony in North America, underwent changes during the 1800s. Although Canada remained loyal during the American Revolution, a desire for greater autonomy made itself felt not long afterward. This sentiment was partly due to the example of successful rebellion just to the south. It was also caused partly by a great wave of immigration during the early 1800s. Armed uprisings took place in 1837 to 1838. Although they failed, they convinced the British authorities that flexibility was called for. In 1840, Upper Canada (now Ontario) and Lower Canada (now Quebec), along with other territories in the east, were joined together as the United Provinces of Canada. However, the United Provinces were not self-governing.

More independence came in the 1860s. Canadian politician John Macdonald became the leader of the country's freedom movement. Thanks largely to his efforts, not to mention British fears that a disgruntled Canada might grow closer to the United States, the home government in London passed the British North American Act in 1867. The act conferred upon Canada dominion status. Dominion status entitled Canada to its own constitution and parliament. The constitution created a confederation of Upper Canada, Lower Canada, Nova Scotia, and New Brunswick.

The British monarch was still the head of state, the constitution technically remained under British control until 1982, and for the time being, foreign affairs were still controlled by Britain. Still, in most respects, Canada was self-governing. John Macdonald became the first prime minister. In 1870 to 1871, Canada began to assume control over the western provinces, such as Manitoba and British Columbia, then Alberta and Saskatchewan. Later, Great Britain would use this scheme of dominion status to give similar autonomy to Australia and New Zealand.

THE HAITIAN REBELLION

BACKGROUND OF THE HAITIAN REBELLION

One of the key moments in the spread of the Atlantic revolutions to Latin America and the Caribbean was the Haitian Rebellion (1791–1804). It was the only large-scale slave revolt to succeed in the New World. The Haitian Rebellion was inspired in large part by the American Revolution and caused directly by events related to the French Revolution.

The island of Haiti, known then as Santo Domingo, had been colonized by the Spanish and the French. Each ruled half of the island, whose economy was based mainly on sugar production. The French half was populated by a mix of French colonists, Creoles (those of French descent, but born in the colonies), free blacks (known as *gens de coleur*), and over half a million black slaves. When the French Revolution began in 1789, it threw French Haiti into chaos, mainly because the white colonists and freed blacks, all of whom competed over Haiti's sugar economy, quarreled. In 1791, the slaves of Haiti seized this opportunity to rebel.

TOUSSAINT L'OUVERTURE AND THE FREEING OF THE HAITIAN SLAVES

By 1793, the leader of the Haitian Rebellion was François Toussaint L'Ouverture, often referred to as the "Black Washington." Although a slave, L'Ouverture was literate and well-read. He was also a talented military commander who won victory after victory. By 1798, he had not only freed all the slaves in French Haiti, but he had crossed into Spanish-controlled Santo Domingo and liberated the blacks there as well. At this point, L'Ouverture hoped to make of Haiti a country for free blacks. It would be friendly to France, but also independent.

NAPOLEON'S INTERVENTION IN HAITI

Unfortunately for L'Ouverture, the French government had no intention of allowing Haiti to go free. Over the next four years, the French debated the Haitian question. Then, in 1802, Napoleon Bonaparte, who had, in 1799, become leader of France, decided to send troops to Haiti to retake it for the home country. Ironically, while a young officer in France's revolutionary army, Napoleon had been a great admirer of L'Ouverture, but now the two men were political enemies.

HAITIAN INDEPENDENCE AND ITS LONG-TERM EFFECTS

The French managed to capture L'Ouverture, who was put in chains and sent back to France, where he died in prison. However, the French failed to conquer Haiti. Unused to fighting in tropical conditions, the French could not quell the Haitian rebels. Moreover, yellow fever killed over 40,000 French troops. Finally, in 1804, Napoleon decided to give up the effort to reconquer Haiti. The French went home in disgrace, and the independent nation of Haiti was born.

The Haitian Rebellion had the effect of helping to inspire rebellion elsewhere in Latin America. It also had one other far-reaching geopolitical impact. Because of his frustration with the fighting in Haiti, Napoleon chose to abandon the effort to maintain major French colonies in the New World. Up to this point, France had been the master of a vast part of central North America: the large territory known as Louisiana, stretching from the Great Lakes to the Mississippi Delta. In 1803, Napoleon, seeking to rid himself of this territory, sold it at a bargain price to the United States. President Thomas Jefferson accepted the offer eagerly. Unlike Napoleon, he recognized that the Louisiana Purchase would give the United States control of the North American continent, and with it, the opportunity to become a truly powerful nation. By helping to convince Napoleon to sell Louisiana, the Haitian Rebellion played a part in bringing about a major shift in global power.

THE LATIN AMERICAN WARS OF INDEPENDENCE

CAUSES OF LATIN AMERICA'S WARS OF INDEPENDENCE

Not long after the Haitian Rebellion, revolution spread to virtually all of Latin America. From 1810 to 1825, Mexico, Central America, and South America gained their independence from Spain and Portugal. As with the American Revolution, reasons for the Latin American uprisings included a growing sense of national identity and local resentment of Spanish and Portuguese economic policies. Also important was the frustration that the European-descended, or *criollo* ("creole"), upper and middle classes felt toward the rigid social hierarchy of Latin American societies, which prevented them from realizing their goal of upward social and economic mobility. Even before the revolutions began, tensions were brewing.

The spark that set off the Latin American revolutions was lit back in Europe, by Napoleon. As part of his campaign of European conquest, Napoleon invaded Portugal and Spain in 1807 to 1809. He toppled the royal governments there and put his own representatives, including his brother, in charge. The Spanish king was placed under house arrest, while the Portuguese royal family fled to Brazil.

These sudden blows to the Spanish and Portuguese monarchies had a swift and profound impact on Latin American politics. Brazil's transition to independence was relatively smooth. Spain's Latin American possessions, however, rose up in rebellion.

SIMÓN BOLÍVAR AND THE LIBERATION OF SPANISH SOUTH AMERICA

The most influential revolutionary was Simón Bolívar (1783–1830), known throughout Latin America as the "Liberator." A member of the creole upper class in Venezuela, Bolívar was inspired by the ideals of the Enlightenment, frustrated by the inefficiency and injustice of Spanish rule, and personally ambitious.

In 1810, Bolívar took control of the independence movement that was sweeping across the northern provinces of South America: his own Venezuela, Colombia, Bolivia, and Ecuador. Unlike many members of the creole elite, who rebelled against Spain for the sake of their narrow class interests, Bolívar realized that no revolt could succeed unless it attracted all classes. In a bold stroke, he promised to fight for the rights of mixed-race Latin Americans, as well as for the emancipation of slaves. This pledge turned a small and largely unsuccessful upper- and middle-class rebellion into a mass war of independence. The military turning point of Bolívar's wars came from 1819 to 1821, when he managed to gain control over Venezuela and Colombia.

At this juncture, Bolívar joined forces with another freedom fighter, José de San Martín, a general turned revolutionary. San Martín had begun his uprising in 1816. By 1820, he had freed Argentina, Chile, Uruguay, and Paraguay. He then turned to the north, to Bolivia, Ecuador, and Peru, at the same time that Bolívar was turning south, into the same areas. Despite certain political differences—San Martín was more conservative than Bolívar—the two men decided to cooperate. Bolívar was made the overall leader of the movement. By 1824 to 1825, Bolívar had cleared all Spanish and loyalist forces out of Bolivia, Ecuador, and Peru. Spanish South America was free.

BRAZILIAN INDEPENDENCE

In the meantime, Brazil had also become independent. In this case, the decision to free Brazil came from above, rather than below. In 1820, the King of Portugal went back to Europe to reclaim his throne. He left his son, Prince Pedro, as regent. However, the king also gave his son the following advice: "My son, if Brazil starts to demand independence, make sure you are the one to proclaim it. Then make sure to put the crown on your own head." Indeed, in 1822, when Brazilians began to agitate for their freedom, Pedro declared independence, created a constitutional monarchy, and proclaimed himself Pedro I.

THE MEXICAN WAR OF INDEPENDENCE

Mexico and Central America waged wars of independence from 1810 to 1823. Mexico's revolution was complicated by the inability of various social classes to cooperate. The Mexican War of Independence was begun in September 1810 by the priest Miguel Hidalgo, who, unfurling the flag of the Virgin of Guadalupe, called for revolution against Spain. Hidalgo was killed in 1811, but his fight was carried on by another priest, José Maria Morelos. Hidalgo and Morelos fought not just for independence from Spain, but also social justice. They wanted equal rights for Indians, mestizos, and slaves (whom they planned to set free). They wanted constitutional rule. Hidalgo's and Morelos's platform gained mass support from the lower classes. Unfortunately, Hidalgo's and Morelos's goals were opposed not just by the Spanish, but also many upper-class Mexicans, even those who wanted independence. Like Hidalgo, Morelos was killed, in 1815, by conservative Mexicans, not the Spanish.

This meant that Mexico's revolt had to be carried out by the elite, not the lower classes. A conservative colonel, Agustín Iturbide, overthrew Spanish rule in 1820 to 1821. He then tried to establish a dictatorship, with himself as emperor. Iturbide was quickly overthrown, and a Mexican republic was proclaimed in 1823. That same year, the nations of Central America, south of Mexico, established the United Provinces of Central America.

THE CARIBBEAN

Only in the Caribbean did Spain retain any of its American colonies. Until its defeat by the United States in the Spanish-American War of 1898, Spain kept islands such as Cuba and Puerto Rico.

POLITICAL CONSOLIDATION IN LATIN AMERICA

POLITICAL DIFFICULTIES IN NINETEENTH-CENTURY LATIN AMERICA

Shortly before his death in 1830, Simón Bolívar commented pessimistically about the revolutions he had helped to make: "We have achieved our independence . . . at the expense of everything else." In and of itself, freedom did not bring about good government, social justice, or healthy economies. Throughout the nineteenth and early twentieth centuries, Latin America suffered from a number of long-standing and fundamental problems.

First and most immediate was political breakdown. Bolívar had hoped that Latin America would be divided into a small number of sizable states, governed by constitutional rule. Almost right away, Bolívar's large confederations—such as Gran Colombia and the United Provinces of the Río de la Plata—split apart into many smaller states.

Second was the failure of constitutional rule in many of these new Latin American states. Bolívar drafted constitutions for more than a dozen nations, and they were based on fair political and social principles. Latin American constitutions were largely influenced by the Napoleonic law code and the ideals of the American and French revolutions. But they were imposed on Latin American nations somewhat artificially. There was no tradition of constitutional rule in Latin America, and constitutions, civil liberties, and political rights therefore became meaningless.

This failing led to a third problem: the prevalence of dictatorial rule throughout Latin America. It was typical for military or political strongmen, often known as caudillos, to gain control of Latin American governments. They ruled by means of personal charisma, military force, or oppression. Despite the efforts of reformers and liberals such as Mexico's Benito Juárez, who led the country from 1867 to 1872, conservative dictatorship, rather than representative, democratic government, was the rule in nineteenth-century Latin America.

ECONOMIC BACKWARDNESS IN LATIN AMERICA

Another problem was economic backwardness. Hundreds of years of Spanish and Portuguese rule had shaped Latin American economies in certain ways. They were geared to extract raw materials. They generally emphasized monoculture or, at best, the development of only a small set of resources. They required large reserves of slaves or cheap labor. These practices continued. Plantation agriculture continued. Latin American leaders failed to diversify their economies. Profits tended to benefit only the elite (or, as described presently, foreign investors), while the labor was carried out by large numbers of extremely poor peasants and workers. Moreover, Latin American economies were extremely slow to modernize and industrialize. They remained very backward.

SOCIAL AND RACIAL DIVISIONS IN LATIN AMERICA

Social inequality persisted. Although constitutions theoretically did away with the rigid social hierarchies that the Spanish and Portuguese had put in place, people of mixed race, Indians, and blacks were the victims of much informal prejudice. In many areas, such as Mexico's Yucatán peninsula and Brazil's Amazon basin, racial tensions led to uprisings and guerrilla wars. Another social problem was economic inequality: the gap between rich and poor had always been wide, and it remained wide or grew even wider in most Latin American societies during the 1800s. Finally, in Brazil and Cuba, slavery continued to be legal until the 1880s.

Slavery in Brazil.
From the mid-1500s to the end of the 1800s, Brazil was the largest single importer of slaves from Africa. In particular, the Brazilian sugar industry was dependent on slave labor. Not until the 1800s did the Brazilian government make slavery illegal. Shown here are scenes of the sale and punishment of slaves in Brazil.

FOREIGN INFLUENCE OVER LATIN AMERICA

Another problem was the increased influence that foreign countries exerted over Latin American economies, and even politics. This was especially the case with the United States. During the Texas rebellion of the 1830s and the Mexican-American War of 1846 to 1848, U.S. imperialism stripped vast amounts of territory away from Mexico, including Texas, New Mexico, Arizona, and California.

During the 1860s, Napoleon III of France attempted to install a Habsburg emperor, Maximilian, as the ruler of Mexico.

Less dramatically, foreign investors, especially from Britain and the United States, worked hand-in-hand with Latin American elites to control Latin American economies, then pocket the profits. This "dollar diplomacy" gave Britain, then later, the United States, a tremendous amount of influence in the region.

Until late in the 1800s, Spain continued to exercise a role in the Caribbean. Spain retained control over islands such as Puerto Rico and Cuba. Spanish treatment of these colonial possessions was harsh. Slavery persisted in Cuba until the 1880s. Cuban freedom movements began to appear. The most famous voice for Cuban independence was the poet José Martí. Spain responded by placing political agitators and dissidents in concentration camps, the modern world's first such prisons. Spain's influence in this part of the world would end in 1898, with the Spanish-American War.

The United States also exercised political power in the region, viewing the Americas as its sphere of influence. When the Pan-American Union was formed in 1889 to promote cooperation among the nations of Latin America, cynics referred to it as the "Colonial Division of the U.S. State Department." The Spanish-American War of 1898 actually gave the United States an empire of sorts in Latin America, by placing Cuba and Puerto Rico under U.S. protection. The fact that the United States built the Panama Canal during the early 1900s was another sign of U.S. dominance over the region.

LIMITED MODERNIZATION AND INDUSTRIALIZATION IN LATIN AMERICA

Despite all these problems, Latin America did modernize somewhat by the late 1800s and early 1900s. Industrialization came late, but it did come, especially in countries like Mexico and Argentina. Countries such as Argentina, Uruguay, and Chile made it possible for women to gain educations (even, in Chile, law and medical degrees), and extended greater rights to them.

Immigration from Europe and Asia also swelled the populations of Latin American nations. Although countries like Argentina, Brazil, and Chile did not receive the same numbers as the United States, millions settled there during the last half of the 1800s, adding to what was already a diverse social and ethnic mix.

QUICK REVIEW

1. During the American Revolution, "Tories" were

    (A) American colonists who remained loyal to Great Britain
    (B) Canadian volunteers who joined the British armies
    (C) English merchants who sympathized with the American colonists
    (D) Irish mercenaries who fought with the Americans against the British
    (E) American colonists who fought the British, but opposed forming a single nation afterward

2. Who was the first prime minister of Canada?

    (A) Lord Halifax
    (B) William Pitt the Elder
    (C) Alexander Mackenzie
    (D) Brian Mulroney
    (E) John Macdonald

3. The global effect of the Haitian Rebellion was

    (A) to reestablish French control over the Caribbean
    (B) to bring the British into the conflict on the side of the rebels
    (C) to place Haiti in authority over Cuba and Puerto Rico
    (D) to convince France to sell its North American territories to the United States
    (E) to lead the United States to establish a protectorate over Puerto Rico and the Virgin Islands

4. Who was the most important and successful of the liberators of South America?

    (A) José de San Martín
    (B) Simón Bolívar
    (C) Bernardo O'Higgins
    (D) Agustín Iturbide
    (E) Miguel Hidalgo

5. Which Latin American nation made a smooth transition from colony to independent monarchy?

    (A) Brazil
    (B) Venezuela
    (C) Ecuador
    (D) Colombia
    (E) Uruguay

6. Which of the following best describes Mexico's road to independence?

(A) A mass movement of the lower classes led to the formation of a participatory democracy.

(B) A failed mass movement of the lower classes was followed by a successful anti-Spanish rising by Mexican conservatives.

(C) The Spanish quickly and voluntarily granted Mexico its independence.

(D) The Mexican army, aided by the young United States, rapidly expelled the Spanish rulers.

(E) none of the above

7. Who were the caudillos?

(A) Latin American cattle ranchers

(B) Liberal politicians who safeguarded constitutional rule in Latin America

(C) Wealthy plantation owners who dominated Latin American agriculture

(D) Conservative strongmen who established dictatorships in many Latin American nations

(E) Indian warriors who rebelled against Latin American governments

8. Where did slavery persist the longest in the Americas?

(A) the United States and Mexico

(B) the United States and Cuba

(C) Cuba and Brazil

(D) Cuba and Paraguay

(E) Paraguay and Chile

9. What was the chief result of the Mexican-American War?

(A) The United States gained huge amounts of territory, including California.

(B) Mexico took Texas back from the United States for the next 50 years.

(C) The United States installed the Habsburg emperor Maximilian as ruler of Mexico.

(D) The United States set Mexican slaves free.

(E) The United States took the Yucatán peninsula from Mexico.

10. Who among the following was Mexico's most liberal reformer during the nineteenth and early twentieth centuries?

(A) Agustín Iturbide

(B) Lopez de Santa Anna

(C) Porfirio Díaz

(D) Benito Juárez

(E) Emiliano Zapata

ANSWERS:

1. **A**, p. 329
2. **E**, p. 331
3. **D**, p. 332
4. **B**, pp. 332–33
5. **A**, p. 333
6. **B**, p. 333
7. **D**, p. 334
8. **C**, pp. 334–35
9. **A**, p. 335
10. **D**, p. 334

Unit Five: Review Questions

SAMPLE ESSAY QUESTIONS

1. Discuss the wave of revolutions that swept the Atlantic world during the late 1700s and early 1800s. Include the American Revolution, the French Revolution, the Haitian Rebellion, and the Latin American wars of independence. How did these revolutions alter the economic, political, and social patterns of not just the West, but the entire world?

2. Examine the factors that motivated and enabled the Europeans—and the Americans—to enjoy such success in their nineteenth-century campaigns of imperialism. Where were the main arenas of imperial conquest? How did imperialism affect the West, and how did it affect the areas that were conquered and colonized? How did different Western nations handle their colonies?

3. Compare and contrast the efforts of non-Western regimes to reform and modernize during the 1800s. Include in your discussion Qing China, Meiji Japan, and the Ottoman Empire.

MULTIPLE-CHOICE QUESTIONS

1. Why was England the first country to industrialize?

   (A) It already had a developed trade system.
   (B) The depletion of timber caused it to rely more heavily on coal.
   (C) It had a well-developed transportation network.
   (D) It was already heavily urbanized.
   (E) all of the above

2. Which of the following statements would Marxists oppose?

   (A) It is best to skip the capitalist stage and move straight to communism.
   (B) Economic competition is inherently unfair.
   (C) The upper classes exploit the labor of the lower classes.
   (D) Laissez-faire capitalism leads to inequality.
   (E) none of the above

3. Which of the following was NOT a cause of the French Revolution?

    (A) a wide gap between ordinary citizens and the country's elite

    (B) the unfairness of the tax system

    (C) middle class dissatisfaction with the present state of affairs

    (D) a peasant revolt against the middle class

    (E) the influence of the Enlightenment

4. At the Congress of Vienna,

    (A) the peace following World War I was settled

    (B) post-Napoleonic treaties were decided on

    (C) legislators gathered to work out the design for a League of Nations

    (D) the German states were allowed to unify

    (E) all of the above

5. In what major way did democratization in nineteenth-century France and Britain differ?

    (A) Britain's process was more consistent and less violent.

    (B) France's process was more consistent and less violent.

    (C) Women were granted suffrage in Britain, whereas French women were not.

    (D) Women were granted suffrage in France, whereas British women were not.

    (E) none of the above

6. Which of the following countries was not colonized by Western powers?

    (A) Indonesia

    (B) Laos

    (C) Japan

    (D) Cambodia

    (E) Vietnam

7. Why was control over the Suez Canal so contentious in the late 1800s?

    (A) It linked Europe with Turkey.

    (B) It linked the Atlantic to the Pacific Oceans, the United States to Latin America.

    (C) It linked Europe and the Mediterranean with the Red Sea and Indian Ocean.

    (D) It strengthened French control over Egypt.

    (E) none of the above

8. In what ways did African colonization change after 1880?

    I. The competition among Western powers to colonize the continent intensified.

    II. The competition among Western powers to colonize the continent cooled.

    III. The Western powers at the Berlin Conference agreed to certain basic rules.

    IV. Diplomatic crises between colonizing states persisted into the twentieth century.

    (A) I, II, and III

    (B) II, III, and IV

    (C) I, III, and IV

    (D) I and III only

    (E) none of the above

9. In the early 1900s, which countries made up the Triple Entente?

    (A) Great Britain, Germany, and Italy

    (B) Great Britain, France, and Germany

    (C) Russia, Germany, and France

    (D) France, Russia, and Great Britain

    (E) Germany, Italy, and Austria

10. The map on page 322 illustrates that

(A) France controlled Cameroon
(B) Britain controlled Madagascar
(C) Belgium was the only European country to have colonized Central Africa
(D) Germany controlled the most amount of territory in Africa, followed by France
(E) the only African states that were not colonized by European powers in 1914 were Liberia and Ethiopia

11. What internal factors or forces weakened the Ottoman Empire beginning in the 1600s?

(A) rulers who wielded too much power
(B) weak rulers and state corruption
(C) earthquakes and other natural disasters
(D) collapse of the monarchy
(E) none of the above

12. By the early 1800s, Manchu leaders in China

(A) were known for economic efficiency
(B) had yet to peak in terms of economic growth and regional expansion
(C) accepted a vast amount of Western goods in trade
(D) met with popular discontent and widespread reaction against corruption and economic malaise
(E) encouraged opium addiction among the peasants to keep them under control

13. The Chinese Republic was characterized by

(A) political breakdown and decentralization
(B) a flowering of Chinese democracy
(C) a period of peace with Japan
(D) unification of Chinese provinces
(E) the strengthening of imperial power

14. Which of the following was NOT an illustration of the social transformation Japan witnessed during the Meiji Restoration?

(A) A larger middle class developed.
(B) The regime allowed labor unions to form.
(C) The samurai class lost its traditional privileges.
(D) Prefects replaced nobles in regional government.
(E) Commoners could serve in the military.

15. How did the British East India Company gain control of India?

 I. through economic influence
 II. by means of naval power and the use of armies, both along the coast and in the interior
 III. through effective use of native elites and native troops trained in the British style
 IV. by governing via the authority of local Mughal officials

(A) I only
(B) I, II, and III
(C) II, III, and IV
(D) II and III only
(E) all of the above

16. What impact did the Haitian Rebellion have on the outside world?

(A) It caused rebels elsewhere to think twice before staging a coup.
(B) It caused France to work harder toward gaining a stronger colonial foothold in America.
(C) It inspired rebellions elsewhere in Latin America and caused France to abandon its main colonies in the New World.
(D) It encouraged other European powers to colonize islands in the Caribbean.
(E) It caused the southern parts of the United States to strengthen their hold on slaves.

17. As part of his strategy for gaining independence in northern provinces of South America, Simón Bolívar

    (A) fought for the rights of mixed-race peoples and the freeing of slaves
    (B) focused on enlisting the upper-classes, since they held most of the wealth
    (C) drew from Napoleon's tactics
    (D) stressed that he would not work to free the slaves
    (E) held up the justice of Spanish rule as an example elsewhere

18. How did the history of Liberia differ from that of other African countries?

    (A) It was colonized by Europeans long before any other parts of Africa were.
    (B) It was the last African country to be colonized by Europeans.
    (C) Missionaries ran the country's government in the early 1900s.
    (D) It was founded by former slaves with the aid of colonization societies.
    (E) none of the above

19. Which African peoples put up the strongest resistance to European militaries?

    (A) the Asante and the Zulu
    (B) the Bantu and the Swazi
    (C) the Ngoni and the Gaza
    (D) the Dahomeians and the Fulani
    (E) the Ndebele and the Tutsi

20. Why did abolishing the slave trade in Africa help pave the way toward European conquest there in the late 1800s?

    (A) The pattern of African trade changed, causing many states to lose revenue, suffer economic downturns, and become more vulnerable to foreign takeover.
    (B) Fighting for the abolitionist cause, Europeans set a precedent for future interventions in African affairs.
    (C) Europeans began thinking that military invasions of African territory were justified.
    (D) all of the above
    (E) none of the above

ANSWERS:

1. **E**, p. 271	11. **B**, pp. 290–91
2. **A**, p. 276	12. **D**, p. 299
3. **D**, p. 256	13. **A**, p. 303
4. **B**, p. 260	14. **B**, pp. 305–6
5. **A**, p. 261	15. **E**, pp. 310–11
6. **C**, pp. 284, 298	16. **C**, p. 332
7. **C**, pp. 294–95	17. **A**, p. 333
8. **C**, p. 285	18. **D**, p. 321
9. **D**, p. 287	19. **A**, pp. 318–19
10. **E**, p. 322	20. **D**, p. 322

UNIT SIX

The Twentieth Century and Contemporary World Cultures

(1914–present)

Unit Overview

GENERAL REMARKS

The twentieth century ranks as one of the most tumultuous eras in world history. It was also a time of paradox and contradiction, leading one major historian to refer to it as the "age of extremes." It was during the twentieth century that a greater portion of the world than ever before adopted democratic forms of government, but it was also during the 1900s that the most oppressive dictatorships in world history appeared. The 1900s were an era of unprecedented prosperity, but also a time of striking socioeconomic polarity, as the gap between rich and poor widened. The twentieth century witnessed tremendous cultural and scientific advancement, but also the worst wars and the greatest arms buildup in human history.

The first half of the twentieth century was dominated by two great military conflicts: the world wars. Both World War I and World War II caused immense devastation. The latter was the largest, bloodiest, and costliest conflict humanity has ever experienced. The world wars also led to profound changes in the world balance of power, both politically and economically. World War I destroyed several of the great empires of the nineteenth century and weakened all of Europe. World War II completed the process of weakening Europe, dislodging it from its position of global mastery.

The time between the world wars was marked by economic crisis, resulting from the Great Depression, which emanated outward from the United States. The interwar period also saw the emergence of powerful, extremely repressive dictatorial regimes, such as Soviet Russia, Fascist Italy, and Nazi Germany. For a time, it appeared that these "totalitarian" states, and not democratic governments, might be the wave of the future. Starting with the establishment of the Soviet state, communism became an important and influential—although, in the end, seemingly unworkable—alternative to capitalism as a form of economic organization.

During the second half of the twentieth century, following World War II, sweeping trends affected the entire world. One trend, following upon the collapse of Europe's global dominance, was decolonization. From the 1940s through the 1970s, those parts of Africa, Asia, and the Pacific that had been under European (and U.S.) imperial control during the 1800s and early 1900s became free. This wave of national liberation created dozens of new nations around the world. In some cases, decolonization proceeded smoothly and peacefully. In others, national liberation was attained by force or quickly disintegrated into violence and political chaos.

Another effect of World War II and Europe's decline as a global power was a new diplomatic alignment, the Cold War. In the previous century and a half, world affairs had been determined by the workings of the European balance of power. After World War II, political and economic power was concentrated in the hands of two large, evenly matched superpowers: the United States and the Soviet Union. This situation of bipolar equilibrium persisted for four and a half decades. The Cold War divided most of the globe into two hostile camps. It led to a massive nuclear arms race. For almost half a century, the Cold War was the driving force in international affairs worldwide.

Broadly speaking, the twentieth century was a time of political extremes. On one hand, more of the world democratized than ever before. For the first time in world history, major nations began to allow women to vote and participate fully in political life. On the other hand, some of the most dictatorial regimes in the history of humankind emerged. Countless millions of people were imprisoned, abused, tortured, or killed by such governments.

The twentieth century proved to be an era of modernization. Those societies that were already industrialized when the 1900s began—such as the United States, Canada, western Europe, and Japan—became even more adept at scientific and technological innovation, until, after the 1940s and 1950s, they began to move into postindustrial modes of economic organization and production. Such societies are generally referred to as the developed world. A number of other countries, especially in Asia, made great progress in industrializing and modernizing, especially after World War II. The majority of the world's nations, known as the developing world, remain in a less advanced stage of economic and technological progress.

During the late twentieth century, there was an overall rise in the level of wealth and modernization. The economies of the world have also globalized, or grown closer together, to a steadily increasing extent. Despite this, however, the twentieth and twenty-first centuries have also seen the widest gap between prosperity and poverty to appear in many years, if not in world history. Even within developed nations, social and economic polarity is extreme. And the gulf between the developed and developing worlds is especially immense.

The 1980s and 1990s saw the collapse of communism in Europe and the USSR, and with that, the end of the Cold War. The same decades also witnessed a wave of democratization in many parts of the world, as well as the increased globalization of the world economy. Mass communications have made the world, metaphorically speaking, a much smaller and more connected place. This is especially due to the relatively sudden proliferation of computer technology, which has caused an information and communications revolution.

The general direction of the post–Cold War world in the early twenty-first century remains unclear. On one hand, many trends, such as the end of the nuclear arms race, economic globalization, the worldwide prevalence of American popular culture, and the spread of mass communications and computer technology, seem to be drawing the world closer together. On the other hand, ethnic violence, extreme forms of nationalism, religious fundamentalism, fear of biological and chemical weaponry, growing tensions between China and the West, and a cooling of relations between Russia and the United States are all factors that threaten to pull the world further apart in years to come.

BROAD TRENDS

GLOBAL POWER AND INTERNATIONAL RELATIONS

- During the first half of the twentieth century, two world wars profoundly shaped global affairs.
- After 1914, Europe's position of world dominance was badly weakened by World War I. Nonetheless, Europe retained its position of global importance, as well as its overseas empires, for three more decades.
- The United States, after World War I, became the world's richest and most powerful nation.
- World War II completed the process of dismantling Europe's global dominance. The war left world power roughly divided between two superpowers, the United States and the Soviet Union.
- For almost five decades after World War II, most of the world was divided into hostile camps, led by the United States and the Soviet Union. This great geopolitical struggle was known as the Cold War. Although the two superpowers never went to war against each other directly, they used other nations as proxies in their struggle. They also engaged in a nuclear arms race, which ranks as the largest and most expensive weapons buildup in world history.

- From the 1940s through the 1970s, a mass wave of decolonization deprived the European powers of their empires. Former colonies in Asia, Africa, the Pacific, and elsewhere became free. Dozens of new nations were formed.
- During the late 1980s and early 1990s, communism in Eastern Europe and the Soviet Union collapsed. This sudden and dramatic development helped bring an end to the Cold War.
- The years since the Cold War have seen global power completely realigned. The only remaining superpower is the United States. Beyond that, alliances and coalitions are constantly shifting. A rising economic and political power is China, the world's most populous nation.

POLITICAL DEVELOPMENTS

- The level of popular representation in national governments grew in many countries, especially in the Western democracies.
- Women were allowed to vote in the majority of Western nations, then in most countries worldwide.
- During the era between the world wars, democracies tended to be politically weak and economically depressed.
- The strongest and most dynamic governments during the interwar period tended to be the new "totalitarian" dictatorships, which aimed to control as many aspects of their subjects' lives as possible.
- After World War II and during the Cold War, the primary form of political and economic organization in the West (Canada, the United States, and Western Europe) was the democratic state with a capitalist system, although capitalism was modified to varying degrees by social welfare systems.
- A number of regimes, led by the Soviet Union and China, adopted communist economic systems. Their political systems tended to be dictatorial.
- The nations of the so-called Third World, which joined neither the U.S. alliance nor the Soviet bloc during the Cold War, experimented with a variety of political and economic systems.
- During the late 1980s and early 1990s, communism collapsed in Eastern Europe and the Soviet Union. This development ended the Cold War. It also left China as the world's major communist state.
- The globalization of culture and economics has led some scholars to speculate that the nation-state may either fade away altogether or at least cease to be the primary form of political organization. Whether or not this will prove true, regional diplomatic alliances and regional economic blocs, such as the Association of Southeast Asian Nations and the European Union, have become increasingly important during the second half of the twentieth century and the early twenty-first.

ECONOMIC DEVELOPMENTS

- During the first half of the century, the West (Europe, Canada, and the United States) fully industrialized. Certain other parts of the world achieved significant degrees of modernization and industrialization as well (such as Japan, parts of Latin America, and parts of China).
- A number of countries experimented with communist economies (the Soviet Union, then, after World War II, Eastern Europe, China, North Korea, Cuba, Vietnam, and others).
- During the 1930s, the Great Depression, emanating from the United States, had a tremendously negative impact on the economies of most of Europe and Latin America, as well as Asia and Africa, to a lesser degree.
- World War II consumed a huge amount of the world's economic resources during the first half of the 1940s. It is estimated that, at the war's peak, between one quarter and one third of the world's entire productive capacity was devoted directly or indirectly to the war.

- After World War II, a great split between the capitalist West and the communist Soviet bloc emerged. This split prevailed until the end of the Cold War.
- Also after World War II, a different split emerged between the developed world, whose prosperity steadily grew (with a few minor regressions, such as the economic crisis of the 1970s), and the nondeveloped and developing worlds, which lagged behind. Because so many of the nations of the nondeveloped and developing worlds are located near or south of the equator, this disparity is sometimes referred to as the north-south split.
- After the 1950s and 1960s, the economies of the West began to make transitions from industrial economies to postindustrial economies, based less on manufacturing and more on service, information, and advanced technology (especially computers). This trend continues to the present day.
- During the 1970s, a general economic crisis, characterized by energy (particularly oil) shortages, recession, unemployment, and general slowdown struck most of the capitalist West.
- A general rise in overall prosperity took place in Western economies during the 1980s and 1990s. The same was true in China. The Soviet bloc experienced a severe economic downturn during this time.
- The 1980s and 1990s were also an era of greater economic globalization, as international trade, economic regionalization, and the clout of multinational corporations all became increasingly important. This trend still continues, and is steadily accelerating.
- The collapse of communism in Eastern Europe and the Soviet Union has forced a number of countries to make a painful, difficult transition from communism to free-market economies. Most of these countries continue to wrestle with this transition in the early twenty-first century.

CULTURAL DEVELOPMENTS

- Mass media and mass communications technology have transformed the cultural sphere. Cinema, the radio, television, and other electronic media have been used to create high art.
- Mass media and mass communications have also been used to create popular culture (or mass culture): music, literature, and so forth aimed at a popular audience for purposes of entertainment.
- The art world of the twentieth century was characterized by bold experimentation and the distortion, even abandonment, of traditional norms and conventions.
- Especially during the first two thirds of the 1900s, largely because of the demoralizing effects of Europe's decline and the world wars, Western high art tended to be marked by uncertainty and pessimism (in great contrast to the exuberance and energy of popular culture and the mass media).
- Scientific advancement proceeded at a breathtaking pace and scale. Fields that were especially innovative were physics, biotechnology, rocketry, electronics, and computers.
- After World War II, Western culture began to move beyond the "modern" period into a newer "postmodern" era.
- Worldwide, different cultures have begun to mix, interact, and blend to an unprecedented degree. This celebration and acknowledgment of different traditions and styles is generally referred to as multiculturalism.
- Since the 1990s, the proliferation of personal computer technology, particularly access to the Internet and World Wide Web, has led to an information revolution.

GENDER ISSUES

- Women's movements began to campaign for greater equality and the right to vote during the late 1800s and early 1900s.

- By causing large numbers of women to move into the workplace, World War I greatly accelerated the cause of women's equality.
- Most Western nations gave women the vote shortly after World War I.
- Even more so than the First World War, World War II gave millions of women the opportunity to work. Many women also served in the armed forces (almost always in noncombat roles). Their role during World War II significantly boosted women's hopes and chances for more rights and greater equality.
- The development of reliable contraception (especially the birth-control pill) gave women with access to it unprecedented control over pregnancy.
- During the 1960s and 1970s, a great feminist movement, agitating for women's liberation and equal rights, swept Canada, the United States, and Western Europe. Since then, women's movements have sought to achieve more than simple legal equality and the right to vote. Their goals have been to reach full cultural and economic equality, changing social norms and behaviors to create a more positive climate for equal gender relations.
- Progress toward equal treatment of women has been uneven in non-Western parts of the world.

COMPARATIVE ISSUES TO CONSIDER

- Discuss the various ways in which different nations and regions modernized during the twentieth century. Were they industrialized before the 1900s? Did modernization efforts come from the population at large, or were they instituted by the government? Did they have to be put into place by force? Has modernization by force proven effective?
- What kind of impact did the world wars have on the non-Western world? Compare different regions, such as Africa and Asia.
- Compare two or more of the twentieth century's major revolutions, such as the Russian, Chinese, Cuban, or Iranian. Alternatively, compare one or more of these with revolutions in previous centuries.
- Investigate the process of decolonization as it played out in various parts of the world. What role does geography play? How important is the role of the colonizing power, both historically and at the time of independence? Compare the experiences of different regions (for example, India and Africa).
- Look at various national liberation movements during the period of decolonization. What obstacles did various movements face? How did their approaches to liberation and decolonization differ, and how were they alike? Did they use force? If so, how and why? Compare, for example, Gandhi and Ho Chi Minh, or African national leaders such as Kwame Nkrumah, Jomo Kenyatta, Patrice Lumumba, or Nelson Mandela.
- Examine the various effects of nationalism in the modern era. What positive effects has it had? How and in what parts of the world has it had a negative impact?
- Compare the effects of the Cold War on the West, the East, and the so-called Third World.
- How has the rise of Western consumer society and the globalization of the economy affected different civilizations outside Europe? Compare, for example, China with sub-Saharan Africa, or Japan with Latin America.
- In what different ways were women of various societies affected by the world wars? How have they been affected by the major revolutions of the twentieth century (Russian, Chinese, Iranian, Cuban)?
- How does ethnic violence in the late twentieth century compare with the Holocaust?
- Compare the nation-state with regional groupings (diplomatic, economic, military) that have emerged during the late twentieth and early twenty-first centuries.

- Examine Western and non-Western forms of cultural expression. How have mass media and popular culture affected world culture? Which has become more important: multiculturalism or the "Americanization" of contemporary world culture?

KEY TERMS AND CONCEPTS

World War I (the Great War)

the Triple Alliance (Central Powers) versus the Triple Entente (Allies)

the assassination of Francis Ferdinand

the Serbian ultimatum and Germany's "blank check"

the Schlieffen Plan

the Eastern and Western fronts

trench warfare

submarine warfare

tanks and aircraft

the Turkish massacre of Armenian civilians

economic mobilization and the home front

women in the workplace

women and the vote

the Paris Peace Conference

the Treaty of Versailles

Woodrow Wilson and the Fourteen Points

the League of Nations

the "war-guilt" clause

Germany's war repayments

the Great Depression and its worldwide effects

totalitarianism

the February Revolution and the Provisional Government in Russia

Vladimir Lenin and the Bolshevik (Communist) Party

the October Revolution and the establishment of the Soviet Union

Leon Trotsky

Joseph Stalin

the First Five-Year Plan and the collectivization of agriculture

the Great Purges and the gulags

Benito Mussolini and the Italian Fascist Party

the March on Rome

the Weimar Republic

Adolf Hitler and the Nazi Party

Mein Kampf

the Enabling Act

the Nuremberg Laws

the Young Turks

Mustafa Kemal Ataturk and the birth of modern Turkey

Reza Shah Pahlavi

oil in the Middle East

the Arab mandates

the Balfour Declaration

Ibn Saud and the founding of Saudi Arabia

Sun Yat-sen and the Nationalist (Kuomintang) Party

Yuan Shikai

the Chinese Communist Party

the May Fourth Movement and Tiananmen Square

Chiang Kai-shek and the Nanjing Republic

the Long March

Emperor Taisho and democratic reform in Japan

Kita Ikki

the Japanese invasion of Manchuria and China

Emperor Hirohito

Hideki Tojo

the Rape of Nanking

the Indian National Congress (Congress Party)

the Amritsar massacre

Mohandas K. ("Mahatma") Gandhi and nonviolent resistance (satyagraha)

Jawaharlal Nehru

Muhammad Ali Jinnah and the Muslim League

U.S. economic and political influence over Latin America

the Good Neighbor Policy

Mexico and the Institutional Revolutionary Party

Lázaro Cárdenas

Getúlio Vargas

Hipólito Irigoyen

Juan and Eva Perón

World War II

the Allied Powers versus the Axis Powers

collective security

the occupation of the Rhineland

Francisco Franco and the Spanish Civil War

Lebensraum

the Anschluss

the Sudeten crisis, the Munich Conference, and appeasement

the Nazi-Soviet Pact

the invasion of Poland

blitzkrieg

the fall of France

the Battle of Britain

Lend-Lease

Operation Barbarossa

the Greater East Asian Co-Prosperity Sphere

Pearl Harbor

Midway, El Alamein, and Stalingrad

Operation Overlord (D-Day)

strategic bombing

Hiroshima, Nagasaki, and the atomic bomb

the Holocaust ("Final Solution")

the *Einsatzgruppen*

the Wannsee Conference

Auschwitz-Birkenau

the Nuremberg Trials

from balance of power to bipolar equilibrium

superpowers

the Cold War

the Teheran, Yalta, and Potsdam conferences

the partition of Germany

the division of Eastern Europe

the United Nations

the "iron curtain" speech

the Berlin Blockade

the Truman Doctrine, the Marshall Plan (European Recovery Plan), and NATO

George Kennan and the containment strategy

Mao Tse-tung and communist revolution in China

the Korean War

Nikita Khrushchev

the nuclear arms race

mutually assured destruction (MAD) and deterrence

the Third World

the domino theory

the Soviet invasion of Hungary

the Suez crisis

Fidel Castro and the Cuban Revolution

the Bay of Pigs

the Berlin Wall

the Cuban missile crisis

the Prague Spring and the Soviet invasion of Czechoslovakia

the Brezhnev Doctrine

the Sino-Soviet split

détente

the Afghan War

Soviet modernization and industrialization of Eastern Europe

postindustrial economies in Western Europe

the European Coal and Steel Community, the Common Market, and the European Union

Charles de Gaulle

Margaret Thatcher

François Mitterand

Helmut Kohl

decolonization and national liberation

Middle Eastern oil and the Organization of Petroleum Exporting Countries

Gamal Abdul Nasser

the establishment of Israel

the Arab-Israeli conflict

Yasser Arafat and the Palestine Liberation Organization

Menachem Begin, Anwar Sadat, and the Camp David Accords

the intifada

the Iranian Revolution and the Ayatollah Khomeini

Saddam Hussein

the Algerian War of Independence

the African National Congress

Kwame Nkrumah

Jomo Kenyatta

the Mau Mau

Patrice Lumumba

Nelson Mandela

Desmond Tutu

Idi Amin

Mobutu Sese Seko

the AIDS/HIV epidemic in Africa

the independence of India

Indo-Pakistani partition

Indira Gandhi

Sukarno and "Guided Democracy"

Suharto

Ho Chi Minh

the Vietnam War

the Khmer Rouge

the postwar economic recovery of Japan

the Liberal Democrats

Taiwan and the Kuomintang
Kim Il Sung
the Great Leap Forward
the Cultural Revolution
Deng Xiaoping
Augusto Pinochet
the Institutional Revolutionary Party
the Mexico City demonstrations
Ché Guevara
the Sandinistas and the Nicaraguan
 Revolution
the contras
modern versus postmodern culture
Bretton Woods, the World Bank, and the
 International Monetary Fund
the General Agreement on Trade and Tariffs
European Union
the energy crunch and economic crisis of the
 1970s
multinational corporations
the G-7 (G-8)
the World Trade Organization
the North American Free Trade Agreement
economic globalization
the standard-of-living disparity between the
 developed and developing worlds
the north-south split
population growth
the migration of peoples
consumerism
environmental movements and green parties
nongovernmental organizations
terrorism
nationalism and ethnic violence
women's movements, feminism, and women's
 liberation
stream of consciousness
abstract and surrealist art
existentialism
mass media
popular culture
Diego Rivera

Lu Hsun (Lu Xun)
Rabindranath Tagore
Wole Soyinka
Chinua Achebe
Yukio Mishima
Isabel Allende
Salman Rushdie
Albert Einstein and the theory of relativity
quantum physics
rocketry and space exploration
biotechnology, DNA, and genetics
computer technology, the Internet and World
 Wide Web, and the information revolution
Marshall McLuhan and the "global village"
 concept
stagnation in the Soviet Union
Andrei Sakharov, Alexander Solzhenitsyn, and
 the Soviet dissident movement
Lech Walesa and Solidarity
Deng Xiaoping and limited reform in China
Mikhail Gorbachev, perestroika, and glasnost
Chernobyl
the fall of the Berlin Wall and the collapse of
 East European communism
the Tiananmen Square demonstrations and
 massacre
the collapse of the Soviet Union
Boris Yeltsin
the nuclear club and the nonproliferation issue
the Nuclear Non-Proliferation Treaty
weapons of mass destruction (nuclear,
 biological, and chemical weapons)
the Gulf War
the rise of China
nationalist extremism
the Yugoslav wars (Croatia, Bosnia, Kosovo)
the Hutu-Tutsi conflict
East Timor
Israeli-Palestinian conflict and the second
 intifada
environmentalism and the green movement
global warming

CHAPTER 28

World War I

In the late summer of 1914, the nations of Europe went to war. All parties involved expected that the conflict would be short and decisive—that, as the British press was fond of claiming, "the boys" would be "home by Christmas."

Instead, World War I (July 1914–November 1918), known simply to the people who experienced it as the Great War, lasted more than four years. More than 30 nations joined in the fighting. In that time, the war killed up to 10 million soldiers. Between 3 million and 5 million civilians perished as well, mainly of disease and starvation caused by the war, but also as a result of direct military action. Approximately 28 million to 30 million people were wounded or disabled by the war. According to the prices of the time, World War I is estimated to have cost $32 billion (almost $400 billion in current economic terms). At war's end, Europe's economies lay in ruins, even those of the countries that had won. The peace treaties that ended the war also redrew the map of Europe, and that of the world, completely.

It is no exaggeration to say that World War I also shattered Europe politically and culturally. Four great empires—the German Reich, Russia's tsarist regime, Austria-Hungary's Habsburg dynasty, and the Ottoman Empire—were thoroughly destroyed. Even most of the victors, Britain, France, and Italy, were exhausted and demoralized. The barbarity and bloodshed caused by the war brought about a huge shift in European cultural attitudes. The spirit of optimism and faith in progress that had been so prevalent during the nineteenth century vanished, only to be replaced by fear, anxiety, and gloom. The Europeans' view of themselves as models of civilized behavior and cultural superiority was exposed as a foolish illusion. The only major nation in the West to escape this malaise was the United States, which remained comparatively undamaged by the war—and even managed to profit from it economically.

Far-reaching social changes resulted from, or were at least sped up by, the war. These included the final decline of the aristocracy, the rise of the middle and lower classes, the greater democratization of European politics, the complete industrialization and modernization of European economies, and the granting of suffrage to women.

In global terms, World War I brought about a fundamental shift in power. Europe had gained tremendous global might during the last half of the 1700s. In the nineteenth century, it had become the dominant civilization on the planet, and it reached the absolute zenith of its power from 1870 to 1914. After World War I, however, it was becoming clear that Europe would not be able to continue in its position of economic, political, and imperial preeminence for much longer. The United States was on its way to becoming the world's military and economic powerhouse. Europe's imperial possessions were becoming increasingly restless, and although countries like Britain and France held on to their empires for a while longer, the process of decolonization was unavoidable—the only question was when, not whether, it would happen.

Clearly, World War I was much more than a straightforward armed conflict. It truly ended one age and began another. For all these reasons and more, World War I, rather than the calendar year 1900, is generally considered to be, metaphorically speaking, the true beginning of the twentieth century.

BACKGROUND AND BEGINNING

LONG-TERM CAUSES OF WORLD WAR I

Many of the long-term causes of World War I are discussed in Chapter 22. They include competition over empire during the end of the 1800s (especially in Africa); Anglo-German rivalry over empire, industrial competition, and naval superiority; the rising intensity of nationalism in Europe (especially in the Balkans); and the conflicting interests of Italy, Austria-Hungary, Russia, and the Ottoman Empire in the Balkans.

Overlaying all that was the alliance system that had emerged during the late 1800s and early 1900s. Locked into place were two sides: the Triple Alliance (Germany, Austria, and Italy) versus the Triple Entente (France, Russia, and Britain). It should be noted that Italy was a weak link in the former, and would actually change sides during World War I. Also, Britain's commitment to the Triple Entente was informal, although it honored that commitment once war began.

THE ASSASSINATION OF FRANCIS FERDINAND

The war began in the Balkans, famously known as the "powder keg of Europe." The actual spark that exploded the powder keg was the assassination of the Archduke Francis Ferdinand, heir to the Austrian throne, and his wife Sophie, on June 28, 1914, in the Bosnian city of Sarajevo. Austria's 1908 annexation of this Slavic province, with its large Serbian population, had angered not only Russia, but Serbia, which was by now an independent nation with ambitions to grow larger. The killer was a Bosnian student of Serb descent and a member of a terrorist group that received money and arms from Serbia.

AUSTRIA'S ULTIMATUM TO SERBIA AND GERMANY'S "BLANK CHECK"

The assassination caused an international outrage. Austria blamed Serbia for the murders and determined to use them as a pretext to humble its troublesome neighbor once and for all. On July 23, Austria handed Serbia an ultimatum, a list of humiliating demands, and threatened to declare war if Serbia did not agree to all of them.

Because of the European alliance system and a general spirit of nationalist belligerence, this regional quarrel quickly escalated into a continental war. Slavic Russia, "big brother" to the Serbs, was bound to intervene. Kaiser Wilhelm II of Germany backed up his ally with the so-called blank check, an assurance of German support of any action Austria might take against Serbia, even if Russia became involved. France, of course, was pledged to aid Russia in the event of hostilities.

DECLARATIONS OF WAR

On July 28, Austria declared war on Serbia. Russia mobilized for war. Like clockwork, the alliance system went into operation. Between July 28 and August 4, Serbia, Austria, Russia, Germany, France, and Britain entered the war. Ultimately, although blame for the war was later assigned solely to Germany, it can be seen that many factors contributed to the beginning of the war. Likewise, a number of countries bear at least part of the blame for starting the conflict.

COMBAT

THE COMBATANTS: THE CENTRAL POWERS AND THE ALLIES

When the war began, the two sides were as follows. The Allies, as the nations of the Triple Entente now called themselves, consisted of Great Britain, France, and Russia. Many of Britain's imperial possessions and dominions, such as Canada, Australia, New Zealand, and South Africa, also took part. Italy abandoned its former partners and joined the war on the side of the Allies in 1915, because Britain and France promised it Austrian territory. In 1917, the United States would join the Allied war effort; later that same year, Russia would drop out of the war. On the other side were the Central Powers. These were Germany and Austria, the nations of the Triple Alliance, minus Italy. They were joined by Bulgaria and the Ottoman Empire. Many other nations took part in the war, one way or another, but these were the major combatants.

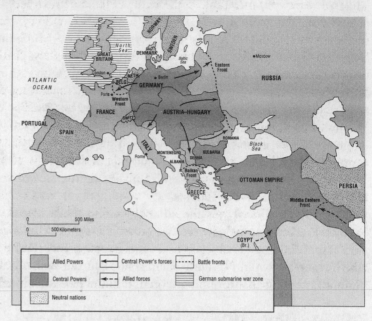

World War I in Europe, 1914–1918.
In western Europe, the basic dynamic of the conflict was determined quite early. Then, thanks to the stalemate of trench warfare, it changed very little until the last months of war. In the east, the conditions of the fighting were much more fluid.

THE SCHLIEFFEN PLAN, THE INVASION OF BELGIUM, AND THE BATTLE OF THE MARNE

Germany's war plan—the Schlieffen Plan—and its failure determined how the first phase of World War I proceeded. Faced with a two-front ground war against France and Russia, not to mention the long-term threat of the British navy, Germany realized that the longer the conflict lasted, the more likely it and Austria were to lose. Therefore, the Schlieffen Plan called for a daring gamble: Germany would send 75 percent of its army against France, in order to capture Paris and knock France out of the war in six weeks. The rest of the army, along with the Austrians, would defend against Russia, which was expected to take months to mobilize fully. To catch the French off guard, the main attack force would move through Belgium, which was neutral.

The illegal invasion of Belgium, which also resulted in the death of many civilians, ensured that Britain would join the war on the side of the Allies. It also stained Germany's reputation badly, enabling Allied propaganda to make a convincing argument that the Germans were aggressors, "barbarians," and "Huns."

The Schlieffen Plan was put into effect in August. By early September, it had failed. The Belgians resisted more stoutly than the Germans had expected. The Russians mobilized more quickly than expected, and the Germans had to divert troops to the east to keep them from invading. Although German troops came within sight of Paris, the French army made a heroic stand at the Marne River. The Battle of the Marne saved Paris and ended the Schlieffen Plan's chances of success. The Battle of the Marne also destroyed any hope that the war would end quickly.

TRENCH WARFARE ON THE WESTERN FRONT

During the rest of 1914, two European fronts, the Western Front and Eastern Front, took shape. The two were very different. In the west, stalemate prevailed. Both sides were evenly matched and armed with the latest in industrial-era weaponry. Artillery, machine guns, and modern rifles had made the battlefield so deadly that traditional tactics, which involved charging the enemy, were no longer feasible. Military technology disproportionately favored the defensive. The result was trench warfare, one of the most horrific styles of combat in human history. By the end of 1914, 500 miles of trenches, bunkers, and barbed wire, separating the Germans from the Allied forces, stretched from the English Channel to the Swiss border. For the next three years, fighting on the Western Front, while exceptionally bloody, resulted in almost no movement at all. Battles such as the Battle of Verdun and the Battle of the Somme, both in 1916, rank among the most futile operations of all time, resulting in hundreds of thousands of casualties, but no useful outcome.

Ordinary life in the trenches could be almost as miserable as combat. Mud, lice, rats, disease, and the smell of dead bodies all combined to make the trench experience maddeningly terrible. Eloquent descriptions of trench warfare can be found in literary works such as Erich Maria Remarque's novel *All Quiet on the Western Front*, Robert Graves's autobiographical *Goodbye to All That*, and the work of Britain's so-called war poets (Robert Owen, Siegfried Sassoon, Stephen Spender, and others). Not until 1917 and 1918 did tactical changes and new weaponry (such as tanks and airplanes) start to bring an end to the painful stalemate of trench warfare.

THE EASTERN FRONT

Fighting on the Eastern Front was very different from that in the west. The front was much longer, extending well over a thousand miles. It was much more fluid, and battles were decisive. Serbia fell to the Austrians. After some initial setbacks, the Germans and Austrians moved quickly and efficiently against the Russians, killing, wounding, and capturing millions of them. The Central Powers also took hundreds of thousands of square miles of Russian territory. From the beginning, the Russians found themselves in terrible trouble. The fact that Bulgaria and the Ottoman Empire joined the war on the side of the Central Powers meant that Russia was cut off from its allies and had to fight the war without supplies or assistance. By 1917, Russia was nearing the end of its capacity to fight.

NAVAL WARFARE AND THE USE OF SUBMARINES

Considering that the naval race between Britain and Germany had been one of the underlying causes of the war, it was ironic that there were almost no traditional, ship-to-ship naval battles during World War I. Britain's Royal Navy imposed a blockade on Germany and Austria. In response, Germany made use of its most effective naval weapon: the submarine, or U-boat. The submarine enabled the German navy to do tremendous economic damage to Britain, which, as an island nation, was at risk of running out of food. However, submarine warfare carried with it the danger of destroying neutral ships or killing civilians from neutral countries, so it was a diplomatically risky course of action. Over time, Germany's success with submarine warfare would backfire, bringing the United States into the war in 1917.

THE GLOBAL DIMENSIONS OF WORLD WAR I

The war also took on a global dimension. The war had begun largely because of empire, and its effects spread to Europe's colonies. Many of Britain's former colonies, now imperial dominions, including Canada, Australia, New Zealand, and South Africa, declared war on the Central Powers and took an active part in European and Middle Eastern combat.

France and Britain mobilized native troops in Africa. Although most of them played a support role, performing construction and garrison duties, some saw combat in the skirmishing that took place in Africa against German colonial troops. The French also brought African troops to the Western Front (in a classic instance of stereotyped prejudice, the Germans feared these soldiers as cannibals). According to one estimate, more than 2.5 million Africans (almost 2 percent of the total population) were involved in the war effort in some way. Britain also mobilized Indian sepoys, Sikhs, and Nepalese Gurkhas for combat in the Middle East.

The fighting itself spread beyond Europe, as well. There were clashes in Africa, including the German colony of Togoland. Japan joined the Allied war effort, then took over Germany's island colonies in the Pacific. Australia seized German New Guinea. The most important non-European theater of war was the Middle East. In 1915, the British, using Australian and New Zealand troops, tried to knock Ottoman Turkey out of the war by landing at Gallipoli, southwest of Istanbul. This campaign proved to be an utter disaster, resulting in 50 percent casualties (and the disgrace of Winston Churchill, whose idea the campaign had been).

More successful was the effort of the officer T. E. Lawrence, better known as Lawrence of Arabia, who persuaded Arab princes to rise up against their Ottoman masters. By 1917 and 1918, the British, in conjunction with their Arab allies, were able to dismantle what was left of the Ottomans' Middle Eastern empire. Before that, however, in 1915, the Ottoman Empire carried out the twentieth century's first campaign of genocide, massacring somewhere between 500,000 and 2 million Armenians.

THE WAR'S LAST STAGES: 1917 AND 1918

The year 1917 was a crucial turning point in several ways. By that time, all the original European combatants were exhausted by the fighting. Frustrated by the stalemate and its inability to win surface battles at sea, the German navy turned more and more to unrestricted submarine warfare, hoping to starve Britain out of the war. Economically, the U-boat campaign worked: by the spring of 1917, Britain was reduced to a six-week food supply. Diplomatically, however, submarine warfare was a disaster, because it caused the Germans to sink ships from the United States, which was neutral, but increasingly sympathetic to the Allies. American opinion turned even more against Germany with the revelation of the Zimmerman telegram, in which Germany tried to convince Mexico to declare war on the United States. In April 1917, the United States declared war on Germany.

On the other hand, Russia was collapsing. The tsarist regime fell in March, and although the new government attempted to continue the war effort, the Russian army was in full retreat and suffering mass desertions. When Vladimir Lenin and the Bolsheviks staged their Communist takeover of Russia in October–November 1917, they immediately took steps to pull their country out of the war. Germany was now free to send large numbers of troops to the Western Front, where the balance of force was already razor thin.

The last year of the war—late 1917 to late 1918—was, therefore, a great military race. The Allies' goal was to get American soldiers across the Atlantic (with German U-boats sinking troop ships) and ready for combat. The German goal was to transfer soldiers from the Eastern Front to the Western Front and use these reinforcements to knock the weary French and British out of the war before the Americans arrived in large numbers. Whichever side could accomplish its goal first would win the war, and it was not clear until the summer of 1918 which side would prevail.

Realizing that time was against them, the Germans launched a massive offensive against northern France, hoping to take Paris, in the spring of 1918. As in 1914, this attack was halted by a determined stand at the Marne River. During the summer, American, Canadian, British, and French troops started to push the Germans back. In the fall, the Germans were in full retreat, all the way to the French border. In early November, strikes and mutinies convinced the Austrian and German governments to surrender. World War I came to an end on November 11, 1918.

THE HOME FRONT

WORLD WAR I AS TOTAL WAR

World War I was a total war, meaning that it required nations to involve their populations and mobilize their resources completely in order to carry on the fight. The last such war in the Western world had been the U.S. Civil War (1861–1865). Europe itself had not experienced such a conflict since the days of Napoleon. Against all their expectations, the nations of Europe—and, to a lesser extent, the United States—found that World War I affected their civilian populations deeply and directly. The home front became a crucial part of every combatant's war effort.

CONSCRIPTION

The most immediately noticeable way in which the home front was affected involved conscription. Even before the war, most European powers had armies of 1 million to 2 million men, larger than ever before in history. But even those numbers did not suffice. Even in Britain, which had a long tradition of maintaining an all-volunteer army, substantial conscription was called for. Eventually, the belligerent nations of World War I drafted more than 70 million men.

ECONOMIC MOBILIZATION AND RATIONING

Entire economies had to be geared for war as well. Industrial wartime production required enormous amounts of raw material: iron, steel, petroleum, rubber, cloth, and much more. The workforce needed to turn out uniforms, weapons, tanks, aircraft, ships, and other wartime necessities was immense. Agricultural production had to be stepped up, in order to feed armies and civilian populations. With so many able-bodied men gone to fight, the strain put on civilian populations—especially women—to keep national economies functioning was incredible. All major combatants centralized their economies somewhat, placing even private enterprise at least somewhat under state control. Food, strategic materials, and consumer goods were rationed, and the rationing grew stricter as time passed.

By the end of 1916 and early 1917, all European nations were suffering terrible shortages. Britain's food supply was almost depleted during Germany's campaign of unrestricted submarine warfare. Germany and Austria experienced the so-called turnip winter in 1916–1917. Russia, cut off from outside help and supplies by Germany and the Ottoman Empire, was so lacking in food and equipment that, by the end of 1916, its soldiers were being sent to the front barefoot and unarmed. They were told to scavenge boots and rifles from soldiers who had died in battle.

RESTRICTIONS ON CIVIL LIBERTIES

Another domestic effect of the war was a certain curtailment of civil liberties, even in democratic nations like Britain, France, and America. All countries imposed censorship on the press, the mass media, and even the mails. Those suspected of espionage or treason could be arrested, tried, and sentenced without due process. In most countries, all political parties agreed to unite behind the war effort and refrain from criticism of the government. Even pessimism or an insufficient display of patriotism could bring a person under suspicion.

WOMEN AND THE WAR EFFORT

Perhaps the most striking effect the war had on the home front involved the role of women. With so many men serving in the armed forces, farms, factories, and workplaces of all types were left understaffed, just as wartime economic pressures required greater, not lesser, production. In all major countries, women stepped up to take the place of men in the workplace. They served as truck drivers, farmhands, factory workers, munitions workers, and in other occupations of all types.

The economic contribution of women to their countries' war efforts was considerable. In Britain, more than 1.35 million women who had never worked before took jobs. In the factories of Germany's most important arms producer, Krupp, women made up 38 percent of the workforce. Even France, highly resistant to the notion of giving women equal rights, granted a minimum wage to female textile workers producing uniforms.

THE PARIS PEACE CONFERENCE

After the war, peace terms were decided at the Paris Peace Conference, which lasted from 1919 to 1920. All decisions were made by the leaders of the victorious Allied nations. All delegates from the defeated Central Powers were excluded. The major players were President Woodrow Wilson of the United States, Prime Minister David Lloyd George of Britain, Premier Georges Clemenceau of France, and Prime Minister Vittorio Orlando of Italy. The Allies drew up five treaties, one for each defeated power: Germany, Austria, Hungary, Bulgaria, and the Ottoman Empire. The most important was the Treaty of Versailles, the agreement reached with Germany and signed on June 28, 1919.

DIPLOMATIC DISAGREEMENTS AMONG THE ALLIED LEADERS

The Paris Peace Conference was characterized by a clash between American idealism and the European Allies' thirst for revenge. As he arrived from America, Wilson's sincere desire was, in his words, to "make the world safe for democracy" and prevent war in the future. These goals were reflected in his famous Fourteen Points, which called for an end to secret treaties, freedom of the seas, free trade, arms reduction, decolonization, the rearrangement of European borders according to the "self-determination" of national groups, and the establishment of an international dispute-resolution body called the League of Nations.

By contrast, Lloyd George and, even more so, Clemenceau, desired to make Germany pay for the war. France also feared Germany, even in defeat, and wanted to keep it from rising up again as a threat to European peace. Italy wanted the Austrian land and German colonies it had been promised by Britain and France. All of the European victors were adamantly opposed to Wilson's goal of decolonization.

THE TERMS OF THE TREATIES

The treaties that resulted were the product of bitter negotiation and compromise. As Wilson wished, the League of Nations was formed. Ironically, since the U.S. Congress did not ratify the treaty that formed it, America never joined it. This decision helped make the League of Nations extremely weak. Many of the other Fourteen Points were discarded or watered down. Taken together, the main points laid out in the five treaties signed by the end of the Paris Peace Conference included

- *Dismantling of Austria-Hungary:* The Habsburg Empire was destroyed. Austria and Hungary became two separate states, and each of them lost a great deal of territory.
- *New nations:* Mainly out of Habsburg territory, but also out of lands lost by Germany and Russia, new countries were created. These included Yugoslavia ("Land of the South Slavs"), Czechoslovakia, Poland, Finland, Latvia, Lithuania, and Estonia. This was done in accordance with Wilson's principle of self-determination.
- *Italy and Austria:* Italy received some of the Austrian territory it had been promised, but not all of it. It gained part of the Tyrol, but not the lands on the Adriatic coast it craved.

- *Population transfer in the Balkans:* Thousands of Turks living in southeastern Europe were expelled and sent to the Ottoman Empire. Likewise, large numbers of Greeks living in the Ottoman Empire were forced to move to Greece.
- *The Middle East:* The Ottoman Empire was stripped of its Middle Eastern possessions, especially the Arab lands. They were placed under temporary French and British control, according to a mandate system (the League of Nations would help supervise these areas, which were to be prepared for eventual independence). This stipulation greatly disappointed the Arabs, who had expected freedom in exchange for their military assistance against the Ottomans during the war. Britain also assumed control over Palestine. In the Balfour Declaration of 1917, Britain had agreed in principle to the creation of a Jewish homeland in Palestine. However, it delayed indefinitely on this question, in order to avoid antagonizing Arabs throughout the Middle East.

GERMANY AND THE TREATY OF VERSAILLES

The most important provisions pertained to Germany. The Treaty of Versailles imposed the following terms:

- *War guilt:* According to the infamous Article 231, Germany was assigned full blame for the war (a review of the causes of World War I should remind the reader that, although Germany deserved a good part of the blame for the war, other nations, such as Serbia and Austria, did much to start it as well). Article 231 was used as justification for the many heavy punishments that the Treaty of Versailles imposed on Germany.
- *Loss of territory:* Germany lost approximately 13 percent of its territory, amounting to 25,000 square miles. This had been home to 6 million people. The provinces of Alsace and Lorraine were given to France. Other provinces went to Denmark, Belgium, and Poland. France and Belgium were allowed to occupy the resource-rich Saar until 1935. The Rhineland, the borderland between France and Germany, was also to be occupied till 1935. Furthermore, it was to be maintained as a demilitarized zone in perpetuity.
- *Loss of colonies:* All of Germany's colonies were stripped from it. They were placed under Allied trusteeship. Only Woodrow Wilson's efforts prevented France and Britain from colonizing them outright.
- *Disarmament:* France and Britain feared a resurgent German army and navy, and therefore disarmed them. Germany was allowed to have a token force of only 100,000 soldiers. It was not permitted to have any military aircraft, submarines, battleships, or heavy artillery.
- *War payments:* Against Wilson's wishes, France and Britain insisted that Germany pay the full cost of the war. This was calculated to be $32 billion. According to the initial repayment schedule (which was later changed several times), Germany would have been making war payments until 1961.

In general, the Paris Peace Conference has to be regarded as having produced a flawed peace. Greed and revenge determined many of the terms of settlement. Ignorance, especially regarding eastern Europe and the Balkans, where the newly created regimes tended to be unstable and weak, played a large role in redrawing the world map. Justified or not, the harsh treatment of Germany, especially the imposition of such heavy economic terms, would make the peace absolutely unacceptable to most Germans, and would be a significant factor in the rise of Hitler and the beginning of World War II twenty years later.

LONG-TERM CONSEQUENCES

STATISTICAL COSTS OF WORLD WAR I

The grim short-term consequences of the war were obvious: 10 million soldiers killed, somewhere between 3 million and 5 million civilians killed, and 28 million to 30 million people wounded. Financially, the cost of the war was $32 billion, or $400 billion in contemporary prices. Countless people, particularly in eastern Europe, where borders shifted constantly during the end of the war and the early 1920s, were made homeless or even stateless. As a final injury, a global epidemic of Spanish flu struck during the closing months of the war. Then and shortly afterward, the Spanish flu killed almost 20 million people worldwide.

LONG-TERM CONSEQUENCES OF WORLD WAR I

The long-term consequences were as follows:

- *Destruction of eastern and central European empires:* The German, Austro-Hungarian, Russian, and Ottoman empires had all fallen.
- *Communism in Russia:* The tsarist regime was replaced by the Soviet Union, a communist state.
- *Instability in eastern Europe:* With few exceptions, the new nations of eastern Europe were inexperienced and weak. Nationalist tensions within many of them were high. During the 1920s and 1930s, only Czechoslovakia would prosper economically and remain democratic. The others experienced economic difficulties, became politically authoritarian, suffered from interethnic strife, or some combination of all these.
- *Social and political transformation:* Although World War I did not cause this trend, it helped to accelerate it. Even before the war, the political power, social influence, and economic clout of the traditional aristocracy had been vanishing, while that of the middle and lower classes had been rising. In almost all countries of Europe—and even elsewhere—the war did much to complete this transformation.
- *Further industrialization and modernization of European economies.*
- *Women's suffrage:* Thanks largely to the economic role they played during the war, when they proved they could do "man's work," women gained a great deal of respect, not just in the workplace, but in the public sphere overall. Perhaps the most important result of this was that, in most Western nations, women gained the vote during or just after World War I. This happened in Scandinavia, the Low Countries, Russia, Britain, the United States, and elsewhere. France and Italy were alone among the major Western powers in resisting this trend; not until the 1940s did French and Italian women get the vote.
- *German resentment:* Almost all Germans regarded the Treaty of Versailles as unfair. Many saw it as altogether illegitimate. Anger about the war payments was universal. Years later, this attitude played an important role in the rise of Hitler and the outbreak of World War II.
- *General decline in European economic and global power:* Although the nations of Europe were still able to maintain the appearance of great powers, they had been badly drained by World War I. Even the victors' economies were in distress, and those of the losers were in shambles. Countries like France, Britain, Belgium, Portugal, and the Netherlands still possessed their overseas empires, but maintaining control over them would become increasingly difficult during the 1920s and 1930s, and even more so after World War II.
- *Sense of uncertainty and anxiety in European culture:* Even before World War I, the prevailing faith in progress that had characterized Europe's cultural and intellectual life during most of the 1800s had been waning (see Chapter 20). The destruction and despair caused by the war, not to mention the gloom surrounding Europe's clear political and economic comedown,

only made this sense of uncertainty and anxiety worse, bringing it to the forefront of European culture.

QUICK REVIEW

1. Which of the following events could BEST be used as evidence to support the argument that Germany was to blame for World War I?

   (A) the assassination of Francis Ferdinand
   (B) the harshness of the Austrian ultimatum to Serbia
   (C) the Germans' "blank check" to Austria
   (D) the Anglo-German naval race
   (E) the Zimmerman telegram

2. Which of the following BEST describes the Schlieffen Plan?

   (A) a massive attack on and rapid defeat of France, then a single-front war with Russia
   (B) a massive attack on and rapid defeat of Russia, then a single-front war with France
   (C) the devotion of equal force and attention to France and Russia at the same time
   (D) a total focus on the strategic threat posed by Britain's Royal Navy
   (E) a flanking move directed against Serbia, which might otherwise knock Austria out of the war

3. Where was the Germans' initial drive toward Paris halted?

   (A) the Aisne
   (B) Verdun
   (C) the Somme
   (D) Ypres
   (E) the Marne

4. Which of the following is most true about combat on the Western and Eastern fronts?

   (A) Fighting on the Eastern Front degenerated into stalemate, whereas conditions on the Western Front were much more fluid.
   (B) Fighting on the Western Front degenerated into stalemate, whereas conditions on the Eastern Front were much more fluid.
   (C) Conditions on both fronts were roughly the same.
   (D) The level of technology on the Eastern Front was significantly higher than on the Western Front.
   (E) There were no aircraft used on the Eastern Front.

5. What was the most useful type of naval vessel deployed during World War I?

   (A) the battleship
   (B) the battle cruiser
   (C) the submarine
   (D) the destroyer
   (E) the aircraft carrier

6. Which of the following non-European peoples served with the Allies during World War I?

   (A) the Gurkhas
   (B) the Hereros
   (C) the Navajo
   (D) the Hottentots
   (E) the Montagnards

7. What British guerrilla leader captured the world's imagination by stirring up Arab revolt against the Ottoman Empire?

  (A) D. H. Lawrence
  (B) Edmund Allenby
  (C) Winston Churchill
  (D) T. E. Lawrence
  (E) Richard Francis Burton

8. Besides submarine warfare, what factor helped to induce the United States to declare war on Germany?

  (A) Germany's attempt to persuade Mexico to declare war on the United States
  (B) German atrocities in Belgium
  (C) German mistreatment of French and British prisoners of war
  (D) Germany's mass slaughter of Slavs and Gypsies in eastern Europe
  (E) Germany's threats to occupy Cuba and Puerto Rico

9. What best describes the relationship between Woodrow Wilson and his fellow Allied leaders, Georges Clemenceau and David Lloyd George, at the Paris Peace Conference?

  (A) Out of gratitude, Clemenceau and Lloyd George agreed to almost all of Wilson's proposals.
  (B) Wilson opposed most of the so-called Fourteen Points supported by Clemenceau and Lloyd George.
  (C) Wilson's thirst for revenge clashed with the lofty idealism of Clemenceau and Lloyd George.
  (D) Clemenceau's and Lloyd George's thirst for revenge clashed with the lofty idealism of Wilson.
  (E) Clemenceau and Lloyd George vetoed Wilson's plan for a League of Nations, but readily agreed to decolonize the French and British empires.

10. After the Paris Peace Conference, Arab leaders

  (A) were content with their new-found independence
  (B) were frustrated by the limited autonomy granted them as mandate states
  (C) were overjoyed by the Balfour Declaration
  (D) were grateful to the Turkish government for standing up on behalf of the Middle East at the conference
  (E) were angry that Middle Eastern affairs had not been discussed at all during the conference

ANSWERS:

1. **C**, p. 353	6. **A**, p. 356
2. **A**, p. 354	7. **D**, p. 356
3. **E**, p. 354	8. **A**, p. 356
4. **B**, p. 355	9. **D**, p. 358
5. **C**, p. 355	10. **B**, p. 359

CHAPTER 29

The Twenty Years' Crisis: The World During the Interwar Period

Many historians have argued that World War I and World War II were simply two halves of the same conflict, separated by twenty years of temporary peace. Whatever the truth of that observation, it is undeniable that the peace that prevailed during the 1920s and 1930s rested on an extremely shaky foundation.

This was certainly the case in Europe, where many of the problems that had been stirred up by World War I were not solved by the treaty settlements that followed. Also, the social, economic, and political forces unleashed by twentieth-century modernization were often too strong for many governments—especially those that had been damaged badly by the war, or those that had just been created by the Paris Peace Conference—to handle. Another factor that affected the fortunes of Europe during the interwar period was the Great Depression. Starting in the United States in October 1929, the Depression began to affect the economies of Europe by 1930 to 1931. The Depression damaged beyond repair many economies and regimes that had already been struggling during the 1920s. As a result, extremism and dictatorship became the rule, not the exception, in European politics during the 1930s.

Elsewhere in the world, powerful political developments were under way. Revolution, modernization, and industrialization caught up with many countries that had not experienced those trends during the 1800s. European colonies in Africa, Asia, and the Middle East began to agitate more actively than ever before for freedom. Nationalism, dictatorship, and militarism became part of political life in much of the non-Western world.

Finally, by the mid-to-late 1930s, the storm clouds of war were gathering. Japanese aggression in Asia, along with German and Italian belligerence in Europe, made it more likely with every passing year that a major conflict would break out. The failure of the Western democracies to prevent such a conflict only served to demonstrate how fragile the peace of the interwar period had been.

POLITICAL EXTREMISM AND ECONOMIC DEPRESSION IN EUROPE

THE FRAGILE PEACE OF THE 1920s

During the 1920s, peace prevailed in Europe, but it was fragile. Also, at the beginning of the decade, peace was not yet complete. From 1919 through 1922, there were revolutions, civil wars, and military clashes in Germany, Russia, Poland, Hungary, and the Balkans. Even afterward, peace was preserved mainly by the fact that European nations were too weak and exhausted to fight. Established at the Paris Peace Conference, the League of Nations provided what little political leadership there was. The League was well-meaning, and accomplished a great deal of humanitarian work. But it was largely ineffective. It had few powers of enforcement. Also, the United States, the strongest and richest country in the world following World War I, refused to join.

Despite a number of treaties during the 1920s that were intended to outlaw war completely (such as the Treaty of Locarno and the Kellogg-Briand Pact), there was very little political will on the part of liberal democracies to take the necessary steps to ensure long-term peace. During the 1920s, the absence of any real threat to peace created the illusion that a permanent state of peace had been reached. That illusion would be shattered during the 1930s.

THE WANING OF DEMOCRACY IN INTERWAR EUROPE

In general, the 1920s and 1930s were not good years for democracy in Europe. In 1920, after the conclusion of the Paris Peace Conference, there were 23 governments in Europe that could be considered democratic. By 1939, on the eve of World War II, there were only 12. Most of the new states of central and eastern Europe fell victim to political extremism, especially during the 1930s, when inflation and, especially, mass unemployment caused by the Great Depression made it difficult to maintain a healthy form of government. Right-wing dictatorship, as well as ethnic discrimination and class tensions, plagued this part of Europe during these years. As described presently, the most famous of these dictatorships emerged in Italy and Germany.

Even in the stronger and better-established democracies, France and Great Britain, times were troubled. During the comparatively easier decade of the 1920s, the economies of both these countries, especially Britain's, were weak, as a result of the draining effect of World War I. Both countries had borrowed a great deal of money from the United States, and relied on German war reparations to make their own payments to the United States. Unemployment, strikes, and deficits became the norm in France during the early 1920s, and in Britain during the entire decade.

The 1930s were even worse, because of the Depression. By 1932, one British worker in four was out of work. France was not as badly hurt as Britain, but it went through hard times as well. Particularly during the 1930s, both democracies suffered from weak political leadership. In Britain, no single party could provide firm governance, and a weak coalition, the National Government, ran Parliament with caution and compromise. Over the course of the decades, the basic elements of a modern welfare state—social security, pensions, unemployment insurance, and so on—were put into place. In France, elections were frequent, and leadership passed from left to right and back again on a regular basis. In both countries, economic weakness and political mediocrity made it more difficult for France and Britain to cope with the growing threat of Hitler's Germany during the 1930s.

COMMUNISM IN THE SOVIET UNION

Unfortunately, the general crisis of democracy in interwar Europe meant that the strongest and most dynamic regimes tended to be the dictatorships, which grew in number and power during the 1920s and especially the 1930s. The first of these new dictatorships to be established was the Union of Soviet Socialist Republics (USSR), or the Soviet Union. This was the communist regime that rose to power during World War I, in October–November 1917. When the tsarist regime of Nicholas II fell in February–March 1917 (see Chapter 28), its place was taken briefly by a moderate Provisional Government that attempted to continue the war against Germany, solve Russia's dismal economic problems, and establish a democratic government. In the fact that its first stage was relatively liberal, the Russian Revolution resembled the French Revolution of 1789.

However, the Provisional Government did not satisfy the desire of the vast majority of the Russian population (80 percent of whom were peasants) for economic stability, land reform, and peace. The party that benefited most from popular discontent was the Russian Communist Party, or Bolsheviks, led by Vladimir Lenin and his second-in-command, Leon Trotsky.

In the fall of 1917, Lenin and Trotsky overthrew the Provisional Government. From then until 1921, they pulled out of World War I, formed the Soviet government, and fought and won the terrible Russian Civil War (which pitted the Bolshevik Red Army against their anticommunist enemies, called Whites). From 1921 till his death in 1924, Lenin tightened his grip on power and attempted to modernize the Soviet Union along Marxist lines. One of his major challenges was that, while Marx had predicted that communist revolution would first take place in a mature capitalist society with a large industrial working class, Russia was a backward, barely capitalist nation with a huge peasantry, but an extremely small working class.

Lenin died in 1924. A half-decade succession struggle followed, during which Joseph Stalin defeated Leon Trotsky for control over the Soviet government. Stalin became one of the most brutal dictators of all time. Even more rapidly and intensely than Lenin had, Stalin modernized the USSR, starting in 1928. His Five-Year Plans were intended to transform the Soviet Union from an overwhelmingly agricultural society into a modern industrial state. The collectivization of agriculture—the placement of all peasants on state-run farms—was meant to rationalize farming, increase governmental control over the countryside, and harness the labor of the peasants (profits generated by agriculture were used to pay for the Five-Year Plans).

Although the USSR did modernize under Stalin, the price was steep. The Five-Year Plans were similar to a state-sponsored industrial revolution, with much of the same social and economic trauma, applied with tremendous ruthlessness. Collectivization resulted in a great famine in southern Russia and Ukraine that killed approximately 4 million to 6 million people. Later in the 1930s, Stalin carried out a huge campaign of terror, the Great Purges, which resulted in the execution of at least 1 million people and the arrest and exile to labor camps (gulags) of at least 5 million to 7 million. Like most modern dictators, Stalin also used propaganda to indoctrinate his subjects and instituted an extravagant cult of personality to glorify himself. The Stalinist experience is an extreme example of how rapid modernization, brought about from above by dictatorial leadership, can both benefit and torment a country.

FASCISM IN ITALY

In Italy, dictatorship came from the right. After World War I, Italy was rocked by economic depression and political turmoil. Strikes, communist agitation, and constant turnover in the government brought the country to the edge of chaos. The middle and upper classes, frightened of social breakdown and left-wing revolution, looked for a strong leader to restore stability. They turned to Benito Mussolini, the right-wing, anticommunist leader of the Fascist Party.

Fascism, Mussolini's invention, is a difficult political concept to define. It can best be described as right-wing radicalism or revolution from the right. This makes it different from ordinary right-wing conservatism, which seeks to prevent change. Fascism seeks to bring about change. It is anticommunist, but also anticapitalist and antidemocratic. Fascism is also often characterized by hypernationalism and a state-sponsored campaign of racial and ethnic bigotry.

In October 1922, after his March on Rome, Mussolini convinced King Victor Emmanuel III to place him in charge of the government.

For the next twenty-one years, Mussolini would govern Italy, becoming increasingly dictatorial. Mussolini coined a new term to describe his style of rule: totalitarianism, a twentieth-century form of dictatorship in which the regime, using modern technology and bureaucracy, attempts to control every aspect of its subjects' lives. Compared to other totalitarian rulers, such as Stalin and Hitler, Mussolini was a mild dictator. Still, he imposed censorship and controls over culture, placed political enemies and dissidents in prison, used propaganda to create a cult of personality, and had thousands of people killed.

On the other hand, Mussolini also tried to modernize Italy. He built modern highways, sponsored literacy campaigns, fought the Mafia, and brought medicine and technology to backward parts of his country. His chief claim to fame was to have made Italy's notoriously inefficient trains run on time. His economic policy was based on the principle of syndicalism, a form of state-controlled capitalism in which labor unions were completely suppressed. In fascist economies, corporate leaders, rather than practicing free trade, are required to cooperate directly with the government. For a time, during the 1920s, Mussolini was considered by many to be an effective, even admirable, leader, despite his dictatorial tendencies. During the 1930s, however, the Depression undercut his modernizing efforts. He became more dictatorial and, in foreign policy, more aggressive (see Chapter 30). Also during the 1930s, Mussolini drew closer to the new fascist-style regime to emerge in Europe: Nazi Germany.

NAZISM IN GERMANY

Germany's road to dictatorship was longer than Italy's, and the results were infinitely worse. From 1919 to 1933, Germany was governed by a democratic regime, the Weimar Republic, which replaced the empire of the kaisers. The Weimar Republic was dogged by economic trouble (hyperinflation during the early 1920s wiped out the value of the German mark), the burden of war payments, widespread resentment of the Treaty of Versailles (which the Weimar regime had been forced to sign), crushed national pride because of defeat in World War I, and the rise of extremist political parties.

From the left, the German Communist Party became a powerful threat. From the right, there appeared Adolf Hitler's Nazi Party: an anticommunist, antidemocratic party that, after Mussolini's rise to power in Italy, consciously imitated fascism in many ways. The Nazi Party was also obsessed with the notion of racial purity. They hated all minorities, but especially Jews, whom they viewed as "subhuman" and the source of all of Germany's troubles. In 1923, Hitler and the Nazis made a failed attempt to take over the German government. During the short time he spent in prison afterward, Hitler wrote his infamous memoir, *Mein Kampf* (*My Struggle*).

By the late 1920s, it seemed that the Weimar Republic had solved most of its problems and established a reasonably solid democracy in Germany. The Depression, however, ended all of that. The effects of the Depression reached Germany in 1930. By 1932, 6 million Germans—40 percent of the workforce—were unemployed. Industrial production plummeted by 40 percent. The economic pain gave a political boost to Germany's extremist parties, the Communists and the Nazis, destroying the Weimar Republic's ability to govern moderately and democratically. A series of elections in 1932 made the Nazi Party the largest in Germany. In January 1933, Hitler was appointed chancellor of Germany.

Having risen to power by legal means, Hitler established himself as an absolute dictator within months. In February 1933, the Reichstag building, seat of the German government, was burned down. Hitler took advantage of the resulting panic to declare a state of emergency and pass the Enabling Act (March 1933), which suspended the Weimar constitution and gave Hitler the power to rule by decree for four years (a limit Hitler had no intention of obeying).

With blinding speed, Hitler outlawed all other political parties (especially his archenemies, the Communists), took control of the press and mass media, banned labor unions, imposed a system of state capitalism similar to Mussolini's, built concentration camps such as Dachau for political opponents and dissidents, and established a secret police, the Gestapo. He managed to end German unemployment by means of a giant program of public works and highway building, as well as a massive increase in arms production.

The Nazi regime also began to act against the Jews and other racial "undesirables." Jews were forced out of various professions (such as law, civil service, and university teaching), their businesses were boycotted, and they were physically harassed. Before World War II, the most drastic official measures taken against the Jews were the Nuremberg Laws of 1935. These stripped German Jews of their citizenship and forbade Jews and German non-Jews to marry or have sexual relations of any kind.

In terms of foreign policy, Hitler pursued a highly aggressive diplomatic line. As described in Chapter 30, Hitler's belligerence was the principal reason that the fragile peace of the 1920s began to shatter during the 1930s.

NATIONALISM AND MODERNIZATION IN THE MIDDLE EAST

Even before World War I, the Middle East had been on the threshold of great change. Modernization was coming to the Ottoman Empire, thanks to the actions of the Young Turks. Secularization, science, and technology were becoming a more important part of modern life. In those parts of the Middle East that were controlled by outside powers, the force of nationalism was rising. Then, by toppling the Ottoman Empire, World War I brought even greater changes to the region.

THE YOUNG TURKS, WORLD WAR I, AND THE COLLAPSE OF THE OTTOMAN EMPIRE

The transformation of the Ottoman Empire into the modern Turkish state had its roots in the efforts of the Young Turks, who had seized power in 1908 (see Chapter 23). These pro-Western, modernizing officers and politicians had already started to carry out reform before World War I. During the war, the Turks joined the Central Powers and thus shared defeat with Germany and Austria. The Ottoman Empire suffered more than 300,000 casualties and saw their Middle Eastern possessions, stirred up by the British adventurer Lawrence of Arabia, rise in revolt. It surrendered in October 1918.

ATATURK AND THE BIRTH OF MODERN TURKEY

After the war, the Turks lost most of their Middle Eastern territories to France and Britain (discussed presently). Greece, with Allied permission, was threatening to seize Turkey's western provinces. In the midst of this crisis, a new leader emerged: Mustafa Kemal, a colonel who had fought bravely against the British landing at Gallipoli in 1915. Kemal formed a new government in the city of Ankara, drove the Greeks from the Turkish mainland, and negotiated a new treaty with the Allies. In 1923, the last sultan fled the country. The Ottoman Empire was no more. In its place, Kemal established the Turkish Republic and became its first president. He took the title Ataturk, meaning "father of the Turks."

From 1923 till his death in 1938, Ataturk labored to create a modern, secular state in Turkey. He wrote a constitution, and, despite the fact that he was quite authoritarian, he made the pretense of acting like a democratic ruler. Industrialization, Western dress, and Western education were encouraged. Turkish was written in the Roman alphabet. Church and state were separated, and *shar'ia*, the Islamic law code, was replaced by a European legal system. Women were no longer required to wear the veil. They received the right to vote in 1934, and they were encouraged to become educated and join the workforce. To this day, Turkey's status as the most Westernized, most secular state in the Middle East, next to Israel, is a direct legacy of Ataturk's policies.

PERSIAN INDEPENDENCE AND MODERNIZATION

Persia went through a change similar to that of Turkey, becoming the modern state of Iran. From 1794 to 1925, Persia was ruled by the Qajar dynasty. In reality, however, the country had been divided into two spheres of influence: Russian in the north, British in the south. After World War I, the British presence in Persia increased. Its strong presence had much to do with the fact that oil had been discovered there shortly before the war, in 1908. Resentment of foreign domination grew steadily, and a nationalist backlash was inevitable. In 1921, an army officer named Reza Khan led a mutiny against the Qajar rulers. He also expelled the British. By 1925, he had gained control of the country. He now called himself Reza Shah Pahlavi, establishing a new royal dynasty. Like Mustafa Kemal Ataturk in Turkey, Reza reformed his country, which he renamed Iran. Although he was not as much a foe of the Islamic clergy as Ataturk was, he westernized Iran, boosted education, did away with the veil for women, and, in general, secularized the nation. He was quite authoritarian.

EGYPT, NORTH AFRICA, AND ARABIA

The political fate of the rest of the Middle East was mixed. Egypt and North Africa remained in British, French, and Italian hands, although nationalist sentiment there was growing. For the time being, the Arabian peninsula remained under Turkish control. The other Arab states that had been under Ottoman rulership before the war ended up under French and British control. Because there was no single Arab nation, the Arab lands were divided into mandates, or states that would be supervised partially by the League of Nations. Syria and Lebanon were assigned to France, and Iraq, Jordan, and Palestine fell to Britain.

This arrangement angered most Arabs, who had thought that, by helping the British fight the Turks during World War I, they would gain full independence afterward. Another thing that enraged the Arabs was the Balfour Declaration of 1917, which publicly stated the British government's intention to create a Jewish homeland in Palestine—whose population, during the late 1910s, was 90 percent Arab.

Change came to all these areas during the 1920s and 1930s. Despite the fact that the British allowed only limited Jewish emigration to Palestine, in order to keep from provoking the Arabs, thousands of Jews flooded into the region, many of them illegally. By 1939, the Jewish proportion of the population had risen from 10 to 30 percent.

During the early 1920s, the Arab prince Ibn Saud drove the Ottomans out of the Arabian peninsula. Over the next decade, Ibn Saud united the many Arabian tribes living in the region. In 1932, he founded the kingdom of Saudi Arabia. As the only major Arab state that enjoyed full independence, Saudi Arabia was important in and of itself. However, it became immensely more important after 1938, when Standard Oil, the U.S. corporation, discovered huge oil reserves at Dahran. Almost overnight, Saudi Arabia became wealthy and strategically vital.

MILITARISM AND REVOLUTION IN ASIA

SUN YAT-SEN AND THE BIRTH OF THE CHINESE REPUBLIC

Just prior to World War I, in 1911, revolution in China had overthrown the imperial dynasty of the Qing. In its place was the Chinese Republic, governed by the Nationalist (Kuomintang) Party. Sun Yat-sen, often regarded as the father of modern China, was president.

YUAN SHIKAI AND THE DISINTEGRATION OF THE CHINESE REPUBLIC

Quickly, however, the republic disintegrated. In 1912, Sun was forced to give up the presidency to General Yuan Shikai, in order to gain the support of the armed forces. In the face of Yuan's growing traditionalism and dictatorialism, Sun and the Kuomintang found themselves in opposition to the government. In 1913, Yuan disbanded the Kuomintang-dominated parliament. In response, the Kuomintang began a revolution. It failed, and Sun fled to Japan. Yuan ruled until his death in 1916. Military officers continued to govern in Beijing until the early 1920s.

The rest of China slipped into anarchy. Warlords and bandits took control of vast stretches of the country. In 1920, Sun and the Nationalists returned to the mainland, establishing a base at Canton and throughout southern China. The Chinese Communist Party (CCP), founded by radicals at Beijing University in 1921, became a major force. A deadly external threat came from Japan, whose imperial ambitions grew during and after World War I. Japan already controlled Korea and had a sphere of influence in southern Manchuria. Because it had aided the Allies in World War I, Japan also had their blessing to expand that sphere after the war.

Political control was not the only issue over which these groups would struggle. During these years, there was a great clash between traditional values and the desire for modernization. The military government in Beijing attempted to revive Confucian principles, while younger students and intellectuals embraced progressive concepts such as democracy, technology, and science. The clearest example of popular activism came on May 4, 1919, when thousands of students came to Tiananmen Square in Beijing to protest against the military government. The immediate cause of the May Fourth Movement was the government's willingness to allow Japan to annex Shantung Province, Germany's former concession in China. Underlying that specific issue, however, was the desire for political and social reform. As for China's other major political actors, the CCP was progressive in its outlook, while the Kuomintang was torn between the past and the future.

THE CHINESE CIVIL WAR: NATIONALISTS VERSUS COMMUNISTS

By the mid-1920s, the real political forces in China were the Nationalists and the Communists. From 1923 through April 1927, both parties had cooperated to drive warlords and foreign powers out of China. Sun Yat-sen died of cancer, leaving the leadership of the Kuomintang to Chiang Kai-shek, a Western-educated officer who was also farther to the right than Sun had been. By early 1927, the Nationalist-Communist alliance, in its Northern Expedition, had gained control of all China south of the Yangtze River, including the major cities of Shanghai and Nanjing.

At this point, Chiang turned against the Communists. In April 1927, he murdered thousands of Communists in Shanghai. Most of the rest of the party was driven far to the north, under the revolutionary Mao Tse-tung (Mao Zedong). Chiang completed the Northern Expedition in 1928, gaining control over Beijing. That same year, he established the Nanjing Republic, a Kuomintang-dominated regime that combined Westernization with mild authoritarianism. Chiang proclaimed his allegiance to Sun's Three People's Principles, and made some attempts to create a constitutional government and an industrial economy. However, general backwardness, the foreign threat of Japanese imperialism, and warlord anarchy hampered Chiang's efforts.

Full-scale civil war against the Communists would also become a problem. Against incredible odds, Mao Tse-tung kept the CCP alive, leading it on the Long March (1934–1935), far to the north. At Yenan, the Communists established a base from which they would launch military operations against the Nationalists during the late 1930s. Mao's central strategy was to make communism appealing to China's vast peasant masses, rather than concentrating on the small industrial working class in the cities.

In 1937, Japanese forces would land on the Chinese mainland, starting a three-way conflict among China's Nationalists, Mao's Communists, and the invading Japanese.

JAPAN DURING THE 1920s

At the beginning of the twentieth century, Japan seemed to have the potential of evolving into a democratic parliamentary monarchy in the Western style. During the 1920s, the powers of the Diet increased, and political parties became more meaningfully competitive. Universal male suffrage and a bill of rights were granted in 1925. The media grew freer. The emperor, Taisho, actively supported these democratic reforms. The economy continued to industrialize and modernize.

On the other hand, traditional forces remained in place. The upper-class elite retained its oligarchical outlook. Nationalism ran high. Japan's imperial tendencies grew more intense. Even though the economy was strong and modern, most of Japan's industrial might was concentrated in the hands of a small number of corporate conglomerates called *zaibatsu*. By the 1930s, the four largest *zaibatsu* (including Mitsubishi) controlled 21 percent of banking, 35 percent of all ship-building, 38 percent of the merchant marine, and 21 percent of the mining industry. The effect of this system was to keep wealth in the hands of a tiny number of rich and powerful industrialists and capitalists, rather than benefiting the entire population. Also, because the *zaibatsu* enjoyed substantial governmental support, economic policy was largely under state influence, in a way not unlike the system of state capitalism practiced in Fascist Italy and Nazi Germany.

JAPANESE MILITARISM AND THE INVASION OF MAINLAND ASIA

Increased imperial aggression and the effects of the Great Depression derailed Japanese democratization during the 1930s. Almost overnight, Japan's exports plummeted more than 50 percent. Farmers and workers alike were badly hurt. Nationalist sentiment skyrocketed, and anti-Western feelings sharpened. The right-wing nationalist Kita Ikki became a celebrity with his slogan, "Asia for the Asians," calling for the expulsion of colonizing powers such as Britain and France from Southeast and South Asia.

In September 1931, Japan seized all of Manchuria from China, turning it into a puppet kingdom, Manchukuo, ruled by Henry Pu-yi, who had been China's last emperor before 1911. Shortly afterward, Japan withdrew from the League of Nations. In 1932, Japan's prime minister was assassinated by right-wing extremists. Moderates and leftists were persecuted informally during the mid-1930s. By 1941, the Japanese military, under Hideki Tojo, had gained control of the parliamentary government. The military was able to dominate the young emperor, Hirohito, who had taken the throne in 1926.

The Japanese began a full-scale war in Asia in 1937. After a military clash with Chinese forces at the Marco Polo Bridge in July, the Japanese decided to seize as much of mainland Asia as possible. Proclaiming a "New Order" in Asia, the Japanese invaded in full force, committing dreadful atrocities against the civilian population. The "Rape of Nanjing" in December 1937 included the massacre of 200,000 to 300,000 noncombatants, including women and children. The Japanese war against the Chinese would continue throughout the 1930s and all during World War II. In 1938 and 1939, the Japanese clashed with the Soviets on the Siberian borderland, but were turned back. The war then spread to Southeast Asia, as Japan attempted to drive out the French and British, establishing its own empire, which it referred to as the Greater East Asian Co-Prosperity Sphere.

NATIONALIST MOVEMENTS IN SOUTH AND SOUTHEAST ASIA

In South and Southeast Asia, most of which remained under British and French colonial rule, nationalists and anti-imperial aspirations became widespread. In Vietnam, Burma, Indonesia, and elsewhere, anticolonial agitation was stepped up. Typically, such an effort involved an uneasy alliance of Western-educated, middle-class modernizers with intellectuals and students inspired by the communist ideals of Marx and Lenin. It was similar to the temporary joining of the Nationalists and Communists in China—and, as in China, these alliances typically broke apart.

GANDHI, NEHRU, AND THE INDIAN NATIONAL CONGRESS

The most successful and most sustained freedom movement appeared in British-controlled India. The moving force here was the Indian National Congress (later the Congress Party), founded in 1885. After World War I, the dominant figure of the independence movement was Mohandas K. Gandhi. Because it had loyally supported Britain in World War I, mobilizing 1.2 million soldiers, India hoped it would gain greater autonomy after the war, perhaps even dominion status, like Canada, Australia, and New Zealand. But demonstrations and protests, organized largely by Gandhi, led to clashes with the British. In 1919, at Amritsar, British troops fired on unarmed protestors, killing 379 and wounding 1,137. This Amritsar massacre led to chaos. The British imposed a strict crackdown, and Gandhi went to prison.

For the rest of the 1920s, India balanced on a political knife-edge. The British began to make concessions, such as the Government of India Act (1921). The act allowed 5 million Indians to vote and created a new Parliament, in which two thirds of the members would be Indian, elected by popular vote. On the other hand, the earlier repression of the British prompted the Congress Party to demand more. India could very well have erupted into bloody revolution. That it did not was due mainly to Gandhi's political and spiritual guidance.

Whether free or in prison, Gandhi—by now known increasingly as Mahatma, or "Great Soul"—preached the policy of nonviolent resistance to British authority. Based partly on Hindu religious principles, this policy was called *satyagraha*, or "hold to the truth." An example of *satyagraha* in action came when the British imposed a high tax on the salt they sold to India. Rather than protest violently, Gandhi led 50,000 people on a 200-mile march to the seashore, where they began to make salt illegally by drying out seawater. When the British arrived, Gandhi allowed himself to be arrested peacefully.

Gandhi was freed in 1931. He continued to work with the Congress Party, but as a guiding force rather than a politician. The political leader of the Congress, and Gandhi's working partner, was a younger lawyer and intellectual, Jawaharlal Nehru. The spiritual, traditional Gandhi and the modern, secular Nehru pressed the British for greater reform. In 1935, the British granted a liberal constitution that was a long step forward on the path toward eventual self-rule. In 1937, Gandhi and Nehru began their "Quit India" campaign, trying to convince the British to leave altogether. The advent of World War II delayed the British withdrawal, but India would gain its freedom in 1947, soon after the war.

MUHAMMAD ALI JINNAH AND THE MUSLIM LEAGUE

The Congress Party was not the only force pressing for Indian independence. India's Muslims had their own freedom movement. Although during World War I, with the Lucknow Pact of 1916, Muslims and Hindus had pledged to work together for greater autonomy from the British, they began to go separate ways during the 1920s. By 1930, a Muslim League, led by Muhammad Ali Jinnah, had formed. It paralleled the Congress Party's independence efforts, but its aims were different. The Muslim League called for the creation of a separate Muslim state called Pakistan, or "land of the pure." The failure of the Muslim League and the Congress Party to resolve their differences peacefully would lead to great bloodshed when independence was finally achieved in 1947. It would also lay the foundation for the bitter Indo-Pakistani rivalry that still persists.

DICTATORSHIP IN LATIN AMERICA

OUTSIDE INFLUENCES ON LATIN AMERICA

Before World War I, modern nations in Latin America, while politically independent, had been economically dominated by outside influences. British and U.S. investors had gained a great deal of control over enterprises in Latin America. Most Latin American nations relied on the export of one or two raw materials or agricultural products. Chile was a source of fertilizer and copper; Peru mined copper as well. Chile and Brazil sold steel. Oil was being taken out of Mexico, Bolivia, Argentina, and Peru. Argentina produced wheat and beef. Central America grew bananas and other fruit. As it had for centuries, sugar came from the Caribbean and Brazil. Brazil was the source of 75 percent of the world's coffee supply.

In exchange for foreign capital and industrial know-how, political elites in Latin American countries would allow foreigners much influence in their local politics. The great mass of the population did the work and saw very few of the resulting profits.

THE UNITED STATES' SPHERE OF INFLUENCE IN LATIN AMERICA

World War I had the effect of increasing the United States' role in Latin America's political and economic life. With their economies weakened by the war, countries like France and Britain no longer had the funds to invest in Latin America. U.S. corporations like the United Fruit Company became major forces in Latin America.

Strategically, the United States viewed Latin America as its sphere of influence. This had been the case since the late 1800s. The United States had gained possessions like Puerto Rico and the Virgin Islands, as well as a protectorate over Cuba, after the Spanish-American War of 1898. U.S. Marines had occupied Haiti. Just as the British had taken control of the Suez Canal after investing in it, America established a military presence in Panama after constructing the canal there. Instability in Mexico (discussed presently) convinced the United States to militarize the border there. The United States sponsored dictators, such as Vicente Gómez of Venezuela and Fulgencio Batista of Cuba, in order to preserve order. A sense among Latin Americans that the people of the United States—the *yanquis*, or "yankees"—were imperialists grew steadily.

THE GOOD NEIGHBOR POLICY

During the mid-1930s, President Franklin Roosevelt attempted to reduce the United States' influence over Latin America. His Good Neighbor Policy of 1935 was intended to accomplish this goal and thereby improve relations with the region. As a token of goodwill, Roosevelt withdrew U.S. Marines from Haiti. For the first time in three decades, the United States had no troops in Latin America.

THE GREAT DEPRESSION'S EFFECTS ON LATIN AMERICA

Unfortunately, the United States affected Latin America in yet another way during the 1930s. The effects of the Great Depression on the region were devastating. Since Latin American economies were so dependent on exports to the United States, the inability of the United States to purchase Latin American goods caused tremendous damage. Exports were cut almost in half. As in many parts of Europe, the economic pain brought about by the Depression had a negative effect on politics. It helped to incline Latin American politics toward extremism and dictatorship.

As discussed in Chapter 27, there was a long-standing tradition of authoritarian rule in Latin America. This trend continued into the 1920s and 1930s, when there were few, if any, genuine democracies in Latin America. The three largest and wealthiest nations—Mexico, Brazil, and Argentina—all became dictatorial, to one degree or another, during these years.

MEXICO AND THE INSTITUTIONAL REVOLUTIONARY PARTY

Mexico had been beset by political troubles since the death of the liberal reformist Benito Juárez in 1872. Mexico was embroiled in revolution at the turn of the century, as rebels like Emiliano Zapata and Pancho Villa fought the dictatorial leader Porfirio Díaz and his successors. Villa's raids across the border had prompted U.S. military intervention just before World War I. Not until 1920 was order restored, by the Institutional Revolutionary Party (PRI). Its very name a contradiction in terms, the PRI went to great lengths to appear democratic. Its constitution granted universal suffrage and the right to strike. However, the PRI leadership was an oligarchy that chose a president every six years, than arranged an election that guaranteed victory to its candidate.

Under this mild form of authoritarian rule, the upper classes prospered and the country modernized. However, the middle class was small and narrow, while the large lower classes— workers and peasants—lagged far behind the elite. Things improved somewhat under Lázaro Cárdenas, who became president in 1934. His land reform, in which more than 40 million acres were taken from the upper class and distributed among the peasantry, made him popular with the lower classes. Cárdenas also stood up to the United States by nationalizing the oil industry. Roosevelt lived up to his Good Neighbor promises and refrained from intervention. In exchange, Cárdenas compensated U.S. companies for their losses, then formed PEMEX, Mexico's state-run oil enterprise.

AUTHORITARIANISM IN BRAZIL

Authoritarianism became genuinely dictatorial in Brazil. Before 1930, Brazilian government was dominated by wealthy landowners, most of whom owed their power and riches to coffee. The Depression, however, gutted the coffee trade and plunged the country into crisis. In 1930, Getúlio Vargas, a cattle rancher, became president and ruled as dictator until 1945. Vargas governed from the far right, in direct imitation of Fascist Italy and Nazi Germany. He censored the press and authorized his secret police to use torture against his political opponents. On the other hand, Vargas modernized the Brazilian economy, diversifying it and freeing it from its dependence on coffee. He also turned Brazil into Latin America's most industrialized nation. Nonetheless, he was forced out of office by his army in 1945.

DICTATORSHIP IN ARGENTINA

Argentina became a military dictatorship during the 1930s. In 1916, Hipólito Irigoyen of the Radical Party was elected president in 1916. His platform had consisted of a number of reform measures intended to improve the lot of the lower and middle classes. Under Irigoyen, labor unions became more active. However, landowners and the upper class sabotaged Irigoyen's efforts. In 1930, on behalf of the propertied classes, the army ousted Irigoyen. The military government lasted throughout World War II, but its efforts to go back to the old export-based economy failed. Labor unrest increased, and the radical lower classes, the *descamisados* ("shirtless ones"), grew louder and more belligerent. Shortly after World War II, in 1946, General Juan Perón, along with his charismatic wife Eva, would appeal to the lower classes in order to come to power—then establish his own dictatorship.

QUICK REVIEW

1. Which of the following best applies to the League of Nations between the world wars?

   (A) The League provided strong leadership and effectively kept the world at peace.
   (B) The League was effective at functions such as providing famine relief and dealing with refugee issues, but was otherwise weak.
   (C) U.S. leadership of the League enabled it to stop aggression in Ethiopia, Spain, and China.
   (D) No major European powers remained in the League by the middle of the 1930s.
   (E) From within, Adolf Hitler manipulated the League into granting Germany a number of territorial concessions.

2. Which of the following best describes the Communist takeover of Russia in 1917?

   (A) The Communists came to power after assassinating the royal family.
   (B) Defeat in World War I demoralized the country so badly that the population overthrew the tsar and voted the Communists into power.
   (C) Recognizing its limitations, the Provisional Government voluntarily stepped down from power, handing government over to the Communists.
   (D) Taking advantage of widespread radicalism and popular discontent with the Provisional Government, the Communists staged a successful armed insurrection.
   (E) The Communists won the majority of seats in parliamentary elections.

3. Who is generally considered to be the father of modern Turkey?

   (A) Mustafa Kemal Ataturk
   (B) Selim III
   (C) Enver Pasha
   (D) Suleiman the Magnificent
   (E) Reza Khan

4. Which Middle Eastern state became independent AND discovered vast oil reserves, both during the 1930s?

   (A) Egypt
   (B) Jordan
   (C) Syria
   (D) Palestine
   (E) Saudi Arabia

5. Who succeeded Sun Yat-sen as leader of the Nationalist Party?

   (A) Mao Tse-tung
   (B) Yuan Shikai
   (C) Chiang Kai-shek
   (D) Zhou En-lai
   (E) Lu Hsun

6. What was the Long March?

   (A) the epic retreat of the Chinese Communists, thousands of miles to the north
   (B) the Chinese Communists' massive offensive against Beijing
   (C) the years-long propaganda campaign the Chinese Communists waged in the countryside, to capture the hearts of the peasantry
   (D) the years-long propaganda campaign the Chinese Communists waged in the cities, to capture the hearts of the working class
   (E) the Chinese Communists' last-ditch defense of the city of Guangzhou

7. Before World War II, the most notorious atrocity committed by the Japanese military was

(A) the strategic bombing of Bangkok
(B) the execution of British prisoners taken at Singapore
(C) the torture of Nepalese noncombatants in Kathmandu
(D) the massacre of Chinese civilians after the capture of Nanjing
(E) the refusal of Red Cross packages to U.S. officers captured at Guadalcanal

8. What is the best description of *satyagraha*?

(A) a fusion of Marxist ideology and Hindu theology directed against British rule
(B) the policy of nonviolent resistance, mixed with Hindu principle, preached by Gandhi
(C) the policy of nonviolent resistance, mixed with Muslim principle, preached by Gandhi
(D) a fusion of Marxist ideology and Muslim radicalism, advocated by Muhammad Ali Jinnah
(E) Gandhi's ethical justification for the use of violence in resisting British rule

9. The violent suppression of demonstrators by British troops at which city almost plunged India into full-scale civil war?

(A) Lucknow
(B) Amritsar
(C) Meerut
(D) Calcutta
(E) Mysore

10. In which Latin American state did the Institutional Revolutionary Party control politics for most of the twentieth century?

(A) Brazil
(B) El Salvador
(C) Mexico
(D) Guatemala
(E) Bolivia

ANSWERS:

1. **B**, p. 364   6. **A**, p. 370
2. **D**, p. 365   7. **D**, p. 370
3. **A**, p. 367   8. **B**, p. 371
4. **E**, p. 368   9. **B**, p. 371
5. **C**, p. 369   10. **C**, p. 373

CHAPTER 30

World War II and the Holocaust

World War II (September 1939–September 1945) was and remains the largest, costliest, and deadliest armed conflict in human history. Beyond that, its long-term global impact continued to be felt in world politics, economics, and diplomacy for five decades.

Before the war ended, sixty-one nations joined the fighting. They were divided into two coalitions, the Axis Powers and the Allied Powers. The major combatants were as follows:

- The Axis Powers: Nazi Germany, Fascist Italy (joined the war in June 1940; left the war in July 1943), and Japan
- The Allied Powers: Great Britain, France (left the war in June 1940), Canada, Australia, New Zealand, the Soviet Union (joined the war in June 1941), and the United States (joined the war in December 1941)

The war was waged over two thirds of the entire planet. Every continent except Antarctica and South America saw fighting on the ground, and naval engagements ranged over every major body of water. Much more so than World War I, World War II was truly a global war.

Economically, World War II has been calculated to have cost $1.6 trillion in 1940s dollars, or at least $4 trillion to $5 trillion in contemporary terms. By the war's midpoint, somewhere between one quarter and one third of the world's entire economic capacity was directly dedicated to war production.

Concerning the grimmest statistic of all, it is estimated that somewhere between 55 million and 60 million people were killed during the war. In keeping with one of the most distressing trends of the twentieth century—increased civilian involvement in war—almost half of these casualties were noncombatants. World War II involved yet another ugly trend of the twentieth century, genocide. Twelve million victims—6 million Jewish, 6 million non-Jewish—perished in the German campaign of racial extermination known as the Holocaust.

In addition to its immediate effects, World War II also resulted in a complete shift in the balance of global strength. World War I had begun the process of toppling the powers of Europe from their position of dominance. World War II finished it. When the war was over, only two nations, the United States and the Soviet Union, which became known as the superpowers, had the military and economic might to affect the course of world events. The great geopolitical struggle between these two new superpowers, the cold war, played the dominant role in shaping global diplomacy, military affairs, and international trade for four and a half decades. World War II also destroyed the imperial might of the European powers. From the 1940s through the 1970s, a massive wave of decolonization swept through the non-Western world, and dozens of nations in Africa and Asia became free.

In addition, World War II changed the patterns of international trade, shifted global wealth to the superpowers (especially the United States), spurred a boom in technological and scientific innovation that would be put to civilian use long after the war was over, brought women into the workplace, and had countless other social, economic, and cultural effects. For these and many other reasons, World War II can be considered not only the most massive military enterprise in world history, but also the most influential.

THE ROAD TO WAR

Unlike the First World War, whose origins were quite complex, World War II resulted from a fairly straightforward pattern of aggression on the part of Nazi Germany, Fascist Italy, and militaristic Japan. Especially in Europe, aggression met with a weak and passive response from the major democracies. Hamstrung by the Depression, anxious to avoid another global conflict, or simply hoping that each aggressive move would be the last, countries such as France, Britain, and the United States did very little to stand up to the dictatorships. This policy of letting the aggressors have what they wanted, in the hope that they would demand no more, became known as appeasement. The League of Nations proved almost useless when it came to dealing with foreign-policy crises. A timetable of the various steps on what is often referred to as the road to war follows:

- 1933:
  —Hitler withdrew from the League of Nations.

- 1935:
  —Hitler openly began to rebuild the German army and navy, violating the disarmament clauses of the Treaty of Versailles.
  —Mussolini, seeking imperial glory, invaded Ethiopia. This caused an international outcry. The League of Nations imposed sanctions, but these were not enforced. The League's efforts did not prevent Italy's takeover of Ethiopia, which was completed in 1936. They only served to draw Mussolini closer to Hitler.
  —The Soviet Union, fearful of Germany, concluded an alliance with France. Both countries agreed to protect Czechoslovakia. France also signed a treaty to protect Poland. This policy of antifascist cooperation was known as collective security.

- 1936:
  —In another violation of the Treaty of Versailles, Hitler sent German troops into the Rhineland, which was supposed to remain a demilitarized zone permanently. France and Britain protested, but took no action. This set a precedent, in which Hitler would act and the democracies would appease him.
  —Mussolini completed his conquest of Ethiopia.
  —The Spanish Civil War (1936–1939) started. It began with Francisco Franco's military uprising against the democratically elected, left-leaning government. Because Franco was allied with Spanish fascists, Mussolini and Hitler gave him money, weapons, and troops. Stalin attempted to aid the Spanish government. He expected France and Britain to help him in doing so, and was deeply disappointed when they did not. This eroded Stalin's trust in the Western democracies and proved to be a great blow to collective security. Aside from the USSR, only a contingent of antifascist volunteers, the International Brigades, helped the Spanish government against the rebels. More than 600,000 people would be killed, and Franco's rebellion would eventually succeed. He became the dictator of Spain, ruling until his death in 1975.

- 1937:
  - —In Japan, the military gained control of the government.
  - —Germany, Italy, and Japan signed the Anti-Comintern Pact, pledging to oppose international communism. This signaled the formation of their alliance, the Axis Powers.
  - —Japan invaded mainland China, taking much of the coastline. The Japanese army committed terrible atrocities in China, including the "Rape of Nanking," in which hundreds of thousands of civilians, including women and children, were slaughtered.
  - —Hitler made public his desire for Lebensraum ("living space") for Germany. His campaign of expansion would begin the next year.

- 1938:
  - —Germany annexed Austria in the Anschluss ("union").
  - —Hitler announced his plans to take over the Sudetenland. This territory, formerly Germany's, had been given to Czechoslovakia after World War I. More than 3 million Germans lived there. After a serious war scare, Mussolini and Hitler met with Neville Chamberlain, Britain's prime minister, and Edouard Daladier, the French premier, at the German city of Munich. The Czechoslovaks were not invited; neither were the Soviets, who, with France, had promised to protect Czechoslovakia from aggression. Britain and France agreed to let Germany have the Sudetenland in exchange for Hitler's promise to expand no further. Although Chamberlain claimed to have guaranteed "peace in our time," the Munich Agreement was appeasement at its worst. It also destroyed collective security: Stalin, angry and betrayed by the events in Munich, chose not to trust Britain and France any further.
  - —Japan and the Soviet Union clashed in Siberia. This conflict was unofficial, although the battles were quite large. The Soviets drove the Japanese back from their border.

- 1939:
  - —Germany took the rest of Czechoslovakia. This demonstrated to the rest of the world how foolish France and Britain had been to believe Hitler's promises.
  - —Germany took western Lithuania.
  - —Italy invaded Albania.
  - —The Japanese and Soviets fought another short, undeclared conflict in Siberia.
  - —Hitler began to make claims on Polish territory that had formerly belonged to Germany. Realizing that this was where Hitler would act next, France and Britain promised to guarantee Poland's safety.
  - —Wishing to avoid a two-front war, Hitler sought to reach an agreement with Stalin before invading Poland. In August, Stalin, no longer trusting Britain and France, agreed to sign a nonaggression pact with Hitler. This Nazi-Soviet Pact kept the USSR neutral and opened the way for Hitler to invade Poland.
  - —On September 1, 1939, Germany invaded Poland. This began World War II.

THE AXIS ASCENDANT, 1939–1941

During the first half of the war, the Axis powers were triumphant. In Europe, the only major powers opposing Germany were France and Britain. The USSR had agreed to remain neutral, and the United States, sunk into isolation, stayed out of the fighting as well. In Asia, Japan expanded its war against China to include a greater war of conquest against British, Dutch, and French colonies in Southeast Asia.

NEW TECHNOLOGY AND WORLD WAR II

In terms of combat and technology, World War II was very different from the First World War. During the latter, the new military technology of the industrial era had favored the defensive. The result, at least on the Western Front, had been the hellish stalemate of trench warfare. By the time World War II had begun, military technology had developed in such a way as to make warfare more rapid and more dynamic.

At sea, naval aircraft, the aircraft carriers to transport them, new landing craft that allowed large numbers of marine troops to invade faraway islands and beachheads, and long-range submarines gave the combatants a truly global reach. On the ground, new artillery and, especially, the tank gave armies a tremendous offensive punch, as well as the ability to move quickly. In the air, giant strategic bombers would be able to fly thousands of miles and drop unheard-of quantities of explosives, further increasing offensive capacity and extending global reach.

All this new technology would help to make World War II a faster-paced, more decisive conflict, fought on a much grander scale, than World War I. It also had the deeply unfortunate effects of making warfare significantly more deadly and involving civilian populations to a degree never before imagined.

The necessity to develop better and more effective military technology during the war had a tremendous effect on civilian technology long after the war was over. Among the many innovations that came out of the Second World War to play a large role in postwar life were radar, jet aircraft, synthetic materials (such as nylon), rocketry, atomic energy, and computer science.

BLITZKRIEG, THE INVASION OF POLAND, AND SITZKRIEG

The war began with Germany's invasion of Poland, in September 1939 (although it must be remembered that Japan had been fighting China since 1937). The new offensive character of war was apparent right away. Germany's innovative method of warfare, Blitzkrieg ("lightning war"), used tanks and airplanes to penetrate deeply and quickly into enemy territory. Blitzkrieg was terribly effective. Within weeks, the war in Poland was over—especially because the USSR invaded the eastern half of the country, in accordance with the Nazi-Soviet Pact between Hitler and Stalin.

In contrast to Germany's fast action, Britain and France, although they declared war, did very little. With an outdated First World War mentality, the Allies waited for Germany to attack them, believing that, as in 1914, the defense would prevail. While Britain and France marked time, Germany prepared its attack. The winter of 1939 to 1940 was nicknamed *Sitzkrieg*, or "phony war."

GERMANY'S INVASION OF WESTERN EUROPE AND THE FALL OF FRANCE

In April 1940, Hitler launched his assault on western Europe. The next several months were stunningly successful. Denmark, Norway, Luxembourg, Belgium, and the Netherlands were all defeated in weeks, if not days.

Most amazing of all was the fall of France. The Germans attacked France on May 10. By June 22, the largest and most powerful democracy on the European continent had surrendered. The French had been confident that their great chain of border fortifications, the Maginot Line, would protect them. The German Blitzkrieg sidestepped the Maginot Line and sent tanks streaming into northern France. The defeat of France shocked the world. It also left Great Britain in the seemingly hopeless position of fighting Germany and Italy (which joined the war in June) by itself.

THE BATTLE OF BRITAIN

From the summer of 1940 to the spring of 1941, Germany concentrated its attention on Britain. Meanwhile, Italy launched attacks in the Mediterranean, trying to take Greece, Yugoslavia, and

Egypt (which was still under British protection). Hitler's attempt to knock Britain out of the war failed. The Royal Navy protected the British Isles from an actual invasion. When Hitler tried to win the war from the air, the Royal Air Force defended England's skies against his bombers in the Battle of Britain.

Britain held out due to the skill of its air force, its use of radar, and economic aid from Canada and the United States (although the United States was neutral, the government of Franklin Roosevelt was sympathetic, and its Lend-Lease program of economic assistance kept Britain and, later, the USSR well supplied throughout the war).

INVASIONS IN THE EAST AND OPERATION BARBAROSSA

In the spring and summer of 1941, Hitler decided to shift his focus from Britain to eastern Europe. Italy's wars in Greece, Yugoslavia, and North Africa had gone wrong, and Germany had to assist in all these areas. One of Hitler's most skilled tank commanders, Erwin Rommel, was sent to Africa to fight the British in Egypt.

Hitler also had a larger intention in mind: the invasion of the Soviet Union, the plan for which he called Operation Barbarossa. Although the USSR and Germany had carefully observed their pact of neutrality since August 1939, Hitler, having eliminated France from the war, felt confident enough to fight the USSR, even though Britain had not yet been defeated.

On June 22, 1941, Germany invaded the Soviet Union, starting the largest ground war in history. From this point onward, 60 to 75 percent of the German armed forces would be fighting on this eastern front. At first, it looked as though the USSR would fall with almost the same speed that France had. German forces surrounded Leningrad, the USSR's second largest city, placing it under the worst siege in modern times. They drove deep into Ukraine and southern Russia. They also reached the outskirts of Moscow, the capital. A last-ditch defensive effort in December halted the German advance, but only barely.

JAPANESE AGGRESSION IN SOUTHEAST ASIA

In the Pacific, fighting between China and Japan continued. Japan's war effort widened in 1940 and 1941, as French, Dutch, and British misfortunes in Europe made their Southeast and South Asian possessions vulnerable. When France fell in 1940, Japan began to threaten its colony in Indochina. Japan's eventual goal was to establish its Greater East Asian Co-Prosperity Sphere over the entire Chinese coast, all of Southeast Asia, India, Indonesia, and perhaps Australia and New Zealand.

By the summer of 1941, Japan's takeover of Indochina and increased aggression toward Southeast Asia compelled the United States, already upset at Japanese atrocities in China, to impose economic sanctions. Without steel, oil, and other raw materials from the United States, the Japanese war effort on the Asian mainland would be badly damaged, and Japan viewed the embargo as an act of war. In late 1941, Japan began to plan a military assault against the United States.

PEARL HARBOR AND JAPAN'S ASSAULT ON THE SOUTH PACIFIC

On December 7, 1941, just as the Soviets were halting the Germans outside Moscow, Japan launched its surprise attack on the U.S. naval installation at Pearl Harbor, Hawaii. At the same time, the Japanese bombed and invaded U.S. bases throughout the Pacific and on the Philippines.

By the spring of 1942, the Japanese were masters of the South Pacific and Southeast Asia, having captured Hong Kong, Indochina, Thailand, part of Burma, the Malaysian Peninsula (including the great British base of Singapore), the Philippines, Indonesia (the Dutch East Indies), and hundreds of small Pacific islands. However, the effect of the Japanese attack was to bring the United States into the war, both in the Pacific and in Europe (several days after Pearl Harbor, Germany joined Japan in declaring war on the United States).

Because Pearl Harbor, however devastating, was not a knockout blow, what the Japanese had managed to do was to rouse one of the world's largest countries—with great humanpower resources and the most productive economy on earth—and involve it in the war. In the long term, neither Japan nor Germany would be able to match America's capacity for military industrialization or mass conscription of troops.

THE ALLIED QUEST FOR VICTORY, 1942–1945

THE SHIFTING BALANCE OF WORLD WAR II

The second half of the war, 1942 through 1945, had a much different character than the first. Most obviously, a different set of countries was involved. France had dropped out, but the USSR and the United States had joined in. Just as important, a different set of factors came into play. The advantage of the Axis Powers lay in the skill and quality of Germany's and Japan's armed forces. The advantages of the Allies, especially once the Soviets and Americans became involved, were geographic size, huge reserves of humanpower, large economies, and abundant natural resources.

This distribution of advantages and disadvantages meant that the longer the war lasted, the more likely it became that the Allies would win. Realizing that time was working against them, Germany and Japan had been trying to gain decisive victories between 1939 and the end of 1941. Germany's failure to take Moscow and Japan's failure to cripple America permanently with its initial sweep through the Pacific ended the Axis's chances of ending the war quickly. Although Germany and Japan still held the advantage when 1942 began, all of the long-term trends were against them.

THE TURNING POINT: 1942

A handful of battles during the summer and fall of 1942 completely changed the tide of the war. If the Axis had won these encounters, they might well have been able to force a favorable end to the war. By losing all three, Japan and Germany wasted vast amounts of irreplaceable troops, weapons, and equipment—and lost the strategic initiative they had enjoyed since 1939. These battles were

The European and Mediterranean Theaters of Combat, World War II, 1942.
From September 1939 until the autumn of 1942, the Axis Powers—Germany, Italy, and Japan—succeeded in seizing the military initiative and keeping it. By the middle of 1942, Nazi Germany had reached the height of its power. The areas shaded in gray mark territory that was controlled directly by Germany before the war, belonged to its allies, or had been conquered by it during the war. Not long after this point, primarily because of defeats at El Alamein and Stalingrad, the tide of war turned against the Germans and their partners.

- Midway (June 1942), a naval battle in which the U.S. Navy destroyed a huge portion of the Japanese aircraft-carrier fleet
- El Alamein (fall 1942), where the British turned back the drive of Erwin Rommel's German tanks toward Egypt and the Suez Canal
- Stalingrad (August 1942–February 1943), a mammoth, savage clash along the Volga River, where the Soviets prevented the Germans from capturing all of south Russia and their oil reserves in the east

With these victories, the Allies had held on long enough for their advantages—larger populations and economies—to become decisive.

THE SHIFTING TIDE: 1943 AND 1944

In 1943 and 1944, the Allies determined the direction and pace of the war effort. In the Pacific, the Americans pushed the Japanese steadily westward. Australia, India, Burma, and large parts of China remained free and joined in the fighting. Guerrilla uprisings in Thailand, Vietnam, Indonesia, the Philippines, and elsewhere hurt the Japanese badly.

On the European and Mediterranean fronts, Britain and America took control of North Africa, then used it as a platform from which to invade Italy, depose Mussolini's Fascist government, and knock Italy out of the war. From the east, the Soviets pushed the Germans out of their country, into eastern Europe, and toward Berlin.

In June 1944, in the famous D-Day invasion (technically known as Operation Overlord, or the Normandy Invasion), British, Canadian, and American troops, ships, and aircraft crossed the English Channel and landed on the coast of France. On land, Hitler now faced Allied threats from three directions: the eastern front, the Italian peninsula, and now western Europe.

WAR AT SEA AND IN THE AIR

At sea, the British and Americans neutralized the last weapon with which Germany had any real chance of threatening their war effort: the submarine fleet, which became ineffective by mid-1943.

In the air, the Allies had complete control of the skies by late 1943. From that point forward, British and American aircraft were able to bomb German-held Europe with impunity. After the summer of 1944, American forces had gone far enough across the Pacific that U.S. bombers were able to pound Japan from the air constantly. This practice of strategic bombing caused immense damage and killed tens of thousands of civilians. It remains one of the most controversial aspects of the Allied war effort.

THE END OF WORLD WAR II

In 1945, the Axis surrendered. Germany gave up the fight first. Caught between the Anglo-American Allies in the west and the Soviet advance from the east, Hitler chose to commit suicide on April 30. Germany officially surrendered in early May.

Despite the fact that it had no hope of winning, Japan continued its struggle against the Allies. The U.S. Navy and Marines closed in on the Japanese home islands, while U.S. bombers continued their assault from the skies.

America's new president, Harry Truman (who took the Oval Office upon the death of Franklin Roosevelt in April 1945), greatly feared that an invasion of the Japanese islands would cost millions of American and Japanese lives. He hoped to win from the air, but conventional bombardment did not seem to be forcing the Japanese to surrender. In July, an international team of scientists working for the Allies tested the first operational atomic bomb in New Mexico. Truman chose to use the A-bomb against the Japanese.

After warning Japan's government that the United States had a new weapon of terrible power, Truman acted. On August 6, 1945, a B-29 bomber named *Enola Gay* dropped an atomic bomb on Hiroshima. The initial blast killed at least 78,000 people and destroyed the entire city center; tens of thousands more died later, of burns or radioactive fallout. When the Japanese government ignored Truman's next request for surrender, the Americans dropped a second bomb on August 9, on the port of Nagasaki. The following week, the Japanese agreed to a cease-fire. They surrendered officially on September 2.

THE HOLOCAUST AND OTHER WAR CRIMES

WAR CRIMES AND CRIMES AGAINST HUMANITY

The most grisly aspect of World War II involved the many war crimes committed during the 73 months of fighting. Of the 55 million to 60 million people who died during the war, approximately half were civilians. A good number of those were killed by means that fell outside the bounds established by international law or acceptable military behavior. Many of these atrocities were horrendous enough that the phrase "war crime" seemed inadequate to describe them. It was after World War II, therefore, that the phrase "crimes against humanity" entered the world's legal vocabularies.

The Axis Powers were not the only nations to kill civilians. The Red Army committed many crimes—rape, plunder, wanton destruction of civilian property—as the Soviets advanced through eastern Europe and Germany. The American and British policy of strategic bombing, both over Japan and German-held Europe, caused tremendous civilian suffering. Some commentators, including many Germans and Japanese, have argued that strategic bombing can be considered a war crime (it should be noted that this is a minority opinion). Of course, America remains the only nation that has ever used an atomic or nuclear weapon in wartime, and the question of whether it was necessary to use it against Japan continues to be a matter of controversy.

JAPANESE WAR CRIMES

Nonetheless, it was the Axis that committed war crimes and crimes against humanity systematically and on a large scale. In Asia, Japan was guilty of a wide variety of atrocities. Even before World War II, Japanese forces had raped, pillaged, and butchered civilian populations in many Chinese cities, most notably Nanjing in December 1937.

As the "Greater East Asian Co-Prosperity Sphere" widened during World War II, Japanese soldiers continued to terrorize civilian populations, not just in China, but throughout all of Southeast Asia. On a number of occasions, Japanese armies killed large numbers of American, British, and Asian prisoners of war, against all legal conventions pertaining to military conduct. Prisoners of war were also used as subjects for Japanese scientific experiments, especially for testing biological and chemical weapons. Finally, the Japanese military administration officially instituted the practice of rounding up so-called comfort women from Korea and Southeast Asia. These women were forced to serve as prostitutes for Japanese soldiers. After the war, the U.S. military authorities held a series of Tokyo Trials, during which Japanese civilian and military officials were tried for these crimes.

NAZI ATROCITIES IN GERMANY

More famous and more extensive than Japanese crimes against humanity were those committed by the Germans. Even before the war, the Nazis already operated an extensive apparatus of terror, which included the formation of a secret police (the Gestapo) and the establishment of concentration camps (such as Dachau). Dissidents (including Protestant and, especially, Catholic religious figures who protested Nazi policy) had been imprisoned, even executed, since the early 1930s.

As the war began, then progressed, the Nazis began to "euthanize" medical patients with incurable diseases, venereal diseases, or tuberculosis. They eliminated homosexuals, people who were mentally disabled, and political dissidents. They performed medical and scientific experiments on human subjects, typically to the point of mutilation and death (Jews and Soviet prisoners of war were used most often).

NAZI RACIAL POLICY AND GENOCIDE

Most infamous were the Nazi campaigns of genocide. The Nazis targeted a number of ethnic and cultural groups. Roma (Gypsies) and Slavs were among the peoples the Nazis considered to be "subhuman" or "undesirable."

Most of all, the Nazis hated the Jews. After Hitler's rise to power in 1933, the Nazis passed a number of anti-Semitic policies that grew worse over time. The worst were the Nuremberg Laws of 1935, which deprived all German Jews of their civil rights. Before the war, however, violence against the Jews was not yet official policy, even though, in reality, thousands of Jews and Jewish residences and businesses were being harassed, beaten, and vandalized during the late 1930s, on the eve of World War II. The worst of these moments came in November 1938, on Kristallnacht ("Night of Broken Glass"), when Jewish shops, synagogues, and homes throughout Germany and Austria were attacked or burned in a single night.

It was during the war that Nazi anti-Semitic policy escalated to the point of genocide. There were 11 million Jews in Europe before the beginning of the war. In 1939 and 1940, as the Germans brought more and more of Europe under their control, Nazi authorities began to round Jews up and detain them, either in ghettos or preexisting concentration camps like Dachau. It was sometime in 1941 that the order for genocide came down from above. Although no written orders survive, it is certain that, ultimately, the command was issued by Hitler himself.

THE HOLOCAUST

Nazi genocidal policy is popularly referred to by the name given to it by the Jews: the Holocaust. The Nazis themselves referred to it as the "Final Solution." Whatever its name, it evolved according to the following steps:

- 1939–1940:
  —Jews were forced to wear the yellow star to identify themselves.
  —Polish Jews were rounded up and placed in ghettos.
  —Other European Jews were imprisoned in concentration and transit camps.
  —Some Jews were sporadically executed or died by random violence.

- 1941:
  —In preparation for Germany's invasion of the Soviet Union, Hitler issued secret orders for the immediate execution of Communist Party members.
  —In July, an order "to make preparations for the general final solution of the Jewish problem within the German sphere of influence in Europe" was handed down to the SS (the Nazi Secret Police).
  —The Nazis organized "special action squads" (*Einsatzgruppen*) to follow the German army into the Soviet Union, round up Jews, and execute them by shooting.
  —Dissatisfaction with the "special action squads" grew. This method of execution was considered to be too slow, too wasteful of ammunition, and too hard on the morale of the executioners. Because the "special action squads" only buried the bodies instead of destroying them, the danger that the victims could later be found remained.

—Limited experiments with carbon monoxide and other gasses were carried out at various concentration camps in an attempt to find an "efficient" way to kill large numbers of victims. Experimental cremation methods were also tested.

—Late in the year, construction of new camps, designed principally for execution and cremation, began.

—A cyanide-based insecticide, Zyklon-B, was chosen as the most efficient means of extermination.

- 1942:

—In January, fifteen Nazi officials met in the suburbs of Berlin. Here, at the Wannsee Conference, it was decided to use special camps, already under construction in German-held Poland, for the express purpose of eliminating Jews and other undesirables. Among these camps were Majdanek, Chelmno, Belzec, Sobibor, and Treblinka. The largest and most infamous was Auschwitz-Birkenau.

—The special extermination camps went into operation.

- 1943–1945:

—Jews from all over Europe were shipped to the extermination camps. Other victims were taken there as well. Victims were gassed, their bodies were processed, their remains were cremated.

—Soviet liberation of camps in Poland began in 1944. Auschwitz-Birkenau was liberated in early 1945.

—Camps in the west were liberated by the British and Americans.

In the end, the Final Solution resulted in 12 million deaths. Of Europe's 11 million Jews, approximately 6 million were killed. In addition, 6 million non-Jewish victims perished.

It was mainly to punish these crimes that the Americans, British, and Soviets staged an important set of court cases, the Nuremberg Trials (1946), to try the remaining Nazi military and political leadership. It was during the Nuremberg Trials that the term "crimes against humanity" was coined. In 1948, in a collective effort to avoid such atrocities in the future, the United Nations General Assembly adopted the Universal Declaration of Human Rights.

QUICK REVIEW

1. The term *appeasement* best applies to which of the following episodes?

   (A) the Soviet support of the Spanish Republic against Franco's revolt in 1936

   (B) Ethiopia's resistance to Italy's 1935 invasion

   (C) France's and Britain's 1938 agreement with Germany at Munich, regarding the Sudetenland

   (D) France's and Britain's willingness to defend Poland in the fall of 1939

   (E) the Soviet takeover of Estonia, Latvia, and Lithuania in 1939 and 1940

2. The diplomatic effect of Italy's invasion of Ethiopia was

   (A) to strengthen ties between Italy and Germany

   (B) to boost the prestige of the League of Nations

   (C) to show how France and Britain could stand up against Fascist aggression

   (D) to convince the USSR to join Japan in an anti-European alliance

   (E) to draw Italy into a closer partnership with Austria

3. Which two countries' armies clashed in Siberia in 1938 and 1939?

    (A) Japan's and India's
    (B) Japan's and Mongolia's
    (C) Mongolia's and Nepal's
    (D) Mongolia's and the USSR's
    (E) the USSR's and Japan's

4. The failure of collective security convinced Stalin to

    (A) resign all his political posts
    (B) sign a treaty of neutrality with Nazi Germany
    (C) declare war on Nazi Germany
    (D) conclude an alliance with Poland
    (E) take over Czechoslovakia in an effort to protect the Soviet border

5. Which countries were NOT officially involved during the first month of World War II?

    (A) Poland, Italy, France
    (B) the United States, the Soviet Union, Great Britain
    (C) the Soviet Union, Poland, Romania
    (D) Italy, the Soviet Union, the United States
    (E) the United States, France, the Soviet Union

6. Above all, what did France erroneously trust to keep it safe from German invasion?

    (A) the French air force
    (B) the Maginot Line
    (C) the Vosges Mountains
    (D) the Belgian army
    (E) the threat of Soviet invasion from the east

7. What city experienced the worst siege not just of World War II, but of the entire modern era?

    (A) Leningrad
    (B) Krakow
    (C) Stalingrad
    (D) Dresden
    (E) Nagasaki

8. What was the Greater East Asian Co-Prosperity Sphere?

    (A) an association of British colonies in Southeast Asia
    (B) a military alliance that resisted the Japanese attack on Southeast Asia
    (C) a free-trade zone whose economic activity was disrupted by Japanese invasion
    (D) the name given by the Japanese to the Asian empire they conquered in the 1930s and during World War II
    (E) the formal name of the Dutch colony in Indonesia

9. If the Axis Powers had won World War II, which of the following Allied operations would they most likely have punished as a war crime?

    (A) British and U.S. strategic bombing of German and Japanese cities
    (B) the D-Day landings in northwestern France
    (C) Soviet conduct during the battle of Kiev
    (D) the U.S. and British takeover of Sicily
    (E) the sinking of Japanese aircraft carriers by U.S. pilots at Midway

10. Japanese war crimes included which of the following?

   I. abuse of Chinese and Southeast Asian civilians

  II. execution of U.S., British, and Australian prisoners of war

 III. forced prostitution of women from Korea and Southeast Asia

 IV. the use of prisoners as subjects in chemical- and biological-weapons experiments

(A) I only

(B) I, II, and III

(C) II and III only

(D) II, III, and IV

(E) all of the above

ANSWERS:

1. **C**, p. 378

2. **A**, p. 377

3. **E**, p. 378

4. **B**, p. 378

5. **D**, p. 379

6. **B**, p. 379

7. **A**, p. 380

8. **D**, p. 380

9. **A**, p. 383

10. **E**, p. 383

CHAPTER 31

The Cold War and the New Bipolar Order

The end of World War II brought about a fundamental shift in global power. For well over 200 years, the ability to shape world events had been concentrated in the hands of the European powers. The constantly shifting balance of power among six or seven European nations had determined the course of geopolitics around the globe. With Europe devastated by the war, however, only two nations possessed any kind of genuine military, political, and economic strength: the United States and the Soviet Union. This reduced the European balance of power to a new equation, referred to by political scientists and diplomatic historians as bipolar equilibrium—an alignment in which two nations, matched relatively evenly, share global power. Because these two nations were orders of magnitude stronger and wealthier than any great power had been before them, they were referred to as superpowers.

The popular name given to the state of bipolar equilibrium that existed between the United States and the USSR from 1945 to 1991 is the Cold War (the term was coined by one of Franklin Roosevelt's advisers, then popularized by an American journalist). For almost five decades, the rivalry between capitalist America and the socialist Soviet Union divided the world into hostile camps. It gave birth to a massive arms race that, because it was nuclear, brought into the world the deadliest weapons ever seen. The great wave of decolonization that took place after World War II (see Chapter 32) was deeply affected by the Cold War, as newly free nations often had to choose between allying with one superpower or another. Although the United States and the USSR never went to war with each other, dozens of small and medium-sized conflicts were fought worldwide between 1945 and the end of the Cold War, killing an estimated total of 50 million people, more than half of them civilian.

The Cold War finally ended in the late 1980s and early 1990s, with the collapse of communism in Eastern Europe and the breakup of the Soviet Union. For more details on these topics, see Chapter 34.

WARTIME DIPLOMACY

DIVISIONS AMONG THE WARTIME ALLIES

The wartime alliance between the United States, Great Britain, and the Soviet Union had been a marriage of convenience. Although the United States and Britain were mutually sympathetic, they cooperated with the USSR and its dictator, Joseph Stalin, only because they needed Soviet help to defeat Hitler. Even during the war effort, many tensions had arisen between Franklin Roosevelt and

Winston Churchill on one hand, and Stalin on the other. It was clear to all that things would only get worse after the war ended.

THE WARTIME CONFERENCES

The issues that concerned the wartime allies were dealt with most clearly at three summit conferences, at which all three heads of state met in person. These were the Teheran Conference (November 1943), the first time Roosevelt, Churchill, and Stalin all met face-to-face; the Yalta Conference (February 1945); and the Potsdam Conference (July 1945), at which the leadership was somewhat different. Roosevelt had died, and was replaced by Harry Truman. Churchill had been voted out of office; his place was taken by Clement Attlee. The questions that were dealt with at the wartime conferences included the following:

- *Second front:* The USSR, which fought the vast majority of the German army, desperately wanted the British and Americans to open up a second front in western Europe, in order to share the burden of fighting the Germans. Not until the Teheran Conference was an agreement about the second front reached. It was decided to invade France in June 1944; this led to Operation Overlord, or the D-Day invasion of Normandy.
- *Japan:* Fearing the potential deadliness of a direct attack on the Japanese islands, and not knowing that the atomic bomb would be invented in time to use in the war, Roosevelt was anxious to secure Soviet help against Japan. At Yalta, Stalin agreed to declare war on Japan once the Germans were defeated. He demanded territory—Sakhalin Island and the Kurile Islands—and the division of Korea into communist and noncommunist zones (he made the same request about Japan, but was refused).
- *Division and denazification of Germany and Austria:* What to do with the fallen foe, Germany, was decided at Yalta. It was to be divided into four sectors, British, French, U.S., and Soviet. Berlin itself, which fell into the Soviet zone, was likewise divided, and the British, French, and U.S. parts of Berlin were guaranteed highway, air, and rail access to the west. Austria was partitioned in a similar manner. Both countries were to undergo a process of denazification, in which former Nazis were to be removed from public offices and positions of authority. Germany was to repay $20 billion in reparations. The division of Germany lasted until the end of the Cold War. Austria was allowed to join together as a single, independent nation in 1955.
- *United Nations:* Just as Woodrow Wilson had created the League of Nations after World War I, Franklin Roosevelt hoped to establish a new international body, stronger and more effective than the League had been. This body was to be called the United Nations. At Yalta, Roosevelt convinced Churchill and Stalin to accept the idea in principle. Organizational and practical details were worked out later.
- *Fate of Eastern Europe:* By far, this was the most sensitive issue raised at the wartime conferences, especially Yalta and Potsdam. In the process of defeating Germany, Soviet troops were occupying all of Eastern Europe and much of central Europe. It was becoming clear that Stalin hoped to turn this territory into a Soviet sphere of influence. Roosevelt and Churchill were deeply concerned about Stalin's intentions. But Stalin had 11 million troops in the region, and to press him too hard on this question was to risk having him drop out of the war before Germany was defeated. At Yalta, Roosevelt and Churchill came up with an awkward compromise. They agreed that the USSR would have a certain amount of informal influence in certain East European nations. In exchange, they asked the Soviets to promise to allow free elections throughout Eastern Europe. Stalin agreed, then broke his promises. This caused great anger between Truman and Stalin at Potsdam. Some historians view Yalta as a moment when Roosevelt and Churchill betrayed Eastern Europe; others argue that there was little they could have done, considering the military realities of the situation.

BRETTON WOODS AND INTERNATIONAL AGREEMENTS ON THE WORLD ECONOMY

Before the end of the war, the Roosevelt administration began to lay the groundwork for U.S. leadership in the postwar global economy. Pursuant to this aim, in July 1944, representatives of forty-four Allied countries met in Bretton Woods, New Hampshire, to commit themselves to the goals of economic development, monetary stability, and free trade.

Participants established the International Bank for Reconstruction and Development (World Bank) and the International Monetary Fund (IMF) to rebuild Europe and lend assistance to Latin American, Asian, and African countries. To promote monetary stability, exchange rates were tied to the U.S. dollar, which in turn was anchored to the gold standard. The USSR refused to join the so-called Bretton Woods System for ideological reasons, but by doing so, it isolated itself economically from countries of the "First World."

THE COLD WAR BEGINS, 1945–1949

THE EUROPEAN FOCUS OF THE EARLY COLD WAR

Because of the tensions described previously, the Cold War can be said to have started even before World War II was over. The Potsdam Conference, held after Germany's defeat but while Japan was still fighting on, was an extremely unfriendly meeting. The first stage of the Cold War can be considered to have lasted from 1945 to 1949. Although there were concerns about other parts of the world, such as Japan, Korea, and China, the focus of the Cold War during these early years was primarily European, as well as Mediterranean. For Europe itself, of course, this was a bitter comedown. From being the shaper of world events, Europe—reduced to the superpowers' battleground— was now shaped by them.

The Cold War Division of Europe, 1957.

From 1945 until 1989, the Cold War divided the nations of Europe—with only a few exceptions—into two camps, one dominated by the Soviet Union, the other led by the United States and its European allies. By the mid-1950s, the so-called Iron Curtain had descended over Europe. The nations of the West were joined by the North Atlantic Treaty Organization, a military alliance, and many also joined in the European Economic Community. The Eastern bloc was held together by the Soviet-imposed military alliance known as the Warsaw Pact, as well as COMECON, an economic union led by the USSR.

THE SOVIET ABSORPTION OF EASTERN EUROPE

From 1945 through 1948, the USSR took over Eastern Europe. It installed pro-Soviet, communist governments in the eastern half of Germany, as well as Poland, Czechoslovakia, Hungary, Romania, and Bulgaria. Yugoslavia became communist as well. But, under its charismatic leader, Josip Tito, Yugoslavia pursued an independent course and broke with the USSR in 1948. Albania, also communist, was allied with the Soviets until after Stalin's death; after the mid-1950s, it isolated itself from both superpowers. It was in response to the rise of communism in Eastern Europe that, in March 1946, Winston Churchill warned of the permanent division of the continent in his famous "iron curtain" speech.

All of this was a violation of the Soviets' promises at Yalta. In addition, the USSR was threatening Iran and Turkey in 1945 and 1946. At the same time, the Yugoslavs were sponsoring a communist rebellion in Greece. This brought the Soviet bloc perilously close to the oil fields of the Middle East, as well as the important waterways of the eastern Mediterranean.

Stalin's policy during these years was simple: to gain as much territory as possible without a fight. Although they kept it as secret as possible, the Soviets had been hurt badly by the war. They had lost 25 million to 30 million dead. One third of their entire economy had been destroyed. The USSR could not afford to fight the West. On the other hand, Stalin wanted as much of a buffer zone in Eastern Europe as he could get, in order to protect his country from ever suffering again as it had during World War II. Also, because the United States had atomic weaponry and the USSR did not, Stalin felt even more vulnerable. His goal was to push the Americans as hard as he could, up to the point where they pushed back. The clearest example of this came in 1948, during the Berlin Blockade. In March, the Soviets suddenly cut off highway and railroad traffic between West Berlin and the western zones of Germany. It was easy to do this without provoking an actual war. When the United States began to fly airplanes to West Berlin, however, Stalin was faced with a choice: allow the flights to continue or shoot the aircraft out of the skies, which would certainly start a war. Stalin backed down, having reached the limit of what the United States would allow.

THE U.S. RESPONSE: CONTAINMENT

Until the period between 1947 and 1949, the United States had no coherent strategy for the emerging Cold War. In 1947, however, as the threat of communist takeover in Greece and Turkey worsened, Truman decided to act. That March, the United States began to assist Greece and Turkey. It also proclaimed the Truman Doctrine, which promised "moral and material aid to any and all countries whose political stability is threatened by communism."

Later in 1947, in the summer, the United States unveiled the European Recovery Plan (or Marshall Plan), the brainchild of the secretary of state, General George Marshall. If the Truman Doctrine represented America's political commitment to the Cold War, the Marshall Plan was its economic commitment. Remembering how, during the Depression, economic suffering had driven many European nations to political extremism, Marshall argued that poverty and homelessness in postwar Europe might drive governments to turn to communism. The Marshall Plan pumped over $13 billion into Europe, for purposes of economic reconstruction. Even the nations of Eastern Europe were invited to take part in the Marshall Plan, but the USSR forbade them to do so.

Finally, in 1949, due to reasons discussed in the next section, the Truman Administration made a military commitment to the Cold War. This was the formation of the North Atlantic Treaty Organization (NATO), which bound the United States, Canada, Britain, and nine other West European states into a formal strategic alliance (the number of NATO members has grown steadily over time). During the Cold War, U.S. forces stationed in Western Europe acted as a so-called trip wire, whose presence would automatically guarantee U.S. involvement in any war that resulted from a Soviet attempt to invade Western Europe.

Taken together, all these items were elements in the United States's overarching strategy for dealing with the USSR. This strategy was called containment. This term was coined by the American diplomat George Kennan, one of the U.S. government's few experts on the Soviet Union. In telegrams to Washington from the U.S. Embassy in Moscow, as well as a famous article, "Sources of Soviet Conduct" (which he wrote under the pseudonym "Mr. X"), Kennan argued that the USSR would expand as far as it could, as long as it did not have to fight. Soviet expansion, therefore, could be halted by "long-term, patient, but firm and vigilant containment."

Containment did not necessarily mean war, but could also consist of economic and diplomatic support for an area that the communists seemed ready to move into. The advantage of this approach was that it provided a means by which Soviet expansion could be kept in check without risking combat. There were, however, several drawbacks. Containment gave the initiative to the Soviet Union: it acted, then the United States reacted. There was no end in sight, meaning that containment would have to be pursued for years, if not decades. It would cost immense amounts of money, especially as the arms race between the two countries escalated. Moreover, as described presently and in Chapter 32, the containment strategy affected—and not for the better— how America chose its allies in the developing (or "third") world of Africa, Asia, and Latin America.

EUROPE DIVIDED

The Soviets, of course, resisted the Americans' efforts to "contain" them. In response to the Marshall Plan, the USSR formed its own Eastern-bloc economic union, the Council for Mutual Economic Assistance (COMECON). It also developed its own military bloc, the Warsaw Pact, to oppose NATO.

By the end of the 1940s, Europe was sharply divided between noncommunist and communist camps, with only a few nations remaining neutral. It was at this point, however, that Europe ceased to be the only battleground—or even the primary battleground—of the Cold War. From 1949 onward, the Cold War would become an increasingly global affair.

THE COLD WAR GLOBALIZES, 1949–1968

GLOBALIZATION OF THE COLD WAR: 1949

Nineteen forty-nine was a key year in the globalization of the Cold War. In Europe, NATO was established. In the USSR, the Soviets tested their first atomic bomb, eliminating America's advantage in military technology—and starting a four-decade arms race. In China, the civil war between Chiang Kai-shek's Nationalists and Mao Tse-tung's Communists, which had been raging since the end of World War II, came to an end. The Nationalists fled to the island of Taiwan. On the mainland, Mao and the Communists established the People's Republic of China (PRC). They also allied with the USSR. In a matter of months, the Cold War had expanded unimaginably: the two most populous nations on earth, and the two largest nations on the Eurasian landmass, were now joined together under the banner of communism. And one of them was armed with atomic weapons.

THE KOREAN WAR

Increasingly, the new arena of the Cold War would become Asia, Africa, and Latin America. The first sign of this was the Korean War (1950–1953). After World War II, the Korean peninsula had been divided into two zones: a northern communist sector and a southern noncommunist sector. In 1950, encouraged by Mao's victory in China (and promised assistance by Stalin and, especially, Mao), the communist dictator of North Korea, Kim Il Sung, invaded South Korea.

America's policy of containment would not allow it to stand by while South Korea was swallowed by the communist north. Under the auspices of the United Nations, the United States fought the North Koreans (as well as huge numbers of Chinese "volunteers" who unofficially joined the war). By 1953, the invasion had been turned back, and a cease-fire provided for the continued split of Korea at the original line of division. This was the first major conflict of the postwar period, and it killed more than 1.25 million Koreans and Chinese. Many of the Koreans were civilians.

THE DEATH OF STALIN AND THE RISE OF KHRUSHCHEV

During the 1950s and 1960s, new realities dominated the Cold War. The first was a change in Soviet leadership. Stalin died in 1953. He was succeeded by Nikita Khrushchev (1953–1964), then Leonid Brezhnev (1964–1982). Although Khrushchev was not as brutal a dictator as Stalin had been, and could be friendly to the West (unlike Stalin, he traveled abroad frequently and visited the United States), he was extremely unpredictable in foreign affairs. Brezhnev was more predictable, but could be quite aggressive.

THE NUCLEAR ARMS RACE

A second reality was the nuclear arms race. From 1945 to 1949, the United States enjoyed a brief monopoly on atomic weapons. This changed after 1949, when the Soviets tested their first atomic bomb. During the 1950s and early 1960s, the United States had more atomic weapons than the USSR, but its advantage narrowed with every passing year. By the mid-1960s, both superpowers had reached a state of nuclear parity. Each had large numbers of atomic weapons that could be dropped by aircraft or fired from submarines. Both sides also had the rocket technology to launch intercontinental ballistic missiles (ICBMs), loaded with nuclear warheads, directly at each other. Both superpowers were locked in an arms race, in which the quantity of nuclear weapons constantly increased. Other countries, such as Britain, France, and China, also possessed small nuclear arsenals.

This situation made traditional military planning obsolete. It also made international diplomacy incredibly tense. Any quarrel that got out of control—for example, in the way that the assassination of Francis Ferdinand in 1914 had—could result not just in a world war, but in a nuclear exchange that would destroy, at the least, both superpowers and, quite possibly, the entire world. Over time, a loose strategic arrangement known as mutually assured destruction (MAD) was reached. Both superpowers informally acknowledged that any nuclear exchange would be equally harmful to both sides. As long as neither side tried to build an anti-ballistic missile (ABM) system to defend itself, or so many ICBMs that it could destroy the other side's missiles *and* still have enough to continue fighting, both sides could assume that the other would not commit an action that was so provocative or sudden it could trigger a real crisis. With a few exceptions, this uneasy arrangement frightened both the United States and the USSR into keeping the peace during most of the Cold War. The foundation of U.S. nuclear policy was the concept of deterrence, whereby the USSR would be deterred from attacking the United States or Western Europe, because of America's commitment to retaliate by using its large nuclear arsenal.

THE CONCEPT OF THE THIRD WORLD

The third reality, which has already been commented on, was the increasingly global nature of the Cold War. Positions in Europe were so entrenched by the 1950s that little change was possible without risking all-out conflict. In Africa, Asia, and Latin America, however, many nations were modernizing, giving birth to industrial economies, or freeing themselves from European colonialism (see Chapter 32). These countries were generally politically unaligned, and the superpowers competed for influence over many, if not most of them.

For this reason, it was common during the Cold War to refer to the developing world as the Third World, because the nations of the Third World were not inherently part of the Soviet-led communist bloc or the U.S.-led west. The Soviets and Chinese enthusiastically tried to spread communism to many parts of Africa, Asia, and Latin America. In its effort to contain communism, the United States intervened in many of these areas. This gave rise to a way of thinking known as the domino theory: the belief that if one country in a region became communist, all countries in the region would "fall" to communism, like a row of dominoes collapsing. Over time, this approach frequently led the United States to choose unsavory allies in the Third World. Whether a political leader or party was democratic or popular mattered less than whether he or it was communist or anticommunist. Sadly, America supported many dictatorial or authoritarian leaders in the Third World, simply because they opposed communism.

THE 1950s

Major Cold War events of the 1950s include the rise of Khrushchev in the Soviet Union. He liberalized the USSR somewhat, especially by condemning the dictatorial excesses of Stalin in a famous speech in 1956. He also declared that the USSR was willing to have a more peaceful relationship with the United States. On the other hand, Khrushchev was capable of ruling with a firm hand. When Hungary tried to leave the Soviet bloc in 1956, he responded with a brutal invasion.

Also in 1956, Egypt's nationalization of the Suez Canal resulted in a major diplomatic crisis, in which the French and British—who owned the controlling shares in the Canal—were humiliated by a Soviet-American agreement to allow the nationalization to proceed (see Chapter 32). The Suez crisis was the most obvious sign possible that Europe's place of diplomatic dominance had been lost forever to the superpowers.

In 1957, the "space race" began, when the USSR launched the first human-made object, *Sputnik*, into space. Because rocket technology was so intimately connected with the nuclear arms race, the Soviet Union's temporary superiority in this area greatly frightened the West.

The last major development of the decade was the Cuban Revolution of 1959. That year, Fidel Castro and his followers overthrew the dictator of Cuba (see Chapter 32). Shortly after coming to power, Castro became a communist and allied himself with the USSR. Because Cuba was only ninety miles off the U.S. coast, this greatly altered the strategic equation of the Cold War.

HEIGHTENED TENSIONS DURING THE EARLY 1960s

The most dangerous phase of the Cold War came during the early 1960s. From 1960 to 1962, the superpowers came closer to all-out war than at any other point in time. Because both sides had a full-scale nuclear capacity, any such war would have been globally devastating. Ironically, the United States and the USSR were preparing for major peace talks in the summer of 1960. In May, however, an American spy plane, the U-2 piloted by Francis Gary Powers, was shot down over the Soviet Union. This incident increased tensions dramatically—although because the Soviets had known about American spy flights for years, whether or not they were truly upset or using the incident as anti-American propaganda remains unclear.

In April 1961, the United States' newly elected president, John F. Kennedy, gave his approval to the Bay of Pigs operation, in which the Central Intelligence Agency supported an anticommunist Cuban force's attempt to invade Cuba and depose Castro. The Bay of Pigs operation failed miserably and embarrassed the United States badly. Also in April 1961, the USSR sent a human pilot, Yuri Gagarin, into space for the first time in history. This triumph contrasted greatly with the Americans' failure at the Bay of Pigs.

At this point, if not beforehand, the Soviets decided to pressure America in two ways simultaneously: by renewing their aggression in Berlin and installing nuclear missiles in Cuba. In August 1961, the USSR sealed East Berlin from West Berlin by building, literally overnight, the infamous Berlin Wall. To show American determination to keep West Berlin free, Kennedy made a famous visit there shortly thereafter, declaring, "I am a Berliner."

In early 1962, the Soviets secretly began to ship rockets to Cuba and put them into place. By October, American spy planes had discovered what the Soviets were doing. The resulting Cuban Missile Crisis (1962) presented the U.S. government with a painful dilemma. Invading Cuba or trying to destroy the missiles from the air would almost certainly start a war with the USSR. Allowing the missiles to be installed was unacceptable. Kennedy chose to blockade Cuba with the U.S. Navy, forbidding any Soviet ship to proceed to the island.

The blockade was perhaps the most harrowing moment of the entire Cold War. For days, the entire world watched to see if a war, and perhaps a nuclear exchange, would result. Instead, the Soviets backed down. Khrushchev agreed to remove the missiles he had already shipped to Cuba, in exchange for America's promise never to invade the island, as well as America's agreement to remove nuclear missiles from Turkey.

THE MID-TO-LATE 1960s

During the rest of the 1960s, direct relations between the United States and USSR cooled down considerably, largely because both sides were frightened at how close to nuclear war they had come. In 1963, both sides agreed to sign the Nuclear Test Ban Treaty. That same year, a "hot line," or "red phone," was installed between the Kremlin and the White House to facilitate communications. In 1964, Khrushchev was overthrown, and Brezhnev took his place as Soviet leader. Blander and less erratic than Khrushchev, Brezhnev was more of a hard-line politician. At home, he was less liberal. Within the Eastern bloc, he was authoritarian. When, during the "Prague Spring" of 1968, Czechoslovakia embarked on a campaign of liberalizing reforms, Brezhnev sent in a Warsaw Pact invasion force to take over the country. In the process, he issued the Brezhnev Doctrine, stating that the USSR had the right to intervene in the affairs of its East European allies. However, Brezhnev seemed less likely to threaten outside the Soviet Union's declared sphere of influence. The "space race" that paralleled the arms race reached a climax, and ended in American dominance, in 1969, when the United States became the first and, thus far, only nation to land a crewed spacecraft on the moon.

In the wider world, the Cold War dynamic was changing. One of the most important developments was the growing rift between China and the USSR, or the Sino-Soviet split. Although both nations were communist, Mao and Stalin's successors disagreed about what path international communism should take. Mao also resented the Soviet leadership's patronizing, "older-brother" attitude toward the "younger" communist power. The Chinese also felt that many of the Russians, being white, treated them as racial inferiors. By the early 1960s, tensions between China and the USSR were already apparent. By the end of the 1960s, the Sino-Soviet border was a militarized zone, and occasional episodes of violence broke out.

THE VIETNAM WAR

Another development of the 1960s was that the superpowers, rather than fight each other directly, intervened in the many civil conflicts and anticolonial wars going on in the Third World. The longest and most famous of these conflicts took place in Vietnam. During World War II, the communist leader Ho Chi Minh had led forces against the Japanese. After the war, he asked the Allies to help free his country from French rule. Instead, the United States assisted in the French effort to defeat Ho Chi Minh.

After the French failed in 1954, the United States continued to oppose the Vietnamese communists. The United States supported a government in South Vietnam that was anticommunist, but also authoritarian and deeply unpopular with most ordinary Vietnamese. By the 1960s, the American effort to prop up the South Vietnamese government had become an all-out military commitment. America's involvement in Vietnam resulted from the domino-principle mindset that came with the containment strategy. By the late 1960s, the United States had more than 500,000 troops in Vietnam. In the early 1970s, the fighting spread to Laos and Cambodia. The U.S. military pulled out of the war in 1973, having lost 58,000 lives. Hundreds of thousands of Vietnamese had died during the conflict. In the end, by the spring of 1975, all of Vietnam became communist. For more, see Chapter 32.

THE LATE STAGES OF THE COLD WAR, 1968–1991

DÉTENTE DURING THE 1970s

From 1969 through 1979, the Cold War entered a more peaceful period known as *détente*, a French diplomatic term referring to the relaxation of tensions. The United States, wearied by the Vietnam conflict and plagued by economic recession at home, was relieved to scale back hostilities. The USSR's reasons for agreeing to détente include a similar economic downturn, the need for U.S. grain shipments to feed its population, and fears that America was growing closer to China (by the early 1970s, the United States had become aware of the Sino-Soviet split, and President Richard Nixon skillfully exploited this by visiting China in 1972).

Détente did not mean that Cold War tensions disappeared completely. Wars and conflicts in Africa, Asia, and Latin America still raged, with the United States and USSR typically sponsoring opposing sides. The arms race continued, and nuclear arsenals grew larger. Nonetheless, for almost a decade, the Soviets and Americans established a working relationship. At times, there were moments of genuine cooperation. The United States sold grain to the USSR. Both powers cooperated in the enforcement of the Nuclear Non-Proliferation Treaty (1968–1969), whose purpose has been to prevent the spread of nuclear weaponry to nations that are not part of the "nuclear club" (the United States, the USSR, Britain, France, and China). The United States and USSR signed the first arms-control treaties, such as SALT (1972) and the Anti-Ballistic Missile Treaty (1972). In the Helsinki Accords of 1975, the Soviet government agreed to guarantee its people basic human rights. The superpowers even cooperated in space, during the Apollo-Soyuz mission (1975).

THE EARLY-TO-MID 1980s: THE COLD WAR RESUMES

The spirit of détente ended in 1979. That year, the Soviet invasion of Afghanistan, which threatened the oil supplies of the Middle East, as well as the Indian Ocean coastline, badly damaged relations between the superpowers. The Afghan War would last for ten years and turn into a Vietnam-like nightmare for the Soviets. It also destroyed détente. In 1980, the United States elected President Ronald Reagan, who, over the next eight years, swung American foreign policy far to the right.

In terms of the arms race and the risk of nuclear war, the period between 1979 and 1987 was more perilous than any other part of the Cold War, with the exception of the Cuban missile crisis of 1962. Arms-control negotiations were abandoned, and the arms race escalated tremendously. By 1986, each side was spending roughly $300 billion per year on new weaponry. Third World brush-fire wars, terrorist campaigns sponsored by the USSR and its allies, and covert operations carried out by the CIA or the KGB all increased in number.

Both the USSR and the United States publicly expressed extreme hostility toward each other. Each boycotted Olympic Games hosted by the other (Moscow in 1980, Los Angeles in 1984). Reagan referred to the Soviet Union explicitly as the "evil empire." Because the nuclear weaponry of the 1980s was faster, more accurate, and more destructive than ever before, the chances that a diplomatic crisis could quickly result in a full-scale exchange that would destroy the entire planet were increasingly greater.

THE COLD WAR ENDS, 1987–1991

However, from the late 1980s to the early 1990s, the Cold War came to a peaceful end. This process is described in more detail in Chapter 34. The main reasons have to do with the steady internal collapse of the USSR. Brezhnev died in 1982 and was followed by two leaders who died in rapid succession. By this point, the Soviet economy was failing, and the political system was extremely corrupt.

When Mikhail Gorbachev became the leader of the USSR in 1985, he attempted to reform it completely. One thing he realized was that the Soviet Union no longer had the economic ability to keep up with the United States in the arms race.

From 1987 onward, Gorbachev entered into arms control negotiations with the American government. He also allowed the nations of Eastern Europe to free themselves from Soviet domination in 1989 and 1990. The Berlin Wall, the most tangible symbol of the "iron curtain" that had divided Cold War Europe, came down. Unexpectedly, in 1991, the Soviet Union itself collapsed. After forty-six long years, the Cold War was finally over.

QUICK REVIEW

1. What diplomatic alignment did the Cold War replace?

   (A) Europe's traditional balance of power
   (B) the unipolar domination of global power by Germany
   (C) Asiatic hegemony
   (D) global anarchy
   (E) a similar condition of bipolar equilibrium

2. Which of the following is true about armed conflict during the Cold War?

   (A) The United States and Soviet Union declared war on each other several times.
   (B) There were almost no armed conflicts at all during the Cold War.
   (C) There were no armed conflicts during the Cold War.
   (D) Approximately 50 million people died in various small-to-medium conflicts.
   (E) Several tactical nuclear exchanges took place during the Cold War.

3. What was the overall strategy pursued by Stalin and the Soviet leadership during the half-decade following World War II?

   (A) to cooperate with the United States peacefully in building an equitable global order
   (B) out of weakness, to allow the United States a free hand in shaping postwar Europe
   (C) to concede control of Asia to the United States, but gain full control of Europe
   (D) to achieve dominance over as much of Europe as possible, even if it meant risking war with the United States
   (E) to push for as many concessions as possible from the United States, both in Asia and Europe, but not at the risk of war

4. Which communist states in Eastern Europe broke away from the Soviet bloc before the 1980s?

   (A) Yugoslavia and Bulgaria
   (B) Yugoslavia and Albania
   (C) Yugoslavia and Romania
   (D) Yugoslavia and Hungary
   (E) Yugoslavia and East Germany

5. What was the Truman Doctrine?

(A) Truman's commitment to lend aid to countries threatened by communist takeover

(B) Truman's promise that the United States would go to war to protect any nation from communist takeover

(C) Truman's oath to protect Poland from absorption into the Soviet bloc

(D) Truman's declaration of war on North Korea

(E) Truman's public refusal ever to use atomic weapons after Hiroshima and Nagasaki

6. Which of the following helped to make 1949 such an important turning point in the Cold War?

(A) Fidel Castro led the Communists to victory in Cuba.

(B) The Korean War began.

(C) The USSR tested its first atomic weapon.

(D) Tito withdrew Yugoslavia from the Soviet bloc.

(E) John F. Kennedy was assassinated.

7. What made the launching of *Sputnik* and the flight of Yuri Gagarin MOST troubling to the United States?

(A) The blows to national prestige they represented.

(B) Triumphs in the "space race" were technologically linked to progress in the nuclear arms race.

(C) Gagarin's landing on the moon gave rise to fears that the USSR would make territorial claims there.

(D) Both *Sputnik* and Gagarin's spaceship were armed with advanced laser weaponry.

(E) Both *Sputnik* and Gagarin's spaceship were used to take reconnaissance photographs of U.S. missile silos.

8. Which of the following is associated with Khrushchev's leadership of the Soviet Union?

I. the brutal suppression of the Hungarian uprising

II. official denunciation of Stalin's dictatorial excesses

III. a declared willingness to establish friendlier relations with the nations of the West

IV. a sudden increase in the power of the KGB

(A) I only

(B) I or II only

(C) I and IV only

(D) I, II, and III

(E) I, III, IV

9. The Brezhnev Doctrine was

(A) the USSR's official protest against U.S. conduct in Vietnam

(B) the USSR's denunciation of Maoist China, as the Sino-Soviet split worsened

(C) the USSR's condemnation of NATO's nuclear-arms buildup

(D) the USSR's formal outlawing of all dissident activity within its borders

(E) the USSR's ideological justification of its military intervention in Czechoslovakia.

10. Détente means:

(A) a heightening of tensions

(B) a relaxation of tensions

(C) containment

(D) counterespionage

(E) exposing the enemy

ANSWERS:

1. **A**, p. 388
2. **D**, p. 388
3. **E**, p. 391
4. **B**, p. 391
5. **A**, p. 391

6. **C**, p. 393
7. **B**, p. 394
8. **D**, p. 394
9. **E**, p. 395
10. **B**, p. 396

CHAPTER 32

Divergent Forms of Development in the Postwar World, 1945–1991

Although the postwar decades were dominated diplomatically by the Cold War (see Chapters 31 and 34), individual parts of the world underwent a variety of political and social changes.

One preeminent trend was economic and technological modernization. However, this trend applied unevenly to various parts of the world. The societies of the West, the United States, Canada, and Western Europe, were already the most developed and industrialized in the world, and therefore had the capacity to modernize more quickly and more thoroughly than any other. These societies became immensely prosperous and advanced, moving into a postindustrial era by the end of the twentieth century. As for regions such as the Middle East, Africa, Asia, and Latin America, modernization, in most cases, was slower in coming. The labels typically given to these regions, the "developing world," "less developed countries," or "nondeveloped world," indicate that they lagged behind the nations of the West in moving toward prosperity. Many countries in the developing world have still not achieved that prosperity, even in the twenty-first century.

The postwar world was also an era of decolonization. World War II completed the process of weakening the grasp that several European nations still had on their empires. From the 1940s through the 1970s, countries such as Britain, France, Belgium, and the Netherlands were convinced or forced to free their colonies in the Middle East, Africa, and Asia. Moreover, many regions that had not been colonized per se, but had been economically or politically dominated by outside powers, began to assert themselves in the postwar era. This made the so-called Third World—the developing or newly liberated nations of Asia, Africa, the Mideast, and Latin America—increasingly important in global politics and economics. Unfortunately for many of these states, decolonization has sometimes caused as many problems as it has solved. Not all newly liberated countries were able to develop healthy forms of government and economic organization. Also, many of them were caught up on one side or the other in the politics of the Cold War, as the United States and Soviet Union dueled for influence throughout the Third World.

To this day, many imbalances and inequities between the West and the developing world still persist from the Cold War era. In particular, the great disparity in technological development and the vast gap between the West's affluence and the ghastly poverty of many parts of the Third World remain in place and continue to cause political and economic tension.

RECOVERY IN POSTWAR EUROPE

Europe found itself in a paradoxical situation during the postwar era. On one hand, World War II had toppled it from its position of global dominance. It had been divided by the superpowers into a Cold War battleground. It lost its remaining colonies. On the other hand, after the damage caused by World War II was repaired, most of Europe came to enjoy a level of prosperity never before known there. This was certainly the case in Western Europe, which became one of the wealthiest and most technologically advanced societies on earth. Even in communist-controlled Eastern Europe, which remained more backward than the West, the devastation caused by the war was overcome. And, albeit more crudely and more slowly than in Western Europe, Eastern Europe's standard of living and level of modernization rose from the 1950s onward.

WORLD WAR II'S EFFECTS ON EUROPE

Wartime damage had been extensive. Millions were dead. One third of the Soviet economy had been destroyed. German cities lay in ruins. At least 50 million people were homeless, and more than 16 million were refugees or "displaced persons" without a country. The migration and dislocation caused by World War II was tremendous. Poverty was horrendous. Shortages of food, clothing, consumer goods, and housing threatened to plunge Europe into utter chaos.

In another blow to European prestige, French, British, and other empires began to agitate for and win their freedom during the late 1940s and afterward. These campaigns and wars of decolonization will be discussed at greater length subsequently. It should be noted, though, that they caused the nations of Europe great stress and strain. For example, Algeria's war of independence caused the French government to collapse in 1958.

SOVIETIZATION IN EASTERN EUROPE

Despite all this, economic recovery began surprisingly quickly. In the east, as a result of the sheer political will of Stalin and the plundering of its new East European satellites (especially the Soviet-controlled zone of Germany), the USSR recovered to prewar economic levels within a decade. The USSR went on to create Soviet-style economies throughout the Eastern bloc. Economies were nationalized and centrally planned. Massive industrialization campaigns began. Collectivization, while not as brutally implemented as it had been in the USSR during the 1930s, brought agriculture under state control. The Soviet-imposed system known as the "socialist division of labor" required each East European nation to specialize in the production of certain goods or natural resources.

In both the USSR and Eastern Europe, there was substantial economic growth after the 1940s and early 1950s. Social welfare systems, which provided education, medical care, pensions, and other basic services to all citizens, were put in place. However, East European economic production was characterized by poor quality. Consumer goods were constantly in short supply, because so much emphasis was placed on weapons production during the arms race against the United States. Because Soviet and East European production was carried out without any regard whatsoever for the environment, the ecological damage caused by a half-century of East European industrialization was nothing short of catastrophic—and remains a problematic legacy. Moreover, the entire system was maintained by means of political repression. Especially under Stalin, Soviet control over Eastern Europe was harsh. There were periods of liberalization, but they were sporadic and temporary. The price of going beyond what the Soviets were willing to allow was demonstrated by the Soviet invasions of Hungary (1956) and Czechoslovakia (1968). Not until the end of the 1980s would the Eastern bloc experience real freedom (see Chapter 34).

RECOVERY IN WESTERN EUROPE

Economic recovery was even more dramatic in Western Europe. It is common for historians to refer to the boom of the 1950s and 1960s as the "miracle." As a first step, the European Recovery Plan (better known as the Marshall Plan) infused more than $13 billion into the economies of Western Europe. This helped to rebuild the war-torn nations of Europe. It helped prevent the spread of communism. It also rewarded the United States, because this first dose of economic aid created healthy markets eager to buy U.S. goods.

The "miracle" continued throughout the next two decades, as European economies went beyond rebuilding to improving and innovating. A particular star here was West Germany, which rose from the ruins of war to become Europe's economic powerhouse. Ironically, Great Britain, one of the victors of World War II, took a longer time than most European nations to recover (mainly because it had spent so much money fighting the war). Industrial growth was high. Moreover, technological innovation allowed West European economies to move beyond industrial production to service, or postindustrial, modes of economic activity (in this, the West Europeans were following a trend set by the United States).

As in Eastern Europe, most West European nations put into place social welfare systems, or improved on the ones that had been created during the 1920s and 1930s (for instance, Britain instituted social security and a National Health Service from 1946 to 1948). Although they were not socialist or communist, many West European nations began to experiment with economic systems that were not purely capitalist, either. This blend of capitalist and social-welfare (even mildly socialist) practice began to be called the "third way."

PROBLEMS IN WESTERN EUROPE

Not all developments in Western Europe were positive. Europe was caught in the crossfire of the superpowers' nuclear arms race. For a long time, Germany refused to come to grips with the Holocaust or its Nazi past. Democracies like France and Italy, mired for decades in widespread official corruption, experienced frequent government turnover. In 1968, France was rocked by a massive wave of worker and student protests in Paris that paralleled uprisings that same year in Mexico City, Prague, and universities throughout the United States. Mild authoritarianism and anti-unionism persisted in countries like Spain, Portugal, and Greece until after the mid-1970s. Great Britain wrestled with nationalist aspirations, then, after the late 1960s, terrorism in Northern Ireland.

ECONOMIC UNION IN WESTERN EUROPE

One way in which the West Europeans made up for their loss of global might was to devise various forms of union. Over time, the principle of union has enabled Europe to boost its economic strength, increase its diplomatic clout, and (less successfully) work together to prevent the outbreak of war or political extremism.

At first, efforts to unite European nations were economic. In 1952, six nations (Belgium, Luxembourg, the Netherlands, Italy, France, and West Germany) joined together to form the European Coal and Steel Community. In 1957, leaders of these six countries agreed to form even stronger economic ties when they signed the Treaty of Rome, which established the European Economic Community, also known as the Common Market. The goal of the EEC was to eliminate internal tariffs and encourage the free movement of money, goods, services, and labor. Eventually renamed the European Union, the group expanded (Britain, Ireland, and Denmark joined in 1973, and others were admitted later) and strengthened its ties. By the mid-1990s, it would include fifteen members and be moving toward monetary union and intensifying its efforts to integrate more of its policies (see Chapter 35).

Other regional organizations binding Western Europe together include the North Atlantic Treaty Organization (NATO, formed in 1949) and the Council of Europe (also 1949).

ECONOMIC CRISIS DURING THE 1970s

An economic crisis struck the Western world—the United States as well as Europe—in the early 1970s. The significant devaluing of the U.S. dollar, the currency on which so much European trade was dependent, hurt Europe. In August 1971, the United States was forced to detach its ailing currency from the gold standard. This move led to monetary instability across Western Europe. The oil embargo of 1973, imposed by the nations of the Middle East (from which Western Europe bought 70 percent of its oil), badly damaged the economies of Europe and the United States.

Both Western Europe and the United States suffered from inflation, recession (the rare combination of inflation and the stagnation caused by recession was given the nickname stagflation), and unemployment.

WESTERN EUROPE DURING THE 1980s AND 1990s

During the 1980s, many West European nations moved to the right, in an effort to escape the malaise of the 1970s. The elections of leaders such as Margaret Thatcher in Great Britain and Helmut Kohl in West Germany (discussed subsequently) were part of this general trend. The same can be said about the election of Ronald Reagan in the United States. Even France's first socialist president, François Mitterand, was forced to make various concessions to the right.

In many West European countries, there was a partial retreat from the social-welfare systems of the past, as leaders such as Thatcher privatized state-run sectors of the economy. Overall, economies throughout Western Europe recovered during the 1980s and 1990s. To be sure, unemployment, poverty, socioeconomic inequality, and racial prejudice (stirred up by the large influx of non-European and East European immigration into Western Europe) were problematic. Still, by the end of the Cold War, Western Europe was a region in which economic prosperity, healthy democratic government, and technological advancement could be taken largely—although not universally—for granted.

Major leaders of postwar Europe included Charles de Gaulle, president of France during the late 1950s and 1960s. France's only military hero of World War II, de Gaulle was fiercely independent and resisted American domination of European affairs as much as possible. Konrad Adenauer, chancellor of West Germany (1949–1963), played a large part in making Germany a respectable member of the international community after World War II. Chancellor Willy Brandt (1969–1974), also of West Germany, became famous for his policy of *Ostpolitik*, or détente with Eastern Europe. Margaret Thatcher, the first female prime minister of Great Britain (1979–1990), moved British politics and economics to the right, dismantled and privatized much of Britain's nationalized social-welfare apparatus, and worked closely with Presidents Ronald Reagan and George Bush of the United States in opposing Soviet communism. In France, president François Mitterand (1981–1995) made the socialists, rather than the communists, the respectable voices of the French left wing. Chancellor Helmut Kohl (1982–1998) of West Germany led his country to economic dominance during the 1980s. His enduring mark on German history is his reunification of East and West Germany in October 1990, after the collapse of communism in Eastern Europe.

DECOLONIZATION AND THE EMERGENCE OF THE DEVELOPING WORLD

THE RISE OF THE THIRD WORLD

One of the most powerful trends of the postwar era was the surge in importance of the developing world, also referred to by its Cold War designation, the Third World. This Third World consisted of nations in Latin America, Asia, Africa, and the Middle East that had lagged behind the countries of the West in economic and political development, or had been kept under the political and economic thumb of foreign powers, or had been directly colonized.

DECOLONIZATION AND NATIONAL LIBERATION

Even before World War II, some steps had been taken to decolonize. Britain was forced to give home rule to Ireland in 1922, thanks largely to a serious armed uprising that began there in 1916. In 1931, the Statute of Westminster transformed the British Empire into the British Commonwealth, whose members were entitled to varying degrees of autonomy. Both France and Britain began to allow some of their Middle Eastern mandates and protectorates greater freedom, if not actual independence, during the 1930s.

After World War II, decolonization became a major agent of change in Asia, the Middle East, and Africa. The war pried loose the grip that countries such as Britain and France had been able to keep on their empires, even after the debilitating effects of World War I. From the 1940s through the 1970s, dozens of new nations came into being, after having attained their freedom from their imperial masters.

Another change that took place throughout the developing world during the Cold War era was the overthrow (or attempted overthrow) of dictators and oligarchies, many of which had been installed or supported by foreign governments or economic interests. This was especially the case in Latin America, the countries of which were nominally free, but often influenced heavily by the United States. These political conflicts were often referred to as struggles for national liberation, just as actual decolonization campaigns were.

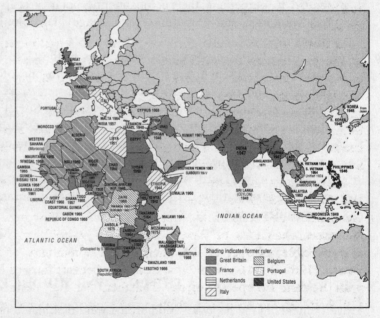

Decolonization and National Liberation in Africa and Asia After 1945.
World War II dealt the final blow to the European powers' ability to maintain control over their colonial empires. From the 1940s through the 1970s, a great wave of decolonization and national liberation swept Africa and Asia. Freedom was attained in a variety of ways—sometimes peacefully, sometimes by force.

PATTERNS OF DECOLONIZATION

The means and results of decolonization varied from country to country. Specific cases will be discussed in the geographical sections that follow. There was no set pattern to decolonization. Whether or not a newly liberated nation succeeded in building a healthy political and economic system depended on, among other things, the following questions:

- Had a newly decolonized nation had to fight a war to become free?
- How enlightened had the colonizing power been? Had it educated a native elite, leaving behind politicians, economists, and trained personnel with practical skills? Did the colonizing power assist actively with the transition to freedom? As a general rule, Britain had a good record in this respect. To a certain degree, France did as well, but it had more problems with decolonization than Britain did.
- Were there serious ethnic, cultural, or religious divisions within a newly liberated country? In many cases, the presence of a colonizing power had acted as a restraining force, keeping such tensions under control. Decolonization often released these tensions, leading to violence.
- Did a country have natural resources to exploit? Did the government exploit them efficiently? Former colonies that could not compete on the international market often suffered severe economic difficulties. Also, a newly liberated nation that did not diversify its economy, but continued to rely on monoculture or the extraction of a small set of resources, tended to perpetuate the socioeconomic polarity (gap between rich and poor), economic backwardness, and environmental damage that colonialism and imperial economics had caused.
- Did a newly liberated country take sides in the Cold War? If so, did it choose to, or was it forced to? Often, former colonies turned to one of the superpowers for economic and political support. Because their former masters were generally aligned with the United States, and because the Marxist rhetoric of the Soviet Union (and, as time passed, China) sounded appealing, many newly liberated countries turned, at least for a while, to the USSR (or, less frequently, China). In other cases, strategic considerations led one or both superpowers to intervene in the affairs of a decolonized nation. After the Cold War ended, left behind in many Third World countries were thousands of small arms and light weapons— and a persistent flow of deadly weapons that continues to fuel interethnic and intertribal animosities today.

THE MIDDLE EAST

GENERAL PATTERNS IN THE POSTWAR MIDDLE EAST

Developments in the postwar Middle East were dominated mainly by the following factors:

- *The independence of former colonies and mandates.*
- *The region's strategic and economic importance as the world's key source of petroleum.* Two thirds of the world's crude oil is produced in the Middle East. The Organization of Petroleum Exporting Countries (OPEC), founded in 1960, is dominated by states from the Middle East. Unfortunately, the wealth derived from oil has not led to the elimination of poverty or socioeconomic inequality. The major reserves are not located in the most heavily populated countries. Also, even within oil-producing states, profits have tended to land in the pockets of the upper class.
- *Contradictions between the urge to modernize and a desire on the part of many Middle Easterners to preserve Islamic tradition.* Islamic fundamentalism has been dominant in countries such as Iran (after 1979) and Afghanistan (after 1989). Its influence in other

Middle Eastern states varies, depending on specific circumstances, but it is considerable. One of the most difficult questions facing the Islamic states of the Middle East is how to balance the cultural and religious heritage of Islam with progressive social and political practices such as democracy, freedom of religion, freedom of journalistic and artistic expression, secular law codes, and gender equality. How women are treated, how they dress, how much reproductive freedom they have, whether they may go out in public, what types of educations or jobs (if any) they may have—all these are questions that especially depend on how this issue is resolved.

- *The destabilizing effect of the Arab-Israeli conflict since 1948.* This remains an intractable, painful, and divisive issue, even into the twenty-first century.
- *The competition between the United States and the USSR for influence in the region during the Cold War.* The two Middle Eastern states firmly in the U.S. camp were Turkey and Israel. All others switched sides, back and forth, depending on where they thought their advantage lay.
- *The persistence of dictatorship, authoritarian rule, or human rights abuses, even in countries that are technically democratic.*

AUTONOMY AND MODERNIZATION IN THE MIDDLE EAST

Even before World War II, the various protectorates and mandates of the Middle East had been gaining freedom or greater autonomy. Shortly after the war, Saudi Arabia, Iraq, Jordan, Syria, and Lebanon were all free. Egypt and North Africa would become independent during the 1950s and 1960s. Egyptian officers staged a coup against the pro-British king in 1952. Libya, taken from Italy by France and Britain during the war, was also freed in 1952. Morocco and Tunisia gained their freedom from France in 1956. Algeria, the African colony France was most unwilling to set free, had to fight a bitter war of independence from 1954 to 1962.

Turkey and Iran, already independent during the interwar period, continued on their paths toward modernization. More than any other Islamic state, Turkey has remained dedicated to secularism and westernization. It has integrated itself into European markets, as well as the NATO alliance. This has enabled Turkey to serve as a gateway between the Western world and the Middle East. Iran did much the same, but to a lesser extent, and only until 1979, when its pro-Western government was overthrown.

EGYPT UNDER GAMAL ABDEL NASSER

Independence, oil-based wealth, and geostrategic importance made the states of the Middle East more assertive in the 1950s and 1960s. The most famous example of this new Arab nationalism appeared in Egypt, which became an independent republic in 1952. By 1954, Colonel Gamal Abdel Nasser had taken control of the government.

A great booster of modernization, Nasser was an equally great proponent of pan-Arabism. He labored to create a United Arab Republic that would link all Arab nations together in a cooperative commonwealth. This effort failed, but Nasser was successful in modernizing his country. He also stood up to the West, nationalizing foreign-owned or foreign-controlled industries and businesses.

In 1956, Nasser took the bold step of declaring Egyptian ownership of the Suez Canal. The move prompted the Suez crisis, in which French, British, and Israeli troops tried to seize the canal. The United States and USSR, however, wishing to avoid a serious armed conflict in the region, forced the British, French, and Israelis to withdraw, leaving the canal in Egyptian hands. The end result was a huge blow to the diplomatic prestige of France and Britain.

Because Nasser was anti-British, he chose to strengthen ties with the Soviet Union, at least temporarily. Soviet advisers and engineers brought technology and weaponry to Egypt; they also constructed the Aswan Dam, the world's largest. However, when the Soviets attempted to exert too much control over Egyptian politics, Nasser expelled them.

Nasser died in 1970. He was succeeded by Anwar el-Sadat, who drew Egypt closer to the United States and, in 1978, became the first Arab leader to recognize the state of Israel. Sadat was assassinated by Islamic militants in 1981. Since then, Hosni Mubarak has served as Egypt's president.

THE ESTABLISHMENT OF ISRAEL

Along with freedom and independence, the most dramatic postwar development in the Middle East has been the establishment of the state of Israel as a homeland for the world's Jews. In 1917, Britain, which gained control over Palestine at the end of World War I, agreed in principle to create a Jewish state there, but delayed this decision during the 1920s and 1930s in order to avoid Arab unrest.

After World War II and the horrors of the Holocaust, however, international sympathy for the Jews, along with strong U.S. support, led to the establishment of the state of Israel, in May 1948. Immediately, this stirred up Arab outrage and plunged the Middle East into war. The Israelis had to fight a war in 1948 simply to keep the state that had been given them. This had the effect of displacing millions of Palestinian Arabs, who scattered to Jordan, Lebanon, and throughout the Middle East.

In 1964, the Palestinian diaspora gained a semblance of leadership with the foundation of the Palestine Liberation Organization (PLO), a terrorist group and political movement led by Yasser Arafat.

THE ARAB-ISRAELI CONFLICT

The Arab states fought several wars against Israel, most notably the Six-Day War in 1967 and the Yom Kippur War in 1973. Each time, Israel, with a supremely trained, highly motivated army and strong backing from the United States, defeated the Arab coalitions decisively, taking much territory away from several Arab states in the process. PLO terrorism was frequent; most infamously, a PLO squad assassinated members of the Israeli Olympic team in 1972.

Not until 1978, when Anwar al-Sadat of Egypt, encouraged by U.S. President Jimmy Carter, agreed with Israeli Prime Minister Menachem Begin to recognize Israel in exchange for the return of the Sinai Peninsula, was there an end to outright war in the region. Following Egypt's lead, a number of moderate Arab states began to recognize Israel during the 1980s.

However, problems remained. Throughout the 1980s, the Palestinian population of Israel staged a continuous uprising called the intifada. These demonstrations and protests often led to bloodshed. At the same time, various terrorist groups acted against Israel as well. This placed Israel in a difficult position: in order to avoid utter social collapse and a total breakdown of security, it— despite being a democracy, theoretically committed to human rights— routinely felt compelled to use violence against civilian agitators who, although hostile and sometimes dangerous, were poorly armed and often minors.

In 1993 and 1994, the Israelis and Palestinians signed historic peace agreements, one of which called for Palestinian self-rule in parts of Israel. The United States attempted throughout the 1990s to mediate between the two sides and to keep the peace process alive. Nonetheless, tensions remained high, and the peace effort collapsed in 2001, amid violence from both sides.

POLITICAL AUTHORITARIANISM IN THE MIDDLE EAST

As a general rule, Middle Eastern regimes have tended to be authoritarian or dictatorial. Many Middle Eastern states, such as Morocco, Jordan, and Saudi Arabia, are monarchies. Strongman dictatorships are also common, as in Syria (under Hafez Assad and his family), Libya (Colonel Muammar Qaddafi), and Iraq (President Saddam Hussein).

Even in democracies such as Egypt and Turkey, the perceived need to combat Islamic extremism has led to a certain heaviness of political control: elections are not completely open, civil rights are somewhat constrained, and the media are not entirely free. Israel's democracy has been compromised by the harshness with which it has put down terrorism and the intifadas of the 1980s and 2001.

IRAN

The most powerful dictatorships in the Middle East are those of Iran and Iraq. Since the 1920s, Iran had been ruled by the secular, modernizing Pahlavi shahs. The last shah of Iran, Mohammad Reza Pahlavi, ruled from 1941 to 1979. The Shah used Iran's oil wealth to industrialize and modernize. Like the Turkish government, the Shah's regime opposed Islamic traditionalism, encouraging Western dress, Western education, the unveiling of women, and the eradication of Islamic law. The Shah became an ally of the United States.

Unfortunately, the Shah relied on repression to carry out his modernization campaign: dissidents were ruthlessly suppressed by the secret police (SAVAK), and the regime was decidedly antidemocratic. By 1979, the Shah was in poor health, and his popularity had plummeted. He left the country to seek medical treatment, but died of cancer in 1980.

In the meantime, in 1979, the Shiite cleric Ayatollah Ruhollah Khomeini, an Islamic fundamentalist the Shah had exiled years before, returned to Iran and took control of the country. This Iranian Revolution transformed the country into an anti-Western (particularly anti-U.S.), theocratic dictatorship. Famously, the new regime held American hostages captive for a number of months in 1979 to 1981. At the same time, Iran went to war with neighboring Iraq. The Iran-Iraq War lasted from 1980 to 1988, and devastated both countries. Khomeini died in 1989. The theocracy he created remains in place, although reformers gained a majority of seats in Parliament in 2000, and the current president, Mohammad Khatami, is a moderate Muslim cleric.

IRAQ

Iraq came under the control of Saddam Hussein in 1979. Although his title is "president," Hussein is one of the most powerful dictators of the Middle East. Originally sponsored by the United States because of his opposition to Iran, Hussein turned his brutality against his own people, his neighbors, and the United States. During his war with Iran, he used poison gas, drafted teenaged children to fight in his armies, and killed many civilians. He viciously persecuted his nation's Kurdish minority.

In 1990, he invaded the oil-rich state of Kuwait and appeared ready to do the same to Saudi Arabia. In the first major conflict of the post–Cold War era, the United States led a military coalition that pushed Hussein out of Kuwait in the Gulf War (1991). Casualties were estimated to be over 85,000. Beginning in 1991, United Nations trade sanctions were put in place, in an effort to force Hussein to comply with the terms of the 1991 cease-fire agreement, which include the abolishing of chemical and biological weapons programs. Since then, the United States and Great Britain have continued to bomb Iraqi air-defense sites.

AFRICA

DECOLONIZATION IN AFRICA

Decolonization began in Africa mainly during the 1950s and 1960s, somewhat later than it did in the Middle East or Asia. Colonized after most other parts of the world, anticolonial backlash started in Africa correspondingly later. Before World War II, native political groups in Africa had been founded mainly for the purpose of improving living conditions or working within the political systems imposed by the colonizing powers.

After World War II, however, those groups began to agitate for actual independence. By the late 1990s, Africa would contain 46 countries. Its population would grow from 300 million in the 1960s to around 800 million by 1990. All African nations are still affected by the colonial legacy in terms of security and economic stability.

NATIONAL LIBERATION IN NORTH AFRICA

The Islamic states of North Africa became free during the 1950s. As described previously, Egypt declared independence in 1952, as did Libya. Morocco and Tunisia gained freedom from France in 1956. The long and painful Algerian War of Independence (1954–1962) against France completed the process of lifting the colonial yoke from North Africa.

As opposed to sub-Saharan Africa, North African states had several advantages when it came to decolonization. They were largely, although not completely, homogeneous in terms of religion, ethnicity, and language. They had existed as meaningful political units for a long time, making the transition to nation-state easier. Their colonizing powers also left behind technology and industrial infrastructures (railroads, telegraphs, canals, etc.) that proved economically useful, especially in Algeria and Egypt.

INDEPENDENCE IN SUB-SAHARAN AFRICA

The nations of sub-Saharan Africa, with a population of around 250 million in 1945, had more of a struggle when it came to creating successful independent states. Major freedom movements began this struggle during the 1940s. One of the oldest was South Africa's African National Congress (ANC), which had existed since 1912, but became much more radical after World War II. In the Gold Coast, Kwame Nkrumah founded the Convention People's Party almost immediately after the war was over. Also important was Jomo Kenyatta's Kenya African National Union, founded in the late 1940s.

For the most part, these movements were nonviolent political parties, led by intellectuals and labor activists. There were, however, exceptions. One of the most famous was the Mau Mau movement among Kenya's Kikuyu people. In contrast to Kenyatta's approach to decolonization, the Mau Mau killed more than 100 Europeans and 1,700 Africans during the 1950s. Regions in which violence became a major part of the decolonization process included Zimbabwe (Rhodesia), South Africa, Rwanda, Zaire (the Belgian Congo), Angola, and Mozambique.

The first sub-Saharan colony to gain its freedom, in 1957, was the British-controlled Gold Coast, which, under Nkrumah's leadership, renamed itself Ghana. France freed its colonies in sub-Saharan Africa during the period from 1958 to 1962: Guinea, Senegal, Upper Volta (now Burkina Faso), Madagascar, Mali, Mauritania, Niger, Gabon, Dahomey (now Benin), the Central African Republic, Chad, Côte d'Ivoire, the Republic of the Congo (not to be confused with the Belgian Congo), and Cameroon. After freeing Ghana in 1957, Britain waited until 1961 to 1966 to begin a massive wave of decolonization: Nigeria, Sierra Leone, South Africa (1961), Uganda, Kenya (1963), Botswana, Zambia, Gambia, Lesotho, and Tanzania (the union of Tanganyika and the island of Zanzibar). Spain freed Equatorial Guinea in 1968.

VARYING TRANSITIONS TO FREEDOM

For the most part, decolonization in the parts of Africa that had been British and French went smoothly. Both Britain and France (to a lesser extent) took great care to prepare their colonies for freedom by educating native elites, allowing greater native representation in transitional governments, and minimizing the possibility of interethnic conflict. On the whole, violence was kept to a minimum or avoided altogether, even in Kenya, where the Mau Mau movement had raged.

Not all went well, however. In Rhodesia, a white-controlled government declared independence from Britain in 1965. The new government harshly repressed black natives, who responded with violence. Only after a savage fifteen-year conflict was Rhodesia placed under native rule, in 1980, when the country renamed itself Zimbabwe. For decades, there were also serious problems involved with South African independence from Britain (discussed presently).

The worst transitions to independence were made by Belgium's and Portugal's colonies. Here, the imperial masters had been particularly exploitative (especially in the Belgian Congo), and neither Belgium nor Portugal took steps to prepare their colonies for independence. Guinea-Bissau gained freedom from Portugal in 1974, but only after a vicious guerrilla war. Angola fought a war of liberation against its Portuguese masters from 1961 to 1975. Then, even after achieving independence, Angola was torn apart by the continuation of the violence that had been stirred up by the anti-Portuguese war.

A similar situation prevailed in the Portuguese colony of Mozambique, which fought against Portugal from 1965 to 1975, then experienced civil war after being granted independence.

Belgium pulled out of Rwanda in 1962, leaving behind two tribes, the Hutu and Tutsi, that hated each other deeply. Earlier, the Belgians had freed the Congo, after years of having exploited it terribly. Postindependence violence in the Congo was so pervasive from 1960 to 1964 that the United Nations had to intervene. The prime mover in the campaign for Congolese independence, the Marxist Patrice Lumumba, was assassinated by political rivals in late 1965.

SOUTH AFRICA AND THE EXPERIENCE OF APARTHEID

As in Rhodesia/Zimbabwe, but for much longer, decolonization in South Africa was tainted by the clash between white and black citizens of the newly free country. The government that had declared freedom from Britain was controlled by the white minority, largely descended from Dutch Boers. These Afrikaners still practiced the policy of apartheid, or extreme racial segregation. South Africa is one of the world's richest sources of gold and diamonds. Therefore, from the 1960s through the 1990s, the white government of South Africa turned its nation into the wealthiest, most modern, and most industrialized nation on the continent.

Apartheid, however, made South Africa one of Africa's most repressive nations as well. By the 1980s, internal unrest, economic problems, and international revulsion were placing extreme pressure on the South African government to abandon the policy of apartheid. Groups like the Zulu Confederation and the African National Congress opposed the white government. The ANC's leader, Nelson Mandela, gained the status of sympathetic dissident during his long imprisonment (1964–1990) by the white authorities. His wife, Winnie Mandela, continued the struggle on his behalf. Another moral figure in the anti-apartheid movement was Bishop Desmond Tutu, a black clergyman in the Anglican Church and a Nobel Peace Prize recipient. Finally, in 1990, the government released Nelson Mandela. In 1994, free elections resulted in the ANC's victory. Mandela became the country's president.

VARYING METHODS OF MODERNIZATION

During the postwar period, free African nations took many paths toward modernization. Some leaders, such as Jomo Kenyatta, attempted Western-style capitalism. Others were attracted to Marxism and various types of socialism, such as Julius Nyerere of Tanzania, Kwame Nkrumah of Ghana, Patrice Lumumba of the Congo, and Sékou Touré of Guinea. Pan-Africanism was a utopian goal of several of these leaders. In 1964, Nkrumah presided over the foundation of the Organization for African Unity (OAU). An African Economic Community was founded in 1991.

PROBLEMS FACING INDEPENDENT AFRICA

Unfortunately, many of Africa's original aspirations proved difficult, if not impossible, to attain. Very few African nations managed to achieve democratic governments, open societies, and economies that led to prosperity for all (or even many) citizens. Some of the problems that have interfered with African modernization include the following:

- *Dictatorship:* Despite beginning as democratic systems, many of Africa's governments degenerated into strongman regimes, at least temporarily. Among the most notorious of African dictators was Idi Amin, whose brutal rule over Uganda (1971–1979) was notoriously savage. Other authoritarian regimes included those of Nigeria's military rulers and Mobutu Sese Seko of Zaire (1965–1997).
- *Corruption:* Dictatorial or not, many African regimes also tended to function according to unlawful systems of patronage, nepotism, and graft.
- *Failure to modernize and diversify economies:* Rather than industrialize and diversify, many African regimes have chosen to generate wealth simply by continuing to export the natural resources their former colonial masters took from them. This has enabled foreign investors to gain a great deal of control over African politics. It has also kept profits in the hands of political rulers, rather than spreading wealth among the population at large.
- *Foreign debt:* The fact that most African regimes owe massive amounts of money to Western nations makes it even more difficult for them to direct wealth toward the well-being of their own people.
- *The Cold War:* As with the rest of the developing world, many African nations became pawns in the global chess game between the United States and the USSR.
- *Rapid population growth and food shortages:* Africa has one of the world's fastest-growing populations. Because Africa is the world's second-largest continent, it is not actually over-populated. Its problem is that the *rate* of population growth has outstripped the rate of economic growth. Political regimes have not developed the economic ability to distribute food, goods, and wealth to all people. This population growth has tended to result in large numbers of people suffering from poor medical care and lack of food. Famine has been a persistent problem in certain parts of Africa, especially the Sahara. Somalia and Ethiopia have particularly suffered from food shortages. A 1991 survey reported that only 22 percent of land suitable for cultivation was in fact in production.
- *The HIV/AIDS pandemic:* From the 1980s onward, the HIV virus, which seems to have originated in Africa, has caused millions of deaths. Containing the spread of the virus has proven impossible, and African nations are too poor to afford the medicines needed to treat large numbers of AIDS victims.
- *Lack of cultural or linguistic unity:* In Africa, the lines that determine a nation's political borders are, in most cases, meaningless when it comes to determining where people of a certain ethnicity or language group live. Most borders were drawn by European colonizers for their own benefit and convenience. Therefore, within most African nations, there is a dizzying array of ethnicities, languages, cultural practices, and religions. In the Democratic Republic of the Congo, for example, there are more than 200 distinct tribes, and 75 languages are spoken. Often, the only common tongue is that of the former colonial power. This makes it difficult for a single state to govern all its people fairly.
- *Intertribal and interethnic conflict:* Frequently, the preceding problem becomes serious enough that it breaks out into violence, even all-out warfare. Since the colonial period, nearly all the wars in Africa have been fought within national borders, not between different countries.
- *Uncontrolled flow of small arms and light weapons:* Although this is a problem throughout the developing world, it is particularly dire in Africa. Small arms feature prominently in

armed conflicts, postconflict situations, and everyday life. Thousands of children have been forcibly drafted into militias and paramilitaries.

- *Treatment of women:* In Africa's more developed countries, and especially in the cities, women have attained a certain degree of economic and social equality—such as the right to an education, the right to work, and the right to legal divorce and birth control. However, progress has been slow, and has not enjoyed much success in the many rural parts of Africa. Women are still dominated by men in many parts of Africa. Where they can work, they often have low-status, low-paying jobs. Less than 20 percent of students are women. In less-developed areas, wives are still subservient to husbands, and marriages are arranged. In many regions, polygamy is still permitted. One infamous practice, clitoridectomy, is still in effect in certain parts of Africa.

ASIA

Among the nations of the developing world, those of Asia seem to have been the most successful in terms of building stable governments and attaining economic prosperity. Regional organizations, notably the Association of Southeast Asian Nations (ASEAN, formed in 1967), have boosted economic, social, and cultural development and cooperation among their members. Nonetheless, political repression, interethnic and interreligious strife, socioeconomic inequality, and periodic economic crises have caused problems as well. The Cold War also played a role in creating tensions.

THE PHILIPPINES

In South and Southeast Asia, decolonization campaigns began almost immediately after World War II. Some were ended quickly, others dragged on. Almost all involved some degree of violence. The first colony in the region to be freed was the Philippines, which, during the war, had been promised independence from the United States. Freedom was granted voluntarily in 1946. The United States hoped that this would provide an example to colonial powers such as France and Britain.

INDIAN AND PAKISTANI INDEPENDENCE

India and Pakistan gained their independence next. In this case, Britain handed over power freely. In 1945, the British viceroy, Lord Louis Mountbatten, was ordered to prepare to transfer government to "responsible Indian hands" by 1948. Riots and disturbances, mainly consisting of clashes between Muslims and Hindus, sped up the British timetable.

On August 15, 1947, India and Pakistan were given their independence. Although the British did not have to be expelled by force, independence led to violence nonetheless. The transfer of population between Hindu India and Muslim Pakistan, along with religious violence along the border, cost at least a million lives. In January 1948, Mohandas "Mahatma" Gandhi, the spiritual leader of the Indian freedom movement, was assassinated by a Hindu extremist who opposed his rhetoric of tolerance between the two faiths.

Despite their difficult beginnings, both nations survived. Pakistan has become a modern Islamic republic and a major regional power. However, the original goal of its founder, Muhammad Ali Jinnah, has not been attained. Jinnah dreamed of a democratic republic that, while carrying out progressive and modern policies, could remain true to Muslim principles and traditions. Instead, Pakistan has been plagued by corruption, political repression, and military rule. It has also been caught up in a costly and dangerous diplomatic rivalry with its neighbor, India. Both countries developed nuclear-weapons capability during the 1990s, making this conflict even tenser.

MODERN INDIA

India has turned itself into the world's largest democracy. On the other hand, it has also suffered from sprawling inefficiency, an inability to balance population growth with economic growth, and interethnic and interfaith strife. The dominant political force in free India was the Congress Party, led by Jawaharlal Nehru, who served as India's prime minister from 1947 until his death in 1964. Unlike Gandhi, who had favored traditional Hindu values (although not religious bigotry) and economic simplicity, Nehru wanted to secularize India and turn it into a modern, educated industrial power.

Diplomatically, Nehru negotiated a difficult position: neighbor to a hostile China and even more hostile Pakistan, and not wishing to be a client of the Soviets, the British, or the United States, Nehru maintained a friendly, cooperative relationship with the USSR, without actually falling into the Soviet camp. Like Sukarno of Indonesia (discussed presently), Nehru preserved his country's status as a nonaligned nation.

From 1966 to 1975, then again from 1977 to 1984, Nehru's daughter, Indira Gandhi, was prime minister of India. She continued her father's policies of modernization and political nonalignment. Religious strife was her downfall. Her government's actions against the Sikh minority of Punjab caused much strife. In 1984, Sikh soldiers in her own bodyguard assassinated her. From 1984 to 1991, her son, Rajiv Gandhi, led the Congress Party and served as prime minister. He was assassinated by Sri Lankan separatists. Since 1991, India's democratic government has continued to struggle with the same problems that Nehru and his descendants did.

SOUTHEAST ASIA

After freeing India, Britain let go of its other Southeast Asian colonies. Burma became independent in 1948, Malaysia in 1957, Singapore (which had been attached to Malaysia) in 1965. Hong Kong remained in British hands until 1997, when it was returned to mainland China.

INDONESIA

Less willingly than the British, the Dutch and French were forced out of Southeast Asia. Even after World War II, the Netherlands retained control over the Dutch East Indies, or Indonesia. After the war, the charismatic leader of the Indonesian Nationalist Party, Sukarno, began to agitate for freedom, and a war of national liberation began in 1945. Afraid that continued combat would lead to a communist takeover of the region, the United States persuaded the Dutch to hand over freedom.

The new nation of Indonesia was born in 1949, with Sukarno as its leader. A huge archipelago, Indonesia is one of the world's largest and most populous nations. It is linguistically and ethnically diverse, although 80 percent of the population is Muslim. At first Sukarno governed this vast nation democratically, but became authoritarian as time passed. In the late 1950s, he dissolved the constitution in favor of a policy he called "Guided Democracy." He also drew closer to the Indonesian Communist Party. In 1965, the army, allied with conservative Muslims, staged a coup against Sukarno. It turned into a popular uprising, in which as many as half a million people—mainly Communists—were killed. Sukarno was weakened by the coup, then forced out of office in 1967.

From 1967 to 1998, Indonesia was governed by a military strongman, General Suharto. A dictatorial ruler with a record of frequent human-rights abuses, Suharto promoted economic growth, anticommunism, and alliance with the United States.

VIETNAM, LAOS, AND CAMBODIA

The French attempted for almost a decade to hold on to their colony of Indochina (Vietnam, Laos, and Cambodia). In September 1945, however, the Vietnamese nationalist and communist Ho Chi

Minh declared independence. Encouraged by the U.S. promise of freedom to the Philippines and proud of his movement's record of anti-Japanese resistance during World War II, Ho Chi Minh hoped that freedom would be granted without a struggle.

Instead, the French, with U.S. support, fought Ho Chi Minh until 1954, in an effort to maintain control over Indochina. Defeated by Vietnamese expertise in guerrilla warfare and jungle fighting, the French withdrew. At the Geneva Conference of 1954, Laos, Cambodia, and Vietnam were given their independence. Vietnam was temporarily divided into a northern communist-dominated zone and a southern noncommunist zone.

Elections were to be held as soon as possible, but the French-educated, Catholic, U.S.-backed leader of South Vietnam, Ngo Dinh Diem, refused to allow elections, because he knew that the Buddhist, anti-French peasant masses would vote against him. Frustrated, Ho Chi Minh and the North Vietnamese communists began to fight the south in 1959.

By the early 1960s, the United States was providing substantial military support for South Vietnam. Despite the uselessness of conventional military methods against the North's guerrilla-warfare skills and the obvious hatred of most Vietnamese for the southern government, the United States continued its military intervention for years. In 1968, the United States suffered a serious public-relations setback when the communists staged the Tet Offensive, catching the Americans and South Vietnamese forces off guard. America began to scale back its war effort, but not until January 1973 did the United States agree to withdraw all of its troops. In April 1975, the communists captured the South Vietnamese capital and unified the entire country under their rule.

MILITARISM AND AUTHORITARIANISM IN SOUTHEAST ASIA

Military or authoritarian government became the rule throughout much of Southeast Asia. The communist Khmer Rouge movement in Cambodia took power and carried out a hideous reign of terror that claimed as many as 2 million victims. The U.S.-backed regime of Ferdinand Marcos, which governed the Philippines until the early 1980s, violated civil rights and was extravagantly corrupt. To a lesser degree, the same was true for the regime the United States supported in South Korea (discussed presently). Myanmar (Burma) and Thailand came under military rule. As noted previously, Indonesia was heavily authoritarian. Even prosperous and ultramodern Singapore, under prime minister Lee Kuan-yew, emphasized conformity and tradition over freedom and civil liberties.

JAPAN AFTER WORLD WAR II

Modernization came to the major nations of East Asia. Japan became the region's surprise power-house. Just as West Germany, one of the defeated powers of World War II, became the economic dynamo of postwar Europe, Japan, a losing nation, developed Asia's most powerful economy. At its peak during the 1980s, the Japanese economy was the world's third most productive, after the United States' and West Germany's. Per capita income was among the world's highest, and social services such as education and health care were excellent.

After World War II, Japan was occupied by the U.S. armed forces, which presided over democratic constitutional reform (1947) and the demilitarization of the country. The United States viewed Japan as a strategic anchor of its Cold War policy in Asia, and invested in it heavily, both militarily and economically. Politically, Japan became a parliamentary democracy; although the emperor retained his symbolic role, the Diet (parliament) ran the government.

The Liberal Democratic Party came to dominate party politics, and, although Japan's democratic system never ceased to function, the Liberal Democrats' tremendous influence over the Diet has led some commentators to view Japan as slightly oligarchic. Much of Japan's postwar success depended on its population's dedicated work ethic and, through the 1980s, its willingness to place the needs of Japanese society above the desires of the individual.

The 1990s, however, brought not only an economic recession and revelations of deep-seated government corruption, but also changes in social attitudes. Younger generations are becoming less willing to submit their individuality to a general spirit of conformity, to work as selflessly as their parents and grandparents, or to accept traditional social roles. A desire for greater gender equality, in a society where women have generally been expected to play secondary and supporting roles, has begun to take hold of Japan as well.

TAIWAN, SOUTH KOREA, AND THE "LITTLE TIGERS"

Like Japan, but to a lesser extent, Taiwan (the Republic of China) and South Korea have developed prosperous and free societies. From the 1950s through the 1970s, neither Taiwan nor South Korea was truly democratic. Instead, they were anticommunist regimes that, while parliamentary, concentrated power in the hands of one dominant party. In the case of Taiwan, this was the Nationalist Party (Kuomintang) that had been defeated by Mao's Chinese Communist Party in 1949. Chiang Kai-shek remained in control of the Kuomintang—and thus Taiwan—until his death in 1975. By the end of the 1970s, Taiwan began to democratize.

South Korea remained authoritarian until 1989, when free elections began to be held. Despite their less than democratic nature, both Taiwan and South Korea became allies of the United States because of their staunch anticommunism. They also became economic success stories; along with Hong Kong, Singapore, and Thailand, they became known as the "little tigers" for their economic strength (as distinct from the great "tiger" of the Japanese economy).

Both Taiwan and South Korea were extremely important to the United States' Cold War strategic posture. In 1950 to 1953, the United States spearheaded the United Nations coalition that kept South Korea safe from North Korean invasion. In the 1970s, even though the United States was forced to disclaim its formal recognition of Taiwan in order to establish formal ties with the People's Republic of China on the mainland, the U.S.-Taiwanese relationship has remained strong, both politically and economically.

NORTH KOREA

Communism in East Asia came to North Korea after World War II, when the country was divided by the Americans and Soviets. From the 1940s onward, North Korea has remained one of the most isolated and rigidly dictatorial societies on earth. Its longtime leader, Kim Il Sung (1948–1994), was an uncompromising Stalinist and ruthlessly oppressive. To the present day, North Korea still holds to its communist system, although economic collapse and its insistence on maintaining a huge military have placed the population in imminent danger of mass starvation.

THE PEOPLE'S REPUBLIC OF CHINA

The People's Republic of China, established by Mao Tse-tung's Chinese Communist Party (CCP) in 1949, has been the most populous communist nation on earth for more than five decades. Like the rest of East Asia, China has modernized—although not as consistently or successfully.

China was ruled by its founder, Mao, from 1949 until his death in 1976. At first, Mao seemed to want to carry out pragmatic social and economic reform. His New Democracy of the early 1950s was greeted with some enthusiasm, as were his initial land reforms. His first Five-Year Plan (1953–1958), done in imitation of the USSR's five-year plans, led to industrial growth. Collectivization of agriculture began in 1955, but was (at first) carried out in a more gradual and more humane fashion than Stalin's collectivization campaigns of the late 1920s and early 1930s.

On the other hand, Mao's radical transformation of society, which included persecution of dissenters and so-called class enemies (members of the bourgeoisie or aristocracy), was harsh. Moreover, Mao's aspirations became overly ambitious by the end of the 1950s, and he began to press too quickly and too radically for further modernization. In 1958, Mao began the Great Leap Forward. It included a rapid industrial buildup, even more grandiose than the First Five-Year Plan. More important, in the sphere of agriculture, it intensified collectivization and called for an utterly unrealistic increase in the production of foodstuffs. The trauma, stress, and confusion caused by the Great Leap Forward led to utter chaos and breakdown in the industrial sector. Even worse, harvests failed and agriculture collapsed altogether. The famines that resulted in 1959 and 1960 killed millions (the best estimate is 15 million). The Great Leap Forward was halted in 1960, but not before the damage was done. The Great Leap Forward caused splits within the CCP leadership, and opposition to Mao grew.

In 1966, Mao embarked on yet another program of radical modernization, this time in the sphere of society and culture. This was the Great Proletarian Cultural Revolution, which lasted a decade, until Mao's death in 1976. The Cultural Revolution has been interpreted by historians as a policy used by Mao and his wife, Jiang Qing (the movement's primary architect), to strike at their political enemies. It also represented Mao's and Jiang's sincere desire to instill absolute revolutionary purity within Chinese society and culture. Censorship was absolute, and indoctrination was crushingly heavy. The one acceptable source of all wisdom was *The Little Red Book,* a collection of Mao's sayings. Young communist activists, known as Red Guards, rampaged throughout the country, denouncing and putting on trial any person—university professors, factory foremen, heads of collective farms, writers or journalists, even politicians—whom they considered to be untrue to revolutionary communist ideals in any way. Victims were demoted, harassed, often arrested and sent to labor camps for "reeducation"—and sometimes executed. Even members of the CCP elite were not immune to the Cultural Revolution. Among the key CCP figures arrested during this time was Deng Xiaoping, general secretary of the Party, and, years later, supreme leader of China.

The Cultural Revolution ended only with Mao's death in 1976. A power struggle followed Mao's passing. By 1978, Deng Xiaoping, having defeated Mao's widow and her allies (known afterward as the "Gang of Four"), had come to power. For Deng's policies, see Chapter 34.

LATIN AMERICA

DICTATORSHIP AND ECONOMIC EXPLOITATION IN LATIN AMERICA

Since Latin America had freed itself from colonial domination during the 1800s, national liberation and modernization in this region tended to involve the struggle against dictatorship at home and the political and economic influence of the United States.

The Great Depression, despite its generally negative impact, did have the effect of forcing nations of Latin America to diversify their economies somewhat. World War II also forced a number of the interwar period's dictators out of power. However, despite some temporary progress toward economic modernization and democratization during the late 1940s and early 1950s, many Latin American countries reverted to exploitative economies and dictatorial government from the late 1950s through the early 1980s. Moreover, in Latin America, "modernization" often led to a concentration of wealth in the hands of a narrow social stratum and weak social justice for the working classes and indigenous peoples.

Military governments and right-wing dictatorships appeared throughout Latin America during these decades. By the mid-1970s, only Colombia, Venezuela, and Costa Rica could be considered truly democratic.

ARGENTINA AND THE PERÓNS

In 1943, military rule was established in Argentina. By 1946, the charismatic Juan Perón had come to dominate the military government by appealing to the poor. His wife Eva, whose appeal among the lower-class *descamisados,* or "shirtless ones," was great, was helpful to him in this. During the 1950s, Perón became increasingly right-wing, even fascistic. He was overthrown by the army in 1955 and fled to Spain.

Perón's popularity remained so high, however, that he was able to return in 1973 and become president until his death in 1974. A brutal military regime ruled from 1976 to 1983. This regime ruthlessly purged leftists, intellectuals, and dissidents, causing at least 30,000 to "disappear" over a decade and a half.

BRAZIL AND CHILE

Brazil and Chile also had military regimes from the mid-1960s through the mid-1980s. In Chile, General Augusto Pinochet (backed by the U.S. Central Intelligence Agency) led a 1973 coup against the left-wing government of Salvador Allende—who, in 1970, had become one of the few Marxist politicians to come to power by means of a democratic election. Pinochet remained in charge until the late 1980s. Like the military dictators of Argentina, Pinochet held the reins of power tightly, using force and violence to eliminate enemies and dissidents.

MEXICO

Mexico, although nominally democratic, was really an authoritarian oligarchy run by the Institutional Revolutionary Party (PRI). Its ability to keep the Mexican economy—based increasingly on oil exports—healthy during the 1950s and 1960s made the PRI's less than democratic nature acceptable to most Mexicans. By the end of the 1960s, however, economic stress, as well as the rising resentment of Indians, Mayans, and other minorities, who felt they were being treated as second-class citizens, stirred up discontent with the government.

In 1968, a series of strikes, protests, and student demonstrations in Mexico City (much like similar political disturbances in Paris, Prague, and U.S. universities that same year) showed how the PRI's democratic facade was wearing thin. By the 1980s, the Mexican government was starting to reform gradually, but not completely.

FIDEL CASTRO AND THE CUBAN REVOLUTION

Dictatorship from the other end of the political spectrum, the left, appeared in Cuba. In January 1959, the revolutionary movement led by Fidel Castro overthrew the right-wing dictator Fulgencio Batista. Within months, Castro had begun to nationalize industry and carry out land reform. His goals were to modernize, industrialize, increase literacy rates, and eliminate socioeconomic inequality. Castro, along with his second-in-command, the Argentine radical Ernesto "Ché" Guevara, also wanted to combat what they considered to be U.S. imperialism in Latin America. Accordingly, the Cuban revolutionaires declared themselves to be Marxists and turned to the Soviet Union for assistance.

Because of its proximity to the United States, Cuba became a Cold War hotspot from 1961 onward, as demonstrated by the Bay of Pigs incident (1961) and the Cuban Missile Crisis (1962). Domestically, the Castro regime's record is mixed. It is undeniable that Cuba has modernized under Castro, and the gap between rich and poor that had prevailed under Batista narrowed considerably. Educational levels have improved, and women (at least officially) are treated with greater equality than they had been earlier. However, Castro's regime has been rigidly dictatorial and has violated human rights for more than four decades.

LATIN AMERICA AS COLD WAR BATTLEFIELD

Many problems plagued Latin America during the 1970s and early 1980s. Almost all of the military dictatorships found themselves heavily in debt, especially to the United States. Latin America had also become a great Cold War battlefield. Cuba, both on its own and on behalf of the USSR, consistently attempted to export Marxist revolution throughout Latin America. The Soviet Union did the same. For its part, the United States, fearing the spread of leftism directly to its south, made a practice of supporting any Latin American regime that opposed communism. Unfortunately, pro-U.S. regimes in Latin America tended to be right-wing and dictatorial.

One of the clearest examples of how Cold War politics were played out in Latin America during these years was the Nicaraguan Revolution. In 1979, the Marxist, Soviet-supported Sandinista movement overthrew the right-wing Somoza dictatorship that had ruled Nicaragua (with U.S. support) since 1937. In response, the U.S. government began to support a right-wing, counterrevolutionary guerrilla movement known as the contras. In essence, the struggle between the Sandinista government and the contra movement, both of whom were responsible for political abuses, was a proxy war between the Soviets and the Americans.

DEMOCRATIZATION IN LATIN AMERICA

During the late 1980s and early 1990s, a wave of democratization swept Latin America. Much of it was tied to economic improvements, but just as much was due to the cooling down of the Cold War, which reduced the superpowers' anxiety about influence in the region. In addition, the Organization of American States (OAS), a regional organization of approximately forty countries, has promoted democratization, peace, and security in the region.

Argentina's dictatorship fell in 1983, and a free election peacefully handed power over in 1989. Brazil's dictatorship collapsed in 1985. Mexican elections in 1988 prompted the PRI to loosen its monopoly on power. The controversial Pinochet lost power in Chile in 1989.

One of the few exceptions to this trend was Cuba, where Castro's communist regime remained in power, despite the fall of communism in Eastern Europe and the USSR. Latin America's transition to democracy is still not complete. Corruption, backsliding toward authoritarian practice, the widespread economic dependence on illicit drug trafficking (especially in Colombia), and economic instability have troubled many of the region's new democracies. Nonetheless, the struggle to move toward democracy—or continue in that direction—continues.

QUICK REVIEW

1. Which of the following was NOT associated with the Western world's economic malaise of the 1970s?

   (A) oil shortages
   (B) the uncoupling of the U.S. dollar from the gold standard
   (C) levels of unemployment higher than at any time during the twentieth century
   (D) inflation
   (E) recession and general slowdown

2. What was Jawaharlal Nehru's overall policy direction for India?

   (A) to put Gandhi's dream of a spiritually pure, nontechnological India into action
   (B) to cement a firm military alliance between India and the United States
   (C) to modernize, secularize, and democratize India
   (D) to gain more territory for India at the expense of China
   (E) to create a theocratic regime governed by Hindu principles

3. In which Middle Eastern nation did a Shiite theocracy succeed a secular, modernizing monarchy?

(A) Iraq
(B) Jordan
(C) Syria
(D) Saudi Arabia
(E) Iran

4. Which of the following INCORRECTLY matches an African nation and an important political figure associated with it?

(A) Congo—Patrice Lumumba
(B) Kenya—Idi Amin
(C) Ghana—Kwame Nkrumah
(D) Tanzania—Julius Nyerere
(E) South Africa—Nelson Mandela

5. Where has the HIV/AIDS epidemic proven to be the worst social problem?

(A) North America
(B) South America
(C) Southeast Asia
(D) the former Soviet Union
(E) sub-Saharan Africa

6. The loss of which colony during the 1960s caused the French government to collapse?

(A) Algeria
(B) Tunisia
(C) Laos
(D) Quebec
(E) Vietnam

7. What Marxist regime devastated Cambodia, killing well over a million people?

(A) the Khmer Blanc
(B) the Sihanouk Serpents
(C) the Angkor Brigade
(D) the Khmer Rouge
(E) the Viet Cong

8. Which of the following is NOT among the economic powerhouses known during the 1980s and early 1990s as the "little tigers"?

(A) Singapore
(B) Vietnam
(C) Hong Kong
(D) Taiwan
(E) South Korea

9. What role did Jiang Qing play in Chinese politics?

(A) She served as a moderating influence on Mao Tse-tung.
(B) She was the prime mover behind the Great Proletarian Cultural Revolution.
(C) She overthrew Mao Tse-tung.
(D) She supported Deng Xiaoping's rise to power.
(E) She became the most eloquent voice among China's anticommunist dissidents.

10. What Central American nation, during most of the 1980s, became a battleground between the U.S.-backed contra rebels and the Soviet-supported Sandinista government?

(A) Nicaragua
(B) Guatemala
(C) Costa Rica
(D) El Salvador
(E) Honduras

ANSWERS:

1. **C**, p. 402   6. **A**, p. 400
2. **C**, p. 412   7. **D**, p. 413
3. **E**, p. 407   8. **B**, p. 414
4. **B**, p. 408   9. **B**, p. 415
5. **E**, p. 410   10. **A**, p. 417

CHAPTER 33

Social Developments, Cultural Changes, and Intellectual Trends

The twentieth and twenty-first centuries have witnessed an explosion of social, cultural, and intellectual changes. Scientific and technological advancement has become faster paced than ever before. The world's population has grown with breathtaking speed. Thanks to modern transportation and communications, that population has become increasingly interconnected. The gradual globalization of the world's economies has tied the fortunes of each country almost literally together.

Different parts of the world have experienced a bewildering variety of transformations during the 1900s. As a general rule, however, the changes of the twentieth and twenty-first century can be said to have proceeded along four basic tracks:

- In Western Europe, the United States, and Canada—the West—movement has been toward stable democratization, greater economic prosperity, thorough urbanization, commitment to social equality and individual liberties, and the creation of social welfare systems. Scientific and technological achievement has been tremendous. Western nations have developed postindustrial economies that emphasize services, consumerism, and cutting-edge technology (especially biotech and computers).
- Prosperous nations in Asia—the so-called "tigers," such as Japan and, to a lesser extent, Taiwan, South Korea, Indonesia, and Singapore—have made great strides toward economic and technological modernization. They have urbanized greatly and developed a variety of social services. Their economies are postindustrial and high-tech. In many respects, Japan has equaled or surpassed the West (even though its phenomenal economic growth slowed during the 1990s). However, these societies, although nominally democratic, have been relatively slow to embrace, or even tolerate, the diversity and individualism that have been the hallmarks of Western societies during the late 1800s and 1900s.
- The Soviet Union and Eastern Europe modernized economically, especially during the postwar era. They urbanized and developed social welfare services. Technological and scientific advancement was considerable. However, Soviet and East European economies remained industrial rather than postindustrial, and, in terms of technological finesse (especially with regard to computers), were cruder than Western economies. Moreover, until the collapse of communism in this region from 1989 to 1991, political systems were dictatorial and repressive. Even after the collapse of communism, it has been difficult for this region to move toward democracy and economic prosperity.

- The developing nations of Asia, Africa, the Middle East, and Latin America are all, to one degree or another, striving to attain advanced economic systems, modern societies, and representative forms of government. Some have made great progress, attaining a relatively high level of prosperity or functioning democracies, or both. Others are mired in backwardness, poverty, civil war, and dictatorship. Most are somewhere in between. Perhaps the most distinctive case is the People's Republic of China. Communist China has the geography, population, and military capacity of a major power, and its economic growth has been considerable from the 1980s onward. The government is still authoritarian, however, and social and economic progress remains very uneven, as does technological and scientific advancement.

With regard to historical labels, it is common to speak of the modern period (ca. 1800–1945) of having come to an end, at least in the more developed Western world. The postwar era and the early twenty-first century are generally referred to by historians as either the contemporary era or the postmodern era. The modern era was characterized by industrialization, the formation of the nation-state as the primary form of political organization, and the struggle for representative government and economic equality. The postmodern era is characterized by postindustrial and global forms of economic organization, multiculturalism and the blurring of national lines, and an extreme form of individualism that takes for granted the political and social equality won during the modern era.

One can argue convincingly that this description suits the Western world well. It is more difficult to fit the label "postmodern" to the less developed nations of Africa, Asia, Latin America, and the Middle East, many of which are still in the process of modernizing. This unevenness of social, political, and economic development is, in and of itself, a major characteristic of twentieth- and twenty-first-century world history.

ECONOMIC GLOBALIZATION

INTERNATIONAL TRADE BEFORE WORLD WAR II

Systems of international trade had existed long before the twentieth century, and the scope and volume of that trade grew steadily between World War I and the Great Depression of the 1930s. The Depression sparked a wave of protectionism, as countries sought to shield their own industries and farms by imposing high tariffs on other nations' goods. The most notorious example of protectionism was the United States' Smoot-Hawley Tariff Act (1930). This act is widely considered to have spread the Depression to Europe, Latin America, and Asia by destroying the ability of these regions to export goods to the United States. World War II altered the patterns of international commerce in obvious ways.

FOUNDATIONS OF THE POST–WORLD WAR II ECONOMIC SYSTEM

True globalization of the world economy began after World War II. President Franklin Delano Roosevelt, guided by the economic principles of John Maynard Keynes (and the convictions of Woodrow Wilson before him), believed that free trade was the key not only to economic prosperity, but also world peace. Nations whose economies interacted equitably, he felt, would be less likely to go to war.

As discussed in Chapter 31, Roosevelt met with delegates from Allied nations at Bretton Woods, New Hampshire, in 1944. It was here that the International Bank for Reconstruction and Development (World Bank) and the International Monetary Fund (IMF) were created. In 1958, the first round of the General Agreement on Tariffs and Trade (GATT) was held, to establish the working rules governing imports, exports, and economic interaction among participating nations. The Soviet Union and the Eastern bloc refused to join this "Bretton Woods System," which meant their economies were cut off from much of the rest of the world's. Until the international economic crises of the 1970s, currency exchanges were fixed to the value of the U.S. dollar, the world's strongest. In turn, the U.S. dollar was based on the gold standard.

PROSPERITY AND MODERNIZATION IN THE WEST

Over time, great prosperity came to the United States, Canada, Japan, and the nations of Western Europe. One way in which Western Europe staged its economic recovery was through economic union (European Coal and Steel Community, European Economic Community, Economic Community, European Union), as described in Chapter 32. The reconstruction of war-torn Western Europe—particularly in West Germany—was nothing short of incredible. The same was true with Japan.

ECONOMIC DEVELOPMENT IN THE NON-WESTERN WORLD

The rest of the world developed unevenly. In Latin America and Africa, many governments relied on the export of small sets of natural resources or crops, just as they had done as colonies or economic dependents during the 1800s. The Middle East benefited from its dominance in oil production. The Organization of Petroleum Exporting Countries (OPEC), formed in 1960, consists mainly of Mideastern nations. OPEC has been one of the most successful and influential international economic coalitions in history.

The Soviet Union, its East European allies, and Communist China tended to remain economically isolated from the Western world, although not completely.

Many nations in Asia, such as Japan, Taiwan, South Korea, Indonesia, and Singapore, were quick to adapt to global capitalism. As Western Europe did, many Asian nations joined together in regional economic associations. Although the Association of Southeast Asian Nations (ASEAN), formed in 1967, was largely diplomatic in nature, it also tightened economic ties. The Asia-Pacific Economic Cooperation Group (1989) did the same.

ECONOMIC CRISIS DURING THE 1970s

A general economic crisis struck most of the world during the 1970s. OPEC's oil embargo severely affected the energy-dependent economies of the West. Recession and inflation plagued the United States and Western Europe. Although the USSR had its own oil reserves and was therefore safe from OPEC's embargo, general inefficiency, food shortages, the cost of the arms race, and governmental corruption sapped the economies of the Eastern bloc. In 1971, President Richard Nixon rocked the international community by taking the U.S. dollar off the gold standard.

MULTINATIONAL CORPORATIONS

Despite all this, Western economies recovered during the mid-to-late 1980s. Part of this recovery involved the growing strength of multinational corporations: huge conglomerates that, although technically "from" a single country, maintained factories, subsidiaries, and distribution networks all over the world, employing foreign workers and selling directly to foreign markets.

For years, the activities of these multinational corporations had been laying the groundwork for further globalization of the economy during the 1980s and 1990s. Critics say that multinational corporations have hurt indigenous populations by exploiting their labor, harming their environments, and preventing their own economies from producing homegrown industries and manufactured goods.

ECONOMIC GLOBALIZATION DURING THE 1990s

The 1990s brought about a high tide of economic globalization. Chronologically, and somewhat causally, this coincided with the collapse of Soviet and East European communism, as well as the democratization of much of the developing world, especially Latin America. The strength of multinational corporations increased. The explosion of computer technology and Internet activity facilitated the electronic transfer of money. Meetings of the Group of Seven, or G-7 (the Group of Eight, or G-8, after 1998, when Russia joined), an informal association of the countries with the world's largest economies—the United States, Canada, Great Britain, Japan, Germany, France, and Italy—became more frequent and increasingly influential.

In 1995, the GATT regulations were upgraded and strengthened by the formation of the World Trade Organization (WTO), whose purpose is to regulate the economic interaction of the more than 100 nations that belong to it.

In particular, regional economic unions became increasingly important. In 1994, the United States, Mexico, and Canada created a zone of free movement of money, goods, services, and labor by means of the North American Free Trade Agreement (NAFTA). Moves are afoot to enlarge this zone to include all of the Americas, through the auspices of the Organization of American States (OAS).

Asian nations have tightened their ties as well. By far the boldest experiment in economic integration, however, is Western Europe's. In 1991, the nations of the European Union agreed to the Maastricht Treaty, which provides for the formation of a common monetary system, the creation of a single currency (the "euro"), the establishment of a European Central Bank, and common policymaking in the fields of immigration, environmental protection, and even foreign affairs and security issues. It took until the mid-1990s for the nations of the EU to ratify the terms of the Maastricht Treaty, and friction between member states regarding the details of integration continues. Still, in 1999, 11 EU states (12 by 2000) agreed to join the Economic and Monetary Union. In 2002, these states will abandon their own currencies for the euro.

COSTS AND BENEFITS OF GLOBALIZATION

The costs and benefits of economic globalization are mixed. On one hand, it can be said that globalization has created great wealth and led to increased prosperity, at least in a broad sense and in certain parts of the world. Proponents of globalization continue to argue, with some justification, that free trade helps to preserve peace.

On the other hand, the fact that the economies of all (or at least most) nations influence each other so much means that negative trends in one region—financial crisis in Mexico in 1994 or Asia in 1997, for example, or Russia and Brazil in 1998—can adversely affect the entire world. In addition, it is questionable whether all nations will be willing to subject their individual economic policies to the dictates of international bodies like the WTO. There have already been bitter disputes over this issue, especially between developing and developed countries. Moreover, various nongovernmental organizations (NGOs) have advocated for greater transparency in terms of rule making, as well as the need to take into account social justice and environmental protection concerns.

Finally, globalization threatens to lead to a constant state of economic change and instability. Seeking profits, multinational corporations tend to move to wherever they can produce more cheaply. This means relocating to whatever city or country will provide them with the least expensive labor force, the most advantageous tax benefits or exemptions, and the most lenient environmental regulations. This can also mean the lowering of wages, the sudden unemployment or layoff of local labor forces, and a great deal of social stress. Agriculture has also been greatly affected by globalization, as farmers in one country find themselves competing with cheap food being imported from other parts of the world. Some critics of globalization also point to its homogenizing effects on culture and fear that their own indigenous cultures are being crushed under the force of foreign (in particular, American) popular culture and values.

Whether or not economic globalization will continue remains to be seen. It most likely will. What also remains to be seen is whether the benefits of globalization will eventually outweigh the costs. This is much harder to predict, and will remain a major issue into the twenty-first century.

SOCIAL TRENDS AND MOVEMENTS

BASIC FEATURES OF WESTERN SOCIETIES

Social change during the twentieth century was so rapid and thorough that it is difficult to generalize about it. By and large, Western nations and other developed states can be said to have evolved the following social features (albeit imperfectly or gradually in many cases):

- Elimination of legal distinctions between social classes.
- The replacement of aristocratic social elites by a professional, white-collar class that attains its elite status through earned wealth or educational status (often referred to as meritocracy or technocracy).
- Creation of a large, stable middle class.
- Access to at least a minimum standard of living and adequate level of material well-being, even among lower classes.
- Urbanization, as well as suburbanization.
- Establishment of a social-welfare system that includes unemployment insurance, pensions, and health care (at least for the elderly, if not the population as a whole).
- Universal educational system.
- Equal political rights for all adult citizens, including females.
- Equal treatment of all citizens before the law.
- Equal rights for minorities (still an ongoing process, even in areas as advanced as the United States, Canada, and Europe).
- The participation of nongovernmental organizations (NGOs) in the political process. NGOs represent the interests of various groups in society. They act on behalf of their constituents in pressuring governments to set policy, implement policy, and provide social services to populations in need.

STANDARD-OF-LIVING DISPARITY BETWEEN THE WEST AND THE DEVELOPING WORLD

With varying degrees of success, countries in the developing regions of Africa, Asia, Latin America, and the Middle East attempted to bring about many of these same changes. Some managed to do so by the end of the century, others did not.

One of the most pressing issues affecting the entire globe is the vast standard-of-living disparity between the developed world and the developing world. Many political scientists and sociologists refer to this as the "north-south split," because of the fact that most of the world's advanced, postindustrial societies are located in the northern third of the globe.

The gap between the developed and developing worlds causes diplomatic friction, interferes with the smooth and equitable globalization of the world economy, and perpetuates tremendous socioeconomic inequality. An extremely small number of people in the developed nations possess the majority of global wealth, use up the bulk of the world's resources, eat a massive share of the world's food, and are responsible for most of the world's energy consumption and pollution. For example, in 1998, the United States alone consumed 25 percent of the world's energy consumption, but its population makes up only 5 percent of the total world population. This trend has been in place during the entire twentieth century. It showed no signs of reversing as the century ended.

MAJOR TRENDS

Other important trends of the 1900s and early 2000s:

- *Population growth:* At the beginning of the twentieth century, the world population was 1.6 billion. At the century's end, that number had risen to 6 billion. Even in the developed world, where birthrates have tended to decline, population has tended to increase. In the developing and less developed worlds, population growth has literally exploded. China and India each have populations of more than 1 billion. The rate of growth in Africa has averaged more than 3 percent per year. Latin America went from 165 million in 1950 to 400 million in the mid-1980s. Cities such as Mexico City, Shanghai, and Buenos Aires are among the most densely populated in the world. Ironically, however, the true problems resulting from population growth—the overconsumption of food and energy and overproduction of waste and pollution—have more to do with the developed world, where population growth is slower or even.

- *Migration:* This pattern dates back to the last half of the nineteenth century, when millions of immigrants from Europe (and a smaller number from China) flooded to the United States, Canada, Argentina, and Chile. This same trend continued throughout the early 1900s, until the United States instituted stricter immigration policies. The movement of peoples continued after World War II, however, and even intensified. During the late 1940s and 1950s, Europeans that had been made homeless by the war, as well as refugees and displaced persons (largely from Eastern Europe, where Nazi genocide, then Soviet occupation, led to massive population transfers), moved throughout the continent, mainly to Western Europe. All throughout the postwar period, economic opportunity, violence in the developing world (caused largely by brushfire conflicts related to the Cold War), and political repression have led millions of people to leave Asia, the Middle East, Latin America, and Africa for Western Europe and North America. Even as France and Britain dismantled their empires, many of their former colonial subjects migrated there from Algeria, India, sub-Saharan Africa, the Caribbean, and elsewhere. Refugees have fled from Asia and Latin America to the United States and Canada, from Africa and the Middle East to Europe. Guest workers from the Middle East (especially Turkey) and elsewhere began to be admitted to Western Europe; by the 1980s, there were more than 15 million of them. Most recently, the collapse of communism in the former Soviet bloc, as well as ethnic conflict in the former Yugoslavia, has led to a rush of migration from Eastern to Western Europe. Migration has often provided a much-needed labor force and enriched the cultural diversity of the host nation. However, especially when economic times are tight, it has stirred up xenophobia, typically among right-wing extremists.

- *Rise of the consumer society:* In developed societies, inexpensive, mass-produced goods tend to be available to almost all people, even the lower classes. At the same time, fewer and fewer people in these societies tend to earn their living by means of agricultural or even industrial production. Consumer societies therefore tend to be based on service, or postindustrial, economies.

- *Social activism and the rise of nongovernmental organizations (NGOs):* Demonstrations, protests, and strikes have been important in bringing about social, political, and economic change ever since the French Revolution of 1789. During the twentieth century, however, social activism has become an increasingly important force. This has especially been the case in the postwar era, when social movements, student groups, and nongovernmental organizations (NGOs) have lobbied for or protested against various policies and issues. Perhaps the most famous wave of social activism came during the 1960s and early 1970s, when social activism helped to bring about civil rights for African Americans in the United States, an end to the Vietnam War, a temporary wave of reform in communist Czechoslovakia, and a loosening of the PRI's monopoly on power in Mexico, among other things. Such social activism played a key role in the peace movements and anti–nuclear-arms movements of the 1970s and 1980s. Social activism was crucial to women's liberation and the environmental movement, both described in more detail presently.

- *Environmentalism:* Ever since the Industrial Revolution, there has always been a spirit of environmentalism, striving to preserve the natural world from overdevelopment or complete destruction. Conservation efforts can be dated back to Henry Thoreau, Ralph Waldo Emerson, John Muir, and other turn-of-the-century figures. The modern environmental movement, however, is a product of the post–World War II era, when it became clear that pollution and worldwide industrial development posed a dire threat to the earth's ecological well-being. Green movements began during the 1960s, both in North America and Western Europe. A major boost was given to environmental movements by the publication in the United States of Rachel Carson's *Silent Spring* (1962), warning of the dangers connected with the use of the insecticide DDT. The celebration of Earth Day in 1970 also popularized the environmental movement. International NGOs working on behalf of the environment, such as Greenpeace and the World Wildlife Fund, have become globally famous and influential organizations. In many West European countries, political parties whose primary concern is the environment, "green" parties, actually play an important role in national politics. For example, in the 1998 parliamentary elections in Germany, the Green Party gained enough seats to be asked to join the governing coalition as junior partners with the Social Democrats.

- *Terrorism:* The first major conflict of the twentieth century, World War I, was sparked by the action of a terrorist. Ever since, it has become more and more common for political movements to achieve their goals by means of violence and assassination. Especially in the post–World War II era, terrorist activity has escalated. Major terrorist groups include the Palestinian Liberation Organization (PLO), the Irish Republican Army (IRA), the Red Brigades (a communist organization in Italy), the Baader-Meinhoff Group (a Marxist group in Germany), and a variety of anti-Israeli groups such as Hamas and Hezbollah. The first major terrorist attack of the twenty-first century, and the one which is likely to have the greatest impact on world affairs, is the September 11, 2001 attack on the United States. Terrorists linked to Osama bin Laden hijacked a number of aircraft and flew them into the World Trade Center and Pentagon, killing over 3,000 people.

- *Rise in extreme nationalism, ethnic hostility, and religious fundamentalism:* Unfortunately, even as much of the world has democratized and decolonized during the postwar era, economic tensions and diplomatic realignments caused by the end of the Cold War have led to the renewal of religious and ethnic tensions that had previously been kept in check. Examples of this trend include the rise of Islamic fundamentalism in Iran and Afghanistan; the poor treatment of Roma (Gypsies) in Eastern Europe; the rise of anti-immigrant sentiment in Europe; similar anti immigrant feelings in the United States; the persistence of right-wing extremists, and even neo-Nazi movements, in Europe; the massacre of 800,000 Tutsis by their tribal rivals, the Hutus, in Rwanda in 1994; and the wars of separation in the former Yugoslavia during the 1990s, particularly Serbia's genocidal campaigns of "ethnic cleansing" in Bosnia and Kosovo.

WOMEN AND THE SHIFT IN GENDER RELATIONS

One of the most important trends of the twentieth century—affecting slightly more than half of the world's entire population—is women's liberation (also referred to as feminism). Progress here came mainly in the Western world, although other regions have also moved forward, if slowly and partially.

EARLY WOMEN'S MOVEMENTS

An active women's movement dated back to the late 1800s and early 1900s, as American and European suffragettes—including Susan B. Anthony, Elizabeth Cady Stanton, and Emmeline Pankhurst—lobbied for the right to vote. However, before World War I, only a few small countries, such as Finland and Norway, granted suffrage to women. Women during this time were also fighting for equal access to colleges and universities.

WORLD WAR I AND THE INTERWAR PERIOD

As described in Chapter 28, World War I brought large numbers of middle-class women into the workplace (not just working-class women, who had been employed in low-wage, low-status positions since the days of the Industrial Revolution). This boosted women's claims to equal rights in many Western nations.

Between 1917 and 1920, women got the vote in Russia, Sweden, Great Britain, Germany, Poland, Hungary, Austria, Czechoslovakia, and the United States. Among the major European nations, only Italy and France failed to give women the vote before World War II. Women had also gained a stronger foothold in the workplace, even though the number of working women decreased during the 1920s and 1930s (except in the USSR, where Stalin's industrialization campaigns and the collectivization of agriculture put large numbers of women to work). Fascist Italy, Nazi Germany, and militarist Japan were all extremely hostile to the notion of gender equality.

WORLD WAR II AND ITS EFFECT ON WOMEN

Famously, World War II brought women into the workplace in even greater numbers than the First World War had. The image of "Rosie the Riveter," while somewhat exaggerated, became a potent symbol of women's role in U.S. wartime economic production. In the Soviet Union, women made up nearly 40 percent of the national workforce. Moreover, large numbers of American, Canadian, and British women served as military nurses and military personnel (although not combat troops) during World War II. In the USSR, women served in the military, and in some limited but important cases, saw active duty in combat.

Although there was a temporary dip in female employment after World War II, the war had served the purpose of permanently cementing women's place in the working world. Moreover, France and Italy gave women the vote in 1945.

WESTERN WOMEN DURING THE LATE 1940s AND 1950s

During the postwar era, as Japan, Western Europe, the United States, and Canada moved on to ever-higher levels of economic advancement, women took an increasingly larger role in the workplace and public life. The same was true—and to an even larger degree—in Eastern Europe and the Soviet Union. However, during the late 1940s and 1950s, it was still generally considered that a woman's roles were mainly those of homemaker, childbearer, and caregiver to children. Even those women who worked suffered widespread gender discrimination: sexual harassment, unequal wages, lack of access to positions of leadership, and so on. One of the first systematic attempts to analyze women's place in modern society was the French philosopher Simone de Beauvoir's *The Second Sex* (1949), which investigated the deep-seated cultural and biological reasons for male domination of women.

FEMINISM AND "WOMEN'S LIB" DURING THE 1960s AND 1970s

A giant step toward equality was taken by women in the Western world during the 1960s and 1970s. This was the era of feminism, or women's liberation (popularly known in the United States as "women's lib"). Major figures here were Gloria Steinem, as well as Betty Friedan, whose book, *The Feminine Mystique* (1963), joined de Beauvoir's *The Second Sex* in providing an intellectual foundation for the movement.

The goal of the women's movement was not just to achieve legal equality, but also to eliminate cultural stereotypes about women as the "weaker sex" and to remove social barriers that blocked the way toward true equality. Achievements of the women's movement include better and more varied career opportunities, better pay, equal access to higher education, equal treatment for women's athletics, the right to birth control, the right to legal abortion, the right to divorce, and a greater role in political life.

CONTEMPORARY GENDER ISSUES

Problems still remain, however. Informal discrimination and sexual harassment have not been eliminated. Access to the highest levels of business and political life is still not complete (this is commonly referred to as the "glass ceiling").

Moreover, women are still relegated to traditional and secondary roles in many non-Western societies. Although it is a stereotype to say that women are not treated equally in Asian, African, Middle Eastern, and Latin American societies, the fact remains that Islamic fundamentalism, conservative Catholicism, machismo, old-fashioned views of women as inferior (or wives as servants, even property) constrain women more commonly in these regions than they do in the West. Notably, the Taliban, the Islamic fundamentalist group that took control of much of Afghanistan after the Soviet withdrawal in 1989, has deprived women of most individual rights and introduced stiff penalties for breaking rules, such as those against going out in public unescorted by a man.

THOUGHT, CULTURE, AND SCIENCE

The hallmarks of twentieth-century thought and culture are rapid change and incredible diversity. Other major trends have included multiculturalism—the interaction and fusion of the world's various ethnic, artistic, and intellectual traditions—and the effect of technology and mass media on cultural and artistic production. Scientific and technological advancement has proceeded at a breathtaking pace.

PESSIMISM AND UNCERTAINTY IN WESTERN CULTURE

After World War I, art and literature in the Western world tended to be dominated by the themes of uncertainty and anxiety that had begun to appear by the late 1800s and early 1900s (see Chapter 20). The psychological theories of Sigmund Freud, as well as the philosophical implications of scientific findings such as Albert Einstein's theory of relativity and the new field of quantum physics, had dampened the overall optimism of the mid-to-late 1800s.

The demoralization caused by World War I increased the spirit of pessimism and relativism (the belief or attitude that there are no objective standards or truths). The best-selling nonfiction book in interwar Europe was German philosopher Oswald Spengler's *The Decline of the West*. The prose and poetry of T. S. Eliot and Franz Kafka dealt with the dehumanization caused by life in a modern, industrialized, bureaucratized era. By experimenting with stream-of-consciousness prose, authors like Virginia Woolf, Marcel Proust, and James Joyce attempted to capture the workings of the human mind on the written page. Abstract painters such as Pablo Picasso distorted reality to demonstrate that objects and concepts could be seen from a variety of perspectives. Surrealists like Salvador Dalí placed realistic objects in unrealistic situations to confuse the viewer's sense of reality.

After World War II, the philosophical and literary school of existentialism, championed by the playwright Samuel Beckett and the philosophers-novelists Albert Camus and Jean-Paul Sartre, proposed that humanity was not guided by any deity, special destiny, or objective morality. Alone in the universe, the individual must learn to create a worthwhile, ethical existence for himself or herself without the benefit of religion or the hope of any life beyond the earthly one.

MASS MEDIA

Mass media came to play an increasingly important role in cultural life. Radio, film, the inexpensive production of mass quantities of books, television, and computers have brought music, drama, literature, information, and more into the lives of a greater variety of people than had ever before been able to enjoy such things. In addition, in the hands of creative directors and filmmakers, cinema has been used to create genuinely great art.

On the other hand, critics of mass media have argued that they tend to cheapen or "dumb down" cultural production by catering to the taste of the masses. In addition, mass media have been used for political purposes, such as propaganda and indoctrination ("brainwashing"), especially in dictatorial societies. Even in free societies, critics say, mass media have become powerful tools in the hands of corporate entities, brainwashing people not for political purposes, but in order to advertise goods and make a profit.

Another effect of mass media has been to westernize the popular culture of virtually the entire world. Even before World War II, the lure of American jazz and Hollywood movies was immensely seductive. After World War II, when America dominated world markets and mass-media technology, Disney, McDonald's, and Coca-Cola, among others, became economic and cultural symbols recognizable not just in the United States, but almost literally in every corner of the globe.

ARTS AND LITERATURE IN THE NON-WESTERN WORLD

The twentieth and twenty-first centuries have also seen the literary and artistic traditions of the non-Western world achieve a status equal to—and in some cases surpassing—those of the West. In addition to maintaining their own indigenous traditions, non-Western authors and artists have come to adopt Western forms of writing, painting, and composing, often adapting, modifying, and adding native elements to them.

Mexican painter Diego Rivera created powerful murals that vividly expressed the plight of the working poor, as well as that of Mayans and other indigenous peoples in his country. Chinese author Lu Xun (Lu Hsun) wrote hard-hitting stories about his nation's economic domination by outside powers, as well as the Chinese government's inability and unwillingness to provide for the well-being of the lower classes. Indian poet Rabindranath Tagore, the first non-Westerner to win the Nobel Prize for literature, dazzled not just his own people, but readers throughout the world with his lyrical, mystical verse based on Hindu religious concepts.

Non-Western voices in the artistic world grew even bolder and more eloquent after World War II. Common themes included the growing pains associated with decolonization, the difficulty of resisting Western (especially U.S.) cultural hegemony, the clash of Western and non-Western culture, and political opposition to one's own politically repressive regime. In *The Interpreters*, Nobel laureate Wole Soyinka writes about political corruption in his native Nigeria; he also calls attention to dictatorial practices there. Fellow Nigerian Chinua Achebe has taken on themes of decolonization and political dictatorship equally boldly, especially in *Things Fall Apart*. Ama Ata Aidoo describes the place of women in contemporary Ghana in, for example, *Changes: A Love Story*.

Cry, the Peacock is Anita Desai's famous treatment of women's lives in India. In Japan, Yukio Mishima, a traditional (but also gay) nationalist, angrily opposed U.S. influence (what he called "coca-colonization") over the non-Western world, as well as what he saw as the destruction of Japan's cultural values. His ritual, samurai-style suicide in 1970 elevated him to cult status.

In Latin America, authors such as Gabriel García Márquez and Isabel Allende pioneered magical realism: a richly textured style featuring thickly detailed storytelling.

In the Islamic world, novelist Naguib Mahfouz won the Nobel Prize for his *Cairo Trilogy*, a vibrant portrait of postwar Egypt. The Indian-born, English-speaking Muslim Salman Rushdie, a great literary experimenter, came to world attention in 1988 with *The Satanic Verses*, an irreverent treatment of Islamic orthodoxy. Both Mahfouz and Rushdie fell afoul of Muslim traditionalists. Mahfouz was stabbed by an Islamic extremist outside his Cairo residence in 1984. Rushdie was declared a heretic by the Ayatollah Khomeini of Iran, who openly called for Rushdie's assassination and forced him to go into hiding for years.

SCIENCE AND TECHNOLOGY

Scientific and technological advancement during the twentieth and twenty-first centuries has been constant and spectacular. During the first half of the 1900s, the Western world fully industrialized, moving into a world in which petroleum and electricity were its primary sources of energy.

Also in the Western world, great innovation has been made in all fields of science. But progress in certain areas has been most noteworthy. Physics was revolutionized at the beginning of the 1900s. First, Albert Einstein developed the theory of relativity, making the first major changes to the system of science and mathematics that had been synthesized by Isaac Newton in the late 1600s and early 1700s. Following Einstein's work on relativity came the birth of quantum physics, along with atomic theory. Major figures here included Max Planck, Niels Bohr, Werner Heisenberg, and Enrico Fermi. The work of the quantum physicists and atomic theorists has completely altered our understanding of astronomy and subatomic particles. It also made atomic weaponry and nuclear energy possible.

Rocketry and space science is another field that emerged during the 1900s. Pioneers of rocket science included the American Robert Goddard and Russia's Konstantin

Apollo 15 Mission to the Moon, August 1971.
To this date, the United States is the only nation that has landed manned spacecraft on the moon. The first moon landing came on July 20, 1969. The Apollo 15 mission, pictured here, was one of the several landings that followed. In recent years, trends in space exploration have included the deployment of unmanned probes deep into the solar system (and beyond), long-term space station missions, space shuttle flights, and the use of remote-controlled technology to explore hostile environments such as the surfaces of other planets.

Tsiolkovsky. The new science matured during World War II, thanks largely to the efforts of German scientists. The nuclear arms race between the United States and the Soviet Union spurred a parallel space race. The USSR was the first to launch a human-made object into space (1957) and the first to put a human being into space (1961). The United States, however, was the first (and only) nation to reach the moon (1969). The move toward a permanent presence in space was encouraged by the USSR's work in developing orbital laboratories and the United States' invention of the space shuttle. Rocket science has also made satellite communications possible.

Another field of special significance during the twentieth and twenty-first centuries is biotechnology and genetic science. The field of genetics was born during the late 1800s, thanks to the efforts of the Austrian monk Gregor Mendel. The great breakthrough in genetic science, however, came with the discovery of DNA by James Watson and Francis Crick in 1953. Since then, scientists have gained an unprecedented wealth of knowledge about how the human organism works. Combined with amazing advances in computer technology, genetic theory has allowed truly incredible medical advances. In the late 1990s, it also gave human beings the power to clone living beings—a practice that is and will continue to be highly controversial.

Undoubtedly the most significant advancement in postwar science and technology was the invention of the computer. The computer arguably was the most significant postwar technological advancement. Computers and their components (such as microchips) have altered the way people communicate, transact business, analyze data, keep records, and perform medical procedures.

One major computer innovation was the development of the Internet. The Internet was originally created in the 1960s for U.S. defense research purposes as a way to integrate government, business, and academic computer networks. By the end of the 1990s, a World Wide Web (WWW) had connected millions of users in what Marshall McLuhan, a Canadian sociologist, had predicted in the 1960s would eventually form a "global village." Although a "digital divide" exists between those people who have better access to computer technology in the Northern Hemisphere and those who have poorer access south of the equator, the worldwide trend is toward wider access to computers and related equipment.

QUICK REVIEW

1. What international organization has played the most influential role in determining the production level and price of oil in the post–World War II era?

   (A) ASEAN
   (B) the Common Market
   (C) OPEC
   (D) the EEC
   (E) the WTO

2. What function does NAFTA serve?

   (A) It creates a free-trade zone that links Canada, the United States, and Mexico.
   (B) It serves as an agreement between Mexico and the United States, preventing illegal immigration from south to north.
   (C) It attempts to regulate the flow of illegal drugs throughout North America.
   (D) It establishes a set of tariffs and trade barriers between Canada and the United States.
   (E) It establishes a free-trade zone that links all the nations of North and South America.

3. In which of the following cities did major demonstrations and social protests break out in 1968?

   (A) Madrid, Glasgow, and Bogotá
   (B) Paris, Mexico City, and Prague
   (C) Quito, Paris, and Bucharest
   (D) Mexico City, Rangoon, and Ottawa
   (E) Bangkok, New York, and Lisbon

4. What measures have many northern and western European nations adopted to make up for their diminished diplomatic and economic clout in the post–World War II environment?

   (A) They have constructed their own strategic nuclear forces, jointly controlled by all nations in the region.
   (B) They have created a military alliance that excludes the United States and Russia.
   (C) They have engaged in a new campaign of imperial conquest.
   (D) They have agreed to join together in an economic union, which will use a common currency.
   (E) They have gained control over the mass media and entertainment industries.

5. In what country has an environmental political party attained a meaningful role at the national level?

   (A) Great Britain
   (B) Belgium
   (C) Spain
   (D) Italy
   (E) Germany

6. Which of the following was among the last Western nations to give women the vote?

   (A) France
   (B) Great Britain
   (C) the Netherlands
   (D) Finland
   (E) Russia

7. The effect of the theory of relativity on Western cultural and intellectual life was

   (A) to stimulate popular interest in science
   (B) to restore a spirit of optimism to arts and letters
   (C) to increase the sense of uncertainty reflected in arts and letters
   (D) to convince artists and writers that there was a single objective truth
   (E) to drive artists and writers to the political left

8. Mass media have been used for purposes of

   (A) advertising
   (B) propaganda
   (C) high art
   (D) entertainment
   (E) all of the above

9. Where was the first non-Westerner to be awarded the Nobel Prize for literature from?

   (A) Nigeria
   (B) India
   (C) Japan
   (D) Iran
   (E) Peru

10. The discovery of what substance in 1953 dramatically furthered the progress of genetic research?

   (A) DNA
   (B) amino acids
   (C) RNA
   (D) hemoglobin
   (E) chlorophyll

ANSWERS:

1. **C**, p. 421	6. **A**, p. 426
2. **A**, p. 422	7. **C**, p. 427
3. **B**, p. 425	8. **E**, p. 428
4. **D**, p. 422	9. **B**, p. 428
5. **E**, p. 425	10. **A**, p. 430

CHAPTER 34

The Collapse of Communism and the End of the Cold War

One of the most dramatic changes of the twentieth century was the collapse of communism in the Soviet Union and Eastern Europe (1989–1991), as well as the end of the Cold War. If the twentieth century, as a historical era, began not with 1900 but the outbreak of World War I in 1914, one can argue that it ended not in 1999 or 2000, but in 1991, the year the USSR ceased to exist.

The end of the Cold War came about because of a combination of diplomatic negotiation, the United States' widening lead in the arms race, increased unrest throughout Eastern Europe, and the internal disintegration of the Soviet Union.

The collapse of the Soviet Union and its East European satellites has been a great blow to communist movements worldwide. Within two years, nine communist regimes—including history's first—had ceased to exist. The Soviet Union broke apart into 15 independent nations. Communist governments continued to exist, most notably in China, Cuba, Vietnam, and North Korea. As a global force, however, communism was greatly diminished after 1991. As for the many nations that have ceased to be communist, their painful transitions to other forms of government and economic organization are described in Chapter 35.

The end of the Cold War has brought about a tremendous shift in the balance of global power. The Cold War had been a condition of bipolar equilibrium, in which military and political might was concentrated in the hands of two superpowers. From 1991 onward, the world has been in the unprecedented situation of having only one superpower—the United States—capable of diplomatic, strategic, and economic action on a truly global scale. How long this situation might persist, and what it means for world affairs, is discussed in Chapter 35.

THE COMMUNIST WORLD DURING THE 1980s

COMMUNIST BLOCS DURING THE 1980s

The first thing to note about the "communist world" during the 1980s is that, by this time, there were several communist "worlds." The Soviet Union, the oldest and largest communist regime, was still paramount. It also dominated the six nations of the Warsaw Pact: Poland, Czechoslovakia, Hungary, Romania, Bulgaria, and East Germany.

Cuba remained an ally of the USSR, but was an increasingly independent actor. China, the world's second largest center of communism, rivaled the USSR and was hostile to it. Albania, Yugoslavia, Vietnam, and North Korea were all communist, but tended to remain unaligned.

THE END OF *DÉTENTE* AND THE ARMS RACE OF THE 1980s

The 1980s were a turbulent time for the Soviet Union and its Eastern bloc. Internationally, the period of détente had come to an end in 1979, with the USSR's invasion of Afghanistan. Another point of tension was the Sandinista revolution in Nicaragua (1979). As described in Chapter 32, the Soviets supported the Sandinistas, while the United States sponsored their enemies, the contras. The latest arms treaty between the United States and the Soviet Union, SALT II (1979), went unratified.

The arms race escalated during the early 1980s, and although it was not clear to the American public or ordinary Soviets, the United States was pulling far ahead in terms of technological expertise. Although both sides had roughly equal quantities of warheads, the United States had weapons systems that were faster, harder to destroy, and more accurate. These included the cruise missile, the MX missile, and submarine-launched missiles. President Ronald Reagan began to make plans for a space-based defense system, the Strategic Defense Initiative (SDI), popularly known as "Star Wars." During the early 1980s, Cold War tensions were higher than they had ever been before, with the exception of the early 1960s.

STAGNATION IN THE SOVIET UNION

In the Soviet Union itself, the political system was corrupt, and the economy was failing. From the late 1970s until Leonid Brezhnev's death in 1982, and also under the two leaders who followed him until 1985, the USSR went through a period of stagnation. Shortages of consumer goods were extreme. An ever-increasing percentage of the Soviet gross national product went toward the arms race. The war in Afghanistan was a disappointing failure, killing thousands of young Soviet soldiers, all for nothing.

The dissident movement—a community of protestors, humanitarians, and intellectuals that had formed during the 1970s—grew larger, louder, and more determined during the 1980s. Among the most famous of the Soviet dissidents were writer Alexander Solzhenitsyn (who had been expelled from the country during the 1970s) and the husband-and-wife team of physicist Andrei Sakharov and Elena Bonner.

UNREST IN EASTERN EUROPE

The Eastern bloc became dangerously restless during the 1980s. Although nations like Bulgaria and East Germany remained unswervingly loyal, others did not. Although Romania continued to be part of the Warsaw Pact, its dictator, Nicolae Ceausescu, insisted on having a certain degree of autonomy in diplomatic and domestic affairs (his relative independence from the USSR, however, did not mean that he was liberal; in fact, Ceausescu was one of the most brutal of Eastern Europe's rulers). Hungary legalized limited capitalism and reformed its economy as much as the Soviets would allow it to. In Czechoslovakia, an important dissident group, Charter 77, formed under the leadership of playwright Vaclav Havel.

It was in Poland, however, that Soviet rule over Eastern Europe met its gravest challenge. In 1980, economic shortages and labor disputes led to the creation of the trade union Solidarity. At first, Solidarity's goal was simply to improve the conditions of Poland's working class. Very rapidly, under the leadership of Lech Walesa, Solidarity became a political movement as well as a trade union. Joined by intellectuals and Catholic clergy, Solidarity became a focal point for protest and outrage against the Soviet-backed communist regime, as well as the USSR itself.

In December 1981, Poland's communist regime declared martial law. This state of martial law remained in effect until the end of the decade. In the meantime, Walesa was arrested, and Solidarity was driven underground. However, throughout the 1980s, the Polish resistance agitated against the communist regime and the Soviet Union. Over the course of the decade,

Solidarity's illegal activities made it increasingly difficult—and expensive—for the USSR to maintain control over Eastern Europe.

CHINA UNDER DENG XIAOPING

China was much more fortunate than the Soviet Union. As noted in Chapter 32, China underwent a painful modernization process under Mao Tse-tung. Mao's death in 1976 led to great changes. In 1978, after a power struggle, Deng Xiaoping came to power in China, having defeated the so-called Gang of Four (which included Mao's widow, Jiang Qing).

Like Mao, Deng was a modernizer. He instituted a "four modernizations" program, focusing on industry, agriculture, technology, and national defense. However, while Mao had been idealistic, inflexible, and revolutionary, Deng was pragmatic, willing to compromise, and gradual. Although a communist, Deng was more concerned with China's well-being and growing strength than he was with absolute commitment to abstract Marxist ideals. Famously, he commented that whether a cat is black or white makes no difference, as long as it catches mice.

In opposition to Mao's militant anticapitalism, Deng allowed limited free-market reform in China. Under the slogan, "create wealth for the people," Deng permitted private enterprise, small business, and limited capitalist exchange. Economically, the result was clear: China experienced fabulous economic growth throughout the 1980s. Wages and standards of living improved considerably. There was, however, a social and cultural effect as well. With greater wealth came the desire for greater freedom. This was a luxury that even Deng was not prepared to allow. By the end of the 1980s, China would have to deal with this growing problem.

GORBACHEV AND THE ATTEMPT AT SOVIET REFORM

THE RISE OF GORBACHEV

In March 1985, Soviet communism was on the threshold of major changes. That month, Mikhail Gorbachev, a young, dynamic, reform-minded politician, became leader of the USSR. His assumption of power followed the long, stagnant Brezhnev period, as well as two and a half years of gerontocracy (rule by the old), when elderly and dull senior members of the Communist Party had taken control of the government.

Gorbachev inherited a Soviet Union in crisis. The economy was worsening. The political system was riddled with corruption and apathy. The deadly accident at the nuclear reactor in Chernobyl, Ukraine, in 1986, demonstrated clearly the inefficiency of the Soviet system. The Afghan War raged on, killing more Soviet troops, draining the country's finances, and accomplishing nothing. Unrest in Eastern Europe was worsening. Beyond that, the non-Russian republics of the Soviet Union were starting to become independence-minded, threatening to break up the USSR itself. In terms of military affairs, although it took care not to reveal it publicly, the Soviet government knew the USSR was falling behind in the arms race—and did not have the economic resources to catch up with the United States.

PERESTROIKA

At home, Gorbachev's response to all these problems was to attempt a thorough reform of the Soviet system. In his famous policy of perestroika ("restructuring"), Gorbachev tried to strengthen the Soviet economy. He emphasized local control over central planning. He allowed limited free enterprise and loosened rules regarding private property. He set into place some of the foundations of a free-market economy. In many ways, much of perestroika was similar to what Deng Xiaoping was doing in China during the 1980s. The major difference was that, while economic liberalization led to prosperity in China, it did not do so in the USSR. This was largely due to ingrained inefficiency in the Soviet system, dating back to the Stalin period. It also had to do with the fact that Deng dealt better with conservative opposition in China than Gorbachev did in the Soviet Union.

GLASNOST AND POLITICAL REFORM

Another difference between Gorbachev's liberalization and Deng's was that Gorbachev allowed political and cultural liberalization at the same time. Gorbachev's policy of glasnost ("openness") provided for greater freedom of the press and media, frank discussion of the Soviet Union's clouded past (especially the Stalin period), public criticism of contemporary problems, and exposure of political corruption or workplace abuses. Gorbachev's hope was that glasnost, greater social and cultural freedom, would motivate the Soviet population to carry out perestroika in the political and economic spheres.

Gorbachev also carried out political reforms. He allowed competitive elections in 1987 (although all candidates were members of the Communist Party or ran as individuals). A nationally elected parliament, the Congress of People's Deputies, met in 1989. In 1990, Gorbachev legalized non-Communist political parties.

GORBACHEV, THE WEST, AND THE COOLING OF THE ARMS RACE

To the rest of the world, Gorbachev turned a friendly face. Realizing that the USSR could not continue to compete with the United States in the arms race, Gorbachev sought to reduce tensions between the superpowers. To Western leaders such as Reagan and British Prime Minister Margaret Thatcher, Gorbachev portrayed himself as (in Thatcher's words), "a man one can do business with." For the first time since 1979, relations between the Soviet Union and the West cooled rather than heated.

A diplomatic breakthrough came in 1987, when Reagan and Gorbachev negotiated the Intermediate Range Nuclear Forces (INF) Treaty, which removed short- and intermediate-range nuclear weapons from Europe. Afterward, Gorbachev met regularly with Reagan and George Bush, the next U.S. president, concluding a series of agreements that limited the number and type of various nuclear and conventional weapons. These agreements were long steps forward in ending the Cold War.

GORBACHEV AND EASTERN EUROPE

Moreover, Gorbachev began to loosen the Soviet Union's grip on Eastern Europe. Publicly, he called for economic reform and greater observance of human rights throughout the Eastern bloc.

Gorbachev's stance toward Eastern Europe gained him a great deal of approval in the West, and

The Fall of the Soviet Union and Formation of the Commonwealth of Independent States, January 1992.

In late 1991, Mikhail Gorbachev was forced to dissolve the USSR. At that time, leaders of the former republics of the Soviet Union, with the exception of Estonia, Latvia, Lithuania, and Georgia, chose to form the Commonwealth of Independent States as a way to maintain ties and attempt a smooth transition from Soviet rule.

contributed to his being awarded the Nobel Peace Prize in 1990. However, it also weakened the USSR militarily and diplomatically. The consequences of this development are discussed in the next section.

THE WALLS COME DOWN: THE COLLAPSE AND PERSISTENCE OF COMMUNISM, 1989–1991

THE DILEMMAS OF SOVIET REFORM

By the end of the 1980s, Gorbachev was faced with two dilemmas, one at home, the other abroad. In the USSR itself, perestroika was not bringing about the economic and political improvements Gorbachev had expected it to. Gorbachev remained true to his communist principles and was unwilling to reform beyond a certain point. Many of the liberals and moderates who had originally supported and admired Gorbachev were disappointed by perestroika's failures. In addition, many of those liberals and moderates who had hoped that Gorbachev would go even further in his reforms now began to look for leaders who would do so.

On the other hand, Gorbachev had made enough changes and eliminated enough abuses that he had badly upset hard-liners and stalwart Communists. Therefore, Gorbachev was losing support from both conservatives and liberals by the late 1980s and early 1990s.

LIBERALISM IN EASTERN EUROPE

The foreign-policy dilemma concerned Eastern Europe. How liberal should Gorbachev be with the Eastern bloc? To crack down would take more money than the Soviets had to spend. It would renew tensions with the West and plunge the Soviets back into an arms race they could not afford. It would destroy Gorbachev's positive reputation abroad.

On the other hand, to allow Eastern Europe too much freedom might result in its complete breakaway. As it happened, Gorbachev was prepared to run that risk. Worse, however, was the prospect that Eastern Europe's desire for freedom might prove contagious and infect the non-Russian parts of the Soviet Union.

With regard to the Warsaw Pact nations of Eastern Europe, Gorbachev chose to allow them to go their separate paths. In a famous joke, the Soviet foreign minister stated that the USSR was replacing the Brezhnev Doctrine (which declared the right of the Soviets to intervene in East European affairs) with the "Sinatra Doctrine," according to which each East European country could "do it 'My Way.'" When dissident movements in East European nations began to press for greater freedom in 1988 and 1989, Gorbachev informed East European communist leaders that the Soviet Union would not go to the financial expense or take the political risk of supporting them militarily, in the event of crisis.

FREEDOM IN EASTERN EUROPE AND THE FALL OF THE BERLIN WALL

Gorbachev's new stance toward Eastern Europe helped stir up the massive wave of liberalization and freedom that swept over the region in 1989 and 1990. In Poland, Solidarity, which had emerged from underground in 1988, was made legal in 1989. That summer, Solidarity was allowed to take part in nationwide elections, winning a huge victory and bringing a noncommunist leadership to power. The Hungarian Communist Party opened the country's borders to the West, then voted itself out of existence.

November 1989 was the great climax. In Czechoslovakia's "Velvet Revolution," Vaclav Havel's dissident movement, Civic Forum (formerly Chapter 77), swept to power. Bulgaria's communist leadership resigned. Most striking of all, however, the East German Communist Party, the strongest and most hard-line in Eastern Europe, collapsed. In the freedom movement's most celebrated, most triumphant event, the Berlin Wall—which, since 1961, had been the most hated symbol of the Cold War—was opened. Shortly afterward, it was torn down altogether.

In December, Romania's communist leader, Nicolae Ceausescu, was executed, in one of the few violent episodes involved with the collapse of East European communism. Later, in October 1990, the map of Europe would be dramatically redrawn by the unification of Germany, brought about principally by the efforts of West Germany's chancellor, Helmut Kohl.

CHINA AND THE TIANANMEN SQUARE DEMONSTRATIONS

Even China was affected, at least partially, by the events in Eastern Europe. In May 1989, Chinese students, who had serious aspirations for greater freedoms, began to stage demonstrations at Tiananmen Square, in central Beijing. There was a deliberate historical significance here: it was the seventieth anniversary of the May Fourth Movement, which, in 1919, had gathered at the square, in order to demand progressive reforms. Inspired by that long-ago event, as well as ongoing developments in Eastern Europe and the USSR, Chinese students hoped to bring about positive change in their own country. However, the government refused to grant any concessions. By the end of May, the authorities sent in troops and tanks, crushing the Tiananmen Square demonstrations by means of force. Here, at least, the leadership chose not to run the risk of being overthrown.

DEMOCRATIZATION IN LATIN AMERICA AND SOUTH AFRICA

Other pro-freedom parallels in non-European parts of the world include the general move toward democratization in Latin America during the late 1980s and early 1990s. In South Africa, the system of apartheid was breaking down during these same years. In 1990, Nelson Mandela, leader of the African National Congress, was released from prison, where he had been held since 1964.

THE COLLAPSE OF THE SOVIET UNION

With Eastern Europe gone, the Soviet Union now had its own problems to cope with. Popular discontent with Gorbachev was growing in 1990 and 1991, as the economy failed to improve. Non-Russian parts of the Soviet Union—especially Georgia, Ukraine, the republics of Central Asia, and the Baltic nations of Estonia, Latvia, and Lithuania—were now agitating openly for their freedom (in Lithuania's case, freedom was declared in 1990, and Gorbachev responded by sending in tanks).

Liberal politicians, such as Boris Yeltsin, began to oppose Gorbachev, calling for greater reforms and a complete break with communism. From the other end of the political spectrum, unbeknownst to Gorbachev, conservative, hard-line communist elements within the government were plotting against him.

Finally, in August 1991, the hard-line communists struck. They staged a three-day coup, placing Gorbachev under house arrest and attempting to take over the government. Thanks to popular resistance and the bold leadership of Boris Yeltsin, who called for all citizens to oppose the coup, the takeover failed. Gorbachev was brought back to power, but only for a few months. Unlike in Eastern Europe, where "revolution from below" spurred the collapse of communist regimes, in the USSR it was political leaders who acted as the architects of the country's demise.

During the fall and early winter, the various republics of the USSR, including Russia itself, decided to go their separate ways, and Gorbachev was too weak to stop them. In early December 1991, Yeltsin (President of the Russian Republic) and the leaders of Ukraine and Belarus declared the formation of a new, post-Soviet confederation, the Commonwealth of Independent States. In effect, this declaration made the USSR irrelevant. Bowing to the inevitable, on December 25,

1991, Gorbachev resigned as leader of the Soviet Union. At the same time, he declared an end to the USSR itself. Soviet Communism, whose birth in 1917 had been one of the major events of the early twentieth century, did not live to see the twenty-first.

QUICK REVIEW

1. What kind of geopolitical alignment has the end of the Cold War brought into being?

   (A) the traditional form of balance of power
   (B) a concentration of world might in the hands of three evenly matched powers
   (C) a state of affairs in which only one nation can be considered a true superpower
   (D) a repetition of the Cold War's bipolar equilibrium
   (E) complete anarchy

2. Which of the following was among the communist regimes that survived the Cold War?

   (A) North Korea
   (B) Bulgaria
   (C) Albania
   (D) Czechoslovakia
   (E) Yugoslavia

3. Which of the following did NOT happen to the Soviet Union during the 1970s and 1980s?

   (A) Stagnation weakened the entire nation's economic system.
   (B) The political leadership became increasingly corrupt.
   (C) The military fell behind the U.S. armed forces in terms of technological ability and computer skills.
   (D) A wave of political reformers instituted sweeping change throughout the governmental structure.
   (E) The dissident movement became increasingly vocal.

4. Vaclav Havel was associated with the freedom movement in what country?

   (A) East Germany
   (B) Romania
   (C) Bulgaria
   (D) Hungary
   (E) Czechoslovakia

5. Lech Walesa's role in ending the Cold War was

   (A) to declare martial law in Poland
   (B) to lead the trade union and social movement known as Solidarity
   (C) to form an armed resistance group that sabotaged the communist regime
   (D) to negotiate the withdrawal of Soviet tank forces
   (E) to invite the Soviet army into Poland to put down civic disturbances

6. Which statement best characterizes the rule of Deng Xiaoping in China?

   (A) Deng pursued a pragmatic course of limited free-market reform and tight political control.
   (B) Deng maintained a Marxist, centrally controlled economic stance, but allowed a great deal of social and political liberalization.
   (C) Deng proved even more dictatorial than his predecessor, Mao Tse-tung.
   (D) Deng moved rapidly to democratize China.
   (E) Deng brought about surprisingly little change in China.

7. Which of the following would be considered a feature of perestroika?

(A) the Soviet Union's continuation of the war in Afghanistan
(B) greater centralization of the USSR's central-command economy
(C) increased levels of free-market economic activity allowed by the regime
(D) delegation of greater authority to the KGB
(E) a crackdown on liberal elements in the media

8. What was the principal reason Gorbachev sought a more peaceful relationship with the West?

(A) genuine concern for the safety of all European peoples
(B) personal cowardice
(C) desire to win the Nobel Peace Prize
(D) realization that the Soviet economy could no longer keep pace with the arms race
(E) CIA control over Gorbachev's government

9. Which of the following CORRECTLY places events in chronological order?

(A) Hungary's opening of its borders, the formation of Solidarity, the fall of the Berlin Wall, the unification of Germany, the collapse of the USSR
(B) the formation of Solidarity, Hungary's opening of its borders, the fall of the Berlin Wall, the unification of Germany, the collapse of the USSR
(C) the formation of Solidarity, the fall of the Berlin Wall, Hungary's opening of its borders, the unification of Germany, the collapse of the USSR
(D) the formation of Solidarity, Hungary's opening of its borders, the fall of the Berlin Wall, the collapse of the USSR, the unification of Germany
(E) the fall of the Berlin Wall, the unification of Germany, Hungary's opening of its borders, the formation of Solidarity, the collapse of the USSR

10. What effect did the liberation of Eastern Europe in 1989 to 1990 have on the Soviet Union itself?

(A) It provided an example for non-Russian peoples within the USSR who wanted to set themselves free.
(B) It stifled freedom movements within the USSR.
(C) It drained badly needed finances from the Soviet economy.
(D) It greatly boosted Gorbachev's prestige at home.
(E) It provoked a war between Poland and Soviet Ukraine.

ANSWERS:

1. **C**, p. 432	6. **A**, p. 434
2. **A**, p. 432	7. **C**, p. 434
3. **D**, p. 433	8. **D**, p. 435
4. **E**, p. 433	9. **B**, p. 436
5. **B**, p. 433	10. **A**, p. 436

CHAPTER 35

Integration or Fragmentation? Globalism in the Late Twentieth and Early Twenty-First Centuries

Are the nations of the world growing closer together, or further apart? Enduring symbols of the late 1900s and early 2000s would include the sight of McDonald's golden arches in cities such as Nairobi or Shanghai, as well as the all-pervasive presence of mass media and the Internet in literally every corner of the planet. One might argue that these are signs of global integration.

However, other images of the latest turn of the century would seem to be indications of global fragmentation. Ethnic cleansing in the former Yugoslavia. Genocidal butchery in Rwanda. The breakdown of peace talks between Israelis and Palestinians. All of these would appear to signal that world communities are growing apart, rather than growing together.

The fact of the matter is that, globally speaking, there are, at the same time, centripetal and centrifugal forces acting on the nations of the world, simultaneously pushing them together and pulling them apart. Which of these forces will prevail as the twenty-first century progresses remains to be seen.

DIPLOMACY AFTER THE COLD WAR

DIPLOMATIC AMBIGUITY AFTER THE COLD WAR

In 1992, U.S. President George Bush said that the collapse of the Cold War had brought about a "new world order." The U.S.-Soviet arms race ended, as did the bipolar division of most of the world into two hostile camps. In this way, the nations of the world were free to emerge from underneath the nuclear umbrellas of the superpowers and associate with each other as they pleased. The risk of nuclear annihilation decreased dramatically, and, as described in Chapter 34, the end of the Cold War coincided with a general rise in the level of democratization worldwide.

On the other hand, the end of the Cold War has left the world without a defining diplomatic framework. Instead of two superpowers, only one, the United States, remains. The fact that other countries are now free to join together or clash with each other as they wish has made international relations much more unpredictable. New diplomatic alignments appear and disappear. Many old alliances have broken or weakened. Others have had to be redesigned. For instance, what purpose does NATO have in Europe, now that the threat of Soviet invasion has been removed?

POST–COLD WAR HOSTILITIES

Furthermore, during the Cold War, any conflict, anywhere, carried with it the risk of superpower involvement and, with that, the possibility of nuclear war. In its way, then, the Cold War had something of a restraining effect, which contained certain ethnic and cultural pressures, especially within the superpowers' spheres of influence. With the restraining effect of the Cold War removed, many of those hostilities have emerged, breaking out of control in Yugoslavia, Rwanda, Indonesia, and elsewhere (discussed subsequently). In addition, the post–Cold War years have witnessed the gradual spread of nuclear-weapons capability beyond not just the official "nuclear club," but also the few nations that were known during the 1970s and 1980s to have nuclear weapons (also discussed subsequently).

CHINA AND RUSSIA

Other factors creating tensions during the post–Cold War era include the strained relationship between the United States and China, the largest remaining communist power on earth. China is not yet a superpower, but its economic growth has been rapid throughout the 1980s and 1990s, and it possesses the humanpower and geographical size eventually to become truly powerful on a global scale. Although the Clinton administration pursued a policy of engagement with China during the 1990s, trade disputes and diplomatic disagreements between the United States and China have been frequent.

In recent years, the United States' friendly relationship with Russia has cooled a bit. Russia was led by Boris Yeltsin during most of the 1990s, then by a former KGB operative, Vladimir Putin. Russia is still struggling to build its own democratic institutions and to regain its economic footing. It has begun to reassert its sphere of influence in parts of the former USSR, including the Caucasus (especially Chechnya), Belarus, and Ukraine. On the other hand, its leaders clearly do not want to seem overly aggressive or remain isolated from other parts of Europe. Although Russia is, for the moment, too weak to renew its superpower hostility—or nuclear arms race—with the West, it is still an important force in Europe and Asia.

At the time, the end of the Cold War was thought to have brought about a lasting global peace. It has not. Although it would be too much to say that it has brought about global anarchy, it is undeniable that the post–Cold War years have called for new and creative ways of thinking about diplomacy. As one U.S. government official said of the post–Cold War world during the mid-1990s, "We have slain the dragon; but we now live in a jungle filled with a bewildering variety of poisonous snakes."

SECURITY CONCERNS

WAR AFTER THE COLD WAR

The end of the Cold War has by no means brought about an era of peace. For example, the Iraqi invasion of Kuwait and the resulting Gulf War (1990–1991) between Iraq and the U.S.-led coalition resulted in a major conflict. War raged in Yugoslavia during the 1990s. In 1999, NATO bombed Yugoslavia in an effort to stop Serb aggression against the Albanian population of the Serbian province of Kosovo.

Just as important, a large variety of brushfire wars, small armed conflicts, and civil disturbances have raged throughout the decade following the end of the Cold War, resulting in the deaths of hundreds of thousands. Many of these have been motivated by ethnic hostilities that had been kept in check during the Cold War (see subsequent discussion).

WEAPONS OF MASS DESTRUCTION

Other security issues that have become troublesome during the post–Cold War era involve nuclear weaponry. From 1987 onward, the United States and Russia have made great progress in restricting, even scaling back, the production and testing of nuclear weapons. However, recent tension between the two countries has slowed this process down. Beyond that, there have been worries that, given the conditions of extreme economic and political breakdown in Russia, nuclear weapons, or at least weapons-grade atomic material, might be stolen or smuggled out of the former Soviet Union and end up in the hands of terrorists or outlaw governments.

Even more worrisome is the issue of nuclear proliferation. Only five countries belong to the "nuclear club," the group of nations legally permitted to possess nuclear-weapons capability: the United States, Russia, China, France, and Great Britain. Most nations of the world have signed the Nuclear Non-Proliferation Treaty. Generally, the treaty's effectiveness and longevity have been remarkable. In addition, in 1996, the United Nations General Assembly adopted the Comprehensive Nuclear Test-Ban Treaty, although it has yet to enter into force.

Nonetheless, several countries, most notably Israel, developed nuclear arsenals during the 1970s and 1980s. In 1998, India and Pakistan, deadly enemies, each tested nuclear weapons, adding new peril to an already dangerous diplomatic situation. How long nuclear proliferation can continue to be contained is one of the most pressing questions of the new century.

The same can be said for other weapons of mass destruction, such as biological weapons (various germs, viruses, and bacteria, packaged in a delivery system) and chemical weapons (such as nerve gas and water-based toxins). These are relatively easy weapons to manufacture and deliver, and extremely difficult to defend against. During the Cold War, both superpowers abided by international agreements banning the use of biological and chemical weapons. Whether or not certain states—such as Iraq or North Korea—choose to honor such agreements, now that the Cold War is over, is an open question.

THE PROLIFERATION OF SMALL ARMS

At the other end of the weapons spectrum are small arms: pistols, rifles, submachine guns, and automatic rifles. During the Cold War, some 50 million people were killed, mainly in the developing world, because of small-scale conflicts of various types. This trend has continued since 1991. Certain parts of the world, such as Africa, Southeast Asia, and Latin America, are awash with small arms. A huge illegal trade in these weapons thrives. Societies in which large numbers of civilians, noncombatants, and members of paramilitary groups—as opposed to regular military forces— have access to heavy weaponry are inherently unstable.

CHINA AND TAIWAN

Over the past few decades, citizens of mainland China and Taiwan have informally established enduring trade ties and strong family bonds across the Taiwan Straits. Formally, however, there have been many diplomatic clashes and instances of military brinksmanship between China and Taiwan. A number of foreign policy experts warn that tensions between the two could eventually lead to war. To complicate matters, the United States could possibly side with Taiwan in such a conflict. Official U.S. policy since 1979 has been to recognize the communist People's Republic of China as the only legitimate government of China and to maintain no formal diplomatic ties with Taiwan.

However, Taiwan, which, in the mid-1990s, held direct presidential elections for the first time, began to assert its independence more boldly, infuriating Chinese leaders. In 1996, China fired missiles in waters near Taiwan as a note of caution. The United States came to Taiwan's aid by sending aircraft carriers to the region. Relations between the two countries were hurt further when, during the NATO assault on Yugoslavia, a U.S. bomber accidentally dropped explosives on the Chinese embassy in Belgrade.

In 2000, the U.S. Congress granted China permanent normal trade relations, despite strong opposition to the Chinese government's human rights abuses. But that same year, China expressed outrage at the United States' plans to build a national missile defense, which the former sees as a threat to its nuclear deterrence posture. Diplomatic tensions between the United States and China flared in April 2001 after China took hostage the crew of a damaged U.S. Navy surveillance plane that had collided with a Chinese jet, then landed in Chinese territory. The Bush administration appears to be pursuing a policy of containment, rather than one of engagement, with China.

NATIONALIST EXTREMISM, ETHNIC TENSIONS, AND RELIGIOUS FUNDAMENTALISM

One of the forces that the Cold War tended to keep under control was nationalist and ethnic extremism. The collapse of the superpower rivalry has, in many cases, released national, ethnic, and religious pressures, allowing them to boil out of control.

NATIONALIST EXTREMISM IN THE WEST

Even in Western Europe, with its democratic governments and tradition of respecting civil rights, there is a certain level of ethnic tension. Since 1975, the island of Cyprus has been divided between Turks and Greeks, with a United Nations force needed to keep the peace. In countries such as Britain, Germany, France, Switzerland, and Italy, the millions of Turks, Middle Easterners, Africans, Pakistanis, Indians, and Caribbean islanders who live and work there (many of them as guest workers) suffer varying degrees of prejudice and discrimination. Right-wing and neo-Nazi groups harass minorities and call for their deportation, especially in times of economic distress. Likewise, much the same applies to the United States, where anti-immigration sentiment sometimes rises up in opposition to America's "melting-pot" tradition.

EAST EUROPEAN NATIONALISM AND THE BREAKUP OF YUGOSLAVIA

In Eastern Europe, ethnic tensions are even higher than in the West. Each East European state is home to substantial minority populations, many of which have long histories of conflict. Even the East European states that have made the most progress toward democratization have found it difficult to ensure that the rights of national minorities—Romanians living in Hungary, for example, or Slovaks in the Czech Republic, or Russians in the Baltic States—are protected. One group that is heavily discriminated against throughout Eastern Europe is the Roma, better known as Gypsies.

The most striking examples of ethnic hostilities in Eastern Europe are the various wars in the former Yugoslavia. With the collapse of communism in 1989 and 1990, Yugoslavia, an artificial nation created after World War I to unite the southern Slavs—Serbs, Croats, Bosnians, Slovenes, Montenegrins, and Macedonians—began to break apart. Complicating the matter was the fact that these groups practice three religions, Roman Catholicism (Croatians and Slovenes), Eastern Orthodoxy (Serbs, Montenegrins, Macedonians, the Serbian minority in Bosnia), and Islam (the majority of Bosnians). There is also a sizable Albanian minority in Serbia and Macedonia, most of whom are Muslims. All these peoples have a long history of conflict. However, from 1945 until 1980, the communist government of Josip Tito held these conflicts in check and encouraged multicultural coexistence. Even during the 1980s, the various peoples of Yugoslavia lived together reasonably amicably.

After 1989, ethnic tensions began to reemerge. Such tensions were due partly to the stress and strain of communist breakdown, but also to the efforts of nationalist politicians (such as the Serbian leader Slobodan Milosevic), who deliberately whipped ethnic hostility out of control for their own purposes. Slovenia, Macedonia, and Croatia declared independence in 1991.

The first Yugoslav war resulted from Serbia's attempt to take territory from Croatia. When Bosnia declared independence in 1992, the Serbian minority there rose up in arms, with assistance from Milosevic and the Serbian government. Their goal was to create a "Greater Serbia."

From 1992 to 1995, while the Serbian-Croatian war came to an end, a second war raged in Bosnia. Serb forces took three quarters of Bosnia. Even worse, Bosnian Serbs, with full support of Milosevic's Serbian government, carried out the policy of "ethnic cleansing." This form of genocide involved the forced deportation of Bosnian Muslims from territories the Bosnian Serbs wanted for themselves. It also included mass executions and the systematic rape of large numbers of women. The Serbian campaign of ethnic cleansing was the worst military atrocity committed in Europe since the Nazi Holocaust. The failure of the United Nations and the European Community to deal effectively with the crisis was not only embarrassing, but called into doubt the ability of international organizations to cope with international conflict in the post–Cold War era. The war in Bosnia was finally ended by the U.S.-sponsored Dayton Accords, in the fall of 1995, when the Serbs backed down under the pressure of U.S. airstrikes and a renewed Croatian offensive.

Another round of fighting came in 1998 and 1999, when Milosevic and the Serbs began another campaign of ethnic cleansing, this time against the Albanian minority living in the Serbian province of Kosovo. For three months in 1999, NATO, in its first-ever military action, bombed Serbia until Milosevic relented. Although, technically, a state of peace exists in the former Yugoslavia, ethnic resentment and bitterness boils just beneath the surface.

ETHNIC VIOLENCE IN AFRICA, ASIA, AND THE MIDDLE EAST

Other notorious examples of ethnic violence include the Hutu-Tutsi conflict in Rwanda. In 1994, these two tribes fought each other. In the process, the Hutu killed approximately 800,000 Tutsi men, women, and children. The long-standing effort of the people of East Timor, a Pacific island illegally annexed by Indonesia in 1975, to free themselves has led to great bloodshed. Indonesian suppression of the East Timorese has verged on the genocidal since the 1970s. In 1999, the reign of terror Indonesia visited upon the tiny island was so bloody that it prompted United Nations intervention. Along with a severe currency crisis, the disturbances and scandals connected with East Timorese independence also played a role in toppling Suharto, the dictator who had ruled Indonesia since 1967.

Perhaps the longest-lasting, and still problematic, ethnic clash is that of the Israelis and the Palestinians. The Oslo Accord of 1993, in which PLO leader Yasser Arafat and Israeli prime minister Yitzhak Rabin agreed to pursue peace, led to more than half a decade of relative calm in the Middle East. Negotiations came to a deadlock, however, and tensions began to mount once again. In 2001, those tensions broke out into open conflict, as the Palestinians began a second uprising, or intifada.

RELIGIOUS FUNDAMENTALISM

Religious fundamentalism has experienced a revival during the late 1900s and early 2000s. In India, religious conflict among Hindus, Muslims, and Sikhs continues. Although its government is currently (but slowly) reforming, policy in Iran is still shaped largely by Islamic fundamentalism. In Afghanistan, Islamic fundamentalism has led to the creation of a strictly theocratic government under the Taliban. Religious differences are at the heart of the Israeli-Arab conflict in the Middle East, and largely at the heart of the ethnic tensions plaguing the former Yugoslavia.

Ethnic and religious tensions and violence have to be counted among the fragmenting factors threatening to tear the world apart, rather than bring it together.

ENVIRONMENTAL ISSUES

Despite the existence of vibrant and active environmental movements since the 1960s, environmental problems still remain. In several ways, they have become more pressing during the 1990s and early 2000s.

ENVIRONMENTALISM IN THE DEVELOPED WORLD

In the developed world—the United States, Canada, Western Europe, Japan, and others like them—strict environmental regulations have been put into place from the 1970s onward, in an attempt to ensure clean air and clean water for all. Recycling has become common practice. Endangered species have received greater protections. Growing concern about the depletion of the ozone layer led to the elimination of chlorofluorocarbons (CFCs). The ongoing debate about the effect of carbon dioxide and other "greenhouse gasses" on planetary climate patterns—that is, global warming—has raised awareness about this issue.

CONSUMPTION AND POLLUTION IN THE DEVELOPED WORLD

However, the developed world's economies continue to modernize. With that, the rate of consumption among the populations of these countries continues to escalate. This group—a small segment of the world population—eats more, generates more trash, burns more gasoline, uses more electricity, consumes more wood and paper products, and releases more additives and emissions into the air and water than the rest of the people in the world combined.

MODERNIZATION AND ENVIRONMENTAL PROBLEMS IN THE DEVELOPING WORLD

Added to this issue is the modernization of the developing world. As large parts of Asia, Africa, Latin America, and the Middle East industrialize and attempt to catch up with the developed world, their rates of energy use and resource consumption have been increasing. These countries also do not have the same clean-air, clean-water, and other regulations in place that nations in the developed world do.

THE FAILURE OF INTERNATIONAL ENVIRONMENTAL REGULATIONS

On the whole, international agreements to take greater care of the environment have met with limited success. A prime example of this is the Kyoto Summit (1997), where over 150 nations gathered to discuss environmental issues, especially the potential dangers of global warming. Although an agreement was hammered out, it is still contentious, and many countries, including the United States, have not ratified it. A particular point of conflict is the question of whether or not industrializing countries of the less developed world should be compelled to abide by the same clean-air regulations that nations of the developed world do.

ENERGY SOURCES

Another failure has been the inability or unwillingness to develop clean, sustainable sources of energy. Continued reliance on fossil fuels such as coal and especially petroleum has not only led to periodic shortages and economic difficulties, but to continued air pollution. Hydroelectric generation of electric power has its limits. Experiments with wind and solar power—potentially the cleanest sources of power possible—have not been supported by governments or corporations (at times, the latter, whose profits are dependent on oil-based technologies, have actively opposed such experiments).

The only alternative source of energy that has met with any success is nuclear power. This, however, carries with it serious risks, as nuclear accidents at Three Mile Island (1979) in Pennsylvania and Chernobyl (1986) in Ukraine—where 8,000 people were killed immediately and hundreds of thousands were made sick or born deformed afterward—have demonstrated.

Although a variety of environmental issues will confront the nations of the world in the twenty-first century, perhaps the most dangerous, and the one that threatens all countries equally, is global warming.

REGIONALISM, GLOBALIZATION, AND MULTICULTURALISM

Trends that would seem to encourage the integration, rather than fragmentation, of world communities include regionalism, economic globalization, and multicultural interaction. All are prominent features of contemporary life. However, they also have their limits.

THE UNITED NATIONS

Regional and international organizations and agencies serve to unite the efforts of countries around the world, or in specific parts of the world. The United Nations, despite certain failures and flaws, has provided a forum for dispute resolution among the countries of the world since 1945. It oversees peacekeeping missions, monitors the observance of human rights and international treaties, and organizes humanitarian efforts, cultural preservation, and many other activities.

In terms of punitive measures, such as economic embargoes, peacekeeping, and peacemaking, the United Nations' record is mixed. It has many successes to its credit, but events in Bosnia, Rwanda, Central Africa, and Sierra Leone have embarrassed it greatly.

NONGOVERNMENTAL ORGANIZATIONS

A relatively recent trend has been the proliferation of nongovernmental organizations (NGOs). These nonprofit groups harness the effort of volunteers and activists locally, nationally, and around the world to work on various causes. Among the best known NGOs are Greenpeace, the World Wildlife Fund, Amnesty International, Human Rights Watch, the National Organization for Women, Planned Parenthood, and the National Rifle Association.

REGIONAL ORGANIZATIONS AND ALLIANCES

Regional organizations that have fostered international cooperation include the Organization for Security and Cooperation in Europe, the Association of Southeast Asian Nations, the Organization for African Unity, and the Organization of American States. Western Europe has made the greatest efforts to regionalize its economic, military, and political activities. In addition to the European Union (more presently) and the OSCE, many European nations belong to the NATO alliance and the Council of Europe.

TECHNOLOGY AS AN INTEGRATING FORCE

Various cultural and technological factors seem to be bringing nations and regions closer together. Mass media technology has greatly increased people's awareness of other parts of the world. Enhanced means of communication—improved telephone networks, satellite transmissions, and, above all, the Internet and World Wide Web—have made it more possible than ever before for greater numbers of people to be continually in touch with other people in all parts of the globe. Cheaper and quicker modes of transport have enabled people to travel, work, study, or live abroad in greater numbers than ever before. The celebration of art, literature, music, and traditions from all parts of the world—multiculturalism—has become extremely prominent during the 1990s and early 2000s. Cultural fusion and interaction have given multiculturalism even more of a boost.

ECONOMIC GLOBALIZATION

The globalization of the world economy continues. The European Union has already removed barriers to the movement of people, goods, money, and services among its member nations. In 2002, most of its members will begin to use a single currency, the euro. The North American Free Trade Agreement, in operation since 1994, is likely to serve as a model for similar agreements elsewhere. The World Trade Organization, formed in 1995, aims to bring the operations of the global economy under a single set of laws, rules, and practices.

However, economic globalization is not complete, nor is it self-evident that the trend is completely positive. Some of the flaws and potential dangers connected with globalization are discussed in Chapter 33. Not all nations belong to the WTO, and even member states quarrel with each other—and with the WTO's rulings. The great gap between the developed and developing worlds still remains, and at least in some respects, it is widening.

QUICK REVIEW

1. Which of the following nations are suspected or known to possess nuclear weapons?

   (A) Canada, Brazil, Israel
   (B) Brazil, Italy, Russia
   (C) Israel, India, Pakistan
   (D) Pakistan, Zimbabwe, Great Britain
   (E) China, Mexico, France

2. What was the first major armed conflict of the post–Cold War era?

   (A) the Gulf War
   (B) the U.S. assault on Grenada
   (C) the NATO bombing of Belgrade
   (D) U.S. intervention in Somalia
   (E) the Soviet invasion of Afghanistan

3. Over what island's independence are China and the United States most likely to quarrel in the future?

   (A) Hong Kong
   (B) Taiwan
   (C) Quemoy and Matsu
   (D) Sri Lanka
   (E) the Philippines

4. What ethnic group has met with widespread discrimination and regular violence throughout Eastern Europe since the collapse of communism?

   (A) Germans
   (B) Jews
   (C) Kosovar Albanians
   (D) Serbs
   (E) Roma (Gypsies)

5. What politician is MOST responsible for stirring up the nationalist hatreds that led to the Yugoslav wars of the 1990s?

(A) Franjo Tudjman
(B) Alija Izetbegovic
(C) Slobodan Milosevic
(D) Richard Holbrooke
(E) Josip Tito

6. International revulsion toward Indonesia's bloody suppression of what province's freedom movement helped lead to the toppling of Suharto's regime?

(A) East Timor
(B) West Timor
(C) Java
(D) Bali
(E) Srivijaya

7. The Kyoto Accord of 1997 was intended to deal with the problems associated with

(A) the illegal trade in small arms
(B) the HIV/AIDS epidemic
(C) the growing number of biological-weapons programs
(D) the climatic trend known as global warming
(E) the spread of nuclear weapons

8. Which of the following is NOT a nongovernmental organization (NGO)?

(A) Greenpeace
(B) the National Rifle Association
(C) Amnesty International
(D) Habitat for Humanity
(E) the European Union

9. Which of the following would be considered an integrating trend in global development today?

(A) the worldwide proliferation of Internet technology
(B) religious fundamentalism in Afghanistan
(C) discrimination against Turkish guest workers in Germany
(D) all of the above
(E) none of the above

10. In which country did the worst genocide committed in post–Cold War Africa take place?

(A) Sierra Leone
(B) Rwanda
(C) Angola
(D) Mali
(E) Nigeria

ANSWERS:

1. **C**, p. 442
2. **A**, p. 441
3. **B**, p. 443
4. **E**, p. 443
5. **C**, p. 444

6. **A**, p. 444
7. **D**, p. 445
8. **E**, p. 446
9. **A**, p. 447
10. **B**, p. 444

Unit Six: Review Questions

SAMPLE ESSAY QUESTIONS

1. Compare and contrast the global effects of World War I and World War II. How did each shape not just Europe and the United States, but the entire globe?

2. Discuss the beginning of the Cold War, then its major moments from the late 1940s to the early 1990s. How did the Cold War evolve into a truly global phenomenon?

3. Have the forces of integration been prevailing during the post–Cold War era? Or have the forces of fragmentation proven stronger? Provide concrete examples of both.

MULTIPLE-CHOICE QUESTIONS

1. Which of the following was NOT a social change that stemmed from World War I?

   (A) The aristocracy declined in power across Europe.
   (B) The middle and lower classes grew in stature.
   (C) Europeans came to view themselves as models of civilized behavior.
   (D) Europeans' spirit of optimism faded.
   (E) Women were granted the right to vote in most countries.

2. Where did fighting spread beyond Europe during World War I?

   I. New Guinea
   II. Turkey
   III. Hawaii
   IV. Togoland

   (A) I, II, and III
   (B) II, III, and IV
   (C) I and III only
   (D) I, II, and IV
   (E) II only

3. Which of the following was NOT a provision decided at the Paris Peace Conference (1919–1920)?

   (A) breaking up Austria-Hungary
   (B) independence for Palestine
   (C) creation of Yugoslavia
   (D) assigning Germany full blame for World War I
   (E) stripping Germany of its colonies

4. The interwar period in Europe was marked by

   (A) economic depression and weakness within most democratic governments
   (B) strong support for the policy of collective security
   (C) growth in the number of democracies, particularly in eastern Europe
   (D) an economic boom and the strengthening of capitalism
   (E) almost complete decolonization of Africa

5. In which of the following sequences are Soviet leaders placed in the correct chronological order, according to the years they ruled?

(A) Stalin, Lenin, Brezhnev, Khrushchev
(B) Khrushchev, Lenin, Stalin, Brezhnev
(C) Brezhnev, Stalin, Khrushchev, Lenin
(D) Lenin, Khrushchev, Stalin, Brezhnev
(E) Lenin, Stalin, Khrushchev, Brezhnev

6. Fascism can best be described as

(A) left-wing radicalism
(B) socialistic
(C) laissez-faire
(D) right-wing radicalism
(E) moderate

7. Reza Shah Pahlavi of Iran was similar to Mustafa Kemal of Turkey in that he

(A) was a democratic ruler
(B) proclaimed himself sultan
(C) secularized his country
(D) turned his country into a theocracy
(E) introduced a bill of rights

8. Which of the following statements accurately describes civilian participation in World War II?

(A) Nearly half of the war's casualties were civilians.
(B) Only Jewish civilians were killed in great numbers.
(C) Most civilians remained far from the battle scenes.
(D) The warring parties tended to respect international conventions concerning the treatment of noncombatants.
(E) In the United States, a smaller percentage of women worked outside the home than during World War I.

9. In the 1940s, what was Japan's long-term goal in the Pacific?

(A) It planned to take over the United States.
(B) It wanted to control the Chinese coast, all of Southeast Asia, India, Indonesia, Australia, and New Zealand.
(C) It wanted to regain the Kurile Islands from the USSR.
(D) It had no other goal but to strengthen trade with its immediate neighbors.
(E) It wanted to work jointly with Germany in creating a Pacific Rim empire.

10. How did World War II change the patterns of international trade?

(A) No countries traded with Germany after the war.
(B) The World Trade Organization was created soon after the war ended.
(C) The war diminished the European powers' control over world markets.
(D) The USSR began trading more with Western Europe.
(E) The United States stopped trading with Asian countries.

11. Which of the following is an example of bipolar equilibrium?

(A) the Ottoman Empire's hegemony over the Balkans
(B) the North Pole and South Pole during the vernal equinox
(C) French-Italian diplomatic struggles during the late nineteenth century
(D) the United States' and Soviet Union's rivalry during the Cold War
(E) the Austrians' and Hungarians' power sharing within the Habsburg Empire

12. How did Deng Xiaoping's reforms in China differ from those of Mikhail Gorbachev's in the Soviet Union?

    (A) Deng allowed political and cultural liberalization, whereas Gorbachev did not.
    (B) Gorbachev allowed political and cultural liberalization, whereas Deng did not.
    (C) Gorbachev finessed conservative opposition to his reforms better than Deng did.
    (D) Deng's reform plans laid the ground-work for a free-market economy, whereas Gorbachev avoided economic reform.
    (E) Deng gave China's outlying provinces greater autonomy, whereas Gorbachev suppressed all attempts by non-Russian republics to gain more autonomy.

13. What kind of role did many of the so-called Third World nations, including Angola and Vietnam, play in the Cold War?

    (A) They maintained a position of absolute neutrality, remaining on the sidelines.
    (B) They naturally and automatically gravitated toward the Soviet-led communist system.
    (C) They were naturally and automatically attracted toward the American-led democratic nations.
    (D) They became diplomatic and military battlegrounds, over which the two superpowers competed for influence.
    (E) They exerted a great deal of influence over the superpowers' military and diplomatic policies.

14. Which of the following sequences is in the correct chronological order?

    (A) Cuban missile crisis, Suez Canal crisis, Soviet invasion of Afghanistan, U.S. troop withdrawal from Vietnam
    (B) Soviet invasion of Afghanistan, Suez Canal crisis, Cuban missile crisis, U.S. troop withdrawal from Vietnam
    (C) Suez Canal crisis, Cuban missile crisis, U.S. troop withdrawal from Vietnam, Soviet invasion of Afghanistan
    (D) Cuban missile crisis, Suez Canal crisis, U.S. troop withdrawal from Vietnam, Soviet invasion of Afghanistan
    (E) U.S. troop withdrawal from Vietnam, Cuban missile crisis, Suez Canal crisis, Soviet invasion of Afghanistan

15. According to the map on page 435, which of the following countries did NOT become a member of the Commonwealth of Independent States?

    (A) Belarus
    (B) Moldova
    (C) Russia
    (D) Ukraine
    (E) Estonia

16. Which of the following statements best describes Europe's political turn to the right during the 1980s?

    (A) Leaders such as Prime Minister Margaret Thatcher in Great Britain privatized state-run sectors of the economy.
    (B) Leaders such as Chancellor Helmut Schmidt of West Germany promoted the strengthening of the social welfare net.
    (C) Officials became more xenophobic.
    (D) Labor unions were given more economic rights.
    (E) Taxes were increased.

17. What advantages did North African states have over countries of sub-Saharan Africa in terms of decolonization?

    I. They were ethnically and religiously more homogeneous.

   II. Their colonizing powers had left behind technology and industrial assets that still proved to be useful.

 III. They had been states for a longer time than those in sub-Saharan Africa.

 IV. More of their people shared a common language.

    (A) I, II, and III
    (B) II, III, and IV
    (C) II and IV only
    (D) all of the above
    (E) none of the above

18. Why did apartheid in South Africa end during the 1990s?

    (A) White leaders began to realize how unjust the policy really was.
    (B) The African National Congress called for its dismantling.
    (C) It never succeeded in segregating Africans from whites.
    (D) It had succeeded in its goals by then.
    (E) White leaders decided that the policy was hurting the country's economy and international reputation.

19. Which of the following factors has NOT interfered with African modernization?

    (A) the AIDS/HIV epidemic
    (B) lack of cultural or linguistic unity within African states
    (C) negative population growth
    (D) corruption
    (E) interethnic conflict

20. In Latin America, modernization has often led to

    (A) greater social equality
    (B) better control over illegal drug trafficking
    (C) diversified economies
    (D) a concentration of wealth in the hands of political and economic elites
    (E) the establishment of communist regimes

ANSWERS:

1. **C**, p. 352	11. **D**, p. 388
2. **D**, p. 356	12. **B**, p. 434
3. **B**, p. 359	13. **D**, p. 393
4. **A**, p. 364	14. **C**, p. 394
5. **E**, p. 365	15. **E**, p. 435
6. **D**, p. 365	16. **A**, p. 402
7. **C**, p. 368	17. **D**, p. 408
8. **A**, p. 383	18. **E**, p. 409
9. **B**, p. 380	19. **C**, p. 410
10. **C**, p. 400	20. **D**, p. 415

UNIT SEVEN

Model Advanced Placement World History Examinations

Answer Sheet for Model Advanced Placement Examination I

SECTION I: MULTIPLE-CHOICE QUESTIONS

Sample: 1. The first person to reach the South Pole was
A) Roald Amundsen
B) Robert Scott
C) Christopher Columbus
D) Vitus Bering
E) Charles Lindbergh

1. Ⓐ Ⓑ Ⓒ Ⓓ Ⓔ

Box A is filled in because the correct answer for the sample question 1 is A.

1. Ⓐ Ⓑ Ⓒ Ⓓ Ⓔ   15. Ⓐ Ⓑ Ⓒ Ⓓ Ⓔ   29. Ⓐ Ⓑ Ⓒ Ⓓ Ⓔ   43. Ⓐ Ⓑ Ⓒ Ⓓ Ⓔ   57. Ⓐ Ⓑ Ⓒ Ⓓ Ⓔ
2. Ⓐ Ⓑ Ⓒ Ⓓ Ⓔ   16. Ⓐ Ⓑ Ⓒ Ⓓ Ⓔ   30. Ⓐ Ⓑ Ⓒ Ⓓ Ⓔ   44. Ⓐ Ⓑ Ⓒ Ⓓ Ⓔ   58. Ⓐ Ⓑ Ⓒ Ⓓ Ⓔ
3. Ⓐ Ⓑ Ⓒ Ⓓ Ⓔ   17. Ⓐ Ⓑ Ⓒ Ⓓ Ⓔ   31. Ⓐ Ⓑ Ⓒ Ⓓ Ⓔ   45. Ⓐ Ⓑ Ⓒ Ⓓ Ⓔ   59. Ⓐ Ⓑ Ⓒ Ⓓ Ⓔ
4. Ⓐ Ⓑ Ⓒ Ⓓ Ⓔ   18. Ⓐ Ⓑ Ⓒ Ⓓ Ⓔ   32. Ⓐ Ⓑ Ⓒ Ⓓ Ⓔ   46. Ⓐ Ⓑ Ⓒ Ⓓ Ⓔ   60. Ⓐ Ⓑ Ⓒ Ⓓ Ⓔ
5. Ⓐ Ⓑ Ⓒ Ⓓ Ⓔ   19. Ⓐ Ⓑ Ⓒ Ⓓ Ⓔ   33. Ⓐ Ⓑ Ⓒ Ⓓ Ⓔ   47. Ⓐ Ⓑ Ⓒ Ⓓ Ⓔ   61. Ⓐ Ⓑ Ⓒ Ⓓ Ⓔ
6. Ⓐ Ⓑ Ⓒ Ⓓ Ⓔ   20. Ⓐ Ⓑ Ⓒ Ⓓ Ⓔ   34. Ⓐ Ⓑ Ⓒ Ⓓ Ⓔ   48. Ⓐ Ⓑ Ⓒ Ⓓ Ⓔ   62. Ⓐ Ⓑ Ⓒ Ⓓ Ⓔ
7. Ⓐ Ⓑ Ⓒ Ⓓ Ⓔ   21. Ⓐ Ⓑ Ⓒ Ⓓ Ⓔ   35. Ⓐ Ⓑ Ⓒ Ⓓ Ⓔ   49. Ⓐ Ⓑ Ⓒ Ⓓ Ⓔ   63. Ⓐ Ⓑ Ⓒ Ⓓ Ⓔ
8. Ⓐ Ⓑ Ⓒ Ⓓ Ⓔ   22. Ⓐ Ⓑ Ⓒ Ⓓ Ⓔ   36. Ⓐ Ⓑ Ⓒ Ⓓ Ⓔ   50. Ⓐ Ⓑ Ⓒ Ⓓ Ⓔ   64. Ⓐ Ⓑ Ⓒ Ⓓ Ⓔ
9. Ⓐ Ⓑ Ⓒ Ⓓ Ⓔ   23. Ⓐ Ⓑ Ⓒ Ⓓ Ⓔ   37. Ⓐ Ⓑ Ⓒ Ⓓ Ⓔ   51. Ⓐ Ⓑ Ⓒ Ⓓ Ⓔ   65. Ⓐ Ⓑ Ⓒ Ⓓ Ⓔ
10. Ⓐ Ⓑ Ⓒ Ⓓ Ⓔ   24. Ⓐ Ⓑ Ⓒ Ⓓ Ⓔ   38. Ⓐ Ⓑ Ⓒ Ⓓ Ⓔ   52. Ⓐ Ⓑ Ⓒ Ⓓ Ⓔ   66. Ⓐ Ⓑ Ⓒ Ⓓ Ⓔ
11. Ⓐ Ⓑ Ⓒ Ⓓ Ⓔ   25. Ⓐ Ⓑ Ⓒ Ⓓ Ⓔ   39. Ⓐ Ⓑ Ⓒ Ⓓ Ⓔ   53. Ⓐ Ⓑ Ⓒ Ⓓ Ⓔ   67. Ⓐ Ⓑ Ⓒ Ⓓ Ⓔ
12. Ⓐ Ⓑ Ⓒ Ⓓ Ⓔ   26. Ⓐ Ⓑ Ⓒ Ⓓ Ⓔ   40. Ⓐ Ⓑ Ⓒ Ⓓ Ⓔ   54. Ⓐ Ⓑ Ⓒ Ⓓ Ⓔ   68. Ⓐ Ⓑ Ⓒ Ⓓ Ⓔ
13. Ⓐ Ⓑ Ⓒ Ⓓ Ⓔ   27. Ⓐ Ⓑ Ⓒ Ⓓ Ⓔ   41. Ⓐ Ⓑ Ⓒ Ⓓ Ⓔ   55. Ⓐ Ⓑ Ⓒ Ⓓ Ⓔ   69. Ⓐ Ⓑ Ⓒ Ⓓ Ⓔ
14. Ⓐ Ⓑ Ⓒ Ⓓ Ⓔ   28. Ⓐ Ⓑ Ⓒ Ⓓ Ⓔ   42. Ⓐ Ⓑ Ⓒ Ⓓ Ⓔ   56. Ⓐ Ⓑ Ⓒ Ⓓ Ⓔ   70. Ⓐ Ⓑ Ⓒ Ⓓ Ⓔ

SECTION II: FREE RESPONSE QUESTIONS

Write your answers on a separate sheet of paper.

Model Examination I

SECTION I: MULTIPLE-CHOICE QUESTIONS

Time: **55 minutes for 70 questions**

> *Directions:* Each of the following questions has five suggested answers. Choose the one that is best in each case.

1. Which of the following is an accurate statement about both the Americas and West Africa before 1500?

   (A) Polytheism was the dominant belief system.
   (B) Sorghum and rye were the main food staples.
   (C) Large domesticated animals allowed for extensive agricultural production.
   (D) Trade in bananas and salt was most prevalent.
   (E) A written language was in wide use at the time.

2. Postindustrial modes of economic activity focus MAINLY on providing

   (A) manufactured goods
   (B) services
   (C) raw materials
   (D) plastics
   E) hand-crafted products

3. Why are the years between the mid-1400s and the late 1700s considered a period of major socioeconomic transformation in Europe?

   I. Protestant forms of worship emerged.
   II. Europe's population grew considerably.
   III. Europeans invented gunpowder.
   IV. Agricultural techniques improved.

   (A) I, II, and III
   (B) II, III, and IV
   (C) I and III
   (D) I, II, and IV
   (E) all of the above

4. Which of the following factors did NOT contribute to major worldwide population growth from 1700 to 1800?

   (A) a decline in infant mortality rates
   (B) the widespread introduction of state-supported systems of health care
   (C) a decline in the number of deadly epidemics
   (D) the introduction of American food crops to Europe and Africa
   (E) the growth in the amount of land under cultivation

5. Who among the following was a democratically elected leader of a Marxist government in Chile?

(A) Salvador Allende
(B) Ché Guevara
(C) Augusto Pinochet
(D) Juan Perón
(E) Fidel Castro

6. The Holy Inquisition was created to

(A) track down and punish heretics and religious nonconformists
(B) canonize followers of Christ
(C) build great cathedrals in capital cities of Europe
(D) fight the Muslims in the Middle East
(E) find the Holy Grail

7. How did decolonization in British and French colonies differ from that in colonies once ruled by Belgium and Portugal?

(A) British and French officials better prepared their colonies for freedom and kept violence to a minimum.
(B) Belgian and Portuguese officials better prepared their colonies for freedom and kept violence to a minimum.
(C) British and French officials threatened violence, whereas Belgian and Portuguese officials did not.
(D) Belgian and Portuguese officials allowed native representation in transitional governments.
(E) Decolonization proceeded in about the same manner for all of these colonies.

8. The "Eastern Question" from the 1820s onward

I. forced Great Britain and France to support the East European powers against the Turks
II. took into account how destroying the Ottoman Empire might result in the rise of a hostile power in the area
III. led European powers to act cautiously toward the Ottomans
IV. recognized that the Ottoman Empire was no longer a real threat to Europe

(A) I, II, and III
(B) II, III, and IV
(C) I and III only
(D) II and IV only
(E) all of the above

9. Which invention, above all, allowed the Industrial Revolution to take place?

(A) the cotton gin
(B) electricity
(C) the internal combustion engine
(D) the steam engine
(E) the paddle wheel

10. How were trends in New Spain and Brazil similar during colonization?

(A) Neither used slaves.
(B) Both European conquerors decimated native American populations.
(C) The societies both became ethnically homogeneous.
(D) Copper mining was a critical part of the economy in both colonies.
(E) all of the above

11. Which people were the victims of the twentieth century's first genocide, in 1915?

(A) Jews
(B) Tutsis
(C) Armenians
(D) Kosovars
(E) Serbs

12. Which of the following statements accurately describes the role of oceans in the development of human societies?

   I. Oceans have, at times, kept societies apart.
   II. Oceans have served as an effective means of transport.
   III. Oceans have stimulated the emergence of networks of trade, technology transfer, and cultural exchange.
   IV. Using oceans, humans could travel completely around the world by the sixteenth century C.E.

   (A) I and II
   (B) I, II, and III
   (C) II and III
   (D) III and IV
   (E) all of the above

13. Why was Mali a powerful state in northern Africa by the 1300s?

   (A) It was known for its huge military forces.
   (B) It profited by cooperating with European slave traders.
   (C) Mali was a center of Christian worship.
   (D) It was a major center of trade and religious instruction and possessed large deposits of gold and metal ore.
   (E) It controlled the African spice trade and was the center of Buddhist worship.

14. Why were the Europeans the first to explore the entire world?

   (A) Other peoples lacked the necessary navigational ability.
   (B) The Europeans invented the science of astronomy.
   (C) The Europeans had larger ships, strong weapons, and a powerful economic incentive.
   (D) The Christian religion encouraged exploration, whereas Islam discouraged it.
   (E) none of the above

15. What is the world's largest desert?

   (A) the Takla Makan
   (B) the Kalahari
   (C) the Sahara
   (D) the Mojave
   (E) the Gobi

16. Which country is the world's largest democracy, by population?

   (A) the United States
   (B) Germany
   (C) Russia
   (D) India
   (E) Indonesia

17. Which of the following is a suitable comparison of the political systems in China and western Europe from 1000 to 1200?

   (A) China was unraveling politically, whereas in western Europe the trend was toward unification.
   (B) Leaders in both regions were beginning to colonize parts of Africa at the time.
   (C) Chinese lands were divided into several states, just as Europe was ruled by various monarchies.
   (D) Both regions were undergoing a process of democratization.
   (E) Chinese law instituted civil rights, while Western law focused on protecting the feudal system.

18. Mohandas K. Gandhi

   I. preached a policy of nonviolence in India's nationalist movement
   II. was a Buddhist monk
   III. called for the overthrow of British power by whatever means was necessary
   IV. worked with Jawaharlal Nehru in gaining independence for India

   (A) I, II, and III
   (B) II, III, and IV
   (C) I and IV only
   (D) II and III only
   (E) III and IV only

19. How did the Boers treat Africans?

(A) The Boers allowed Africans to stay in their ancestral lands.

(B) The Boers educated Africans in newly built schools.

(C) The Boers allied with African tribes against the British.

(D) The Boers worked alongside Africans in designing a democratic system of government.

(E) The Boers treated Africans harshly and forcefully created a segregated environment.

20. As a result of the first Opium War

I. the Qing government was forced to open more ports to foreign trade

II. the Chinese government had to lower tariffs on British goods

III. Hong Kong fell under British control

IV. British law took precedence in designated parts of Chinese territory

(A) I, II, and III

(B) II, III, and IV

(C) I and III only

(D) all of the above

(E) none of the above

21. On the Western Front, combat in World War I was characterized by a particularly brutal form of violence (that more often than not caused a stalemate) called

(A) virtual war

(B) submarine warfare

(C) trench warfare

(D) tank warfare

(E) strategic weapons

22. Which of the following correctly outlines the order of hominid development?

(A) *Homo sapiens sapiens,* Cro-Magnon, australopithecines, *Homo habilis*

(B) australopithecines, *Homo habilis,* Cro-Magnon, *Homo sapiens sapiens*

(C) Cro-Magnon, australopithecines, *Homo sapiens sapiens, Homo habilis*

(D) *Homo habilis,* Cro-Magnon, australopithecines, *Homo sapiens sapiens*

(E) none of the above

23. How were industrialization and imperialism related?

I. Industrialization gave Europeans better weapons to use in conquering other peoples.

II. Industrialization forced Europeans to search elsewhere for more raw materials.

III. Industrialization created more goods, and Europeans felt they needed to open more markets abroad.

IV. Imperialism leads to industrialization.

(A) I, II, and III

(B) II, III, and IV

(C) I and III only

(D) II and IV only

(E) all of the above

24. Which of the following are causes or illustrations of social trauma in late medieval Europe?

I. uprisings and revolts spurred by dissatisfaction with the Church

II. the Black Death

III. the Little Ice Age

IV. rising fear of witches and witchcraft

(A) I, II, III

(B) II, III, IV

(C) I, III, IV

(D) all of the above

(E) none of the above

25. Britain's three Reform Acts

    (A) restructured the agriculture sector
    (B) gave workers more benefits
    (C) brought Northern Ireland under British control
    (D) brought Scotland under British control
    (E) gradually made the country's electoral laws more representative

26. By the end of the 1920s, why had Japan stopped evolving into a democratic parliamentary monarchy?

    (A) The emperor abolished the Diet.
    (B) The Great Depression and heightened militarism stifled democratic impulses.
    (C) The monarchy was abolished, and the Japanese military took control.
    (D) Japan experienced a left-wing revolution.
    (E) The Japanese people were uninterested in liberal democracy.

27. What was the city of New Amsterdam later renamed when it fell under English control?

    (A) Brooklyn
    (B) Philadelphia
    (C) New York
    (D) Boston
    (E) Baltimore

28. How did the Russian Revolutions of 1917 resemble the French Revolution?

    (A) Both involved a communist takeover.
    (B) During both, the main organizers were peasants.
    (C) In both, the first stage was more liberal than later stages.
    (D) For both, the goal was the founding of a democratic republic.
    (E) Leaders in both revolutions were bankrolled by wealthy capitalists.

29. The Bretton Woods System was created to

    (A) promote international environmental protection efforts
    (B) promote international free trade
    (C) protect Western militaries
    (D) prevent a nuclear war
    (E) engage the Soviet bloc in arms control talks

30. During Japan's feudal period

    (A) the emperor was the symbolic head of the country
    (B) the shogun held effective power
    (C) the samurai class was transformed into a new aristocracy
    (D) all of the above
    (E) none of the above

31. What major mitigating factor changed the economic prospects for East Africa during the early 1500s?

    (A) the depletion of metal deposits
    (B) the arrival of European colonists
    (C) lack of rainfall
    (D) civil war
    (E) invasion by Berber warriors

32. Which of the following ranks as the most remarkable aspect of the reign of Akbar the Great?

    (A) his construction of the Taj Mahal
    (B) his mighty victories in battle
    (C) his many wives
    (D) his dedication to the ideal of religious tolerance
    (E) his establishment of the Mughal Empire

33. What political characteristic did Mexico, Brazil, and Argentina share during the 1920s and 1930s?

(A) All became democracies.
(B) All were governed by authoritarian regimes.
(C) All were monarchies.
(D) All were ruled by Getúlio Vargas.
(E) All had experienced communist revolutions.

34. Which eighteenth-century war in Europe spun off so many conflicts elsewhere and had so many global effects that it is sometimes considered a "world war"?

(A) the Thirty Years' War
(B) the War of the Spanish Succession
(C) the Seven Years' War
(D) the War of the Polish Succession
(E) the War of the League of Augsburg

35. In the nineteenth century, which two countries competed to gain control over Central Asia?

(A) Japan and China
(B) Germany and Russia
(C) Britain and Russia
(D) Japan and Britain
(E) France and Russia

36. How did the harshness and ruggedness of the terrain in the Andes Mountains affect the way that societies there evolved?

(A) People were forced to cooperate with each other and work out a division of labor.
(B) Very few buildings were erected.
(C) Culture was very primitive.
(D) There was much fighting over scarce resources.
(E) Individual families tended to remain isolated, retarding the development of sophisticated societies.

37. What benefits did the discovery of agriculture bestow upon early societies?

(A) a greater ability to affect the environments in which they lived
(B) a more reliable way of obtaining a more diverse supply of food
(C) the ability to establish permanent communities, and the reasons to do so
(D) an increased tendency to cooperate and form more cohesive societies
(E) all of the above

38. What impact did the Europeans have on West and Central Africa from the late 1400s and after?

  I. Those tribes that cooperated with the Europeans in the slave trade gained in strength.
 II. Some tribes, like the Asante, received firearms from the Europeans in exchange for slaves.
III. Trade networks were redirected.
 IV. Some West African tribes raided Central Africa for goods and slaves to sell to the Europeans.

(A) I, II, and III
(B) I and III only
(C) II and IV only
(D) all of the above
(E) none of the above

39. Why was the 1904–1905 Russo-Japanese War significant?

(A) Russia was able to secure its foothold in Manchuria for the first time.
(B) It marked the first time that European powers fought in Asia.
(C) It marked the first time in the imperial era that non-Westerners had defeated a European power in a full-scale military conflict.
(D) It was the bloodiest war to date.
(E) Japan's defeat in the war transformed it from a militaristic nation to a more pacifistic one.

World Human Population Growth: 1 C.E.–1999

Year	Population
1 C.E.	200 million
1650	500 million
1850	1 billion
1930	2 billion
1975	4 billion
1999	6 billion

40. According to the chart above, during which of the following intervals did world population grow at the most rapid rate?

(A) 1 C.E.–1650
(B) 1650–1850
(C) 1850–1930
(D) 1930–1975
(E) 1975–1999

41. In what way did Sukarno of Indonesia and Nehru of India share a similar diplomatic approach?

(A) They both fell strictly under the Soviet sphere of influence.
(B) They both fell strictly under the American sphere of influence.
(C) They both remained largely non-aligned in terms of Cold War diplomacy.
(D) They sided with Western Europe against the Americans.
(E) They both considered China their main patron.

42. What was the major difference between slaves and indentured servants in the New World?

I. Slaves worked outdoors only, whereas indentured servants worked indoors.
II. Indentured servants placed themselves in bondage voluntarily, whereas slaves were forced into bondage.
III. Indentured servants were set free once their debts were paid, whereas slaves could only be freed if their masters wished.
IV. There was no practical difference between the two categories.

(A) I and II only
(B) I, II, and III
(C) II and III only
(D) III only
(E) IV only

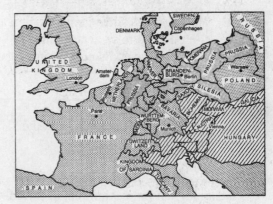

43. Which of the following is depicted by the map above?

(A) the spread of French revolutionary ideology across Europe
(B) the Napoleonic Empire at its peak
(C) the resurgence of the Habsburg Empire under Franz Josef I
(D) the map of Europe as determined by the Congress of Vienna
(E) Europe as it was after the Crimean War

44. Many technological innovations stemmed from World War II, including

(A) nylon
(B) atomic energy
(C) computer science
(D) radar
(E) all of the above

45. Which crop dominated Korean and Vietnamese agriculture in the 1400s?

(A) rice
(B) ginseng
(C) soybeans
(D) sugarcane
(E) wheat

46. In what ways did Mustafa Kemal change Turkey?

(A) He instituted the Islamic law code.
(B) He abolished suffrage for women and forced them to wear the veil.
(C) He westernized its culture and legal system.
(D) He set the country on the road to peace with Greece.
(E) He agreed to rule alongside the sultan.

47. Which of the following is an example of a technological innovation that occurred roughly simultaneously in two different regions of the world?

(A) In both the Middle East and China, toolmakers began to mix copper and tin to create bronze sometime between 4000 and 3000 B.C.E.
(B) Peoples in Europe and the Middle East invented the wheel at the same time.
(C) Both the Sumerians and the Celts invented writing, sometime between 3500 and 3000 B.C.E.
(D) Both the Egyptians and the Celts invented beer at the same time.
(E) Both the Franks and the Flemish invented paper at the same time.

48. The Tanzimat reforms in the Ottoman Empire

(A) created the janissaries
(B) attempted to modernize the empire to a limited degree
(C) called for a religious jihad
(D) strengthened the military
(E) gave officials in North Africa more autonomy

49. How did the collapse of Han China resemble the Roman Empire's loss of its European lands?

(A) Both were later devoured by the Byzantine empire.
(B) Their leaders began to rely on astrology to guide their decision making.
(C) Both fell as a result of depletion of natural resources.
(D) Outside invaders contributed to the collapse of both empires.
(E) Both collapsed due to lack of technological innovation.

50. Which statement below does NOT accurately reflect the condition of women between 1000 and 1450?

(A) Upper-class women in Europe tended to receive educations and manage household affairs in estates and castles.
(B) Among the Japanese aristocracy, several women became renowned as authors of novels.
(C) Certain societies in West Africa were matrilineal, rather than patrilineal.
(D) In Islamic societies, women of the lower classes were, in practice, less restricted by religious law than those of the upper class.
(E) The revival of Confucianism allowed Chinese women to gain greater rights and higher status.

51. The Tokugawa Shogunate

    I. promoted democracy
    II. encouraged interaction with the outside world
    III. failed to spur economic growth
    IV. encouraged more social mobility

    (A) I, II, and III
    (B) II, III, and IV
    (C) II and IV only
    (D) all of the above
    (E) none of the above

52. Which of the following broad changes made the sixteenth century different from the fifteenth century?

    (A) The slave trade began.
    (B) The Renaissance spread to Russia and other regions to the east.
    (C) Absolutism reached its peak in Europe.
    (D) Systematic sugar production was introduced in the New World.
    (E) Triangular trade came abruptly to a halt.

53. How did European and Japanese feudal systems differ?

    (A) Japanese feudalism relied on serfdom, whereas the European system did not.
    (B) European knights had no code of conduct similar to the Japanese ethos of Bushido.
    (C) Gunpowder was restricted in Japan, and affected Samurai less than it did knights in Europe.
    (D) Gunpowder weapons quickly ended the dominance of Japanese samurai, whereas European knights were not affected by such weapons
    (E) Japanese feudalism was more repressive than European feudalism

54. Which of the countries below was the last to grant suffrage to women?

    (A) United States
    (B) Canada
    (C) Great Britain
    (D) France
    (E) the USSR

55. Why was the Indian National Congress formed?

    (A) It served as the new legislature.
    (B) It formed to organize those who advocated Indian independence.
    (C) It was allowed to share governmental power with the British rulers.
    (D) It formed once India gained independence from Britain.
    (E) Its goal was to launch a guerrilla war against the British colonizers.

56. Which Asian religion was founded by Siddhertha Guatama?

    (A) Confucianism
    (B) Jainism
    (C) Hinduism
    (D) Eastern Orthodoxy
    (E) Buddhism

57. Which of the following accurately describes India's ethnic composition in the 1300s?

    (A) Northern parts tended to be populated by Indo-European Aryans, the southern by darker-skinned Dravidians.
    (B) Northern parts tended to be populated by darker-skinned Dravidians, the southern by descendants of the Aryans.
    (C) India's middle provinces were largely Arab.
    (D) India was dominated by Pakistani peoples.
    (E) India was ethnically homogeneous at that time.

58. What did Johannes Gutenberg invent that transformed Europe?

    (A) the steam engine
    (B) the movable-type printing press
    (C) the flying buttress
    (D) the spinning jenny
    (E) the steel plow

59. Which faith is dominant in Indonesia?

    (A) Christianity
    (B) Buddhism
    (C) Hinduism
    (D) Islam
    (E) Polytheism

60. In what ways were the civilizations in Mexico and Central America before 1000 C.E. more sophisticated than those in North America?

    (A) In the former, social structure was more complex, astronomical knowledge was greater, and architectural skills were more advanced.
    (B) In the former, Christianity was already practiced.
    (C) Mexican and Central American civilizations never practiced human sacrifice.
    (D) The former civilizations adopted democracy.
    (E) In no ways, because the North Americans had more advanced social structures.

61. In what way were the student demonstrations in Tiananmen Square in May 1919 similar to those in May 1989?

    (A) The students called for democracy.
    (B) The students called for an end to the communist regime.
    (C) The students wanted to see Mao overthrown.
    (D) The students called for a cultural revolution.
    (E) The students advocated the regime's new pro-capitalist policy.

62. The Hindu concept of samsara is BEST described by which of the following statements?

    (A) a belief that the wicked are punished by everlasting torment after death
    (B) a belief that one's soul lives, dies, and is reborn many times, until it is pure enough to escape the cycle of rebirth
    (C) a doctrine that justifies the caste system of India
    (D) a declaration of nonbelief in the old Vedic gods and goddesses
    (E) a belief that all actions, good and evil, have consequences in future lives to come

63. Why are the 1600s and early 1700s in Europe considered a period of scientific revolution?

    (A) Isaac Newton developed a unified system of physics and mathematics.
    (B) The scientific method was revived and used widely.
    (C) Scientists discovered that living things are made of cells.
    (D) The telescope was invented.
    (E) all of the above

64. Which of the following helps explain why the Mongols were successful at military conquest?

    (A) They outnumbered their enemies.
    (B) They were more barbaric than their enemies.
    (C) They used guns when other peoples lacked them.
    (D) They organized their armies efficiently.
    (E) They used camels instead of horses in their battles.

65. How do most historians characterize the motives of the United States in its annexation of the Philippines?

(A) The United States took the Philippines purely for economic reasons.

(B) The United States annexed the Philippines for strategic purposes and because it felt American rule there would benefit the natives.

(C) The United States wished to keep the Russians from gaining control of the islands.

(D) The Filipinos requested that the United States take control of the islands, so annexation was not truly an imperial action in this case.

(E) The United States took the Philippines in order to encourage the spread of Christianity.

66. Which of the following BEST encapsulates Confucian thought?

(A) Political power is given to rulers by the gods; therefore, rulers may treat their people as they please.

(B) Husbands and wives should share the responsibility for family leadership equally.

(C) Social harmony is attained when superiors treat those below them with kindness, while inferiors respect those above them.

(D) Only members of the aristocracy are capable of cultivating the qualities of etiquette and grace.

(E) Society functions best when people are free to realize their individuality.

67. Which of the following places in East Africa experienced the greatest fusion of Arab, African, and Indian cultures in the nineteenth century?

(A) Alexandria

(B) Basutoland

(C) Madagascar

(D) Zanzibar

(E) the Gold Coast

68. Which of the following statements accurately characterizes Islamic culture during the tenth through thirteenth centuries?

(A) The level of scientific knowledge was much higher than in Christian Europe.

(B) Omar Khayyám composed the poetic cycle known as the *Rubaiyat*.

(C) Muslim philosophers, physicians, and architects had a great impact on the development of medieval European culture.

(D) Muslim scholars were conversant with the learning of the ancient Greeks.

(E) all of the above

69. How did the adoption of parliamentary monarchies change how average people lived in the 1700s?

(A) They were given fewer freedoms.

(B) They enjoyed more social mobility and greater freedom of religion.

(C) They were all given the right to vote.

(D) Poverty vanished.

(E) Economic equality was achieved.

70. At the Berlin Conference (1884–1885)

I. Otto von Bismarck presided over the proceedings

II. European leaders set parameters for intervening in eastern Europe

III. European powers established rules for making new claims in Africa

IV. Socialist parties adopted an international manifesto

(A) I, II, and III

(B) II, III, and IV

(C) I and III only

(D) II and IV only

(E) I and IV only

SECTION II: FREE-RESPONSE QUESTIONS

Part A: Document-Based Question

Time: **10 minutes to read documents; 40 minutes to complete essay**

Directions: The following question is based on the accompanying documents. This question is designed to test your ability to work with historical documents. As you analyze the documents, take into account both the sources of the documents and the authors' points of view. Write an essay on the following topic that integrates your analysis of the documents. DO NOT SIMPLY SUMMARIZE THE DOCUMENTS INDIVIDUALLY. You may refer to relevant historical facts and developments not mentioned in the documents. Some documents have been edited. (Write your answer on a separate sheet of paper.)

---

1. The appearance of new inventions and new forms of science and technology often generates strong feelings within societies at large. The documents that follow speak to some of those feelings. Based on these documents, what general conclusions can you draw about how various societies adapt to scientific and technological change?

DOCUMENT 1

Source: Charlotte Brontë, English novelist, upon viewing the Crystal Palace at London's Great Exhibition (1851).

Yesterday I went for the second time to the Crystal Palace. . . . I must say I was more struck with it on this occasion than at my first visit. It is a wonderful place—vast, strange, new, and impossible to describe. . . . Whatever human industry has created you find there, from the great compartments filled with railway engines and boilers, with mill machinery in full work, with splendid carriages of all kinds, with harness of every description, to the glass-covered and velvet-spread stands loaded with the most gorgeous work of the goldsmith and silversmith. . . . It may be called a bazaar or a fair, but it is such a bazaar or fair as Eastern genii might have created. It seems as if only magic could have gathered this mass of wealth from all the ends of the earth.

DOCUMENT 2

Source: Victor Hugo, "This Will Kill That," *The Hunchback of Notre Dame* (1830).

Our readers must excuse us if we stop a moment to investigate the enigmatic words of the archdeacon: "This will kill that. The book will kill the edifice."

First of all, it was the view of a priest. It was the fear of an ecclesiastic before a new force, the printing press. It was the frightened yet dazzled man of the sanctuary confronting the illuminating Gutenberg press. . . . It signified that one great power was following upon the heels of another great power. It meant: The printing press will destroy the Church.

But besides this first thought, there was a second . . . but it no longer belongs to the priest alone, but to the scholar and to the artist as well. Here was a premonition that human thought had advanced, and, in changing, was about to change its mode of expression, that the important ideas of each new generation would be recorded in a new way, that the book of stone, [in which carvings and sculptures had provided the illiterate with a language of images and symbols], so solid and enduring, was about to be supplanted by the paper book, which would become more enduring still. In this respect, the vague formula of the archdeacon had a second meaning: That one art would dethrone another art. It meant: Printing will destroy architecture.

DOCUMENT 3

Source: Ito Hirobumi, young samurai from Japan, in letter to British official (1866).

Hitherto there have been a great number of stupid and ignorant persons in our provinces, who still adhered to the foolish old learning. They were unaware of the daily scientific progress of the Western nations, being like the frog at the bottom of a well. But lately they have learned. The eyes and ears of the stupid having thus been opened, the desirability of opening our country to foreign knowledge has become clear.

DOCUMENT 4

Source: Mohandas K. Gandhi, leader of Indian independence movement, *Gandhi: His Life and Message* (1954).

The incessant search for material comforts and their multiplication is such an evil, and I make bold to say that the Europeans themselves will have to remodel their outlook if they are not to perish under the weight of the comfort to which they are becoming slaves.

DOCUMENT 5

Source: Matteo Ricci, sixteenth-century Jesuit priest, showing a map of the world to the people of Canton during his visit to China (1578).

Of all the great nations, the Chinese have had the least commerce, indeed, one might say that they have had practically no contact whatever, with outside nations, and consequently they are grossly ignorant of what the world in general is like. True, they had charts somewhat similar to this one, that were supposed to represent the whole world, but their universe was limited to their own fifteen provinces, and in the sea painted around it, they had placed a few islands to which they gave the names of different kingdoms they had heard of. . . . When they learned that China was only a part of the great east, they considered such an idea, so unlike their own, to be something utterly impossible. . . .

To them the heavens are round but the earth is flat and square, and they firmly believe that their empire is right in the middle of it. They do not like the idea of our geographies pushing their China into one corner of the Orient. They could not comprehend the demonstrations proving that the earth is a globe, made up of land and water, and that a globe of its nature has neither beginning nor end.

DOCUMENT 6

Source: Swiss author Henri Frédéric Amiel, on European industrialization, as seen at London's Great Exhibition (1851).

The useful will take the place of the beautiful, industry will take the place of art, political economy of religion, and arithmetic of poetry.

DOCUMENT 7

Source: Ali Akbar Davar, journalist and Iran's Minister of Public Works, editorial in *The Free Man* (1923).

Until we dedicate ourselves to an economic and technological revolution, nothing will move or change. We shall remain a nation of beggars, hungry and in ragged clothing, and we shall continue to suffer. We have six thousand years of history, but that will not translate into factories, railroads, hospitals, or schools. Schools alone without economic reforms will change nothing, as long as the environment outside the schools continues to reek of poverty. . . . When we have at least 5,000 kilometers of railways, 50 factories, 50 roads linking east and west, dams on the Karun River, and have eradicated locusts, we can then attend to the graduation of 1,000 students from institutions of higher learning.

DOCUMENT 8

Source: William Blake (1757–1827), English Romantic poet, *Milton*.

And did those feet in ancient time
Walk upon England's mountains green?
And was the Holy Lamb of God
On England's pleasant pastures seen?

And did the Countenance Divine
Shine forth upon our clouded hills?
And was Jerusalem builded here
Among these dark Satanic Mills?

Bring me my Bow of burning gold:
Bring me my Arrows of desire:
Bring me my Spear: O clouds unfold!
Bring me my Chariot of fire.

I will not cease from Mental Fight,
Nor shall my Sword sleep in my hand
Till we have built Jerusalem
In England's green and pleasant Land.

Part B: Change-over-Time Question

Time: **40 minutes to complete essay**

> *Directions:* You are to answer the following question. In writing your essay, use specific examples to support your answer. (Write your essay on separate sheets of paper.)

2. Choose one of the following slave trades. Discuss how the dynamic of the slave trade in question changed between the middle of the 1400s and the late 1800s.

   the East African slave trade
   the Arab slave trade
   the Atlantic slave trade

Part C: Comparative Essay

Time: **40 minutes to complete essay**

> *Directions:* You are to answer the following question. In writing your essay, use specific examples to support your answer. (Write your essay on separate sheets of paper.)

3. Compare TWO of the following revolutions. What do they have in common? How are they different?

   the Russian Revolution
   the Chinese Revolution
   the Cuban Revolution
   the Iranian Revolution

ANSWER KEY TO MODEL EXAMINATION I

ANSWERS TO MULTIPLE-CHOICE QUESTIONS

1. **A** (pp. 163, 168–69)
2. **B** (p. 419)
3. **D** (p. 186)
4. **B** (pp.180–81, 195, 248)
5. **A** (p. 416)
6. **A** (p. 116)
7. **A** (pp. 408–9)
8. **B** (pp. 292–93)
9. **D** (p. 271)
10. **B** (pp. 234–36)
11. **C** (p. 356)
12. **E** (p. 41)
13. **D** (p. 133)
14. **C** (p. 200)
15. **C** (p. 39)
16. **D** (p. 412)
17. **C** (pp. 117, 139)
18. **C** (pp. 313, 371)
19. **E** (p. 319)
20. **D** (p. 300)
21. **C** (p. 355)
22. **B** (p. 48)
23. **A** (pp. 277, 281)
24. **D** (pp. 123–24)
25. **E** (pp. 261, 263)
26. **B** (p. 370)
27. **C** (p. 237)
28. **C** (pp. 257, 365)
29. **B** (pp. 420–21)
30. **D** (pp. 216–17)
31. **B** (p. 228)
32. **D** (pp. 222–23)
33. **B** (pp. 372–73)
34. **C** (p. 181)
35. **C** (p. 295)
36. **A** (p. 170)
37. **E** (pp. 52–53)
38. **D** (pp. 201, 227)
39. **C** (pp. 306–7)
40. **E** (p. 424)
41. **C** (pp. 411–12)
42. **C** (p. 240)
43. **D** (p. 260)
44. **E** (p. 379)
45. **A** (p. 147)
46. **C** (pp. 367–68)
47. **A** (p. 54)
48. **B** (p. 291)
49. **D** (pp. 64, 66)
50. **E** (pp. 98, 124, 140, 144, 162)
51. **E** (pp. 218, 304)
52. **D** (p. 229)
53. **C** (pp. 114–15, 145)
54. **D** (p. 426)
55. **B** (p. 313)
56. **E** (p. 90)
57. **A** (p. 150)
58. **B** (p. 127)
59. **D** (p. 152)
60. **A** (pp. 72–73)
61. **A** (pp. 369, 437)
62. **B** (p. 88)
63. **E** (p. 193)
64. **D** (p. 158)
65. **B** (pp. 314–15)
66. **C** (pp. 93–94)
67. **D** (pp. 319–20)
68. **E** (pp. 135–36)
69. **B** (pp. 191–92)
70. **C** (p. 325)

SAMPLE ANSWER TO THE DOCUMENT-BASED QUESTION

For the society that develops or encounters it, the emergence of new technology and new scientific knowledge can appear exciting, or it can appear threatening. In most cases, it seems both. This is because science and technology typically play a powerfully transformative role in most societies—and transformation can be for the better *or* for the worse, depending on one's point of view. The documents provided above demonstrate this clearly. One group of documents shows how different people within one civilization, Europe, view in very different ways the technology that their own culture has produced. A second group of documents expresses negative or ambiguous reactions that non-Western cultures have had to Western science and technology. Yet another group of documents depicts positive responses that non-Western societies have had to that same Western science and technology. Although it would be helpful to have certain other types of documents—texts that give voice to a greater variety of social classes, or that show how non-Western cultures react to technological and scientific developments—this set of documents amply illustrates the point that adaptation to or the transfer of new technology or scientific ideas is by no means a process free of ambiguities and contradictions.

How did Europeans react to technological change? Documents #1, #6, #8, and #2 speak to this question. The first two are closely related: they capture their authors' reactions to the Great Exhibition of 1851, held in London to celebrate the industrial age. The inspiration of the many World's Fairs and World's Expositions that have followed since. London's Great Exhibition was a world-famous spectacle. Its centerpiece, the exhibition hall known as the Crystal Palace, was a genuine marvel. In her personal papers (#1), English novelist Charlotte Brontë, author of *Jane Eyre*, describes her second visit to the Crystal Palace, expressing her admiration for what she sees there. To her, the stunning variety of exhibits is "wonderful," and she is impressed with the fact that "whatever human industry has created you find there." It is interesting that she describes the new inventions of the machine age in magical, exotic, and antique terms: the exhibition resembles a "bazaar," that "Eastern genii might have created," and the whole thing appears to be "magic." This reveals Brontë's point of view to be that of an artist, given to symbology and metaphor, rather than a technical expert. Also, one should note that, as someone not of the peasantry or industrial working class, Brontë is content to view the machines and technological devices she sees as marvels and curiosities, rather than a potential threat, putting her out of work, or as objects of oppression, condemning her to a life of drudgery on an assembly line.

Swiss writer Henri Frédéric Amiel, who also visited the Great Exhibition, had a different opinion. His account (#6) expresses a fear that the new scientific spirit of the industrial age will sap life of art, poetry, religion, and beauty—in short, everything that is *non*rational in life. The result, Amiel predicts, will be a dull, dry existence, devoid of everything that makes being human worthwhile. Reading Amiel's words, it is tempting to think of them as the prose counterpart to the poem by Matthew Arnold, *Dover Beach*, in which the poet sees the industrial world, with no faith and no beauty, as a "darkling plain." One can also think of Amiel's words as a prose counterpart to Document #8, the lines from *Milton* by the English Romantic poet William Blake. As one of the most deliberately nonrational and antiscientific artists of the Romantic movement, Blake, almost half a century before Brontë and Amiel visited the Great Exhibition, anticipated that dire things would come about as a result of the Industrial Revolution he was living through. His reference to "dark Satanic Mills" is a clear reference to factories, mines, and other industrial workplaces, and they are compared unfavorably to the "mountains green," "pleasant pastures," "clouded hills," and "green and pleasant Land" that Blake felt represented a spiritually pure England. Incidentally, unlike Brontë, Blake understood quite well the ways in which new technology could harm people occupationally. His own career, engraving by hand, a painstaking craft, was soon to be made redundant by the mass production of machine-printed books.

A more neutral and ambiguous, but still anxious, attitude toward technological change comes from the realm of fiction—in this case, the passage "This Will Kill That" (#2) from French novelist Victor Hugo's *The Hunchback of Notre Dame*. Here, the archdeacon of Notre Dame reflects on the effect that the invention of the printing press (which, since the book is set in the 1400s, is a recent development) will have on architecture. Why are the two related? Because during the medieval era, when they built cathedrals such as Notre Dame, architects, knowing that the vast majority of the European populace was illiterate, depicted stories, incidents from the Bible, saints, Christ and his family, and a whole host of images and tales in stone carvings and stained glass. Architectural imagery was a mode of communication for hundreds of years, beautiful, effective, and profound. Hugo, writing from the perspective of the future, allows his character the realization that, as the printing press brings about a revolution in thought, literacy, and the spread of ideas, it will spell the end of an older way of conveying information, the "book of stone." Although the archdeacon, a member of the Catholic clergy, is also concerned about the effects that greater freedom of information will have on his Church, Hugo himself seems to have a philosophical, detached attitude toward technological change, simply recognizing that it takes place—and that, although it creates new things and benefits people, it can also destroy or render obsolete things that are good and beautiful.

Documents #5 and #4 represent a second category of text: negative reactions to foreign science and technology. In both cases, the new knowledge comes from the West. The memoirs of Matteo Ricci (#5), the famous priest who made an extended journey to China and the Indies near the end of the 1500s, comment on sixteenth-century China's hostile, or at least indignant, reaction to European geographical knowledge. Of course, Ricci's point of view must be taken into account here: he is a European speaking of foreigners, and is perfectly happy to depict them as less learned than his own people. Also, in speaking of the Chinese as "grossly ignorant of what the world in general is like," Ricci shows that he is unaware of the great voyages of the Chinese mariner Zheng He two and a half centuries beforehand. It would be helpful here to have commentary from some of the Chinese who came into contact with Ricci or visited him in order to see his maps and globe.

Nonetheless, it is true that the late Ming rulers who ruled China when Ricci visited were more complacent and decadent than the early Ming emperors of Zheng He's era. The reaction that Ricci describes is characteristic of the Chinese rulers' conviction that their "Middle Kingdom" was literally at the center of the world, blessed by heaven, and had nothing to gain by learning from the "barbarians" of the West. One is reminded of the Qing Emperor Qianlong's response to the mission of English diplomat Lord Macartney at the end of the 1700s: in essence, "you have nothing we need or desire." During the 1800s, China would pay for the shortsightedness of its leaders. Convinced of its cultural grandeur (which was truly astounding) and its innate superiority, the Chinese government failed to understand that the barbarians of the West, far away from the center of *China's* map, had mastered science and technology that would have been useful for the Chinese to master as well.

Document #4 expresses hostility to Western technology as well, but for different reasons. Mohandas "Mahatma" Gandhi, the father of the Indian independence movement, a moral figure of immense stature, rejects altogether the scientific-technological basis of Western culture. One must remember that, although Gandhi couches this idea in spiritual terms, his point of view is also that of a politician. By condemning the Western or European approach to life, he is also condemning the British, from whom he wants his native India to be free. Still, Gandhi is not insincere here. His spiritual convictions truly were such that he believed that materialism and industrial modernization were soul-deadening. It should be noted, however, that few of the leaders of the Indian independence movement had feelings this strong. For example, Jawaharlal Nehru, Gandhi's partner in the drive for independence (and the eventual prime minister of India), greatly favored industrialization and modernization.

So did the authors of the third group of texts, Documents #3 and #7. In each case, a member of the political elite in a non-Western nation speaks approvingly of Western-style science and industrialization. Each sees modernization as the key to his country's success in the modern age. In a letter to a British official (#3), Ito Hirobumi, a young samurai in mid-nineteenth-century Japan, derides the "great number" of his fellow countrymen who "still adhere to the foolish old learning," comparing their tunnel vision to that of "the frog at the bottom of a well." It is interesting that a member of the samurai class, which was mainly interested in preserving Japanese tradition (and its own privileges), should be so interested in modernization. Since Ito's letter was written only two years before the Meiji Restoration—which deposed the Tokugawa shogunate and restored the emperor to full rule—the most likely reason for his protechnology, proscience outlook (aside from his age) is that he was a member of the clique that supported westernization and staged the restoration. Quite famously, Japan's willingness to learn Western science and adapt itself to Western industrialization was a key factor in saving it from China's fate during the 1800s: economic and political domination by the nations of Europe and the United States.

A similarly pro-Western outlook is revealed in a newspaper editorial (#7) by Iranian journalist Ali Akbar Davar. This is an impassioned text, declaring that Western-style industrialization is not only desirable, but crucial for Iran's growth. Without new science and technology, Davar argues, "we shall remain a nation of beggars, hungry and in ragged clothing, and we shall continue to suffer." Iran, Davar states, needs "factories, railroads, hospitals, and schools." Given the date of his editorial, his protechnology point of view, and the fact that he had a government post (the appropriate position of Minister of Public Works), it seems likely that Davar was a supporter of, as well as a government official under, the Shah of Iran, Reza Pahlavi—who, like Davar, was a proponent of modernization, westernization, and industrialization.

The most obvious of the possible reactions to new science and technology are communicated in these documents. It would be helpful to have other texts in order to get a more complete picture. How did people of the lower classes react to scientific and technological changes? Did they, like the Luddites in early-nineteenth-century Europe, resent new machines? Or did villagers in Africa or peasants in China appreciate electric generators, steel fishhooks, and new medicines? Also, economic data detailing industrial growth in countries like Japan and Iran *after* modernizing rulers such as Meiji and Pahlavi came to power would be instructive. Equally useful would be statistics and education data showing how much the benefits of new science, new technology, and industrialization benefited social classes that were *not* part of the westernizing elite.

SAMPLE ANSWER TO THE CHANGE-OVER-TIME QUESTION

One of the most reprehensible institutions in world history had a lifespan of more than four hundred years. This was the Atlantic slave trade, which began in the mid-1400s and lasted until the late 1800s. During these years, somewhere between 9 million and 12 million African men, women, and children were taken from their homes and forced into bondage. The scale and nature of the Atlantic slave trade changed over time, as described in this essay. Throughout its long history, however, the Atlantic slave trade never failed to have a traumatic impact on the tribes and individuals it victimized. Moreover, its effects on African society, politics, and economics were profound. It completely altered the social, ethnic, and economic development of North and South America. And there is no denying that the Atlantic slave trade was at the heart of Europe's phenomenal rise in wealth and prosperity during these years.

The Atlantic slave trade had its origins in Portuguese exploration of West Africa during the 1400s. As the Portuguese charted the African coast, as part of their attempt to reach the East Indies, they began to trade with and extract resources from the Africans as well. Being cheaper, forcible extraction was preferable to the Portuguese. Among the "commodities" the Portuguese took from Africa were slaves. Starting in 1441, a limited number of slaves—approximately 1,000 per year—were taken from Africa to Europe, mainly as domestic servants and, to some degree, as curiosities.

It was during the early-to-mid-1500s that the Atlantic slave trade began in earnest. Two factors in particular emerged simultaneously, combining to increase radically the Europeans' demand for African slaves. Both had to do with Spanish and Portuguese colonization and exploitation of the New World. First, Spanish and especially Portuguese cultivation of sugarcane, an extremely labor-intensive enterprise, was begun in Brazil and the Caribbean. A large and inexpensive labor force was needed to keep this enterprise going. At roughly the same time, the Spanish, who controlled most of the colonial New World during these years, were ceasing to use Native Americans as forced labor, both in mining and agriculture. To begin with, Spanish and Portuguese guns and germs had devastated the native populations of the Americas. Then, Catholic priests successfully lobbied against the encomienda system, which, until 1542, allowed Spanish conquistadors and officials to use Indians virtually as slave labor. Moreover, the Spanish and Portuguese found Native Americans to be temperamentally unsuited to slavery. Therefore, although the Spanish and Portuguese continued to exploit native Americans as cheap, underpaid labor, they needed a new source of slaves. Africa appeared to be the ideal source. Similarly, as French, Dutch, and English colonists began to settle in the New World during the late 1500s and 1600s, they, too, became dependent on slave labor, especially in the Caribbean.

Whereas something like 60,000 slaves, or 1,000 per year, had been taken from Africa during the 1400s, that number rose to more than 2,000 per year during the 1500s. At least 275,000 slaves were brought to the New World during the sixteenth century. That number would climb even higher, much higher, during the 1600s and especially the 1700s.

The seventeenth and eighteenth centuries were the heyday of the Atlantic slave trade. Every major nation in western Europe had a hand in it, as did the European colonies in the New World, where the slaves were transported. It would be no exaggeration to say that the Atlantic slave trade was one of the key elements in the economic foundation that underlay the mercantilist and early capitalist development of early modern Europe. More than a million slaves were transported from Africa to the New World during the 1600s. At least 6 million were shipped during the 1700s, when the slave trade reached its peak. About 37 percent of all slaves taken to the New World went to Brazil, while 15 percent went to Spanish America. The non-Spanish Caribbean was the destination for 41 percent. Only about 5 percent were taken to the English colonies of North America.

By the end of the 1600s, and especially the 1700s, the Atlantic slave trade had become a crucial element in European economic life and world trade. Until the beginning of the nineteenth century, no major nation banned slavery or the slave trade. The Atlantic slave trade became part of the pattern of economic interaction known as the triangular trade. Manufactured goods from Europe, such as metal goods, cotton cloth, firearms, and alcohol, would be shipped to Africa and traded for ivory, timber, gold, and slaves. The slaves would be taken to the New World and sold for cash, as well as raw materials such as tobacco, cotton, sugar, silver, and furs. These would all be brought back to Europe.

The effects of the Atlantic slave trade on Africa were incalculable. On a personal level, it is obvious that the experience was horrible. A victim of the slave trade would be taken prisoner, either in war or in a slave raid. He or she would undergo the fearsome Middle Passage, during which he or she was crammed in a dark cargo hold for weeks on end with hundreds of other captives. During the early years of the slave trade, as many as 25 percent of those shipped across the Middle Passage died. Although the casualty rate dipped to 10 percent by the 1700s and 1800s, the voyage was still horrendous. Waiting at the end of the Middle Passage, of course, was the shock of a new country and language, the humiliation of being sold, and, ultimately, forced servitude.

As for Africa as a whole, the slave trade altered political, economic, and social life. Entire tribes fell victim to the slave trade. Other African peoples, such as the Dahomeians, the Asante, and the Kongo, cooperated with European slavers. Their economies were based on the slave trade, and they became wealthy from the money slavers paid them. Some, the Asante in particular, insisted on payment in gunpowder weapons, and therefore became very powerful. Because these Africans felt it necessary to raid and make war against their neighbors, in order to have slaves to sell to the Europeans, the Atlantic slave trade stirred up a tremendous amount of intertribal violence in West and Central Africa during the 1700s and 1800s.

Tremendous changes came to the slave trade during the 1800s. At the turn of the century, a number of countries, especially Great Britain, decided to campaign for a ban on slavery and the African slave trade. In 1807 to 1808, Britain made slavery illegal in its own home territory. By 1814 to 1815, with the end of the Napoleonic Wars, Britain convinced most European nations (exceptions included Spain and Portugal) and the United States to end the slave trade. Slavery itself, however, continued to be legal in the United States, Cuba, and Brazil. This meant that the slave trade continued illegally, but it lessened considerably. The British and U.S. Navy patrolled the African coast and the Caribbean, interfering with the slave trade quite effectively. The British and French also did much to destroy the fortresses, outposts, and slave markets that West and Central African peoples like the Kongo, Asante, and Dahomeians maintained on the Atlantic coast. The number of slaves taken from Africa during the 1800s reached a total of approximately 2 million, down from 6 million during the 1700s. The Atlantic slave trade dried up altogether with the ending of slavery in the United States (1860s) and Cuba and Brazil (1880s).

SAMPLE ANSWER TO THE COMPARATIVE QUESTION

Among the major political upheavals of the twentieth century are the Chinese Revolution and the Cuban Revolution. Both were also major moments in the history of the Cold War, with wide-ranging effects on global politics. Because both the Chinese and Cuban revolutions were communist revolutions, and because both governments remain—at least in theory—committed to Marxist principles, even in the twenty-first century, both events have much in common, not simply on the surface, but in substance as well. There are, however, differences in the approaches the revolutions took, in the circumstances under which they took place, and in their long-term results. On the whole, the early histories of the Cuban and Chinese revolutions resemble each other quite closely. As time passes, however, the long-term political fates of China and Cuba appear to diverge more than converge.

The most obvious factor linking the Chinese and Cuban revolutions is their Marxist-Leninist inspiration. Mao Tse-tung, the leader of the Chinese Revolution, had been a committed Communist for decades before his final victory in 1949. For years, he had modeled his movement and his ideology on the example of the Soviet Union, and for approximately a decade after coming to power, Mao remained allied to the Soviet bloc. Although Fidel Castro, the leader of the Cuban movement, was not completely committed to the ideals of communism until after his victory in 1959, his brother Raúl and his adviser, the Argentinian revolutionary Ernesto "Ché" Guevara, were. During and immediately after the revolution, they convinced Castro that Cuba's future lay with communism and alliance with the USSR.

Both Mao and Castro came to power by means of guerrilla war backed by popular support. Mao's forces, located mainly in the north, defeated those of Nationalist leader Chiang Kai-shek, in a bitter four-year civil war that followed immediately after World War II. Mao had adapted his Marxist doctrine in such a way as to make the vast peasant population, as opposed to the industrial proletariat, the focus of his revolution. This was a wise decision, because, as had been the case in Russia, where communism first came to power, the vast majority of the population was made up of peasants, not industrial workers. Radicalizing the peasantry led Mao to power. Likewise, when Castro and his supporters landed in secret to overthrow the regime of Fulgencio Batista, they took refuge in the mountains and built support among the ordinary people who were oppressed by the Batista regime. Making lightning strikes from the mountains and quickly building up a following among the people of the countryside, Castro ascended to power. The one major difference here is that Castro took much less time than Mao to come to power.

Both Mao's and Castro's revolutionary governments emphasized modernization, and both achieved it to a high degree—but at certain costs. Both created better health-care systems, built better educational systems, instituted land reform, raised literacy rates, fostered industrial growth, and brought about a higher degree of social and economic equality. On the other hand, these benefits came at a price. Not only were both regimes dictatorial, but many governmental policies were riddled with inefficiency, and some led to outright disaster. Especially in the agricultural sphere, Cuba's economic policies, dictated by a central-command style, were often poorly run (especially, in the beginning, by Ché Guevara, who, although an effective guerrilla leader, was not a skilled minister of finance). Overreliance on tobacco and sugar as cash crops did not help, and although the new industry the Castro regime built went up quickly, it was typically of shoddy quality. In China, Mao's efforts to collectivize agriculture proved moderately successful at first, then, pushed too far, ended in famine, mass starvation, and ruin. Overall, his modernization campaign, the "Great Leap Forward," wrecked the countryside, created a poor-quality industrial base, caused the death of millions, and traumatized even greater numbers of people.

Another point of similarity between the Chinese and Cuban revolutions is that they gave birth to dictatorial regimes—as had the Russian Revolution in 1917 and the imposition of communism on the nations of Eastern Europe in the late 1940s. Both Mao and Castro were guided by the Marxist principle of the "dictatorship of the proletariat," according to which it is necessary, on a temporary basis, for the new revolutionary government to assume dictatorial powers, in order to prevent the defeated classes—the bourgeoisie and aristocracy—from staging a counterrevolution. Unfortunately, as in almost every instance when a communist regime has come to power, the dictatorship of the proletariat, far from being maintained only on a "temporary basis," was, in both China's and Cuba's cases, extended indefinitely.

A final likeness to be aware of is that both the Chinese and Cuban revolutions played a major role in the Cold War. Both were also part of the process by which the Cold War became truly global, rather than focused primarily on Europe. In 1949, the rise of the Communists to power in China coincided with the Soviet Union's first test of an atomic bomb. These two events, within months of each other, were major victories for the worldwide communist movement. A vast portion of the Eurasian landmass—and its population—was now communist, and the American monopoly on atomic weapons had been broken. The immediate ramifications included the formation of the North Atlantic Treaty Organization (NATO), the Korean War (largely prompted by the highly aggressive Mao), and the McCarthy era in the United States, as right-wingers blamed supposed "traitors" in the State Department for "losing" China. The revolution in Cuba brought communism to America's doorstep. During the early 1960s, with the aborted Bay of Pigs invasion (a tremendous embarrassment to the United States) and the Cuban missile crisis, Cuba's revolutionary regime was at the very epicenter of the Cold War.

Despite all the similarities, however, there are important differences between the Cuban and Chinese revolutions. Moreover, the differences loom larger the farther one gets from the actual years of revolution. Although both regimes put people in prison and executed people for political purposes, the casualties in China's case are astronomically more numerous than in Cuba's. The deaths caused by Mao's collectivization campaigns, the Great Leap Forward, and the Cultural Revolution run into the tens of millions. Mao was truly a totalitarian ruler, with a corresponding number of victims. Castro's authoritarian regime has been responsible for a number of abuses, and no one can claim that freedom of speech or expression prevails in Cuba, even now. But the number of people who have been demoted, fired, arrested, or killed in Castro's Cuba pales by comparison to Mao's China.

In keeping with the foregoing point, there are differences in political rulership. Mao was much more of a dictator than Castro. As noted in the previous paragraph, the difference is one of totalitarianism versus authoritarianism. Ironically, however, Castro—thus far the only ruler post-revolutionary Cuba has ever had—has been relatively constant in his level of repressiveness. On the other hand, China has wavered in its level of repressiveness. Mao died in 1976. After a brief power struggle, the pragmatic reformer Deng Xiaoping took control over the government. Although hardly a democrat, as events in Tiananmen Square showed in 1989, he was much less brutal than Mao. The leadership after Deng's death has varied in its level of repressiveness, but can also be considered less dictatorial than Mao.

Another important difference involves the two revolutions' relationship with the Soviet Union. Although Mao immediately allied with Stalin after coming to power, China's relationship with the USSR was never as close as the West imagined and feared. After Stalin's death, Mao's relationship with Khrushchev cooled somewhat, partly as a result of internal changes in the Soviet Union, but mainly as a result of Chinese resentment at the Soviets' insistence that they were the undisputed leaders of the worldwide communist movement. As the newer, more dynamic communist leader, in charge of the most populous nation on earth, Mao felt that he deserved more than to be treated condescendingly as the "little brother" of the Soviets. By the late 1950s and early 1960s, tensions between China and the USSR were growing, and they became worse all during the 1960s, leading to the famous Sino-Soviet split. By contrast, Castro remained loyal to the Soviet Union for more than three decades, until the Soviet Union itself collapsed. Although there were points of disagreement between Cuba and the USSR, the alliance remained solid until, ironically, the Castro regime ended up outliving the Soviet government.

Finally, the differences between the Cuban and Chinese revolutions can be seen in their long-term results. At the present time, both Cuba and China are tightly controlled by regimes that call themselves communist. However, China, having long ago (under Deng) abandoned pure communism for a state-controlled market system, thrives economically. Whereas Cuba, which remained truer to the Marxist-Leninist style and continued its economic relationship with the Soviet Union, now labors under severe economic difficulties—caused largely by economic inflexibility, the collapse of the USSR (and the end of its economic assistance to Cuba), and the long-standing embargo that the United States has maintained against Cuba. The Chinese Communist Zhou Enlai, one of Mao's closest advisers, was once asked by a journalist what he thought the long-range effects of the French Revolution had been. Zhou replied, "It's too soon to tell." The same answer seems to apply to the Chinese and Cuban revolutions as well.

Answer Sheet for Model Advanced Placement Examination II

SECTION I: MULTIPLE-CHOICE QUESTIONS

Sample: 1. The first person to reach the South Pole was
  A) Roald Amundsen
  B) Robert Scott
  C) Christopher Columbus
  D) Vitus Bering
  E) Charles Lindbergh

1. Ⓐ Ⓑ Ⓒ Ⓓ Ⓔ

Box A is filled in because the correct answer for the sample question 1 is A.

1. Ⓐ Ⓑ Ⓒ Ⓓ Ⓔ   15. Ⓐ Ⓑ Ⓒ Ⓓ Ⓕ   29. Ⓐ Ⓑ Ⓒ Ⓓ Ⓔ   43. Ⓐ Ⓑ Ⓒ Ⓓ Ⓔ   57. Ⓐ Ⓑ Ⓒ Ⓓ Ⓔ

2. Ⓐ Ⓑ Ⓒ Ⓓ Ⓔ   16. Ⓐ Ⓑ Ⓒ Ⓓ Ⓔ   30. Ⓐ Ⓑ Ⓒ Ⓓ Ⓔ   44. Ⓐ Ⓑ Ⓒ Ⓓ Ⓔ   58. Ⓐ Ⓑ Ⓒ Ⓓ Ⓔ

3. Ⓐ Ⓑ Ⓒ Ⓓ Ⓔ   17. Ⓐ Ⓑ Ⓒ Ⓓ Ⓔ   31. Ⓐ Ⓑ Ⓒ Ⓓ Ⓔ   45. Ⓐ Ⓑ Ⓒ Ⓓ Ⓔ   59. Ⓐ Ⓑ Ⓒ Ⓓ Ⓔ

4. Ⓐ Ⓑ Ⓒ Ⓓ Ⓔ   18. Ⓐ Ⓑ Ⓒ Ⓓ Ⓔ   32. Ⓐ Ⓑ Ⓒ Ⓓ Ⓔ   46. Ⓐ Ⓑ Ⓒ Ⓓ Ⓔ   60. Ⓐ Ⓑ Ⓒ Ⓓ Ⓔ

5. Ⓐ Ⓑ Ⓒ Ⓓ Ⓔ   19. Ⓐ Ⓑ Ⓒ Ⓓ Ⓔ   33. Ⓐ Ⓑ Ⓒ Ⓓ Ⓔ   47. Ⓐ Ⓑ Ⓒ Ⓓ Ⓔ   61. Ⓐ Ⓑ Ⓒ Ⓓ Ⓔ

6. Ⓐ Ⓑ Ⓒ Ⓓ Ⓔ   20. Ⓐ Ⓑ Ⓒ Ⓓ Ⓔ   34. Ⓐ Ⓑ Ⓒ Ⓓ Ⓔ   48. Ⓐ Ⓑ Ⓒ Ⓓ Ⓔ   62. Ⓐ Ⓑ Ⓒ Ⓓ Ⓔ

7. Ⓐ Ⓑ Ⓒ Ⓓ Ⓔ   21. Ⓐ Ⓑ Ⓒ Ⓓ Ⓔ   35. Ⓐ Ⓑ Ⓒ Ⓓ Ⓔ   49. Ⓐ Ⓑ Ⓒ Ⓓ Ⓔ   63. Ⓐ Ⓑ Ⓒ Ⓓ Ⓔ

8. Ⓐ Ⓑ Ⓒ Ⓓ Ⓔ   22. Ⓐ Ⓑ Ⓒ Ⓓ Ⓔ   36. Ⓐ Ⓑ Ⓒ Ⓓ Ⓔ   50. Ⓐ Ⓑ Ⓒ Ⓓ Ⓔ   64. Ⓐ Ⓑ Ⓒ Ⓓ Ⓔ

9. Ⓐ Ⓑ Ⓒ Ⓓ Ⓔ   23. Ⓐ Ⓑ Ⓒ Ⓓ Ⓔ   37. Ⓐ Ⓑ Ⓒ Ⓓ Ⓔ   51. Ⓐ Ⓑ Ⓒ Ⓓ Ⓔ   65. Ⓐ Ⓑ Ⓒ Ⓓ Ⓔ

10. Ⓐ Ⓑ Ⓒ Ⓓ Ⓔ   24. Ⓐ Ⓑ Ⓒ Ⓓ Ⓔ   38. Ⓐ Ⓑ Ⓒ Ⓓ Ⓔ   52. Ⓐ Ⓑ Ⓒ Ⓓ Ⓔ   66. Ⓐ Ⓑ Ⓒ Ⓓ Ⓔ

11. Ⓐ Ⓓ Ⓒ Ⓓ Ⓔ   25. Ⓐ Ⓑ Ⓒ Ⓓ Ⓕ   39. Ⓐ Ⓑ Ⓒ Ⓓ Ⓔ   53. Ⓐ Ⓑ Ⓒ Ⓓ Ⓔ   67. Ⓐ Ⓑ Ⓒ Ⓓ Ⓔ

12. Ⓐ Ⓑ Ⓒ Ⓓ Ⓔ   26. Ⓐ Ⓑ Ⓒ Ⓓ Ⓔ   40. Ⓐ Ⓑ Ⓒ Ⓓ Ⓔ   54. Ⓐ Ⓑ Ⓒ Ⓓ Ⓔ   68. Ⓐ Ⓑ Ⓒ Ⓓ Ⓔ

13. Ⓐ Ⓑ Ⓒ Ⓓ Ⓔ   27. Ⓐ Ⓑ Ⓒ Ⓓ Ⓔ   41. Ⓐ Ⓑ Ⓒ Ⓓ Ⓔ   55. Ⓐ Ⓑ Ⓒ Ⓓ Ⓔ   69. Ⓐ Ⓑ Ⓒ Ⓓ Ⓔ

14. Ⓐ Ⓑ Ⓒ Ⓓ Ⓔ   28. Ⓐ Ⓑ Ⓒ Ⓓ Ⓔ   42. Ⓐ Ⓑ Ⓒ Ⓓ Ⓔ   56. Ⓐ Ⓑ Ⓒ Ⓓ Ⓔ   70. Ⓐ Ⓑ Ⓒ Ⓓ Ⓔ

SECTION II: FREE RESPONSE QUESTIONS

Write your answers on a separate sheet of paper.

Model Examination II

Section I: Multiple-Choice Questions

Time: **55 minutes for 70 questions**

Directions: Each of the following questions has five suggested answers. Choose the one that is best in each case.

---

1. The Marshall Plan

   (A) helped the Allies defeat Hitler
   (B) ended the Cold War
   (C) granted the British control over Palestine after World War I
   (D) was meant to end the Vietnam War
   (E) gave Western Europe billions of dollars to rebuild after World War II

2. How did the German experience in colonizing Africa differ from that of the British and French?

   (A) The Germans never colonized Africa.
   (B) The British and French were more brutal in their treatment of the natives than the Germans were.
   (C) German colonies were less desirable, lost money, and involved the Germans in brutal wars against the natives.
   (D) The Germans colonized the northern coast of Africa, while the French and British took the eastern coast.
   (E) The German colonies were the most politically and economically successful in Africa.

3. Which of the following INCORRECTLY matches a belief system with one of its central texts?

   (A) Judaism—the Torah
   (B) Confucianism—the Bhagavad Gita
   (C) Islam—the Qu'ran
   (D) Christianity—the Bible
   (E) Zoroastrianism—the Avestas

4. Which of the following is NOT true about women's liberation movements in the twentieth century?

   (A) Fascist Italy, Nazi Germany, and militarist Japan encouraged women to take jobs in factories to promote economic growth.
   (B) Many countries granted women the vote after World War I.
   (C) During World War II, more women worked outside the home than during World War I.
   (D) Major goals of women's movements have been the achievement of legal equality and the elimination of culturally stereotyped gender roles.
   (E) Achievements of women's movements include equal access to higher education and a greater role in political life.

5. Which of the following is NOT a trend associated with Europe's Industrial Revolution?

   (A) urbanization
   (B) population growth
   (C) a general decline in prosperity
   (D) a general increase in prosperity, especially after the 1840s
   (E) the rapid expansion of the middle class

6. In the early 1900s, what kinds of changes did the Young Turks wish to bring to the Ottoman Empire?

   (A) modernization and secularization
   (B) a return to Islamic fundamentalism
   (C) the revival of the janissary corps
   (D) a strengthening of the sultan's powers
   (E) closer diplomatic ties with the United States

7. What area of North America did the French first explore?

   (A) what is now Louisiana
   (B) what is now Florida
   (C) areas along the Mississippi River
   (D) areas along the St. Lawrence River
   (E) what is now Long Island

8. Existentialists such as playwright Samuel Beckett and novelist Albert Camus believe that

   (A) a single God exists for the benefit of all humanity, and organized religion helps point the way to true morality
   (B) every religion is valid, in that it helps people to reach true divinity
   (C) the individual must learn to create his or her own ethical existence without the hope of an afterlife or the guidance of organized religion
   (D) the universe is uncaring and amoral, and therefore all life is meaningless
   (E) in the absence of a higher spiritual authority, might makes right, and everything is permissible

9. Which of these does NOT accurately describe the state of the earth's continents and oceans before 200 million years ago?

   (A) The earth's waters formed one great ocean.
   (B) Geological forces had split the earth's landmasses into several continents.
   (C) All landmasses were joined together into a single large continent.
   (D) Water covered approximately three quarters of the earth's surface.
   (E) none of the above

10. Oda Nobunaga, Toyotomi Hideyoshi, and Tokugawa Ieyasu are most famous for what?

    (A) their haiku verses
    (B) the unification of Japan
    (C) popularizing Zen Buddhism in Japan
    (D) inventing the tea ceremony
    (E) giving birth to kabuki theater

11. Why did the Russians conquer Central Asia in the 1800s?

    (A) feelings of nationalism
    (B) its bounty of natural resources
    (C) a desire to establish warm-water ports on the Indian Ocean
    (D) to protect its long southern frontier
    (E) all of the above

12. What factors encouraged the wave of democratization in Latin America in the 1990s?

    I. cooperation among members of the Organization of American States
    II. economic improvements
    III. further decolonization
    IV. the end of the Cold War

    (A) I, II, and III
    (B) II, III, and IV
    (C) I, II, and IV
    (D) I and III only
    (E) II and IV only

13. For what reasons did medieval popes launch crusades?

    (A) to spread Christianity to Ireland
    (B) to fight Muslims, convert non-Catholics, and wipe out heresy
    (C) to enable England to conquer French lands
    (D) to grasp control of trade along the Silk Road
    (E) to conquer territory in sub-Saharan Africa

14. Ibn Battuta was

    (A) an Islamic traveler and explorer
    (B) an Islamic theologian
    (C) an Islamic poet
    (D) an Islamic astronomer and physicist
    (E) an Islamic general

15. Why was the encomienda system abolished in 1542?

    (A) That year, slavery was abolished in Spain and Portugal.
    (B) It had allowed the Native Americans to regain control of their former lands.
    (C) The British colonies protested its use.
    (D) There was no longer any use for it.
    (E) The protests of Catholic priests did much to do away with the system.

16. Which continent do most scientists consider to be the birthplace of humanity?

    (A) Asia
    (B) Europe
    (C) Africa
    (D) North America
    (E) South America

17. By the 1750s, which European power had defeated the Mughals?

    (A) France
    (B) Great Britain
    (C) Holland
    (D) Spain
    (E) Italy

18. Which of the following best characterizes the ethnic development of Europe during the Early Middle Ages?

    (A) The entire continent's racial composition was a direct legacy of Latin Romans, from whom all Europeans descended.
    (B) A mix of Celts, Latins, the many peoples the Romans had conquered, and Germanic and Asiatic tribes migrating from north and east contributed to Europe's ethnic composition.
    (C) Most remnants of the Roman legacy, racial and cultural, disappeared, to be replaced by an exclusively Germanic presence.
    (D) The Huns took over Europe, making the racial mix there heavily Asiatic.
    (E) The ancient Celts had the greatest influence on the racial composition of the European continent.

19. Which of the following does NOT belong to a list of common Enlightenment tenets?

    (A) Organized religions are conglomerations of superstitious beliefs.
    (B) Rational thought is capable of gaining a full understanding of the universe and its workings.
    (C) Logic and proper planning can alleviate most of society's problems.
    (D) Human beings should be guided as much by instinct and emotion as by the intellect.
    (E) Freedom of expression and freedom from arbitrary rule are political goals worth striving for.

20. Qing China's principal commodities for foreign trade were

    (A) cotton, silk, and gunpowder
    (B) spices, porcelain, and cotton
    (C) tea, gunpowder, and cloves
    (D) gunpowder, silk, and glassware
    (E) tea, silk, and porcelain

21. What was the Spanish conquistadors' PRIMARY motivation in gaining new territories in the Americas?

    (A) They were mainly concerned with making great profits.
    (B) Above all, they wanted to bring Catholicism to the Native Americans.
    (C) They planned to use the land to build prisons for Spanish felons.
    (D) They hoped to find the "Fountain of Youth."
    (E) none of the above

22. Which of the following statements accurately describes human tool use during the Paleolithic and Mesolithic eras?

    I. Humanity made use of axes, knives, and bows and arrows.
    II. Only stone tools were used.
    III. Humans lived not only in caves, but more advanced dwellings.
    IV. The greatest priority in tool use and design was ensuring a supply of food.

    (A) I and II
    (B) I and III
    (C) II and III
    (D) I, III, and IV
    (E) all of the above

23. Of the statements below, which is the BEST assessment of the Renaissance?

    (A) It strengthened the Papacy by emphasizing Catholic orthodoxy.
    (B) It boldly experimented with non-realistic forms of artistic expression.
    (C) It combined a revival of Greco-Latin learning with a conviction that worldly human existence was worthwhile.
    (D) Its primary emphasis was on painting and sculpture, and therefore there were few Renaissance writers or poets.
    (E) Rigidly secular in its outlook, it ignored religious subject matter almost completely.

24. Which of the following factors helped to prompt or enable the European powers' campaigns of imperialism during the nineteenth century?

    I. economic factors, such as the need for more raw materials and new markets
    II. military issues, such as modern weapons and the need for naval bases
    III. a sense of cultural and racial superiority
    IV. greater scientific knowledge

    (A) I, II, and III
    (B) II, III, and IV
    (C) I and III only
    (D) III and IV
    (E) all of the above

25. Which of the following is an accurate statement about slavery in the New World?

(A) The Portuguese were the first to abolish it.

(B) More slaves were brought to the United States than to Latin America and the Caribbean.

(C) More slaves were brought to Latin America and the Caribbean than to the United States.

(D) The French enslaved entire Native American tribes.

(E) none of the above.

26. Which of the following correctly describes the emergence of the first cities?

(A) No cities appeared before the Bronze Age.

(B) Urban populations were less diverse than rural populations.

(C) Cities allowed for the specialization of labor.

(D) The first cities appeared in China.

(E) Only peoples who had developed a system of writing built cities.

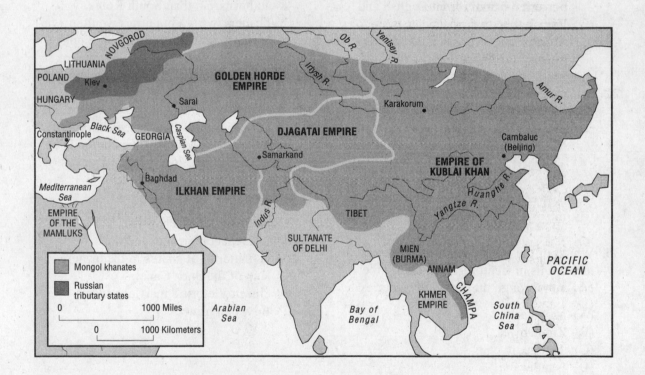

27. What is the central focus of the map above?

(A) the Mongol Empire at its peak

(B) the expansion of Muscovite Russia into Mongol territory

(C) the breakdown of the Mongol Empire into smaller units

(D) the decline and fall of the Delhi Sultanate

(E) the rise of the Khmer Empire

28. The archetypal absolutist ruler of seventeenth- and eighteenth-century Europe was

(A) Henry VIII of England
(B) Louis XIV of France
(C) Ivan the Terrible of Russia
(D) Isabella of Castile
(E) William of Orange

29. What best describes the relationship between Islamic culture and medieval European culture and the Renaissance?

(A) Muslim orthodoxy in Spain prevented the emergence of the Renaissance there.
(B) Muslim scholars and philosophers borrowed heavily from English and French thinkers and scientists.
(C) Muslim science, as well as Muslim translations of ancient Greek writings, were indispensable to the cultural growth of Europe
(D) The Crusades brought European architectural and artistic forms to the Middle East, where they were eagerly absorbed into the local style.
(E) There was very little interaction between the two cultures, because of intense religious hostility.

30. Which of the following was the greatest metropolis in Central Africa during the eleventh through the fifteenth centuries?

(A) Mombasa
(B) Zimbabwe
(C) Timbuktu
(D) Isandlwana
(E) Adowa

31. Which of the following is NOT an example of Ottoman military success between the late 1300s and early 1500s?

(A) the capture of Vienna
(B) the siege of Constantinople
(C) the battle of Kosovo
(D) Suleiman's victory at Mohács
(E) naval mastery over the eastern Mediterranean

32. How have political developments changed in both South Korea and Taiwan since the 1980s?

(A) Both countries have become more authoritarian.
(B) Taiwan has become more authoritarian than South Korea.
(C) Leaders in both countries would now prefer to unite with their communist counterparts.
(D) Both countries have democratized.
(E) none of the above

33. What factor gave Britain justification for interfering in Egyptian politics in the late 1800s?

(A) Lawrence of Arabia's military campaigns there
(B) its control over Palestine
(C) its archaeological expeditions
(D) its majority of shares in the owner-ship of the Suez Canal
(E) Queen Victoria's marriage to an Egyptian prince

World's Major Consumers of Primary Energy (1998) Measured in quadrillions of British thermal units (Btu)

United States	94.57 quadrillion Btu
China	33.93 quadrillion Btu
Russia	25.99 quadrillion Btu
Japan	21.21 quadrillion Btu
Germany	13.83 quadrillion Btu
India	12.51 quadrillion Btu
Canada	11.85 quadrillion Btu
France	10.00 quadrillion Btu
United Kingdom	9.75 quadrillion Btu
Brazil	8.08 quadrillion Btu

34. Based on the data presented in the table, which of the following conclusions might one safely make?

(A) Brazil has a smaller population than Canada does.
(B) The top energy-consuming nations are to be found mainly in the developed world.
(C) Russia is a more efficient consumer of energy than China is.
(D) Japan has a larger population than India does.
(E) Per capita, the people of China are less wasteful of energy than those in the United States.

35. Which of the following is an example of a city built by the Khmer civilization?

(A) Kyoto
(B) Delhi
(C) Angkor Wat
(D) Burma
(E) Malacca

36. How did the demise of the communist regimes in Eastern Europe tend to differ from the collapse of the USSR?

(A) In most East European countries, revolutions were sparked by popular protest, whereas in the USSR, political elites largely caused the collapse.
(B) In the USSR, popular uprisings instigated the ultimate collapse, whereas in Eastern Europe, political leaders decided to change the form of government.
(C) The USSR collapsed purely for economic reasons, whereas in Eastern Europe, communist regimes collapsed mainly as a result of ethnic conflict.
(D) East European regimes collapsed as a result of economic exhaustion, whereas the USSR's breakdown was caused by ethnic warfare.
(E) The reasons for Soviet and East European collapse differed very little.

37. The millet system was

(A) a technique for improving agricultural production in Japan
(B) the Ottoman Empire's method for grouping and governing peoples of various faiths
(C) the Aztec government's system for gathering tribute from neighboring tribes
(D) Tang China's method for keeping trade records
(E) A Zulu form of tactical organization

38. The ancient Athenians used the above structure for what purpose?

(A) as a marketplace
(B) as a government meeting place
(C) as a temple
(D) as a public bathhouse
(E) as a museum

39. Which of the following is an incorrect description of agricultural societies?

(A) Agriculture allowed humans to manipulate their environment as never before.
(B) Women probably played a key role in promoting the transition from hunting and gathering to agricultural societies.
(C) Agriculture promoted permanent settlements.
(D) People began producing their own food nearly 12,000 years ago.
(E) Agricultural societies were less organized than hunter-gatherer societies.

40. The Russian tsar who emancipated the serfs in 1861 was

(A) Nicholas II.
(B) Alexander I.
(C) Alexander II.
(D) Peter the Great.
(E) Catherine the Great.

41. Which of the following is the most accurate statement about the Indian Ocean trade network during the period between 1000 and 1450?

(A) The trade network drew together merchants, travelers, and goods from the Middle East, East Africa, India, Southeast Asia, and China.
(B) The interference of European colonizers and explorers altered the economic patterns of this trade network.
(C) Bitter competition forced the port cities of East Africa out of the Indian Ocean trade network by the 1200s.
(D) China had very little to do with the Indian Ocean trade network.
(E) Arab traders dominated the Indian Ocean trade network throughout this period.

42. Who was the great voyager and explorer of early Ming China?

(A) Yongle
(B) Zheng He
(C) Sun Tzu
(D) Marco Polo
(E) Zhu Yuan-chang

43. What among the following answers best describes the Mississippian culture?

(A) It erected large mounds for ritual purposes and built at least one large city.
(B) It was the earliest civilization to appear in North America.
(C) It was a highly warlike culture, attaining hegemony over most of North America.
(D) It was one of the few monotheistic civilizations in the Americas during the pre-Columbian period.
(E) none of the above

44. Which of the following statements would LEAST likely fit in with the ORIGINAL teachings of the Buddha?

    (A) All human suffering is caused by desire.
    (B) Enlightenment can most effectively be attained by coming to realize the Four Noble Truths and practicing the Eightfold Path.
    (C) Enlightenment leads to a moment of awakening and transcendent consciousness known as nirvana.
    (D) Enlightenment can most effectively be attained by venerating many gods and bodhisattvas.
    (E) none of the above

45. The great oral epic of thirteenth-century Mali, detailing the exploits of a famous chieftain, is which of the following?

    (A) *Son-Jara*
    (B) the *Saga of Geza*
    (C) *Hiawatha*
    (D) the *Epic of Askia Mohammed*
    (E) the *Tale of Shaka*

46. Which of the following statements about European settlements in North America is NOT true?

    (A) The French, more so than the English or Spanish, dominated the fur trade.
    (B) France's principal rival in the New World was England.
    (C) The Spanish once controlled Louisiana.
    (D) The Russians settled along the Pacific coast.
    (E) The French drove the Acadians out of their settlement in Nova Scotia to southern North America.

47. Nikolai Copernicus is best known for which scientific accomplishment?

    (A) for describing the chemical states of matter
    (B) elaborating the theory of elliptical orbits
    (C) devising the first workable microscope
    (D) mathematically proving the heliocentric theory
    (E) inventing the telescope

48. Why did the United States support the Marcos regime in the Philippines?

    (A) because Marcos was strongly committed to democratic principles
    (B) because Marcos was strongly anticommunist
    (C) because Marcos was trying to prevent takeover by a right-wing dictator
    (D) to reward Marcos for observing international human rights standards
    (E) all of the above

49. Which of the following statements can be said to apply to the relationship between the French and American revolutions?

    I. The American War of Independence was inspired by the initial success of the French Revolution.
    II. The cost of military support for the American Revolution was one of the factors that caused the financial crisis that led to the French Revolution.
    III. The Declaration of the Rights of Man and the Citizen was based largely on the ideals of the Declaration of Independence.
    IV. Both revolutions were influenced by the philosophical movement known as the Enlightenment.

    (A) I only
    (B) I and II
    (C) I, II, and III
    (D) II and III
    (E) II, III, and IV

50. In the early twentieth century, what type of people tended to lead independence movements in the Middle East, Africa, and Asia?

(A) peasants
(B) communists
(C) members of the nobility
(D) members of the educated elite
(E) trade-union activists

51. In what key way did early Egyptian civilization resemble societies in Mesopotamia?

(A) They both buried their leaders in pyramids.
(B) They both used cuneiform in preserving their important documents.
(C) They both developed a centralized society ruled by a monarchy and a small caste of priests.
(D) They both created law codes that protected the poor.
(E) They both allowed women to act as priests.

52. What was NOT a consequence of the Mongol invasions?

(A) The Silk Road was destroyed.
(B) Russia fell under Mongol rule for over two centuries.
(C) China was governed by Khubilai Khan.
(D) Mongol armies reached the borderlands of Poland and Hungary.
(E) Much of the Middle East came under Mongol dominance.

53. Which of the following statements about East Africa in the 1800s is inaccurate?

(A) From the late 1700s to the mid-1800s, most of coastal East Africa experienced freedom from external control.
(B) Ethiopia's leaders were Christian.
(C) No major slave markets operated in East Africa.
(D) At one point, more than 40 percent of the population was made up of slaves.
(E) Arabs had gained a great deal of political influence.

54. Which European power colonized Malacca, Goa, and Sri Lanka after the 1500s?

(A) Great Britain
(B) France
(C) Holland
(D) Portugal
(E) Spain

55. Which of the following statements does NOT accurately describe the economic instability Western democratic countries experienced in the 1970s?

(A) Western democracies suffered high levels of unemployment.
(B) Western democracies suffered from inflation.
(C) Western democracies suffered from severe economic depressions.
(D) Western democracies were adversely affected by an oil embargo.
(E) Western democracies were hurt by the devaluing of the U.S. dollar.

56. Which of the following accurately describes both the Han and Roman empires?

(A) Their leaders persecuted Christians up until the collapse of their empires.
(B) Their economic and political instability was largely caused by imperial overreach.
(C) Their leaders were satisfied to maintain their lands and expand as little as possible.
(D) They both tried to conquer the entire Eurasian continent.
(E) They both tried to conquer parts of North Africa.

57. Which of the following was NOT a major characteristic of Middle Eastern political life after World War II?

   (A) widespread democratization
   (B) independence of former colonies and mandates
   (C) tensions between religious fundamentalism and westernization
   (D) the Arab-Israeli conflict
   (E) the persistence of human rights abuses

58. To deter workers from embracing radical ideologies in Germany in the late 1800s, what measures did Otto von Bismarck take?

   (A) He outlawed the sale of all books by Karl Marx.
   (B) He encouraged workers to fight the Jews.
   (C) He imprisoned those who joined the Communist Party.
   (D) He granted universal male suffrage and gave workers many social benefits.
   (E) all of the above

59. Which Hebrew leader united the Kingdom of Israel and is considered to have written many of the songs and poems included in the Book of Psalms?

   (A) David
   (B) Moses
   (C) Joseph
   (D) Jacob
   (E) Abraham

60. Why is 1942 considered the turning point of World War II?

   (A) That year, Italy left the war.
   (B) The United States entered the war that year.
   (C) The Axis Powers lost three pivotal battles, including the Battle of Stalingrad.
   (D) The Allies lost three pivotal battles, including the Battle of Stalingrad.
   (E) The United States dropped the atomic bomb on Hiroshima.

61. Which of the following is true of Simón Bolívar?

   (A) He rose from the lower classes to achieve independence for South America.
   (B) He was instrumental in attaining independence for Mexico.
   (C) He was disdainful of constitutional rule.
   (D) His aristocratic background kept him from supporting freedom for slaves.
   (E) none of the above

62. What factor caused Southeast Asia to experience major political change between 1200 and 1400?

   (A) The Chinese and Mongols conquered parts of Southeast Asia at this time.
   (B) The countries of Southeast Asia adopted Confucianism.
   (C) The peoples of Southeast Asia began to adopt Christian ways.
   (D) Democracy became a leading force in political change.
   (E) all of the above

63. Which of the following best describes the effects of the "agricultural revolution" of the 1700s in Europe?

   (A) Less organic food was grown.
   (B) There were fewer famines and better crop yields.
   (C) Serfdom was abolished.
   (D) Peasants revolted and took control of manors.
   (E) Poverty was eliminated.

64. Why did the European Economic Community form?

   (A) to prepare for economic mobilization in case of war
   (B) to coordinate economic production during World War II
   (C) to oppose U.S. exports
   (D) to encourage the free movement of goods, services, money, and labor inside Europe
   (E) to increase the number of internal tariffs within Europe

65. Which country lost the Spanish-American War, and what happened to it?

   (A) the United States, which was forced to relinquish Cuba
   (B) the United States, which was forced to hand over the Philippines
   (C) Spain, which was stripped of its colonial possessions
   (D) Spain, which lost only Cuba to the United States
   (E) none of the above

66. How were the decolonization processes in Rhodesia and South Africa similar?

   (A) The African population in both countries was treated equitably.
   (B) There was an intense conflict between black and white citizens in both countries.
   (C) In both cases, decolonization resulted in mass genocide.
   (D) French peacekeepers had to be brought in to maintain order.
   (E) Decolonization in both countries required the intervention of United Nations peacekeeping forces.

67. In what way was the Chinese response to the growing presence of Western powers in East Asia during the 1800s different from the Japanese response?

   (A) Japan was forced to grant outside powers economic concessions, whereas China was not.
   (B) The Chinese modernized and industrialized, whereas the Japanese did not.
   (C) The Japanese modernized and industrialized, whereas the Chinese did not.
   (D) China defeated the Western powers in battle, whereas Japan tended to lose.
   (E) China and Japan reacted to Western powers in nearly identical fashion.

68. The Declaration of the Rights of Man and the Citizen

   (A) was adopted by the Constitutional Convention in Philadelphia
   (B) guaranteed basic civil rights and liberties for male citizens in France
   (C) included only people who were property owners
   (D) created a monarchy in Britain
   (E) influenced the Bolshevik Revolution

69. Other than Jews and homosexuals, which groups did the German Nazis target for persecution?

   I. certain ethnic groups, such as Gypsies and Slavs
   II. political dissidents
   III. ethnically pure Germans
   IV. the mentally and physically disabled

   (A) I, II, and III
   (B) I, II, and IV
   (C) II, III, and IV
   (D) I and III only
   (E) all of the above

70. Which of the following devices did China use or invent during the Song dynasty?

   (A) gunpowder
   (B) the magnetic compass
   (C) a chain-driven, water-powered clock
   (D) all of the above
   (E) none of the above

SECTION II: FREE-RESPONSE QUESTIONS

Part A: Document-Based Question

Time: **10 minutes to read documents; 40 minutes to complete essay**

Directions: The following question is based on the accompanying documents. This question is designed to test your ability to work with historical documents. As you analyze the documents, take into account both the sources of the documents and the authors' points of view. Write an essay on the following topic that integrates your analysis of the documents. DO NOT SIMPLY SUMMARIZE THE DOCUMENTS INDIVIDUALLY. You may refer to relevant historical facts and developments not mentioned in the documents. Some documents have been edited. (Write your answer on a separate sheet of paper.)

---

1. One of the most common forms of cultural interchange is the transfer of religious beliefs. As new faiths and spiritual ideas appear in a nation or among a community, reactions to them vary. Based on the documents that follow, what can you conclude about how various religions, missions, and proselytizing efforts have been received in different places at different times?

DOCUMENT 1

Source: Thomas Coryate, English traveler in Turkey, on witnessing Sufi dervishes (1613).

There is a College of Turkish Monks in Galata, that are called [Dervishes], . . . who every Tuesday and Friday do perform the strangest exercise of Devotion that ever I saw or heard of. . . .

A little after I came into the room, the Dervishes repaired into the middle void space, sitting Cross-legged, bending their Bodies low toward the floor for Religion['s] sake, even almost flat upon their Faces . . . the whole company of them were about two and fifty. . . .

[A] certain Singing-man sitting apart in an upper room began to sing certain Hymns, but with the most unpleasant and harsh notes that ever I heard, exceedingly differing from our Christian Church singing, for the yelling and disorderly squeaking did even grate mine ears. . . . [T]hree Pipers sitting in the room with the Singer began to play upon certain long Pipes not unlike Tabors, which yielded a very ridiculous and foolish Music . . . whereupon some five and twenty of the two and fifty Dervishes suddenly rose up bare-legged and bare-footed, and casting aside their upper Garments, some of them having their breasts all uncovered, they began by little and little to turn about the Interpreter of the Law. Afterward they redoubled their force and turned with such incredible swiftness, that I could not choose but admire it.

DOCUMENT 2

Source: Fa-hsien, traveling monk from China, on his reception by Indian Buddhists (399).

When they saw pilgrims from China arrive, they were much affected and spoke thus, "How is it that men from the frontiers are able to know the religion of family-renunciation and come from far to seek the law of the Buddha?" They liberally provided necessary entertainment according to the rules of religion.

[As we reached the Ganges, the local priests exclaimed,] "Wonderful! to think that men from the frontiers of the earth should come so far as this from a desire to search for the law. . . . Our various superiors and brethren, who have succeeded one another in this place from the earliest time till now, have none of them seen men of Han come so far as this before."

DOCUMENT 3

Source: Council of the Aztec city of Huejotzingo, letter to King of Spain (1560).

Catholic Royal Majesty!

When your servants the Spaniards reached us and your captain general Don Hernando Cortés arrived, not a single town surpassed us here in New Spain, in that first and earliest we threw ourselves toward you.

. . . we also say and declare before you that [when] your padres, the sons of St. Francis, entered the city of Huejotzingo, of our own free will we honored them and showed them esteem. When they [told us to] abandon the wicked belief in many gods, we did it. Very willingly we destroyed, demolished, and burned the temples. . . .

But now we are taken aback and very afraid, and we ask, have we done something wrong, have we somehow behaved badly, or have we committed some sin against almighty God?

DOCUMENT 4

Source: Jean Bodin, French philosopher (1530–1596), on Ottoman religious policy.

The King of the Turks, who rules over a great part of Europe, safeguards the rites of religion as well as any prince in this world. He constrains no one, but on the contrary permits everyone to live as his conscience dictates. What is more, even in his seraglio at Pera he permits the practice of four diverse religions, that of the Jews, the Christian according to the Roman rite, and according to the Greek rite, and that of Islam.

DOCUMENT 5

Source: Ashoka, Mauryan emperor of India, *Edicts* (260s B.C.E.).

Whoever honors only his own religion and disparages another man's, whether from blind loyalty or with the intention of showing his own religion in a favorable light, does his own religion the greatest possible harm. Concord is best, with each hearing and respecting the other's teachings. It is the wish of the king that members of all religions should be learned and should teach virtue.

DOCUMENT 6

Source: Dante Alighieri, Florentine poet, *The Inferno*, Canto XXVIII, 28–36 (ca. 1307).

I stood and stared at him from the stone shelf;
he noticed me and opening his own breast
with both hands cried: "See how I rip myself!

See how Mahomet's mangled and split open!
Ahead of me walks Ali in his tears
his head cleft from the top-knot to the chin.

All the other souls that bleed and mourn
along this ditch were sowers of scandal and schism:
as they tore others apart, so are they torn."

DOCUMENT 7

Source: The Regulations of the City of Avignon (1243).

Likewise, we declare that Jews or whores shall not dare to touch with their hands either bread or fruit put out for sale, and that if they should do this they must buy what they have touched.

DOCUMENT 8

Source: Albert Schweitzer, German missionary, doctor, and humanitarian, letter to his sister (April 1913).

Medical knowledge made it possible for me to carry out my intention [of bringing Christ to Africa] in the best and most complete way, wherever the path of service might lead me. . . .

I'm really happy. I feel I've done the right thing in coming here, for the misery is greater than anyone can describe. . . . [T]here are all stages of leprosy. . . . I see a great deal of sleeping sickness. It is very painful for these poor souls. . . . And elephantiasis, that constantly increasing swelling of the limbs. It is dreadful; eventually the legs are so thick that the people can no longer drag them about.

Many heart cases; the people are suffocating. And then the joy when the digitalin works! Evenings I go to bed dead-tired, but in my heart I am profoundly happy that *I am serving at the outpost of the Kingdom of God!*

Part B: Change-over-Time Question

Time: **40 minutes to complete essay**

> *Directions:* You are to answer the following question. In writing your essay, use specific examples to support your answer. (Write your essay on separate sheets of paper.)

2. Choose ONE of the following trade routes. Discuss its global importance, as well as how patterns of economic exchange shifted and altered during the periods designated for each.

   the Indian Ocean trade network (1000–1500)
   the gold trade in West and Central Africa (500–1300)
   the Silk Road (100 B.C.E.–500 C.E.)
   the eastern Mediterranean (500–1300)

Part C: Comparative Essay

Time: **40 minutes to complete essay**

> *Directions:* You are to answer the following question. In writing your essay, use specific examples to support your answer. (Write your essay on separate sheets of paper.)

3. Both in Europe and the Middle East, great efforts were made by religious leaders to create political communities united by faith and governed by spiritual, rather than royal, authority. This was the case with the Catholic popes of medieval Europe and the Islamic caliphs of the Middle East. Did either achieve their goal? Compare and contrast the successes and failures of both.

ANSWER KEY TO MODEL EXAMINATION II

ANSWERS TO MULTIPLE-CHOICE QUESTIONS

1. **E** (p. 401)
2. **C** (p. 324)
3. **B** (p. 93)
4. **A** (p. 426)
5. **C** (pp. 273–74)
6. **A** (p. 293)
7. **D** (p. 237)
8. **C** (p. 428)
9. **B** (p. 39)
10. **B** (pp. 216–17)
11. **E** (p. 295)
12. **C** (p. 417)
13. **B** (pp. 120–21)
14. **A** (p. 136)
15. **E** (p. 234)
16. **C** (pp. 48–49)
17. **B** (p. 223)
18. **B** (p. 69)
19. **D** (p. 194)
20. **E** (p. 215)
21. **A** (p. 239)
22. **D** (pp. 49–50)
23. **C** (pp. 127–28)
24. **E** (pp. 281–82)
25. **C** (p. 230)
26. **C** (p. 53)
27. **C** (p. 159)
28. **B** (pp. 190–91)
29. **C** (p. 126)
30. **B** (p. 164)
31. **A** (p. 135)
32. **D** (p. 414)
33. **D** (pp. 294–95)
34. **B** (pp. 445–46)
35. **C** (p. 152)
36. **A** (p. 436)
37. **B** (p. 209)
38. **C** (p. 62)
39. **E** (pp. 52–53)
40. **C** (pp. 264–65)
41. **A** (pp. 150–51)
42. **B** (pp. 142–43)
43. **A** (p. 168)
44. **D** (pp. 90–91)
45. **A** (p. 133)
46. **E** (p. 238)
47. **D** (p. 193)
48. **B** (p. 413)
49. **E** (p. 256)
50. **D** (pp. 367–69, 408)
51. **C** (pp. 57–59)
52. **A** (p. 159)
53. **C** (p. 320)
54. **D** (p. 202)
55. **C** (p. 421)
56. **B** (pp. 64, 66)
57. **A** (p. 405)
58. **D** (p. 264)
59. **A** (p. 86)
60. **C** (pp. 381–82)
61. **E** (pp. 332–33)
62. **A** (p. 152)
63. **B** (p. 195)
64. **D** (p. 401)
65. **C** (p. 335)
66. **B** (p. 409)
67. **C** (p. 298)
68. **B** (p. 257)
69. **B** (p. 384)
70. **D** (p. 140)

SAMPLE ANSWER TO THE DOCUMENT-BASED QUESTION

One of the fundamental forms of human interaction is the exchange of religious ideas and practices. The simple fact that every one of the world's major faiths is practiced thousands of miles from its point of origin is ample demonstration of this fact. The spread of religions takes place in a variety of ways: missionary activity, forced conversion, the migration of peoples, the wanderings of traveling pilgrims, and the natural expansion of religious ideas among peoples who neighbor each other. Likewise, the ways in which different societies react to new religions varies. The documents included in this question give examples of these different types of reactions. One cluster of documents deals with an all too common response to the appearance or presence of other faiths: hostility and intolerance. Another provides examples of conversion and tolerance that, on the surface, seem voluntary and genuine, but bear closer examination. Finally, a third set of documents describes instances of true tolerance and receptivity.

Sadly, perhaps the most common and most instinctual response to a religion other than one's own is hostility and intolerance, or at least ignorance. Examples abound, such as the government's crucifixion of Christians in Japan during the late 1500s and Spain's expulsion of Jews in 1492. Documents #1, #6, and #7 provide illustrations of this sort of reaction. The account of Thomas Coryate (#1), an English traveler in Turkey, is the mildest of the three, demonstrating not outright hatred or anger, but ignorance and condescension. Upon witnessing a Sufi ritual, the dancing of mystics known as dervishes, Coryate describes the entire affair as "strange." He criticizes the music as "unpleasant and harsh," as well as "ridiculous and foolish." Although he admires the physical dexterity of the dervishes, the religious significance of the dancing is lost on him. Furthermore, it is clear that Coryate automatically assumes the Sufi rite to be inferior to his own Christian faith.

Documents #6 and #7, although falling into the same category as #1, are harsher in tone. The Italian poet Dante, in his famous work *The Inferno*, depicts the Muslim prophet Mohammed and his son-in-law Ali as sinners in hell. The Islamic religion the two founded is, in Dante's eyes, false.

As a false faith, Islam, Dante argues, is a sinful creation that has "torn others apart," or kept people from the truth of Christianity. Accordingly, Mohammed and Ali are punished by having their souls torn apart for eternity. Quite clearly, this passage reflects the extreme hostility that most medieval Catholics felt toward Muslims. Document #7, drawn from the medieval law code of the French city of Avignon, reveals—in the blandest of bureaucratic language—a deeply rooted streak of anti-Semitism. Almost casually, as if it were perfectly logical or natural, all Jews are placed by the Christian authorities in the same category as prostitutes in terms of supposed uncleanliness and undesirability.

A second group of documents, #3 and #4, reveals some of the ambiguities involved with religious conversion, especially when it is carried out by conquest. In a letter to the King of Spain (#3), the council of the Aztec city of Huejotzingo describe how the city's people converted to Catholicism when the priests following the conquistador Hernando Cortés ("the sons of St. Francis," that is, members of the Franciscan order) asked them to. The leaders of Huejotzingo speak of their conversion (not to mention their support of Cortés's invasion) as if it were completely voluntary: "not a single town surpassed us . . . in that first and earliest we threw ourselves toward you," and "very willingly we destroyed, demolished, and burned the temples." But how sincere are these declarations? To begin with, Cortés and his armies brought Spanish rule and Catholicism to Mexico by force. Opposition meant death and ruin. Most likely, the people of Huejotzingo joined Cortés and converted to Christianity because they had no choice. Moreover, it is clear that the council of Huejotzingo is writing the King of Spain because the city is having some kind of trouble or is being accused of having done wrong. In that case, it would be in the interest of the city to appear as loyal as possible. Other documents here would be useful. Could statistics show how many people were killed in Huejotzingo during Cortés's invasion, especially in comparison with Aztec cities that did not submit so quickly and easily? Are there records of the religious attitudes of the ordinary people of Huejotzingo? Perhaps those would show that the city's love for Catholicism was not as heartfelt as Document #3 would seem to indicate.

Similarly, Document #4, an essay by the French philosopher Jean Bodin about the religious policy of the Ottoman sultan during the 1500s, seems to describe a condition of tolerance and acceptance. According to Bodin, the sultan (or "King of the Turks") "safeguards the rites of religion as well as any prince in this world." This was largely true. Islamic doctrine preached tolerance toward the "peoples of the Book"—Jews and Christians, whose religious traditions were historically linked with Islam's—and Ottoman policy grouped people of various faiths into millets, or religious communities, which were free to worship as they chose. The major religions worshiped by the various peoples who fell under Ottoman rule were as Bodin describes: Judaism, Eastern Orthodoxy, Roman Catholicism, and Islam, by far the majority religion. However, what Bodin does not mention is the fact that religious minorities did suffer persecution, mainly unofficial, but occasionally official. Especially in the Balkans and the Caucasus, there were occasional massacres of Christians. Also, Jews and Christians who did not convert to Islam were subject to various regulations, taxes, and other burdens. Since, technically, Muslims could not enslave other Muslims, slaves tended to be Jews and Christians. Bodin's failure to mention all these facts may be due to ignorance. More likely, however, is his purpose for writing about the supposed tolerance of the Ottoman sultan. Bodin was writing for a European audience, and during the 1500s, Europe was tearing itself apart over the religious debates and disputes stirred up by the Protestant Reformation. In particular, Bodin's native France was convulsed with savage wars of religion. It seems likely that Bodin overemphasized the religious tolerance of the Ottomans, in order to provide an example to European Christians. If the Turks, whom the Europeans regarded as savage, rapacious, and decadent, could show religious tolerance, why not the Europeans? It would be interesting to balance Bodin's essay with other documents, especially testimony from Jews or Balkan Christians living under Ottoman rule, to see if the picture they painted of Ottoman religious policy and the millet system would be similar to Bodin's.

A third category of documents, consisting of #2, #5, and #8, depicts instances of religious tolerance and even acceptance. The account of Fa-hsien (#2), a Buddhist monk from China who traveled to India to seek out the roots of his religion during the fourth century C.E., illustrates the wide-ranging spread of Buddhist throughout southern and eastern Asia. It also shows how eager the Buddhists of India were to foster these cross-cultural links. Fa-hsein writes of the excitement and happiness the Indian Buddhists felt upon meeting their Chinese brethren (although it would be helpful to have a corresponding description of the meeting by one of the Indian Buddhists, to see how genuine the excitement and happiness were).

The veracity of Document #5, the *Edicts* of Ashoka, the Mauryan emperor of India during the third century B.C.E., is a matter of record. Ashoka, originally a warrior-king, converted to Buddhism and pacifism while still a young man. A Buddhist ruler in a country that was mainly Hindu, Ashoka chose to support religious tolerance. On a practical level, this was simply good politics, in a country that was such a patchwork of ethnicities, cultures, languages, and faiths. But it was also a matter of genuine conviction for Ashoka, and one can see this in the philosophical manner in which his edict is issued. Ashoka makes the profound point that those who scorn other people's religions do their own religion "the greatest possible harm"—possibly because most faiths contain some kind of commandment or stricture telling their worshipers to treat other people with respect.

The letter of German doctor Albert Schweitzer, a Nobel laureate and famed humanitarian, to his sister (#8) tells of a successful Christian missionary effort in Africa. During the nineteenth and early twentieth centuries, Christian missions to Africa and Asia (especially China) were common. They were not always successful, however. Schweitzer's was extremely successful, as his letter to his sister indicates. Still, the reader would benefit from supplementary documents, especially diaries or records left behind by the Africans with whom Schweitzer interacted. How did they really perceive Schweitzer? Were they truly interested in the Christian faith he preached? Or were they actually interested in the medical skills he brought to Africa? More written records might be able to shed light on those questions. The last question also raises a wider point about missionary work. Traditionally, those missions that proved the most successful were those that brought not just new religion, but also tangible, material benefits, such as medicine, language training, advanced agricultural techniques, new technology, and so on. It is clear that Schweitzer feels that he is advancing the cause of Christianity: he ends his letter with a heavily emphasized statement that he is "serving at the outpost of the Kingdom of God!" However, it seems that he is also aware, consciously or unconsciously, of the fact that a great deal of his appeal to the Africans he preaches to is the medical care he is able to give to them.

SAMPLE ANSWER TO THE CHANGE-OVER-TIME QUESTION

With few exceptions, major trade routes throughout the long preindustrial period of world history were waterborne. The effort of simple overland travel, not to mention transporting large amounts of freight without modern roads or power-driven vehicles, was extraordinarily great, and the expenses were correspondingly high. It was far easier and cheaper to move people and goods by rivers and across lakes and seas.

Perhaps the greatest exception to this rule was the Silk Road, the major overland trade route that stretched over the vast distance between China and the ports of the eastern Mediterranean. Not only did the Silk Road stimulate a tremendous amount of trade and generate great wealth, but it served as a great highway upon which countless travelers moved back and forth across most of the length of the Eurasian landmass. In this way, the Silk Road became a vibrant avenue along which ideas and cultural traditions were exchanged, religious beliefs were brought into contact with each other, and various peoples and ethnicities interacted.

The Silk Road first came into use around 100 B.C.E. From 206 B.C.E. onward, the Han dynasty had strengthened and centralized China. The emperor Wu Ti (140–87 B.C.E.) then subdued or allied with many of the desert and steppe peoples of Mongolia and Central Asia, to China's north and west. This extended China's economic influence far beyond its borders. Moreover, the Han rulers were extremely effective at building roads to facilitate long-distance overland travel. By around 100 B.C.E., an overland route of approximately 4,000 miles—reasonably safe and reliable—stretched from Chang'an in east-central China, through Central Asia, all the way to the Middle East.

The route's name came from China's principal trade commodity, which was silk. For centuries, the Chinese successfully and jealously guarded the secret of silk production, giving Han China one of the most lucrative monopolies in economic history. From the great commercial center of Chang'an, Chinese caravans, loaded with silk and other goods, would move westward, over the North China Plain, through the Pamir and Karakorum mountains, then to the great Central Asian city-states of Samarkand and Bukhara. Silk Road trade made these stopping points important trading centers in their own right, especially because few caravans traveled the entire route. Therefore, cities such as Samarkand and Bukhara provided convenient meeting places for caravans that had arrived from the East and those that had arrived from the West. In addition, Central Asia's local cotton goods and beautifully woven carpets were highly valued.

From Central Asia, caravans would continue on (or go back) to Babylon, Damascus, Edessa, and other great metropolises of Sassanid Persia and the Middle East. Chinese goods also reached Mediterranean ports such as Antioch and Alexandria. By extension, this brought China—and all points in between—into contact with the Roman Empire. From the west, glassware, wool, gold, silver, gems, and wine traveled back toward Persia, Central Asia, and China.

This state of affairs persisted until the 400s and 500s C.E. An immense part of the world was therefore linked, directly or indirectly, by this one route: Europe, the Mediterranean, the Middle East, Persia, Central Asia, China, and, beyond that, Southeast Asia and the Pacific coast. New technologies traveled along the Silk Road, as did new scientific ideas, cultural traditions, and languages. Religions traveled along the Silk Road as well. An eastern Mediterranean denomination of Christianity, Nestorianism, traveled eastward to Central Asia and China. Buddhism came to China from India, along parts of the Silk Road. Then, from China, Buddhism continued to spread—again, largely along the Silk Road—to Mongolia, Tibet, parts of southern Siberia, and parts of Central Asia.

The Silk Road was falling into disuse by the 400s and 500s C.E. To begin with, the Han dynasty collapsed in 220 C.E. For the next three and a half centuries, China experienced a period of civil war and internal decentralization. This affected not only foreign trade, but China's ability to keep the infrastructure that supported the eastern half of the Silk Road intact.

The collapse was gradual, however. Central Asian cities such as Samarkand and Bukhara continued to serve as effective links between east and west. Also, as long as Sassanid Persia and the Roman Empire (or, after the 300s C.E., the Western and Eastern Roman Empires) remained intact, the level of trade in the west remained high enough to make Silk Road travel worthwhile.

After the late 400s, however, conditions in the West changed. The Western Roman Empire fell in 476. During the 500s, the Eastern Roman, or Byzantine, Empire continued trading with China. Indeed, one of the great accomplishments attributed (somewhat mythically) to the emperor Justinian is that his spies stole the secret of silk production, breaking the Chinese monopoly. Still, the level of trade dropped. The same was true for Sassanid Persia. Although interaction between East and West never ended, the Silk Road, for many years, ceased to be the dominant trade route it had been for half a millennium.

As a final point, it should be noted that the Silk Road revived periodically. The Central Asian khanates kept certain parts safe and clear from nomadic incursions. During the 1200s and 1300s, the Pax Mongolica created by the Mongol conquests of much of Eurasia restored the Silk Road to its former glory, especially during the days of Khubilai Khan, when the Venetian merchant Marco Polo made his famous journey along the Silk Road to China. The Silk Road dwindled again, however, after the 1400s, as European explorers established maritime trade routes around the world, forever altering the pattern of global economic interaction.

SAMPLE ANSWER TO THE COMPARATIVE QUESTION

Theocracy, a form of government in which political authority rests in the hands of a society's religious leadership, has proven comparatively rare. Although political authority and spiritual authority have both played vital roles in the history of most societies, they have generally been kept separate, or they have overlapped rather than coincided. However, in many times and places, spiritual authorities have attempted to gain political authority—and, in a few cases, they have succeeded.

From the 900s through the 1400s, the Catholic popes of medieval Europe came very near to attaining this goal. They had tried earlier to assert their political authority, but it was between the tenth and fourteenth centuries that they came closest to succeeding. To the south and east of Europe, the Muslims actually did succeed in creating a theocracy, from the 600s through the mid-1200s. These two periods of time overlap to a great extent, and a comparison of the medieval papacy and the Islamic caliphate yields some interesting conclusions. The foremost is that the Muslims were more successful in joining political and religious authority because the original founders of the Islamic faith spread it themselves, establishing military and political dominance as they proceeded. By contrast, Christianity was, for the medieval Europeans, a legacy of the past, bequeathed by the fallen Roman Empire. Therefore, the Catholic Church was, in effect, attempting to use an older faith as a tool to join together the political chaos of its own era.

From the beginning, early Islamic theology declared that the community of believers, or *umma,* should be joined together under a single political and religious community. During the early 600s, Mohammed's early community was governed by one law and one code of values. As the new faith spread by conquest and persuasion throughout Arabia, then the Middle East, so did that one law and one code of values. This process was not completely smooth. Although the death of Mohammed in 632 did not destroy the new faith, it did raise the issue of who would lead the *umma* afterward. A chain of caliphs, or "successors," was established, but the succession remained unbroken for only a short time. A short but bitter civil war broke out in the 650s between the followers of Mohammed's son-in-law Ali and Mohammed's wife Aisha. The results of the war included the establishment of the Umayyad Caliphate, but also the permanent split of the Muslim faith into two denominations: the Sunni majority and the Shiite minority.

The Umayyad Caliphate lasted until the middle of the 700s. During this time, Islam spread quickly over a vast expanse of territory. The longer-lasting Abbasid Caliphate that followed expanded even farther, through North Africa, to Spain, and eastward, eventually to the borderlands of India. As the new faith expanded, it was the religious authority of the caliphs that created political and military authority as well. The territory governed by the caliphate was united by a single rule, a single law (the Islamic law code of Sharia), a single economic authority, and a single holy language, which was Arabic, the language of Mohammed.

There were, of course, gaps in Umayyad and Abbasid authority. Islam was more prevalent in the cities than in rural areas. Not everyone under Muslim rule converted to Islam (although they were certainly subject to Muslim authority). The Umayyad and Abbasid Caliphates were criss-crossed by a patchwork of ethnic and linguistic differences, covered over by a thin blanket of Arab authority. The worst problem of all was geographic overextension. Although the Abbasid Caliphate survived until the mid-1200s, when Mongol invaders toppled it, it was, already by the 900s, having difficulty retaining control over many of its far-flung territories, such as Egypt, Spain, and elsewhere.

After the collapse of the Abbasid Caliphate, there would never be another political entity that completely united the Muslim faith, especially under a single religious authority. As for the caliphate itself, the Abbasid rulership remains one of the most successful, wide-ranging, and longest-lasting theocracies in world history.

The same cannot be said for the medieval Papacy in Catholic Europe—although it was not for want of trying that the popes failed to attain the same degree of political authority that the Muslim caliphs did.

Unlike Islam, Christian theology was ambiguous on the question of political authority. Believers were to live in this world, but not to be "of" it. Christ himself preached that one should "render unto Caesar what is Caesar's," an indication that Christians should submit to political authority that was not necessarily religious. Certainly early Christians submitted to the will of the Roman Empire, especially after their religion was made legal, then the official faith, during the 300s C.E.

During the first several hundred years that followed Rome's fall in 476, however, the worldly authority of the Catholic Church grew considerably. During most of the early medieval period, roughly 500 to 900 C.E., Europe was plunged into political decentralization, military disorder, and cultural confusion. Amidst the chaos, the Catholic Church stood out as one of the few respectable institutions with some kind of unifying authority. This authority was not merely spiritual, but cultural (the role of the Church in preserving documents, manuscripts, and learning in general was crucial during these years) and somewhat political. The Catholic popes gave legitimacy to political rulers—the most prominent cases being Charlemagne and, after him, the Holy Roman emperors of Germany and Central Europe, whose authority derived partly from the papal stamp of approval.

The heyday of the medieval Papacy came during the High Middle Ages, or roughly from 1000 through the 1200s. During this three-century period, the popes governed Rome and the surrounding region almost as if it were an independent kingdom (the justification for this was a forged document known as the "Donation of Constantine," which the Papacy claimed was the Roman emperor Constantine's will and testament, leaving Rome to the Catholic Church).

Just as important, the Catholic Church, after 1000, made a determined bid to gain even more political power for itself. Indeed, popes such as Gregory VII, who governed the Church during the late eleventh century, and Innocent III, who sat on the papal throne during the early 1200s, argued that the spiritual authority of the popes should be considered superior to that of political rulers, such as kings and monarchs. The ultimate goal of medieval popes was theocratic. They hoped to gather all the nations of Europe together into a single Christian community. This community would be called Christendom, and the popes hoped that it would transcend nationality and language, with religion being the most important unifying factor in Europe. The popes could only have envied the Abbasid caliphs, who, to a large extent, achieved this goal in the Muslim lands.

For a time, the medieval popes were able to make great gains in their struggle for political power. Aside from their rulership of the Papal States, they exerted a sizable influence over the monarchs of Europe. Moral and spiritual authority gave the Catholic Church a great deal of worldly stature in an age when matters of faith were taken extremely seriously. A strong-minded pope could often bend the will of a less determined ruler to his own. The popes also had the power to determine what was acceptable dogma and what was heresy. They had the power to excommunicate, or exclude worshipers from the Catholic Church, thereby (in the terms of Catholicism's belief system) condemning them to eternal damnation unless they submitted to the pope's will. The popes could also begin holy wars, or crusades. Catholic regulations even governed when wars could be fought: no fighting could take place on certain saints' days, holidays, or the Sabbath, and, in most cases, spiritual authority governed military matters. The Church had its own law code, which operated in parallel with the secular law codes of the kingdoms, duchies, and baronies of Europe.

The Catholic Church also became the owner of vast amounts of land throughout Europe. Combined with its right to collect tithes from the general population, this made the Church very wealthy. Another way in which the Church exercised worldly power was its high degree of control over education, thought, and culture. Most institutions of learning were connected in one way or another with the Catholic Church. More broadly, it was dangerous for any scholar or artist to write, say, or produce anything that ran counter to Catholic doctrine. In 1231, the Holy Inquisition, a set of special courts with wide-ranging powers, was established to hunt out and harshly punish heresy and religious nonconformity.

In the end, however, the Catholic Church never attained the ideal of Christendom or the ultimate joining of spiritual authority with political authority. For one thing, it is telling that Church (or canon) law was distinct from worldly law, rather than one and the same, as was the case with the Islamic Sharia. Also, although in specific cases, the popes of high medieval Europe managed to win power struggles against kings and emperors, overall, political authority kept control over its sphere and managed to keep the popes in the spiritual sphere.

By the 1300s, the political influence of the Catholic Church was somewhat on the wane. The "Babylonian Captivity," during which the kings of France kidnapped the pope, then, for several generations, moved the Papacy from Rome to the French city of Avignon, lasted most of the 1300s. It was immediately followed by the Great Schism, during which two popes—the Pope and Anti-Pope, one in Rome, the other in Avignon—claimed authority. The 1400s saw the flowering of Church wealth and corruption, but it was clear that, although the Catholic Church was still powerful in a worldly sense, it would never wrest political power from the kings and emperors of Europe, especially since the latter were finally creating strong, centralized countries. Then, of course, the Protestant Reformation of the 1500s split the spiritual authority of the Church forever, destroying altogether the hope of a united Christendom. At no point was the Catholic Church ever able to imitate the theocratic nature of the Abbasid Caliphate.

INDEX